Fernand Léger
Painting in Space

Fernand Léger

Edited by Katia Baudin

Painting in Space

Museum Ludwig, Cologne

HIRMER

Contents

Foreword

Léger's large-scale painting *Les Plongeurs* (The Divers, 1942) is among the most well-known and popular works in the Museum Ludwig collection. Over three decades, the divers have consistently stood in the limelight, greeting our visitors from their prominent position on the north wall of our spacious staircase—as if made for that spot. Indeed, Peter and Irene Ludwig had this space in mind when they discovered the painting at Art Cologne in 1984 and, accordingly, decided to acquire it for the new building of the Museum Ludwig.[1] Two years later—thirty years ago—the painting was placed in this central location in the newly inaugurated building designed by Busmann + Haberer and situated between the Cologne cathedral and the river Rhine.[2]

That the picture fits so well in this architectural context would certainly have pleased Léger himself, as it was created as a mural for a specific building 6,000 kilometers away from Cologne, in Huntington on Long Island, New York. Léger made the large-scale painting for American architect Wallace K. Harrison's circular living room, and it followed the curve of its rounded wall for forty years.

It is thanks to Katia Baudin that these stories, which had faded into obscurity, have been excavated; she has shone new light on them through her groundbreaking exhibition and accompanying publication. *Les Plongeurs* gave her the impetus to revisit the works of this well-known painter of classical modernism from an entirely new perspective. *Fernand Léger: Painting in Space* is the first retrospective exhibition to survey how Léger took painting off the easel and transferred color to the spaces of daily life. The exhibition's focus on Léger's wall paintings and murals makes clear the central role played by modernist and International Style architecture and architects in Léger's dialogue with three-dimensional space.

As director of a collection-based museum, I am particularly pleased to welcome visitors to an exhibition that has grown out of this very collection, and which manages to unite the core aims of a museum—collecting, preserving, researching, exhibiting, and teaching—in such an effective way, while also finding the perfect balance between high scholarly standards and broad public appeal. *Fernand Léger: Painting in Space* is a special highlight of this anniversary year in which we celebrate the fortieth birthday of our institution.

The organization of such an ambitious exhibition presented a particular challenge to the Museum Ludwig. I would like to extend my thanks, also on behalf of Katia Baudin, to all the individuals and institutions who have helped make this exhibition possible.

First and foremost are the lenders, as the exhibition brings together around 170 works from almost forty different European and American collections, which are listed and acknowledged later in this publication. We would particularly like to single out the Musée National Fernand Léger in Biot, the Centre Pompidou and the Centre National des Arts Plastiques in Paris, the Museum of Modern Art in New York, and the Museu Coleção Berardo in Lisbon for their generous support through major loans, including murals. These presented a particularly complex challenge, as many of them have only rarely, if ever, left their permanent homes and thus required extensive preparation. The cooperation and support from different archives, estates and foundations, including those of Charlotte Perriand, Le Corbusier, Harrison and Nelson Rockefeller, also had a decisive impact on both the exhibition and the catalog, grounding and contextualizing Léger's work.

The publication at hand is more than an exhibition catalog; without a doubt, it will become a standard work on Léger, examining the question of mural painting and the role of architecture in Léger's work for the first time. Katia Baudin has succeeded in persuading leading international experts to reflect on these issues for the catalog, and their contributions are complemented by primary source material. A representative selection of visuals capturing the interplay between Léger, three-dimensional spaces, and key architects completes this publication. We would like to thank the authors as well as the numerous individuals both inside and outside of the museum who worked on this publication, and who are mentioned by name on the Imprint page. Our particular gratitude also goes to the Hirmer Verlag, which enthusiastically included this book in its publications list.

We were privileged to work with major partners on the realization and funding of *Fernand Léger: Painting in Space*. We would firstly like to extend our thanks to the Peter and Irene Ludwig Foundation for their generous support of this exhibition. In addition to their prior extensive support for our acquisitions and exhibitions, the Peter and Irene Ludwig Foundation also made a substantial contribution towards making the exhibition on Léger possible. We are also grateful to RheinEnergie, which has provided us with invaluable support as a trusted partner for our jubilee year.

DS Automobiles recognized the importance of this project that links Germany and France, and made possible the restoration and incorporation of the significant wall mural *Transport des Forces* from the Palais de la Découverte in Paris, for which we extend our thanks. Furthermore, we thank the Friends of the Wallraf-Richartz Museum and the Museum Ludwig for supporting the exhibition financially, thus making an important contribution to the museum's appeal.

One of the first exhibition partners that we were able to welcome on board was the Gesellschaft für Moderne Kunst at the Museum Ludwig, and we would like to thank them for their unconventional help, offered at short notice. We would also like to thank the Bankhaus Sal. Oppenheim and Pesch International Interiors. Last but not least, we thank the Institut Français in Cologne/Düsseldorf for the productive cooperation.

Last but not least, our thanks go to the team at Museum Ludwig, who have mounted the Léger exhibition in our rooms with great dedication and competence. We also wish to thank Kathrin Michel, who assisted Katia Baudin with the preparations as Research and Curatorial Assistant. Our special thanks go to Tino Graß for his successful graphic design of the catalog and the exhibition graphics, which he approached with calm and engaged commitment. We are also most grateful to Meyer Voggenreiter and Nicole Hüttner for managing to develop an exhibition architecture that not only meets the specific demands of Léger's works, but also reflects his own delight in experimentation.

Yilmaz Dziewior
Director, Museum Ludwig

1 This mural was acquired from the Galerie Gmurzynska. Contemporary newspaper accounts make special mention of *Les Plongeurs*. The work was a sensation at Art Cologne that year and is said to have been the most expensive work on offer. More information is contained in the Museum Ludwig's archival files on the painting.
2 The Museum Ludwig was founded in 1976 and was at first housed in the Wallraf-Richartz Museum: this building by architect Rudolph Schwarz now houses the Museum für Angewandte Kunst (The Museum of Applied Arts). In 1986, both museums moved into a larger, new building; since 2001, this building has been occupied solely by the Museum Ludwig. The Wallraf-Richartz Museum is now housed in its own building designed by Oswald Mathias Ungers.

The Wall, The Architect, The Painter Introductory Remarks on *Fernand Léger: Painting in Space*

Katia Baudin

"C'est une entente à trois qu'il faut réaliser:
le mur – l'architecte – le peintre" Fernand Léger, 1933[1]

Fernand Léger: Painting in Space is the first major exhibition to focus on Léger's murals and on the role that architectural and spatial interests play in his work and his overall approach as a painter. The point of departure for this exhibition is the mural *Les Plongeurs* (1942), which the French artist painted for the Long Island home of American architect Wallace K. Harrison, and which was later acquired by Peter and Irene Ludwig for the Museum Ludwig's collection.

Léger (1881–1955), a prolific writer and theorist, generally contrasted the individualistic approach of easel painting with the collective approach of mural painting. Engaging with built spaces through painting was a major concern for the artist, who was an architectural draftsman by training. Léger developed close ties to key figures in modern architecture around the world, including Robert Mallet-Stevens, Le Corbusier, Charlotte Perriand, Paul Nelson, André Bruyère, Carlos Raúl Villanueva, and Wallace K. Harrison. He was an active member of several architectural and applied arts organizations, including Congrès Internationaux d'Architecture Moderne (CIAM), Union des Artistes Modernes (UAM) and the Groupe Espace.

Léger was the architects' ideal artistic collaborator and closest ally, and he welcomed the opportunity to collaborate on their projects. By bringing color to their white, neutral walls, he hoped to ensure the successful integration of modern architecture in society, and generally improve human lives through the social and psychological impact of color. His quest to extend painting beyond the limits of the easel and to integrate it within social spaces and the architecture of buildings is illustrated by a number of projects both realized and unrealized that reflect the various forms of collaboration between Léger and his architect friends.

Fernand Léger: Painting in Space traces the evolution of Léger's exploration of painting in space from the early 1920s until his unexpected death in 1955. The exhibition highlights Léger's temporary and permanent site-specific interventions in the public and private spheres, including houses, apartments, churches, a ship, public buildings, and world's fairs. It also features unrealized, lesser-known and experimental projects. For the first time, individual projects and murals are presented alongside related paintings, drawings, designs, and preliminary studies. Archival and source materials such as photographs, correspondence, and publications locate the projects within their historical context. In addition to its focus on the murals, the exhibition also includes selected early works by Léger in the fields of experimental film, graphic design, and theater and costume design. These projects help set the stage for Léger's mural practice, and demonstrate his interest in extending painting and color beyond the easel's limits.

The present publication aims to do more than "just" accompany the exhibition. Its goal is to contribute to scholarly research on Léger's mural practice and architecture-related projects, and thus to become a standard reference work on this subject. For, although a plethora of publications exist on the painter, none focuses on this central issue in Léger's work. Perusing this Léger reader will certainly be an eye-opener for many. A new Léger emerges, one close in spirit to De Stijl and the Bauhaus, who thrived when collaborating with choreographers, filmmakers, writers, architects, his own students, and others. This Léger called for a rekindling of the attitude and dialogue between painters, sculptors, and architects which gave birth to the great Gothic cathedrals. We discover an artist who transcended borders–literally working around the world–and made some of his most experimental and ambitious proposals when he was over the age of seventy. Many of his ideas were way ahead of their time–a cinematic mural, a polychrome village, a kinetic fountain–and his cut-and-paste method of working and composing his films, photomontages, paintings and murals reflect how current and contemporary Léger remains. The publication also crystallizes the importance of abstraction–which Léger considered particularly suited to mural practice–for an artist usually considered predominantly figurative and object-focused.

The publication is organized in four sections, generally–but not strictly–following a chronological order. Within these sections, we have invited international scholars to examine key aspects and issues: from the influence of stage-related projects, films and graphic design to the impact of the artist's social and political convictions on his practice as a muralist. A particular focus is placed on Léger's intellectual and creative dialogue with key modernist architects, and his ensuing collaborations in the realm of urbanism and architecture. The heart of the publication is doubtless the vast and fascinating selection of primary source documents–photographs, letters, texts by Léger and the other protagonists–few of which have been published in English. These archival documents rhythm the book, and plunge the reader back into Léger's day and age, bringing the painter and his contemporaries to life, and enabling us to view these murals and commissions through their eyes. We gain new insight into the creative process, development, and reception of these works, including some unforgettable behind-the-scenes moments.

Fernand Léger: Painting in Space calls for a reappraisal of Léger's work. It sheds new light on a painter who can truly be considered one of the most important and influential artists of the twentieth century. In his quest to carry painting and color beyond the museum into our everyday lives, Léger helped to make our world a less dreary place–bearing a noble message of hope which has lost none of its pertinence.

Letter from Fernand Léger to Le Corbusier, September 17, 1951

Dear Friend,

Received letter of the 6th.

Naturally, we didn't see each other again before leaving Biot. Marseille is far away and we had to leave. Your letter interests me a lot, but I believe you are mistaken about the Architect-Painter-Sculptor contact.

In my opinion, the request to collaborate should come from the Architect, and then it's in order. And I acknowledge that few major decisions have been made in this order.

I recapitulate my case:

I) Mallet-Stevens - Embassy project 1925
2) Herbst - decoration sports hall
3) Brussels exhibition 1934 or 6
4) Harrisson [sic], N.Y. Nelson Rockefeller apartment 1939
5) The two churches by Novarina - Assy - mosaic and Audincourt 16 stained-glass windows
6) Liège Nedogard
3 mosaic chapels monument to the American dead

That's the record–not much in the way of massive and guiding event–our friendship could have led to something, but nothing! There we are, Old Man, the story of a modern painter dropped into architecture for 30 years. I am impatiently waiting for your colorful layout in Marseille. Would it have been possible to widen your corridor by one meter? It would have become a boulevard!

Your rationalism is tight and impressive. The decisive event will be the behavior of the tenant there. I'm waiting for that as well–what about you?

Amigo Old Man. Building and see you soon

signed: F. LEGER

My regards to Yvonne.

Fondation Le Corbusier, Paris.

–

1 Quoted from "Le mur, l'architecte, le peintre" (1933) in *Fonctions de la peinture* (Paris: Gallimard, 2004), 182, translated as "The Wall, the Architect, the Painter," in Fernand Léger, *Functions of Painting*, trans. Alexandra Anderson (London: Thames and Hudson, 1973), 97: "An agreement between the three parties needs to be reached: the wall - the architect - the painter."

Film, Sets and Graphics

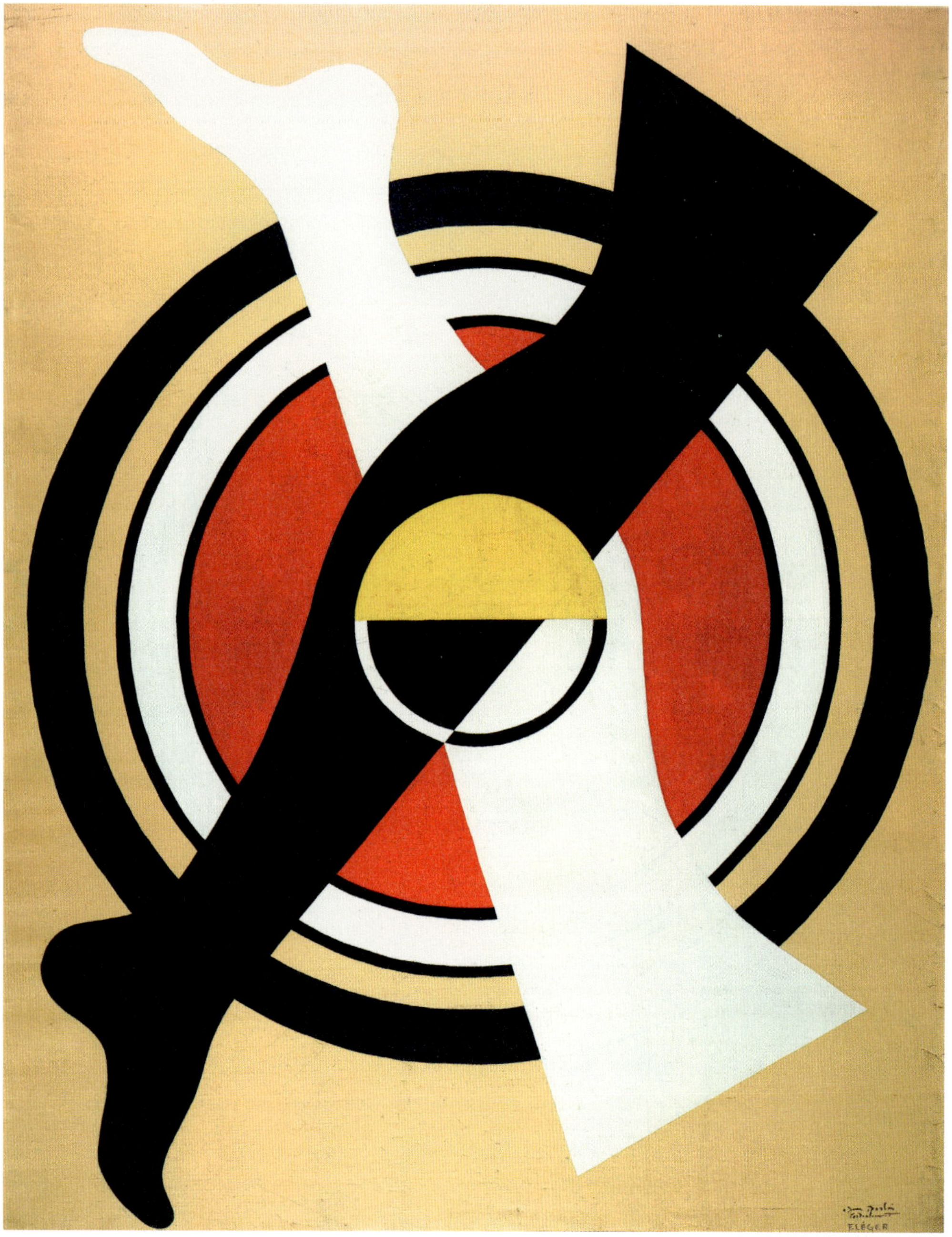

1

1 ***Hommage à la danse***
(Homage to Dance), 1925
Oil on canvas
158.5 × 120.5 cm
Collection Galerie Maeght, Paris

From the Flatness of Painting to the Frontality of Theater and Film
By Giovanni Lista

In the early 1920s, the Cubo-Futurist painting of Fernand Léger's mechanical period led to paintings like *Le Mécanicien* (The Mechanic) or *Les Disques dans la Ville* (Disks in the City), which are triumphs of the flatness of the painted surface, a surface saturated by the close imbrication of geometrized elements that fit together like the gears of a machine. Léger also did the page layout and typography for his friend Blaise Cendrars's novel *La Fin du Monde Filmée par l'Ange Notre-Dame* (The End of the World, Filmed by the Angel Notre-Dame), and then the illustrations for Yvan Goll's poem "La Chaplinade" (The Chapliniad), in which the rhythmic succession of images results in a visual articulation of movement. The alternation or metric succession of static images that takes place materially as the book's pages are read amounts to a mastering of the temporality of visual experience.

In 1921, Léger worked on the animated film *Charlot Cubiste* (Cubist Charlie Chaplin), for which he used flat wooden pieces painted in solid colors to construct a two-dimensional marionette whose movements all take place in a single plane. The film, however, was never completed. Shortly thereafter, Rolf de Maré's Ballets Suédois offered the artist his first opportunity to put his explorations of scenography into practice, explorations focused entirely on a frontal and pictorial approach to the stage, as if it went without saying that the concrete, three-dimensional space of the stage had to be reduced to the "flatness" exalted by his mechanical paintings.

Based on a poem by Ricciotto Canudo and with music by Arthur Honegger, the ballet *Skating Rink*, which premiered on January 20, 1922, is set in the skating rink of a big city. It presents a fleeting encounter between the characters of the Madman and the Woman amid the swirl of skaters. Léger succeeds in imposing his strong and vigorous style, reinterpreting Canudo's pantheistic Unanimism in terms of the vitality and contrasts of the urban crowd. He creates a dynamism of visual dissonances, with sudden changes of tone and abrupt breaks in rhythm. His poetics of theater-as-painting leads him to neutralize the individual and autonomous movement of the dancers, whom he organizes into parallel masses of contrasting colors. In this way, he takes total control of the theatrical event.

Léger used padding to create costumes with highly exaggerated forms, in which the men's square shoulders and extremely bulky torsos contrast with their short legs, made rigid by kneepads. The women's ample costumes are equally rigid; they resemble matryoshkas, those Russian dolls with rounded forms and heavily made-up, expressionless eyes. Movement is incorporated into the costumes themselves through the asymmetry of their geometric motifs, the dynamic slant of their stripes, and the disequilibrium of their large fields of bright solid color, which recall cardboard cut-out silhouettes for children or the enormous advertising posters of the city streets. In the case of the Madman, Léger dismantles the figure's anthropomorphic structure through the asymmetry of the shapes and motifs of his costume: a jacket with an extremely eccentric cut; pants that are visually bisected, with one leg checked and the other striped; a highly elaborate, geometric make-up design; and a bright red scarf. The ballet's characters thus become multicolored elements that glide around the stage, organizing and reorganizing themselves like the pictorial values of a painting, structured by the schemas of a pictural composition in constant motion.

By using techniques that are essentially pictorial, Léger banishes all perspective and forgoes any attempt to organize the depth of the theatrical space. He makes no use of diagonal paths across the stage and avoids any multidirectional movements or internal exchanges between the characters themselves. He seeks only to intensify the ballet's play of shapes and colors by inscribing them on a virtual plane that is lined up in front of an enormous abstract backdrop at the rear of the stage. Conceived in terms of the self-referential interaction of colors and geometric shapes, the curtain, scenic action, and decor are simply stacked one in front of the other like staggered planes. In effect, the scenery is merely a container for the choreographic arabesque that unfolds frontally and with maximum visual intensity.

The ballet *La Création du Monde* (The Creation of the World) has a libretto by Cendrars and a score by Darius Milhaud and was first performed on October 25, 1923; it reflects the craze for African art that developed at the end of World War I. Having ignored African art in his Cubo-Futurist paintings, Léger decided to combine the archaic qualities of African art with the most revolutionary formal innovations of his own work. He began by drawing flattened sketches of the characters, eliminating any effect of relief and suggesting space only through the advance and retreat of the solid fields of color. Into these simplified forms, he then incorporated the compositional elements of his Cubo-Futurist style. The figures of African mythology are realized in a static and abstract manner by collections of elements at right angles, by a clean, uncluttered geometrism of volumes, with simple, solid structures that seek to separate and clarify or even sublimate the formal elements of an archaic primitive art. In this way, the irregularities, life force, and magical aura of African art are neutralized by a highly controlled "style" that is at once modern, monumental, and decorative.

For the backdrop, Léger drew heavy, black-rimmed clouds above a landscape of plates frozen in a kind of geotectonic disequilibrium produced by the cataclysm from before the emergence of life. The various sketches for the three gods, all eight meters tall, clearly reflect the process of taking the disparate elements of African statuary and assembling them like machines. Thus, Léger chose to use the kind of sculpted cardboard costumes previously employed by Picasso, Schlemmer, and Depero to turn the dancers into so many mobile African sculptures. Aiming for complete control and mechanization of the choreographic vocabulary, he dresses the dancers in sumptuous African fabrics that evoke the demigods, then perches them on stilts, thus effectively turning them into marionettes.

The entire stage participates in the logic of the spectacle. Yet Léger makes no attempt to free himself from his obsession with the plane. Although he conceives of the stage as a "visual whole" and thus aligns himself with the defining principle of modern scenography, he neglects to formalize the theatrical space at its most concrete and tangible level, failing to activate the third dimension or any lines that cross the internal physical space of the stage. On the other hand, he increases the closed character of that space by staggering and overlapping the movable screens—the silhouettes, masks, and shields that slowly advance toward the spectators. He also employs a series of borders and side panels with abstract decorative patterns to punctuate the staggered planes that structure the visual rhythm of the spectacle.

The stage openly avows its status as an animated painting, lacking any real articulation of its depth. The scenographic composition seems to be continuously represented on a frontal plane ideally defined by the frame of the stage and subject to the variations of a kineticism that combines the shapes in various ways but always on a plane that is parallel to the stage opening. Léger thus achieves a pictorial definition of the theatrical space that is in every respect identical to that of his Cubo-Futurist paintings, which play with the contrast between two-dimensional surfaces and round forms in motion. Despite the thoroughly "African" dimension of the spectacle, the scenographic formalization hews to the principles of the mechanical theater that were simultaneously being elaborated at the Bauhaus. The rigor of Léger's work for *La Création du Monde* makes it one of the most uncompromising experiments with that pictorialization of the stage that inspired so many productions by the historical avant-garde.

In 1923, Marcel L'Herbier enlisted Léger to design the machines and interiors of the laboratory of Einar Norsen, the deuteragonist of his film *L'Inhumaine* (The Inhuman Woman), which sought to unite in a single work all of the most advanced experiments underway in the decorative arts. Léger produced sketches of interconnected machines in two dimensions. L'Herbier reacted with skepticism to the "representation of an entire mechanical forest in a single plane: trees on wheels with conical trunks and levers for branches. No floors, no walls, no ceilings..."[1] Léger went on to construct the forms of the laboratory, spreading out abstract geometric elements within the space—semicircles, levers, overlapping triangles, rectangles, grids, and rows of indicator lights—which, taken together, represent the laboratory's mechanomorphic structure.

The sequence in which Norsen brings the woman he loves back to life in the laboratory embodies the new dramatic values inherent in scientific mythology and in the energy and splendor of the machine. It is a crescendo of overlapping images, its feverish, pulsating rhythm governed by the metronomic back and forth of a swinging pendulum. And this sequence of *L'Inhumaine* seems to contain the formal template for *Ballet mécanique* (Mechanical Ballet), the film made not long after by Léger and Dudley Murphy.

Completed in September 1924, the film *Ballet mécanique* is an attempt to radicalize the spectacular values of the machine as such. In it, everything—from inert things to the organic life of the human body, from geometric figures to objects in motion—becomes a rhythmic mechanism, a form at once concrete and abstract, swept up in a visual movement that eschews all linear progression. The film's underlying principle is a repetitive dynamism in which all movement is expressed as a segment interrupted and continually resumed. In this way, the image is inscribed in time while still rejecting progression as well as permanence. The kinetic event, which sets up a kind of vital pulse, gives access to nothing more than its own constitutive truth: the machine in action. Léger embraces the linguistic specificity of cinema, laying bare the mechanics of editing in contrast to the *narratum* as a vehicle for expression. Yet at the same time, he eliminates any mobility on the part of the camera, despite the fact that it represents an important element of cinema as a language.

Flattening out the visual field in terms of its depth as well as its breadth, the film uses various effects of fragmentation and mechanization of the image in order to present itself as pure rhythm, accessing matter through a constant pulse that effectively negates the object's instrumental value. Bottles, disks, shiny balls, hats, and saucepans—almost all of them typical objects of the industrial aesthetic exalted by the Purism of *L'Esprit Nouveau*—are treated in the film as simple visual elements. The editing no longer seeks to lend logic and narrative continuity to the image but stands in the service of a quantitative accumulation that provides the rhythms of a composition in motion.

The dazzling close-up becomes an end in itself, since detail follows detail without ever pointing to a larger overall view. The rhythmic sequence involves an alternation between the flickering of the object within the image and the flickering of the image itself, the result of a jerky, metrical editing approach that constantly breaks up the shots. In other words, Léger employs physical objects only in order to transcend them in terms of mechanical energy. At the same time, he reduces editing to a mere vehicle for adding rhythm to the image. The movement of the film is exactly what its title suggests: that of a dance, a dance of machines.

The visual rhythm of the film is primarily that of an elastic movement reverting to its starting point, which takes place both inside and outside the image. Another aspect of its rhythm is supplied by the visual effects, which highlight the mechanical nature of the process of human perception. Léger employs the original technique of stop-motion animation, in which inert objects (in this case bottles of wine) appear to move rather than actually being set in motion.

And he uses balls with reflective surfaces to trick the viewers by presenting a mirror image of their gaze.

Modern painting sought to access the ultimate truth of its own material status by reducing itself to a flatness that echoed the surface of the canvas. Léger endeavored to transpose this principle to theater and cinema. Thus, he rigorously and energetically decomposed these two arts of temporal unfolding into their elementary constituent parts. Despite the fact that he sought to approach theater and cinema in terms of the kinetic values of the machine, he conceived them in a rigid and primitive way. The spectacle was to have the energetic impact of a painting in motion on a grand scale. By eliminating all diagonal lines from the scenic action along with all internal, relational, and multi-directional exchanges between the characters and objects involved in the spectacle, he instituted the strict frontality of a face-to-face encounter that invites the viewer to experience it in an immediate act of sensory perception. In effect, the spectators find themselves deprived of all possibility of retreating or reflecting, since the spectacle addresses them in a primal, archaic, and absolute manner, like Medusa's gaze. Léger sought to return the theater and cinema of the modern age to the force and fascination of their origins, when the act of scenic representation was characterized by mystery, tragic vision, and myth.

1 Reported by Jacques Catelain, the actor who played engineer Einar Norsen in the film; see *Jacques Catelain présente Marcel L'Herbier* (Paris: Vautrin, 1950), 76.

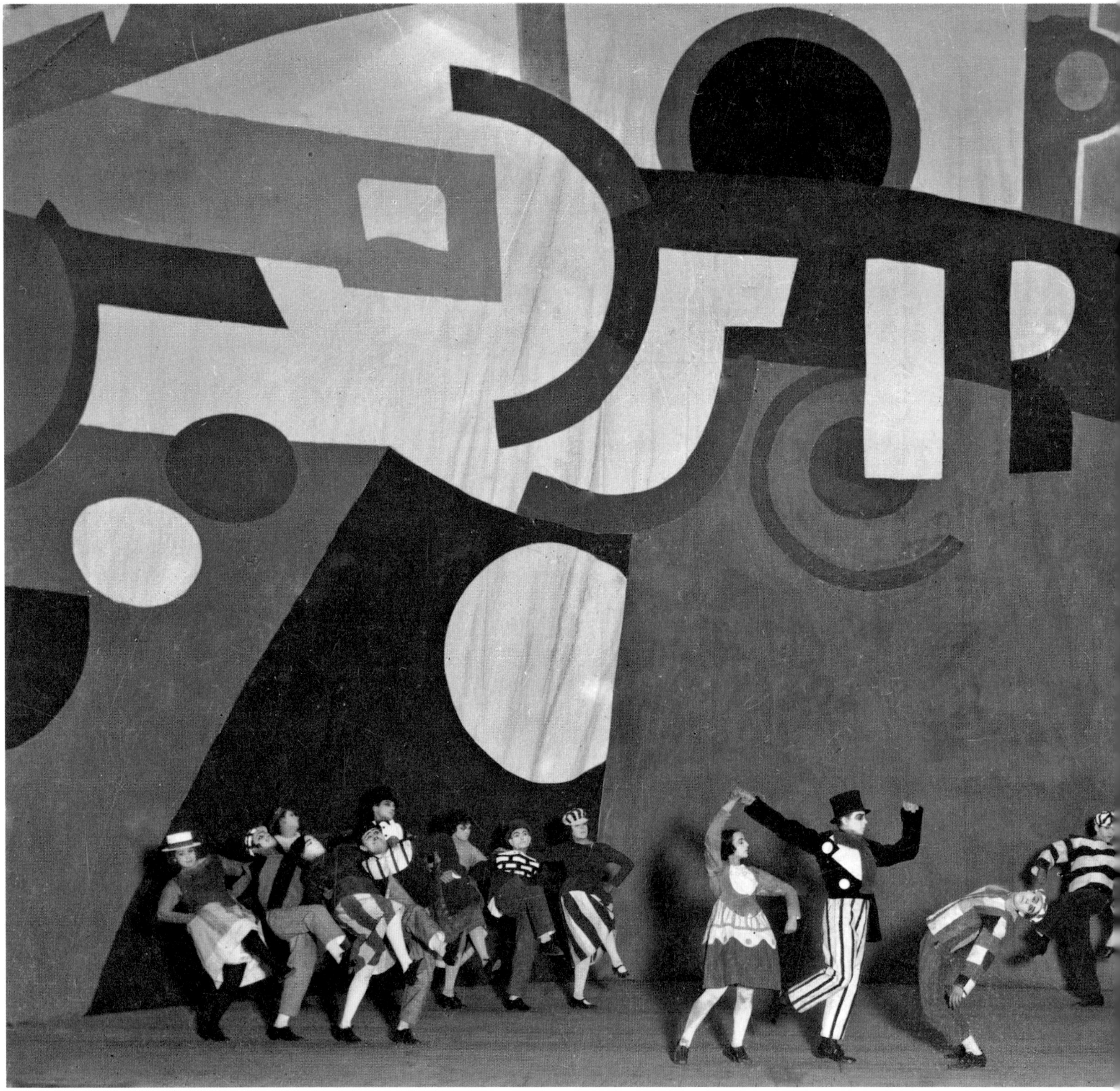

2

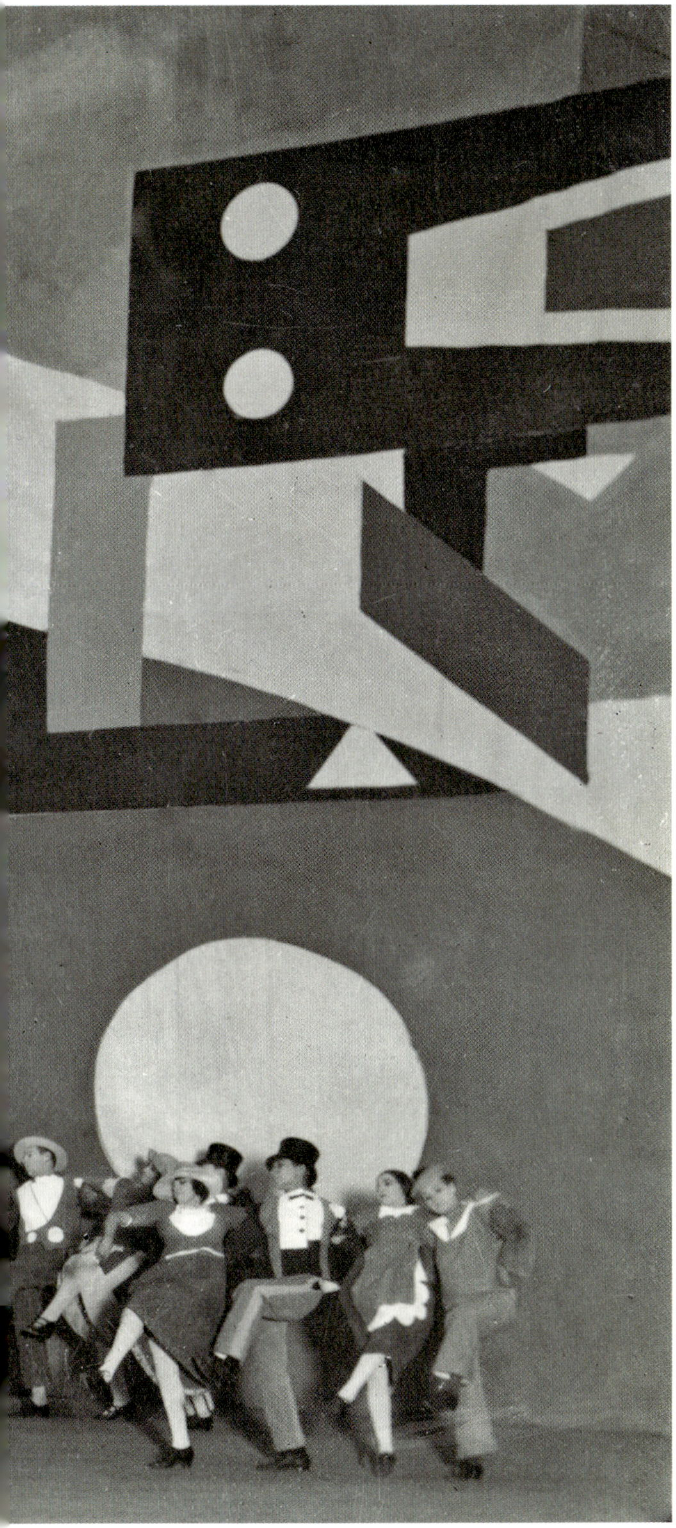

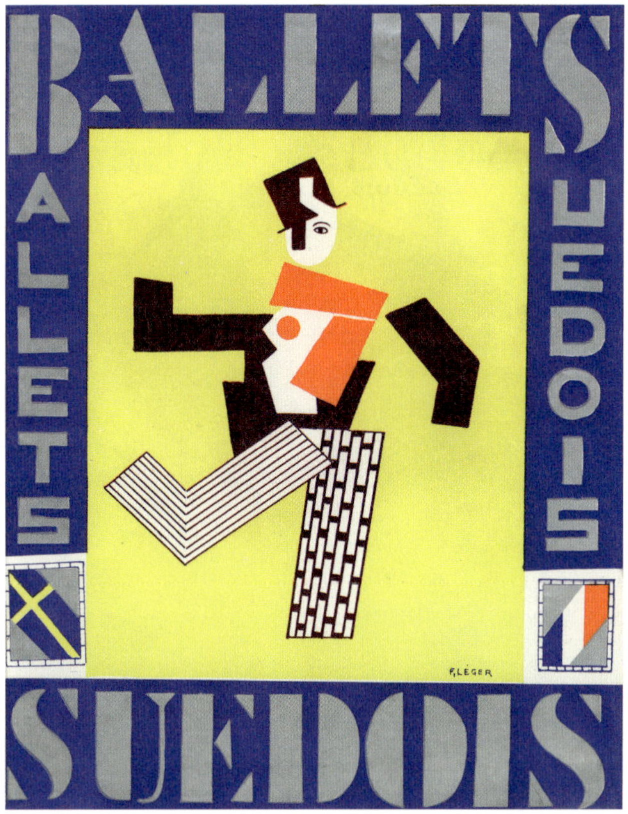

3

2 **Performance of *Skating Rink* by Ballets Suédois, 1922**
Choreography: Jean Börlin;
set design, costumes: Fernand Léger;
music: Arthur Honegger;
libretto: Ricciotto Canudo
Dansmuseet, Stockholm

3 **Cover of program for Ballets Suédois, *Skating Rink,* 1922**
32 × 24.5 cm
Dansmuseet, Stockholm

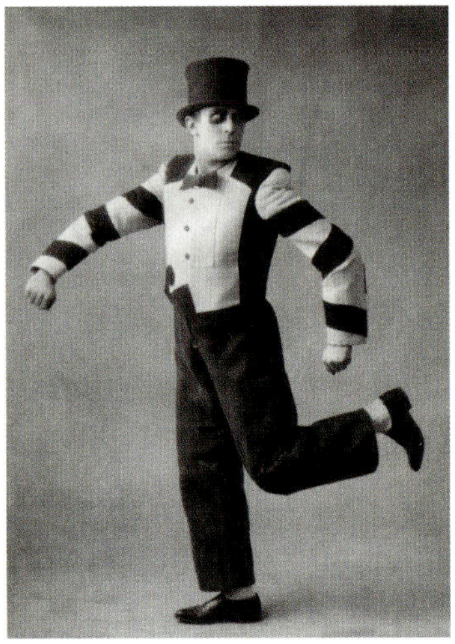
4

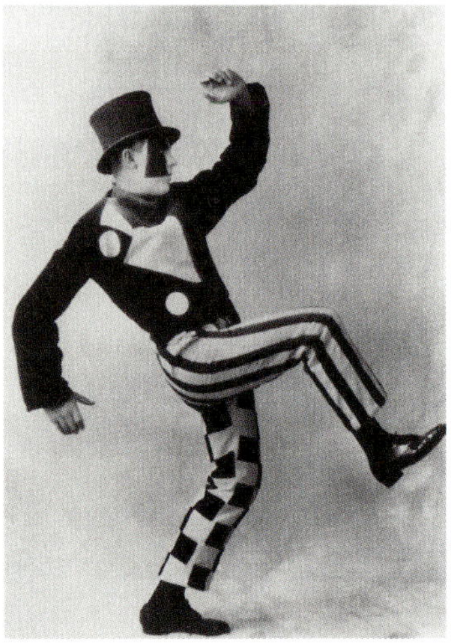
5

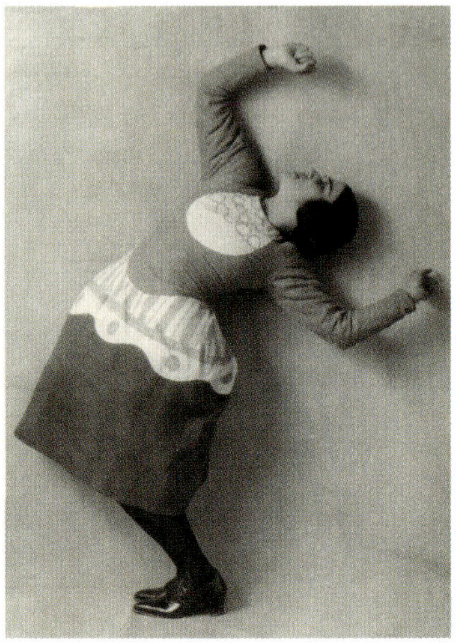
6

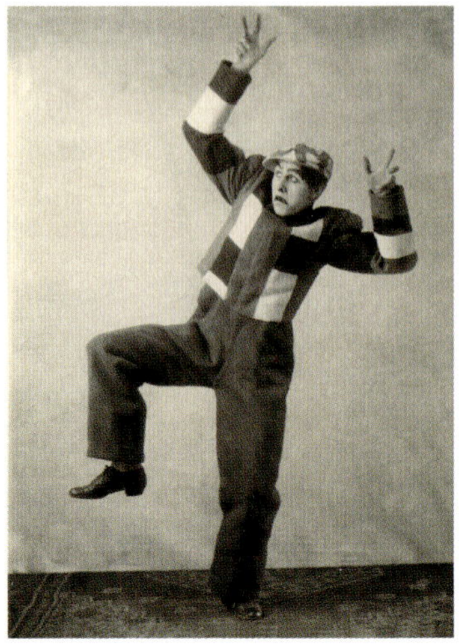
7

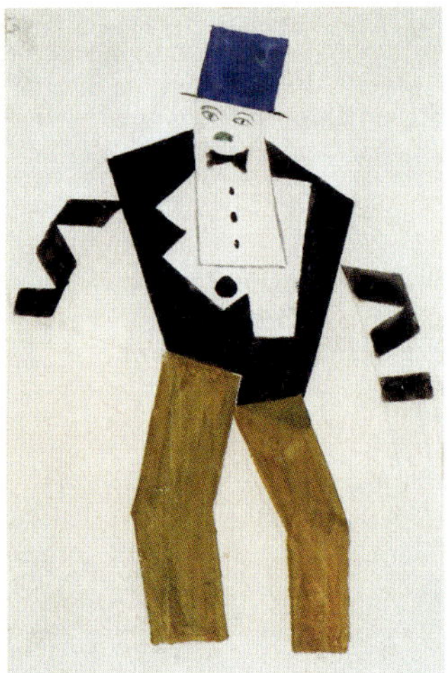
8

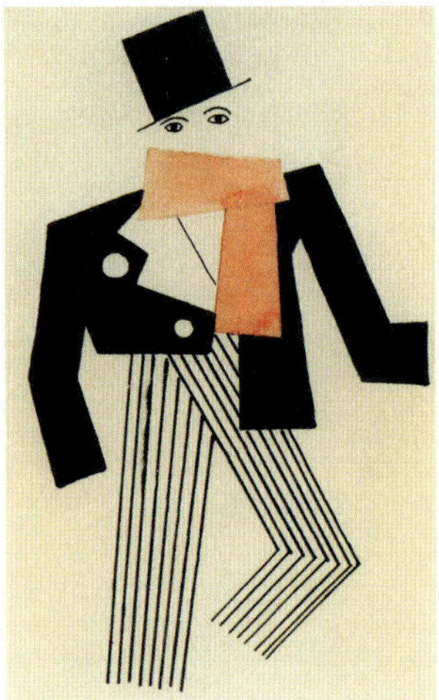
9

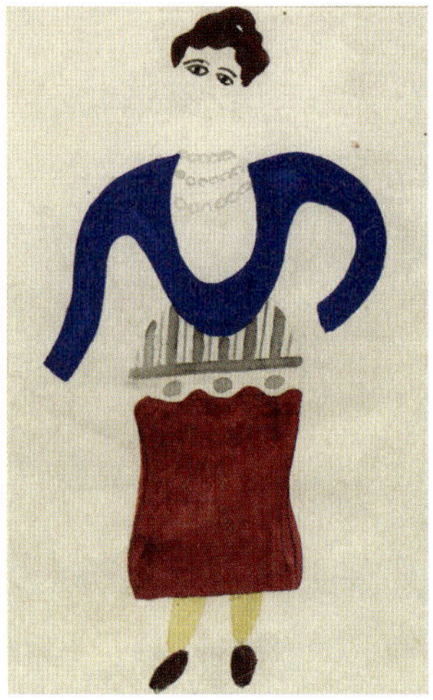
10

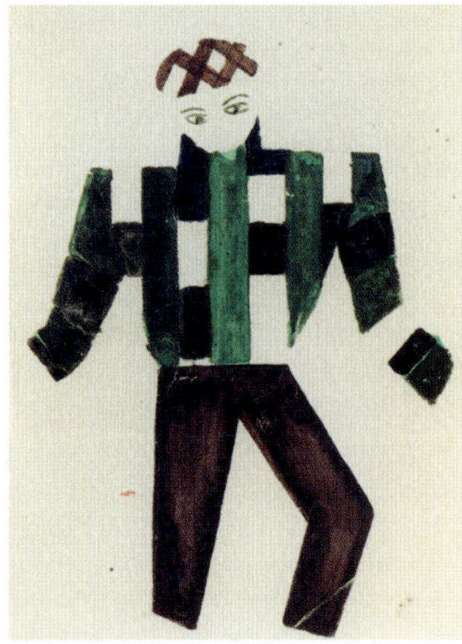
11

4 **Paul Eltorp**

5 **Jean Börlin as the Madman**

6 **Ebon Strandin as the Woman**

7 **Kaj Smith as the Man**

in *Skating Rink*, 1922
Dansmuseet, Stockholm

8 **Costume design for the Man in blue top hat in *Skating Rink*, 1921**
Graphite, watercolor, gouache
and India ink on paper
25 × 16 cm
Dansmuseet, Stockholm

9 **Costume design for Jean Börlin as the Madman in *Skating Rink*, 1921**
Graphite, watercolor, and India ink on paper
30 × 18 cm
Dansmuseet, Stockholm

10 **Costume design for the Woman in red skirt and blue top in *Skating Rink*, 1922**
Graphite, watercolor, gouache
and India ink on paper
25 × 17 cm
Dansmuseet, Stockholm

11 **Costume design for the Man in checked hat and green and brown costume in *Skating Rink*, 1921**
Graphite, watercolor and gouache on paper
22.5 × 14.5 cm
Dansmuseet, Stockholm

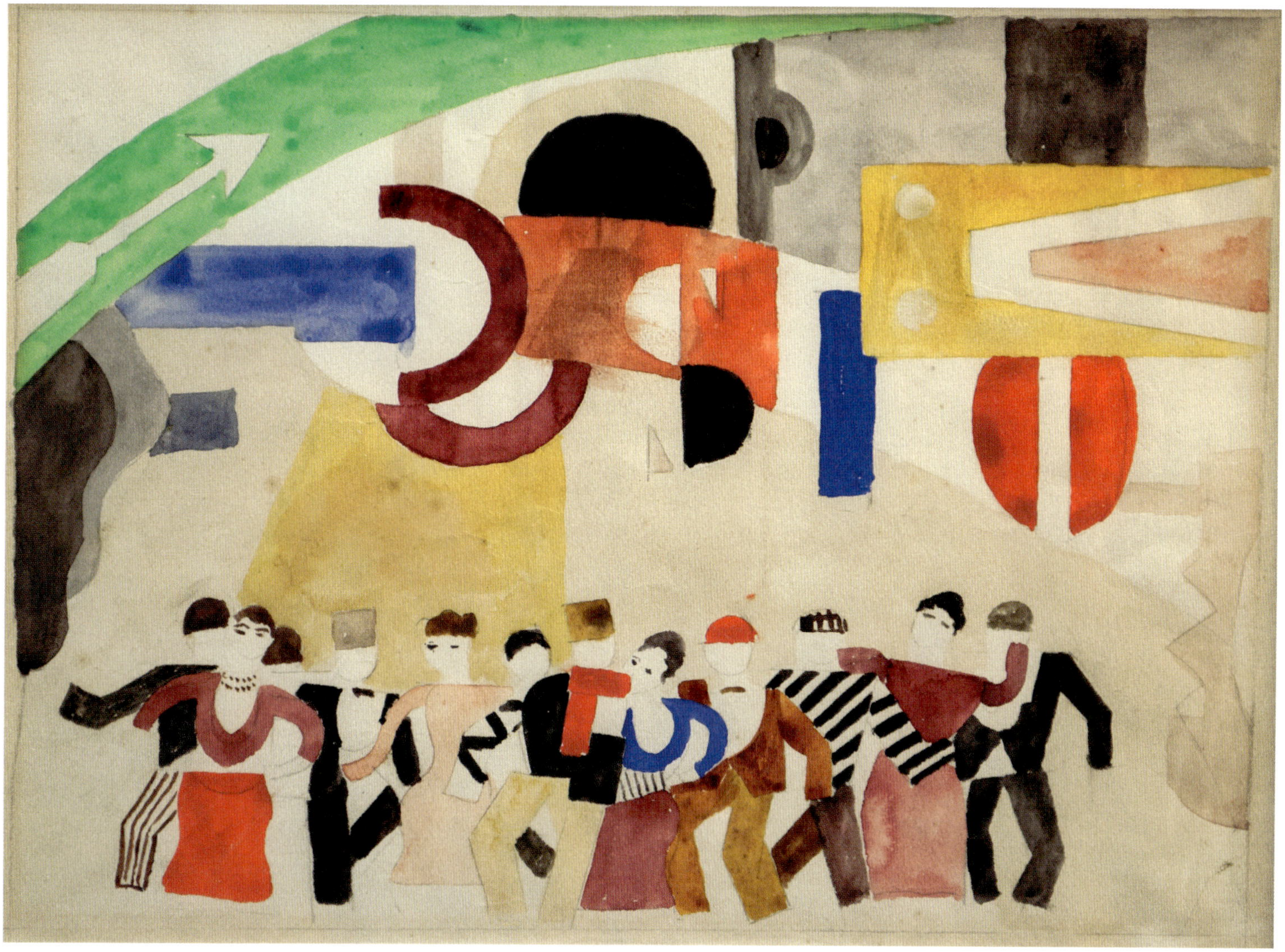

12

12 **Set design for *Skating Rink*, 1921**
Graphite and watercolor on paper
23.5 × 31.5 cm
Dansmuseet, Stockholm

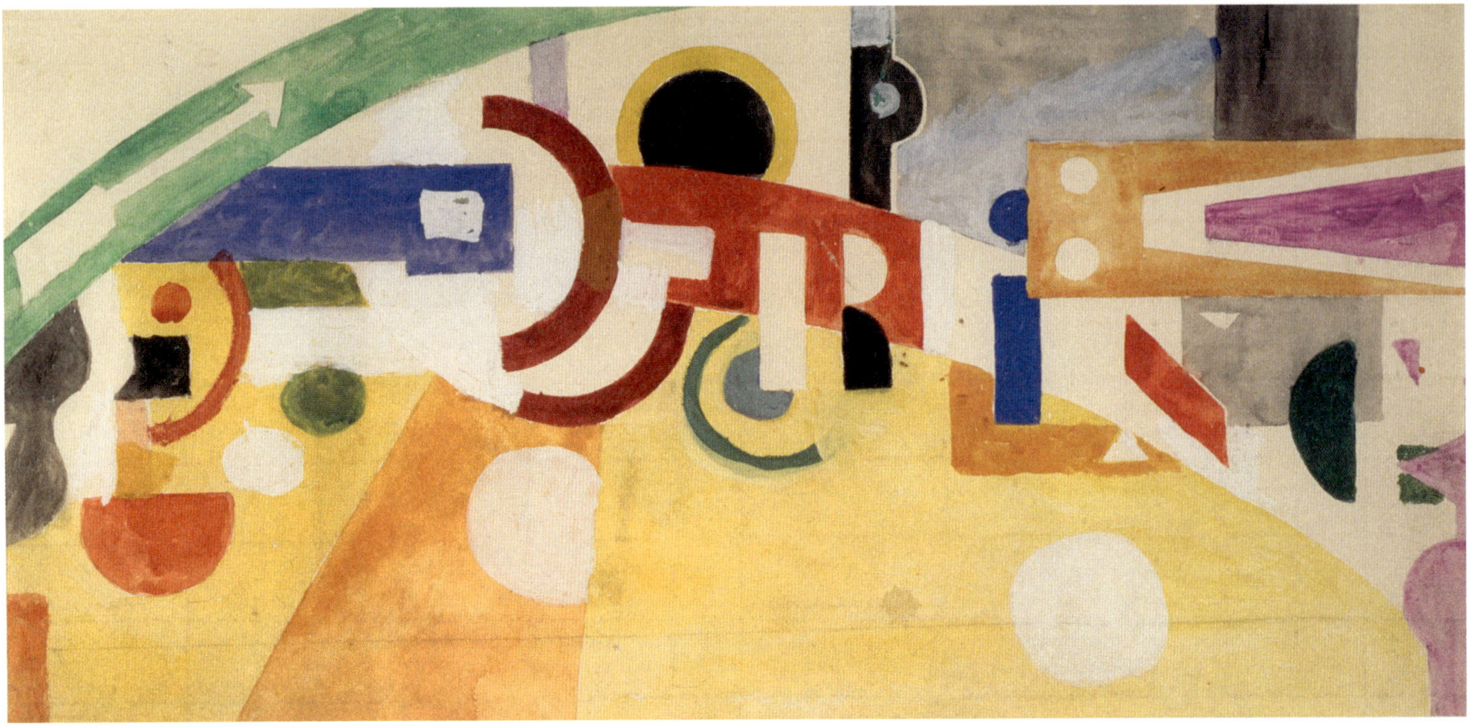

13

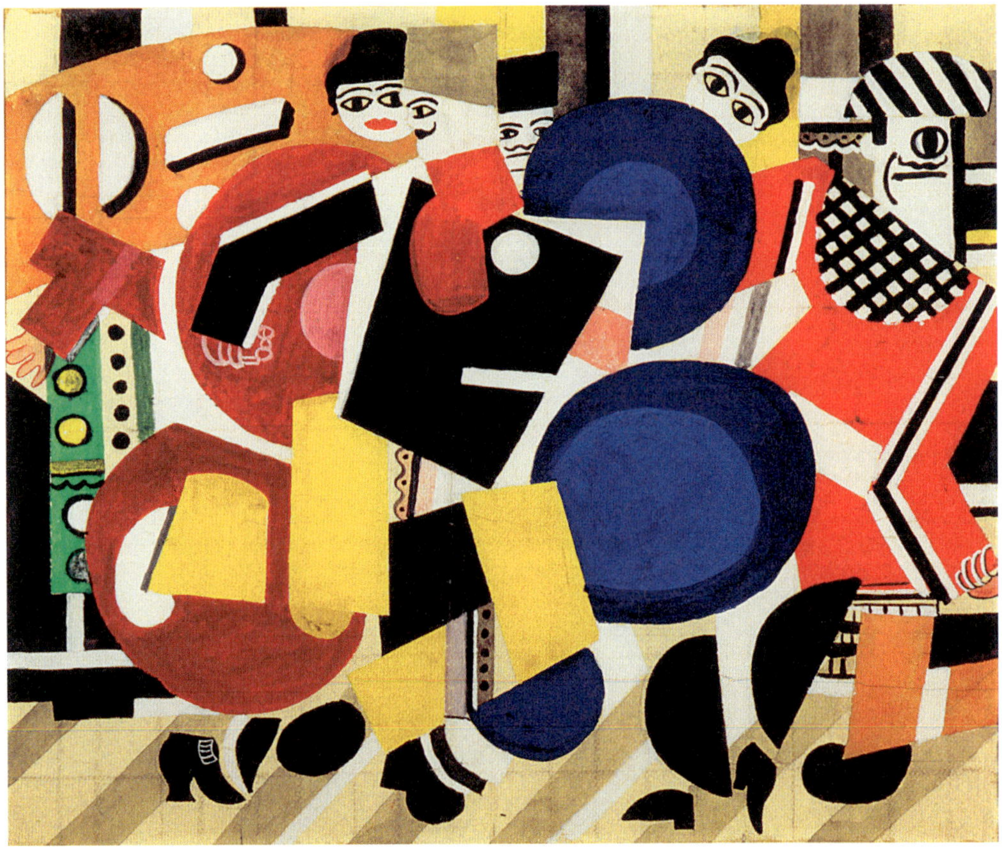

14

13 **Backdrop design for *Skating Rink,* 1922**
Graphite, watercolor, gouache and India ink on paper
29 × 60 cm
Dansmuseet, Stockholm

14 **Curtain design for *Skating Rink,* 1921**
Graphite, watercolor, gouache and India ink on paper
41.5 × 49 cm
Dansmuseet, Stockholm

15 **Sketch for back cover of program Stockholm-Paris, 1923**
Pencil, watercolor, gouache and India ink on paper
32.5 × 24.5 cm
Dansmuseet, Stockholm

16 ***Skating Rink, Danseuses, rideau de scène pour le ballet* (Skating Rink, Dancers, Stage Curtain for the Ballet), 1922–24**
Gouache on paper
22.5 × 24 cm
Collection Galerie Maeght, Paris

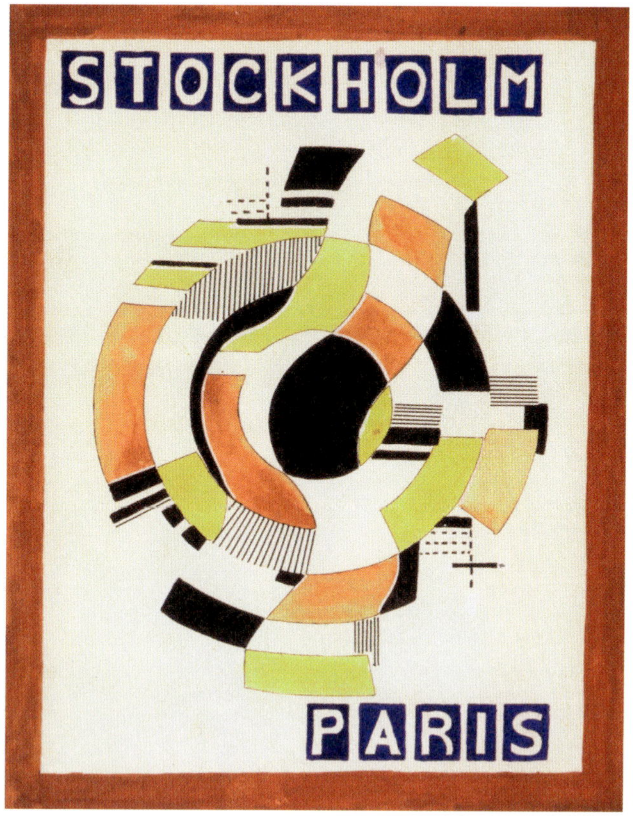

15

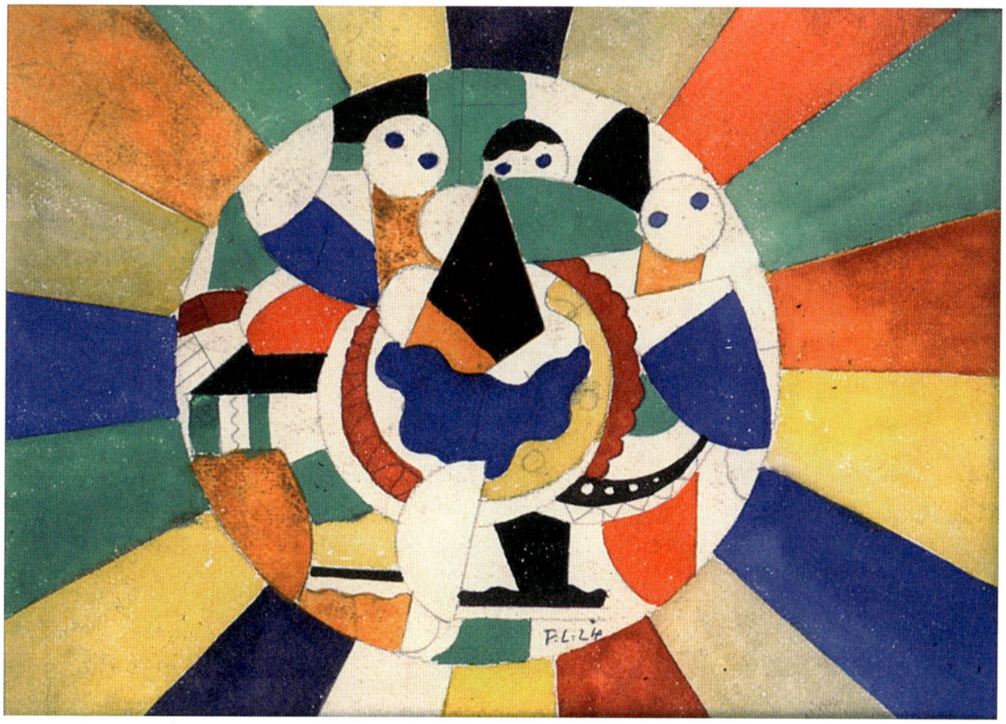

16

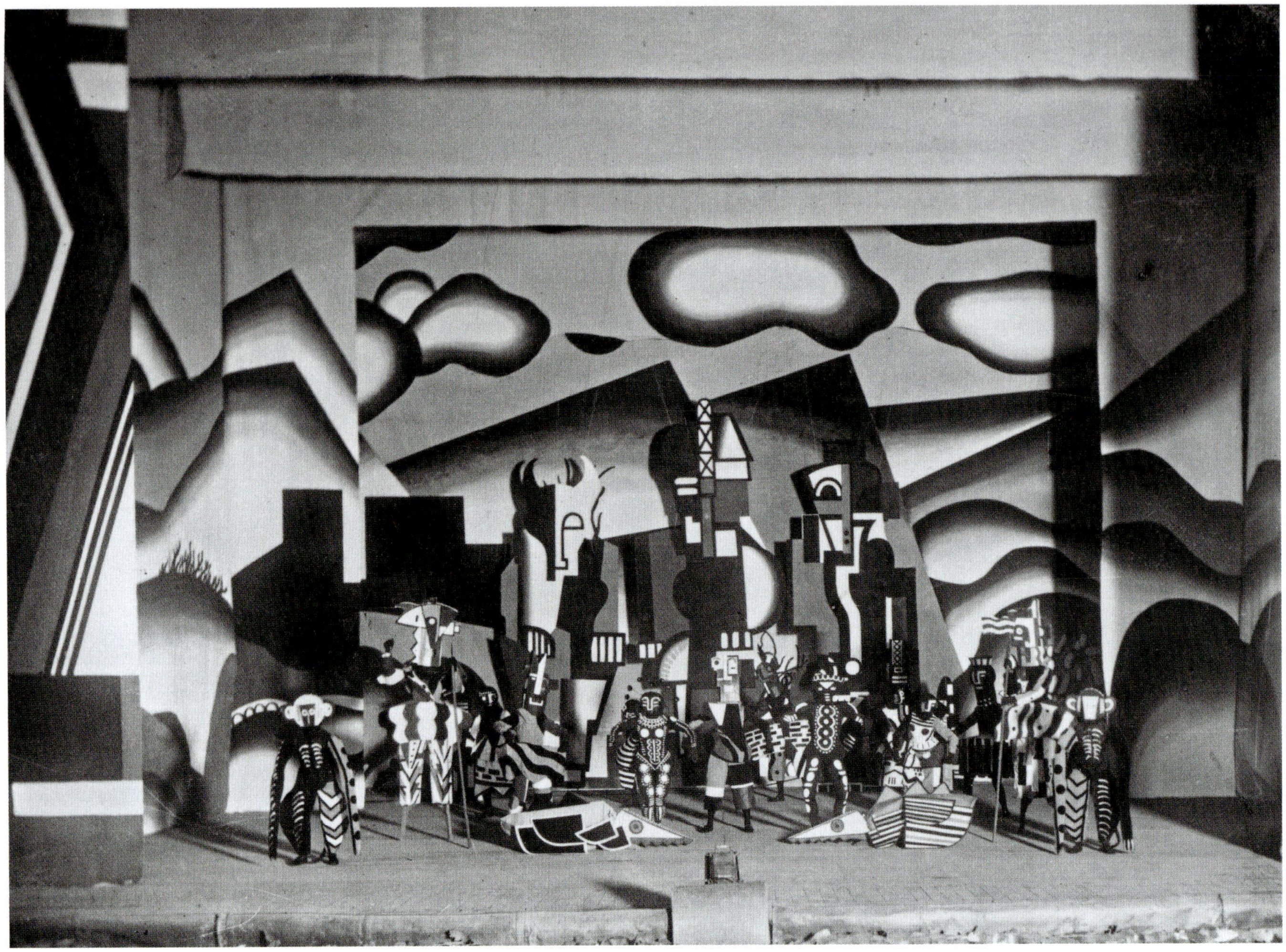

17

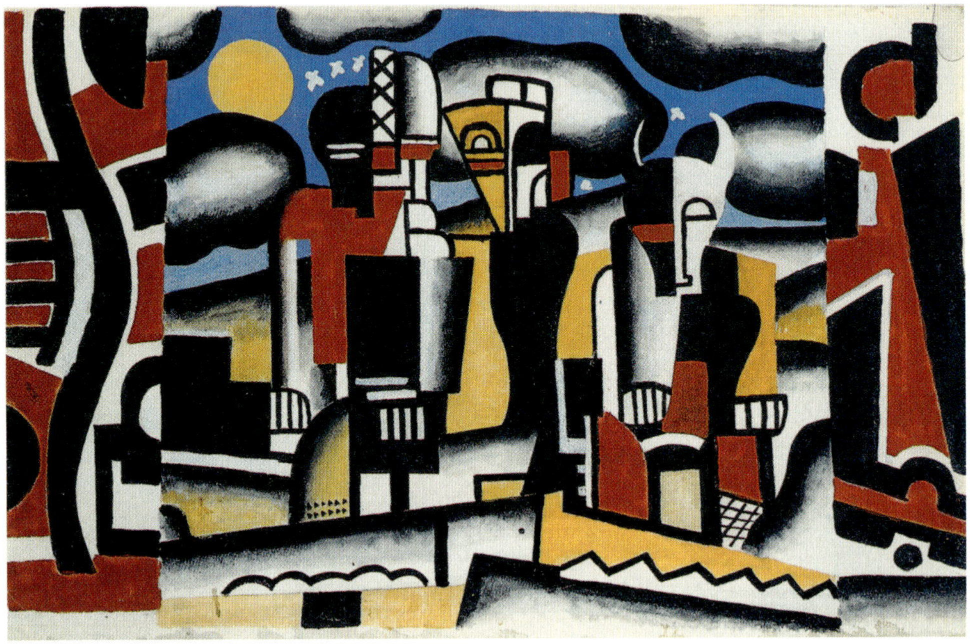

18

17 **Performance of *La Création du monde* (The Creation of the World), 1923**
Choreography: Jean Börlin;
curtains, set design, costumes: Fernand Léger;
music: Darius Milhaud;
libretto: Blaise Cendrars;
dancers: Jean Börlin (the Man),
Ebon Strandin (the Woman)

18 **Set design with godlike figures for *La Création du monde* (The Creation of the World), 1923**
Graphite, watercolor, gouache and India ink on paper
42 × 63 cm
Dansmuseet, Stockholm

19 **The artistic collaborators for *La Création du monde* (The Creation of the World), photographed on the set for *L'Homme et son désir* (The Man and his Desire), Paris, 1923**
(L-R): Jean Börlin, Fernand Léger, below: Darius Milhaud, Blaise Cendrars, Rolf de Maré, Martin Raynal
Dansmuseet, Stockholm

20 **Fernand Léger and Rolf de Maré at the Bal Musette, Paris, 1921**
Dansmuseet, Stockholm

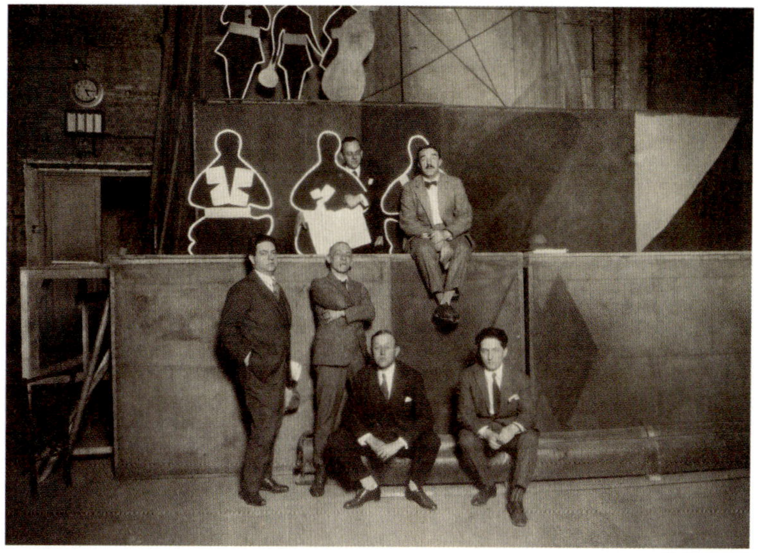

19

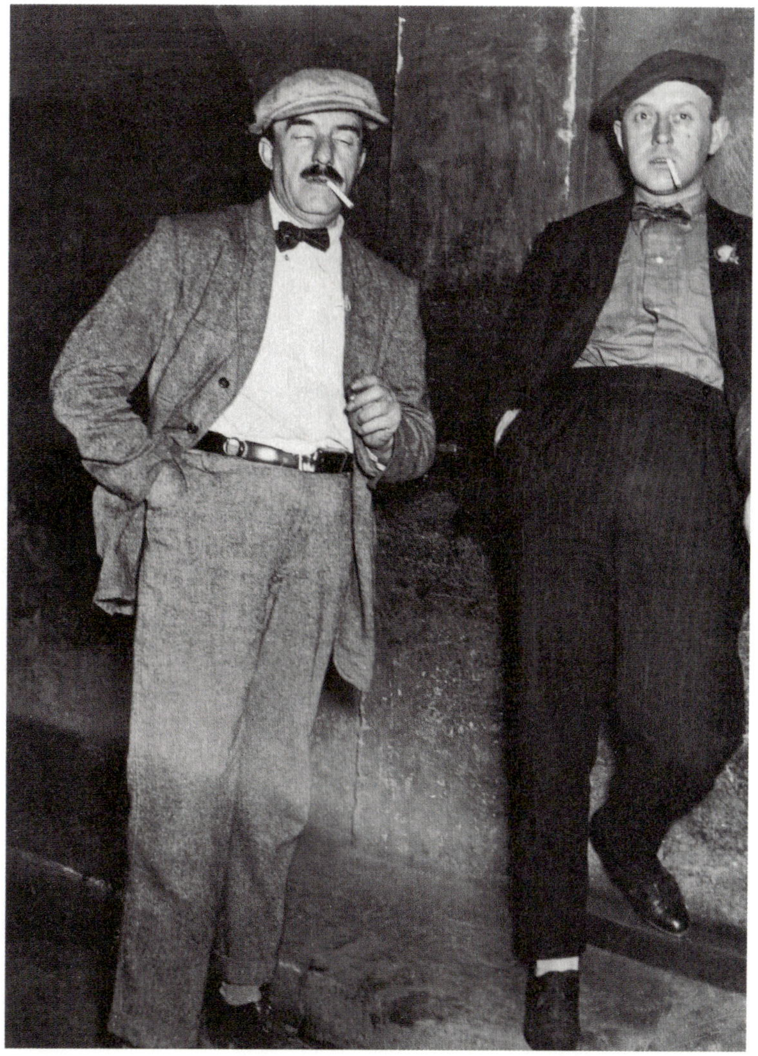

20

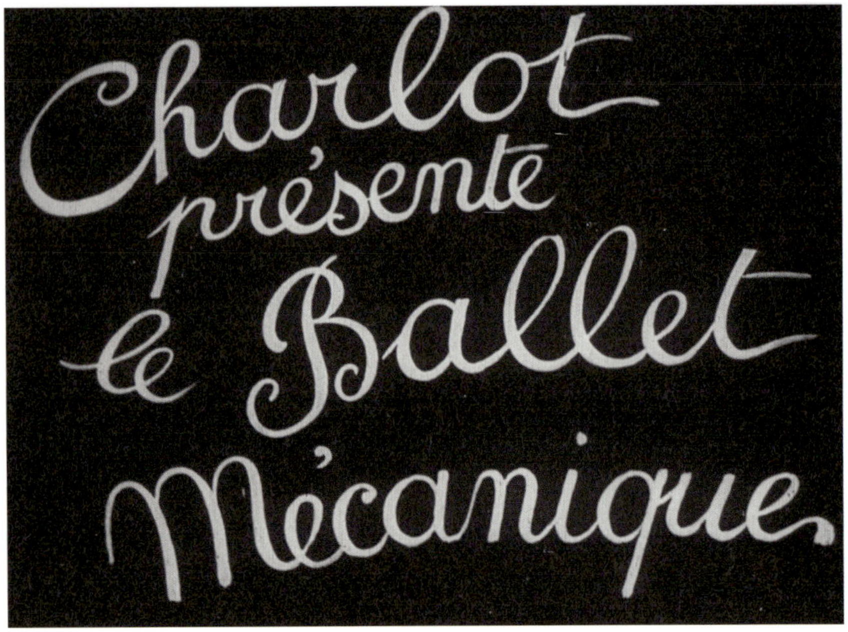

21

21 Fernand Léger in collaboration with Dudley Murphy
Le Ballet mécanique (version Kiesler)
(The Mechanical Ballet, [Kiesler version]), 1923/24
35mm film, black and white, silent
19 min 50 sec
Centre Pompidou, Musée national d'art moderne, Paris

22 Fernand Léger in collaboration with Dudley Murphy
Le Ballet mécanique (version Filmmuseum)
(The Mechanical Ballet [film museum version]), 1923/24
35mm film, black and white, colorized, silent
17 min, Film stills
Centre Pompidou, Musée national d'art moderne, Paris

23 ***Charlot cubiste* (Cubist Charlie Chaplin), 1924**
Montage on wood
70 × 30 × 5 cm
Musée Pierre-Noël, Saint-Dié-des-Vosges

22

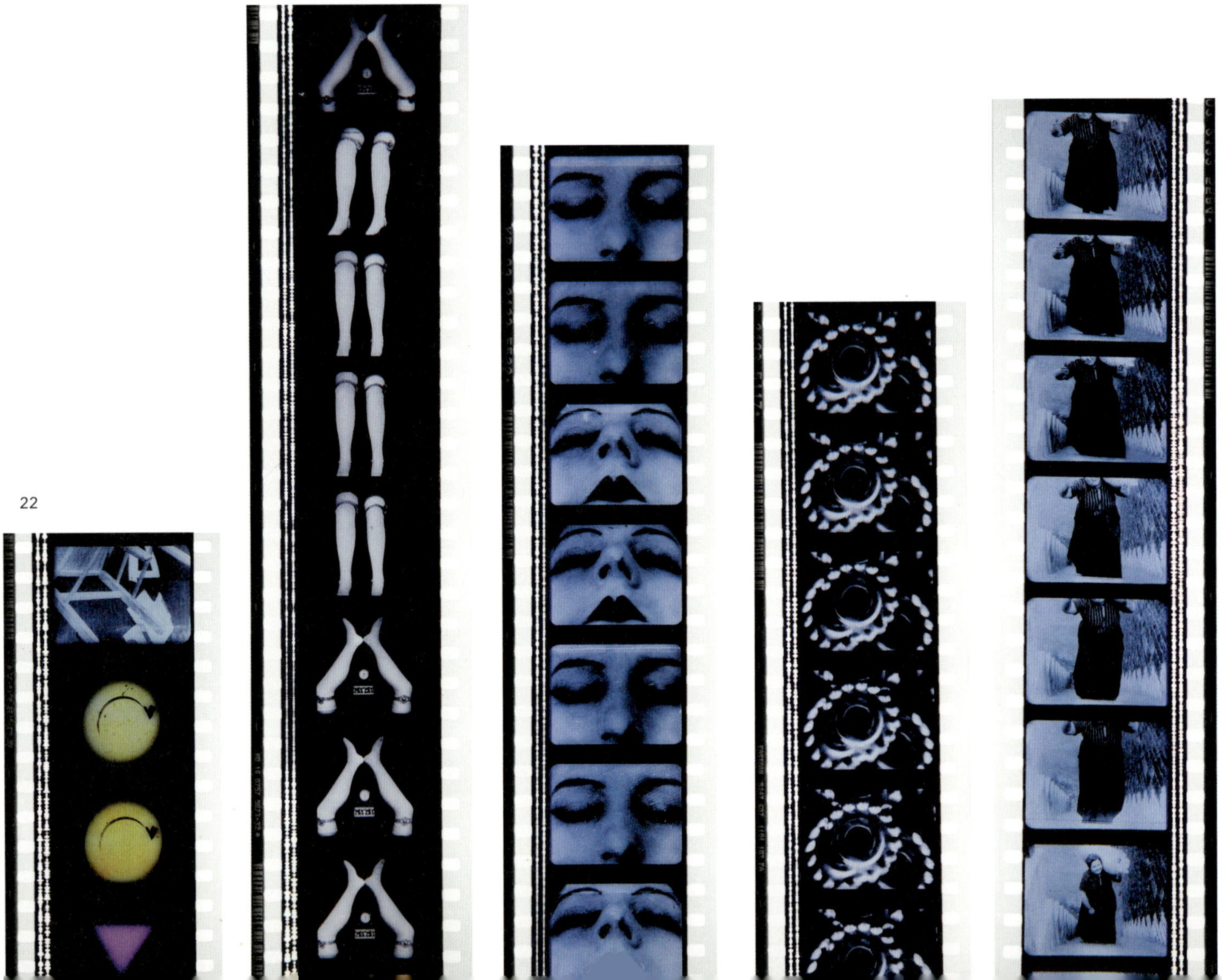

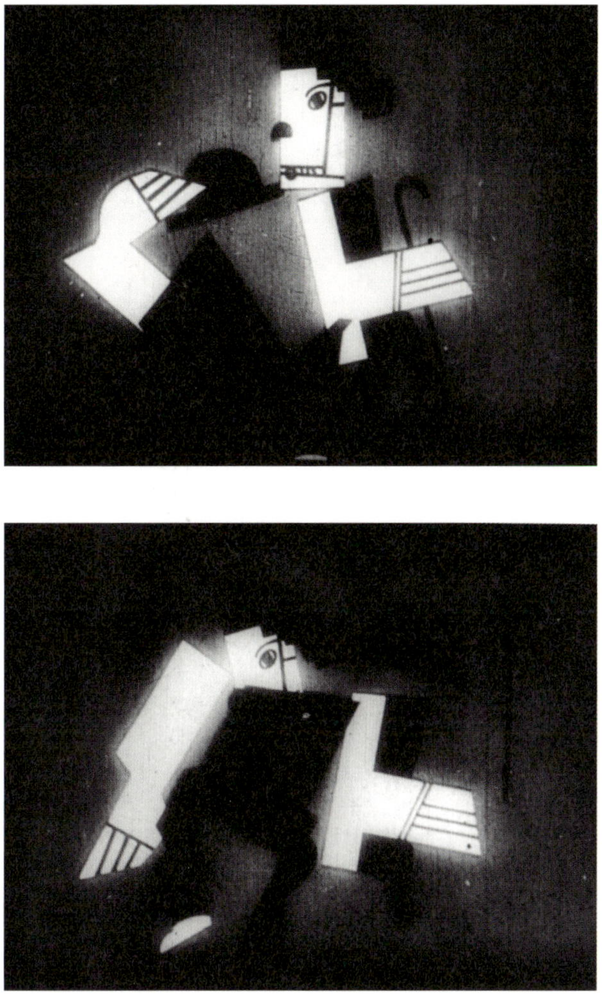

21

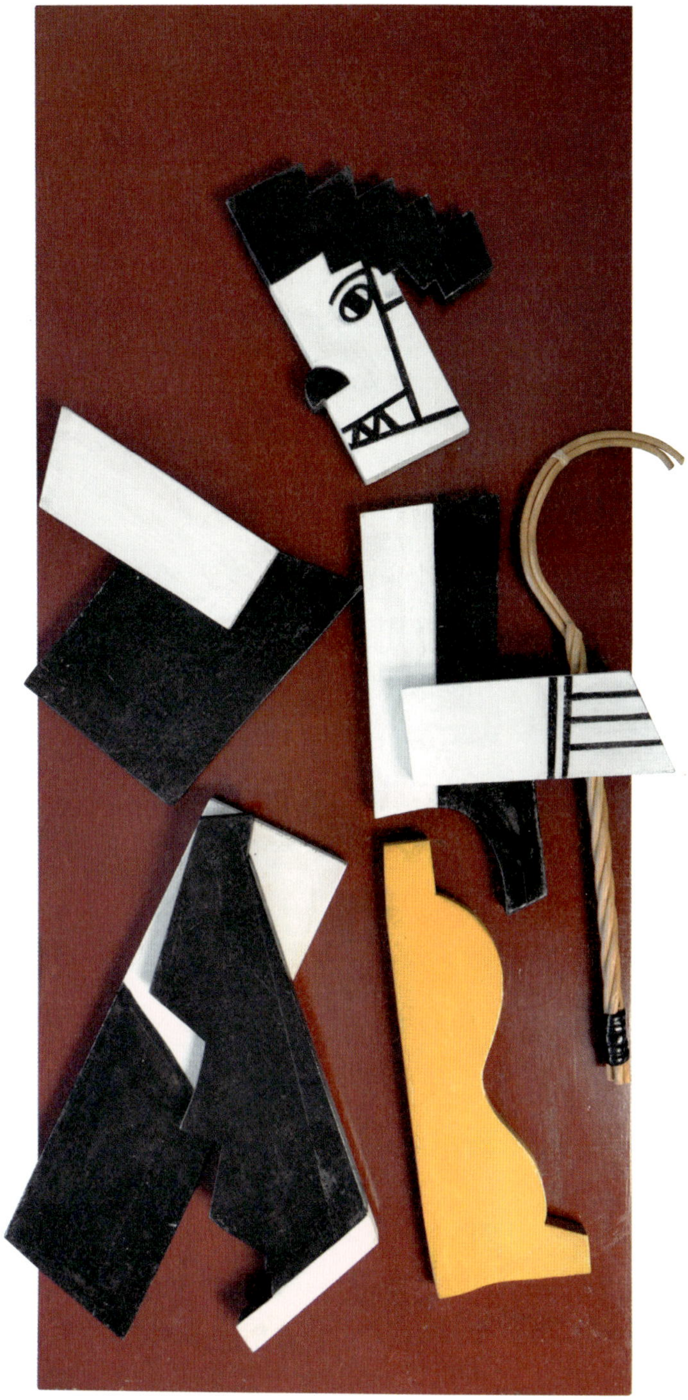

23

TIME
My Ballet Mécanique
From the film by Léger (1926)
Georges Antheil

My Ballet Mécanique is the new **fourth dimension** of music.

My Ballet Mécanique is the first piece of music that has been composed out of and *for* machines, **on earth.**

My Ballet Mécanique is the first piece of music that has found the best forms and materials lying inert in a medium that **as a medium** is mathematically certain of becoming the greatest moving factor of the music of future generations.

My Ballet Mécanique is the first attaining of a form that is *not tonal.*

My Ballet Mécanique is the first music on *earth* that has its very germ of life in the new fourth-demensional phenomena wherein *time functioning in music differs from ordinary time* and also purely physical phenomena that follow it.

My Ballet Mécanique is the first *time-form* on earth.

My Ballet Mécanique is neither tonal, nor atonal. In fact it is of no kind of tonality at all. It has nothing to do with tonality. It is made of time and sound… the two materials, *fundamental materials,* that music is made of.

In music there is *nothing else, except time and sound, and the physical and psychic concept* of these vibrating the human organism.

Anything else is literary, and does not belong to pure music. For instance my Ballet Mécanique has absolutely no forte or piano moments. It is *merely played loud enough to be heard.*

My Ballet Mécanique has nothing to do with fff or ppp. That is literary, mystical, religious, hands pressed to heart.

Music, as I repeat a thousand times, has nothing to do withal this. Musical emotion can have no connection with the literary. It must come out of the finest things within itself.

My Ballet Mécanique comes out of the first and principle stuff of music…. *time-space.*

The whole problem of music today, as the whole world knows, is *form.* I believe that all the forms today are merely parades and arrangements, derived from a tonal nuclei: section C added thereto… all with slight overlappings. Parades. Various formations. Interminglings. In my eyes it is impossible to give further consideration to the tonal forms.

Likewise the atonal, which to me seems quite as tonal as the first tonal laws. I am certain that the people who have decided that they can evolve new forms out of the tonal will find that Beethoven, who did likewise, has finished their work for them long ago. The innocents believe that in the difference between tonality and atonality lies the phenomena out of which new forms will be created.

For it is only out of new phenomena in art, that the nuclei of the new forms lie.

And with this one stroke is all of the modern Central European music eliminated for me.

And because the music of modern France, America, and Italy relies mainly upon its charms (as Strawinsky tells me he always and fundamentally searches) and its intelligence in clearing away the mass of music rubbish that accumulated after Wagner… it is even less interesting to me. I can only recommend it as an antidote to Central Europe… or Central Europe as an antidote to it. Kill one another by the most poisonous methods if you please…

My forms are the first complete forms that have come out of the only forms out of which music can be made—**time.**

Is not **time**, and **time** alone, the **sole** canvas of music? Notes, vibrations, and sounds are merely our drawing pencils… our paint-box. Can you dare to deny that the forms come out of the canvas and not the crayon? Can you dare to deny that the crayon is merely the human instrument for indicating the spaces **existing only upon the canvas… before they are indicated.**

Can you any longer dare to say that music is made of **tone** and not of **time**?

Will you any longer write music in which *time* is merely a by-product of **tonality** or **tone**?

Again I ask you… do you dare to deny that the canvas of music is *time* and not *tonality*… do you mean to say that the very spaces in which you are working, and the finished spaces which is your goal… does not interest you fundamentally, above all other things.

Does not its plan, and its musical phenomena in which it differs from ordinary time… in a word, the root of its miracle, the secret of its existence, the germ of its life, the cool beauty of its plan and mathematics, the tension of its spaces, the beating of our hearts **(for our hearts do not feel… they beat)**, in a word the very *reason* of music, the ultimate *form*… does not this interest you, **except as a by-product.**

Improvisors!

As I have already said, my Ballet Mécanique has under no circumstances, and at no point a single motion or movement that does not come out of *time*.

For the first time on earth *time* has been *used* under its fundamental principles in the single art in which it is fundamentally conceived… or better, in the single art which is fundamentally conceived out of *time*. **Time is the very stuff out of which life is made.**

Originally published as G. Antheil "ZEIT. Mein Ballett Mécanique. Zu dem Film von Léger" in ed. Hans Richter, *G. Zeitschrift für elementare Gestaltung*, vol. 5-6 (April 1926). English translation from eds. Detlef Mertins and Michael W. Jennings, *G. An Avant-Garde Journal of Art, Architecture Design, and Film*, 1923–26 (San Francisco: Getty Research Institute), 216–18.

–

Mechanical Ballet, Film by Fernand Léger and Dudley Murphy, Musical Synchronism by George Antheil (1924)
Fernand Léger

Objects - images - the most usual.

Figures, fragments of figures, mechanical fragments, metals, manufactured objects, flat projection with a minimum of perspective.

The particular interest of the film is centered upon the importance which we give to the "fixed image," to its arithmetical, automatic projection, slowed down or accelerated - additional, likeness.

No scenario - Reactions of rhythmic images, that is all.

Two coefficients of interest upon which the film is constructed:
The variation of the speeds of projection:
The rhythm of these speeds.

An important contribution due to a technical novelty of Mr. Murphy and Mr. Ezra Pound - the multiple transformation of the projected image.

For the sake of variety and contrast some picturesque passages and "cartes postales" which have no value in themselves, but are used for the relation and reaction of the images which follow them.

The film is divided into seven vertical parts (flat, without depth, moving surfaces) which go from slow to rapid.

Each of these parts possesses its own unity due to the similarity of the groupings of similar objects-images, or of the same nature. This merely for the construction and to avoid the breaking up of the film.

To insure variety in each of these parts they are crossed by very rapid horizontal penetrations of similar forms (color).

From one end to the other the film is subjected to an arithmetical constraint, as precise as possible (number, speed, time).

An object is projected to the rhythm of
6 images a second for 30 seconds.
3 images a second for 20 seconds.
10 images a second for 15 seconds.

We persist up to the point when the eye and spirit of the spectator will no longer accept. We drain out of it every bit of its value as a spectacle up to the moment when it becomes insupportable.

This film is objective, realistic and in no way abstract.

I made it in close collaboration with Dudley Murphy. We have asked the composer, George Antheil, to make for it a musical synchronized adaption - thanks to the scientific process of Monsieur Delacomme, we hope to produce mechanically the sound and image absolutely simultaneously.

Originally published as F. Léger, "Ballet mécanique, Film de Fernand Léger et Dudley Murphy, Synchronisme musical de Georges Antheil," in eds. Le Corbusier and Amédée Ozenfant, *L'Esprit Nouveau*, no. 28 (1924): 2336–37.
English translation from *The Little Review* (New York) 10, no. 2 (Fall/Winter 1924/25): 42–44.

–

On Charlie Chaplin (Charlot) (1926)
Fernand Léger

It was Apollinaire who took me to see Charlie Chaplin during one of our leaves.
[…] Here was this "little fellow," who had ceased to be a "little fellow" and become instead a sort of living object–bare, moving, black and white. It was new.

He had nothing of a theater actor about him–it was truly something else. Someone mentioned that he used to be a clown or an acrobat, and then I understood. He appeared–like the source of the only education possible for acing the "mobile image."

The Man-Image–the first man-image–such as to persuade us that he was invented at the same time as the film projector, that they were born together, manufactured together.

"Cinema begins with Charlot."

Originally published as F. Léger, "Charlie Chaplin," in *Chroniques du jour* 7/8 (1926): 243–44.
Excerpts from the English translation by Liesl Yamaguchi in ed. Anna Vallye, *Léger: Modern Art and the Metropolis*, exh. cat., Philadelphia Museum of Art (New Haven and London, 2013), 152–53.

–

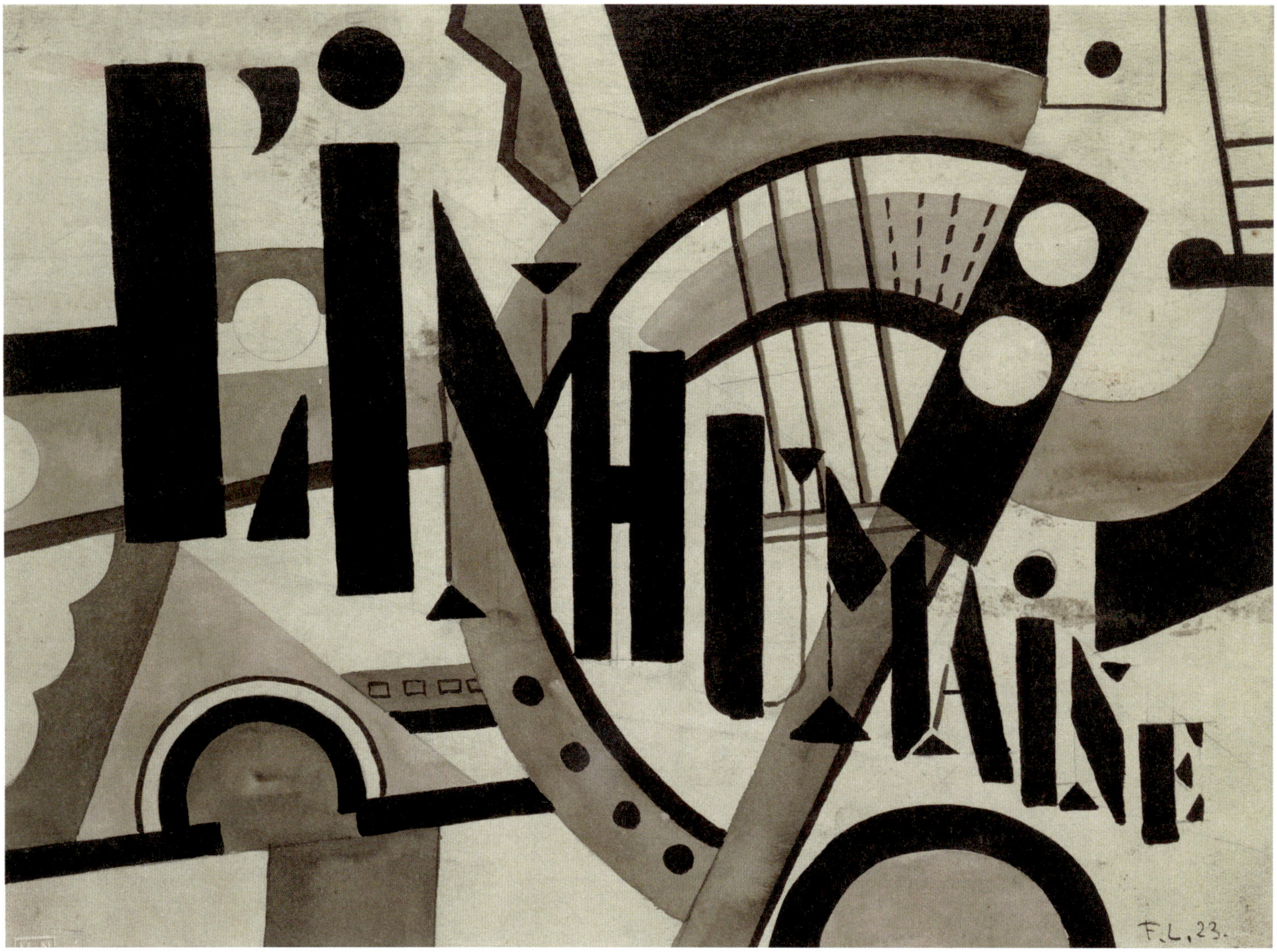

24

24 ***L'Inhumaine* (The Inhuman Woman), poster design, 1923**
China ink, gouache and graphite on paper
25 × 32.2 cm
Musée national Fernand Léger, Biot

25 Marcel L'Herbier
***L'Inhumaine* (The Inhuman Woman), 1923**
Laboratory: Fernand Léger;
exteriors: Robert Mallet-Stevens;
furniture: Pierre Chareau;
garden: Claude Autant-Lara;
sets: Alberto Cavalcanti;
costumes: Paul Poiret;
music: Darius Milhaud;
dancers: Ballets Suédois
35mm film, black and white, silent
132 min
Centre Pompidou, Musée national d'art moderne, Paris

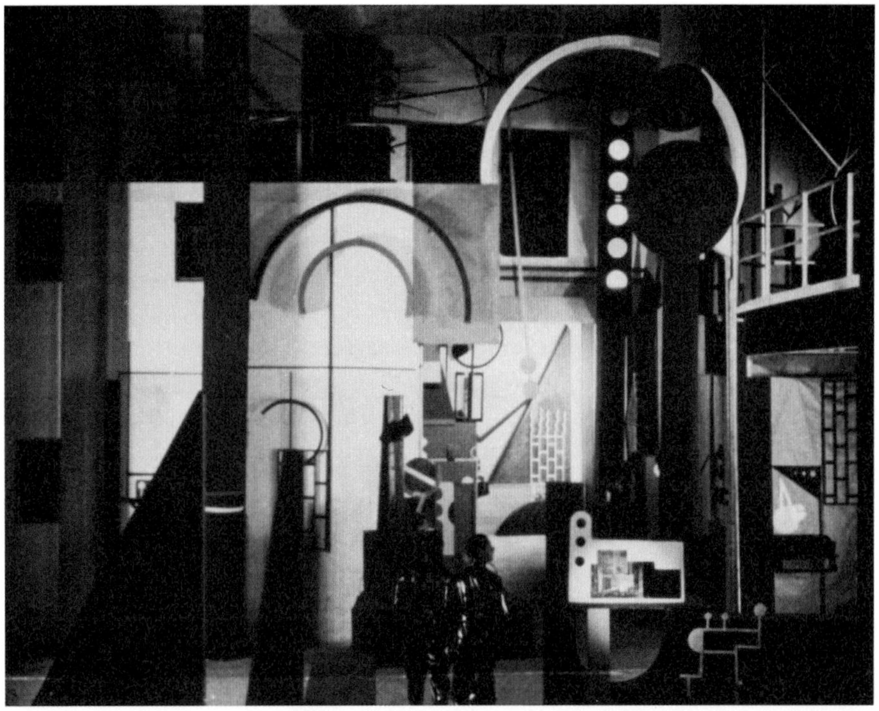

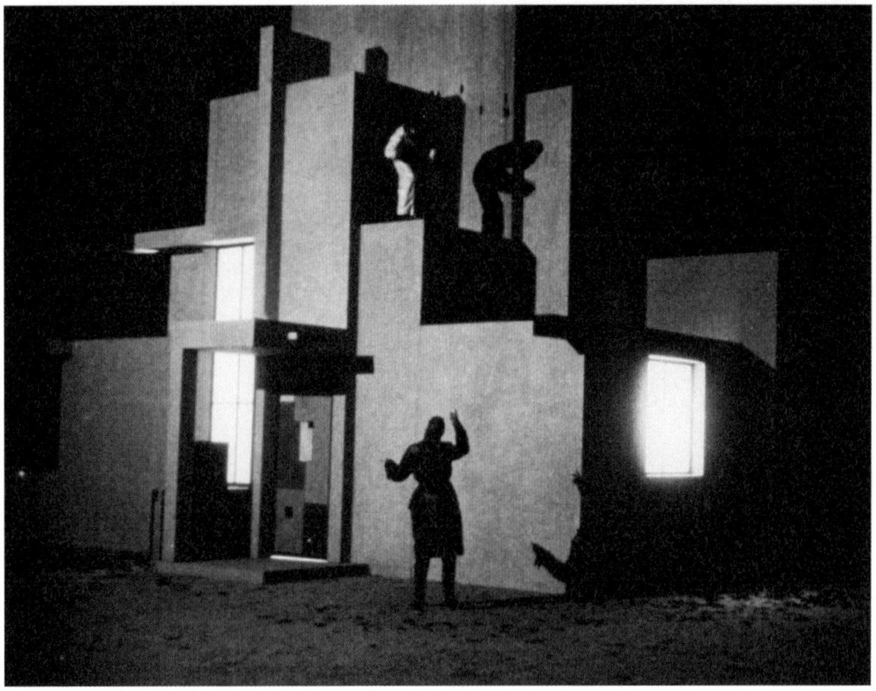

25

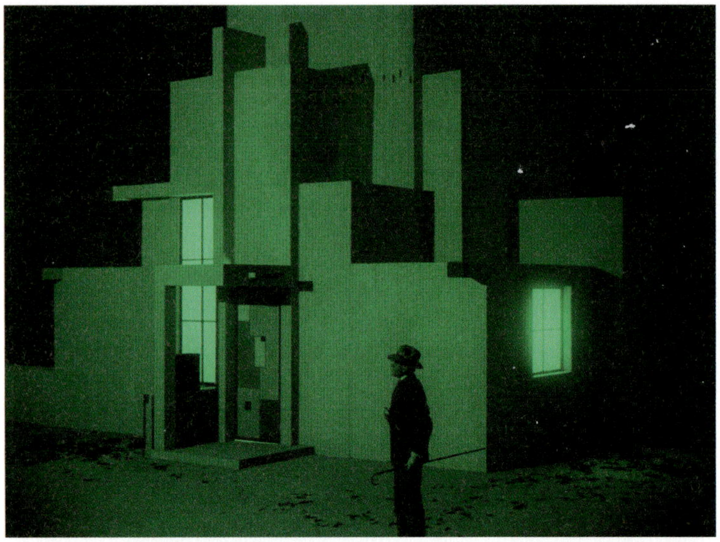

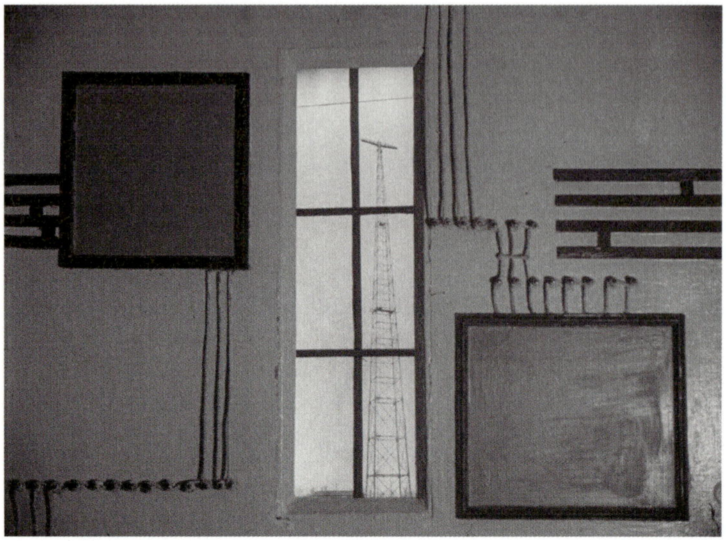

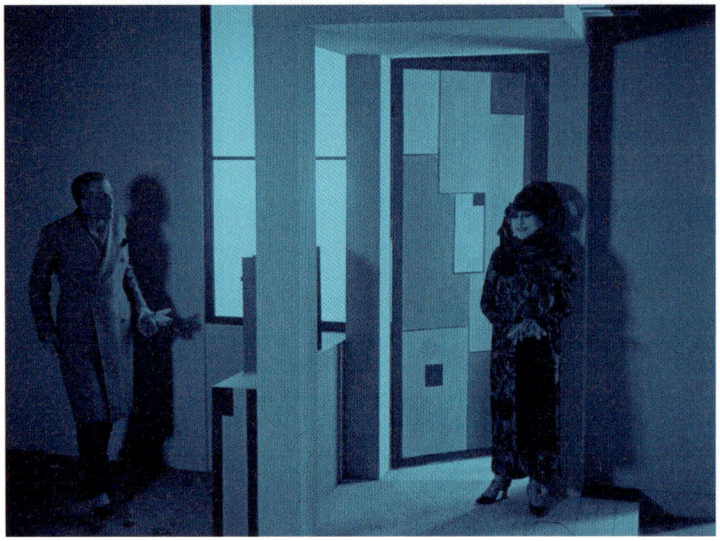

26

26 Marcel L'Herbier
***L'Inhumaine* (The Inhuman Woman), 1923**
35mm film, black and white, silent
132 min

Excerpts from the edition restored and colorized in 2015 (Lobsterfilms)

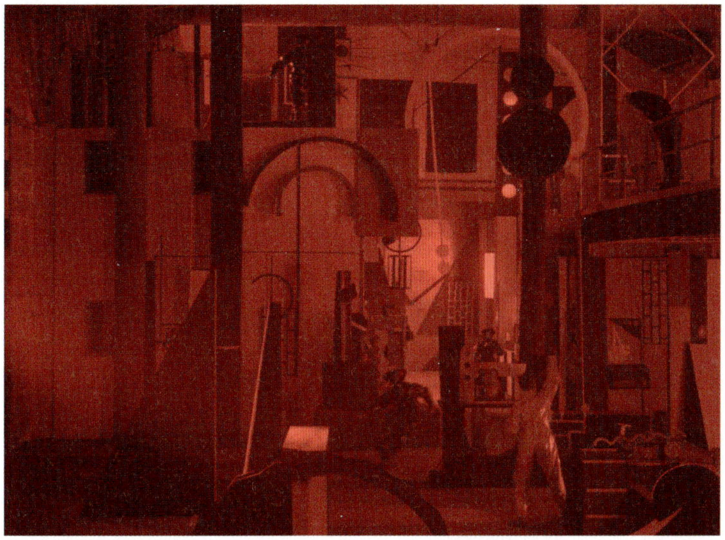
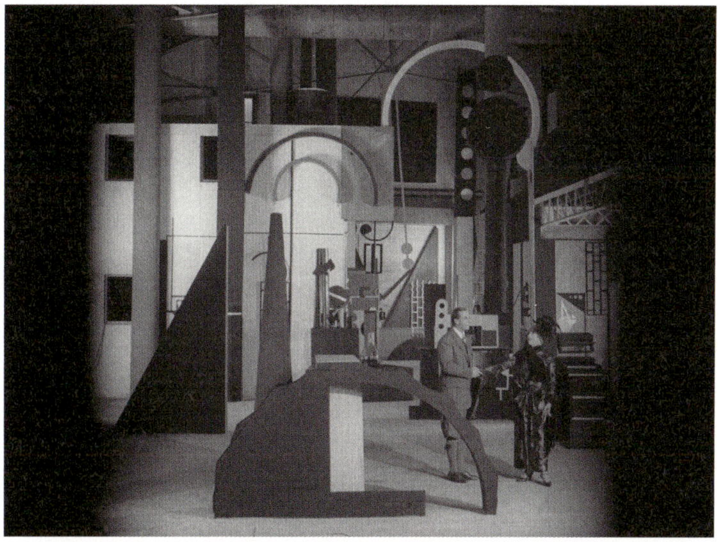
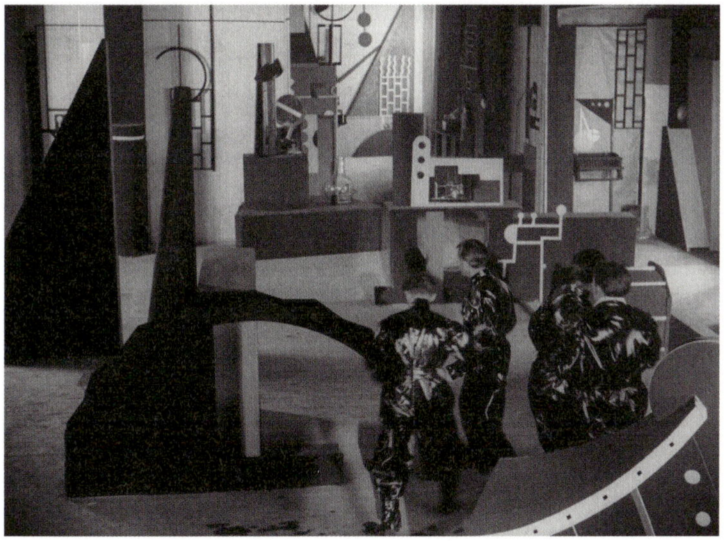
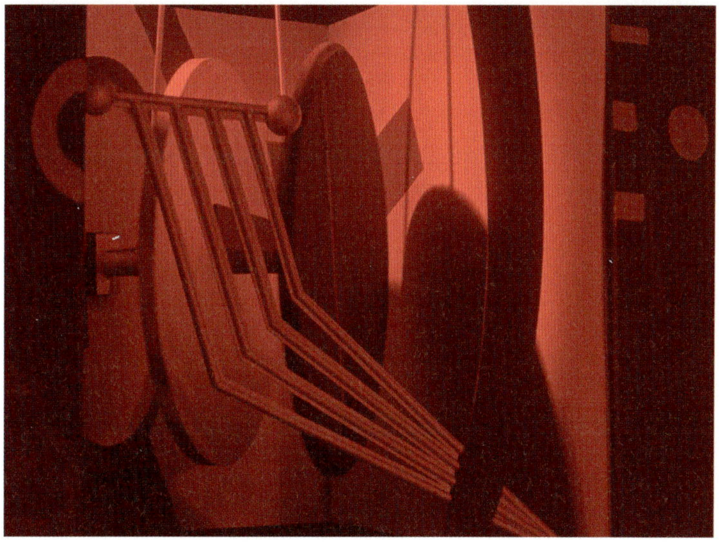

The Spectacle: Light, Color, Moving Image, Object-Spectacle (1924)
Fernand Léger

To have to talk about spectacle is to imagine the world in all its daily visual manifestations (it has become one of the fundamental needs of existence). It dominates all contemporary life.

[…] On the boulevards two men are carrying some immense gilded letters in a handcart; the effect is so unexpected that everyone stops and looks. *There is the origin of the modern spectacle*. The shock of the surprise effect. To organize a spectacle based on these daily phenomena, the artists who want to distract the crowd must undergo a continual renewal. It is a hard profession, the hardest profession.

[…] A spectacle must be fast-moving for the sake of its unity. It cannot go on for more than fifteen or twenty minutes. Let us look at this short time span for "new materials."

We have found what we are competing with; we must renew the man-spectacle mechanically. We can make the materials themselves move, set them in action.

Industry and commerce, swept along in a frantic competitive race, have been the first to grab everything that could serve as an attraction. They admirably sensed that a shop window, a department store must be a spectacle. They had the idea of creating a pervasive, persuasive atmosphere by using only the objects at their disposal.

[…] What is going to be offered to meet this enormous demand?

The music halls, circuses, revues, ballet companies, and gatherings of high or low society are the fields of action (the theater, properly speaking, being outside my subject). However, I will mention Jules Romains's *Six Gentlemen in a Row* as one of the most original theatrical manifestations.

What did one see before our period?

The classical theater was above all theatrical; their means were gesture, declamation, melodrama. As a plastic method, what interests us and moves us is their use of masks; they invented the mask.

The mask dominates classical theater, and the most primitive peoples use it as means of creating spectacle. They realized, with their weak methods, that on stage the human resemblance was a barrier to the lyric state, the state of astonishment.

They wanted to transform the face.

I am going to do my best to tie in this event because it is one the important points of this lecture.

[The mask was devised] to make a break between the visual atmosphere of a room and that of the stage, to make the individual disappear in order to utilize human material, to create fiction on the stage. The human material appeared, but it had the same spectacle value as the object and the décor.

Our present methods are manifold, of course, but on one condition, I repeat, that the individual-as-king is really willing to become a means like the rest. The star artist, with or without the necessary talent, is a frequent obstacle to unity.

[…] Why won't they accept the lesson of the acrobats, the simple, humble acrobats? There are more "plastic passages" in ten minutes of an acrobatic spectacle than there are in many scenes of ballet.

[…] If only they would decide to be choreographers, rather than star performers, if they would agree to become part of a spectacle "with equal billing," if they would accept the role of "moving scenery," if they themselves would direct the advent of the spectacle-object, then a number of entirely new methods would appear that up to now have remained "in the wings." Then you would have the mechanism for unexpected plastic qualities that will be able to come into play and animate the stage.

[…] Let's take a stage with the minimum of depth. Keep to the vertical plane as much as possible; watch in hand, time the length of action (the mechanics of a gesture, a spotlight, or a sound). A plastic movement that is effective for ten seconds becomes poor if it lasts for twelve. The background scenery is movable. The action begins: six actors, "moving scenery," cross the stage turning cartwheels (a lighted stage); they come back, now phosphorescent (on a dark stage). The top of the set is animated by films projected on it—décor for the moving backdrop, it disappears—the apparition of the beautiful, luminous metallic object, it shifts and disappears. Controlled activity of a whole stage where pleasing, extraordinary surprises and unexpected things are continually at play, woven together, and multiplied at the pleasure of the director. If a face appears, it may be stiff, fixed, frozen, rigid, as if it were metal. The human face can play its part, but its "expressiveness" is absolutely null in the spectacle-stage. Heavily made up or masked, transformed, with set gestures, it can contribute variety, but nothing more. Human material may be used in groups moving in a parallel or contrasting rhythm, on the condition that the general effect is in no way sacrificed to it.

[…] Jacques Hébertot is a fabulous director, and I want to pay homage here to Rolf de Maré, the director of the Swedish Ballet, who was the first person in France to have the courage to agree to a spectacle where everything is done with machinery and the play of light, where no human silhouette is on the stage; and to Jean Borlin and his troupe, who are condemned to the role of moving scenery.

In agreeing to perform the Negro ballet *Creation of the World* (*Création du Monde*) he dared to impose on the public for the first time a truly modern stage, at least in terms of technical means. His effort was rewarded with success. The public immediately went along with him completely, while most of the official critics lost themselves in irrelevant remarks. As French propaganda his work was influential. His creations, eight or ten of which were done by artists of the French avant-garde, have gone around the world. He came back from America, where, in spite of the huge difficulties such a trip entails, he will have been the first to have risked and presented over there an entirely French program. There have to be foreigners such as Rolf de Maré and Serge de Diaghilev to recognize the vital French quality in order to present the world.

[…] The French screen has contributed the only truly plastic achievement that has been presented so far.

Abel Gance, assisted by Blaise Cendrars in *The Wheel* (*La Roue*), Jean Epstein in *The Faithful Heart* (*Coeur fidèle*), Marcel L'Herbier in *Gallery of Monsters* (*Galerie de monstres*) and *The Inhuman* (*L'Inhumaine*), Moujoskine in *Keim*, have all obtained, achieved, and successfully presented plastic emotion to the public through the simultaneous projection of "fragments of images" in an accelerated rhythm. They have achieved an equivalent plane through absolutely new technical means; Gance and Cendrars's exploding train, Epstein's street carnival, L'Herbier's circus and laboratories, Moujoskine's jig are the reasons for the success of their films. It is plasticity, it is the image alone that acts on the spectator, and he submits to it, is moved, and conquered. It is a beautiful victory–achieved before an audience that has reacted to and applauded for something other than a sentimental literary intrigue.

The new values are making progress everywhere. The stage and the screen are gradually being liberated.

Spectacle, properly speaking, changes, and we imagine the next advent of new possibilities.

The Eiffel Tower and the Great Wheel, those two enormous "object-spectacles" that dominate Paris, are as much admired as the beautiful Gothic façades.

Everyone regretted the disappearance of the Great Wheel; it was a familiar silhouette. It was better than the Eiffel Tower because of its form. An entire object whose initial form is the circle is always much sought after for its value of attractiveness.

The wheel, lighted and colored, dominates the street carnivals.

The circle is satisfying to the human eye. It is a totality, a whole, there is no break in it.

[…] Those grotesque societies for the protections of the French landscape who presume to stop life and to prevent Cadum Baby* or Brand-X Pills from being inserted into a landscape–but what is a landscape? Where does it begin and end? What court is presumptuous enough to define the elements that make it up?

[…] The visual world of a large modern city, that vast spectacle that I spoke of in the beginning, is badly orchestrated; in fact, not orchestrated at all. The intensity of the street shatters our nerves and drives us crazy.

Let's tackle the problem in all its scope. Let's organize the exterior spectacle. This is nothing more or less than creating "polychromed architecture" from scratch, taking in all the manifestations of current advertising.

If the spectacle offers intensity, a street, a city, a factory ought to offer an obvious plastic serenity.

Let's organize exterior life in its domain: form, color, light.

Let's take a street; ten red houses, six yellow houses. Let's exploit beautiful materials–stone, marble, brick, steel, gold, silver, bronze; let's avoid dynamism completely. A static concept must be the rule; all the commercial and industrial necessities will be developed, instead of being sacrificed–a constant anxiety in society.

Color and light have a social function, an essential function.

The world of work, the only interesting one, exists in an intolerable environment. Let us go into the factories, the banks, the hospitals. If light is required there, what does it illuminate? Nothing. Let's bring in color; it is as necessary as water and fire. Let's apportion it wisely, so that it may be a more pleasant value, a psychological value; its moral influence can be considerable. A beautiful and calm environment.

Life through color.
The polychromed hospital.
The colorist-doctor.
The leprous, glacial hospital is dressed up in multicolor.

We are not in the realm of vague prophecies; we are coming very close to tomorrow's realities.

A society without frenzy, calm, ordered, knowing how to live naturally within the Beautiful without exclamation or romanticism.

That is where we are going, very simply.

It is a religion like any other. I think it is useful and beautiful.

[*Picture used by a toiletry company that advertised widely on billboards in Paris at this time. - Tr.]

Lecture given at the Sorbonne, Paris, May 1924. Originally published as F. Léger, "Le Spectacle: Lumière - Couleur - Image mobile - Objet-Spectacle," in *Bulletin de l'Effort Moderne* (Paris), no. 7 (July 1924): 4–7, no. 8 (Oct. 1924): 5–9, and no. 9 (Nov. 1924): 7–9.
English translation (excerpts) by Alexandra Anderson in Fernand Léger, *Functions of Painting* (New York: Thames and Hudson, 1973), 35–47.

–

27 ***La Roue*** **(The Wheel), poster design, 1922**
Gouache on paper
31.3 × 24.2 cm
Galerie Louise Leiris, Paris

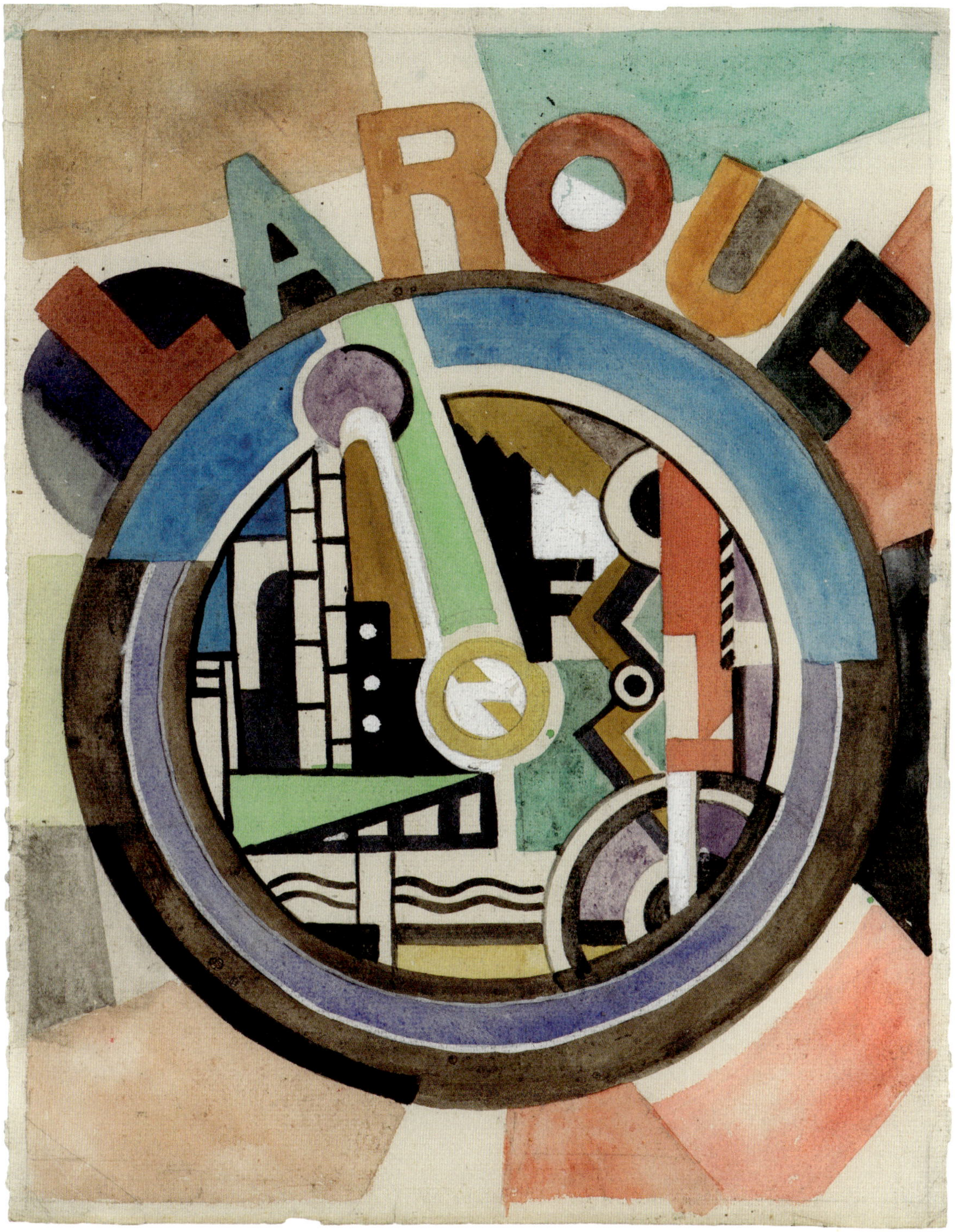

27

Graphics: A Fundamental Source of Inspiration

By Roxane Jubert

"Suddenly after the war, walls, roads, objects became brilliantly colored. Houses were decked out in blue, yellow, red. Enormous letters were inscribed on them. It is modern life, shattering and brutal."– Fernand Léger[1]

"Then the war: a void. Then the epoch: construction, simultaneity, assertion [...] Posters. House fronts devoured by letters. The word steps into the street."– Blaise Cendrars[2]

Graphics and typography have always been a major consideration for art's avant-gardes. Artists, designers, and writers find countless ways of expressing the attraction of visual communication at work in their everyday environment, especially in the urban landscape. This ubiquitous enthusiasm sometimes develops into a veritable fascination, as in the case of the Fernand Léger/Blaise Cendrars duo, Guillaume Apollinaire, László Moholy-Nagy and many others. In his 1937 talk "Color in the World," Léger spoke of the powerful impact the post-World War I period had on him: "Through the open window, the wall across the street, violently colored, comes into your house. Enormous letters, figures twelve feet high, are hurled into the apartment. Color takes over [...] Where are we going? Quite simply, we are going toward a rapid evolution in external plastic life [...] The world courts intensity. Speed is the contemporary law."[3]

Léger's oeuvre is saturated with graphic signs[4] in different forms (figs. 33, 36). They often appear as little brushstrokes, such as the many letters, figures, and obscure remnants of writing that can be found in his drawings and paintings, and in publishing projects which since have become significant exemplars in the history of graphic design, including covers for books and magazines (figs. 29, 30), color compositions, layouts, and *illustrations cinématographiques*, or "cinema illustrations,"[5] among which *La fin du monde* (The End of the World), published in 1919, is a prominent example (fig. 28). Observation of a given setting was a fundamental source of inspiration, and in his works it is important to note the significant relationship he sets up between the individual letter, that tiny common denominator of both language and graphics, and the monumental. He understands the letter as something to be projected spatially, on a wall, in particular via posters (and signage as well). This is a vision of things that chimes perfectly with that of the young graphic artist A.M. Cassandre (the pseudonym of Adolphe Jean-Marie Mouron) when he said in an interview in 1926 that "the poster must become part of architectural forms, filling ever-larger façades and enlivening not only a few fences and houses but also enormous blocks of stone and even vast neighborhoods."[6]

The writings of Léger and Cendrars are studded with remarks revealing their perception of visual communication in genres including typography, lettering, advertising, print, and signboards, as well as in terms of form, line, geometry, and color. No question, these texts—extraordinary testimony to their writers' tremendous enthusiasm for the potent sensory kaleidoscope of the space around them—are compulsory reading for anyone interested in their feel for the sheer immediacy of graphics and its ramifications, and in the decisive impact these had on their daily visual experience. "He marveled at it all," says Cendrars of his friend's passion for posters.[7] The exuberance of Léger's vocabulary, too, demonstrates the extent to which letters, posters, and signs go hand in hand for him with sensations of hugeness, bedazzlement, speed, and violence, and the headlong rush of his writing communicates his enthrallment: "immense gold letters," "huge letters," "[t]he advertising billboard that brutally cuts across the landscape," "the dissonances of some billboard or other," "these amazing fountains of letters and lights," "the hard dry billboard with its violent colors"—and more. He was eloquently putting his message across as early as 1914: "This yellow or red poster, shouting in a timid landscape, is the best of possible reasons for the new painting [...] [it] announces the advent of plastic contrast."[8]

Another graphic source fuels this ardor, one just as fundamental and hardly ever (if at all) taken into account. It has to do with the tragedy of history, and once again Léger himself pithily provides the key, this time in an interview when he mentions Verdun, where he had sketched the battle raging around him (fig. 38):

"The destruction, the walls in ruins, what is left of signs in the streets and on shop fronts: these things become part of compositions in which I strive for a sensation of physical impact with very simple lines and planes. Print and letters from signs crop up in these sketches, but they take on a plastic character, playing a role of their own, functioning like the other visual elements in the establishing of formal signs."[9]

This might well explain the presence—very frequent and, to some extent, mysterious—of exploded letters and fragmentary signs throughout his work (figs. 34, 35). Thus the mid-1910s saw a creative tension develop in his relationship with graphics: on the one hand vividness, structure and vitality, and on the other explosiveness, destruction, and violence. This aspect needs to be highlighted in the interests of an accurate understanding of Léger's oeuvre.

For Léger, typography and graphics as focuses of observation and sources of inspiration seem just as important as their use as a formal vocabulary and creative medium. Moreover, the pull he felt towards visual communication and its effect involved much more than a mere transposition of (typo-) graphic signs and a broadening of the painter's repertoire of inspirational "objects."[10] While Léger very often employed letters and other graphic forms, highlighting their materiality and sheer presence, the influence of his observations on his work would seem to be much more far-reaching and diffuse. Graphics in the public space affected him deeply, to the point of playing a major role in the spatial, dynamic, and kinetic

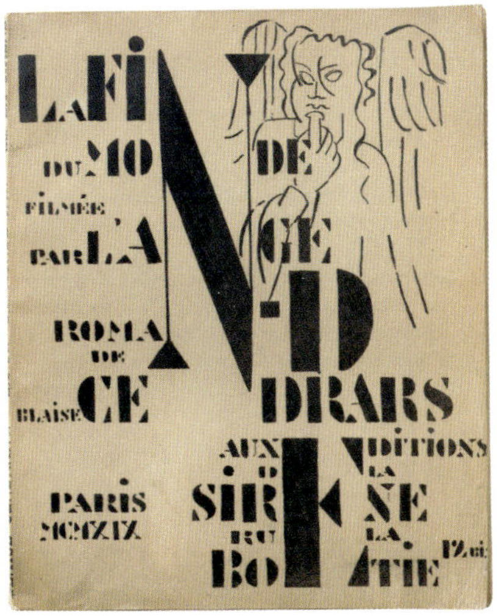

28

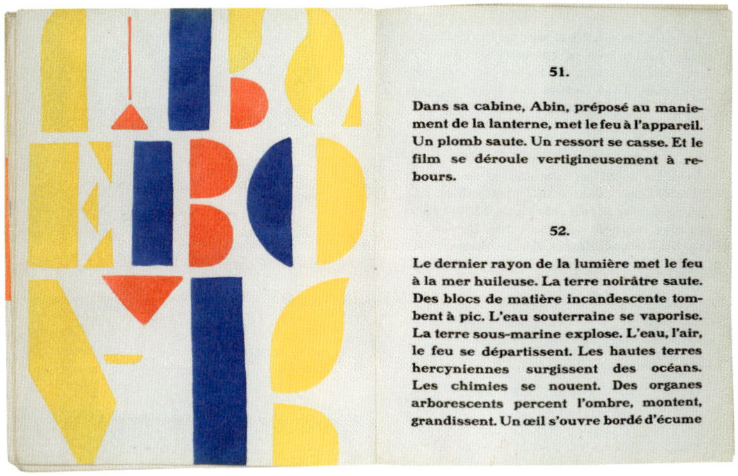

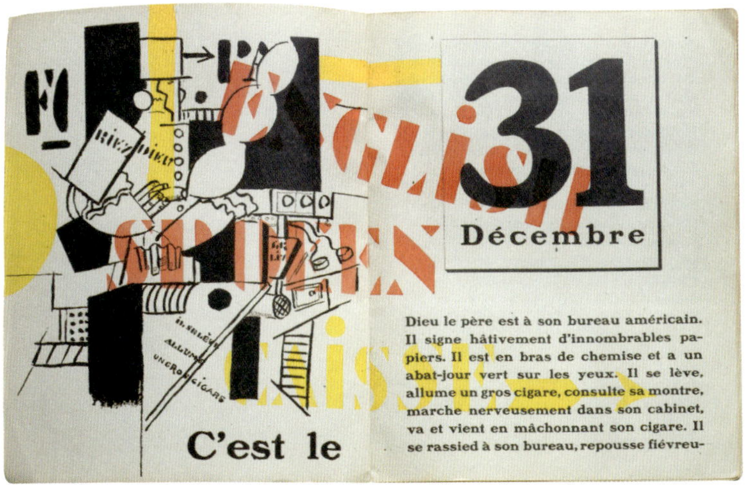

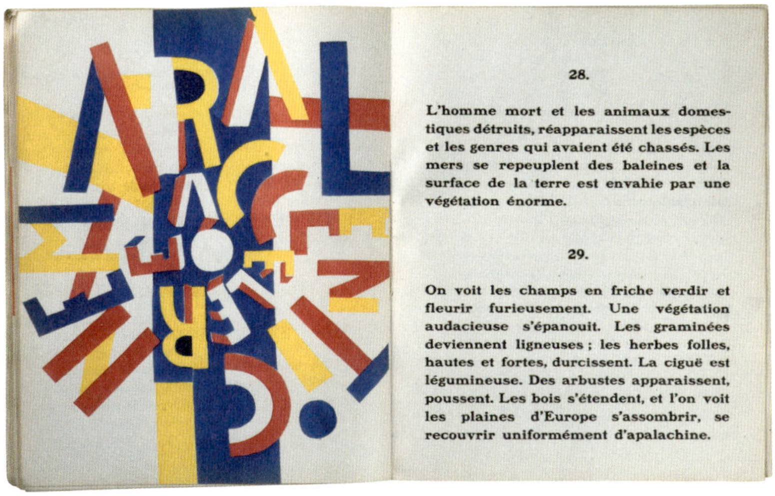

28 Blaise Cendrars
***La fin du monde filmée par l'ange N. D.* (The End of the World filmed by the Angel of Notre Dame), 1919**
Title and double-page spreads with color compositions by Fernand Léger, Paris, Éditions de la Sirène, 1919
Print on Lafuma vellum document paper
31.7 × 25.4 × 0.5 cm
Lille métropole, Musée d'art moderne, d'art contemporain et d'art brut, Villeneuve d'Ascq

29 **Cover for *Broom* magazine, July 1922**
32.5 × 24 cm
Woodcut

30 **Cover for *The Plowshare* magazine, November, 1919**

31 **Cover for first German edition of the poem "Astral. Ein Gesang" by Ivan Goll, 1922**

32 ***Carton d'invitation, exposition d'œuvres de Fernand Léger à la galerie L'Effort Moderne, 1919* (Invitation to an exhibition of works by Fernand Léger at the L'Effort Moderne gallery, 1919)**
Graphic Arts Collection, Princeton University Library

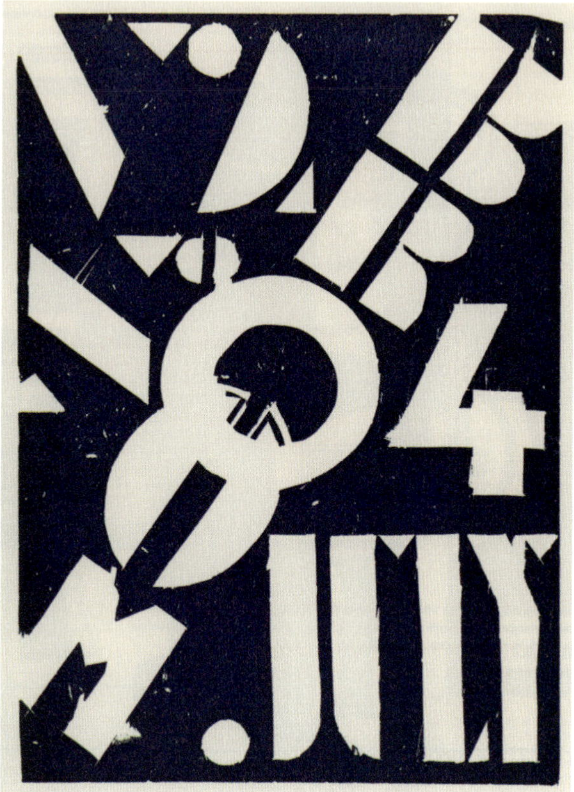

29

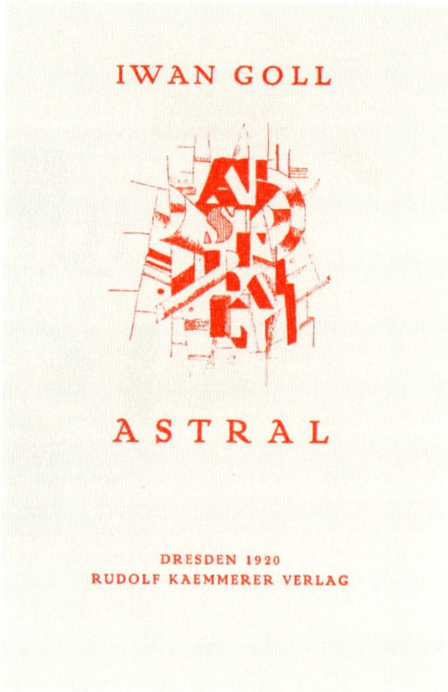

31

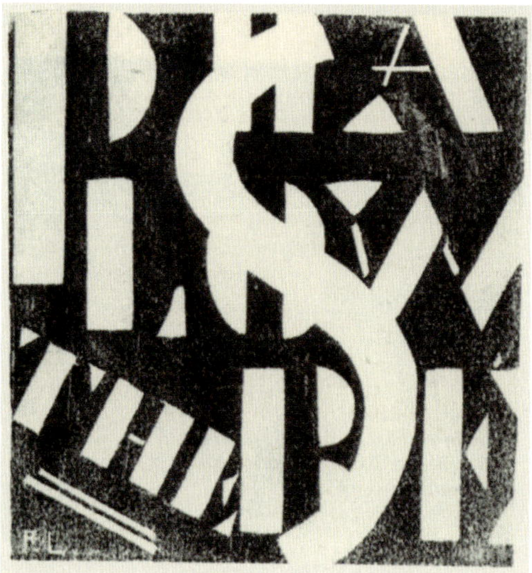

30

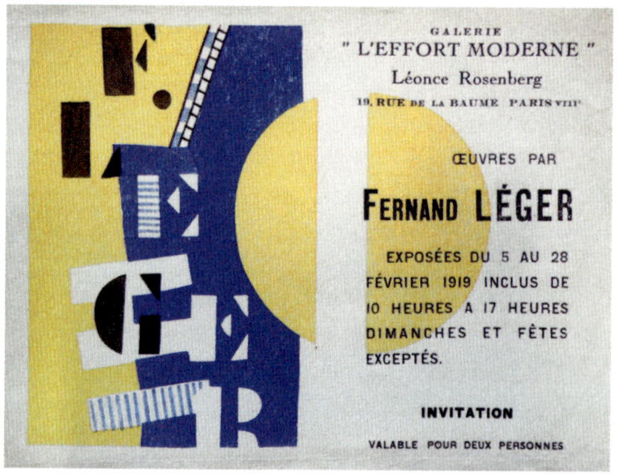

32

aspect of his mix of sensations, his elation, and his visual world. This is evident in the energy and movement of some of his page layouts and (sometimes eddying) typographic compositions (figs. 28, 31), as well as in various pictures and other, non-painterly creations[11] (fig. 13). It is clear, in the light of his artistic output and even more so of his writings, that Léger's sensitivity to visual communication was a fundamental constituent of his work (fig. 184).

For a better grasp of the extent of this reaction to the new graphic environment of the early twentieth century—one shared by many of Léger's contemporaries—we need to go deeper into the narratives and analyses of the period and combine the points of view of painters and writers. Louis Aragon invites us to do just this in a text published in 1918, in which he gives an explicit account of the shift that has taken place:

"Before the advent of the cinema rare were the artists who dared resort to the clangorous harmony of machines and the obsessive beauty of advertising texts, of posters, of evocative upper case [...] Today these courageous precursors—painters or poets—are witnessing their own triumph, they who could be moved by a newspaper or a pack of cigarettes [...] They knew the fascination of hieroglyphs on walls [...] Those letters extolling a brand of soap are like the characters on obelisks or the formulas in a book of spells: they bespeak the destiny of their era."[12]

1 Fernand Léger, "Color in the World" (1937), in *Functions of Painting*, trans. Alexandra Anderson (London: Thames and Hudson, 1973), 119.
2 Blaise Cendrars in a letter dated 1920, quoted by Claude Leroy in "Les Trois rencontres de Léger avec Cendrars," in "Fernand Léger," special issue, *Europe. Revue littéraire mensuelle*, no. 818–19 (June–July 1997): 107.
3 Léger, "Color in the World," 120–21.
4 Some of his canvases have typography, letters and the alphabet as their subject, notably *Le Typographe* (The Typographer, 1918–19) and *Nature morte ABC* (Still Life ABC, 1927) (figs. 33, 36). Even an incomplete listing yields at least two hundred works including letters, created in different media and with different tools: oil on canvas, gouache, watercolor, drawing, pencil and ink on paper, lithography, engraving, drypoint, posters, publishing and illustration, printed programs and invitations, sketches for stage sets (notably for the ballet *Skating Rink* [figs. 12–14]), ceramics, mosaics, tapestries and even a "cinematic mural."
5 The term *illustrations cinématographiques* can be seen written in Cendrars's hand on the sketch for the title page of his novel *La Fin du monde*, reproduced in *Dis-moi, Blaise. Léger, Chagall, Picasso et Blaise Cendrars*, exhibition catalog, Biot/Nice/Vallauris (Paris: Réunion des Musées Nationaux, 2009), 44.
6 Quoted by Henri Mouron in *A. M. Cassandre* (Geneva: Albert Skira, 1985), 18.
7 Blaise Cendrars in *Blaise Cendrars vous parle...*, "Tout autour d'aujourd'hui" series, vol. 15 (Paris: Denoël, 2006), 294.
8 Fernand Léger, "Contemporary Achievements in Painting" (1914), *Functions of Painting*, 12.
9 Fernand Léger, in André Verdet, *Entretiens, notes et écrits sur la peinture. Braque, Léger, Matisse, Picasso, Chagall* (Nantes: Éditions du Petit Véhicule, 2000), p. 74.
10 Regarding the "object" concept, see Fernand Léger, "The New Realism," in *Functions of Painting*, 109–18.
11 See note 2.
12 Louis Aragon, "Du décor," published in the magazine *Le Film* in 1918. For the full article (in a different translation), see Louis Aragon, "On Décor," in Paul Hammond, ed., *The Shadow and Its Shadow: Surrealist Writings on the Cinema* (San Francisco: City Lights Publishers, 2001), 51–54.

In addition to the above article, I refer the reader to some of my earlier writings: "La piste de l'écriture: lettres et fragments d'inscriptions," in Arnauld Pierre, ed., Disques et sémaphores. Le langage du signal chez Léger et ses contemporains, exhibition catalog (Biot: Musée National Fernand Léger, 2010), 52–59; "Un livre haut en couleur: La Fin du monde. Énergie visuelle et cinétique d'une création de Cendrars et Léger," in Hélène Campaignolle, Sophie Lesiewicz, and Gaëlle Théval, eds, Livre/Poésie/Typographie: une histoire en pratique(s), seminar proceedings (2012–13), (Paris: Éditions des Cendres, 2016 [in preparation]); "Signes des avant-gardes: l'alphabet entre construction, système, art et utopie," in Jacques André, ed., Histoire de l'écriture typographique. Le XXe siècle. 1900-1950 (vol. 1) (Gap: Atelier Perrousseaux/Adverbum, 2016 [in preparation]); and "Revolutionizing and Extending the Viewpoint. New visual and spatial experiences transform the field of graphics," in Paulina Kurc-Maj and Daniel Muzyczuk, eds, *A Machine for Communicating: Around the Avant-Garde Idea of New Typography*, colloquium proceedings (Łódź: Sztuki Museum, 2015), Polish version 59–90, English version 72–103.

33 ***Le Typographe*** **(The Typographer), 1918–19**
Oil on canvas
249.6 × 183.5 cm
Metropolitan Museum, New York, promised gift from the Leonard A. Lauder Cubist Collection

34 ***Le Drapeau*** **(Flag), 1919**
Oil on canvas
64.7 × 81 cm
Collection Mr. and Mrs. Howard and Nancy Marks

35 ***La Gare*** **(The Train Station), 1918**
Oil on canvas
56 × 81 cm
Private collection

36 ***Nature morte ABC*** **(Still Life ABC), 1927**
Oil on canvas
65 × 92 cm
Musée national Fernand Léger, Biot,

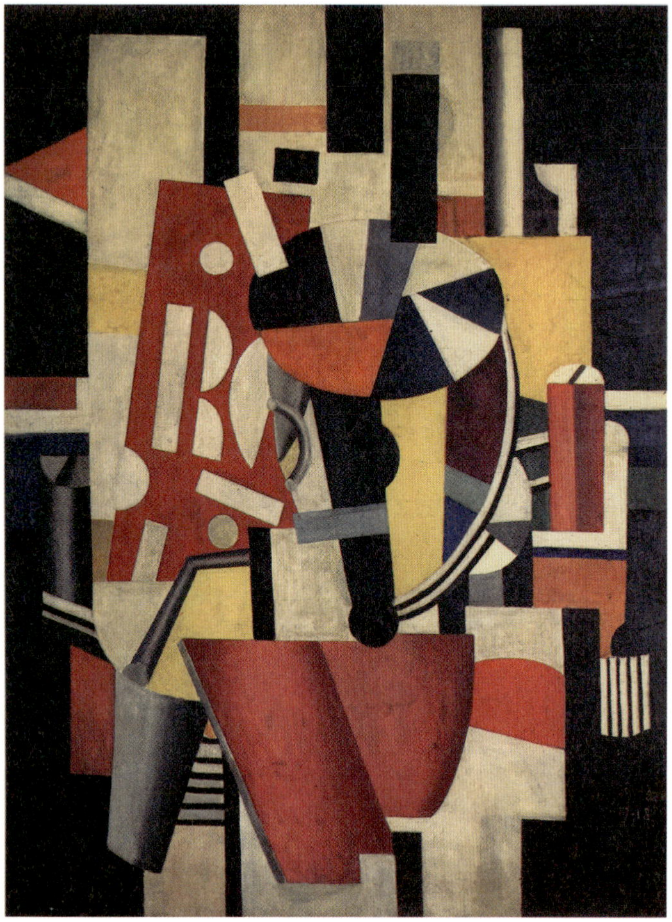

33

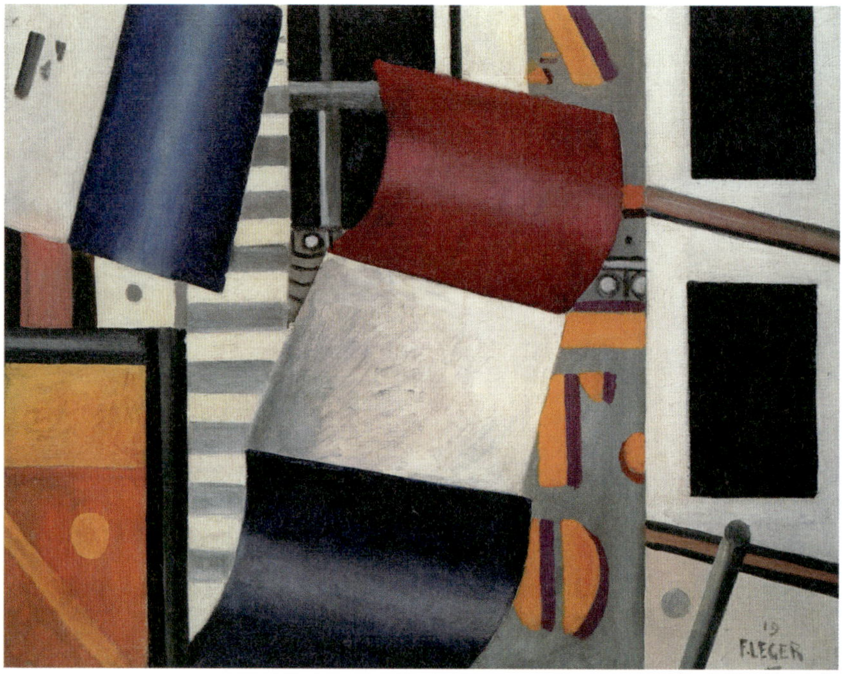

34

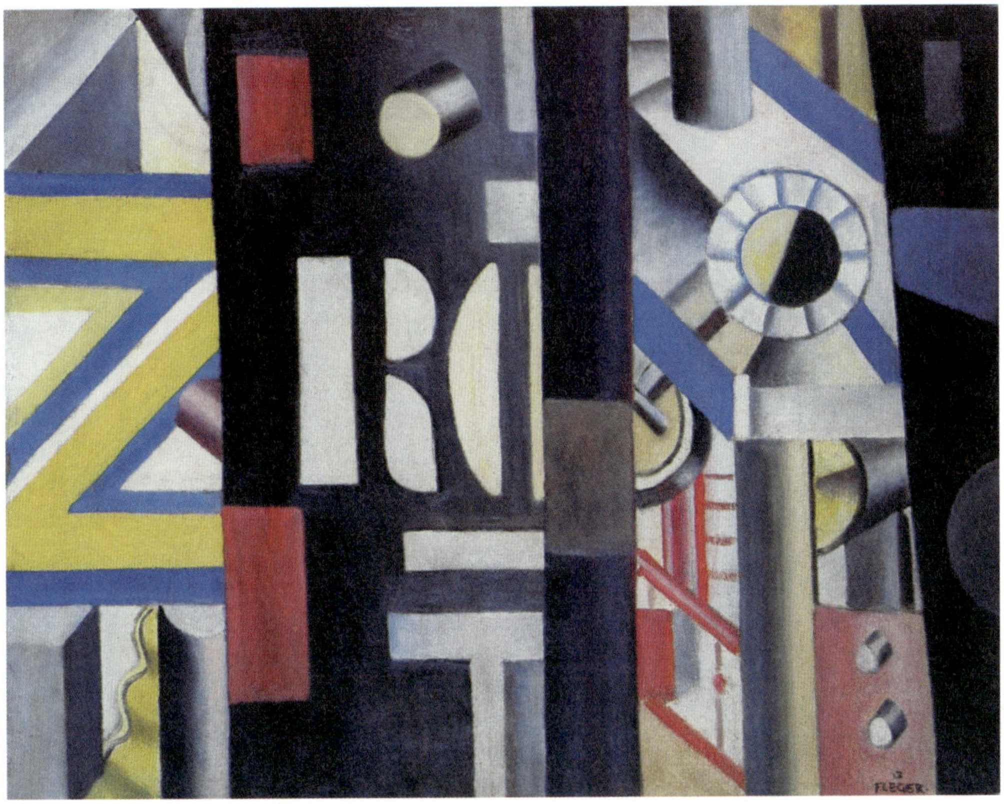

35

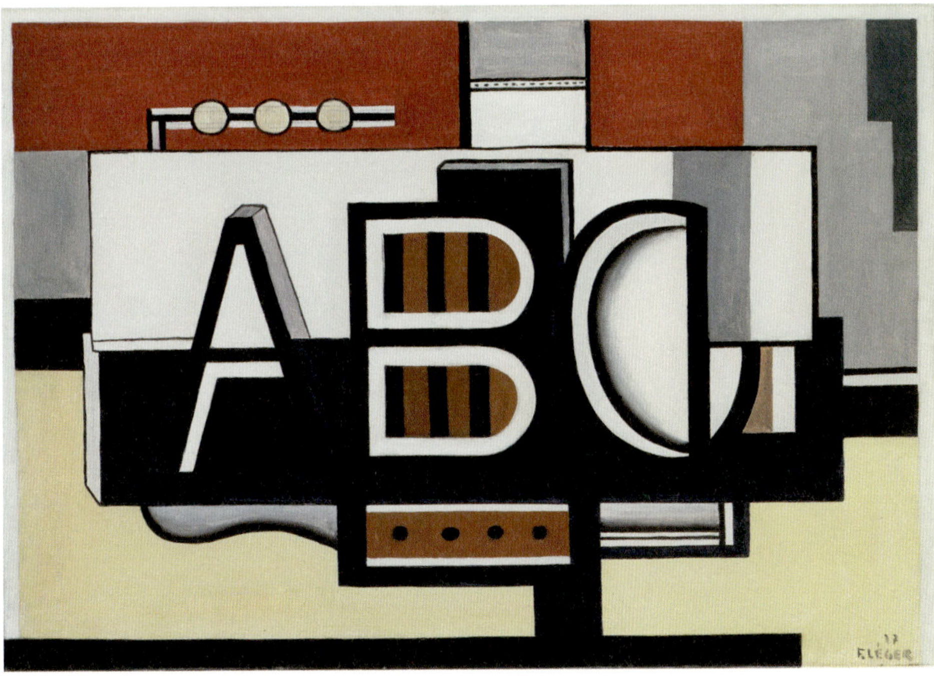

36

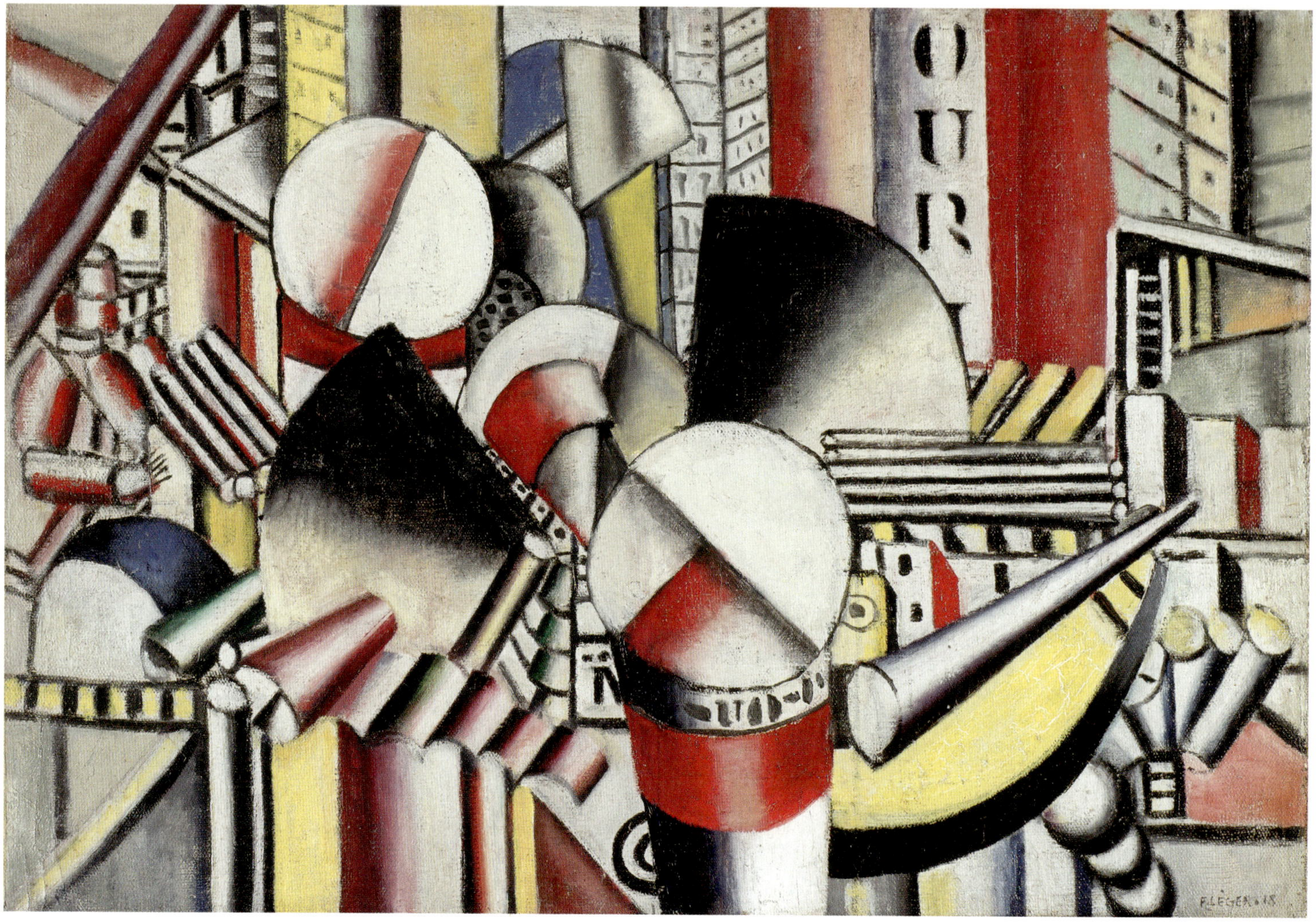

37

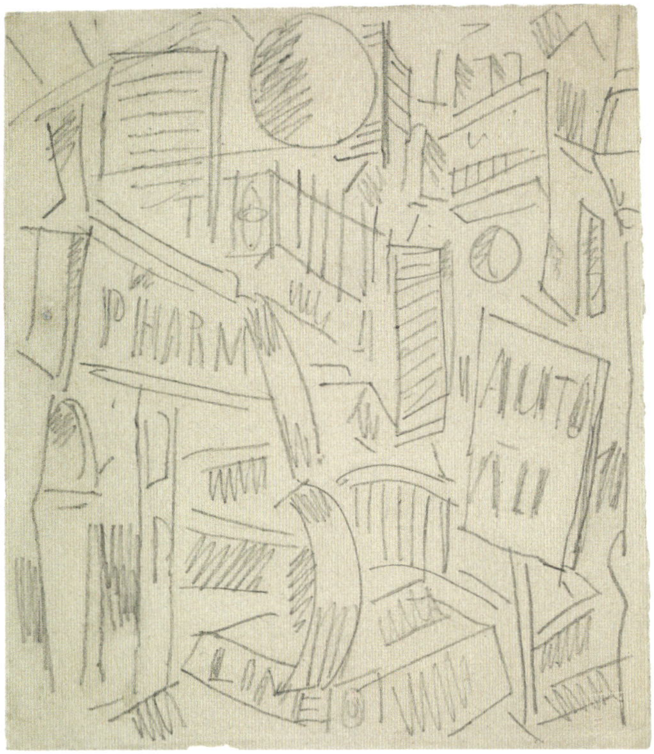

38

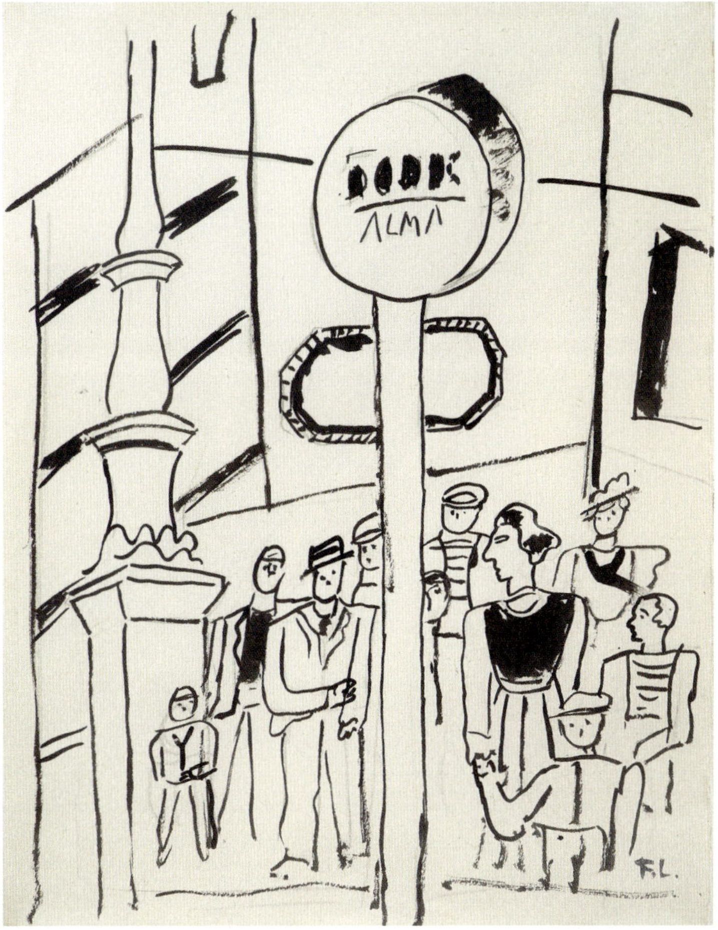

39

37 ***Le remorqueur rose* (The Pink Towboat), 1918**
Oil on canvas
66.5 × 92 cm
Museum Ludwig, Cologne

38 ***Sans titre, Dessin du front, Verdun***
(Untitled, Drawing of the front, Verdun), c. 1915
Pencil on paper
19.4 × 16.4 cm
Musée national Fernand Léger, Biot

39 ***L'arret d'autobus* (The Bus Stop), c. 1919**
India ink on paper
42.5 × 32 cm
Grafische Sammlung Museum Ludwig, Cologne

Painting and Architecture

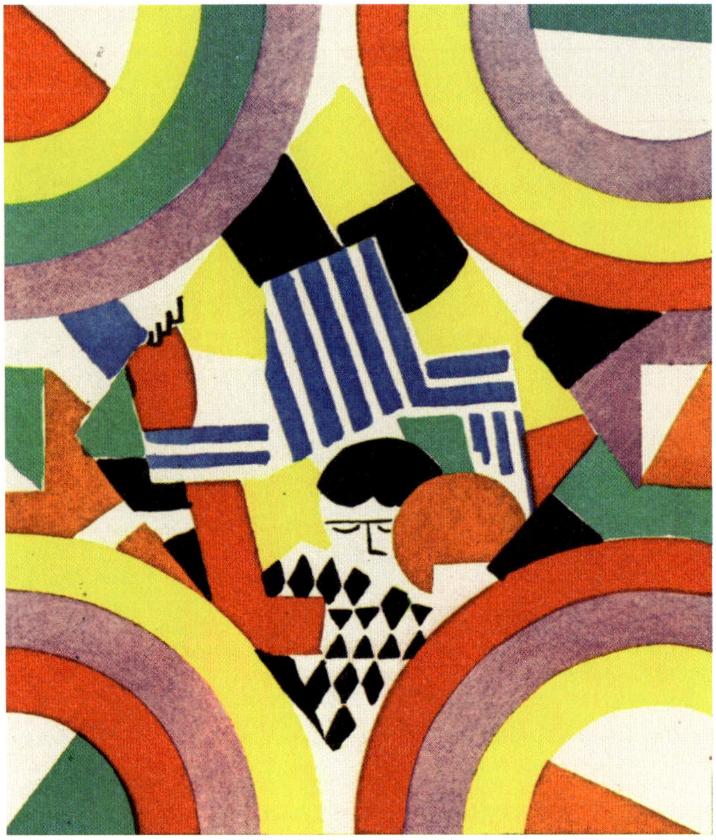

40

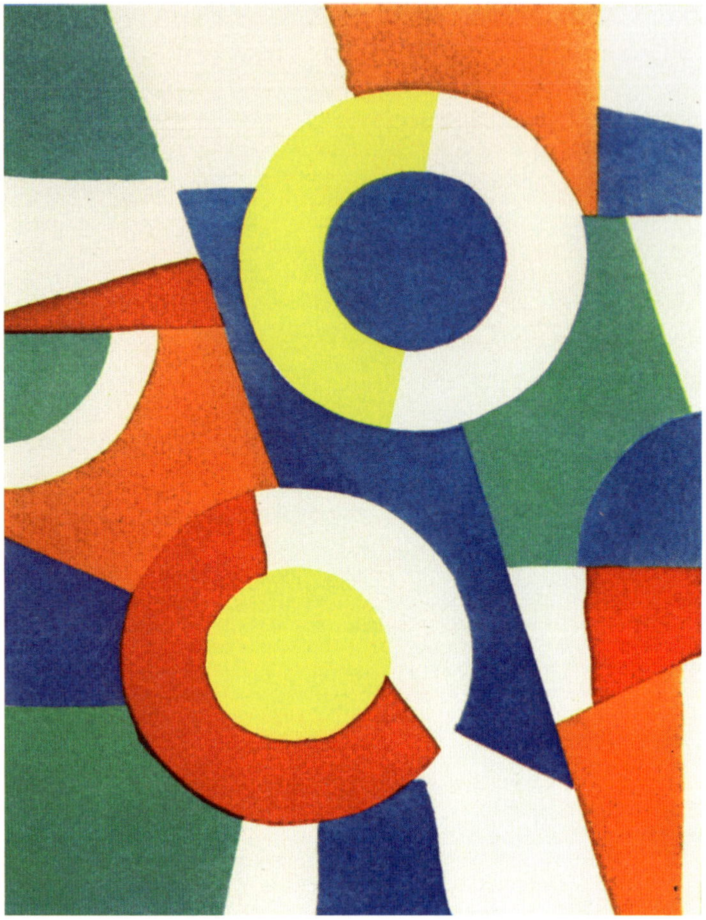

41

40 ***Projet décoratif pour Music Hall***
(Design for decoration of a music hall)

41 ***Projet de fresque (extérieur) (pour un hall d'hôtel)***
(Fresco design for the exterior wall of a hotel lobby), 1922
sheet: 22 × 27 cm
Panel 9 from *L'Architecture Vivante* (Fall/Winter 1924)

42 ***Eléments mécaniques* (Mechanical Elements), 1922**
Pencil, China ink, quill and brush on paper
27.4 × 21.1 cm
Musées royaux des Beaux-Arts de Belgique, Brussels, acc. no. 7338

43 ***Eléments mécaniques* (Mechanical Elements), 1922**
Pencil, China ink, quill and brush on paper
27.2 × 21 cm
Musées royaux des Beaux-Arts de Belgique, Brussels, acc. no. 7339

Decorative Project and Murals by Fernand Léger (1924)
Jean Badovici

CURIOUS BUT POWERFULL INTERPRETATIONS that are fundamentally studies of linear synthesis—they are abstract, geometric harmonies, masterfully colored and essentially decorative.

For a work to endure, it's not sufficient that it be constructed according to accepted principles; one must feel the artist's thought and his domination over the material. It's true that society today is perfectly satisfied to look at images dispassionately. But an artist like Léger strives to rescue it from this danger by disregarding the literal transcription of things. The determination of architectural forms, the selection of surfaces, the relationship among densities, these are the essentials elements for him. He knows that the vertical has dynamic properties opposed to those of the horizontal, which expresses stability and rest, and that specific constants influence the distribution of densities of light and shadow. Color has qualities in and of itself, independent of those lent by the shapes it assumes. Radiant or muted, receding or concentrated, it causes proportions and forms to vary. Léger substitutes a mathematical lyricism for the brute pleasure of the senses. He disciplines colors, mindful not only of their immediate power of suggestion, but also of their more distant and more profound relationships with the givens of our affective experience. He wants to create a physical atmosphere whose suggestive and emotional validity is universal. He mobilizes material constants that, outside of any convention, affect the most general properties of the senses and the spirit. Line is no longer a figurative factor but simply a rhythmic direction. For Léger, "mass must express space and depth constitute a virtually spatial element."

Originally published as J. Badovici, "Project décoratif et fresques, par F. Léger," in *L'Architecture Vivante* (Fall/Winter 1924): 10–11.
English translation by Liesl Yamaguchi in ed. Anna Vallye, *Léger: Modern Art and the Metropolis*, exh. cat., Philadelphia Museum of Art (New Haven and London, 2013), 214.

–

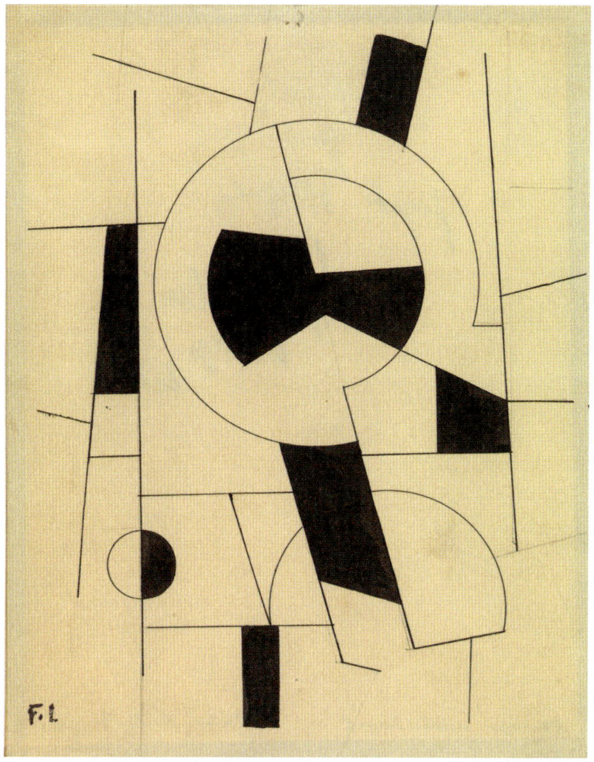

42

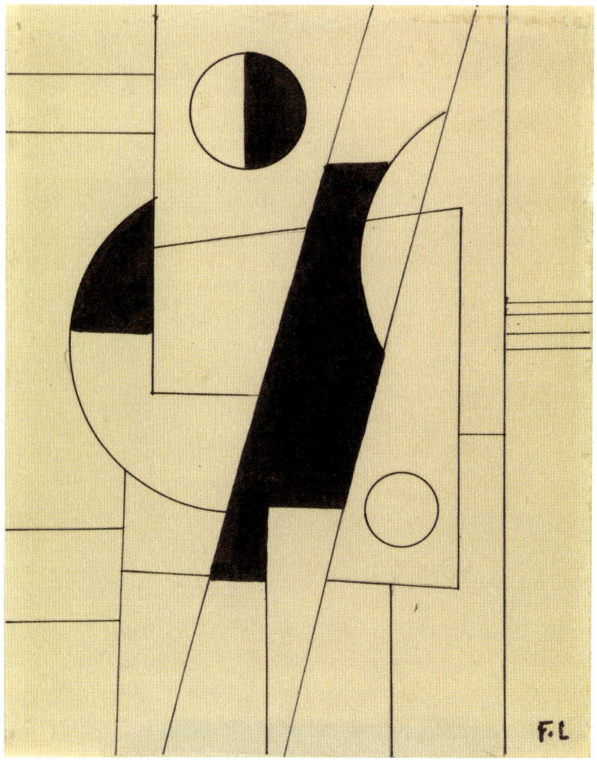

43

Polychromatic Architecture (1924)
Fernand Léger

Architecture is surface and volume. The qualities of volume are inherent: with surface they are relative, living or dead.

Man, set on living in an architectural environment, demands a reasonable quantity of both dead and living surfaces.

Architectural surface is either the horizontal or the vertical plane and is defined by volume.

What then takes place?

A balance of the need, if any, of the architect and his client to 'decorate'. Most men obey the 'decorative' instinct, under the pressure of 'horror vacui'. This 'horror vacui' makes use of the 'decorative' quality to negate itself by means of the living or dead surface. The 'decorative' quality takes the form of color and the object itself: the attributes are there and they can be used.

Architecture is organisation directed towards a rational and beautiful solution of all these values. Today this is a pressing problem and it is considered by active groups of modern artists the whole world over, and especially during the last few years.

In every case their effort and achievement is considerable. Modern artists want to rank the various qualities, they want to re-establish the principle of a plastic hierarchy.

The struggle is sharpest between the manufactured object or the art object (a picture, a relief) and the desire of modern architects to absorb them by their reduction to no more than a means of action in an organised ensemble.

Surface color (a decorative quality) must be used with rigorous discernment to be a 'natural function of architecture'.

In order to create a calm and anti-dynamic atmosphere, a plastic order in color inside or outside, certain knowledge of the relevant values are needed.

Pure color must be viable for internal and external application to maximise its value: thus, a square metre of yellow dominates an area four times its size. Replace it with a piece of red furniture and it too would by power of expansion dominate a considerable area.

The dynamic quality (picture or object) does have the right to a place in this organisation. Man is instinctively attracted by the movement created by an object like a child with something shiny. As for color, the crux is in the quantity. Color and the object have their plastic rationale: to facilitate a calm ensemble where the place for the sharp and unexpected is filled by the people who happen to be there.

In this new environment a man can be seen, for the eye is not distracted by dispersed qualities. Everything is arranged. Against these big calm areas the human face assumes its proper status. A nose, eye, foot, hand or jacket button will become a precise reality. The concept of an intelligent hierarchy of plastic possibilities is extremely modern and constitutes objective realism at its most powerful.

Architecture must take its place in nature without being too obvious. The idea of an object with startling qualities should be confined to the spectacle, and public holidays, being no more than temporary in quality. With an architectural work, the exact opposite holds. Here the quality is permanent, conceived in such way as not to be specific to any period, trend or expression, but simply useful and beautiful through its geometric order most appropriate to the site and inherent requirements.

Originally published as F. Léger, "L'Architecture polychrome," in *L'Architecture Vivante* (Fall/ Winter 1924): 21–22.
English translation by Charlotte Green in *Léger and Purist Paris*, exh. cat., Tate Gallery (London, 1970), 95–96.

–

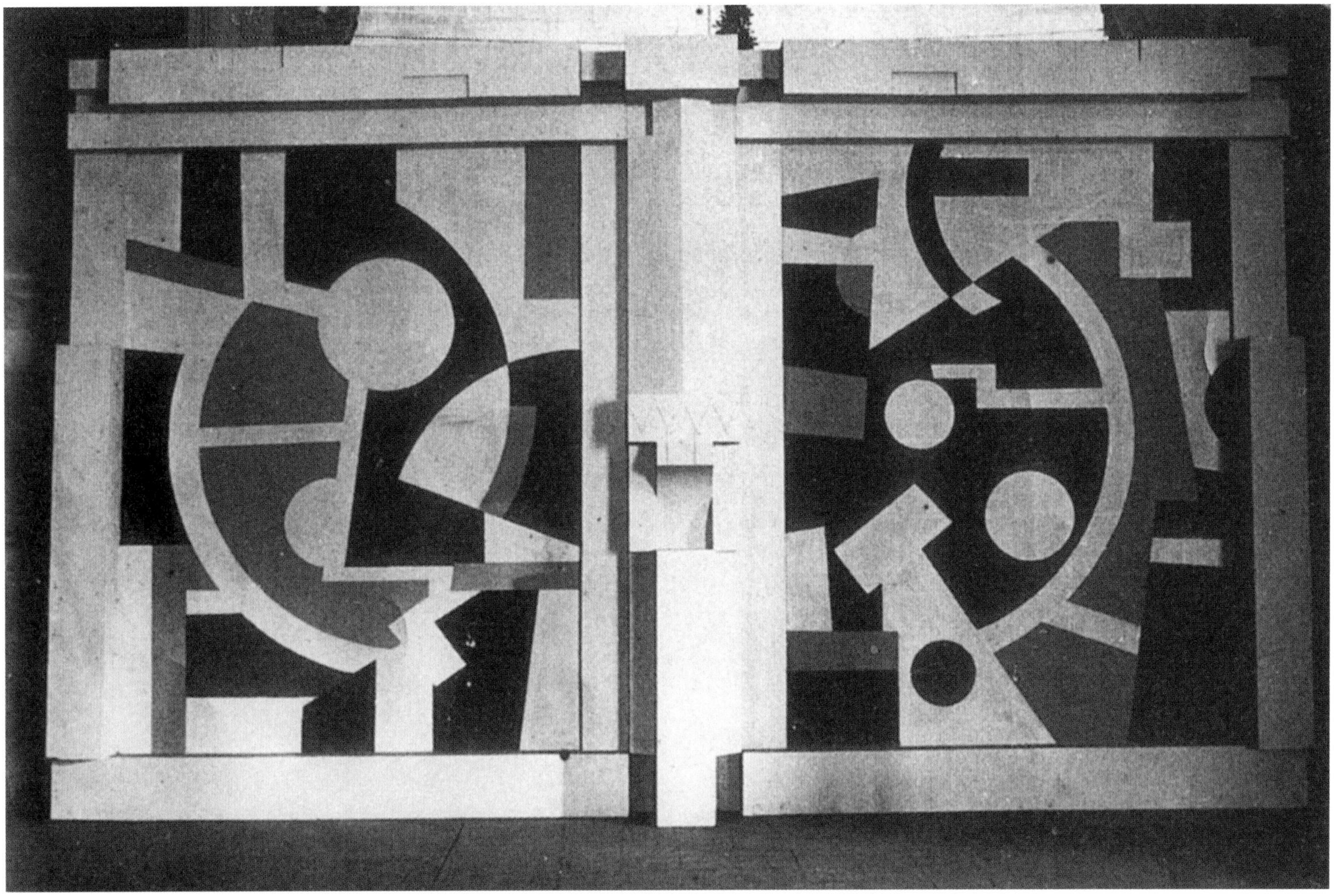

44

44 Fernand Léger and József Csáky
Design for the decoration of an entrance hall for the home of Jacques Doucet presented at the Salon des Indépendants, Paris, 1923
Architect: Robert Mallet-Stevens
Illustration from *L'Architecture Vivante* (Fall/Winter 1924)

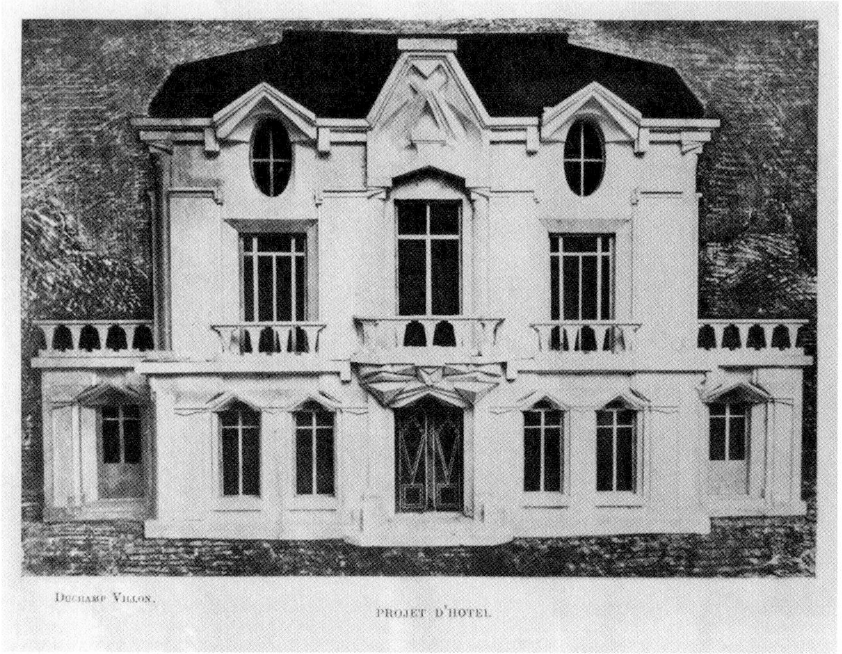

45

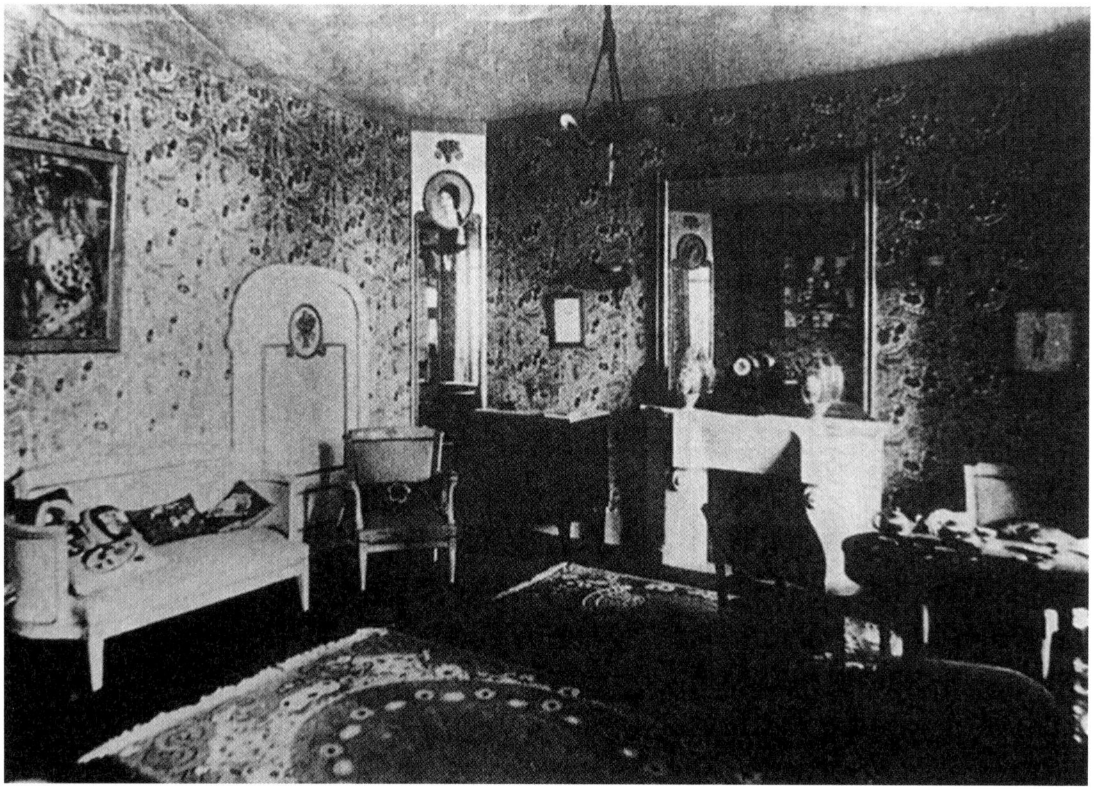

46

45 André Mare et. al.
Model of the Maison Cubiste at the Salon d'Automne exhibition, 1912

46 André Mare et. al.
***La Maison Cubiste* (Cubist House), Le Salon Bourgeois, Salon d'Automne, 1912, Paris**
On the left wall: Jean Metzinger, *Femme à l'Éventail* (Woman with Fan), 1912, reflected in the mirror: Fernand Léger, *Le passage à niveau* (Level Crossing) 1912. Center-left: Marie Laurencin, *Portrait of a Woman*

Between the Easel and the Mural: On the Social Ambitions of Painting in Space
By Anna Vallye

What is architectural painting? One day this question must take its rightful place among what we know to be the paradigmatic quandaries of the international avant-garde between World Wars I and II. Its geographical range, intellectual scope, and long legacy should put it on par with such firmly established vanguard artists' preoccupations as abstraction, the ready-made, mass media, and the *Gesamtkunstwerk*. Like those *others*, the problem of architectural painting was at the heart of the avant-garde project to reinvent the relationship between art and life. That was the crux of it for Léger as well.

Most of us are set in the mold of our youthful fixations, and Léger was no exception. The seed for his seemingly anomalous series of abstract "mural paintings" (executed between 1924 and 1926) and indeed for what would become a life-long interest in the mural genre, may already be found planted in his first published reflections of 1913. In a lecture at the Académie Wassilieff, published as "The Origins of Painting and Its Representational Value" (1913), Léger interprets the much-discussed departure from narrative and figurative representation in Cubist painting as fundamentally driven by the need for a redefined social purpose. In the past, he writes, the social function of painting was to convey an image of communal identity through the "description of great human events."[1] The role of salon or history painting was analogous to that played by the Gothic cathedral in Victor Hugo's famous allegory, "*Ceci tuera cela*" ("This will kill that"), in his novel *Notre-Dame de Paris* (1831/32): The invention of the Gutenberg press had spelled the death of architecture as the image of human thought and communal value cast in stone, henceforth delegating it to the far more nimble and pervasive medium of print. In the same way, Léger claims (citing Hugo) that the "sentimental literary concept" of painting has been made obsolete by the advent of modern "means of production" and reproduction.[2] For popular story-telling today, there is nothing better than the cinema. Stripped of its traditional literary function, modern painting locates a renewed social purpose in its "proper domain," to become an "equivalent," rather than an imitation, of modern life. The "pure" properties of painting (line, form, and color) are better used to capture the "creative spirit" of industrial modernity, a world made new through the accumulated impacts of relentless technological invention.[3]

The question of architectural painting would arise suspended between the two centers of gravity outlined by Léger in that very first essay: aesthetic autonomy and social commitment. That space had a distinct precedent in the history of modern painting. The generation of French artists that came of age before Léger, the so-called Generation of 1885, moved by anarchist, socialist, and other communitarian political currents of the fin de siècle, sought a potential art that could speak to the public realm in a revival of ancient mural traditions.[4] Yet, for these Symbolist and Post-Impressionist painters, a modern mural would have to find its way to public legibility without sacrificing its commitments to higher aesthetic and spiritual values, to the new freedom and independence from social conventions associated with easel painting and the enlightened clientele that cultivated it on the private art market. Thus, the "peculiar space between easel and mural" noted by the art historian T.J. Clark became the interval and interface where modern painting found itself "always pulled to and fro between private (defensive) and public (expository)," between the aesthetic and the social.[5]

"All my life," Léger would write in 1943, "I have been in conflict between the mural idea and the easel painting idea."[6] Indeed, when he penned his first thoughts in 1913, his own painting practice was already poised precisely between the easel and mural modalities, even if he was not yet engaged with the mural as medium. The previous year, he was a participant in two exhibitions at the Salon d'Automne: *La Section d'Or*, a more conventional painting exhibition in one of the galleries, and the Maison Cubiste, a *salon bourgeois* or model domestic interior housed in an architectural setting designed by Raymond Duchamp-Villon, which married painting to the decorative arts in a total environment, an aesthetic subversion of high and low intended to augur the leveling of social differences in utopian communal solidarity (figs. 45, 46).[7] Both projects were the culmination of ardent discussions held in and around the Paris suburb of Puteaux by a group of painters gathered around Albert Gleizes and Jean Metzinger, and including Léger as a frequent participant, engaged in the search for a truly modern painting that would at the same time be integrated into collective and communal life.[8] Deeply informed by Symbolist ideas on the radical communitarian potential of merging fine and decorative art, the Puteaux Cubists found themselves equally drawn to "pure painting" and the architectural environment.[9]

Léger's 1913 essay also demonstrates that he kept abreast of new architectural trends. "Architecture," he wrote, "stripped of all its representational trimmings, is approaching a modern and utilitarian conception... . Architectural art is confining itself to its own means—the relationship between lines and the balance of large masses... ."[10] He likely had in mind the austerely elegant work of younger French architects such as Auguste Perret, whose Théâtre des Champs-Élysées was completed in Paris the same year. Significantly, in restraining or omitting ornament—the architectural version of narrative—modern architecture, to Léger's mind, was following the same path toward formal purity that he had outlined for modern painting.

He would encounter a consummate manifestation of this pure architecture after the war in the work and thought of Swiss architect Charles-Édouard Jeanneret-Gris, better known as Le Corbusier, who became Léger's lifetime friend and collaborator after the two met in Paris in 1920. It was after meeting Corbusier that Léger first seriously contemplated the relationship between painting and architecture through a set of concepts that turned on the problem of color in space —or, as he wrote the following year, "color understood as an architectural element."[11] In 1920, Corbusier co-founded with the painter Amedée Ozenfant and the artist and critic Paul Dermée the extraordinary periodical *L'Esprit Nouveau*, which would become the primary discursive venue for clarifying the particular circuit they aimed to establish between modern aesthetics and society.

One of the key conceptual means for forging that link, put into circulation on the pages of *L'Esprit Nouveau,* was a set of ideas about the psychological impact of artistic form. As the scholar Nina Rosenblatt has demonstrated, the genealogy of those concepts may be traced to late-nineteenth-century discourses of perceptual psychology.[12] Their original source was the German philosophy of *Einfühlung* or "in-feeling," a neologism typically translated as "empathy." Significantly influential for turn-of-the-century avant-gardes across Europe, especially in architecture, empathy theory posited a psychology of aesthetic form based on the hypothesis that in the process of viewing we imaginatively or psychically "project" ourselves into the objects of perception.[13] As the philosopher Robert Vischer, who introduced the concept in 1873, wrote:

"I project my own life into the lifeless form... The perception of exterior limits to a form can combine in some obscure way with the sensation of my own physical boundaries, which I feel on, or rather with, my own skin."[14]

In empathetic reception, the viewing experience of the art-work is understood to be corporeal, and thus spatial, rather than primarily optical. Indeed, Vischer called the sum of such responses our "spatial imagination."[15] It was also entirely independent of any representational content, and solely a matter of the qualitative properties of line, color, shape, and pattern. For French thinkers like Jean-Marie Guyau and Victor Basch, featured on the pages of *L'Esprit Nouveau*, Rosenblatt argues, the psychic effects of empathetic response were fundamentally *collective*, rather than individual. To German theory, the French added, in other words, a "model of the aesthetic subject as a social being, immersed through the physiological facts of life itself within the shifting unities that comprise collective experience."[16] As such, aesthetics could be used to engender the sensations or attitudes of communal unity. Not surprisingly, then, the discourse first nourished the "solidarist" ambitions of the artists' generation of 1885.[17] It returned in the 1920s on the pages of Corbusier's journal as conceptual ground for a new socially or collectively based art of pure form in space.

In Corbusier's thought of that decade, concern for architecture's relationship to the urban and technological conditions of industrial modernity was coupled to a conception of built form astonishing in its elemental abstraction. "Architecture," he famously wrote, "is the masterful, correct and magnificent play of masses brought together in light."[18] He would read Léger's painting in similarly stark terms as a "masterful and magnificent play of colored forces moving on the surface of a wall."[19] As Léger's own ideas focused on the environmental impact of his painting, they too exhibited a concern with color's psychological and ambient effects. Color, he often repeated, is a "vital necessity," key to emotional and even physical health.[20] "A square meter of yellow," he wrote in 1924, "dominates an area four times its size."[21] The set of abstract compositions in vivid primary colors he composed between 1924 and 1926 were tuned to this mode of reflection. He invented for them the rather paradoxical category of "mural paintings" to indicate that they were meant to be viewed as a constituent part of a spatial whole. "Mural painting" was, in his words, "dependent on architecture..., [a] materialization in abstract, flat, colored surfaces, with the volumes supplied by the architectural and sculptural masses."[22]

To the mural typology, Léger counterposed "easel painting," which he saw as an "art object..., isolated, and embodied in a frame."[23] This mural-easel binary was, in part, a translation into terms more familiar to French discourse, as we have seen, of a distinction crucial to the thought of De Stijl artist Theo van Doesburg, whose influence formed the other magnetic pole to that of Corbusier for Léger's reflections on painting in space. Van Doesburg probably met Léger also in 1920, and his abstract *Contra-Constructions*, polychromatic architectural studies, done in collaboration with the architect Cornelis van Eesteren, and exhibited in Paris in 1923, evidently served as the immediate catalysts for Léger's "mural painting" series (figs. 47, 50).[24] Van Doesburg established a fundamental opposition between modern abstract painting and the representational "easel picture." While the latter could only capture an illusion of the third dimension, the former, having taken on the flatness of the wall, formed a "rhythmical unity with architecture" and so "projected" beyond the limits of the frame into real space, becoming "architectonic."[25] Only a logical step would then lead from an "architectonic" canvas, such as van Doesburg's own abstract compositions, to an entire architectural environment orchestrated through color (fig. 48). The 1923 exhibition illustrated that eventuality. "We have given color its rightful place in architecture," proclaimed the De Stijl manifesto that accompanied the show, "and we assert that painting separated from the architectonic construction (i.e., the picture) has no right to exist."[26]

In the end, the *Contra-Construction* was to be but an aesthetic premonition of a social utopia to be brought about through the union of art and life. That *projection* too, to use a play on words not out of keeping with the spirit of the endeavor, bore a distant echo of *Einfühlung*. For, as a consummate avant-garde networker, van Doesburg was well aware of the parallel concept of "pictorial architecture" (*Képarchitektúra*, or *Bildarchitektur* in German) developed by the Hungarian avant-garde artists Lajos Kassák and László Moholy-Nagy, who were conversant with both the Berlin avant-gardes and with German aesthetic philosophy. Abstract art, wrote Moholy-Nagy in 1922, "not only registers contemporary problems, but projects a desirable future order... [It] creates

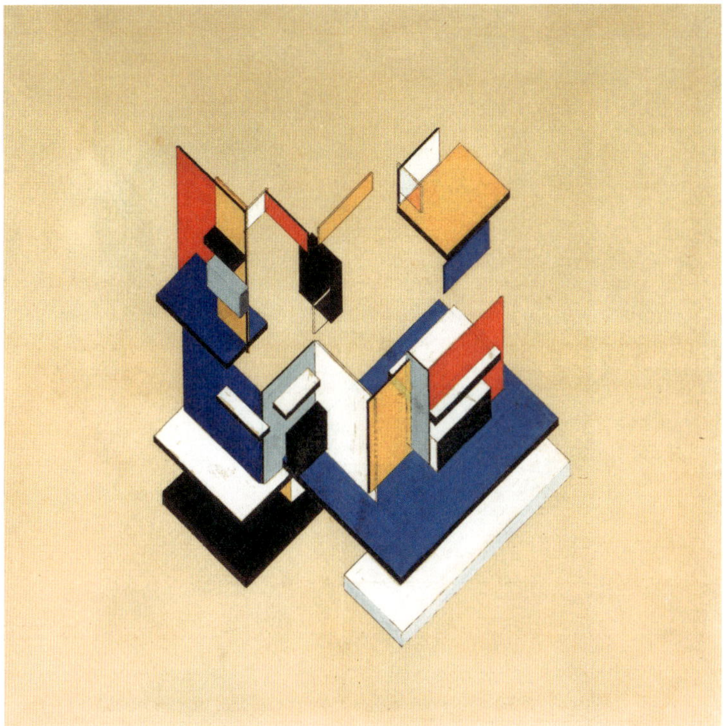

47

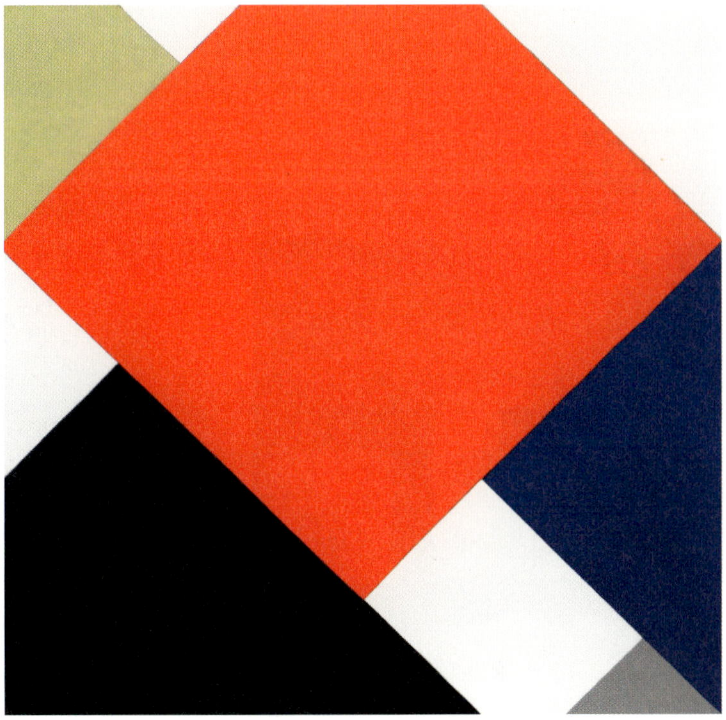

48

47 Theo van Doesburg (Christian Emil Marie Küpper) in collaboration with Cornelis van Eesteren
***Contra-constructie V* (Contra-Construction V. Axonometric Project for a Private House), 1923**
Gouache and ink on paper
57.1 × 57.1 cm
Museum of Modern Art, Edgar J. Kaufmann Jr. Fund, New York

48 Theo van Doesburg (Christian Emil Marie Küpper)
***Contra-Construction de la Maison particulière* (Contra-Construction of the Private House), May 2, 1924**
Gouache
57 × 57 cm
Collection of the Instituut Collectie Nederlands

49 Lajos Kassák
Képarchitektúra **(Pictorial Architecture V), c. 1924**
Oil on cardboard
28 × 20.5 cm
Magyar Nemzeti Galéria, Budapest, acc. no. 70.130 T

50 **De Stijl group exhibition at the Galerie L'Effort Moderne, Paris, October 15 – November 15, 1923**

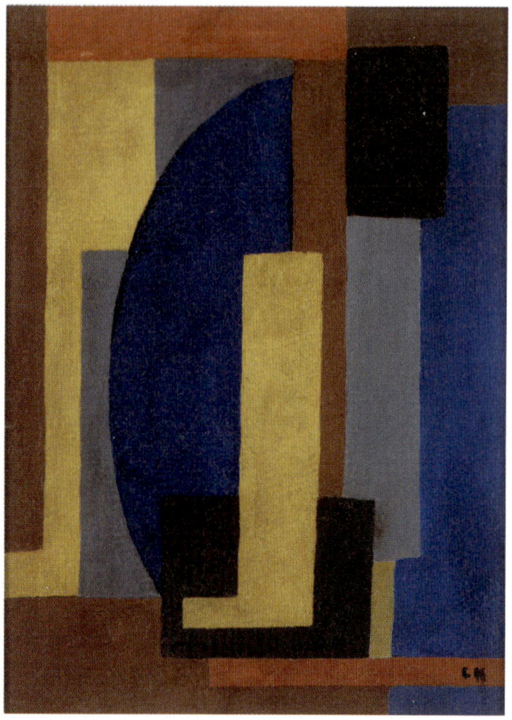

49

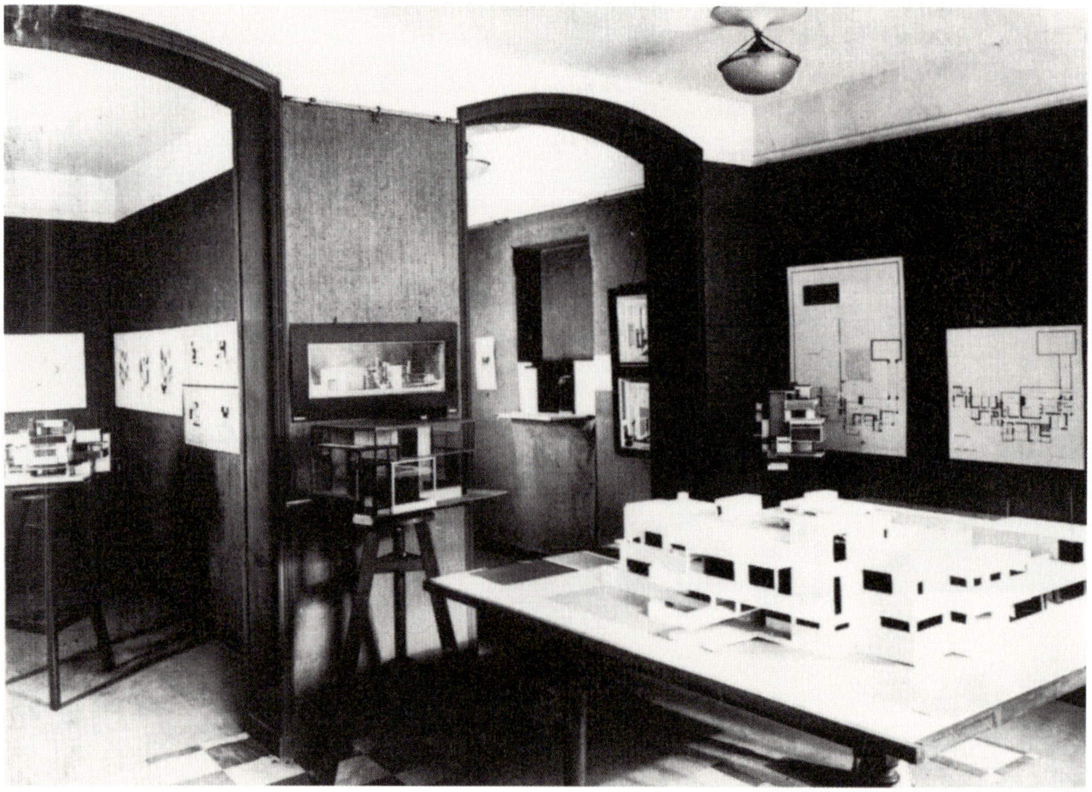

50

new types of spatial relationships, new inventions of forms... as the visual counterpoint to a more purposeful, cooperative human society."[27] His and Kassák's geometric abstractions, formally quite similar to Léger's "murals," were meant to prefigure a "collective architecture of the future" as the analogue of the collective society to come (fig. 49).[28] So, when van Doesburg wrote approvingly in 1929 that Léger "add[ed] to painting a projection,"[29] he was bringing the latter's solution to the old easel-mural quandary of French modernism firmly into the fold of the international avant-garde.

1 Fernand Léger, "The Origins of Painting and Its Representational Value" (1913), in Fernand Léger, *Functions of Painting*, ed. Edward F. Fry, trans. Alexandra Anderson (New York: Viking, 1973), 4.
2 Ibid., 11–12.
3 Ibid., 10. See also Anna Vallye, "The Painter on the Boulevard," in *Léger: Modern Art and the Metropolis*, ed. Anna Vallye (Philadelphia: Philadelphia Museum of Art, and New Haven: Yale University Press, 2013), 10–11.
4 See Daniel Robbins, "From Symbolism to Cubism: The Abbaye of Créteil," *Art Journal* 23, no. 2 (Winter 1963/64): 111–16.
5 T.J. Clark, *Farewell to an Idea: Episodes from a History of Modernism* (New Haven: Yale University Press, 1999), 160. For a discussion of the mural problem in French culture in the mid-century, see Romy Golan, *Muralnomad: The Paradox of Wall Painting, Europe 1927–1957* (New Haven: Yale University Press, 2009).
6 Fernand Léger, letter to Alfred Barr, 20 November 1943, reproduced in Robert L. Herbert, *From Millet to Léger: Essays in Social Art History* (New Haven: Yale University Press, 2002), appendix B, 177.
7 See David Cottington, "The Maison Cubiste and the Meaning of Modernism in Pre-1914 France," in *Architecture and Cubism*, ed. Eve Blau and Nancy J. Troy (Montreal: Centre Canadien d'Architecture / Canadian Center for Architecture; Cambridge, MA: MIT Press, 1997), 17–40.
8 See Christopher Green, *Léger and the Avant-Garde* (New Haven: Yale University Press, 1976), 6–38; Robbins, "From Symbolism to Cubism."
9 The concept of non-representational "pure painting" was formulated, above all, by the influential poet and art critic Guillaume Apollinaire, whose ideas were also important for the Section d'Or artists. See Guillaume Apollinaire, *Les peintres cubistes* (1913), trans. Mrs. Charles Knoblauch as *Aesthetic Meditations on Painting: The Cubist Painters* (Chicago: Margaret C. Anderson, 1922).
10 Léger, "The Origins of Painting," 10.
11 Fernand Léger, "Color in Life (Fragment of a Study on the New Plastic Values)," in Vallye, *Léger: Modern Art and the Metropolis*, 237.
12 Nina Rosenblatt; "Empathy and Anaesthesia: On the Origins of a French Machine Aesthetic," *Grey Room* 2 (Winter 2001): 78–97.
13 See Harry Francis Mallgrave, ed., *Empathy, Form, and Space: Problems in German Aesthetics, 1873–1893* (Los Angeles: Getty Center for the History of Art and the Humanities, 1993).
14 Robert Vischer, "On the Optical Sense of Form: A Contribution to Aesthetics" (1873), in Mallgrave, *Empathy, Form, and Space*, 91–92.
15 Ibid.
16 Rosenblatt, "Empathy and Anaesthesia," 86.
17 Ibid., 84.
18 See Le Corbusier, *Toward an Architecture* (1927), trans. John Goodman (Los Angeles: J. Paul Getty Trust, 2007), 102.
19 Le Corbusier, "Architecture and Fernand Léger" (1929), translated in Vallye, *Léger: Modern Art and the Metropolis*, 216.
20 Léger, "Color in Life," 237.
21 Fernand Léger, "Polychromatic Architecture" (1924), in John Golding and Christopher Green, *Léger and Purist Paris* (London: Tate Gallery, 1970), 96.
22 Fernand Léger, "The Machine Aesthetic, II: Geometric Order and Truth" (1925), in *Functions of Painting*, 64.
23 Ibid. Emphasis in the original.
24 See Vallye, "The Painter on the Boulevard," 30–34.
25 Theo van Doesburg, quoted in Nancy J. Troy, *The De Stijl Environment* (Cambridge, MA: MIT Press, 1983), 30.
26 Cornelis van Eesteren, Theo van Doesburg, and Gerrit Rietveld, "Towards a Collective Construction (Manifesto V of the De Stijl Group)" (1923), in Ulrich Conrads, ed., *Programs and Manifestoes on 20th-Century Architecture* (Cambridge, MA: MIT Press, 2002), 66.
27 Cited in Oliver Botar, *Technical Detours: The Early Moholy-Nagy Reconsidered* (New York: The City University of New York, 2006), 146–47.
28 László Moholy-Nagy, Ernő Kállai, Alfréd Kemény, László Péri, "Manifesto" (1923), translated and reprinted in Krisztina Passuth, *Moholy-Nagy* (London: Thames and Hudson, 1985), 288. See also S.A. Mansbach, ed., "Revolutionary Engagements: The Hungarian Avant-Garde," in *Standing in the Tempest: Painters of the Hungarian Avant-Garde, 1908–1930* (Santa Barbara: Santa Barbara Museum of Art and Cambridge, MA: MIT Press, 1991), 94–95.
29 Theo van Doesburg, "Fernand Léger et le Cubisme," *Sélection: Chronique de la Vie* 5 (1929): 20. Author's translation.

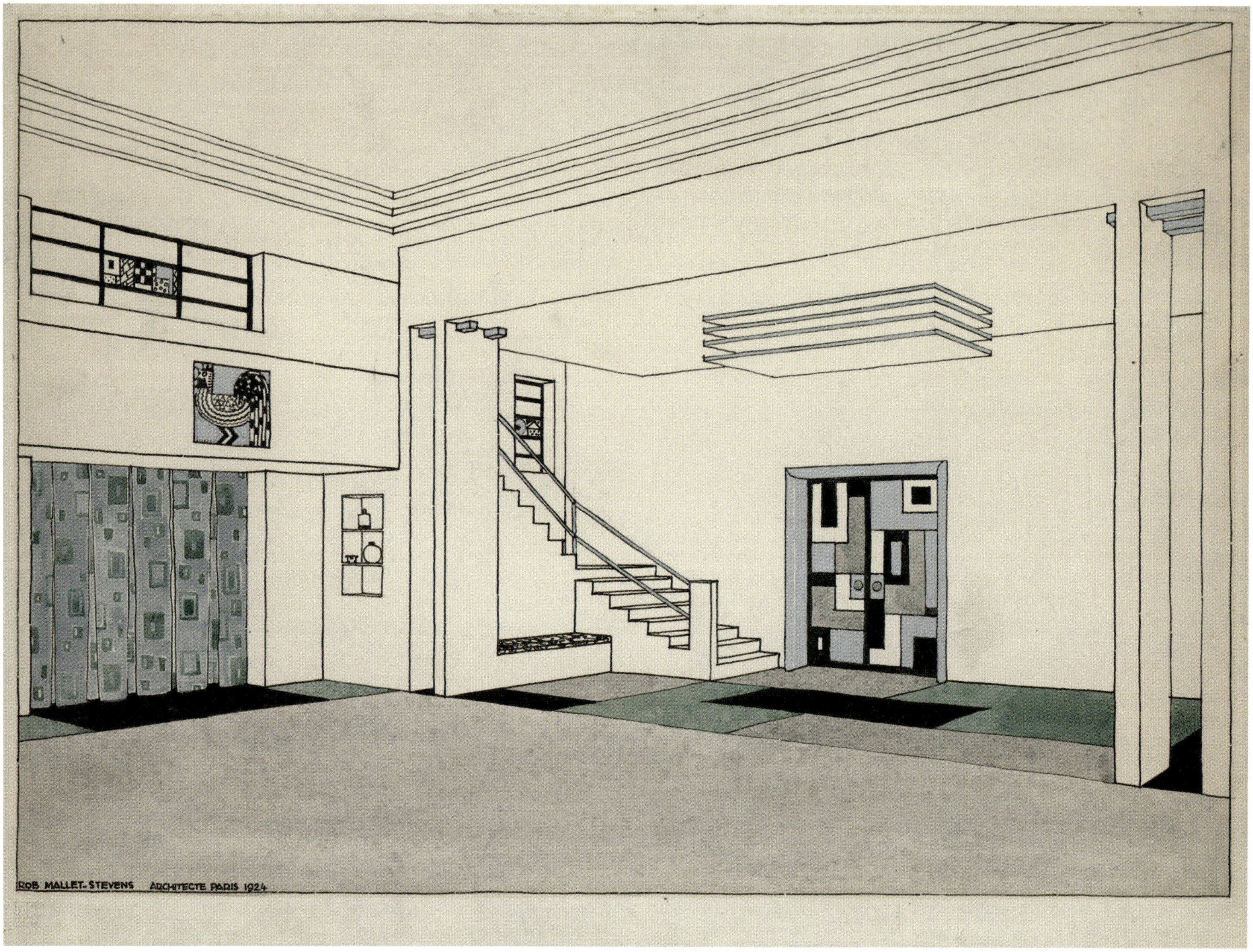

51

51 Robert Mallet-Stevens
Projet pour le hall de l'Ambassade française à l'exposition des Arts décoratifs de 1925
(Design for a hall for the French embassy at the Exhibition of Decorative Arts in 1925), 1924
China ink and gouache on Bristol board
48 × 63.2 cm
Les Arts Décoratifs, Paris

THE "AFFAIR" OF THE ARTS DÉCORATIFS EXHIBITION (1925)
Signed FELS, with citations from Fernand Léger, Robert Delaunay

At the Arts Décoratifs exhibition, various decorators under the direction of Monsieur Mallet-Stevens unveiled plans for a French embassy.

Monsieur Mallet-Stevens has placed in the embassy vestibule two panels by two artists with extremely modern ideas: Monsieur Fernand Léger and Monsieur Robert Delaunay.

These works having since been removed, we have decided to place before the readers of *Les Nouvelles Littéraires* the facts that led up to the suppression of these wall decorations.

[…] M. DELAUNAY – This is what occurred in the hall of that embassy at the Arts Décoratifs following the absurd walkout by the Director of the Fine Arts [Paul Léon], steered by a pallid individual, the assistant president of the Artists-Decorators.

These gentlemen, of whose role I remain unsure, had, on seeing my picture *The City of Paris*, as well as in front of a panel by Léger, chortled with indignation. With due show of respectful piety, I begged to inform them that French art has never been in such rude health.

[…] We ask nothing of them, not even that they purchase an inch of paint for the museums of France, museums abroad having already stocked up. But, at bottom, the ignorance of the people appointed to organize this exhibition is equaled only by their pettiness. In accordance with the letter shown to me by Mallet-Stevens, their sole response was to order the removal of these panels in twenty-four hours.

I will not take down *The City of Paris*.

***

FERNAND LÉGER – Mallet-Stevens had said to me: Here's 80 centimeters wide by 2 meters 40, make me something.

I did a decoration project for a wall painting to be executed in mosaic.

I didn't do a picture.

A hall people walk through should not be decorated with an easel painting, which obeys different laws.

The dimensions were stipulated by the architect.

The architect requires a motif in such and such a place, he wants some color on a white surface.
It would be irrational of me to produce a grisaille for a locale open to the outside.

After being inspected by the jury, the projects were so heavily reworked that the creators themselves could hardly recognize their original plans.

Does an architect have the right to decorate an environment according to his own ideas?

Groult, who did the ambassador's wife's bedroom, put some Marie Laurencins in it.

Were these works presented to the jury?

No. This is nothing more than the thought police, and, moreover, Paul Léon has engineered the affair to the extent that someone has dared to state in front of our works: "That isn't the French spirit!"

Excerpts from text originally published as FELS, "L'Affaire de l'exposition des arts décoratifs," in *Les Nouvelles Littéraires* (June 6, 1925).

–

Letter from Fernand Léger to Robert Delaunay, May 30, 1925

My Dear Delaunay,

I couldn't be with you the other day.
I found your note too late yesterday.
Messrs Rapin and Hairez [?]
have rejected our panels
you probably received a request
to take them down. Don't do anything.
reply that they should talk to
Mr. Mallet-Stevens - for that.
He ordered the work from us
so he should be
responsible for their removal !
I've informed everybody.

Cordially

FLéger

Centre Pompidou, Bibliothèque Kandinsky, Fonds Robert et Sonia Delaunay, DEL 153, Correspondance Fernand Léger, Paris.

–

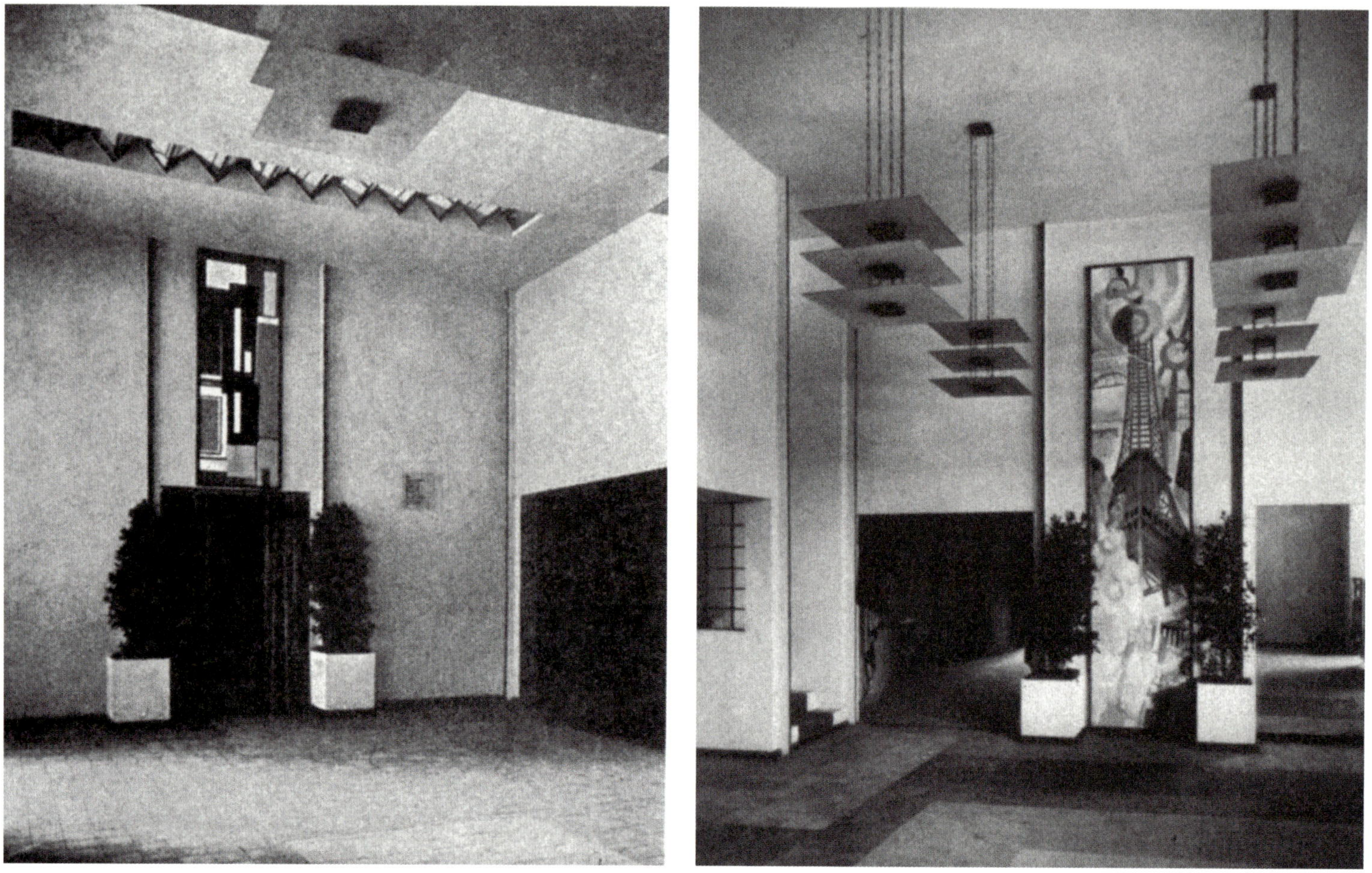

52

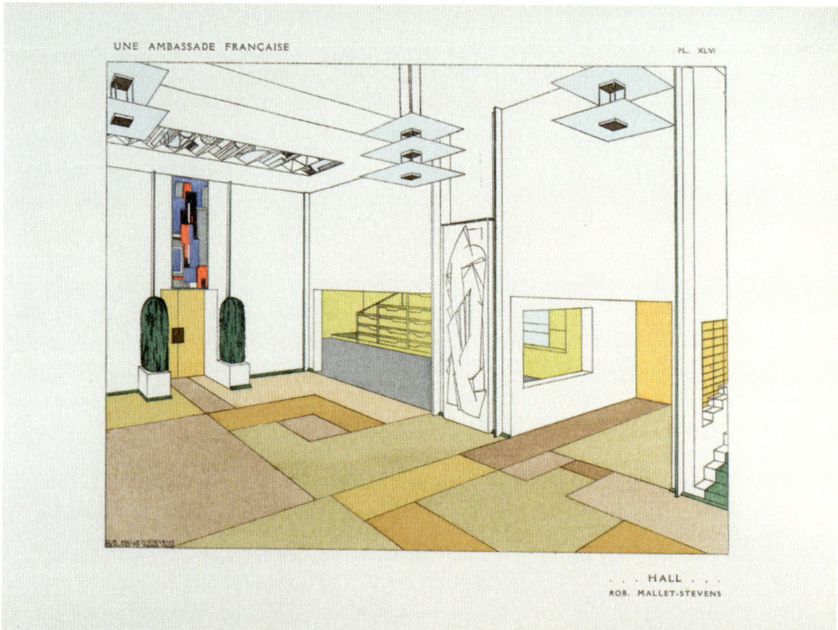

53

52 **Interior view of the lobby of the French embassy at the *Exposition internationale des Arts décoratifs et industriels modernes* (International Exhibition of Decorative and Industrial Modern Arts), Paris, 1925**
Architect: Robert Mallet-Stevens;
mural: Fernand Léger
Illustration from *L'Amour de l'art,* 1925, p. 291

53 ***Une Ambassade française* (organized by the Société des Artistes Décorateurs), Éditions Charles Moreau, 1925**
Stencil print
25 × 32.4 cm
Bibliothèque des Arts décoratifs, Paris

54 **Study for a mural painting, 1925**
Opaque watercolor and black ink
over graphite on vellum
Image: 24.1 × 8.3 cm, sheet: 36.8 × 21.1 cm
Philadelphia Museum of Art, A. E. Gallatin Collection, 1952-61-60

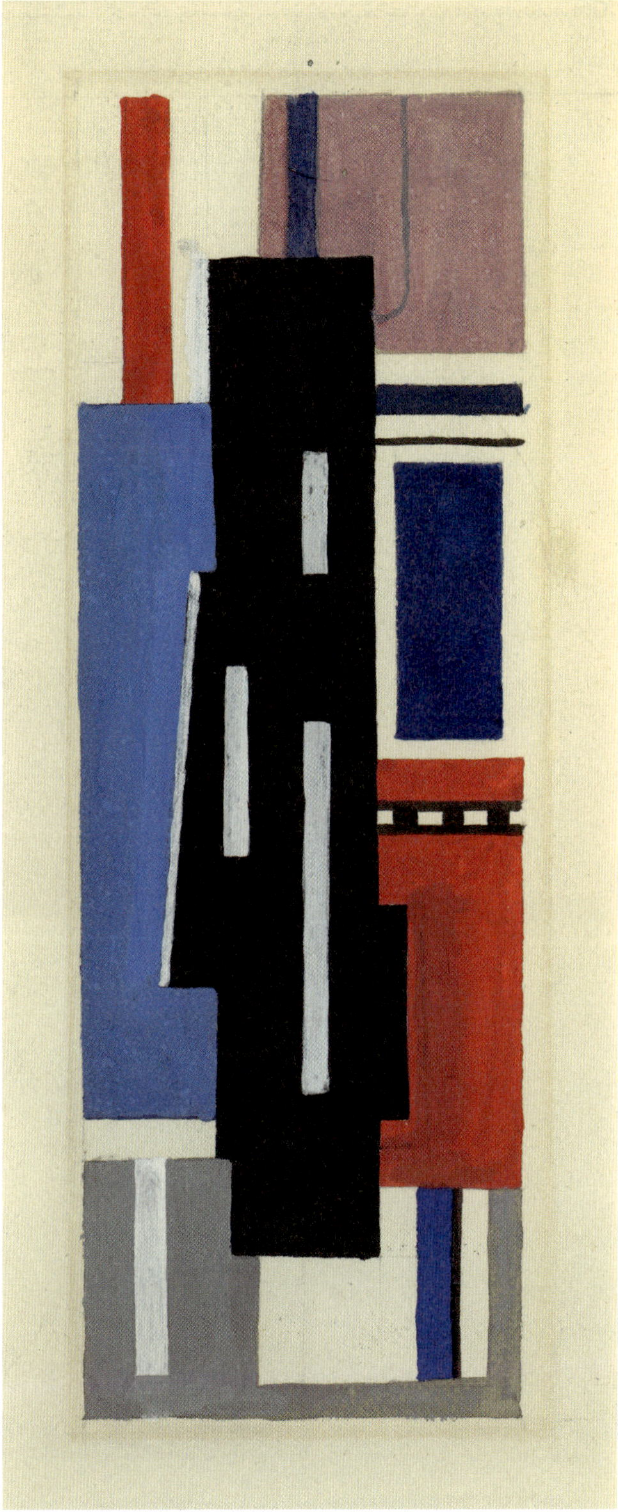

54

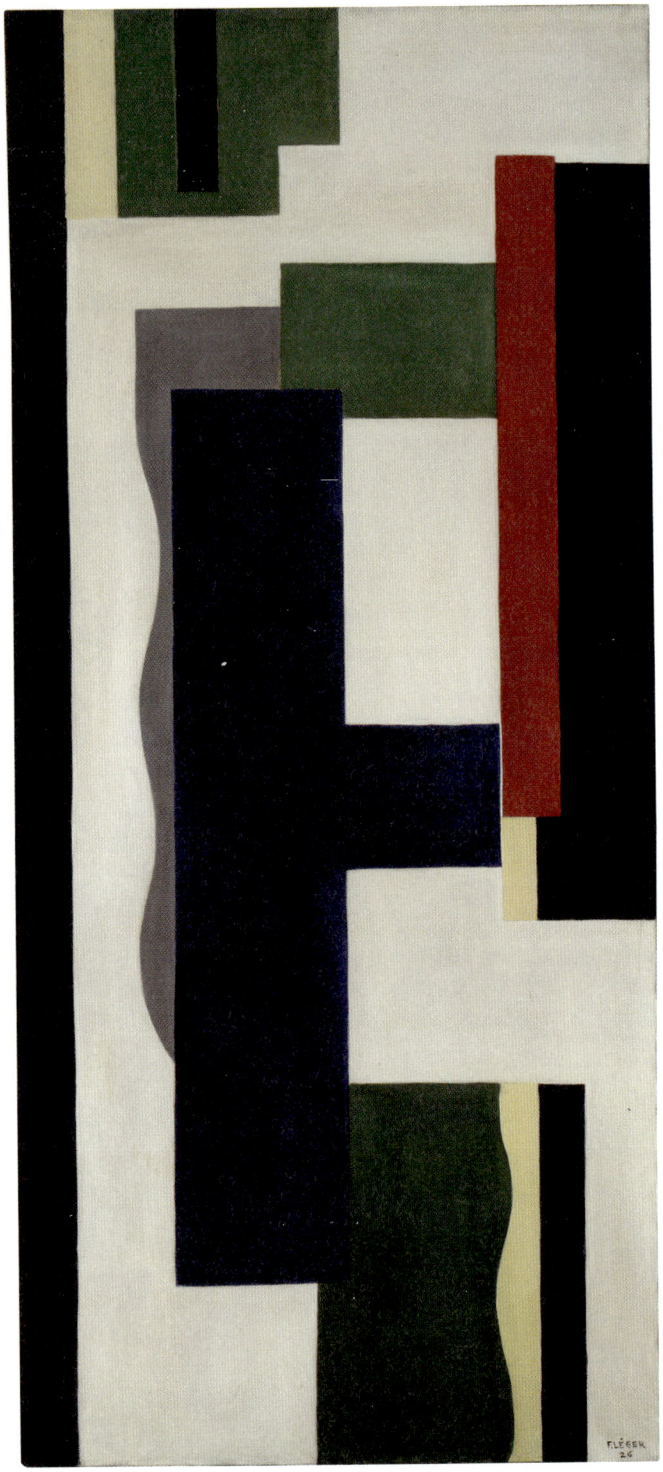

55

55 ***Peinture murale* (Mural Painting), 1926**
Oil on canvas
180 × 80 cm
The Menil Collection, Houston

56 ***Peinture murale* (Mural Painting), 1924**
Oil on canvas
180.3 × 79.2 cm
Museum of Modern Art, New York, acc. no. 49.1965

57 ***Peinture murale* (Mural Painting), 1924/25**
Oil on canvas
180.2 × 80.2 cm
Solomon R. Guggenheim Museum, New York,
acc. no. 58.1507

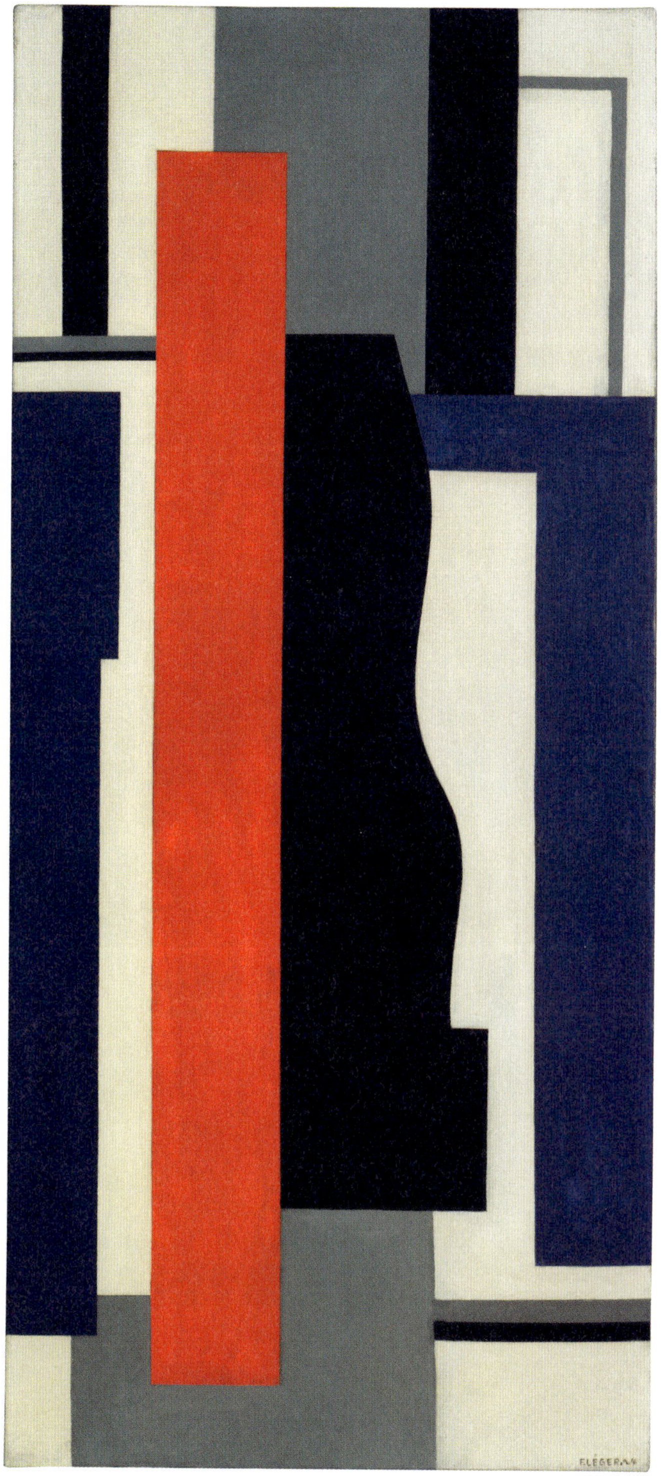

56

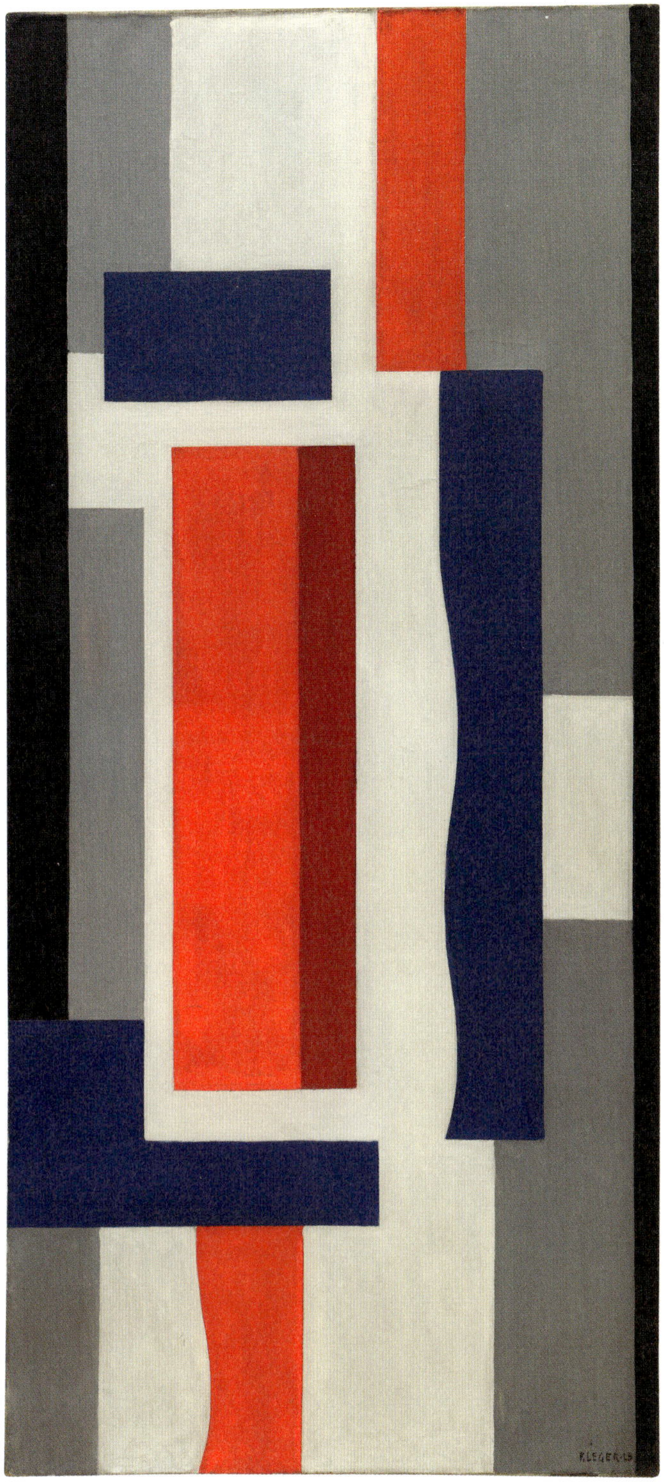

57

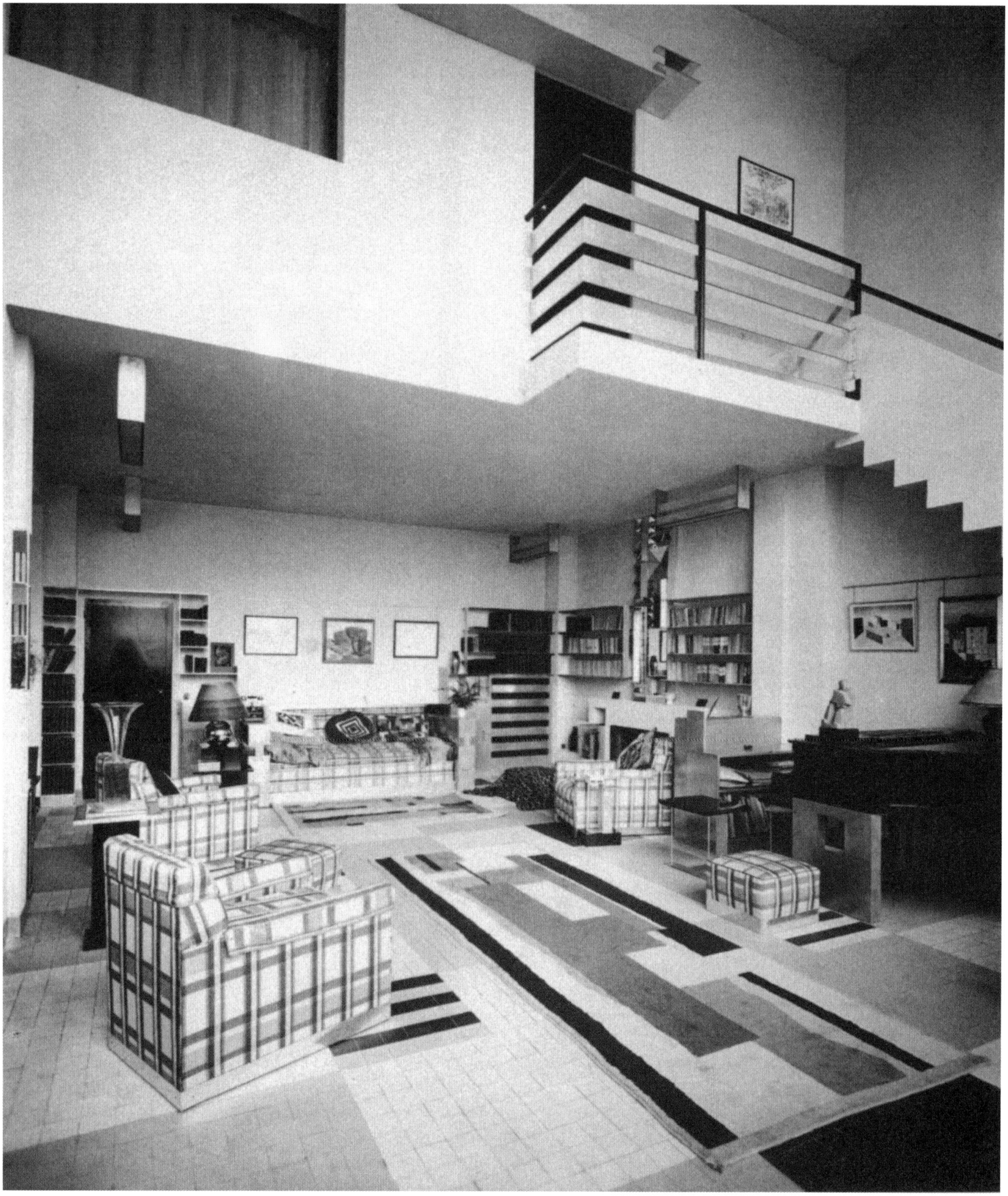

58

58 **Rug by Fernand Léger in the living room of Robert Mallet-Stevens' home, Paris, 1927**

59 ***Tapis pour le grand salon de Robert Mallet-Stevens* (Rug for the living room of Robert Mallet-Stevens' home), 1927**
Wool, knotted
130.5 × 357 cm
Musée des Arts Décoratifs, Paris

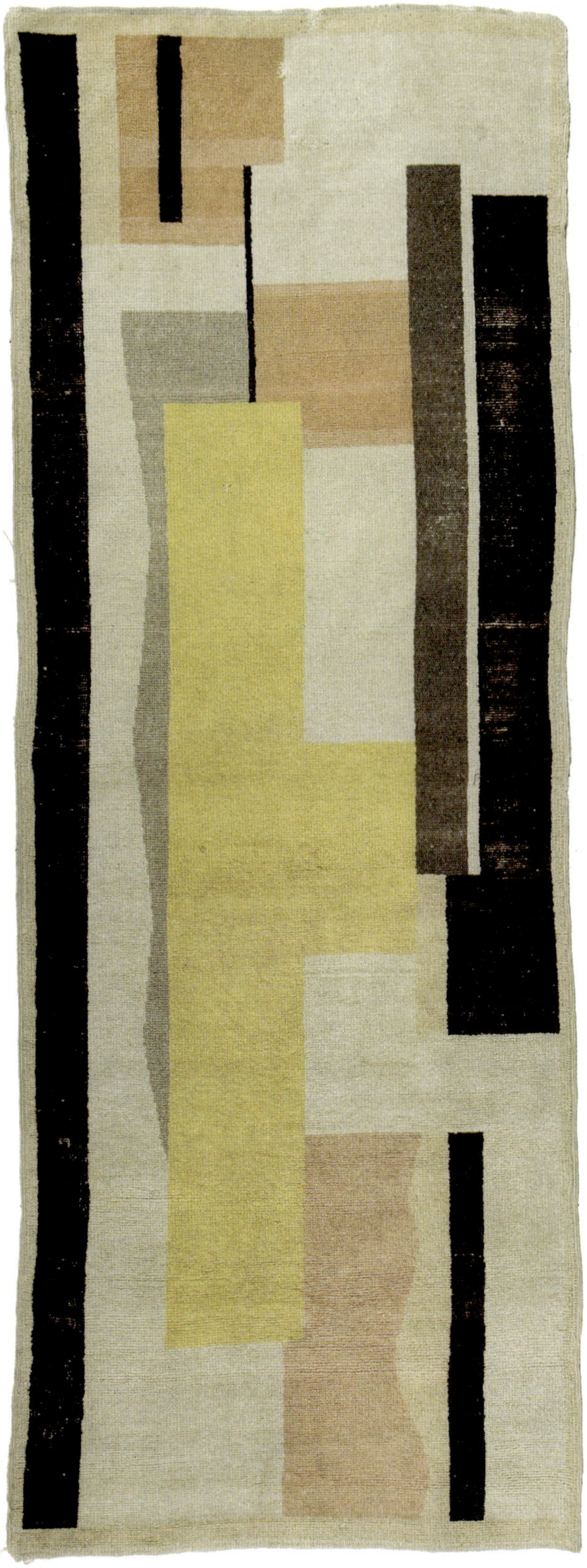

59

60 ***Tapis »blanc«* (white rug), c. 1930, later edition (c. 1950–62)**
Wool, knotted
262 × 138 cm
Private collection

61 **Purist composition, 1926**
Gouache on paper
26 × 13.4 cm
Collection J.-M. Decrop, Hong Kong

62 ***Composition architecturale* (Architectural Composition), 1924–26**
Gouache on paper
54.5 × 38.5 cm
Courtesy Galerie Gmurzynska

63 ***Composition murale* (Mural Composition), 1926**
Oil on canvas
130.4 × 97 cm
Musée national Fernand Léger, Biot

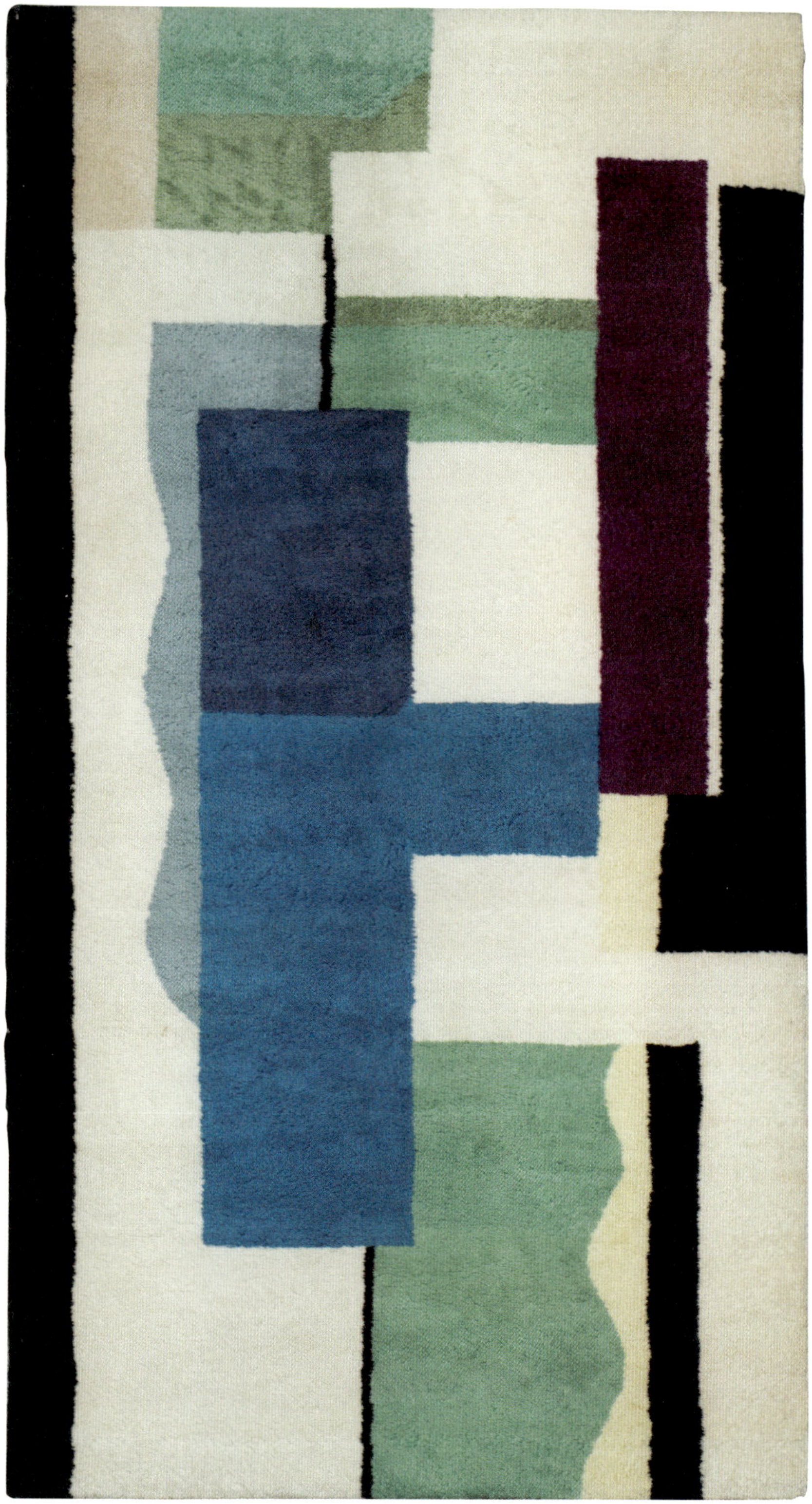

60

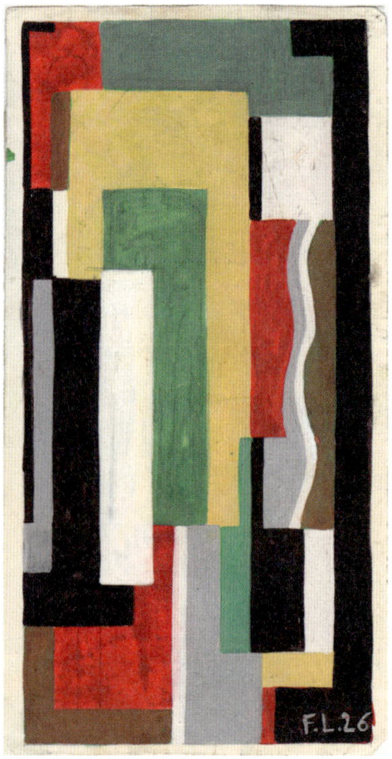

61

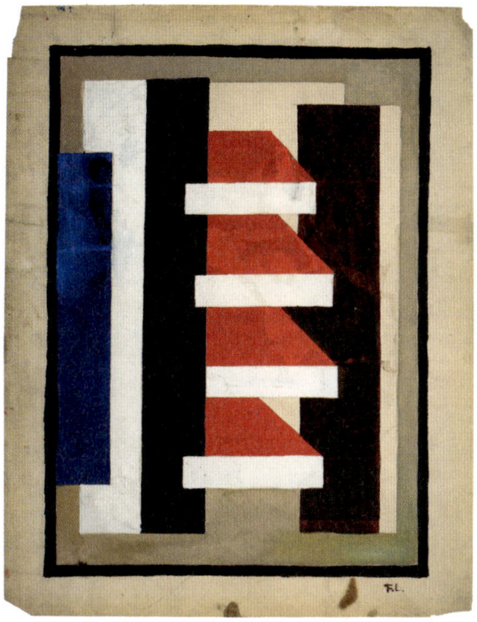

62

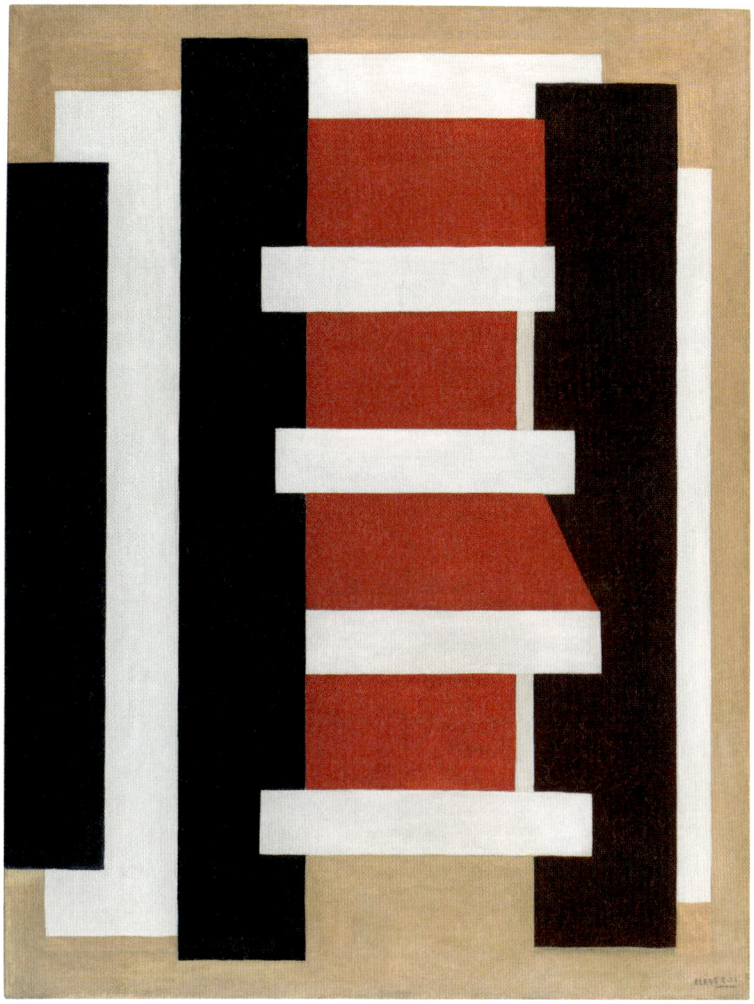

63

64 ***Le Printemps (du cycle: les quatre saisons)***
(Spring [from the "Four Seasons" cycle]), 1928
Oil on canvas
185.3 × 79.8 cm
Kunstmuseum Basel
Gift of Dr. h. c. Raoul La Roche

65 ***L'Été (du cycle: les quatre saisons)***
(Summer [from the "Four Seasons" cycle]), 1928
Oil on canvas
185.5 × 62 cm
Kunstmuseum Basel
Gift of Dr. h. c. Raoul La Roche

66 ***L'Automne (du cycle: les quatre saisons)***
(Fall [from the "Four Seasons" cycle]), 1928
Oil on canvas
185.4 × 80 cm
Kunstmuseum Basel
Gift of Dr. h. c. Raoul La Roche

67 ***L' Hiver (du cycle: les quatre saisons)***
(Winter [from the "Four Seasons" cycle]), 1928
Oil on canvas
185.5 × 76 cm
Kunstmuseum Basel
Gift from Dr. h. c. Raoul La Roche

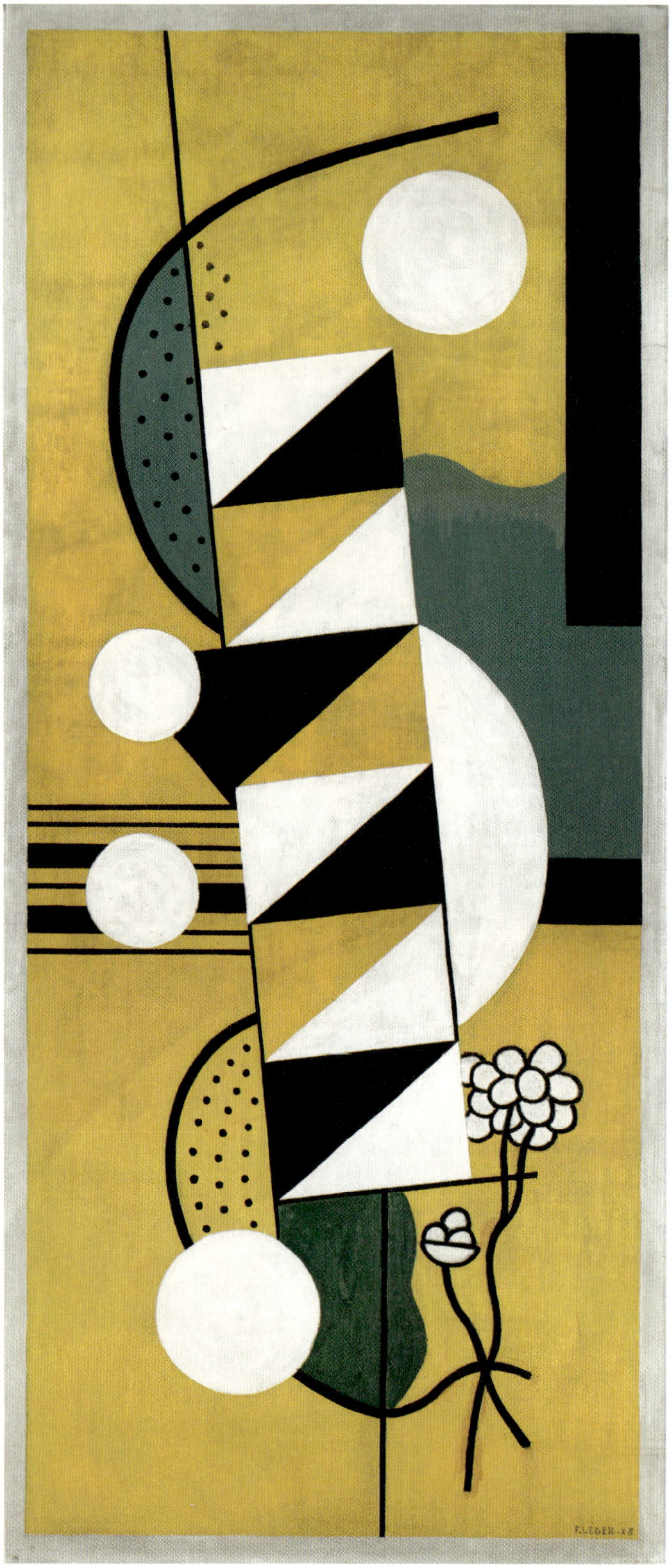

64

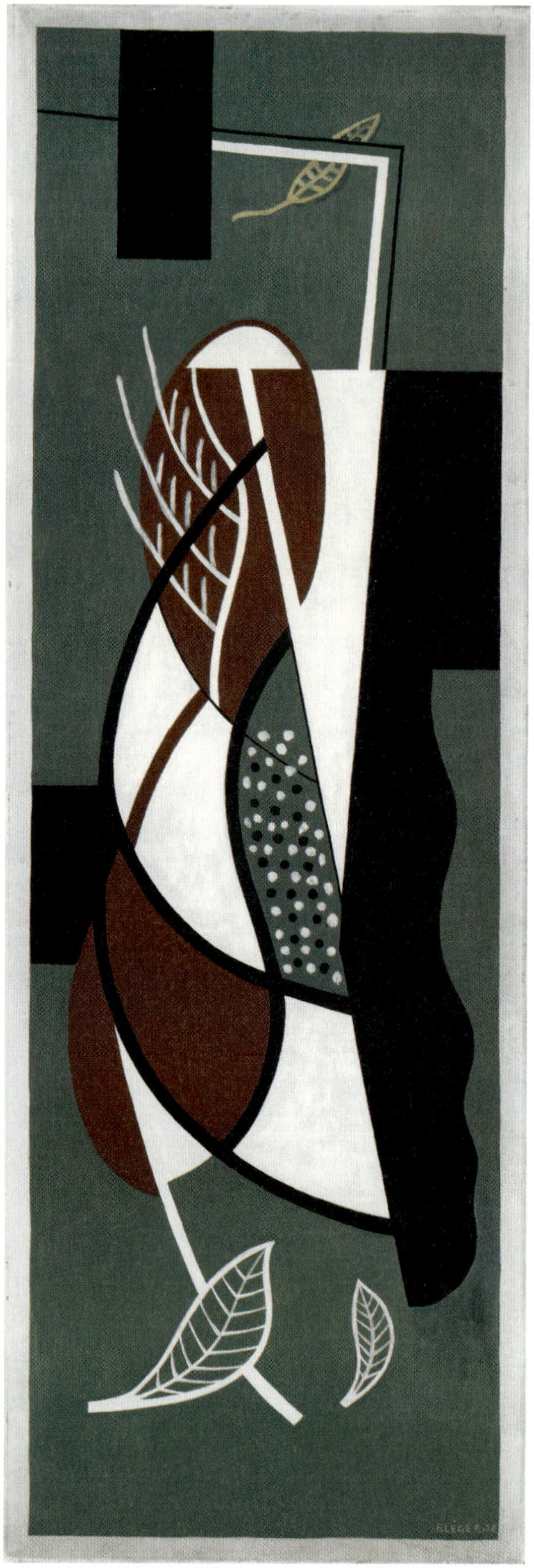

65

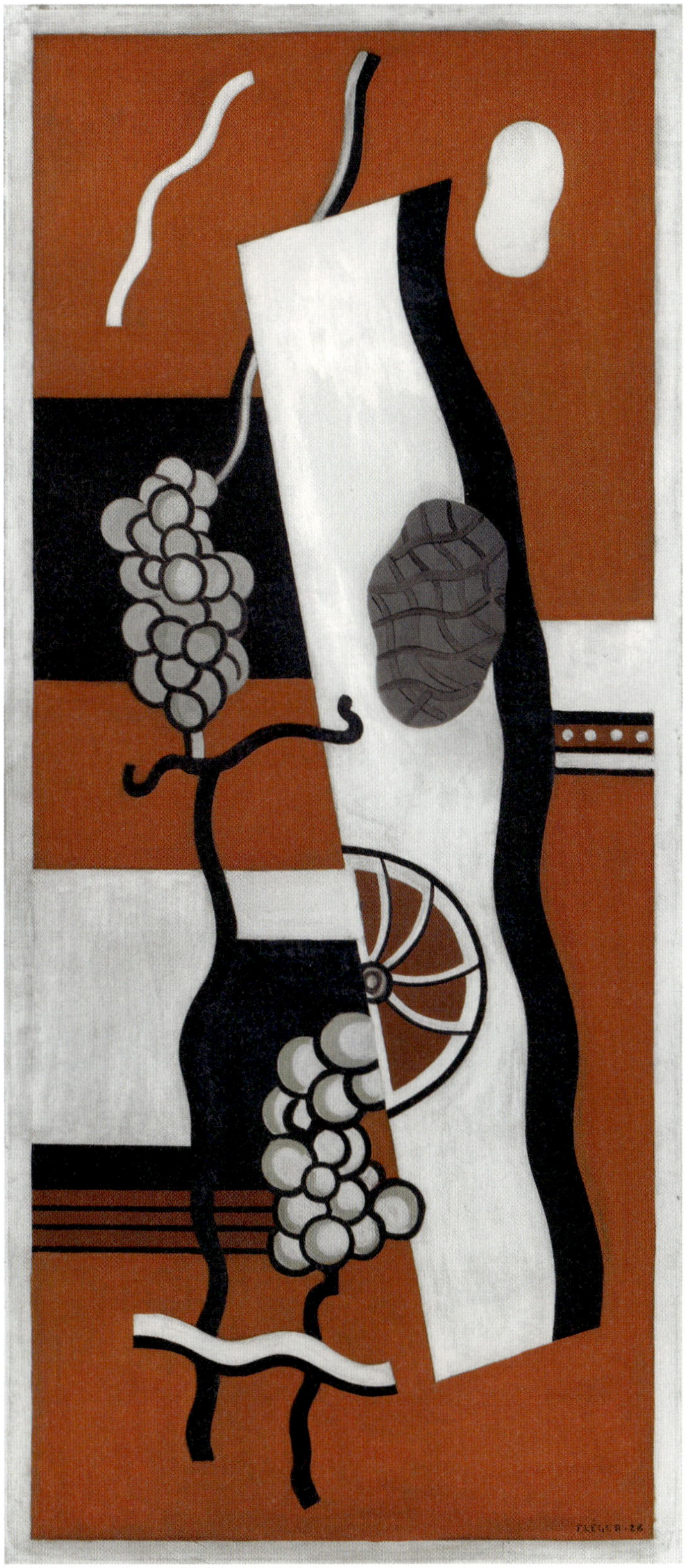
66

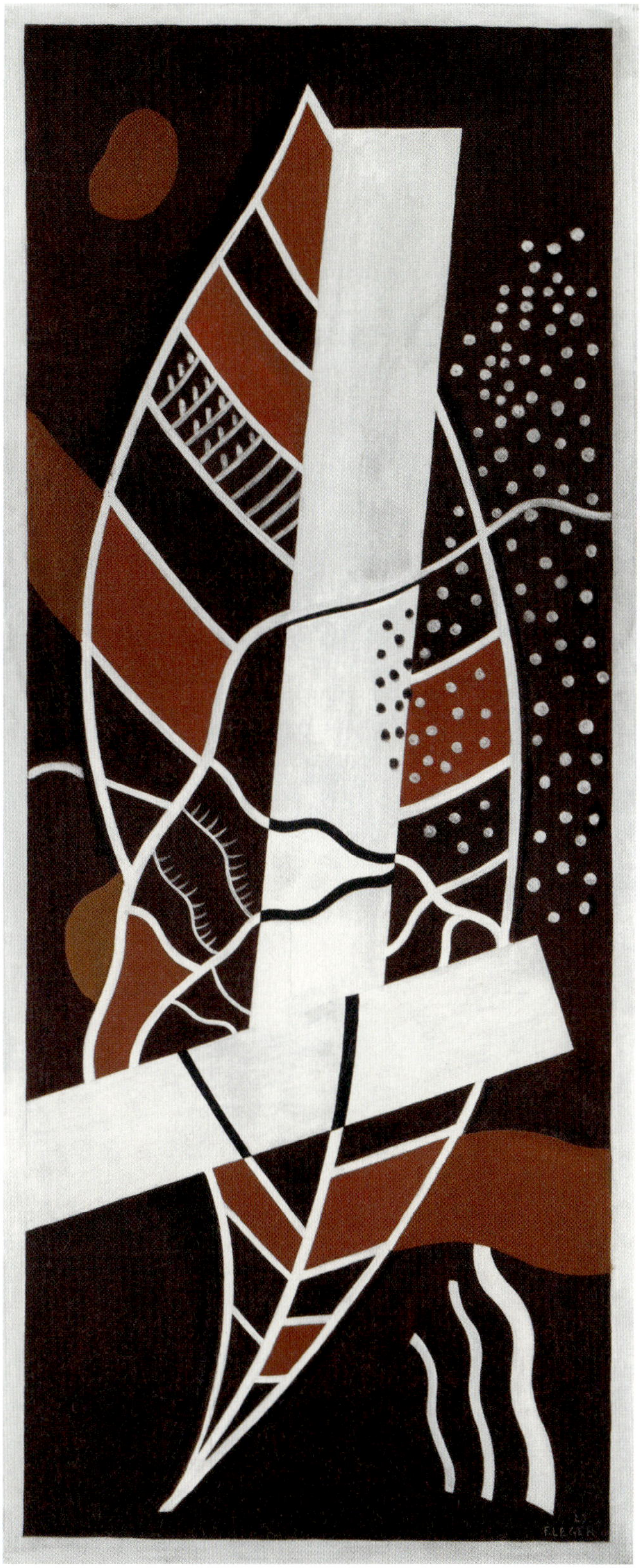
67

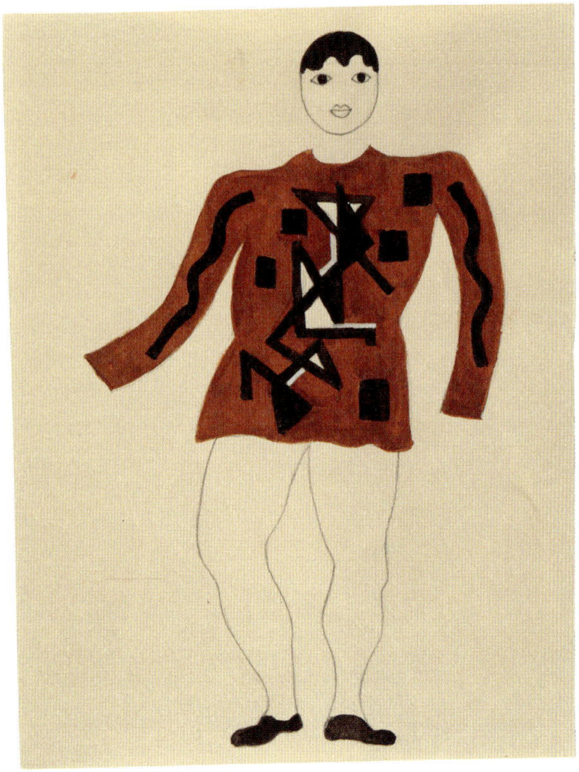
68a

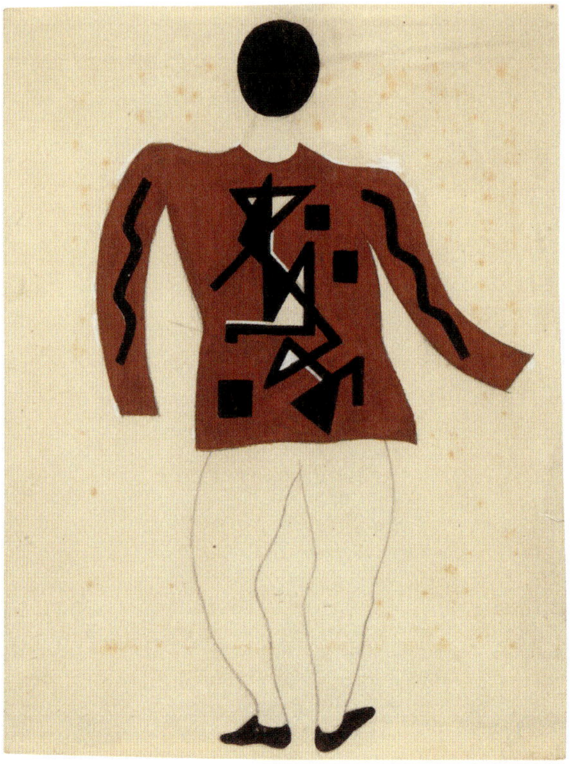
68b

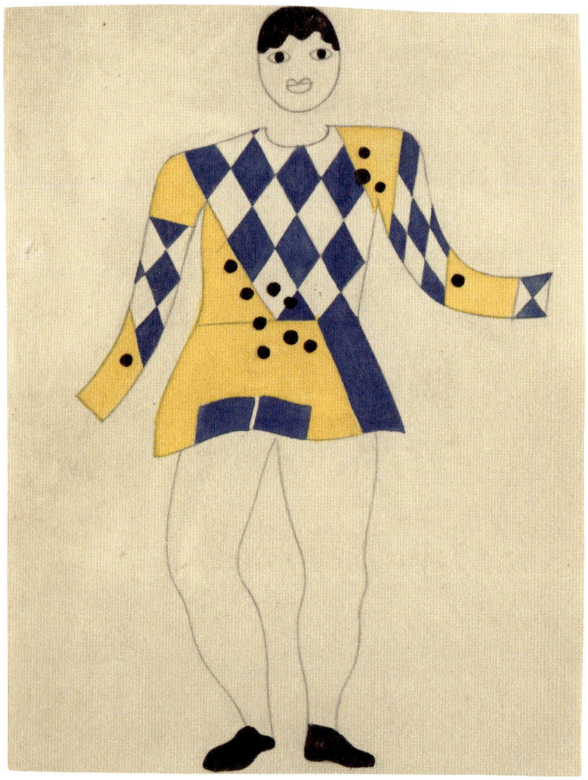
69a

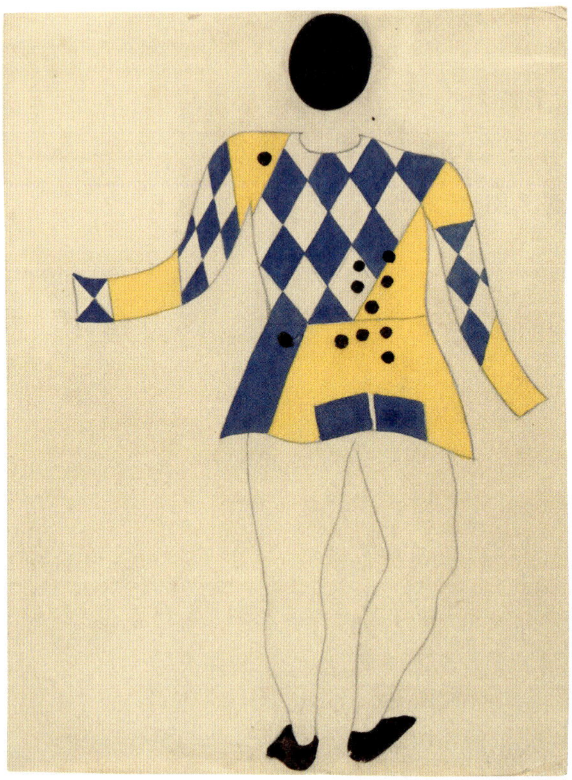
69b

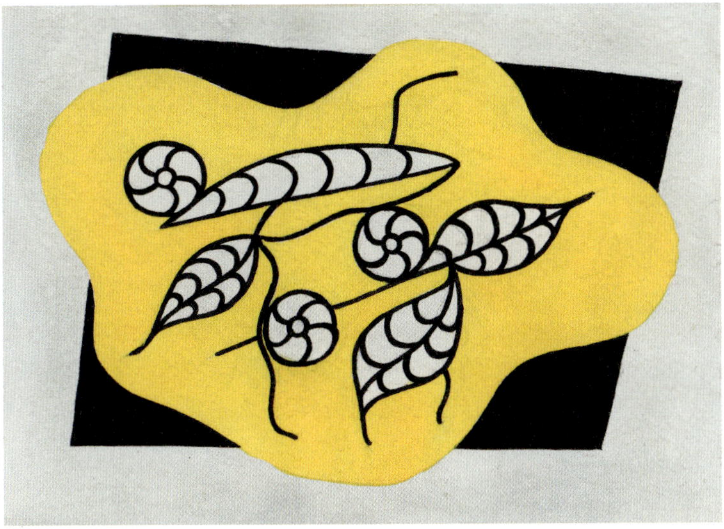

70

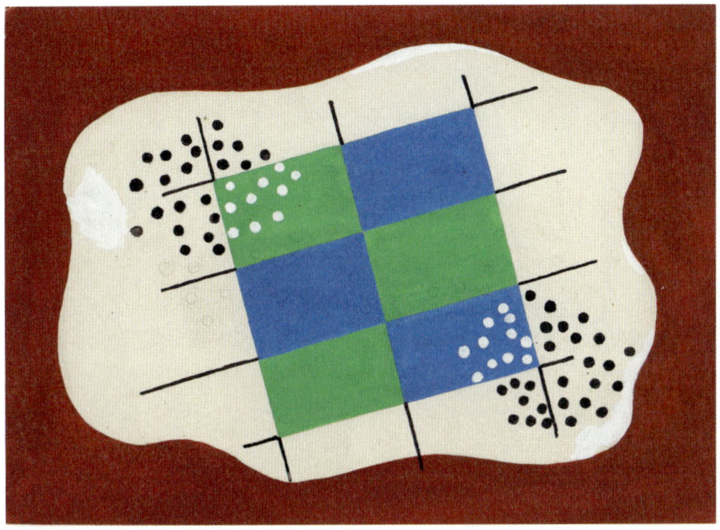

71

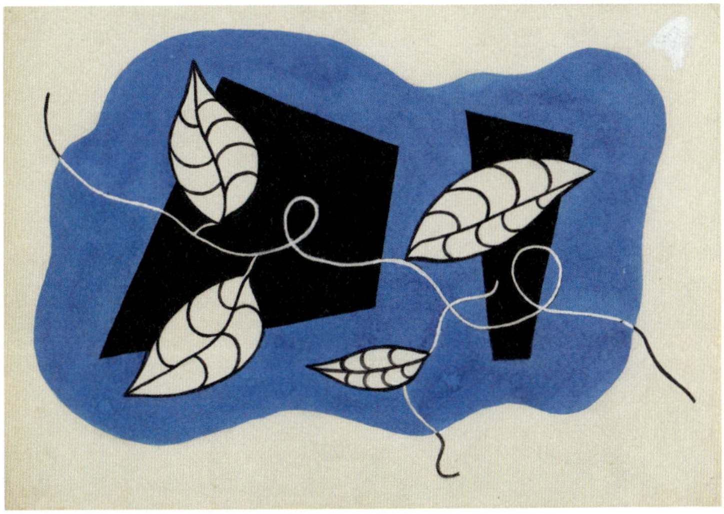

72

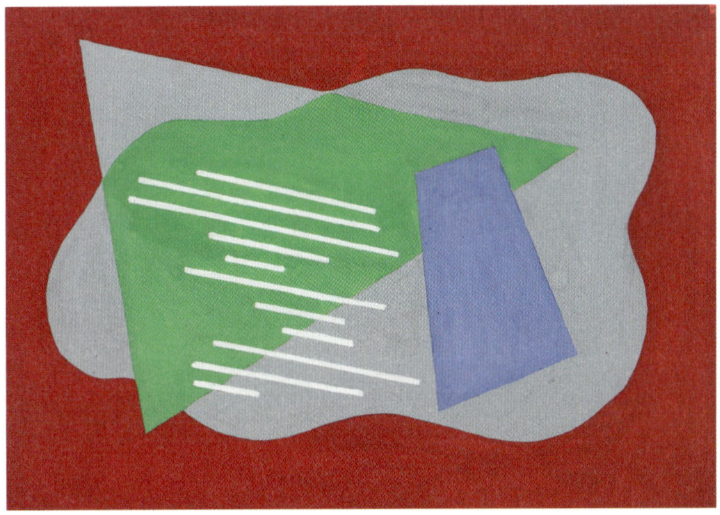

73

68a, b ***Sans titre, projet de costume* (Untitled, study for a costume, realized with assistance from his student Théodora Bücking-Klute), 1929**
Gouache and pencil on paper
30.5 × 22.5 cm
Musée national Fernand Léger, Biot

69a, b ***Sans titre, projet de costume* (Untitled, study for a costume, realized with assistance from his student Théodora Bücking-Klute), 1929**
Gouache and pencil on paper
30.5 × 22.5 cm
Musée national Fernand Léger, Biot

70 **Untitled, study for a rug (realized with assistance from his student Théodora Bücking-Klute), 1929**
Gouache and pencil on paper
30.7 × 23 cm
Musée national Fernand Léger, Biot

71–73 **Untitled, studies for a rug (realized with assistance from his student Théodora Bücking-Klute), 1929**
Gouache and pencil on paper
30.5 × 22.5 cm
Musée national Fernand Léger, Biot

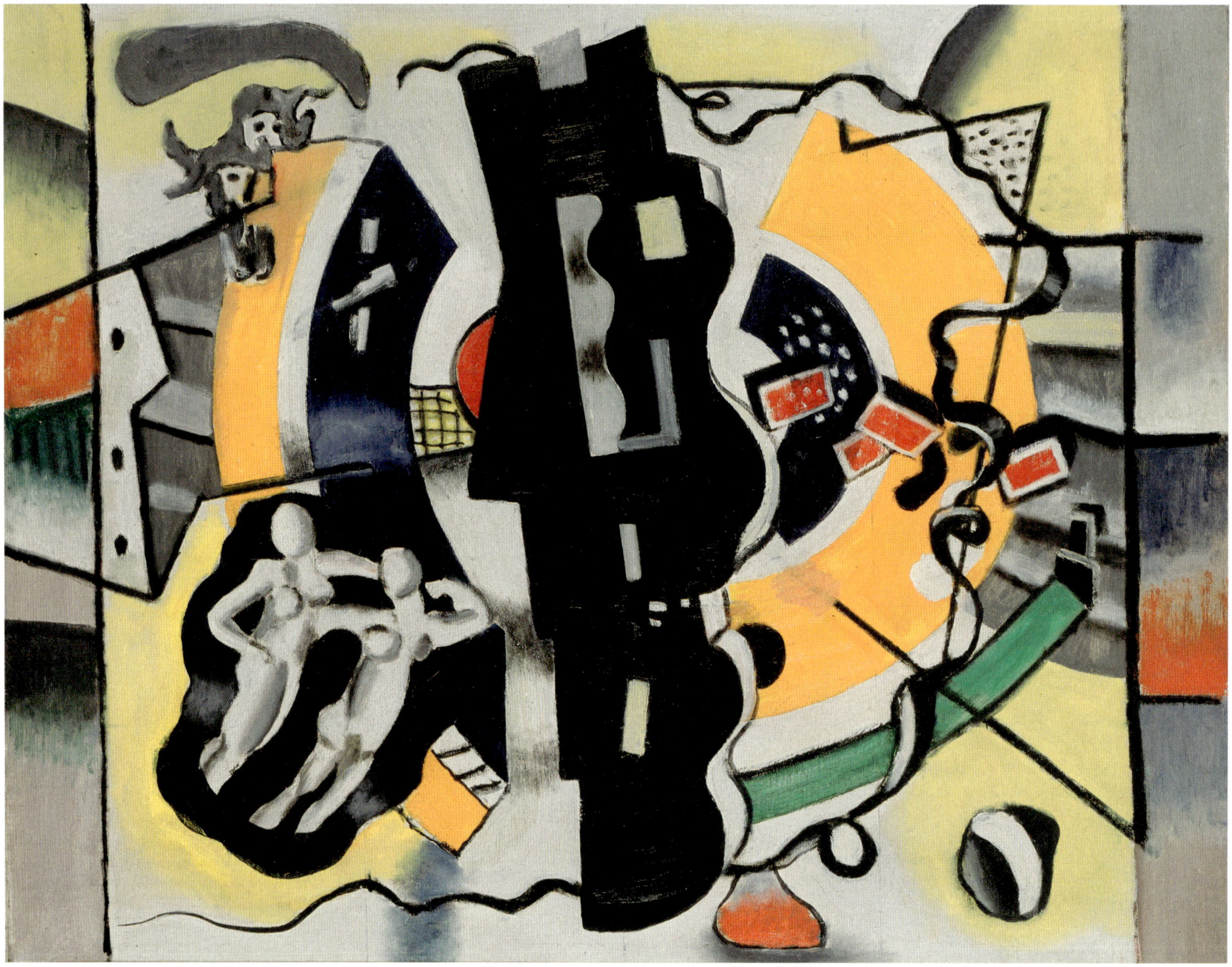

74

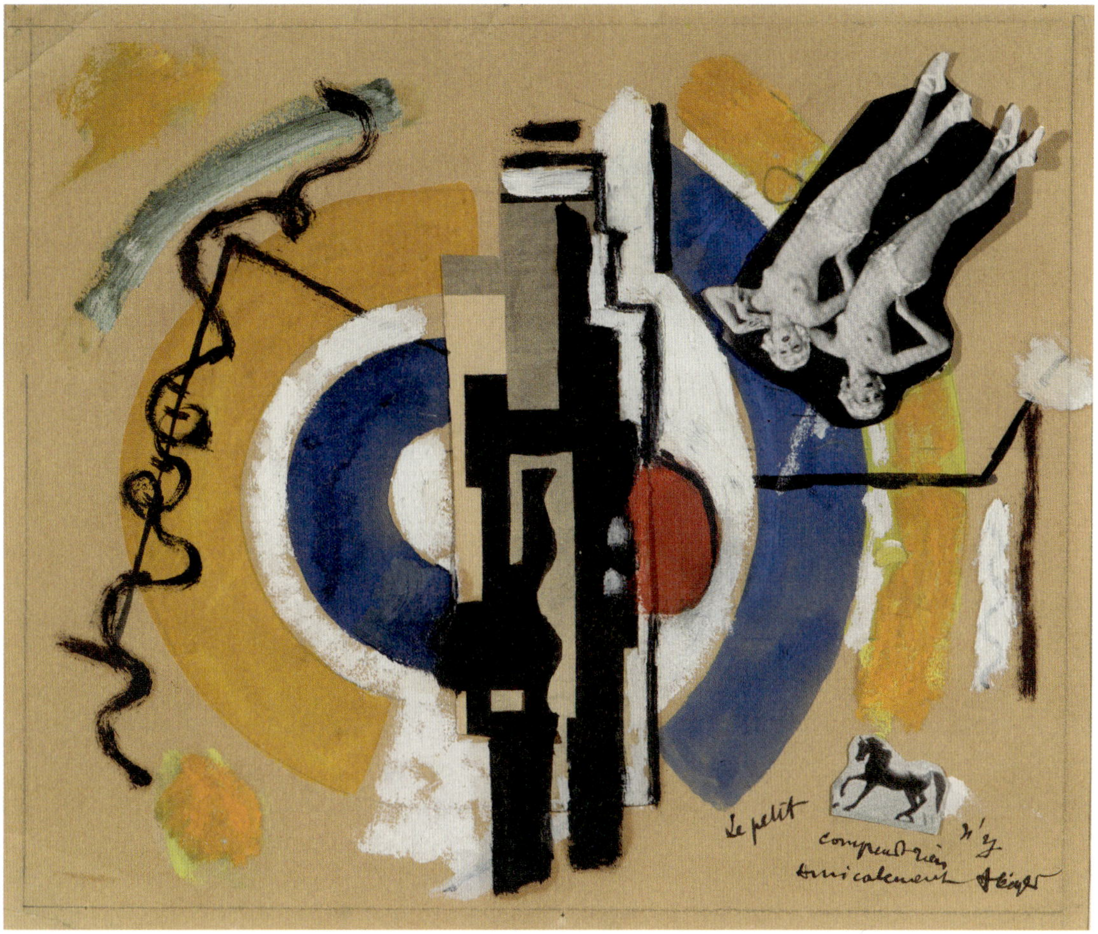

75

74 ***Les gémeaux* (The Twins), 1929/30**
Oil on canvas
73 × 92 cm
Museum Ludwig, Cologne

75 ***Le petit cheval n'y comprend rien***
(The Little Horse Doesn't Understand It), c. 1924/25
Collage, oil and gouache on paper
23 × 26.5 cm
Galerie Louise Leiris, Paris

Léger pasted a preparatory sketch for a carpet in the center of the collage, abstracting its form in the painting *Les gémeaux*. The editor wishes to thank Quentin Laurens, who first established the link between these two works.

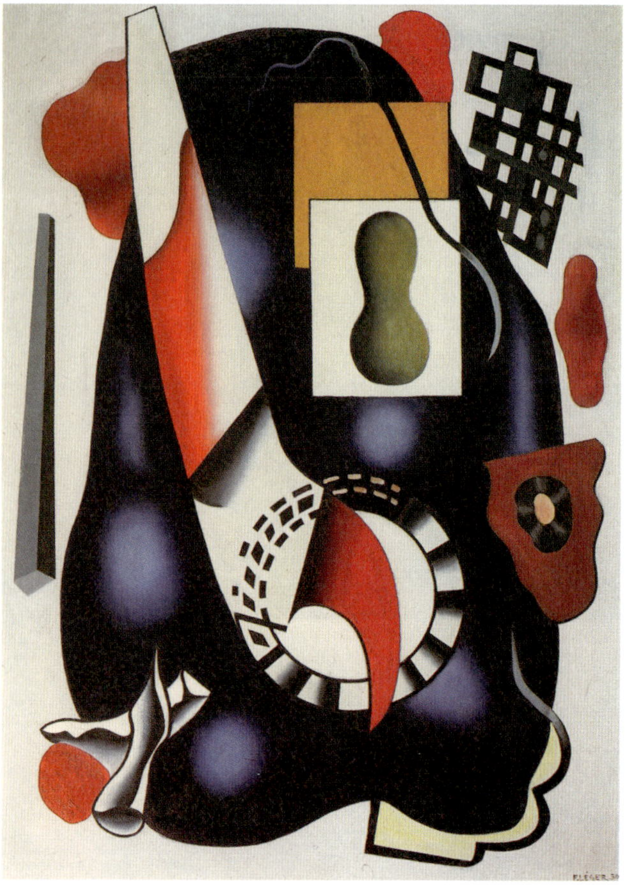

76

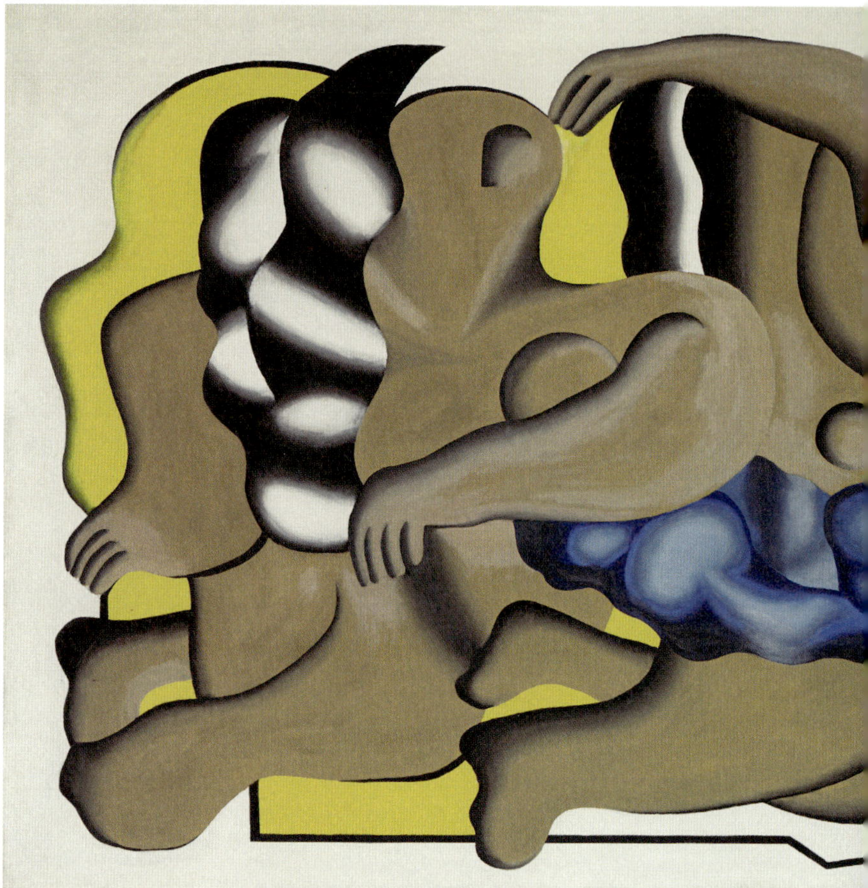

77

76 ***Nature Morte (Composition pour une salle à manger)* (Still Life [Composition for a dining room]), 1930**
Oil on canvas
120.5 × 82 cm
Whereabouts unknown

77 ***Composition I (Décoration pour une salle à manger)* (Composition I [Mural decoration for a dining room]), 1930**
Oil on canvas
141 × 291 cm
Fondation Beyeler, Riehen/Basel
Collection Beyeler

78 ***Nature Morte (Composition pour une salle à manger)* (Still Life [Composition for a dining room]), 1930**
Oil on canvas
120.5 × 82 cm
Private collection

These two still lifes originally formed a triptych with *Composition I (Décoration pour une salle à manger)* installed in the dining room of Dr. Reber in Chailly. The original hanging order is unknown.

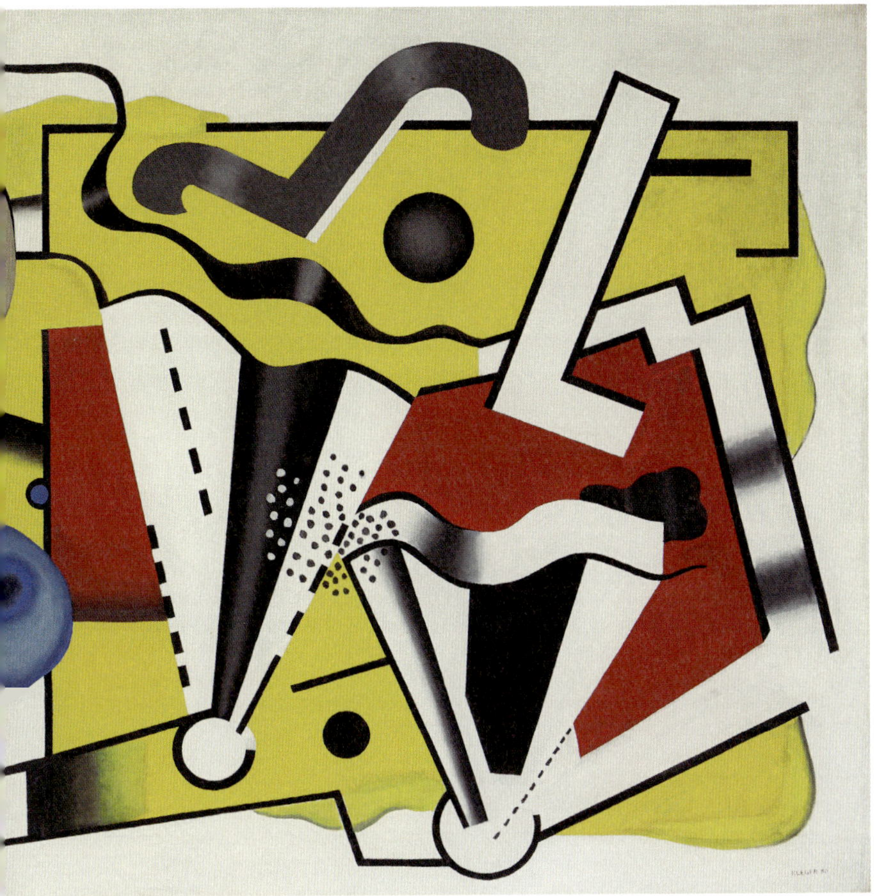

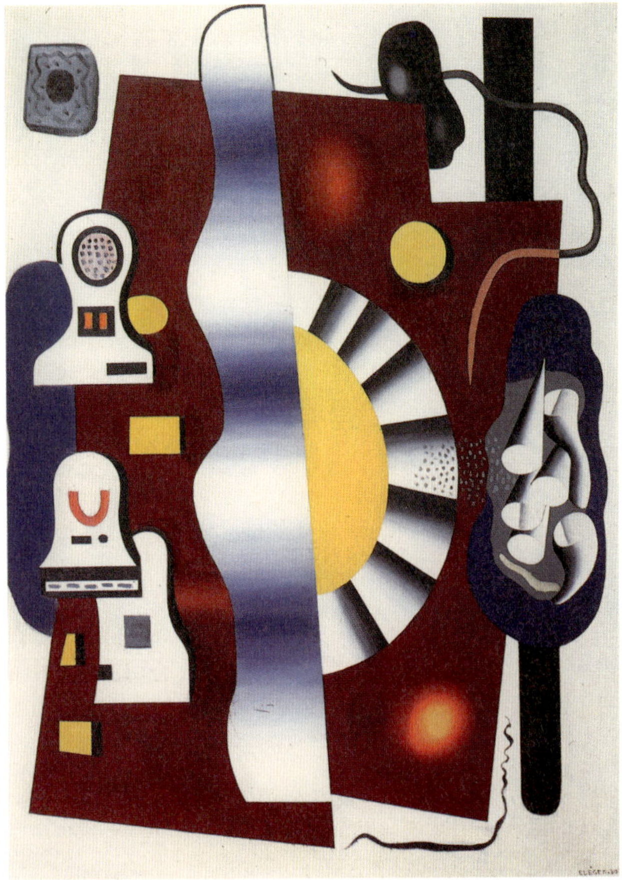

78

MODERN ARCHITECTURE AND COLOR (1946)
Fernand Léger

Color is a natural need, like water and fire. It is a raw material indispensable to life. At every stage in its existence and its history, mankind has associated color with his joys, his acts, and his pleasures.

Flowers have found a place in the home, and the most commonplace objects are covered with color. Dresses, hats, makeup. Everything involving decoration in our daily life has color as its main feature. Functioning in all sorts of ways, indoors and outdoors, color carries the day everywhere. Modern advertising has seized upon it and our roadsides are framed with strident colors that shatter the landscape. Out of this dominant concern has sprung a decorative ethos that rules the entire world.

And so my purpose here is to look into the question of color in modern architecture, and its function, whether dynamic or static, decorative or destructive. A new direction can be envisaged for mural painting in the future.

A wall left bare is a **dead surface**.
A colored wall becomes a **living surface**.

The transformation of walls with color is going to be one of modern architecture's most fascinating challenges now and in the years to come. But for this transformation of the modern wall to be embarked on, color first had to be free.

Personally, in 1912 I successfully placed pure colors in a geometrical setting, in *La Femme en Bleu* (Woman in Blue). After the War, in 1919, I composed the painting *La Ville* (The City) (Philadelphia Museum of Art), using exclusively solid areas of pure color. Technically speaking, this picture was a visual revolution: depth and dynamism could be obtained without light and shade or modulation. The repercussions were first felt in advertising. The tonal purity of the blues, reds, and yellows broke out of this picture and found a place on posters, in store windows, on roadsides, and in signage. Color had been freed. It was a reality in its own right. It had a new impact, completely independent of the objects which, up until now, had been saddled with underpinning it and reining it in. Around the same time, modern architecture began taking an interest in free color, and my friendship with certain modern architects helped me realize that some of the abstract, pure color arrangements I had created between 1921 and 1925–which had no pretensions to being easel paintings–could and should lend themselves to colored architectural adaptation.

Thus colored walls (either as decorative accompaniment or destruction of a wall) were possible. I think it was around this period that the color-architecture relationship took shape.

The 1925 Exhibition was the chance to present this event to the general public:

The embassy project (Mallet-Stevens);
The Esprit Nouveau pavilion (Le Corbusier).

Naturally reactions were very varied, but the deed was done and the consequences are ongoing.

How to create a feeling of spaciousness, of boundaries abolished? Quite simply with color, with walls of different colors.

The apartment I shall call a "dwelling rectangle" is going to turn into an "elastic rectangle."
A light-blue wall recedes, a black wall advances.
A yellow wall disappears (destruction of the wall). The new possibilities are many. A black piano set against a yellow wall, for example, creates a visual shock that can diminish the feeling of spaciousness.

And so, if in this new order of things you arrange your furnishings asymmetrically, and not symmetrically, you are going to accentuate still further the liberation of the interior from a fixed, dead, arrested state that leaves no room for playfulness or whimsy: you enter a realm of total freedom.

The tradition of symmetry is extremely burdensome, and we have all been brought up to obey it.

Where exteriors are concerned, the architectural problem is more far-reaching, but just as new, if not more so.

A given spot can be rendered invisible, weightless, by the orchestration of color. Camouflage has demonstrated astonishing visual effects achieved through the use of color. So why not the organization of a whole street or a city?

An urban center: a built-up area with 1,500 residents becomes a question of interior and exterior polychromy.

Color-light must be distributed and spread.

The example of a modern factory in Rotterdam provides conclusive proof. The old factory was black and gloomy. The new one was bright, colorful, translucent. And what happened was this: no suggestions had been made to the personnel, but the appearance of the men and women workers was transformed. They became cleaner and neater. Unconsciously, they felt that something important had just taken place around them. They were entering a new life. This effect of color-light is not merely an external value: rationally applied, it can transform a whole society.

The psychological emancipation of a person who becomes aware of his three dimensions, his exact volume, and his weight. He is no longer a shadow acting mechanically behind a machine. He is a new human being dealing with a changed daily task. This is the big issue for tomorrow.

The polychrome hospital, treatment with colors: an unexplored domain that is beginning to enthuse young doctors.

Restful green and blue wards for the nervously afflicted, and others, yellow and red, for the depressed and the dispirited.

Thus color has a significant part to play in social life; it still contributes to packaging the monotonous, unavoidable realities of the everyday. It costumes reality: the humblest objects demand that color misleads as to their real purpose.

Let us pursue our endeavors regarding space and liberation in the architecture of the future. Color is a potent means of taking action: it can destroy a wall, embellish it, make it recede or advance; it creates the new space which is the reason for this article.

Modern architecture has its work cut out for it in this regard. Its task is to invent, construct and consummate the great popular monument, the new harmonious opus on which the three major arts–architecture, painting, sculpture–must collaborate.

This collaboration has been totally eclipsed by the rise of easel painting over the last fifty years.

The work of the Primitives–the artists of the Renaissance–was bound up with the wall. The modern era has abandoned the wall for the portable work of art.

A modern picture is an inherently valuable object, absolutely independent of the setting in which it was created. A picture painted in Paris ornaments a wall in Tokyo. Tomorrow it will be sold and will maybe leave for Lisbon. This kind of modern art is essentially speculative and itinerant.

Is a return to Mural Art possible?

Is there any future likelihood of an architect capable of orchestrating the new monument that will express our needs and desires? I think so. In that monument, the feeling of total beauty–the desire for total beauty–that exists in man can be made a reality.

It seems to me that this monument should take the form of a temple to repose and meditation.

This would demand of modern architects a sense of equilibrium and proportion never yet achieved; the architect himself will have to show the painter where he must act dynamically–and the sculptor, too. He will be a leader mindful of the plastic requirements of the creation of the monument.

Perfect beauty rooted in an equilibrium of new plastic forces has never yet been achieved; this is for the architecture of the future.

Published as F. Léger, "L'Architecture moderne et la couleur," in *Formes et Vie*, no. 1 (1951): 24-28.
Published earlier in a slightly modified version as F. Léger, "Modern Architecture and Color," in *American Abstract Artists* (New York: Ram Press, 1946), 207–14.

79 **Compass and Paint Tubes, 1926**
Gouache on paper
26.7 × 36.2 cm
Museum of Modern Art, New York
Gift of Edward M. M. Warburg, acc. no. 4071941

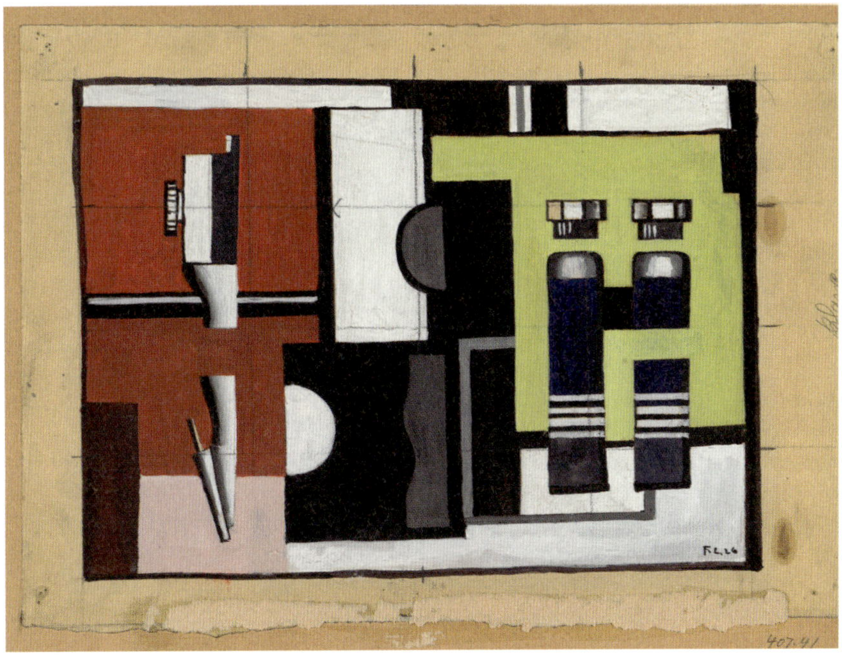

79

Léger - Le Corbusier
By Jan de Heer

For almost his entire career as a painter, Fernand Léger campaigned for painting to be applied in architecture. His friend, the architect and painter Le Corbusier, became involved in the debate from 1923 onwards, mainly taking the opposite stance to Léger's.

Léger and Le Corbusier (1887–1965) first met in December 1920. By then, Léger had been an established member of the artistic avant-garde in Paris for ten years, while Le Corbusier had only just embarked on his career as a painter. The first issue of *L'Esprit Nouveau*, in which Le Corbusier and Amédée Ozenfant launched Purism, had just been published. Léger and Le Corbusier had similar views on modern architecture and the machine aesthetic, but their ideas on painting were very different. Léger regarded Le Corbusier's work as that of a "hanger-on" and described his use of color as "*grise, toute en tonalité*" ("gray, all the same shade"). Nevertheless, the two men had been close friends since the late 1920s. They often vacationed together in Spain and in Le Piquey and Vézelay in France, and they traveled together to Zurich, Athens, and New York on business. Le Corbusier held Léger's paintings in great esteem. He was one of the few artists Le Corbusier invited to show a painting at his Pavillon de L'Esprit Nouveau in 1925, and Léger's was the only work besides his own that hung in Le Corbusier's new home on Rue Nungesser-et-Coli in Paris.

Anyone who reads their articles on painting and architecture in the order in which they were published can discern the unfolding of a debate that went largely unnoticed by readers of the time. The bone of contention was Le Corbusier's idiosyncratic position on architectural polychromy and his associated ideas on easel and mural painting. He had reconsidered his views since becoming a Purist, when he had rejected any decorative application of the arts in architecture. His ideas had since crystallized in response to Léger's mural design for an architectural arrangement in a hall in 1923 and a De Stijl exhibition held later that year in Paris.

Responding to Léger and De Stijl, Le Corbusier summed up the features of Purist architectural polychromy.[1] Polychromy on a building's exterior destroyed form and was therefore out of the question. Inside, however, it was an important factor, not in the form of murals with figures, patterns, or multiple colors, but as a single wall in a single plain color. The interplay between the colored walls would create an architectural polychromy. This was because the prototype of Purist architecture consisted of a primary geometric shape—a bare box with four walls—and because color was seen as subordinate to form. Architectural polychromy was not, therefore, a matter for painters, but for architects (figs. 80, 81).

Léger responded immediately, in January 1924, calling for a polychromatic modern architecture.[2] A year later he specified that he drew a distinction between ornamental art and easel painting.[3] The latter had intrinsic merit, he wrote; it was anti-decorative and opposed the wall, reiterating a statement he had made in 1919. Ornamental art, on the other hand, was determined by the architecture and respected the wall. This was art that collaborated with architecture. In this connection, Léger referred to the "primitive" era prior to the Renaissance. By way of illustration he painted several works entitled *Peinture murale*. He did not in fact acknowledge any difference between architectural polychromy and mural painting. A year later, Le Corbusier also defined the role of easel painting.[4] For him, it should not become involved with the architecture, but should be a discrete meditative world in itself. He did not interpret easel painting as the opposite of the wall, but rather as a hole, an impairment of the wall.

Le Corbusier maintained this position, which left little room for dissension, until the late 1930s, despite Léger's unflagging attempts to convince him otherwise. Slowly but surely, however, he was swayed. At the same time, Léger knew that to execute painting for architecture meant that he had to be dependent on the architect.

In a 1929 article, Le Corbusier praised Léger's dazzling color, which he said was no ornamentation of form, but a force in itself. "This is a new art," he declared, and added, significantly: "And that art existed before, when painting still stood alongside architecture,"[5] referring to the period before the Renaissance.

In 1931, Léger wrote an article about abstract art in which he first set out the statement that would be his mantra for the rest of his life: "Color is a vital element, like water and fire. It is unquestionably an essential requirement."[6] That same year, Le Corbusier issued his Salubra wallpaper collection. He used a much more vivid range of colors than those found in the Purist palette. Clearly, Léger had influenced his choice. Le Corbusier included the quotation from Léger twice in "Polychromie architecturale," which he wrote to mark the launch of his wallpaper collection.[7]

In 1933, Léger gave two lectures, which Le Corbusier attended. In the first, given in Zurich, Léger openly canvassed for collaboration with architects, stating: "In the past, pictorial art was closely bound up with architecture [...] This was the *great* order in antiquity, which I hope to see revived."[8] He aimed to revive the mural. The second lecture was at the CIAM congress in Athens.[9] Before an audience consisting mainly of architects, he attacked bare walls, so prized by modern architects, as unacceptable. He said that architects had thought that they could address the problem by applying color, but he believed that the matter was more complex. And here, again, he offered his services as a painter in the search for a solution.

The debate took a radically different turn in spring 1936.[10] That year Léger and Le Corbusier created their first murals at the home of Jean Badovici in Vézelay (figs. 106, 109). Badovici was more aware than anyone else of Le Corbusier

80 Le Corbusier, Pierre Jeanneret
Polychromie des murs de la salle
(Polychrome wall designs for Villa Cook)
Panel 5 from *L'Architecture Vivante* (1927)

81 Le Corbusier
Color keyboard for Salubra wallpaper collection, 1931

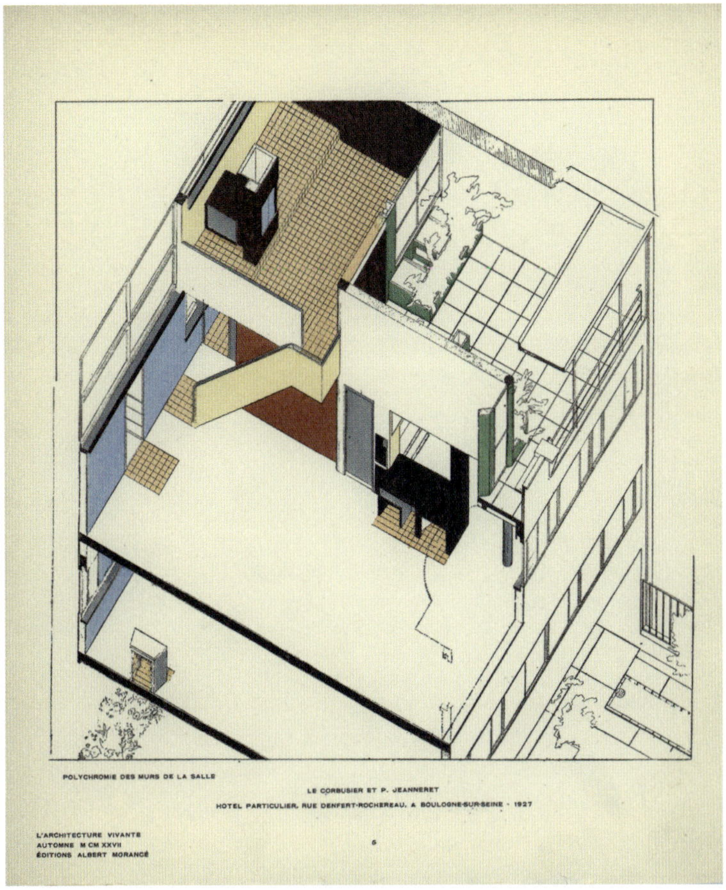

80

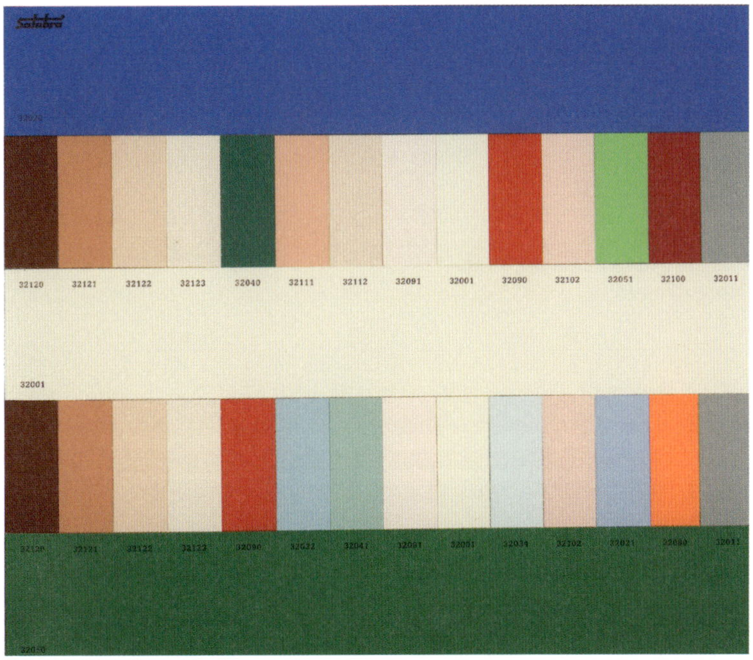

81

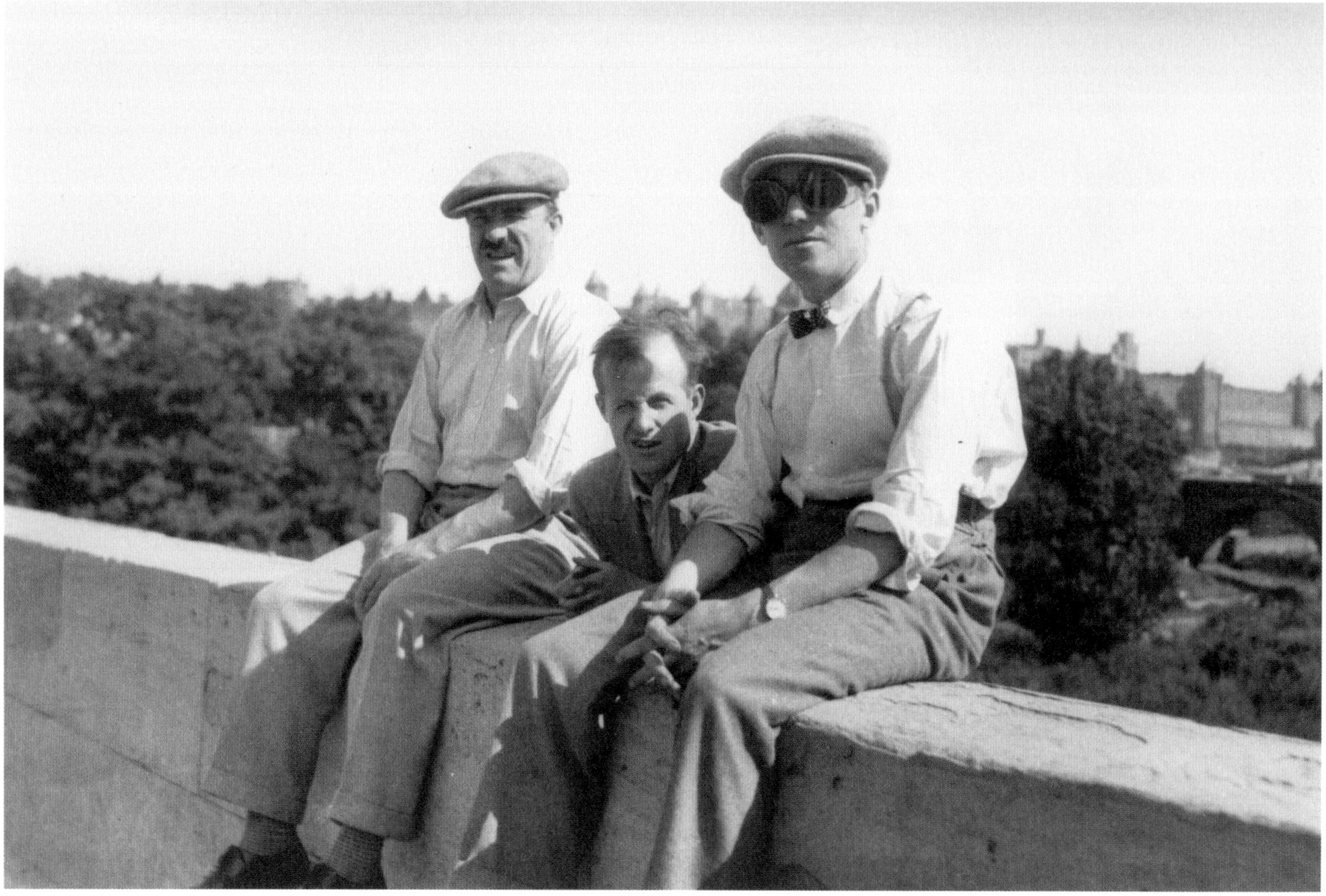

82

82 **Fernand Léger, Pierre Jeanneret and Le Corbusier, 1930**
Fondation Le Corbusier, Paris

and Léger's views. As editor of *L'Architecture Vivante,* he had given them and others a platform to express their views on painting and architecture, publishing their projects in color. He had also attended Léger's lecture in Athens in 1933.

Badovici had bought a medieval house in Vézelay in the 1920s and had renovated it in accordance with modern standards. It was frequently visited by artists from Paris. Badovici managed to persuade Le Corbusier and Léger to design murals for his home when they visited in 1934. This would give renewed impetus to their deadlocked debate. Badovici wanted "the painting to destroy the wall," to put it entirely in Le Corbusier's terms. Léger was commissioned to visually open up the dark inner courtyard behind the house, and Le Corbusier was asked to produce a painting for a wall in a double-height room.

Léger painted an abstract interplay of planes and screens in primary colors. A black plane with figuration in the center camouflaged a door in the wall. Colorful streamers framed the image. The modulation of color, the multiple layers, and the quasi-perspective lines gave the mural an extraordinary spatial effect. Since then, critics have regarded these elements as characteristic of Léger's work.

Le Corbusier's painting was half-hidden behind the mezzanine in the high-ceilinged room. It was visible in its entirety only once one had reached the first floor. Not an abstract image, it showed two bathing women seated in front of a wall with a floating object on the left. The colors were unmodulated: Colored planes filled the space between lines. The spatial illusion was created by the apparent physicality of the women and the object, and the lights and shadows of the architectural setting.

Like Léger, Le Corbusier would emphasize the spatiality and power of his mural to destroy the wall. He was above all struck by the unutterable sense of space—the fourth dimension—that it opened up. He valued the simultaneity of dissimilar objects as a new abstract space: the wall with its mural, the scene with its colors and figures, the medieval house, the modernist renovation.

For both men, the murals signified the start of their later careers. From the early 1940s, Léger was regarded as one of the most important expert modernist mural painters. For Le Corbusier, this marked his final break with Purism. It opened up for him a way to a personal synthesis of arts in which the idea of abstract, ineffable space became the key principle.

1 Le Corbusier, "*L'architecture au Salon d'automne*," *L'Esprit Nouveau* 19 (December 1923).
2 Fernand Léger, "The Machine Aesthetic: The Manufactured Object, the Artisan, and the Artist," in *Functions of Painting* , ed. Edward F. Fry, trans. Alexandra Anderson (London, 1973), 52-61.
3 Fernand Léger, "The Machine Aesthetic: Geometric Order and Truth," in *Functions of Painting*, pp. 62–66.
4 Le Corbusier, "Notes à la suite," *Cahiers d'art* 3 (1926): 46-52.
5 Le Corbusier, "L'architecture et Fernand Léger," *Sélection* 5 (1929): 21–24.
6 Fernand Léger, "Abstract Art," in *Functions of Painting*, 81.
7 Le Corbusier, "Polychromie architecturale," in Jan de Heer, *The Architectonic Colour: Polychromy in the Purist Architecture of Le Corbusier* (Rotterdam: 010 Publishers, 2009), 142–64.
8 Fernand Léger, "The Wall, the Architect, the Painter," in *Functions of Painting*, 93.
9 Fernand Léger, "Discours aux architectes," *Annales Techniques* (Athens, 1933), 1159–62.
10 Christian Derouet, "La première peinture murale de Fernand Léger," *Les cahiers du MNAM* (Paris, 2006), 63–77; Christian Derouet, *Le Corbusier à Vézelay* (Vézelay, 2015).

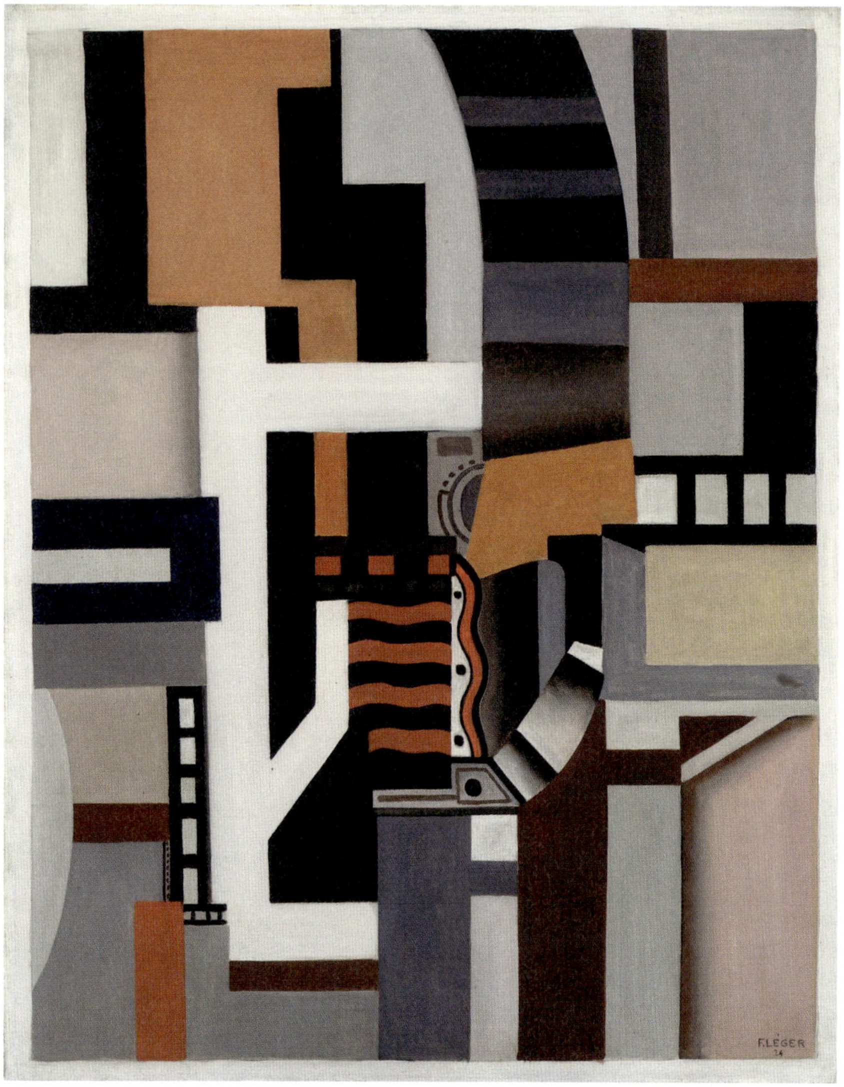

83

83 ***Composition*** **(Composition), 1924**
Oil on canvas
128.4 × 98.4 cm
Indiana University Art Museum
Jane and Roger Wolcott Memorial,
Gift of Thomas T. Solley

84 **Interior view of the Pavillon de l'Esprit Nouveau by Le Corbusier and Pierre Jeanneret at the Exposition internationale des arts decoratifs et industriels modernes, 1925, with *Composition*, 1924 by Fernand Léger**
Panel 50 from *L'Architecture Vivante* (Fall/Winter 1925)

Le Corbusier decided to replace Légers *Composition* by *Le balustre* (The baluster), 1925

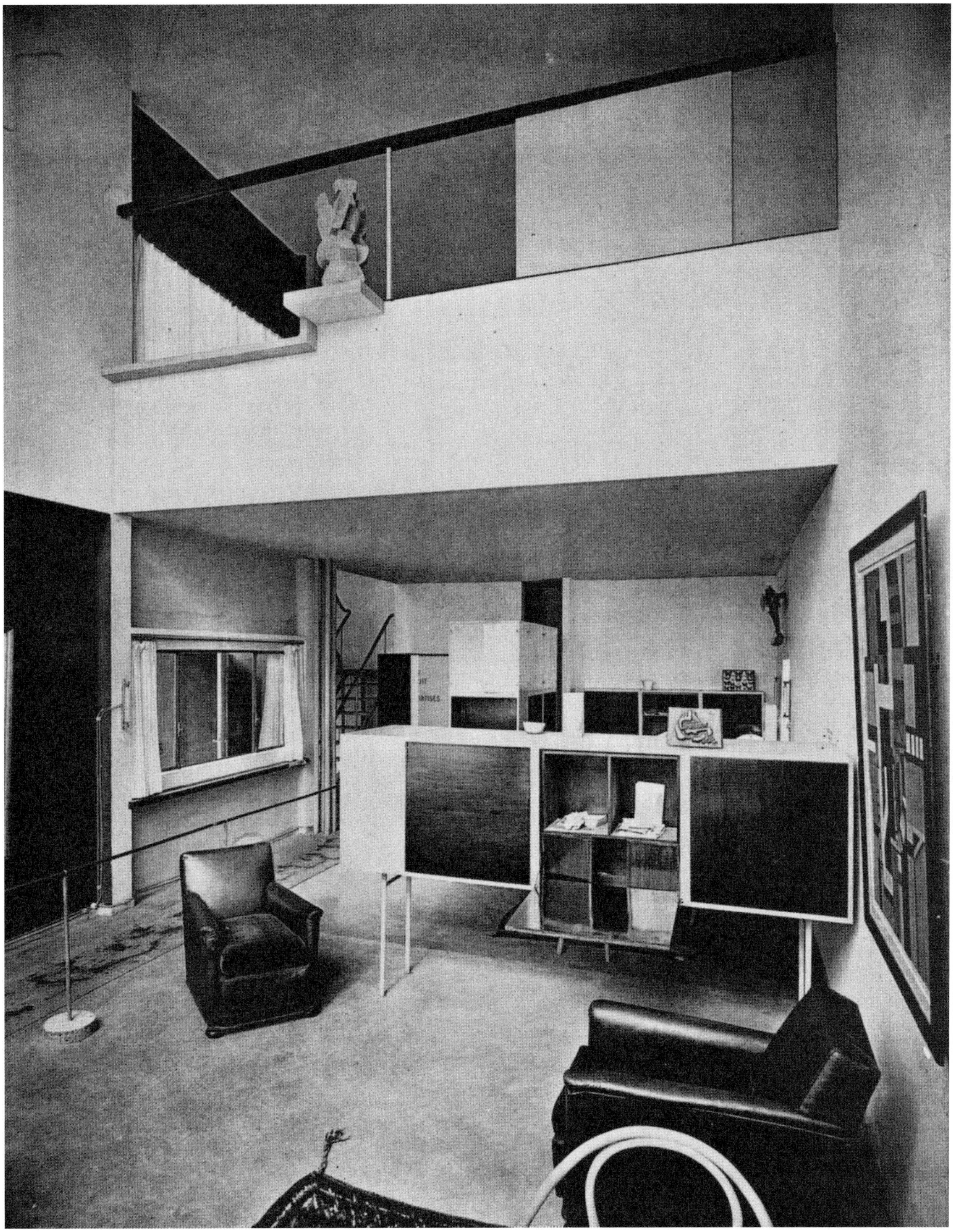

84

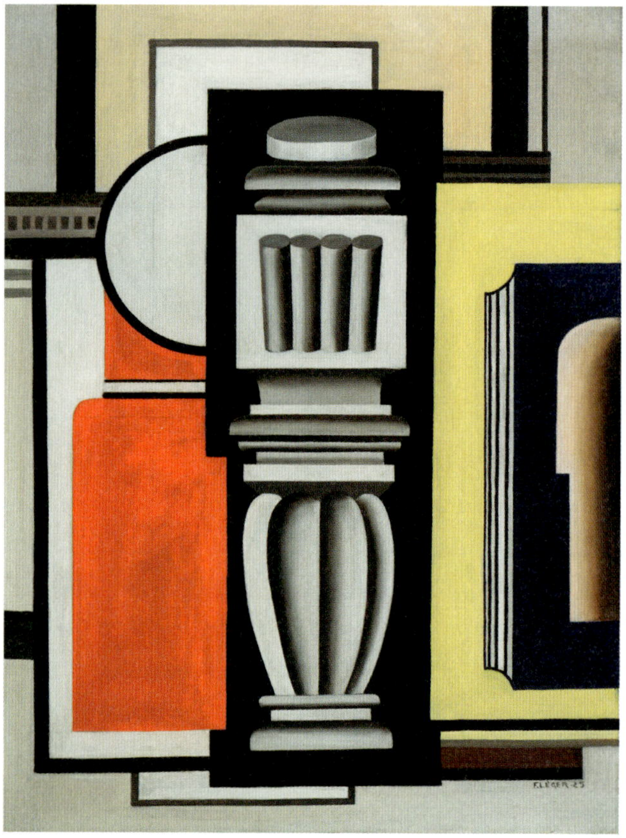

85

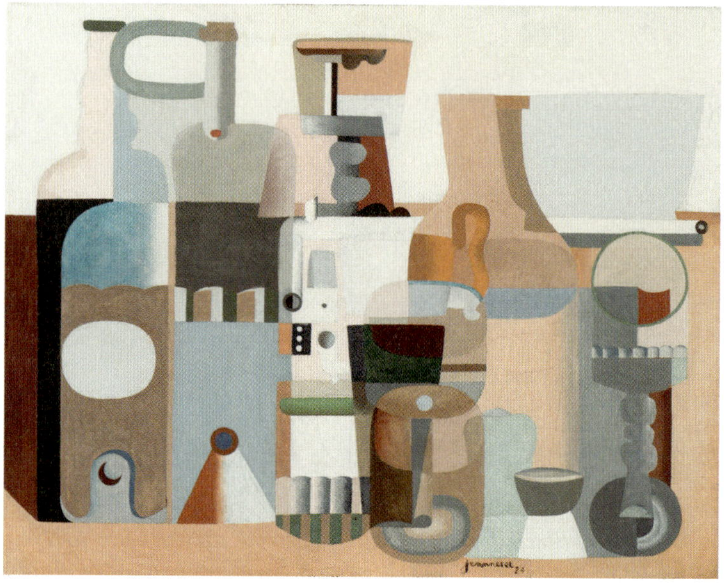

86

85 ***Le balustre* (The Baluster), 1925**
Oil on canvas
129.5 × 97.2 cm
Museum of Modern Art, New York
Mrs. Simon Guggenheim Fund., acc. no. 179.1952

86 Le Corbusier
Nature morte du pavillon de l'Esprit Nouveau
(Still Life of the Pavilion of the New Spirit), 1924
Oil on canvas
81 × 100 cm
Fondation Le Corbusier, Paris

87 **Interior view of the Pavillon de l'Esprit Nouveau, 1925, with *Le balustre* (The Baluster), 1925, by Fernand Léger and *Nature* morte (Still Life), 1924, by Le Corbusier**
Les Arts Décoratifs, Paris

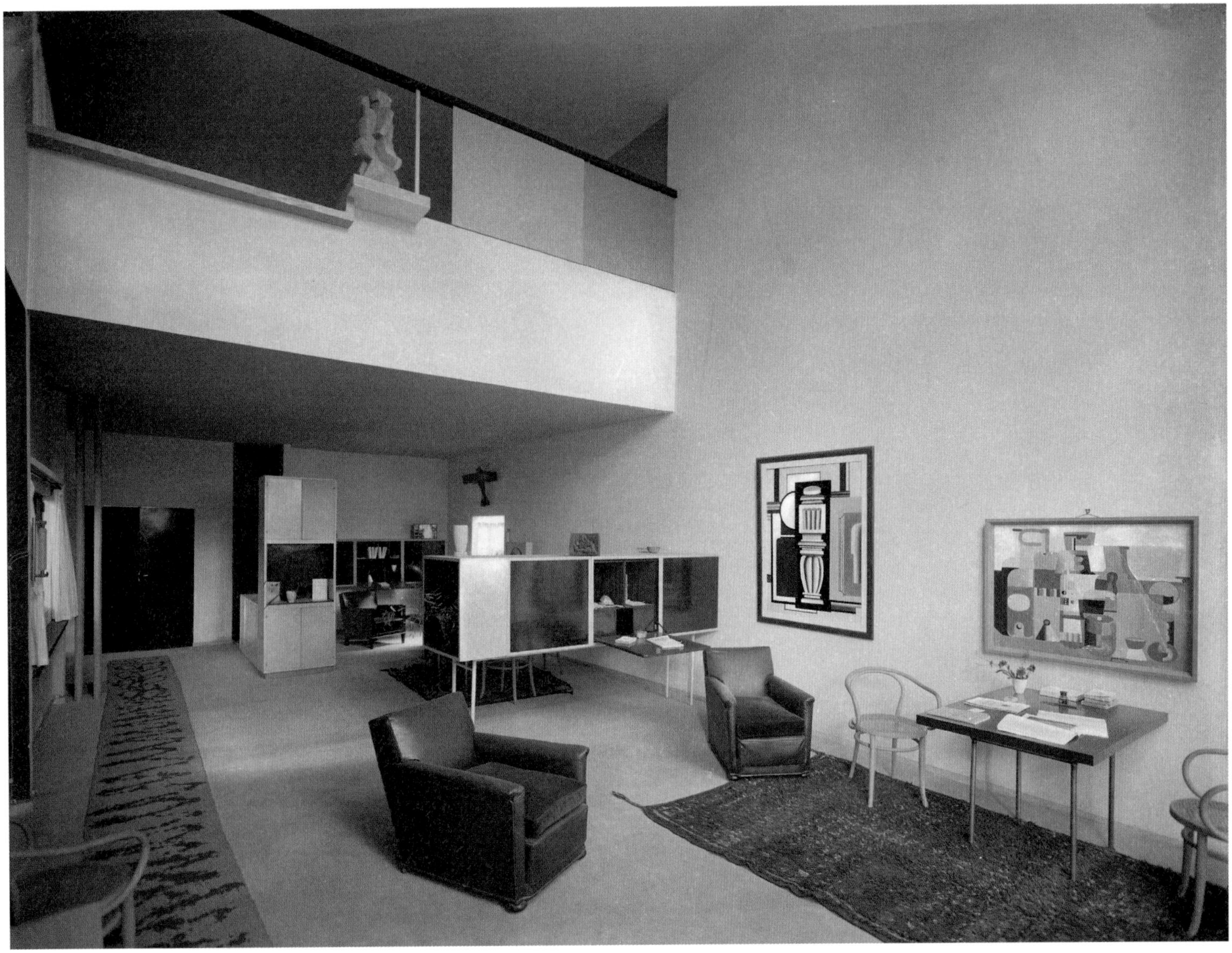

87

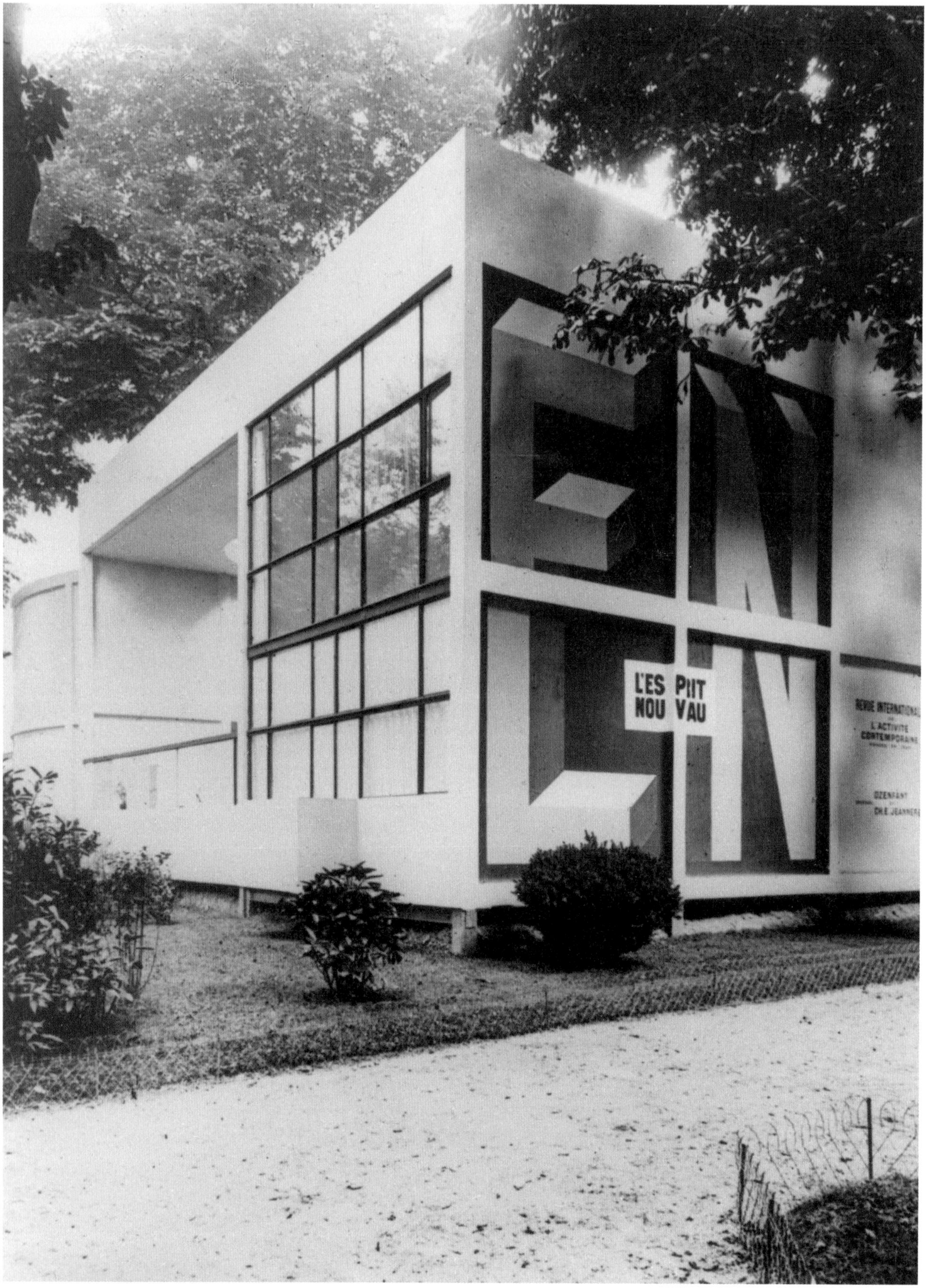

88

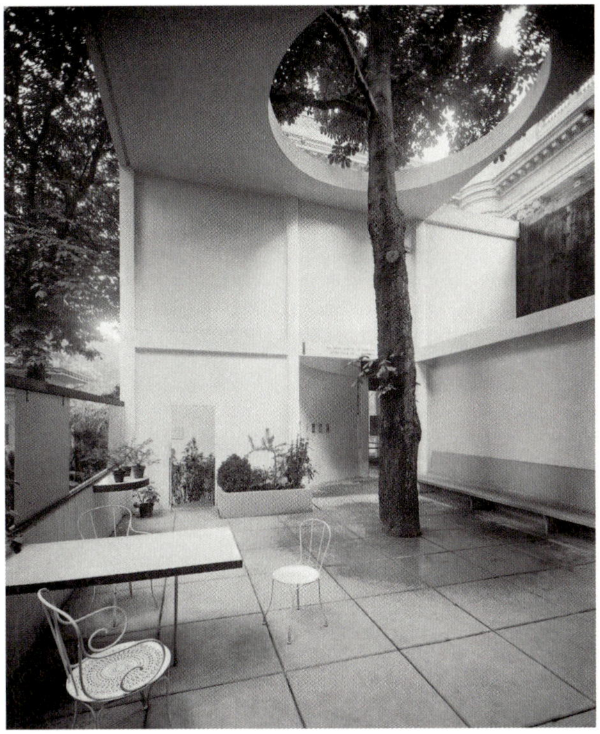

89

88 **Exterior view of the Pavillon de l'Esprit Nouveau at the *Exposition internationale des Arts décoratifs et industriels modernes* (International Exhibition of Decorative and Modern Industrial Arts) in Paris, 1925**
Fondation Le Corbusier, Paris

89 **Terrace of the Pavillon de l'Esprit Nouveau with roof cutout**
Les Arts Décoratifs, Paris

90 Le Corbusier, Pierre Jeanneret
***Pavillon de l'Esprit Nouveau, Paris, étude de façade* (Pavilion of the New Spirit, Paris, design for the façade), 1924**
Black pencil and pastel chalk on paper
60.5 × 111.6 cm
Fondation Le Corbusier, Paris

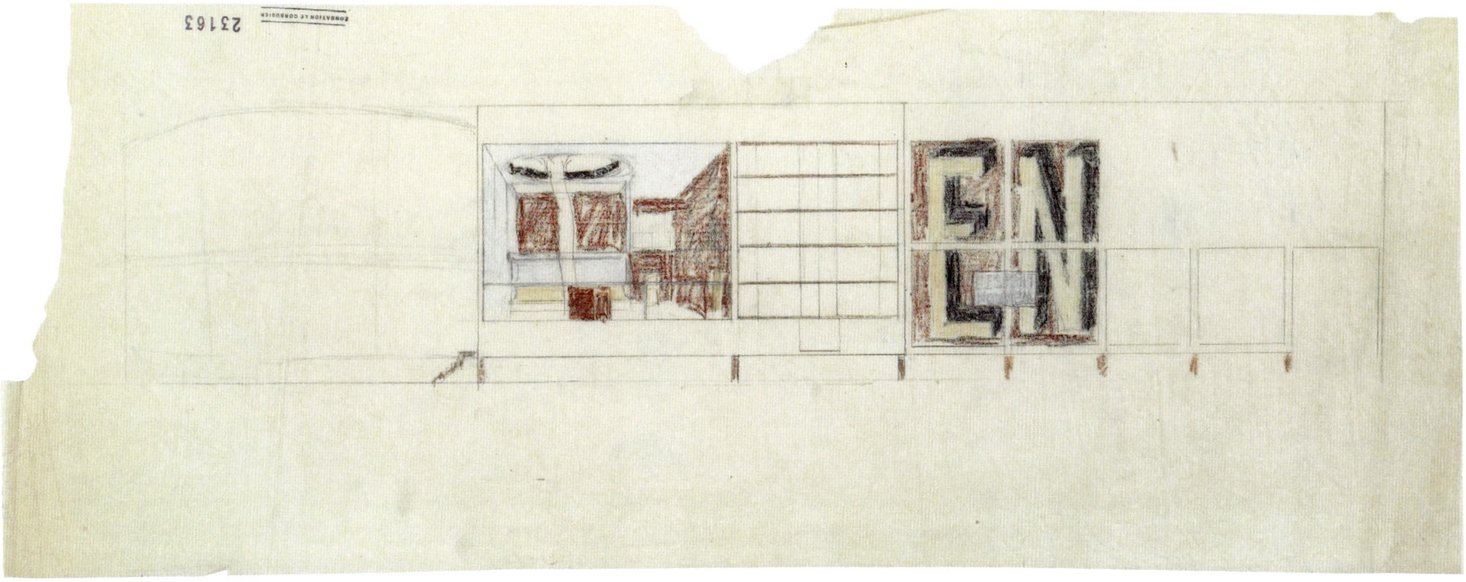

90

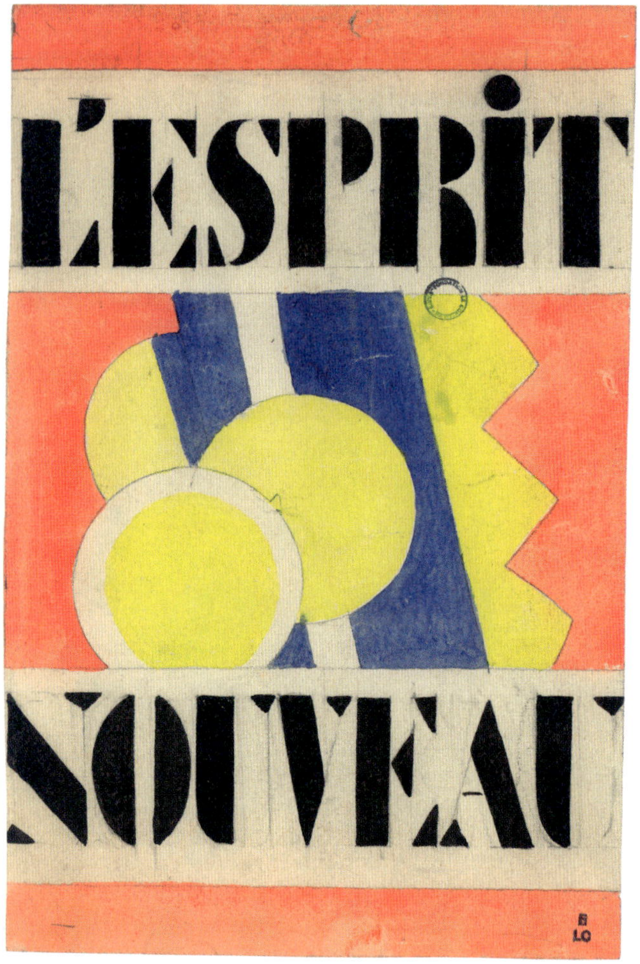

91

91 **Cover design for the magazine *L'Esprit Nouveau*, c. 1922**
Watercolor on paper
25.4 × 16.8 cm
Fondation Le Corbusier, Paris

Architecture and Fernand Léger (1929)
Le Corbusier

LÉGER A red wall, a blue wall, a black floor, a red one, or a yellow one–I see a complete transformation of the interior.

X Right, the red wall is stable, the blue wall recedes, this wall is warm or cold, etc. These are the elements of architectural interiors whose qualities and relationships to one another are not disrupted by the immense world outside.

LÉGER And that is the question that excites me. Imagine designing a bank that way, from color plans!

X Then you agree that colored surfaces should be solid, or nearly so? (For Léger's paintings have just decreed a new fashion in Holland of hatched walls–colored panels with violent gashes crisscrossing capriciously.) In any case, they should not be decorated as you and [Joseph] Csaky attempted at the last Salon des Indépendants?

LÉGER Precisely, that was the mistake: the walls should be discrete entities that enter into the equation as unified wholes.

X A work of art like that would thrill you, you say? But you could not sign such a work at the bottom of the frame.

LÉGER Of course! And so much the better!

And there you have a sign of the times, one whole side of the emerging painting-architecture question. (L.C., *L'Esprit Nouveau*, no. 19 (Winter 1923-24).)

***

Now that he has painted his "mechanical" paintings, Léger is in pursuit of further discovery about the modern world. As a painter, he perceives himself to be powerfully positioned to participate in this great current–more pervasive every day–that is the phenomenon of contemporary architecture: countless new objects are being created under the sign of this new spirit, and the general production of our era is tearing us from the past and propelling us into an imminent new phase.

Léger is mostly a creature of his time–it's an instinct of his; he withers in painting's ivory tower. Life races forward perilously these days, and he wants to be a part of it. At each step there he is, shaken up. He and Cendrars have been for some years now venturing out into this postwar world, sniffing the scent of a new spring.

Picasso and Braque discovered a shattered poetry in the objects of everyday life. Bistro accoutrements–which perhaps we did not question quite enough–expressed the state of our culture in a profound way. In their wake, an elite with newly opened eyes recognized the discovery: a blossoming of magnificent art was the result. Léger and Cendras went elsewhere, their noses tracing other scents. This doesn't seem like much. Nevertheless, they went somewhere else, and a different vision was born. Today its evidence is everywhere, and we are endowed with a different optics.

The great disruption struck Léger at that first Salon de l'Aviation after the war: that astonishing but indisputable appearance of new forms and devices, colors arranged and treated anew, and a powerful impetus toward something.

Then, at the doorway of every Paris outing, we witnessed the emergence of a new backdrop–that of the automobile, that bygone embryo: a few garages and cans of gas, some facades covered in ads… the dull array at the bistro (fake wood, fake marble, the tarred silhouettes of the tin flatware) replaced by a brilliant array of geometric lines. The enterprise was straightforward: it had to *attract the eye*–geometry was reborn!

The painter Léger assesses this painterly event: color no longer clothes forms; to capture the gaze, colors are composed on the fundamental basis of their individual qualities. A great lesson has been outlined for painting.

Today, five or six years later, the racetracks along Napoleon's or Colbert's old routes have become lessons in painting. And everywhere we are tempted to say, "Look, there's a Léger!"

This doesn't seem like much.

Color, instead of *clothing*, acts through its only proper means.

This doesn't seem like much? This is a new art. And this art existed once before, when painting was near to architecture–a masterful and magnificent play of forms brought together in light; masterful and magnificent play of colored forces moving on the surface of a wall.

***

In the dialogue reported above, Léger and his interviewer sensed a truth that was still unsettled at the time–clouded by uneasiness and paradox. The issue has since been settled. We have come to understand the causes behind it. We have decided upon a solution: The new architecture, produced with new techniques and advanced by new aspirations, makes use of a structure in cement or iron, and henceforth *the plan is free*. There is no more Room A in pink or blue, Room B in green or yellow, etc., each enclosed by its four walls supporting the floor above. There are posts here and there, supporting the upper floor; the plan is free; and the lightweight partitions, *not carrying any load*, allow for the diversification of the spaces, the establishment of correspondences, the introduction of functional components to make the space more comfortable. The room units are no longer square; they interpenetrate and continue into one another; some of their walls extend out, others roll up in cylinders, in spirals… and color, with its specific qualities (blue inspiring ecstasy, red stabilizing the plan, etc.), establishes an order, a density, a light, an intense lyricism. It's an achievement of modern architecture. Colored walls enter into the equation as unified wholes.

Léger, who is attuned to architecture, has moved beyond the tumultuous diagonals of the mechanical–tumult will no longer reside in the drawing. Tumult will be born of the advancing or receding movements of colors. This is the dynamic with which he composes. From his architectural education he has retained the right angle, which he uses to order this fore-and-aft circulation of color.

This painting is sister to architecture. There lies its import. But it remains, profoundly, painting.

Such is the link, so imperative that Léger, of all the painters working today, is the one whose paintings demand a new architecture. It's his paintings that require a frame commensurate with the age–one born of it. Whereas the paintings of contemporary masters everywhere support, through their deep, originary laws, the presence of previous architectures. Léger scandalizes. He is the painter of today, for whom a new spiritual expression in architecture is necessary.

Originally published as Le Corbusier, "L'architecture et Fernand Léger," in *Sélection: chronique de la vie artistique*, no. 5 (February 1929): 21–24. Excerpts from the English translation by Liesl Yamaguchi in ed. Anna Vallye, *Léger: Modern Art and the Metropolis*, exh. cat., Philadelphia Museum of Art (New Haven and London, 2013), 215–16.

–

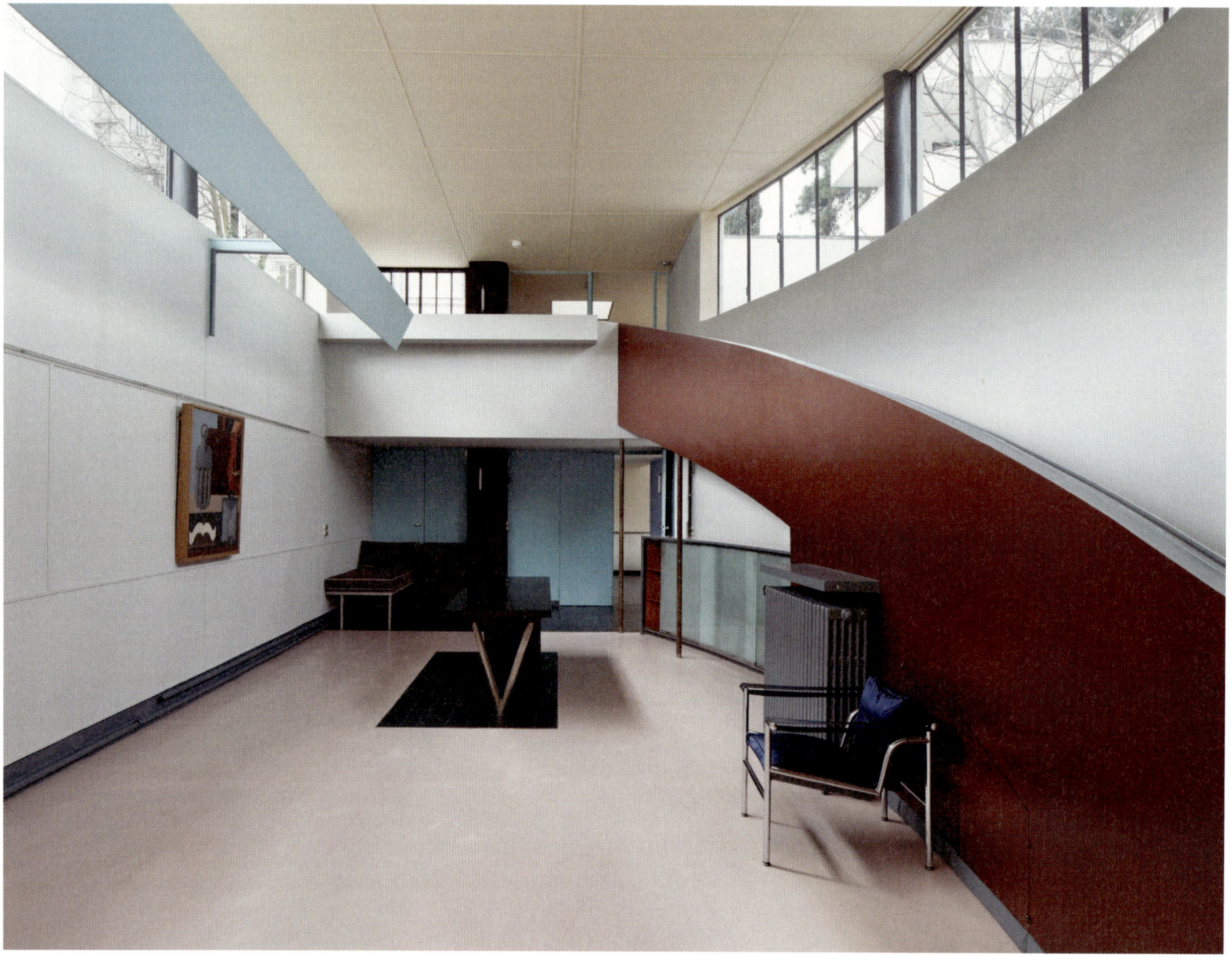

92

92 Le Corbusier
Maison La Roche, 1925, current view
Fondation Le Corbusier, Paris

93 Le Corbusier
Maison La Roche, 1925
Fondation Le Corbusier, Paris

94 Le Corbusier, Pierre Jeanneret
Maison La Roche, perspective
(La Roche house, perspectival view), 1923
Black pencil and pastel chalk on tracing paper
56.9 × 58.8 cm
Fondation Le Corbusier, Paris

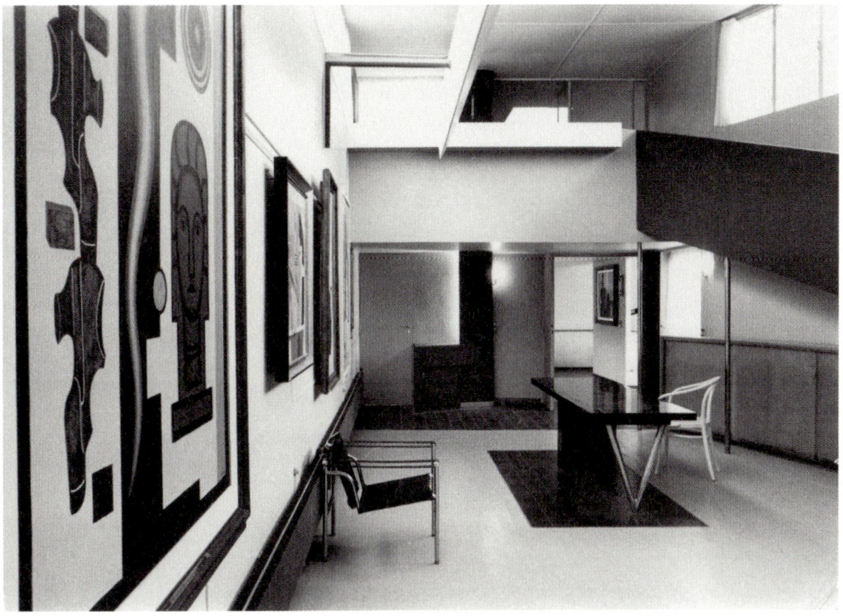

93

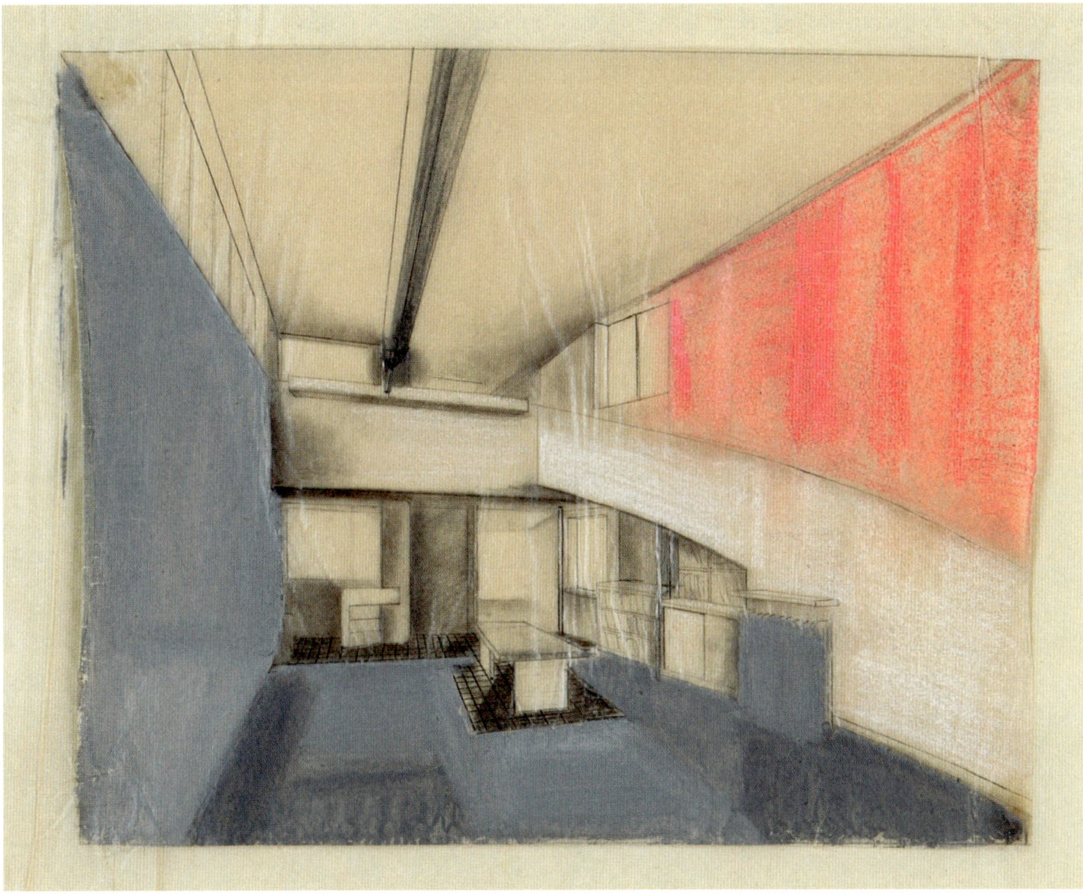

94

Color in Architecture (1948)
Fernand Léger

I met Le Corbusier about 1921 or 1922, I believe in a rather odd way. At the time I lived in Montparnasse, and I used to go occasionally to the terrace of the Rotonde with friends and models of the Quarter. One day one of them said to me: "Just wait, you are going to see an odd specimen. He goes bicycling in a derby hat."

A few minutes later I saw coming along, very stiff, completely in silhouette, an extraordinary mobile object under the derby hat, with spectacles and in a dark suit. It was the outfit of a clergyman and of an Englishman on a weekend. He advanced quietly, scrupulously obeying the laws of perspective. The picturesque personage, indifferent to the curiosity he awakened, was none other than the architect Le Corbusier.

Some time after this vision I made his acquaintance. I can say that our taste met on many common grounds. He also painted. When I saw his painting I was a little disappointed. It was gray and melodious, all in tonalities. At this time I was personally interested in violent and dynamic color. I said to myself: This fellow however is a very likeable sort; it is too bad that we are at the opposite poles in painting. His slant was known as "purism." Since that time his manner has changed greatly.

But aside from all that he was a man of great quality. Of Swiss origin, he had the attentive seriousness of contemporary northerners, entirely divorced from nebulous and literary romanticism. He liked precision, exactitude, simple forms, popular and primitive arts. This was a realm of agreement for both of us. We became good pals.

The approach of the Exposition of 1925 intensified our relationship. The first manifestation of modern architecture appeared under the aspect of a radical cleanup. For a long while no one had known what an interior wall was. It had disappeared in a half-light under curtains, under wallpapers, hangings, and knickknacks. Suddenly it "appeared"; and it was a revelation, a bath of nudism. Le Corbusier made us a present of the white wall. We needed it. A completely white wall is a beautiful thing. Architecture set out once again from zero. It was the great heroic age. An exhibition of modern architecture was even held—I believe at Stuttgart—where not a single picture was admitted, not even a Mondrian. Cult of the void. Voluptuousness of the absolute. Note that before this period poetry and painting had both freed themselves from the subject—from the object—we were living abstract art. The escape was complete. Architecture in its turn was now playing the same part to liberate itself. To break away from secular restraints was a magnificent and dangerous undertaking. Not since the Italian Renaissance had a similar enthusiasm been seen. There were endless discussions about the new space, the habitable rectangle, the asymmetrical order, the "destruction of the wall," the elastic rectangle. All of this bounced around without troubling itself one second whether the good public was of this opinion or not.

At the same time, once intoxicated with the white wall we thought we ought to pay a little attention to it after all. It was at this moment that architects began to look at it from the point of view of color, from the painter's viewpoint. Color was going to be an intimate part of the wall which had just been discovered.

At the Exposition of 1925 we proposed to the public the colored wall. We had recognized that color bound up with light has the effect of rendering distance relative. A light-yellow wall recedes. A dark-chestnut wall advances. Between the two a white wall becomes neutral. The rectangle consequently becomes mobile.

The public proposal of 1925 appeared under the architectural aspect of the creation of a "new habitable space." If you add to that an asymmetrical arrangement of furniture, the revolution is complete. All these problems which we had often raked up together are clearly specified or foreseen in the work of Le Corbusier. He is incontestably the contemporary spirit most lucid in his comprehension and application of all these new ideas.

Color is a natural element, a force of nature indispensable to life. Its function is so various that its powers had to be examined and classified. The year 1925 may be regarded as the beginning of this examination. Before that we were surrounded by disorder and by chance. We can see now a hierarchic border of color running from a delicate shade to a destructive tone. There is a problem of "quantity" which becomes technique. What is the quantity of color necessary in a room for it to be habitable? The same problem exists for a street, for a city.

We have all been brought up in an atmosphere of light and shade. As a child I recall that there was always a great to-do when one put aside the curtains. Light and color was the advent of a long-forgotten truth. The consequences were enormous. The faces, the furniture took on a different look, an entirely different scale. The profusion of objects had made us forget the true dimensions of things. The new law was: Few objects but beautiful objects. A standard till then unknown established itself in this new space. The enthusiasm was international and above all Nordic: Holland, Belgium, Germany, and France began to build houses in this new style.

The Exposition of 1925 came in the nick of time to render spectacular and public what until that time were only scattered realizations. Two pavilions in particular were representative of this new architectural expression: the Pavillon de l'Esprit Nouveau, by Le Corbusier, and Mallet Stevens' project for an embassy. I had paintings in both. One battle took place over a mural panel which I had exhibited in the project for an embassy. It was an abstract painting in pure tones, monumental in spirit and without depth. An undersecretary of state had it removed; a minister had it put back. The battle was on. It still continues.

I am not too sure where to place the origin of the movement: the Dutch would like, it seems, to have been its precursors. In any case the work of Le Corbusier by its clarity, its decision, and its realization without dispute dominates the period. What counts above all for the future is the logical spirit which has understood and established the new data. Intentions, sketches, ingenious as they are, are rapidly absorbed by the constructive spirit. Le Corbusier has had that more than anyone else.

A modern factory at Rotterdam is the van Nelle Factory. The old factory was dark and gray; the new is light and transparent. The laborers who worked in the old factory were slovenly and unhappy. In the new factory–without any hint having been made to them, without any instruction–it was seen that at the end of a certain time, they were more tidy, gayer, better taken care of, better dressed. It was simply the light and color–this new truth–which had brought about the change.

This new architecture has an extremely important psychological and social effect. The future will recognize it. The polychrome hospital, color therapy, new popular monuments, the opportunity of the people to approach beautiful works of art in new appropriate architecture, the urbanization of future agglomerations–all are enormous problems which the destruction of this war renders immediate and urgent. If we run through the books of Le Corbusier, we see that he has touched and foreseen the greater number of these problems. Let us put our confidence in him and in his friends. They will be judged by the test.

Originally published as Fernand Léger, "Color in Architecture," in ed. Stamos Papadaki, *Le Corbusier: Architect, Painter, Writer* (New York: Macmillan, 1948), 78–80.

–

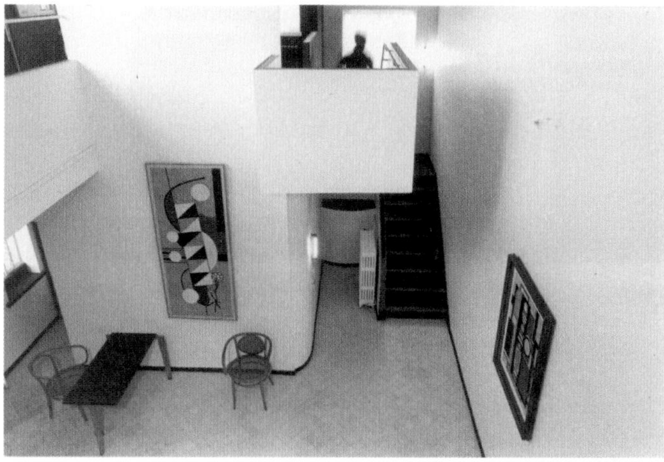

95

95 Le Corbusier,
Maison La Roche, 1925
Fondation Le Corbusier, Paris

In the center: *Le Printemps (du cycle: les quatre saisons)* (Spring [from the "Four Seasons" cycle]) by Fernand Léger, 1928.

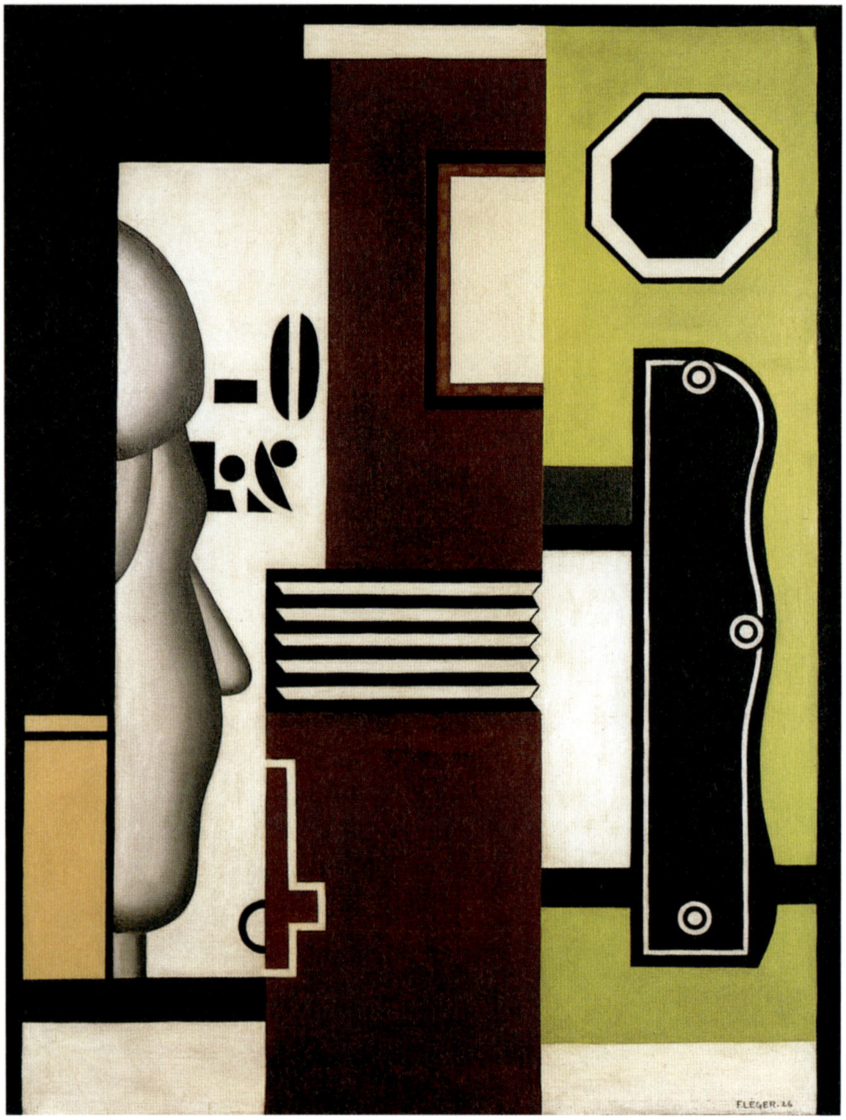

96

96 ***Composition avec profil***
(Composition with Profile), 1926
Oil on canvas
139 × 97 cm
Von der Heydt Museum, Wuppertal

Formerly Le Corbusier collection.

97 **Le Corbusier's dining room,**
Rue Nungesser-et-Coli, Paris, c. 1934
Architects: Le Corbusier and Pierre Jeanneret,
interior design: Charlotte Perriand
Archives Charlotte Perriand

98 Le Corbusier
Nature morte aux nombreux objets
(Still Life of Numerous Objects), 1923
Oil on canvas
114 × 146 cm
Fondation Le Corbusier, Paris

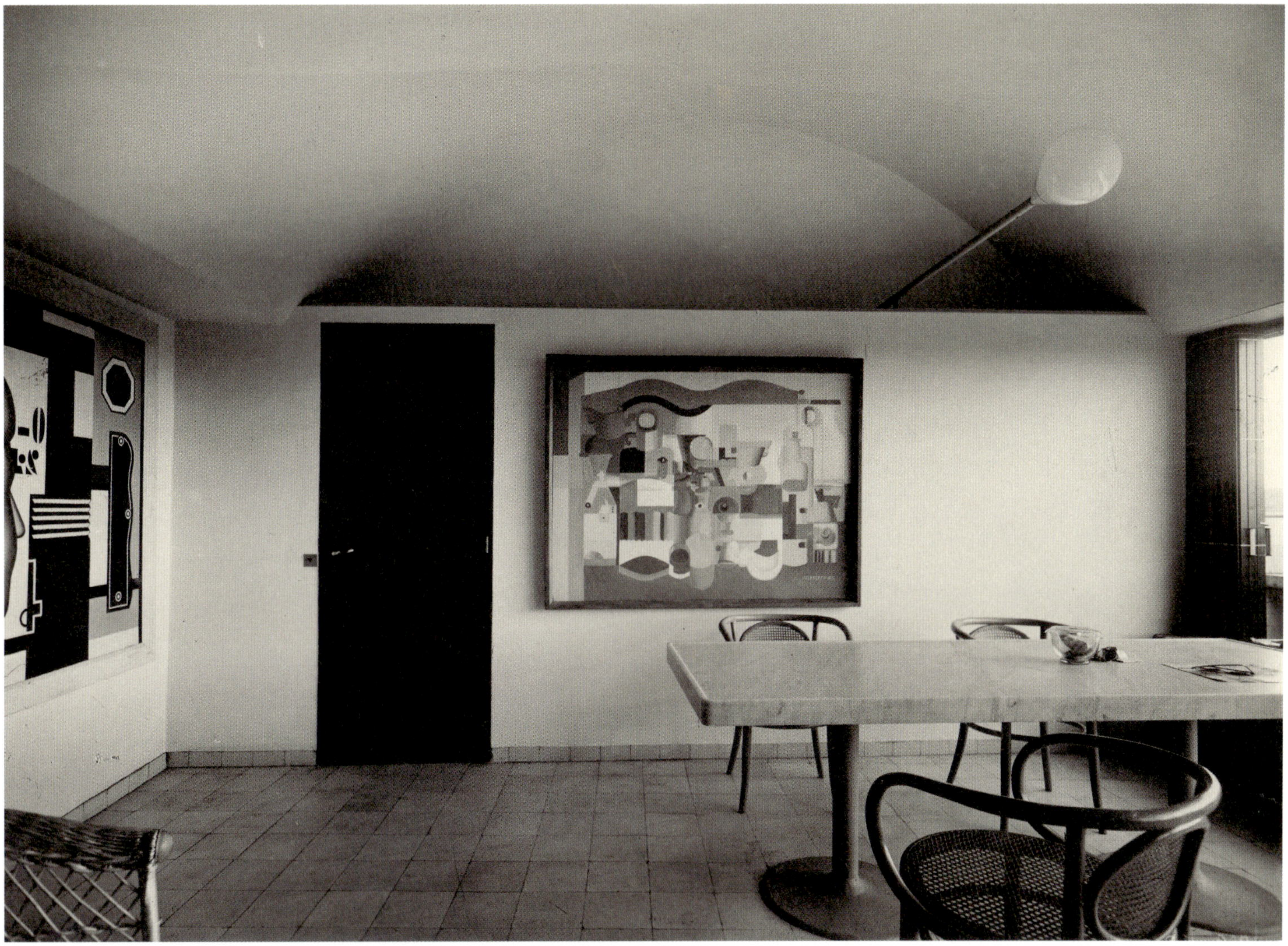

97

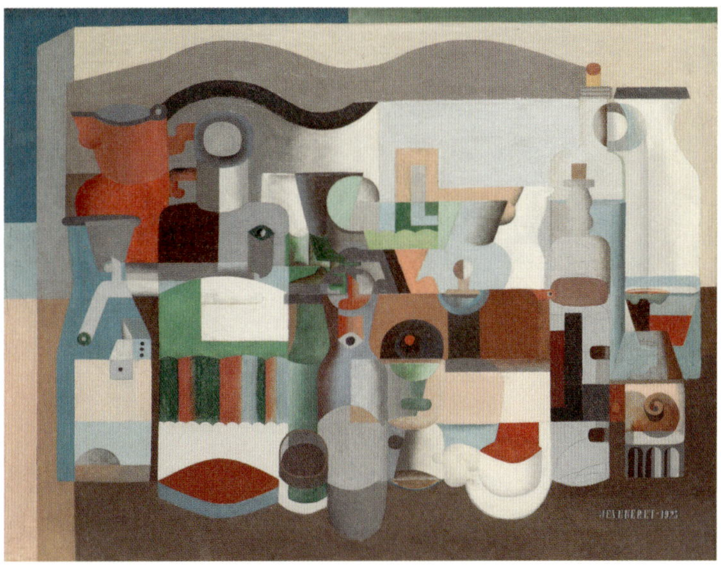

98

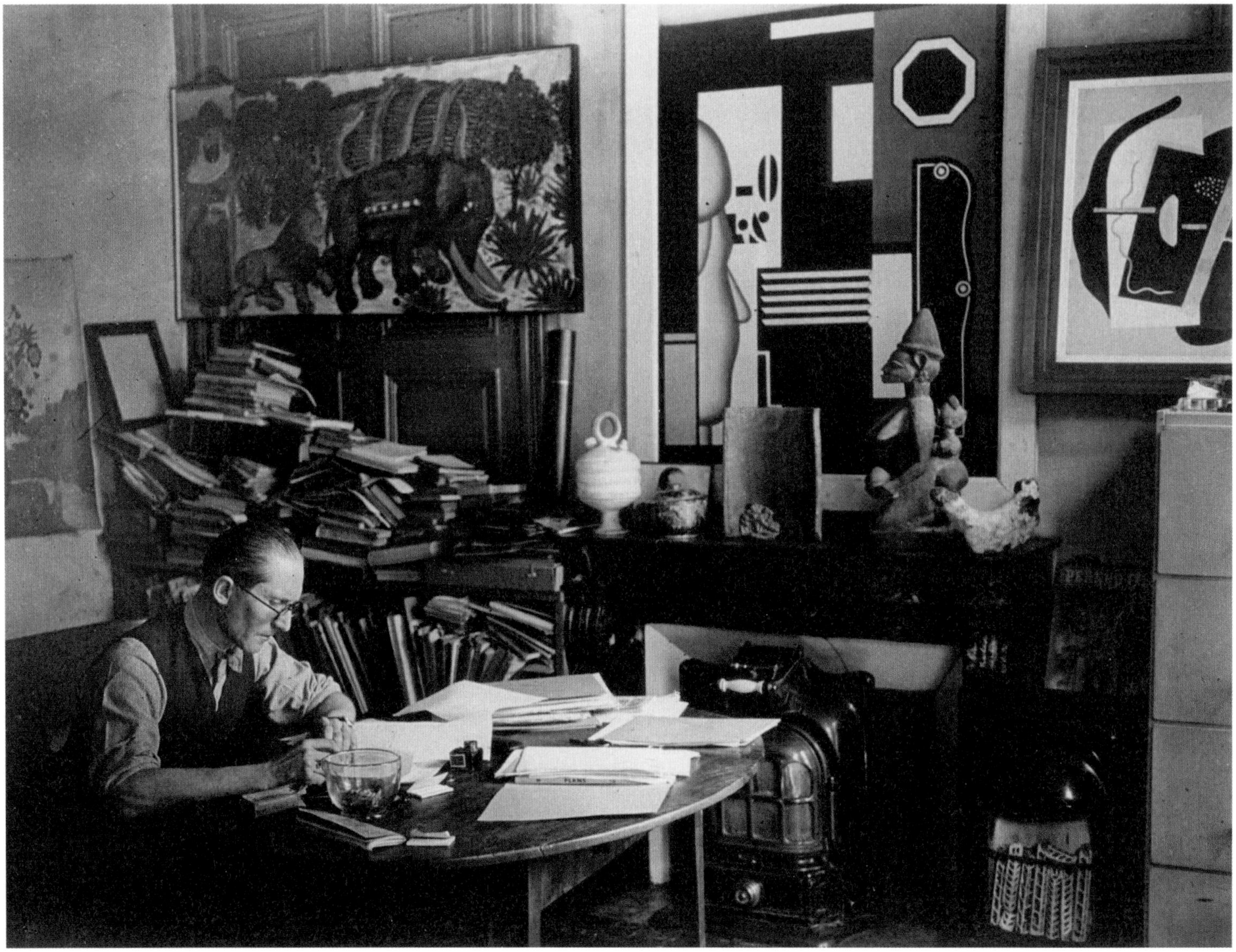

99

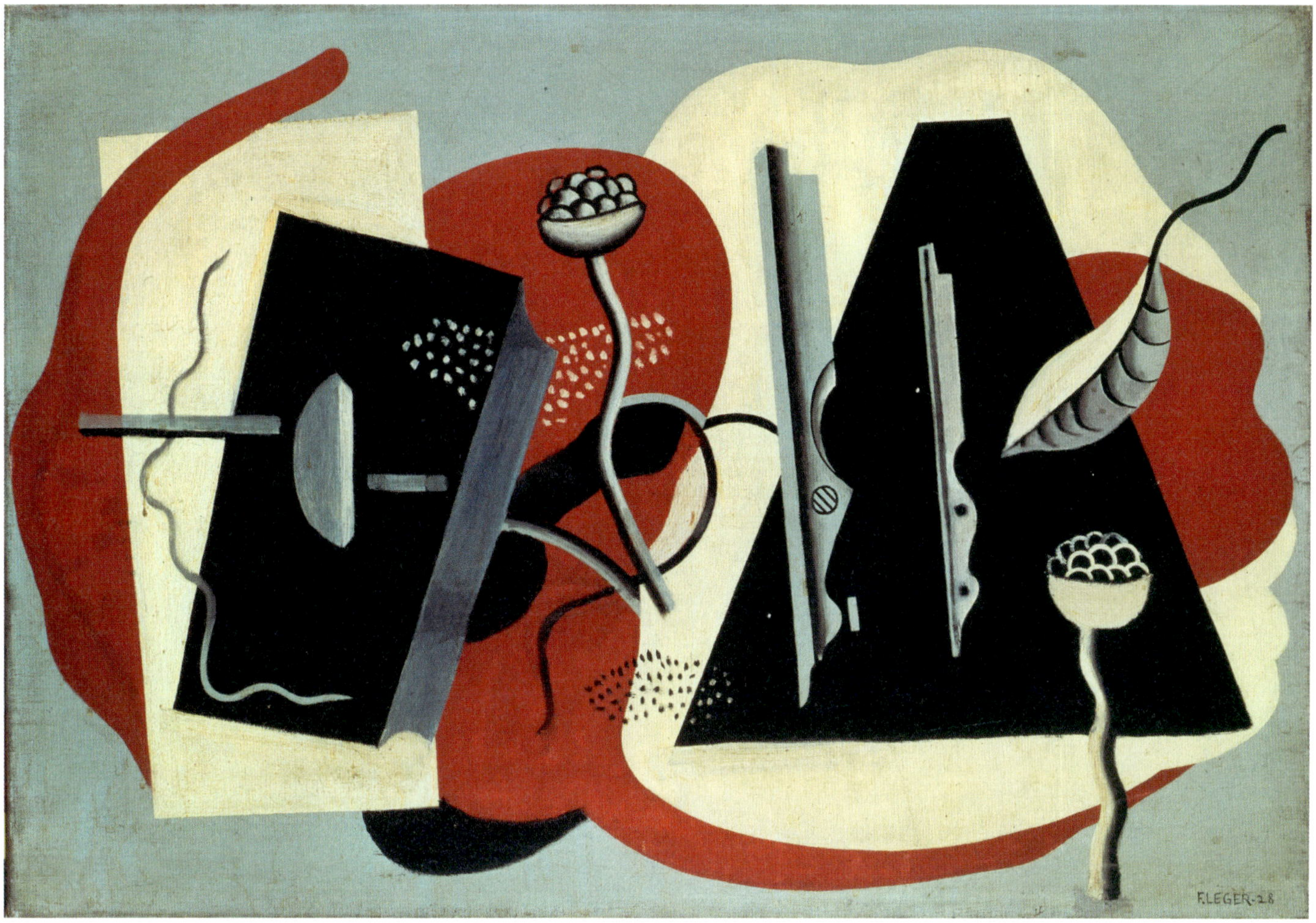

100

99 **Le Corbusier at his desk, Rue Jacob, Paris**
Photographed by Brassaï, 1931, in the background
Composition avec profil (Composition with Profile),
1926, next to Nature morte (Still Life),1928,
both by Fernand Léger
Gelatin silver print
Private collection

100 ***Nature Morte* (Still Life), 1928**
Oil on canvas
69.5 × 96.5 cm
Fondation Le Corbusier, Paris

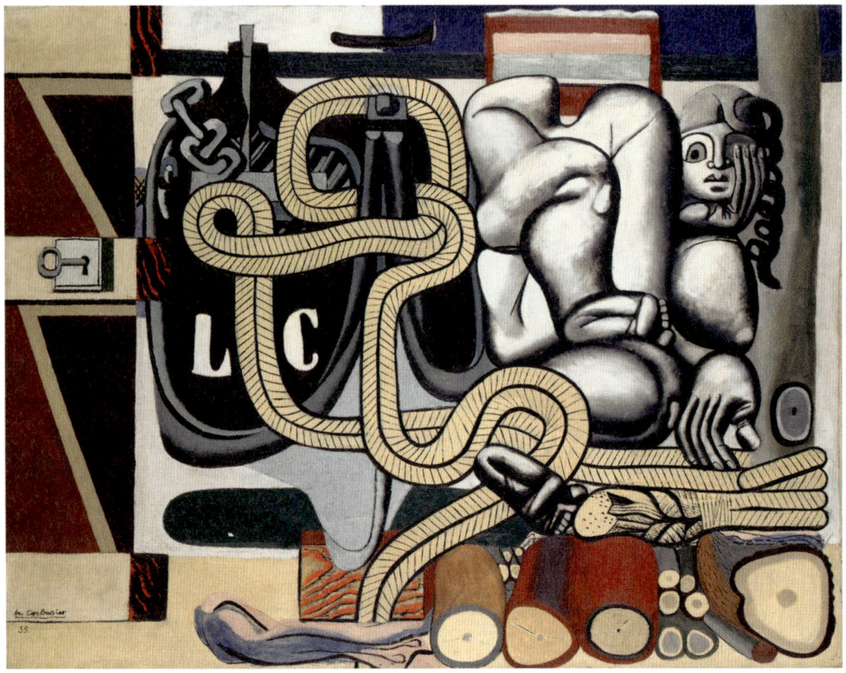

101

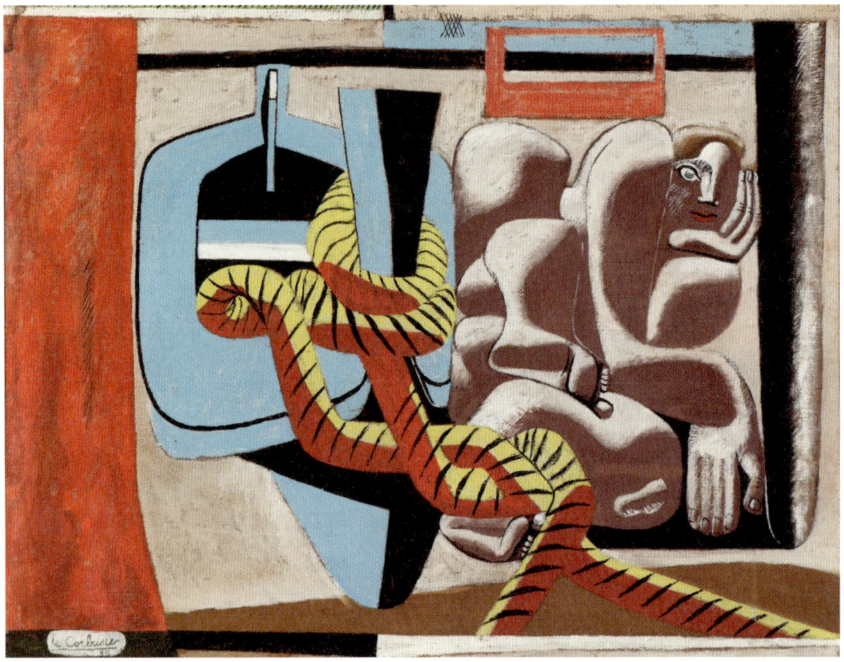

102

101 Le Corbusier
***Femme couchée, cordage et bateau à la porte ouverte* (Reclining Nude, Rope and Boat with Open Door), 1935**
Oil on canvas
129.9 × 162.4 cm
Kunstmuseum Basel
Gift of Dr. h. c. Raoul La Roche

102 Le Corbusier
***Carton pour tapisserie (Marie Cuttoli)* (Design for tapestry [Marie Cuttoli]), 1936**
Oil on canvas
114 × 146 cm
Fondation Le Corbusier, Paris

Like Fernand Léger, Le Corbusier also designed rugs for Maison Myrbor. This work was inspired by Léger's painting "The Bathers."

103 ***La Baigneuse* (The Bather), 1932**
Oil on canvas
98 × 130
Musée national Fernand Léger, Biot

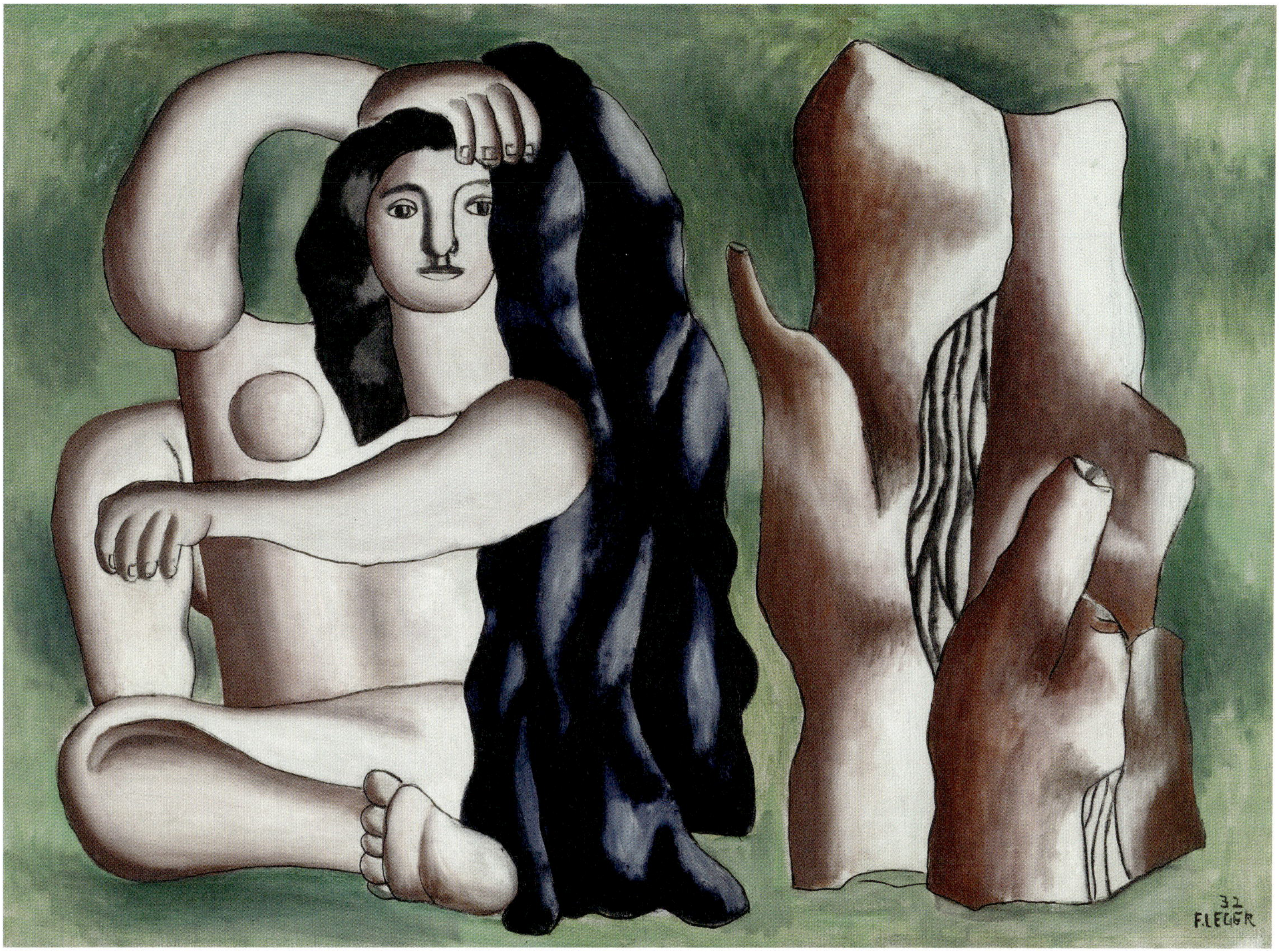

103

The So-called Primitive Arts in Today's Home (1935)
André Bloc

The singular similarities and surprising contrasts achieved by Louis Carré and Le Corbusier in the latter's studio revealed the charm of the unexpected dialogue between the primitive and contemporary arts.

Archaic Greek art adapts quite well to the nearby presence of a Fernand Léger tapestry and a Laurens sculpture, while a Baoulé sculpture from the Ivory Coast fraternizes with a freshly painted canvas by Le Corbusier. For we should not forget that Le Corbusier is a painter. Although his painting does not always excite as much as his architecture, it accounts for the prodigious resources of an artist who does not always bother about his own principles, which are sometimes accepted unquestioningly by his enthusiastic disciples.

André Bloc's preface originally published in Le Corbusier, "Les Arts primitifs dans la maison d'aujourd'hui," in *L'Architecture d'aujourd'hui* (July 1935): 83.

–

104 ***Les Arts Primitifs dans la maison* exhibition, Paris, 1935, organized by Le Corbusier and Louis Carré, View of exhibition**
Fondation Le Corbusier, Paris

105 **Le Corbusier in his studio on Rue Nungesser-et-Coli**
Photographed by Gaston Paris, in front of the tapestry by Fernand Léger *Composition with Three Figures: Return from Greece*. Paris, Exhibition of Primitive Arts in the Home, 1935,

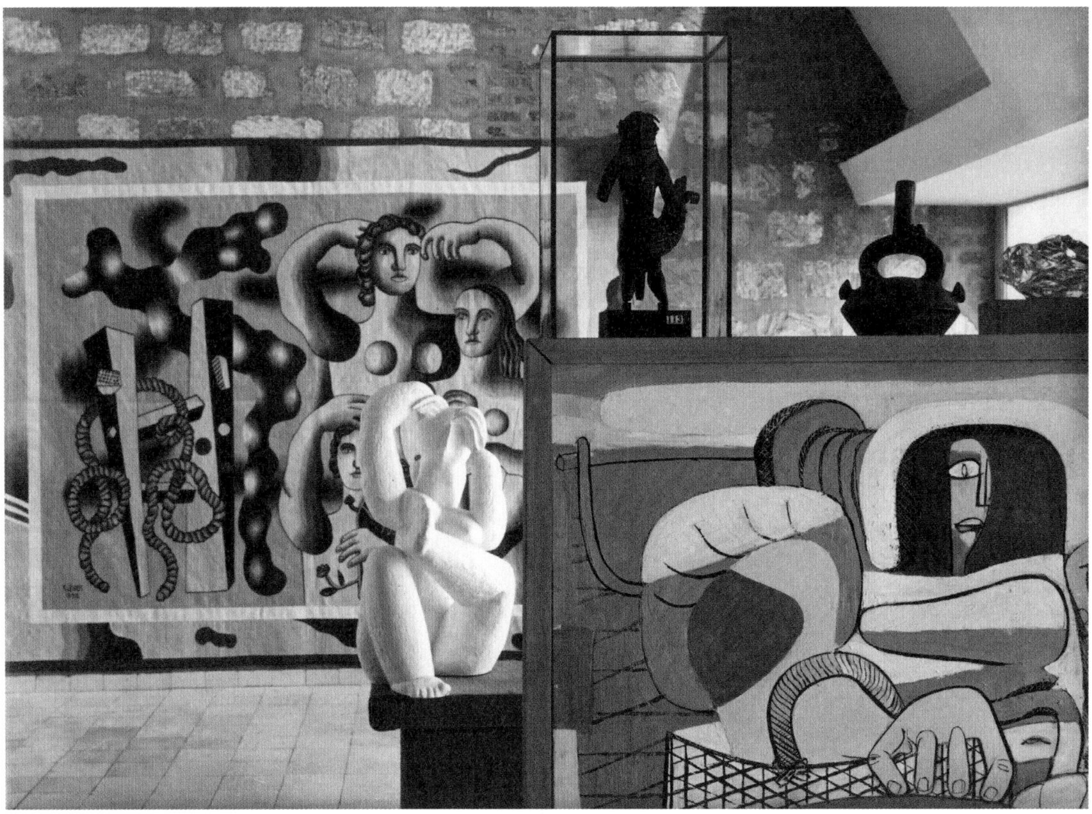

104

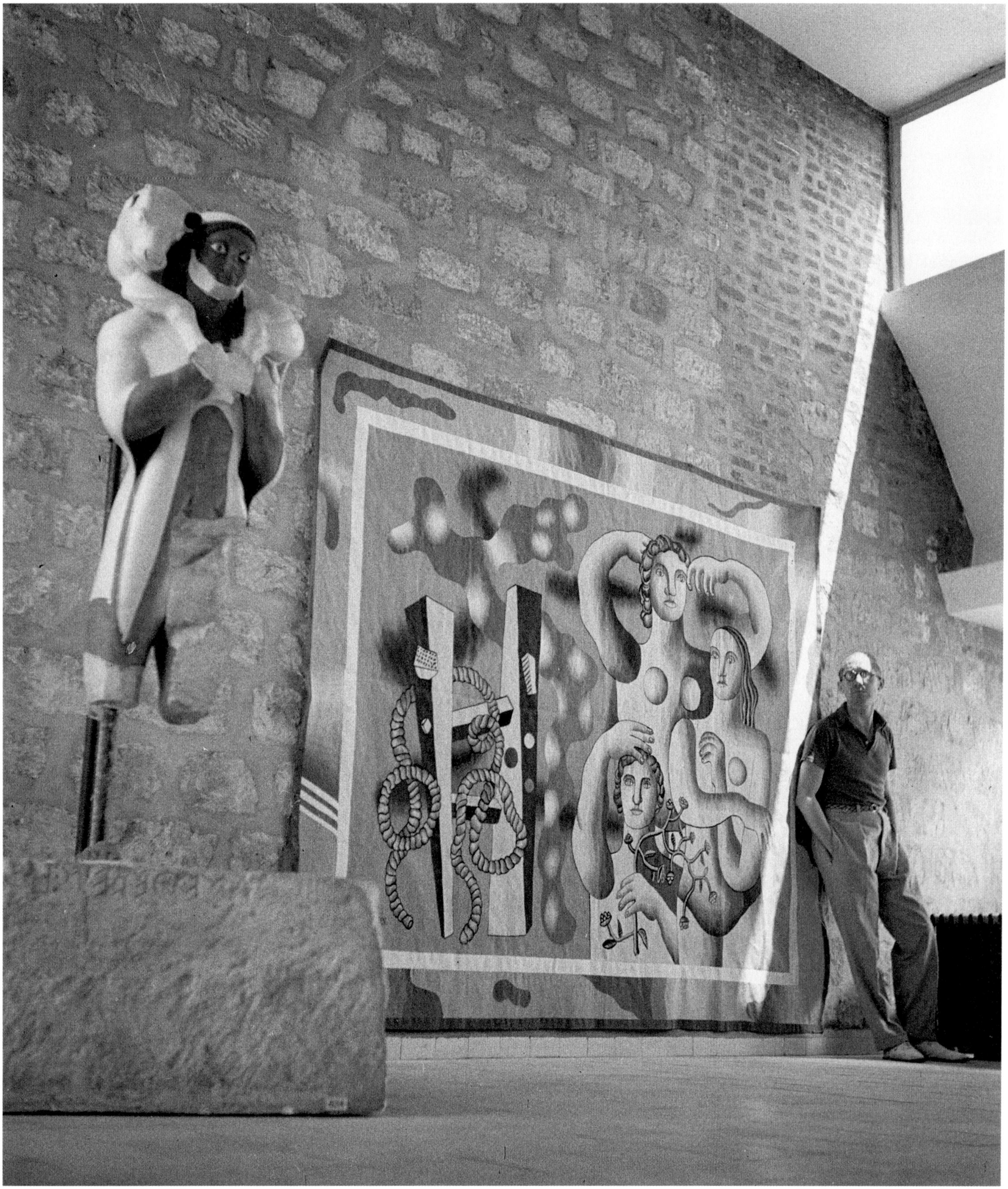

105

WALL PAINTING OR SPATIAL PAINTING (1937)
Jean Badovici

- Fernand, I have before me a bothersome wall, a wall which exasperates me. It is too near, too high, all of this makes me feel sad…

For you, painters, it presents an opportunity, not to decorate it, but to BLOW IT UP, to destroy it with painting, to smash through it, to push it away, and finally to create a little bit of SPACE AROUND IT… That will be your true role in the architecture of tomorrow…

Such were the remarks I made on a building site in a very old house in Burgundy in 1934. A rather shallow courtyard, surrounded by very high walls, proud and bold. In that courtyard there stood Le Corbusier, Fernand Léger, and myself. A discussion broke out: style has let itself go. The mere whiff of a paint tube can kill off a canvas; ingratitude is all around: then there are the reproaches, the indecisiveness of easel painting; architects who longer even want painting. Certain lectures were recalled in which friends embarked on discouraging and unfair propaganda.

But, before the wall, our discussion got down to basics, and—making for fresh pastures—an idea came to us all: THAT OF THE DESTRUCTION OF THE WALL BY PAINTING, which would make the perfect complement to the architecture of the future. One phase is already over and another beneficial possibility is, once again, on the move, and the anticipated form of the future: SPATIAL PAINTING, becomes once again the great pictorial tradition.

Easel painting in its current guise will be liquidated and painting will henceforth enhance architecture as a whole, no longer underlining the wall, as in the past, with the fresco-subject. THE FRESCO WILL BE SPATIAL.

The sadness of the paintings of yesteryear was like that of those posters on the edge of the road that nobody can see, try as one might. Abandoned gardens, birds that no longer sing. And yet discussions that turned a small idea into a big page! We have gleaned such a gorgeous bouquet from the history of fresco! On your knees, the lot of you! Antiquity, the Byzantines, and the Gothics. And all the other Renaissances that testify to the collective role of true fresco painting. LOST, FORGOTTEN.

Tomorrow: stadiums, public buildings, and swimming-pools might again, thanks to SPATIAL PAINTING, become lighter and their volume and heaviness reduced. Their spirit will only be the livelier.

We had reached the elimination of the wall-subject. The WALL-OBJECT will be everywhere. In this trial, the DYNAMIC WALL just follows its natural evolution, it has reached its true goal: PAINTING IN THE OPEN AIR: THE PAINTING OF LIFE… The wall opens an age with a great future. The case of the DYNAMIC WALL will give rise to other possibilities, vaster still, when utility and the intellect will become universal. PAINTING WILL BE USEFUL.

In a new departure, with the Burgundy fresco Léger breaks through the wall by multiplying it, expressing himself through pure planes, with decisive diagonals, which progress through a free, clear space, without "vapors and protective patches."

He has created a nature made of metal, of folding-screens and winding lines that run upwards and reabsorb the wall into a ground whiter than any lake.

A vertical style, bright, without smudges. A spatial style. Architectural, above all. A parade! The wall lives with the intensity of today. Léger has subordinated the wall to the dynamic order of composition—active elements that reinvest the equivalent and solid sensation of its pictorial potential.

Léger revels in the glory of having antagonized the WALL.

[…] As chance would have it, in that same little Burgundy house with the astonishing walls, Le Corbusier has produced his first fresco!

Le Corbusier has tried his hand at this pristine, primitive expression, and, subtle observer that he is, he thus liberates present-day painting from its prostitution. For the real tragedy of painting today is that its acceptance arises from a misunderstanding.

[…] Le Corbusier has recognized how, in nature, objects possess relief: in his fashion, he has invented new oppositions between light and dark. He has created a true mural fresco, dissolving it into a rustic architecture comprised entirely of shade. For the figures he chooses BLUE, glowing like phosphorus, with, as a counterweight, blood red and black. From afar it almost looks like a monochrome. Thus the earliest Greek painters painted with only a single color: Higgionontes, Dimias, and Charmas [sic]. As for Euramis, he later worked with two colors. This was in the 7th century BC.

Le Corbusier's fresco is a far cry from his colorful paintings, distinct from those of Léger, who paints illuminated objects.

[…] This is the impression Le Corbusier's fresco arouses at first sight. And yet this fresco lives in air, like the birds. As with music, the "LINE" is its own melody.

His painting follows his admirable architecture with a determined enthusiasm that gives to his conclusions the moving inflections of a compact, even definitive, "WHOLE."

Talent too is a question of quantity. Talent does not mean carrying out just one thing; it means making a thousand.

It is through experience that genius becomes fecund. It cannot be otherwise. To this Le Corbusier conforms. In his architecture, neither Greek Temple nor Factory, but a human crystal on a human scale. It is towards this that he strives with all his genius. He wants his architecture to be total, elevated to its SUMMUM. From this comes a constant need to paint. And now he has succeeded in painting his first fresco. It is full of intensity.

Situated admirably at a place which, although the nerve center of the house, is also a crossing point, IT IS BY NO MEANS IN THE WAY. The fresco does not impose itself on you, and to see it you really have to raise your eyes.

In the modern era, the mural must bestow wholeness and balance to the architecture of today.

Le Corbusier has grasped that a painting is always a release. It always opens a wall:

a) by its materiality (colors plus lines);
b) by the poem it creates, which is equally evasion of the spirit and equally depth. The subject is constructed in order to attempt, at last, an historical critique.

Paring down his wall fresco like this is Le Corbusier's "SIGN," the reaction of an acute sensitivity that confirms it.

Moreover, Le Corbusier's painting simply enhances today's architecture by clearing and freeing it.

Easel painting that all painters do is like a carriage horse that amazes us by bolting, but which is utterly devoid of any real potential.

Such as he has done in Burgundy, Le Corbusier's debut fresco is the work of a living man. It is the new "HOLY FAMILY" for our day, a composition produced together with his pipe, his matchbox, a bottle of wine, a pack of tobacco. Because Le Corbusier has a feeling for what's in the wind and makes the best of the "TEMPERATURE."

I have often been critical of Le Corbusier. It is hard to reject spiritually exalted accomplishments. But any profound assertion produces a profound negation.

Léger has consecrated the Léger atmosphere, permanently. Le Corbusier changes, throws things over. Whence all the drama of his power: though closely linked to its predecessor, each creation is nonetheless quite separate from it, simply living out its own life.

Excerpts from Jean Badovici, "Peinture murale ou peinture spatiale," in *L'Architecture d'aujourd'hui*, no. 3 (March 1937): 75–78.

–

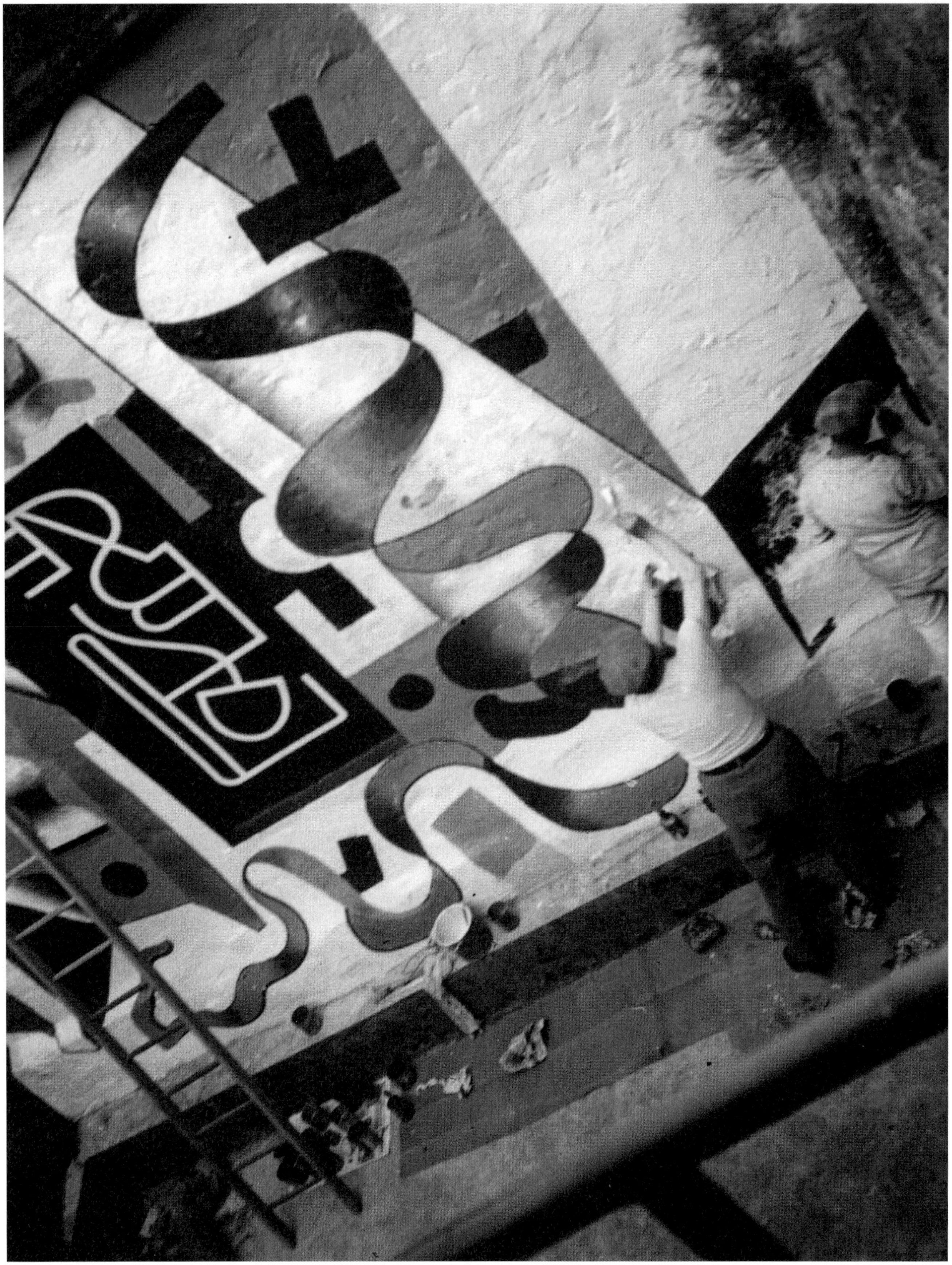

106

106 **Fernand Léger working on *Mur Libre* (Free Wall) in the inner courtyard of the home of Jean Badovici, Vézelay, 1936**
Archives Charlotte Perriand

107 **Completed fresco, left side, in the small 5.5-meter-deep courtyard**
Photograph
6.5 × 6.5 cm
Fonds Badovici, Origine Mireille Rougeot.
MZ Doc 269

108 ***Mur libre* (Free Wall), 1934-36**
Lime, mural painting
388 × 440 cm
Centre Pompidou, Musée national d'art moderne, Paris, permanently installed at the Musée Zervos

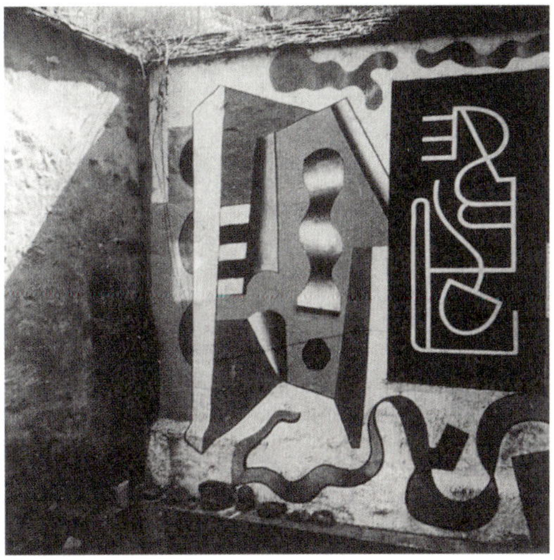

107

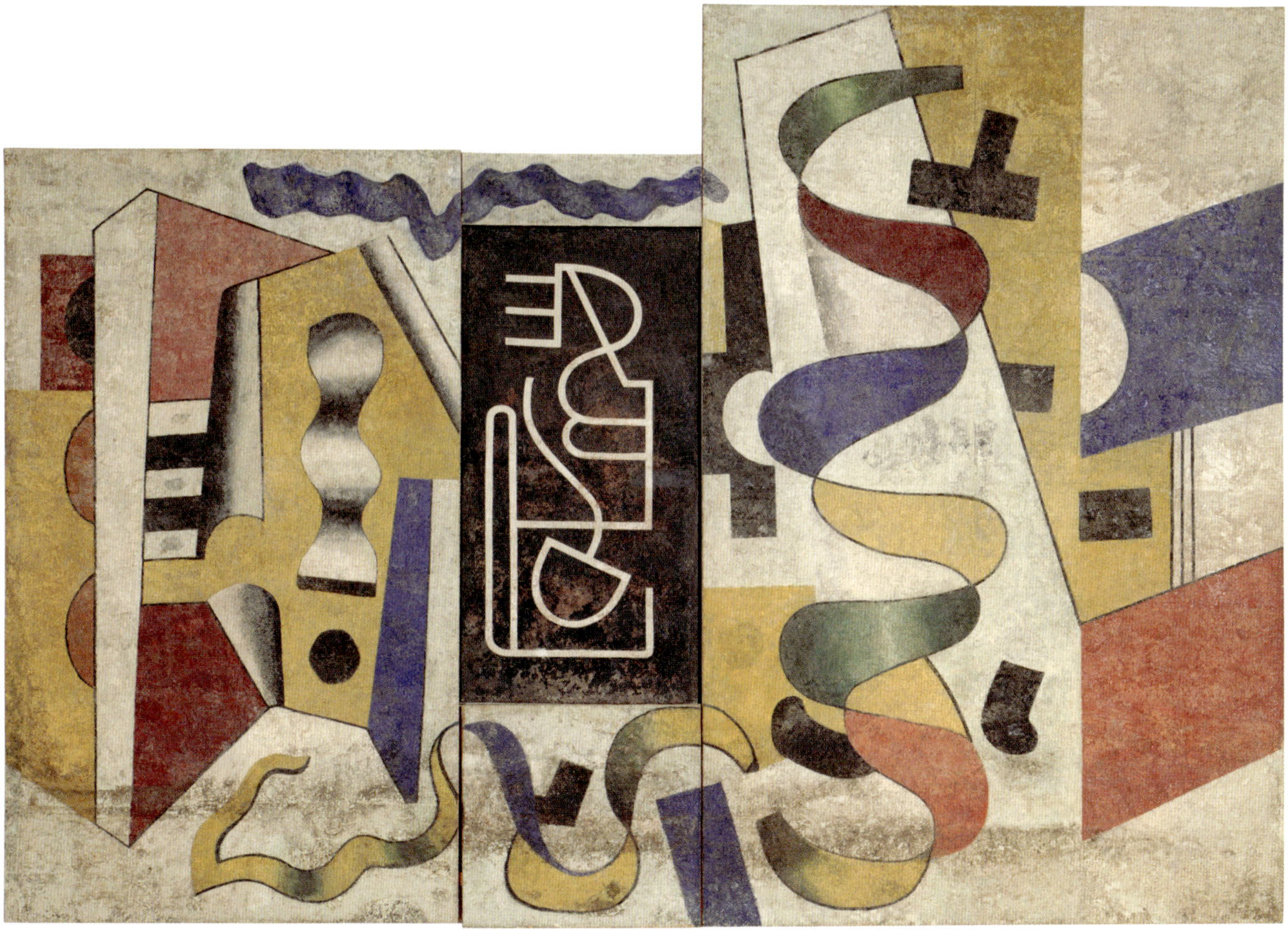

108

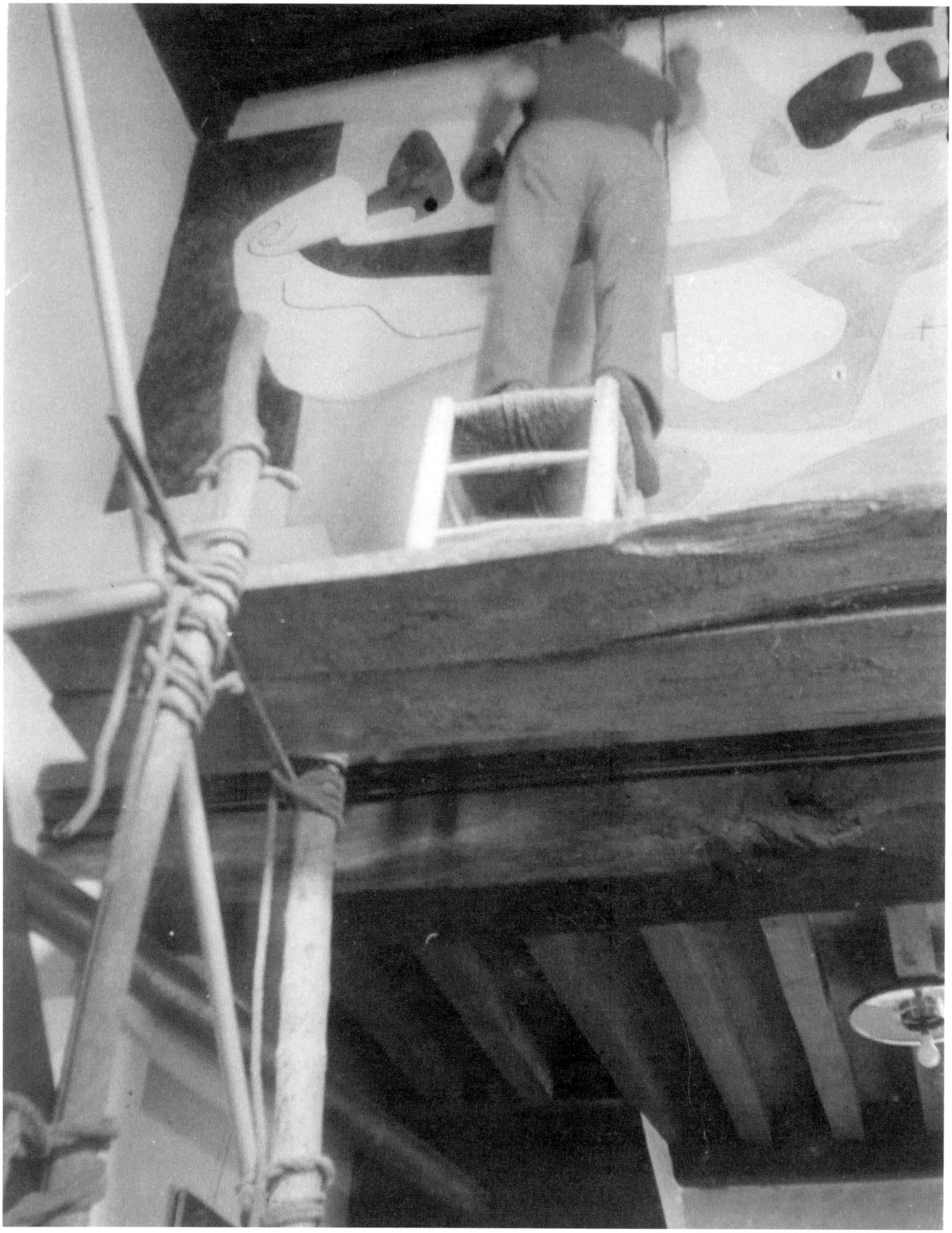

109

109 **Le Corbusier working on his mural painting at the home of Jean Badovici, Vézelay, 1936**
Fondation Le Corbusier, Paris

110 **Fernand Léger and Le Corbusier in front of the Zervos house in Vézelay, 1937**
Archives du Fonds Zervos, 1937

111 Le Corbusier
Mural painting for the home of Jean Badovici, Vézelay, 1936
(fresco removed from wall and mounted on canvas)
253 × 375 cm
Collection Favatier

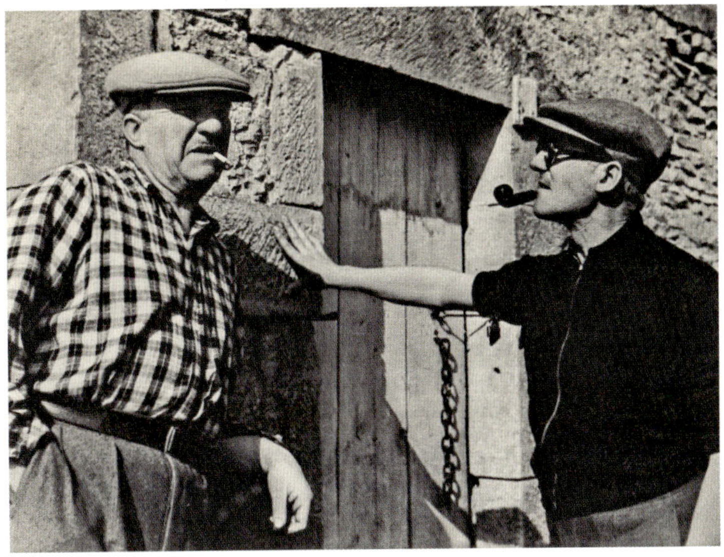

110

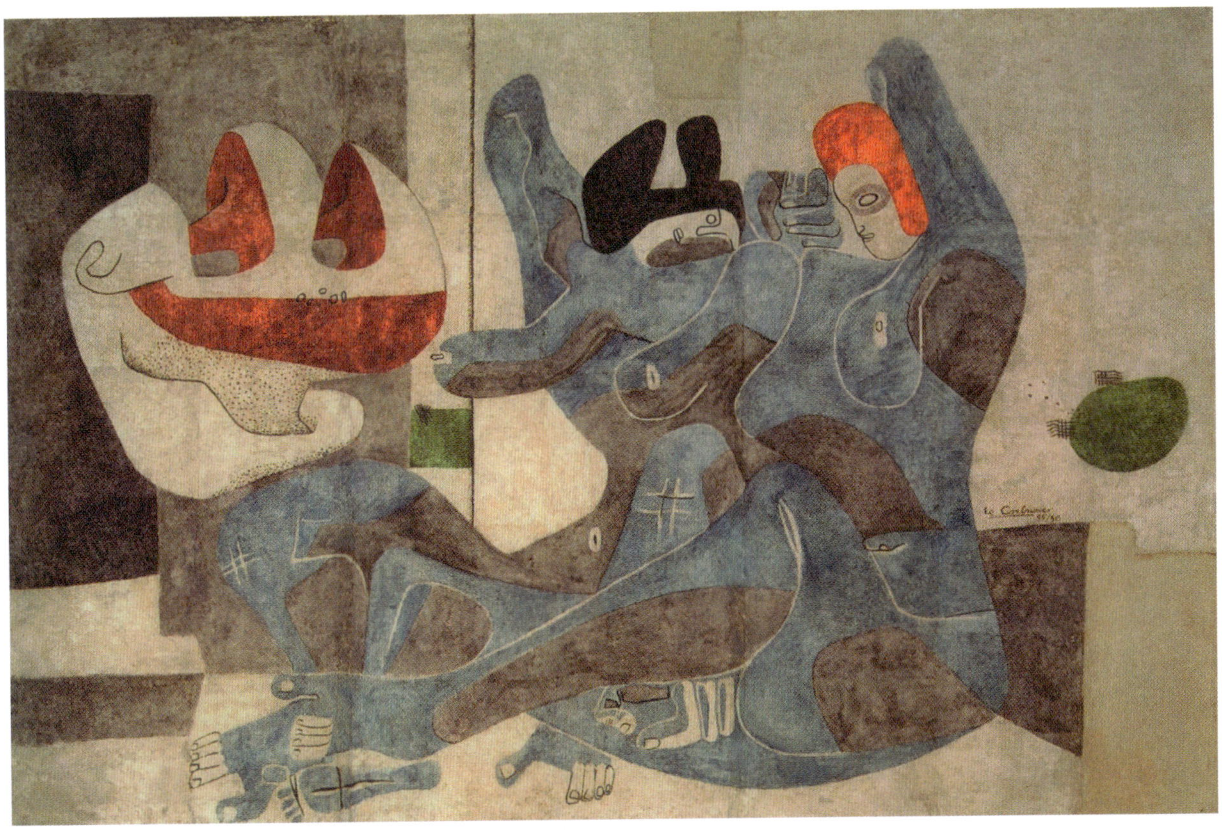

111

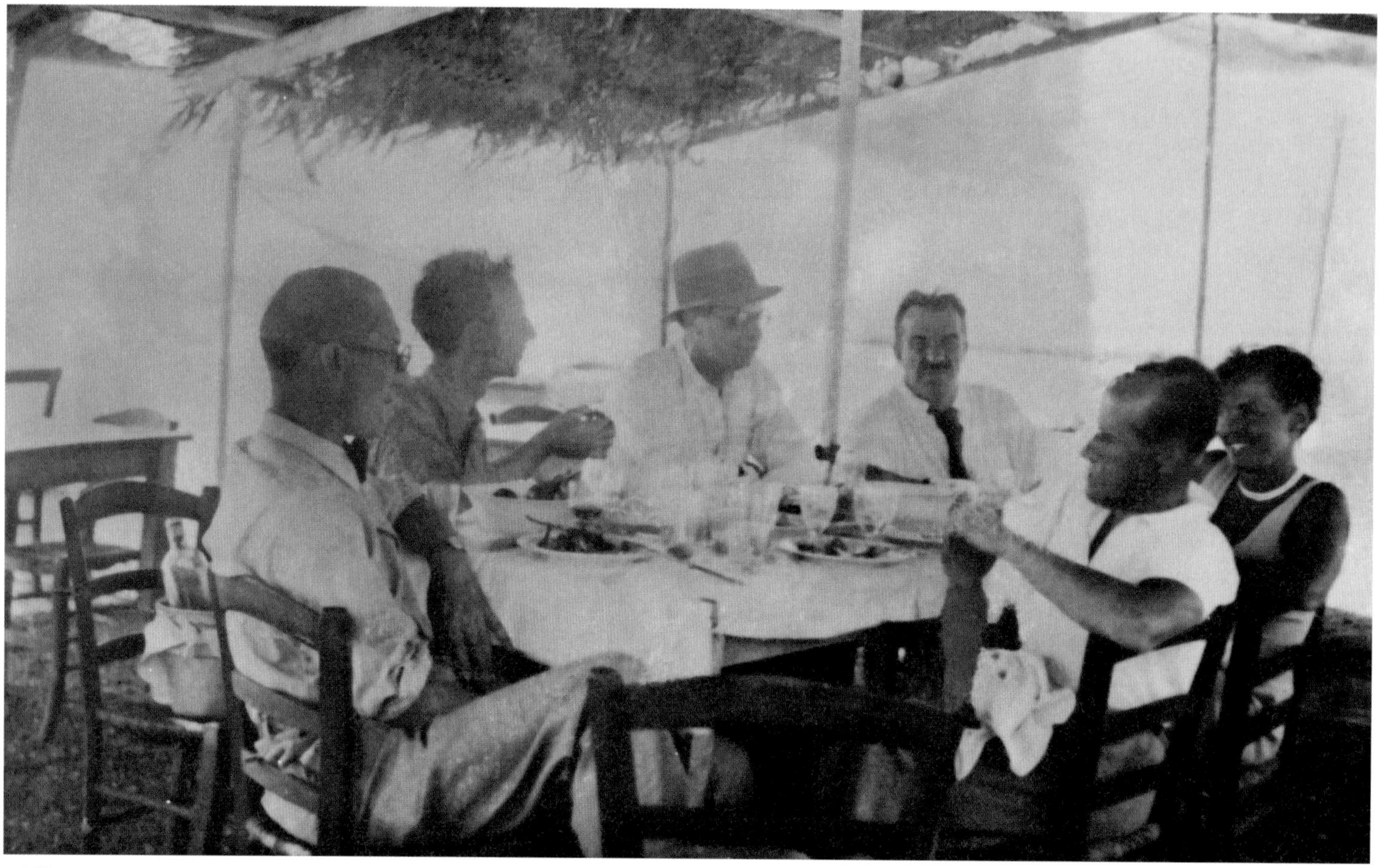

112

112 **(L-R) Le Corbusier, Albert Jeanneret, Matila Ghyka, Fernand Léger, Charlotte Perriand, Pierre Jeanneret in Athens, CIAM IV congress, 1933**
Archives Charlotte Perriand

Speech to Architects (1933)
Fernand Léger

Speed is one of the most demanding laws of the modern world. We are sucked into it in spite of ourselves. It leads to a lack of control as a result of which all the elements in motion travel at different speeds. This is not serious in the case of those that are not connected with each other. But in this mad dash there are events and individuals that need to come together or else they go to waste. We are victims of these missed encounters.

Modern architecture, which I admire, has also been moving at record speed. In the midst of this heroic, burgeoning, creative period, you have vigorously cleared the ground. This was supposed to take the form of the destruction of decoration and, in constructive terms, the use of light as a new architectural element. I shall return to this. Since the war, the world has been seeking a new stability. That of 1912, for example, was good; nothing was happening. Everything was at a standstill. An astute, prudent bourgeoisie had succeeded in imposing, financially and socially, its standard comfort. The individual was slumbering; it felt like the end of something.

Then war came, and then the post-war period, heralding a major renewal, an abrupt fracture. The individual was isolated and fed up, and became aware of his situation. He got together with others to form a group and he became disciplined again. That triggered a move toward extremes of a kind that has never been seen before. That is the current situation.

The generation before yours, the one I belong to, is straddling the two configurations.

It is doubtless this that entitles me to give this lecture and that allows me to take a friendly yet critical look at your work with the requisite detachment. Naturally, it's always risky to criticize the radical impulse of a young, rising generation. But it is also ridiculous to admire and to pretend to be "the young." You have to say what you think, especially to your friends.

We are faced with evidence of a crisis as a result of going too far.

Excessive individual freedom has created this monster, the billionaire, while excessive speculation has created Wall Street, which adopts a purely abstract stance. The billionaire and speculation are at the root of the current crisis.

These men have lost contact with the earth and with people, making a fortune at all costs without heeding the consequences amid a financial tension of a kind the world has never experienced before.

Ask an American on Wall Street what cotton is, for example. He will tell you: "I don't know." Ask him the price of cotton, and he will say, "I know." Ask him how much cotton the entire world needs, he will say, "I don't know." But ask him what his profits are and he will say, "Here they are."

American vertical architecture has also gone too far. In building fifty-story skyscrapers, it forgot that their human contents had to pour out into the street, at around the same time, completely obstructing the traffic. Since everyone has a car, no one can use one anymore.

New York, which for a lot of people is synonymous with "speed," is the city with the slowest traffic in the world.

I shall return to our subject. As I said, modern architecture was thus built "out of light." You went forging ahead without worrying about the damage. It was wonderful, and that's how it had to be.

But I think your heroic period, the warm era, is over. The attempt at cleansing has finished. You need to stop, because you are about to go too far. The cold era is beginning.

You discovered a new architectural raw material, which was "air and light." The materials and decoration that used to smother the architecture of the past disappeared; the heaviness, the volume, and the thickness evaporated. It was a revolution. An elite went along with your heroic era. That's normal. You built houses for people who were already in sympathy with your radical methods. We painters are familiar with this minority. Our works are owned by a few enlightened people scattered around the world. I think I am right in saying that modern architecture up to the present time has also been accepted by a few.

But you want to extend your methods. The word "urbanism" is now meant to dominate the issue of aesthetics.

Urbanism has a social dimension. You are entering a completely different realm, a realm in which your pure and radical methods will have to fight. The tragedy begins right here for us, in this cold period.

You are leaving this elegant minority of supporters in order to deal with ordinary people, who had previously always been surrounded by furniture, hangings and knickknacks covering the walls and windows blocked out through curtains. You stripped bare these simple, slow, timid people and you stuck them, stunned, before "the wall"–this wall that you have just revived and that their fathers and grandfathers had spent all their time concealing. You forced it on them. They were suddenly bathed in light and surrounded by smooth, new surfaces, where it was no longer possible to hide, where shade itself no longer had a place.

The modest ordinary guy, so-called "Urban Man," became dizzy. He was not prepared for this.

From an artistic point of view, I say to you architects, "Well done!" You have created a totally new architecture. But from an urban and social point of view, you have gone too far by going too fast. If you want to practice urbanism, I think you should forget that you are artists. You must concern yourself with social issues. You have to deal with ordinary people and to take them into consideration.

There is a sort of human law according to which everything that is destroyed must be replaced. You have to find "replacement values."

You have revived "the wall." What is going to happen to it? Man does not like revolution. His tastes evolve slowly. His vital rhythm stays more or less the same. He has to eat every day and sleep every night. A tree always takes the same time to grow.

There are "essential" quantities that the ordinary man is always attached to and is particular about. If you destroy them, you have to replace them. The problem is essentially a human one.

Are you sure that you have dealt with the "habitable quantities"?

Here is what I think: between your aesthetic concept, understood and accepted by the minority, and your urban concept, which is everywhere struggling in the face of the incomprehension of ordinary people, there was a fracture and a possibility of continuity. You went so fast that you did not look behind you. If you had turned around, you would have seen that you were not being followed. What are you going to do?

Bare walls are not accepted by working-class people or even middle-class people.

So what's happening is that in this space, in this crack between your two concepts, pseudo-modern architects have appeared, making the required concession and triumphing.

So you have remained isolated in your heroic stance, admirable but with no major project. Your plans remain on the drawing board; why not look around you for the "replacement values"? Sculptors and painters could perhaps help you to solve the problem.

Take your exteriors, for example. I am sure you will agree with me that they age badly. The past styles of architecture were very different due to their decoration, which creates relief and time. Time and wear appear in light and dark, and something strange takes place; over time a monument or house gradually loses its architectural values, its lines melt away, the ground plan disappears and the structure acquires "pictorial value" through the interplay of light and dark colors that time confers on them.

The architecture of the past redeems itself through this patina, which gives it a new and pleasing appearance.

Your new houses cannot hope to have this aged appearance, at least not with the materials currently being used to build them. They do not acquire a patina; they become dirty.

The urban man, the ordinary man who is of interest to you today, saw this. He knows it. You need to find a solution to the problem. And don't forget that all the decoration that you have destroyed formed part of his leisure, his sentimentalism, his inner life. You thought you could solve this problem yourselves by dispensing with color, and by neutralizing a few dead surfaces.

The problem is much more complicated.

If I take the example of a palace, a monument, an eminently popular building, what are you going to do? You have to take into account the instincts and aspirations of the millions of individuals seeking to satisfy, both indoors and outdoors, an obscure but definite ideal. I repeat: it is not about demagogic concessions, but about satisfying average, human, vital needs.

It is necessary for men like you, who have people behind you and alongside you who are expecting something, to pay more attention to them. Put your plans in your pocket, go down into the street and listen to them breathe. You must make contact, immerse yourself in the raw material, walk in the same mud and the same dust.

You are social beings more than artists–you are leaders, followed by millions of individuals prepared to follow you providing you simply grasp the moment of "illumination" between you and them.

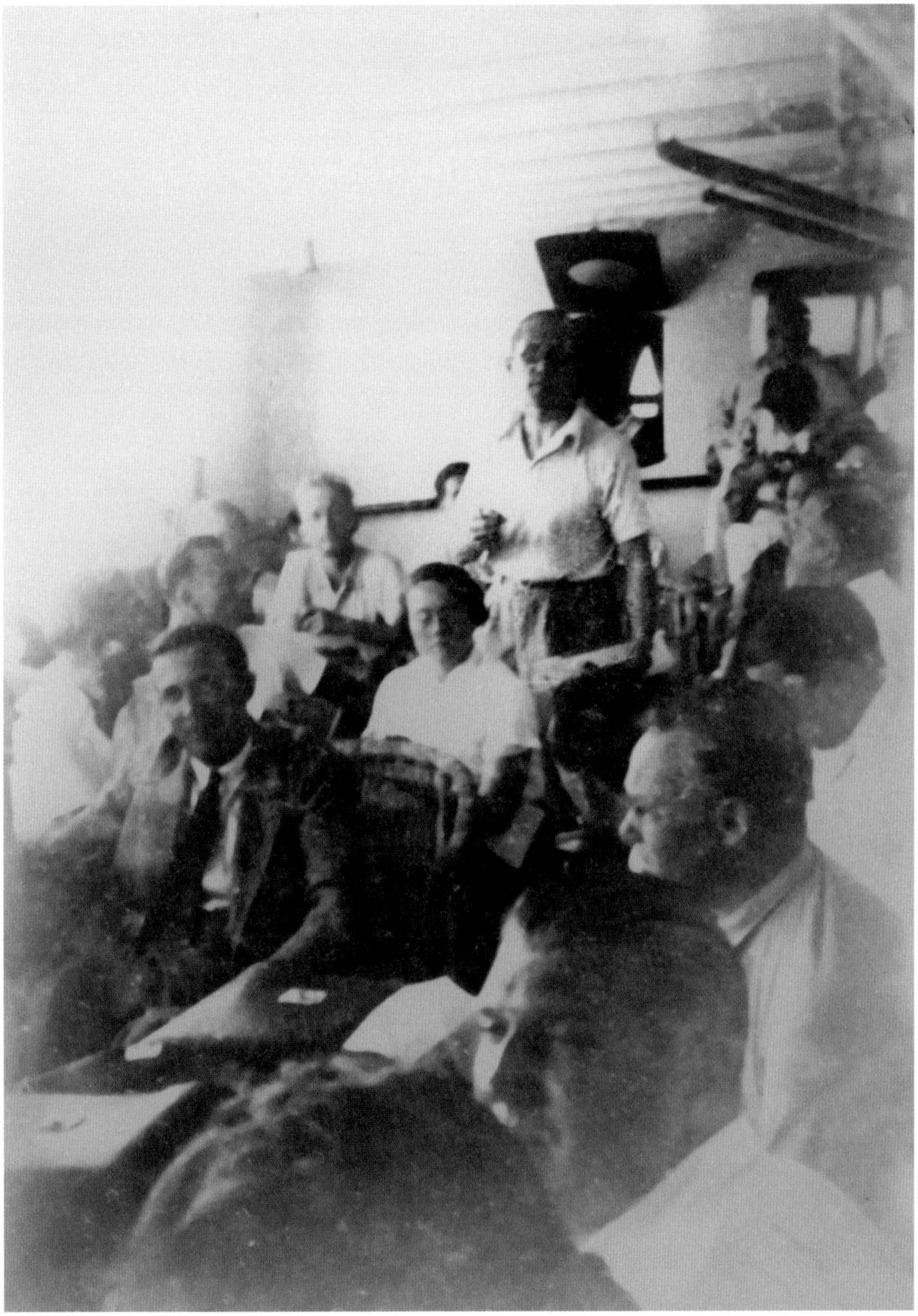

113

113 **Le Corbusier on the *SS Patris II*, CIAM IV Congress, 1933**
Archives Charlotte Perriand

Sculptors and painters are there to solve the issue. I think you are well aware of the magnitude of the problem. It is huge. My generation, which is watching you, understands its importance. Architecture is not an art, but a natural function. It grows on the ground, like animals and plants. It is a function of the human order. Do not forget that. The cathedrals were the product of collaboration—they are still standing and are admired by the entire world; they do not age. They have survived the ages thanks to the collaboration of artists who joined forces to work toward beauty. Your mission is to replace the sentimental and downgraded church by an equivalent work, beautiful in itself and capable of freeing humanity from the grip of religions. You have at your disposal this need for verticality that obsesses everyone, this need for elevation through verticality. You have the round shape—the sphere—that satisfies the mind. These two abstractions are there: make them human and moving, but do not reduce architecture to an aesthetic, linear problem. That would date you.

Architecture must take its place again. The modern monument must be the equivalent of the Byzantine and the Romanesque—as rich and as rooted in duration and time. Do not forget the importance that color plays in the creation of these colossal works.

Color is a raw material that is as necessary to man as water and fire. A beautiful red and a beautiful blue are as necessary to life as a steak. We cannot live without color. It is a human and social value. The road worker chooses his belt because it is blue and his wife her hat because it is red. The effect is more psychological than visual. A hen chooses its color in order to lay and will return to it. The problem of color needs to be solved. Sick people will get better much quicker in a polychrome hospital. The doctor must be a colorist. It is as important socially as music. But because color doesn't make any sound, we have devoted less attention to it. And your stones, your cements, and your metals are dead material if they refuse to share with color.

Together we must insist upon the cult of the beautiful, which an incalculable number of free and emancipated people aspire to. We will all have the honor of erecting the Modern Monument facing the sky that people are waiting for. This is the aim of the collective effort: a new deism of beauty, which will consist neither of vague promises nor a problematic future life, but of beautiful and precise rational objects that you can touch with your finger. Do not forget the lesson of this journey. We are watching out for the country where the ancient religions favored individual fulfillment. They thought that man's supreme strength was to understand the world, virtue, and beauty without the crude help of symbols, and without recourse to gods concealed in the worship of the supernatural, which the Church imposed on a timid and frightened majority. This somber religion is in turn declining.

Despite the worldwide upheaval, it seems to me that this is the right time for us to join forces on this path toward the luminous and pure beauty that we need to create.

Lecture given at the 4th Congrès International d'Architecture Moderne (CIAM IV) in Athens in August 1933, originally published as F. Léger, "Discours aux architects," in *Quadrante* (Milan) 11, no. 5 (September 1933): 44–47, and in *Annales Techniques* (Athens 1933): 1159–62.

–

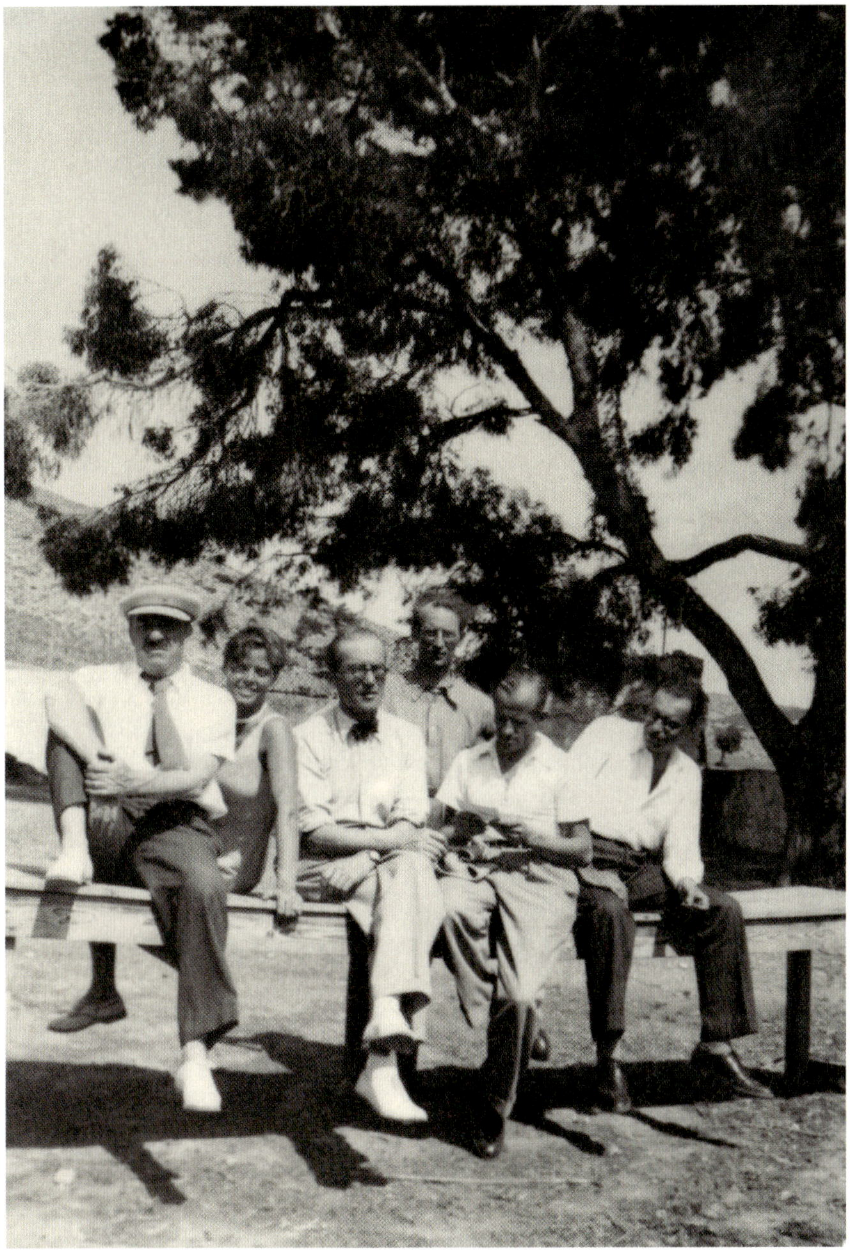

114

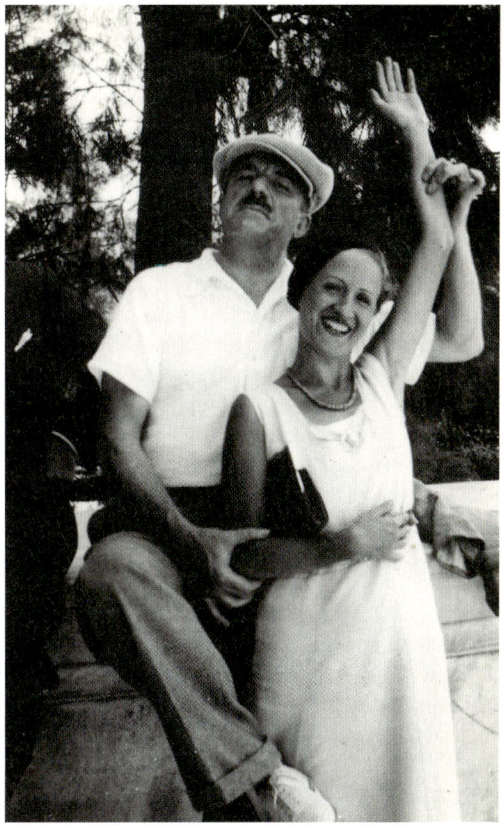

115

114 **(L-R) Fernand Léger, Charlotte Perriand, Le Corbusier, Albert Jeanneret, Pierre Jeanneret, Matila Ghyka in Athens, CIAM IV congress, 1933**
Archives Charlotte Perriand

115 **Fernand Léger and Muncha Sert in Athens, 1933**
Archives Charlotte Perriand

Charlotte Perriand and Fernand Léger: Complicity and Engagement
By Jacques Barsac

Charlotte Perriand first met Fernand Léger in 1930 at a reception at the German Embassy in honor of the Deutscher Werkbund (German Association of Craftsmen):

"My friends and I were invited, and it was there that I met Walter Gropius for the first time, along with the entire Bauhaus team and, most important, the painter Fernand Léger. It was a milestone evening. [...] I left before the end of the reception, flanked by Pierre [Jeanneret] and the towering Léger, in search of a café. It took us all night. I imitated a seal's cry, perched on Parisian dustbins, flapping my arms. We went wild. When I left Léger at dawn, I knew I had made a friend."[1]

The architect Josep Lluís Sert reports:

"Her preference for pure colors drew her to our close friend Fernand Léger, who appreciated the fact that her ideas were similar to his [...] He too adored the colorful objects of the people, the stands at fairs in the Parisian suburbs and their bistros, juke boxes, New York's taxis—he was always talking about these things. Perriand worked with him on the 1937 World's Fair; they shared a common love for all things simple and connected with the people."[2]

From 1932 to 1940, Perriand lived on the top floor of the building next to Léger's studio on rue Notre-Dame-des-Champs in Montparnasse in Paris. "Our big Norman bear,"[3] as she affectionately called him, was twenty-two years older than she. But although they were separated by a generation, they were drawn to each other by their vision of the world and of artists' role in society. Léger told "Bijou" (Simone Herman, his lover during the 1930s) about a vacation Perriand had taken with Pierre Jeanneret:

"They spent an amazing month at an altitude of two to four thousand meters, far from civilization, discovering abandoned villages in the mountains only inhabited by shepherds—terrific people. What a temptation! But exhausting. They camped out in down-filled sleeping bags—they were never cold. I don't think I'd be capable of doing that sort of thing with them and us. They're too good at climbing, and we're not good enough. How incredible that must have been."[4]

Léger followed Perriand's exploits from a distance and with great relish. On returning from her expeditions, she would tell him all about them and show him her photographs, which piqued his imagination. Details from them can be seen in his paintings, like memories: sublimated tree branches, sheep, fragments of landscape, a piece of clothing hung on a tree trunk that serves as a coat rack... Sometimes she took photographs that recalled Léger's view of nature or people.

In the late 1920s and early 1930s, after the great "machinist" and Purist period, Léger, Le Corbusier, Perriand, and Jeanneret turned to nature in search of new creative and philosophical impulses for their work. The consequences of the Crash of 1929, the new disaffection with machines, and the political and economic upheavals led them to ask new questions about art and humanity:

"Léger, Pierre, and I used to go to the Normandy beaches in Pierre's little runabout, spending Saturday evenings and Sundays there. We preferred the beach at Dieppe, and would forage for the best pebbles. [...] We would fill our backpacks with treasures: pebbles, bits of shoes, lumps of wood riddled with holes, horsehair brushes—all smoothed and ennobled by the sea. We sorted them, admiring them, soaking them in water to give them more of a shine, and taking photographs. We called it our *art brut*."[5] (figs. 116, 118)

While she was busy photographing these objects in her studio under the eaves, Léger was drawing stones, roots, trousers, and pieces of meat a few floors below (figs. 119, 120). In 1934, he presented an exhibition of drawings at Galerie Vignon, entitled *Objets* (Objects). Through drawing, painting, and photography, and through found objects treated as sculptures, they reintroduced nature not only into architectural space, but into emotional and intellectual space as well. In this same period, Le Corbusier was also incorporating found objects into his sculptural work; he called them "*objets à réaction poétique*," or "objects that evoke a poetic reaction." This adventure with found objects would later give rise to a new sculptural quality that could be glimpsed in architecture, painting, and furniture. The return to nature would help to renew each artist's creative work.

Like Léger, Perriand was politically engaged. She was a member of the Association des Écrivains et Artistes Révolutionnaires (AEAR, Association of Revolutionary Writers and Artists), and like Léger, Le Corbusier, and Jeanneret, she belonged to the Congrès d'Architecture Moderne (CIAM, International Congresses of Modern Architecture) as well as to the Union des Artistes Modernes (UAM, Union of Modern Artists), which she helped to found. All four went to Athens for the fourth Congrès d'Architectes Modernes in 1933 (fig. 114). As part of a group of young Communist architects,[6] Perriand and Jeanneret tried to persuade the Congress to give a political dimension to the new theses on urbanism that would become the Athens Charter.[7] In Athens, Léger addressed the assembled elite of modern architecture:

"But you want to extend your methods. The word 'urbanism' is now meant to dominate the issue of aesthetics. Urbanism has a social dimension. [...] From an artistic point of view, I say to you architects, 'Well done!' You have created a totally new architecture. But from an urban and social point of view, you have gone too far by going too fast. If you want to practice urbanism, I think you should forget that you are artists. You must concern yourself with social issues. You have to deal with ordinary people and to take them into consideration. [...] Put your plans in your pocket, go down into the street and listen to them breathe. You must make contact, immerse yourself in the raw material, walk in the same mud and the same dust. [...] You went so fast that you did not look behind you. If you had turned around, you would have seen that you were not being followed. What are you going to do?"[8]

Perriand shared this viewpoint. She advocated a dialectic between artists and architects and the user, promoting a Marxist method for analyzing reality that sought to highlight contradictions, which it then attempted to overcome. She wrote to Jeanneret:

"The 'architect's job' is to work for people. One cannot work for people if one doesn't know anything about them and knows nothing about all the different kinds of people who make up our country [...] or about the points they have in common that one can appeal to. We've put ourselves so far ahead that we've forgotten about life and the various ways it expresses itself in reality. We have forgotten—or else simply ignored—what society is actually made of. Humanity is awakening, but we are still standing on the sidelines. The awakening doesn't always line up with the expression we have been looking for. We acknowledge the social phenomenon [...] and [...] remain on the sidelines instead of joining in. [...] Are we gods, that we claim that what we advocate is the absolute truth?"[9]

Perriand challenges the univocal and unidirectional relationship of artists and architects to society, and by extension to art itself.

In 1935, at the same time that Perriand invited Léger to join her in designing *La Maison du jeune homme* (The Young Man's House) for the World's Fair in Brussels (129, 130), she proclaimed in the journal *L'Architecture d'aujourd'hui*, "We will no longer be practicing formalism or constructivism; we will not be endorsing either curves or right angles, stone or cement, blue or red, wood or metal, but we will use each of these in its appropriate time and place, technologically and physiologically."[10] Perriand took a pragmatic approach and expanded her creative palette, returning to the use of wood and slate in furniture and stone or wood in architecture as another way of introducing nature into the home. But she did so without excluding metal, concrete, or prefabricated materials; she championed handcrafted products alongside industrial ones, with the use of traditional or contemporary techniques depending on the overarching plans, the economics of the project, the site, and the available craftspeople, but always in a contemporary rather than a backward-looking spirit. Referring to her collaboration with Léger, she writes: "I raised the idea of mural art with Fernand Léger and he suggested that he try a fresco. Why not use this old technique and incorporate it into contemporary architecture? Léger didn't shrink from anything, and produced a superb panel that I installed in the wall unit."[11]

The wall unit consisted of wall-mounted shelves with found objects, including a whale vertebra, a flint found in the mountains, and an ink stamp that had written on it: "*La guerre est possible*" ("War is possible"). The aim was to permit the "young man" to create his own personal museum without the need for money, using "ordinary, everyday objects or quirky, amusing ones; that way," wrote Perriand, "he will be able to express himself directly."[12] Léger thus produced a fresco that was displayed alongside ready-mades found on walks. Extraordinary artworks and found objects were placed on an equal footing. Léger also produced a large painting on the subject of sports, which dominated the gymnastics area and crowned the entire exhibition (fig. 131).

In *La Maison du jeune homme*, Perriand also created other opportunities for inhabitants and professional artists to express themselves. Behind the work table, she set up a large slate wall on which the "young man" could draw and write down his ideas. He could also write directly on the slate tabletop. To separate the rest area from the gymnastics area, she designed a chest on a flared base that resembled an *unité d'habitation* (housing unit) on *pilotis* (stilts), to which Le Corbusier added a drawing of his Radiant City and his urban planning projects for Paris. The chest thus became a manifesto in praise of modern Corbusian urbanism and its benefits.

Organized by Perriand, *La Maison du jeune homme* realized an ambition also harbored by Léger, who observed in a lecture delivered in 1935: "The collaboration of the four arts—painting—sculpture—architecture—furniture design—can be achieved in our time. It is difficult because of the currently prevailing climate of individualism."[13] But beyond a collaborative dialogue among the arts, the *Maison du jeune homme* also sketched the outlines of a contemporary "human nest," a space for work and rest in which both body and mind could be cultivated and which brought together painting, architecture, urban planning, furniture, music (the chest-manifesto contained a phonograph and radio receiver), as well as scientific information and political reflection (there was a revolving stand with scientific illustrations and photomontages). Like Léger, Perriand urged a decompartmentalizing and transversality of the arts, a comprehensive approach to the human sphere in which art and life would be intimately linked. The dialogue between people and artists—whether painters, sculptors, or architects—was no longer to be a unidirectional face-to-face encounter but a set of ongoing fruitful exchanges, with the users at the center and the artists in a circle around them.

Perriand and Léger seized every opportunity to bring the four arts together and to collaborate on projects that made sense to both of them. As secretary general of CIAM France, Perriand helped to produce propaganda for the new urban planning projects. In 1936, she produced an enormous photomontage entitled *La Grande Misère de Paris* (Extreme Poverty in Paris), in which she decried the living and housing conditions in the capital. When the Front Populaire came to power, she offered her services to Georges Monnet, the

Minister of Agriculture, proposing to create propaganda for the far-reaching reforms he planned to undertake. She covered the walls of the minister's meeting room with huge black-and-white photomontages that immersed the visitors in their subjects in a cave-like environment. The following year, she took on the task of presenting the progressive government's agricultural policies at the 1937 Paris International Exposition; she appealed to Léger to use color and his graphic genius to enhance the impact of the 110 meters of photocollages and graphic works contained in the pavilion. The magnitude of the task was no longer at the scale of architecture but at that of urban space (figs. 154, 155).

Perriand recalled:

"A workshop was made available to us in the ministry courtyard, and we got down to the job at hand. We worked cheerfully and efficiently, our minds in sync; there was total harmony between us, an absolute degree of friendship that I would never find again. [...] Léger, my faithful friend, helped me day in and day out. His quick eye was forever finding shortcuts, juggling letters and colors in a ballet of abstract forms that acted as a foil for the realism of the photographs. Our task was a joy, a celebration, an act of gratitude toward France's country dwellers, who then made up some fifty percent of the population."[14]

Perriand and Léger did not rest content with giving expression to a preexisting discourse; they influenced the content of that discourse in dialogue with the Minister of Agriculture. Léger put his whole heart into the project, delighted to be participating in reforms that were bringing progress to rural areas. He commented: "Hard and detailed work with Charlotte. We're starting with Bloch's *Naissance d'une cité* [Birth of a City], which is scheduled for the end of August–so there'll be no vacation–what a life."[15] With a lively debate underway about the realism being promoted by the Communists, photocollage had the advantage of being somewhat realistic while still allowing Léger the creative freedom that he valued above all else. The Front Populaire presented both Perriand and Léger with the opportunity to combine their ideas with political action and to put their commitment to a better society into practice. According to Perriand, Léger dreamed of painting all the common walls of Paris, and of turning it into the twentieth century's "city of light" by enlisting art school students to bring them to life with brightly colored light projections for the International Exposition.[16] For her part, Perriand wished to turn the banks of the Seine into places of leisure, relaxation, and culture for all. "The joy of living," she observed, "would have won a victory there." In the end, neither of them was able to realize these projects conceived on a city-wide scale.

In 1936, Perriand took part in a competition for the interior design of the office of the Minister of National Education, Jean Zay. She invited Juan Miró to paint a mural and enlisted Léger to design the office floor. For the model, Miró submitted a drawing by his five-year-old daughter, and Léger did a gouache of his design for the floor. Unfortunately, the three did not win the competition (figs. 143, 144).

One of the projects on which Perriand and Léger collaborated was a table for Jean-Richard Bloc, editor of the Communist-leaning anti-fascist journal *Ce Soir,* which included two drawings by Picasso and two by Léger and also functioned as a manifesto (1938). In 1939, Perriand suggested that Léger paint a mural in the bar of a camp of military barracks constructed by the Ateliers Jean Prouvé. The project was never realized. In 1941, she displayed a large black-and-white reproduction of Léger's painting for the project, *Composition aux Deux Perroquets* (Composition with Two Parrots, 1935–39), at her exhibition *Tradition, Création, Sélection* in Tokyo and Osaka; the show presented home furnishings, combining contemporary furniture with that of the *mingei* movement. After the war, she invited Léger, Miró, Calder, and Le Corbusier to participate in the first exhibition of *Formes Utiles, Objets de Notre Temps* (Useful Forms: Objects of Our Time, 1949), a movement of which she was co-founder. The show presented a wide selection of everyday objects alongside paintings, sculptures, and tapestries, which were placed on an equal footing with those objects despite being exceptional artworks (fig. 302).[17]

Léger and Perriand collaborated with Paul Nelson on the polychrome interior design for the France-United States Memorial Hospital in Saint-Lô, whose entrance is dominated by an enormous mosaic by Léger commemorating the friendship between the two countries. They also took part in the presentation in Paris of a model apartment for the Unité d'Habitation apartment complex in Toulon designed by architect Jean de Mailly; it was furnished by Perriand (1951), with Léger lending his painting *La Danse* (Dance, 1942) for the purpose. In 1951, as part of a project directly in line with the exhibition *Formes Utiles, Objets de Notre Temps* (Useful Forms, Objects of Our Time), she invited him to participate in the Triennale in Milan, where she was leading the French section "Furniture and Decoration." Léger painted an enormous mural that lit up the entrance to the French section, financing the project himself by selling lithographs (figs. 300, 301).

In 1953, Léger enthusiastically agreed to participate in the exhibition *Synthèse des Arts. Le Corbusier, Fernand Léger, Charlotte Perriand* (Synthesis of the Arts: Le Corbusier, Fernand Léger, Charlotte Perriand), which Perriand organized in Tokyo in 1955 (figs. 303, 304).[18] She worked with Léger to select his most beautiful available paintings, tapestries, and polychrome sculptures, as well as fifteen models of his windows for the church of Sacré-Cœur d'Audincourt, together with sculptures by Le Corbusier, all of which she arranged around her furniture. Like all of Perriand's and Léger's projects, this exhibition embodied the desire to realize "the collaboration of the four arts–painting–sculpture–architecture–furniture design," an ideal that was equally precious to them both.

In memory of the "big Norman bear" and their twenty-five years of friendship and complicity, Perriand designed an extension for the Musée National Fernand Léger in Biot in 1965 at the request of Nadia Léger and Georges Bauquier. Unfortunately, the project was not completed in its original form. Six months before her death in 1999, Charlotte Perriand paid homage to Fernand Léger with an exhibition entitled *Charlotte Perriand–Fernand Léger, une Connivence* (Charlotte Perriand and Fernand Léger: A Sense of Complicity).[19]

1 Charlotte Perriand, *A Life of Creation: An Autobiography* (New York: Monacelli, 2003), 35-36 (originally published as *Une vie de création*, Paris, 1989).
2 Josep Lluís Sert, *Aujourd'hui, art et architecture*, no. 7 (1956).
3 Perriand, *A Life of Creation*, 96.
4 *Fernand* Léger: *Une correspondance poste restante*, special issue, *Les cahiers du musée d'art moderne* (Paris: Centre Georges Pompidou, 1997): 146.
5 Perriand, *A Life of Creation*, 97. We do not know if the label *art brut* here goes back to the pre-war years or whether Perriand was explicitly seeking to counter the views of Jean Dubuffet, the high priest of *art brut*, who vehemently opposed any tendency to connect it with natural objects. See Pierre Guéguen's article "Art brut," *L'Architecture d'aujourd'hui*, special issue no. 2, 1949: 66.
6 Perriand, Sert, Weissmann, Bossu, Jeanneret, Syrkus, and a number of other young artists came together to form a progressive group at the fourth Congrès.
7 See Jacques Barsac, *Charlotte Perriand: Complete Works, Volume 1, 1903-1940* (Zurich: Scheidegger & Spiess, 2014), 278-83 and 406-19.
8 Fernand Léger, "Discours aux architectes," *Quadrante* 11, no. 5 (1933): 44-47.
9 Charlotte Perriand to Pierre Jeanneret, c. 1936, Charlotte Perriand archives.
10 Charlotte Perriand, "L'habitation familiale, son développement économique et social," *L'Architecture d'aujourd'hui* (1935); in English as "The Family Dwelling: Its Economic and Social Development," trans. John Goodman, in Mary McLeod, ed., *Charlotte Perriand: An Art of Living* (New York: Harry N. Abrams, in association with The Architectural League of New York, 2003), 256.
11 Perriand, *A Life of Creation*, 70.
12 Document describing the architectural portion of *La Maison de Week-end* (The Weekend House), 1934, which included a "wall unit" on the terrace; Charlotte Perriand archives.
13 Fernand Léger, typescript of a lecture given at Yale in 1935, which Charlotte Perriand took with her to Japan in 1940; Charlotte Perriand archives.
14 Perriand, *A Life of Creation*, 84-86.
15 Fernand Léger to Simone Herman, July 1, 1937, in *Fernand* Léger: *Une correspondance poste restante*, 161.
16 Perriand, *A Life of Creation*, 89.
17 See Jacques Barsac, *Charlotte Perriand: Complete Works, Volume 2, 1940-1956* (Zurich: Scheidegger & Spiess, 2015), 244-51.
18 See ibid., 462-85.
19 The exhibition was held at the Musée National Fernand Léger in Biot in 1999. The term *connivence*, or "complicity," was suggested to Charlotte Perriand by the author.

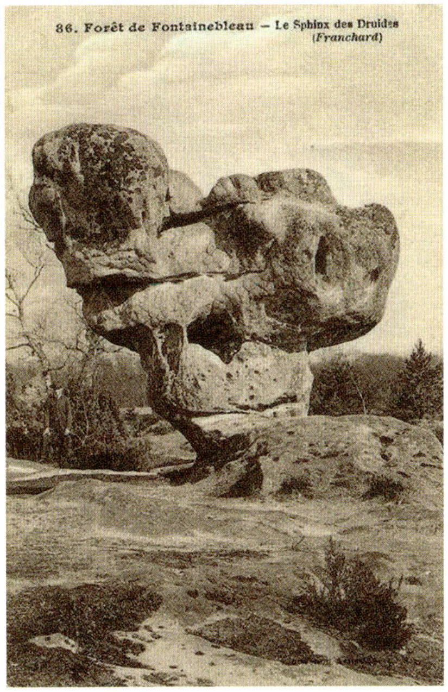

116

Postcard from Fernand Léger
to Simone Herman, March 31, 1935

Belga for ever! Poor cat.
There's a big steak and blue sky.
Charlotte
And a sun! The bear F. L.
It's fantastic miss you. Pierre.

–

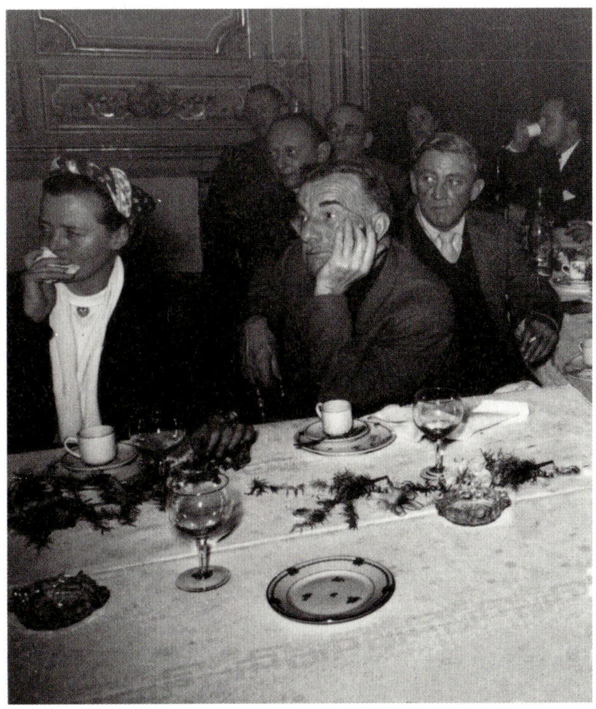

117

116 **Postcard from Fernand Léger to Simone Herman, March 31,1935**
Centre Pompidou, Bibliothèque Kandinsky, Fonds Fernand Léger, B1-B5, 9536, Paris

117 **Charlotte Perriand, Fernand Léger, Paul Nelson at the General Meeting of the board of patrons and editorial committee of *L'Architecture d'aujourd'hui*, 1948**
Archives Charlotte Perriand

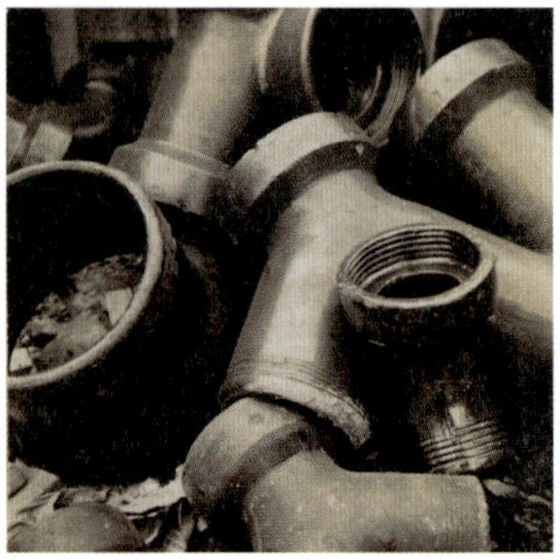
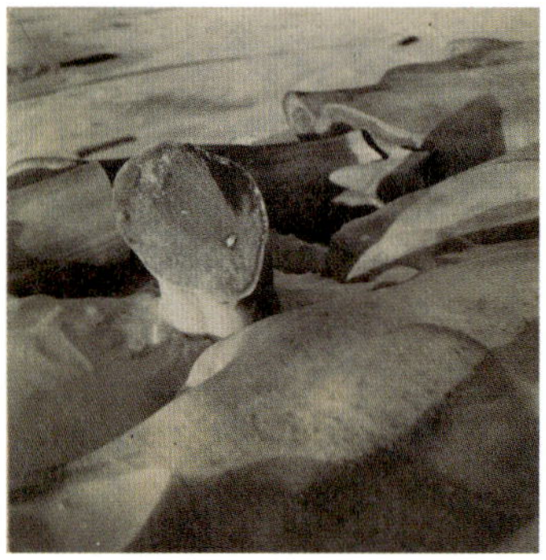
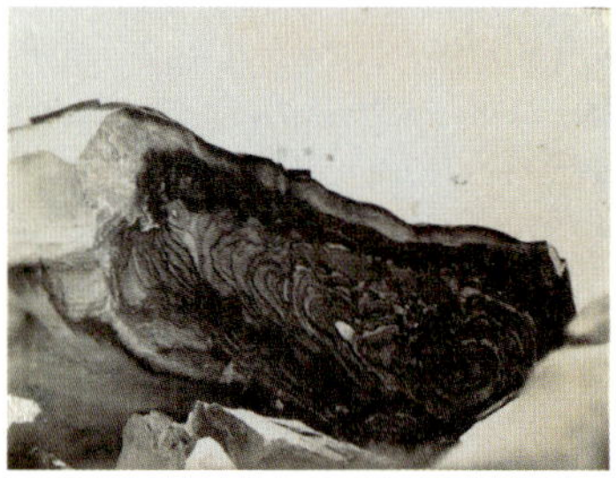
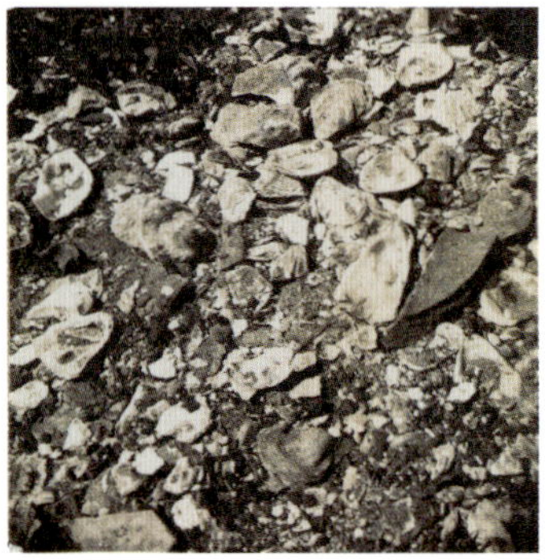
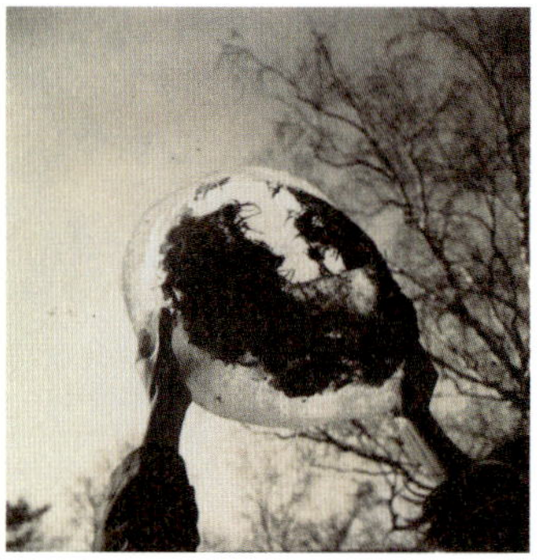
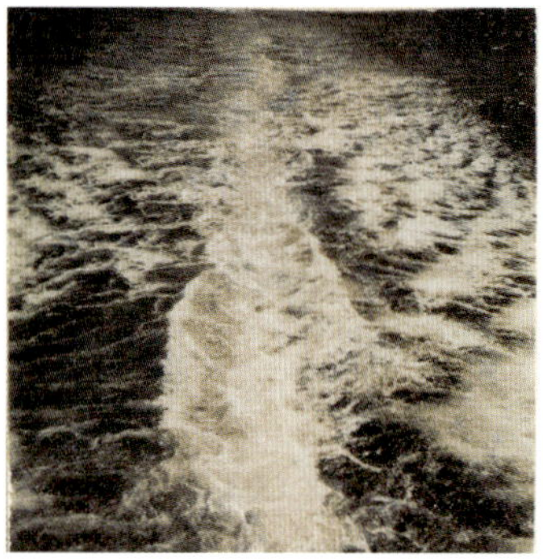
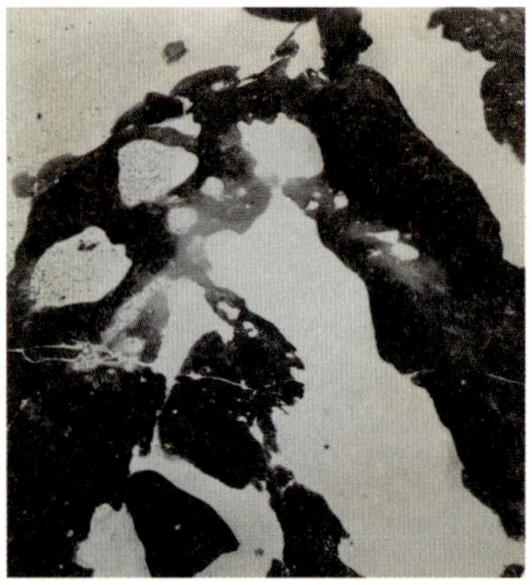
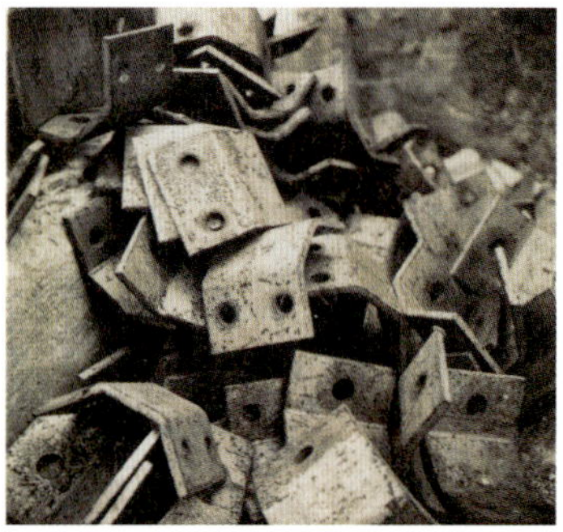
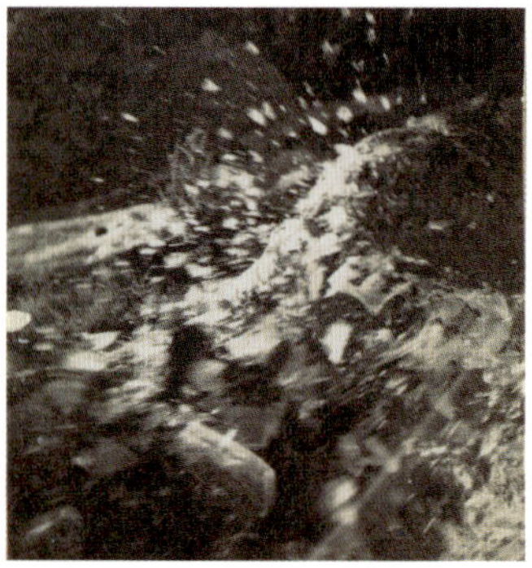
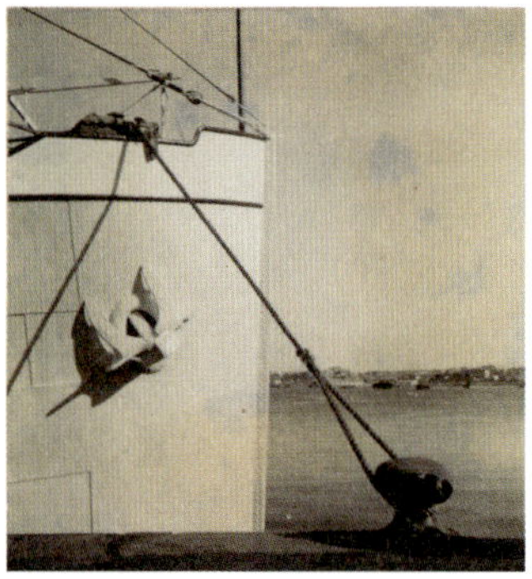
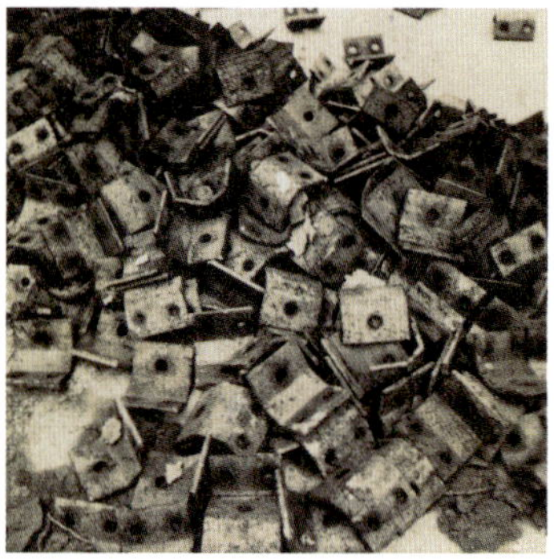
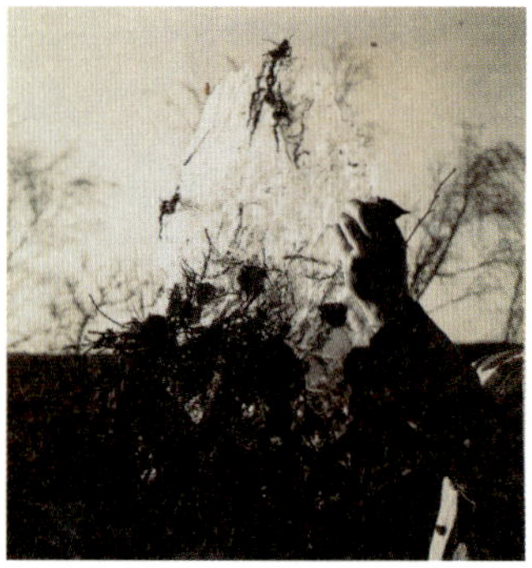

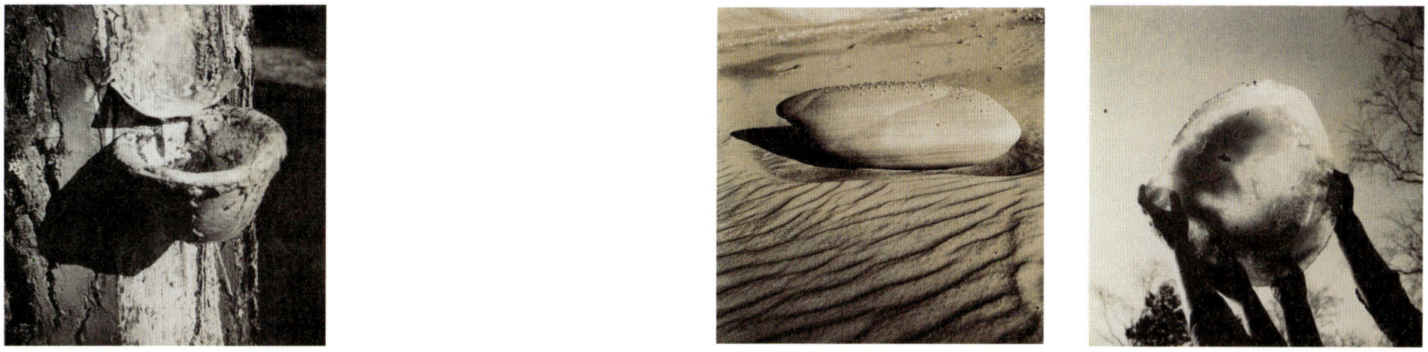
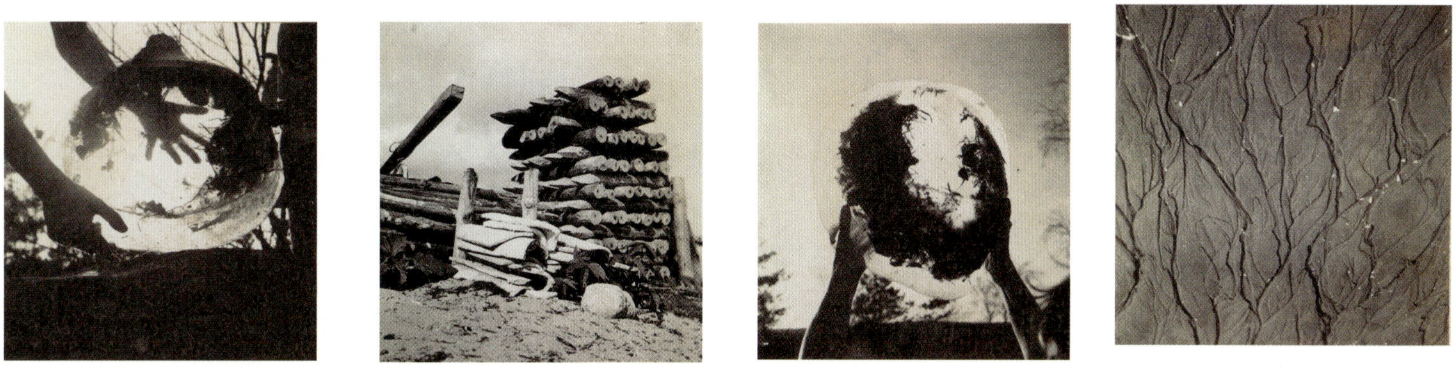
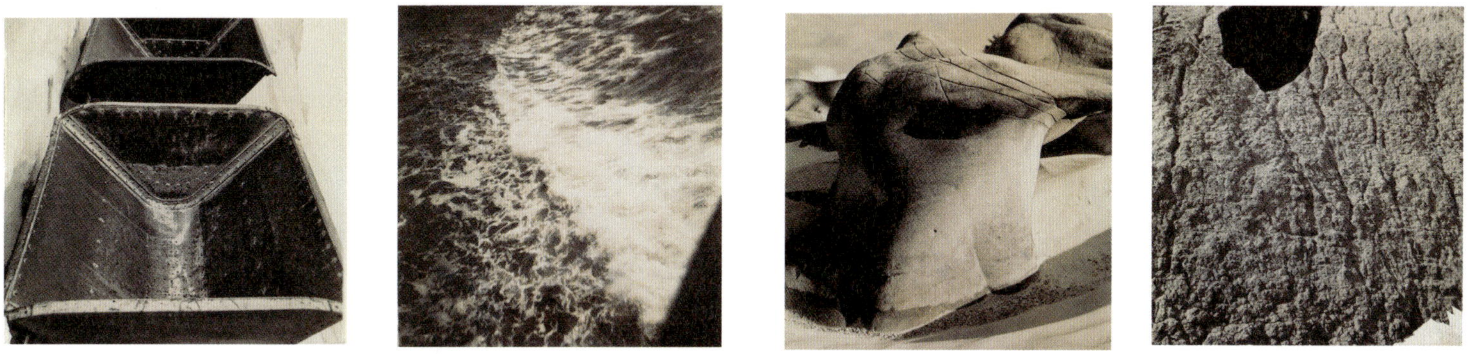
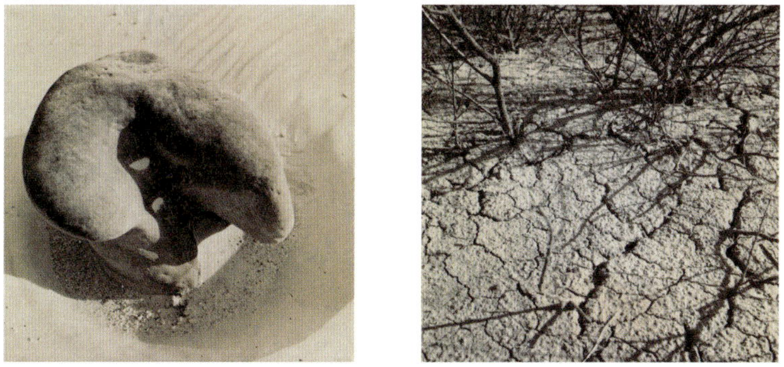

118

118 Fernand Léger, Charlotte Perriand, Pierre Jeanneret
Les Objets à Réaction Poetique
(Objects with Poetic Effect), 1931–36
25 photographs, gelatin silver print on paper
Each: 5.4 × 5.4 cm
Tate: Purchased with assistance from the Photography Acquisitions Committee, Konstantin Grigorishin and the Art Fund 2013

Photographs taken by Charlotte Perriand

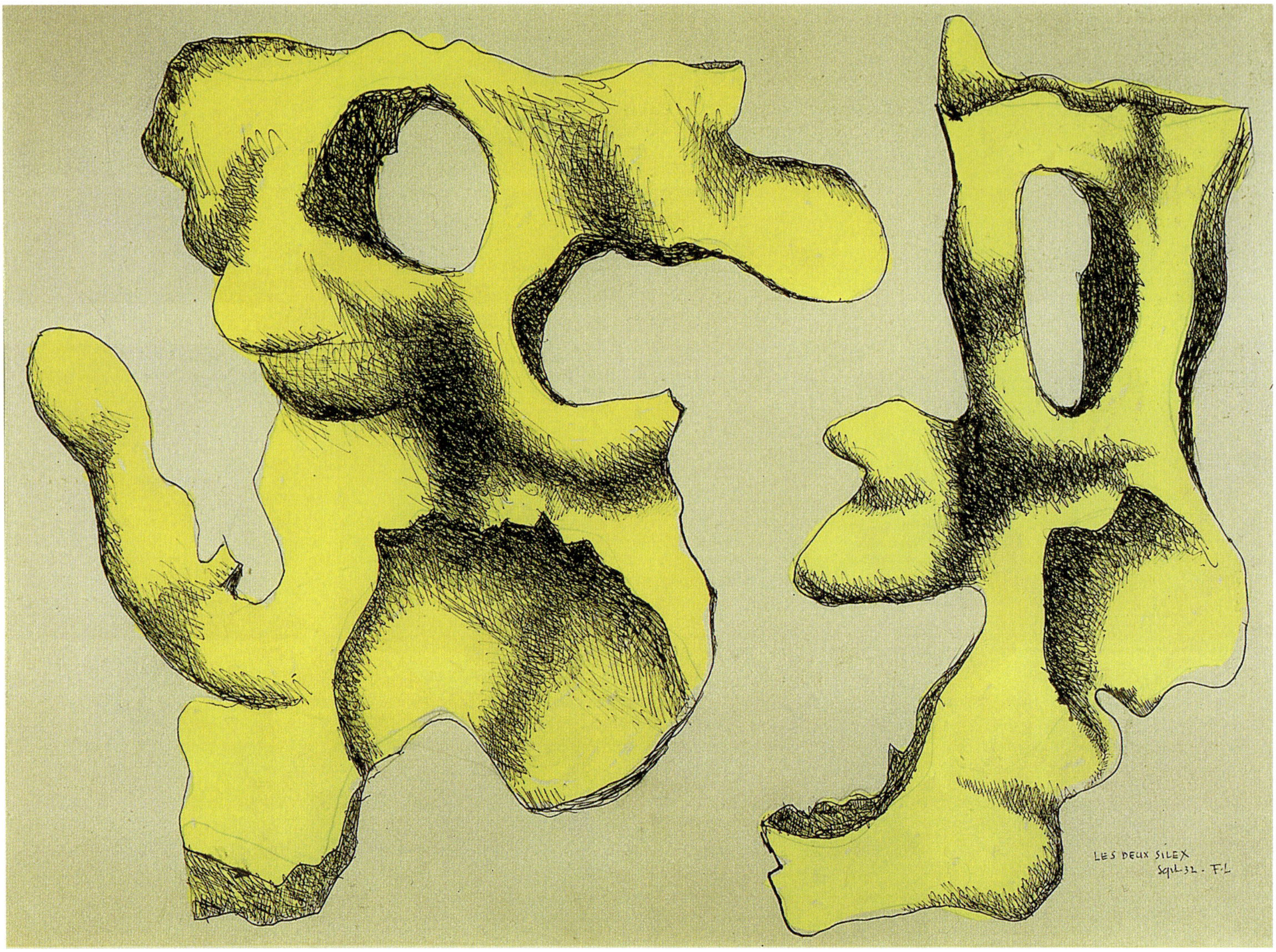

119

119 ***Silex jaune sur fond beige***
(Yellow Flint on Beige Background), 1932
Gouache (drawing) on paper
49 × 67 cm
Musée d'art moderne, Belfort
Donation from Maurice Jardot

120 ***Les troncs d'arbres (Tableau)***
(The Tree Trunks), 1931
Oil on canvas
92 × 65 cm
Musée d'art moderne, Belfort

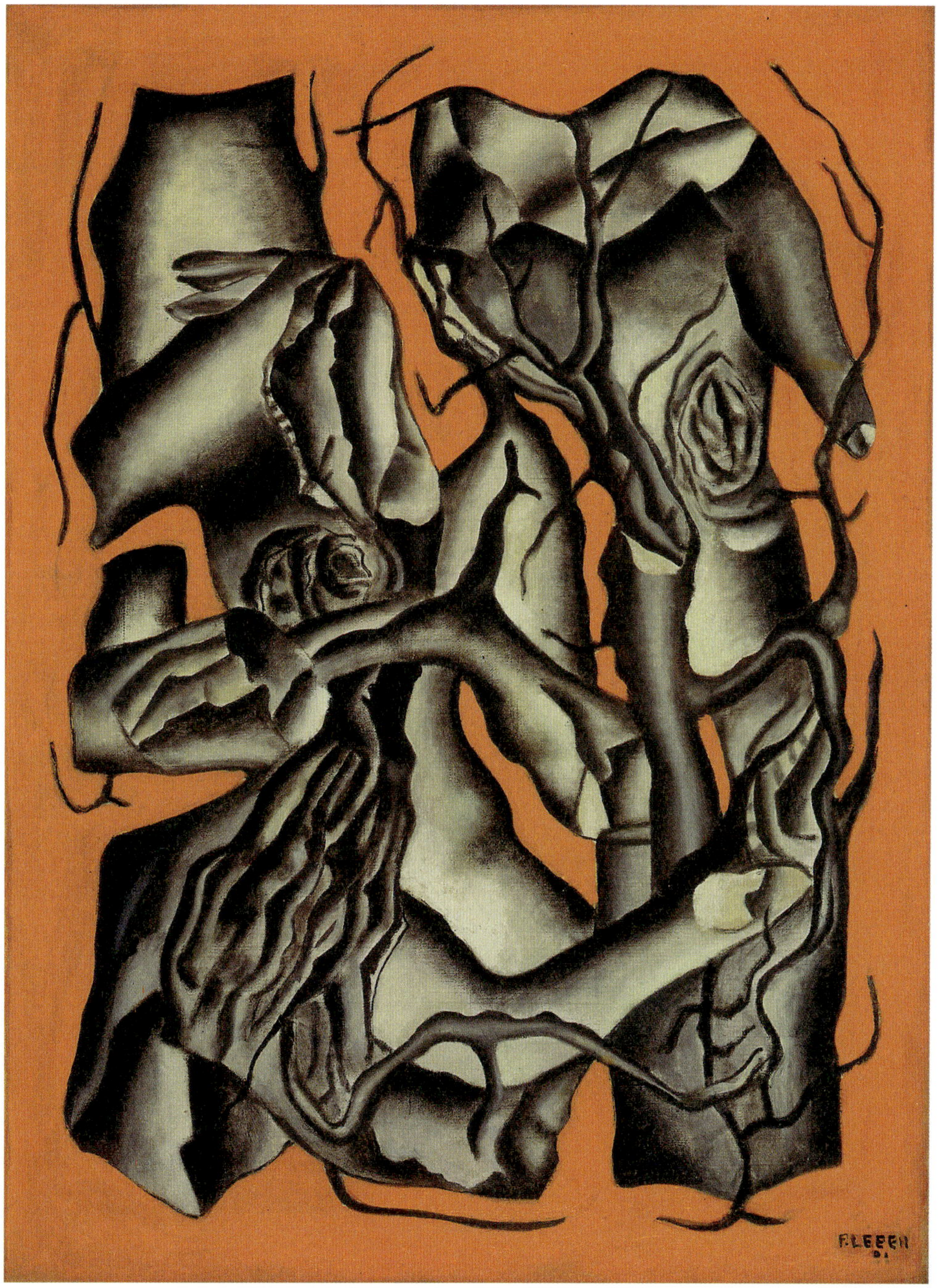

120

Fernand Léger's Remarks on the Object (1935)

This *object*, which was encased in the *subject* matter, becomes free; pure color that could not be asserted independently is going to emerge. It becomes the *leading character* in the new pictorial works.

For instance, I am standing before a landscape composed of trees, of sky, of clouds. I will focus my interest just on the tree, I will study it and extract from it all the visual potential it contains: its bark, with its often expressive design, its branches, whose movement is so dynamic, its leaves of which use can be made in decoration.

This tree, so rich in visual value, *is sacrificed* in the *subject picture*. Isolated, studied separately, it will provide us with material to rejuvenate contemporary pictorial expression.

I have to acknowledge that, in this enthralling story of the object, the cinema, with its close-ups, has allowed us "to advance faster."

[…] Its screen full of fragments of the face—an eye, a mouth, a nostril—it has sparked our visual interest and consolidated existing possibilities.

[…] An isolated cloud, alone in the blue depths of the sky, often has a pattern and relief of a richness that you might not discover when it is part of the landscape. Scientific research also has enabled artists to isolate this new reality. Underwater plants, infinitely tiny animals, a drop of water with its microbes magnified a thousand times by the microscope, can become new pictorial possibilities or permit a development in decorative art.

One then understands that everything is of equal interest, that the human face or the human body is of no weightier plastic interest than a tree, a plant, a piece of rock, or a pile of rope. It is enough to compose a picture with these objects, being careful to choose those that may best create a composition. It is a question of choice on the artist's part. An example: If I compose a picture and use as an object a piece of tree bark, a fragment of a butterfly's wing, and also a purely imaginary form, it is likely that you will not recognize the tree bark or the butterfly wing, and you will ask "What does that represent?" Is it an abstract picture? No, it is a representational picture. What we call an abstract picture does not exist. There is neither an abstract picture nor a concrete one. There is a beautiful picture and a bad picture. There is the picture that moves you and the one that leaves you indifferent.

Based on a lecture delivered in 1935 at the Museum of Modern Art New York and published in *Art Front* II, no. 8 (1935): 10–11 (translated by Harold Rosenberg). English translation (excerpts) by Alexandra Anderson in Fernand Léger, "The New Realism," in Fernand Léger, *Functions of Painting* (New York: Thames and Hudson, 1973), 109–13. The above excerpt also includes passages translated from F. Léger "Un nouveau réalisme, la couleur pure et l'objet," in Fernand Léger, *Fonctions de la peinture* (Paris: Denoël, 1965), 188–89.

–

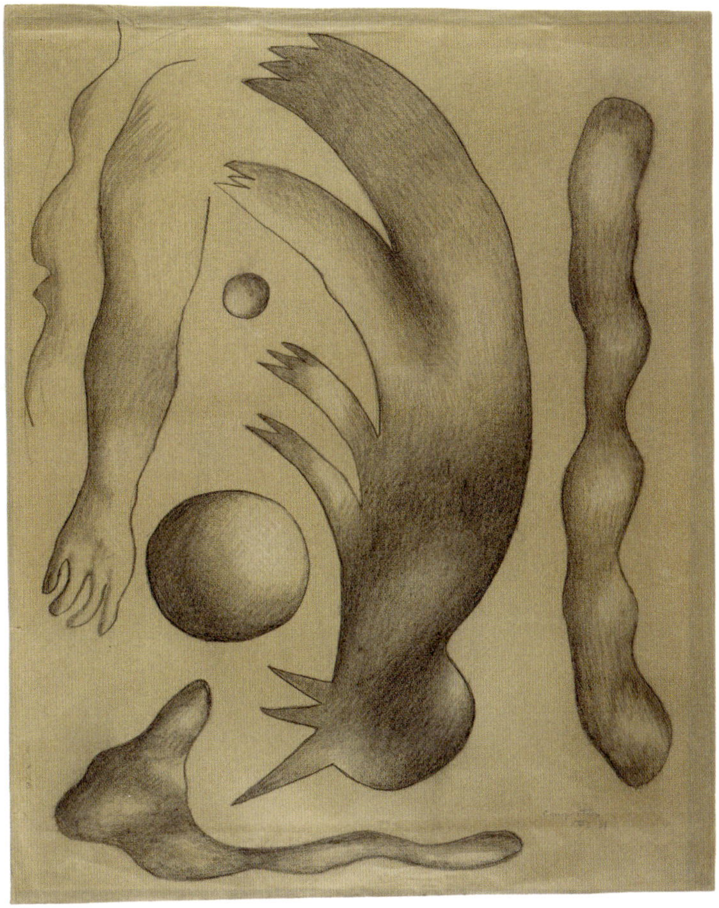

121

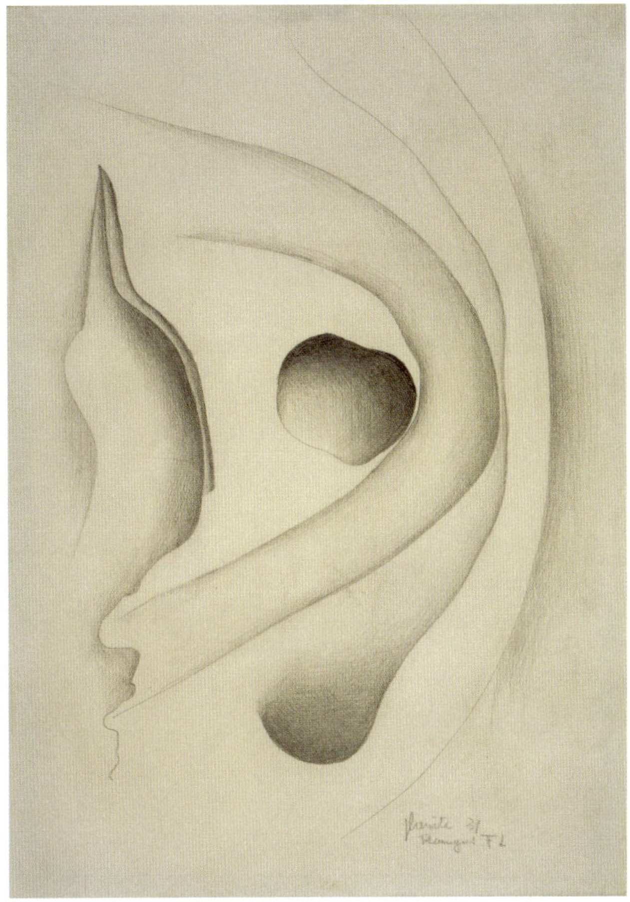

122

121 ***Composition* (Composition), 1931**
White chalk and graphite on grey-green paper
63.2 × 49.5 cm
Centre Pompidou, Musée national d'art moderne, Paris

122 ***Planète* (Planet), 1931**
Graphite on paper
43.5 × 30.2 cm
Centre Pompidou, Musée national d'art moderne, Paris

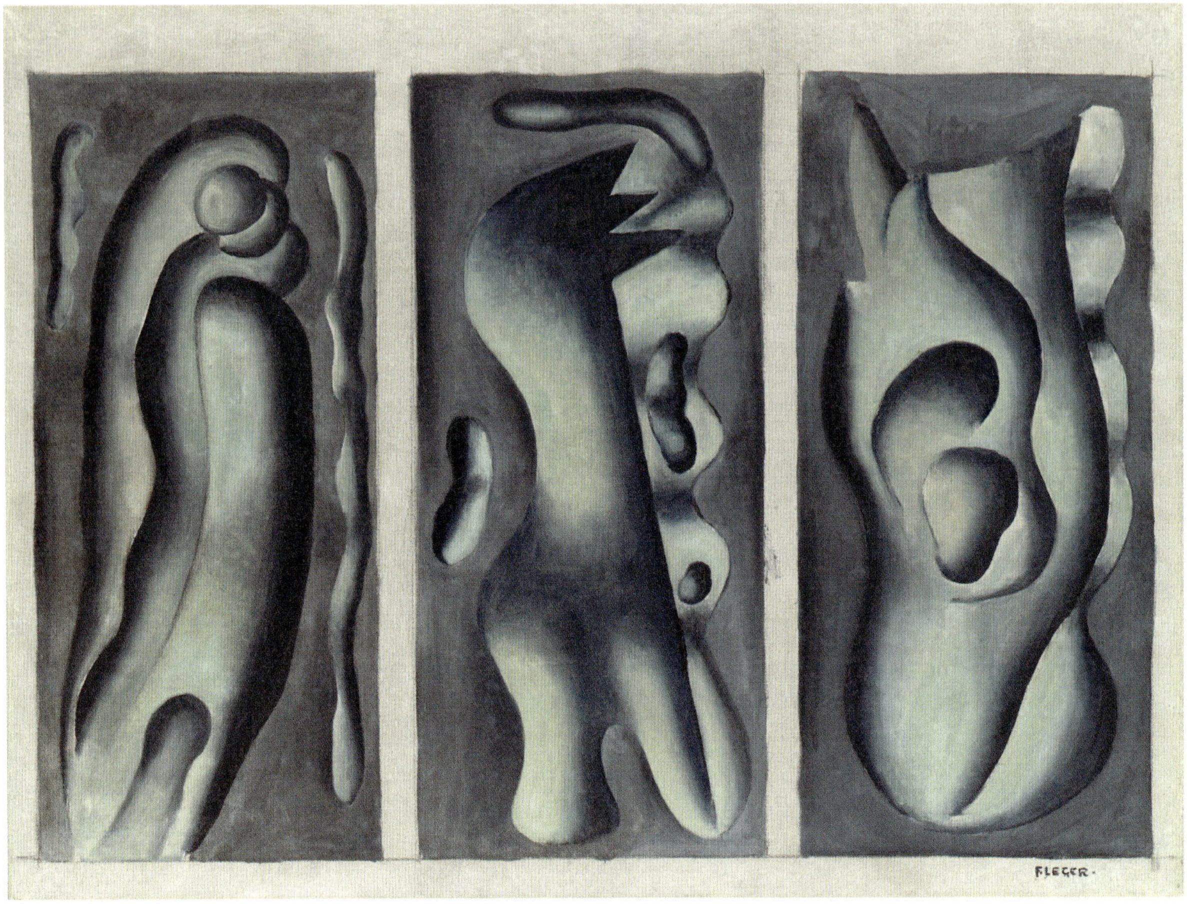

123

123 ***Queues de comètes (Étude pour un paravent)***
(Comet Tails [Study for a Screen]), c. 1930
Oil on canvas
70 × 92 cm
Musée national Fernand Léger, Biot

124 **Fernand Léger in his studio.**
Frontside of the screen in the background, c. 1930

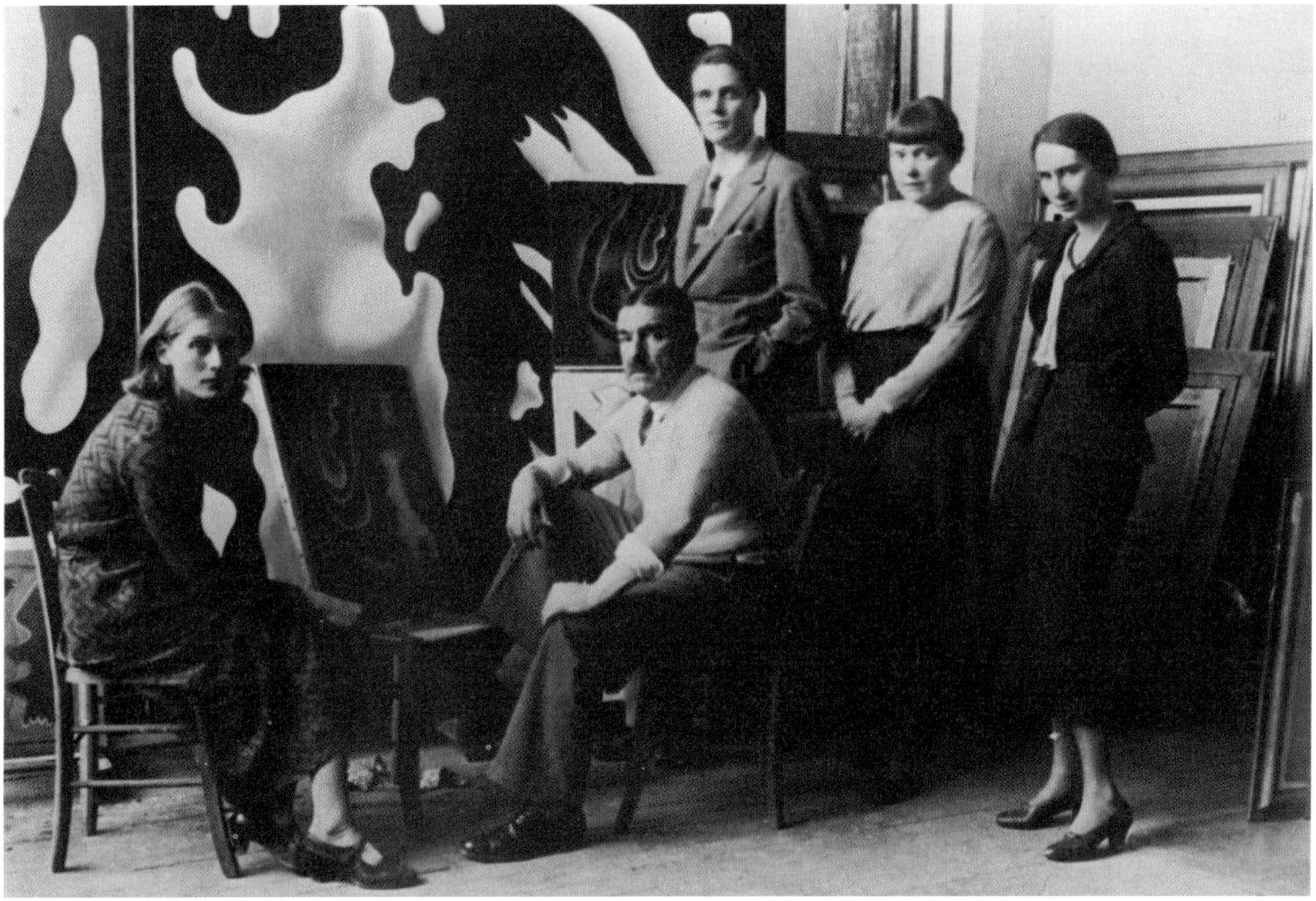

124

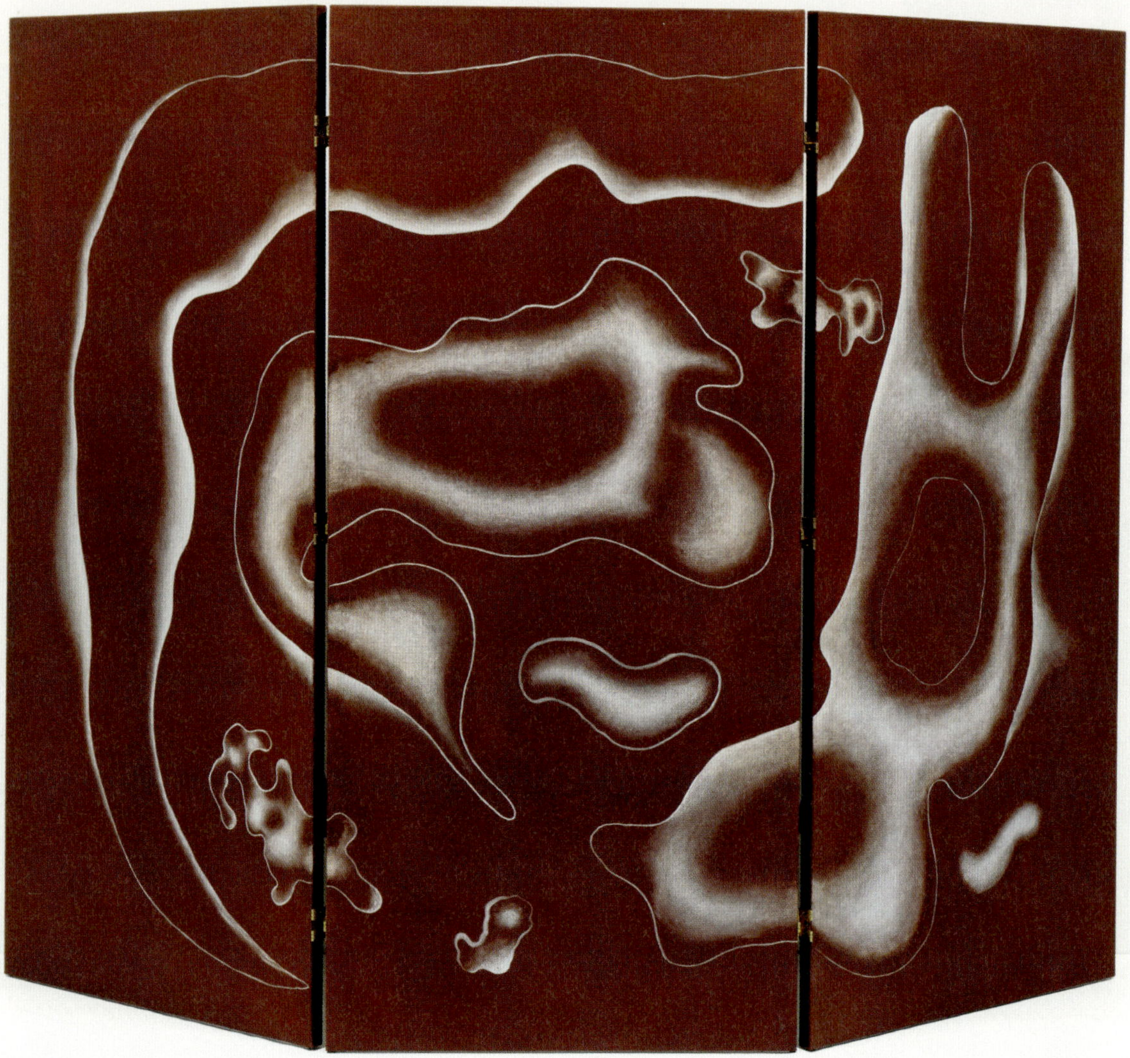

125

125 ***Paravent, Composition sur fond marron, trois feuilles*** **(Screen, composition on brown background, three leaves), back side, c. 1930**
Oil on canvas
201 × 275 cm
Musée national Fernand Léger, Biot

Both sides of a screen for the villa of Gerald and Sara Murphy in Antibes. The two sides were later separated

126 ***Queues de comète sur fond noir (Paravant pour la villa de Gerald Murphy a Antibes)*** **(Comet tails on black background [Screen for the villa of Gerald Murphy in Antibes]), c. 1930**
Oil on canvas
200 × 270 cm
Private collection

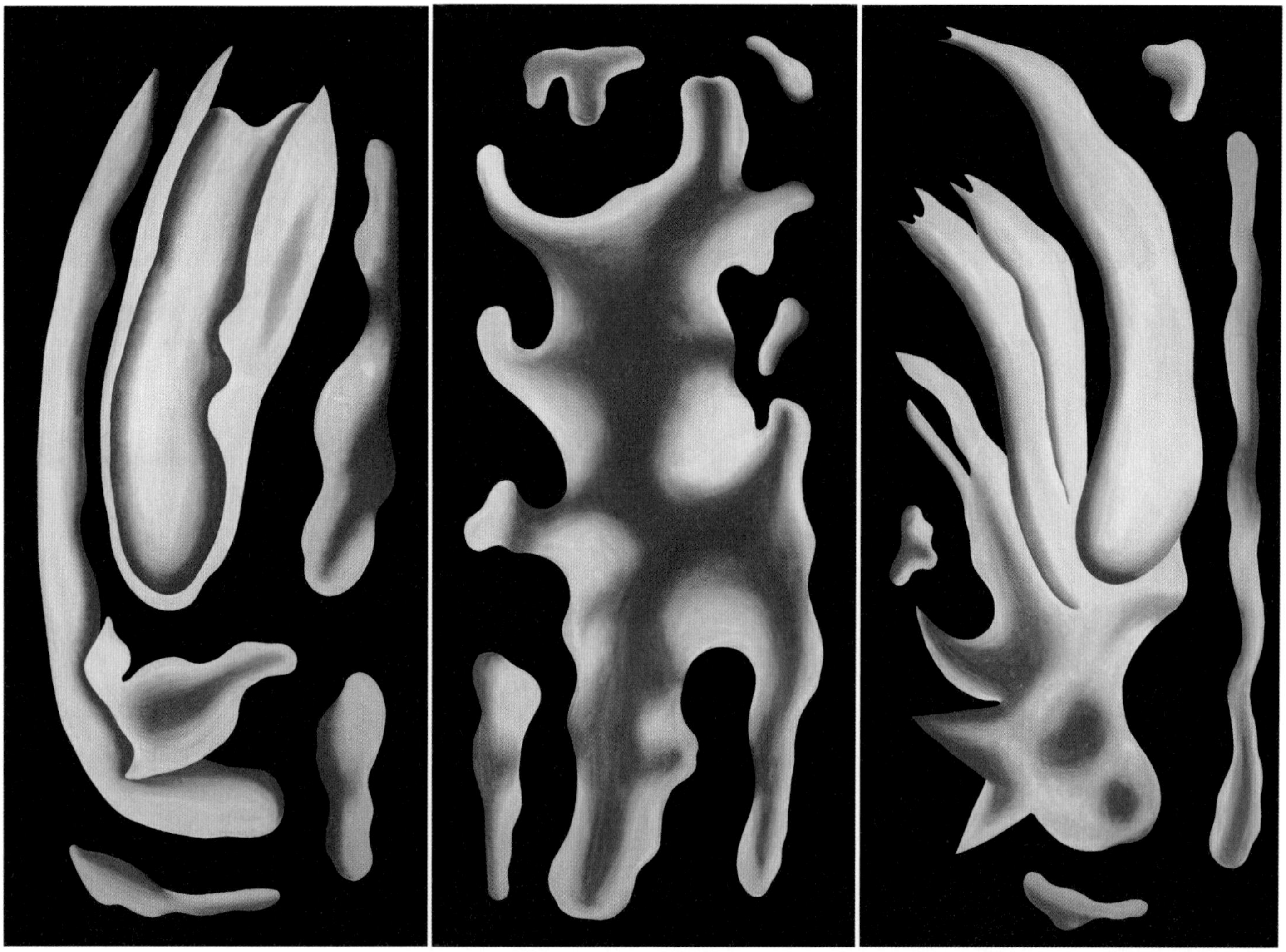

126

127 **Personal album made by Réne Herbst with newspaper articles, photographs, and postcard from Fernand Léger,1935**
Bibliothèque des Arts décoratifs, Paris

128 ***Composition* (Composition), 1935**
Oil on cardboard
38 × 46 cm
Fundación Joan Miró, Barcelona
Gift of Josep Lluís Sert

129 ***La Maison du jeune homme* (House for a Young Man) at the Universal Exhibition in Brussels, 1935**
Architects: Le Corbusier, Charlotte Perriand, Pierre Jeanneret, Louis Sognot, René Herbst
Archives Charlotte Perriand

Study room with *Composition à l'aloës* (Composition with Aloes), 1934/35, by Fernand Léger.

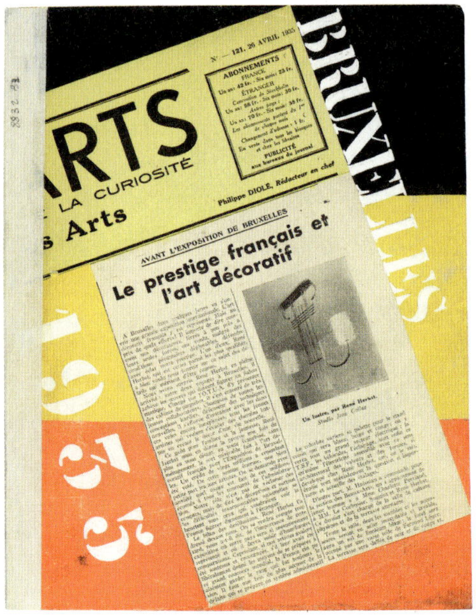

127

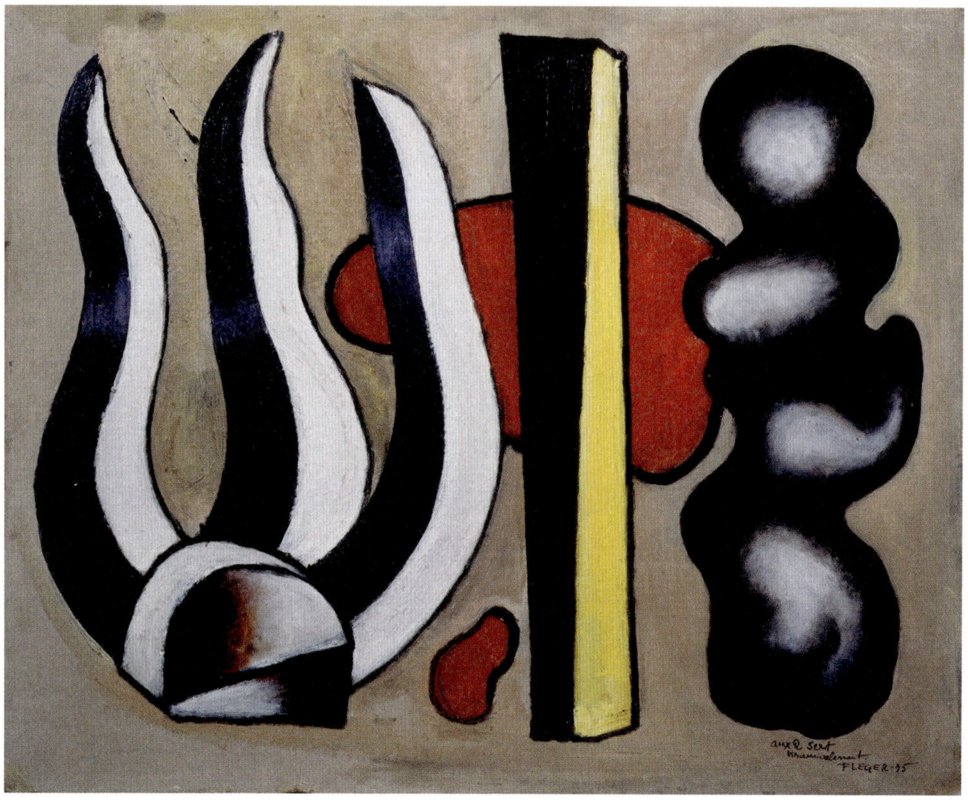

128

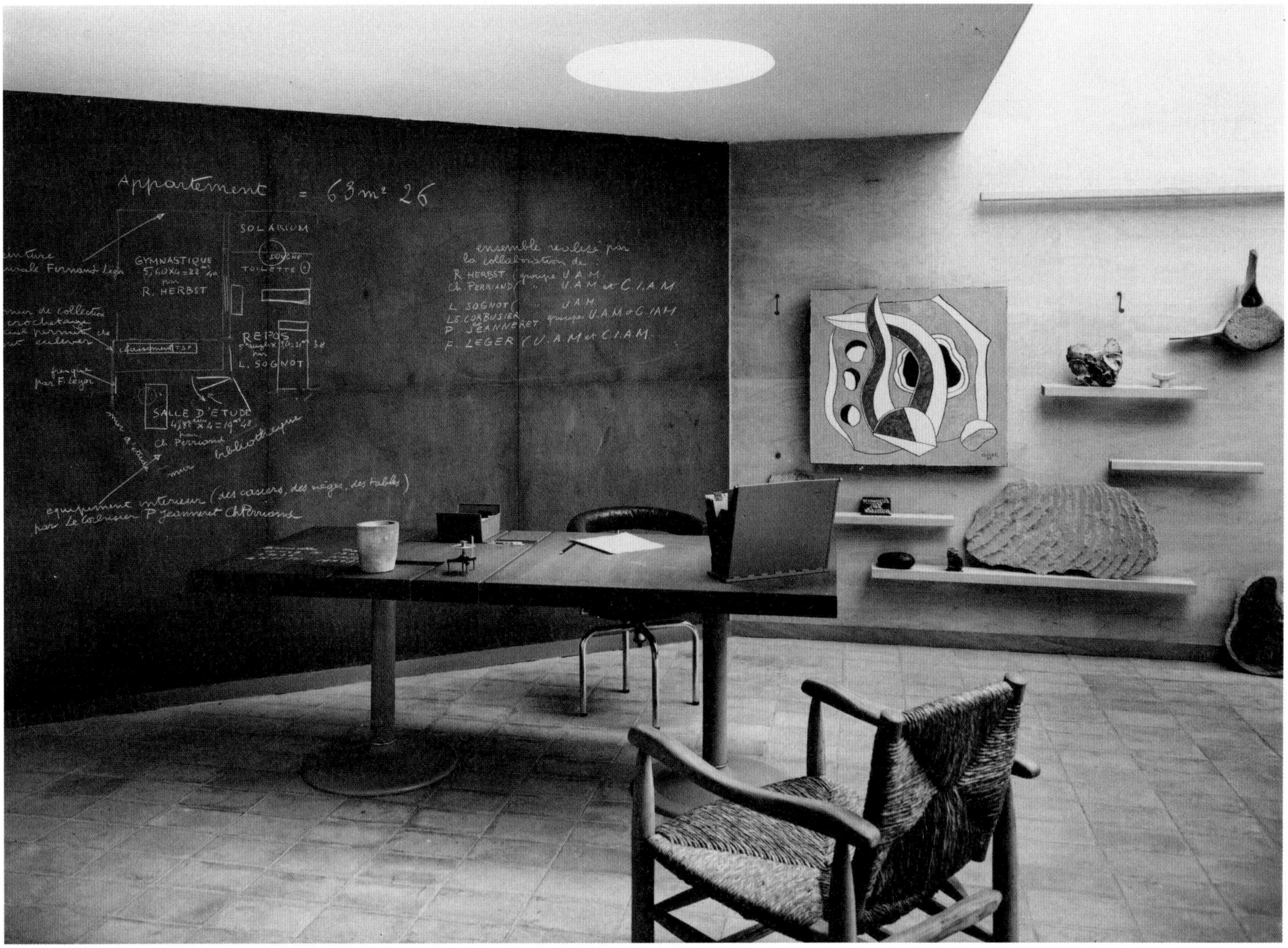
Appartement = 63m² 26
SOLARIUM
GYMNASTIQUE
R. HERBST
DOUCHE
TOILETTE
REPOS
L. SOGNOT
SALLE D'ETUDE
Ch. Perriand
bibliothèque
par F. Léger
équipement intérieur (des casiers, des sièges, des tables)
par Le Corbusier P Jeanneret Ch Perriand
ensemble réalisé par
la collaboration de :
R HERBST (groupe U A M
Ch. PERRIAND (" U.A.M et C.I.A.M
L SOGNOT (" U A M
LE CORBUSIER
P JEANNERET groupe U.A.M et C.I.A.M
F. LEGER (U.A.M et C.I.A.M

129

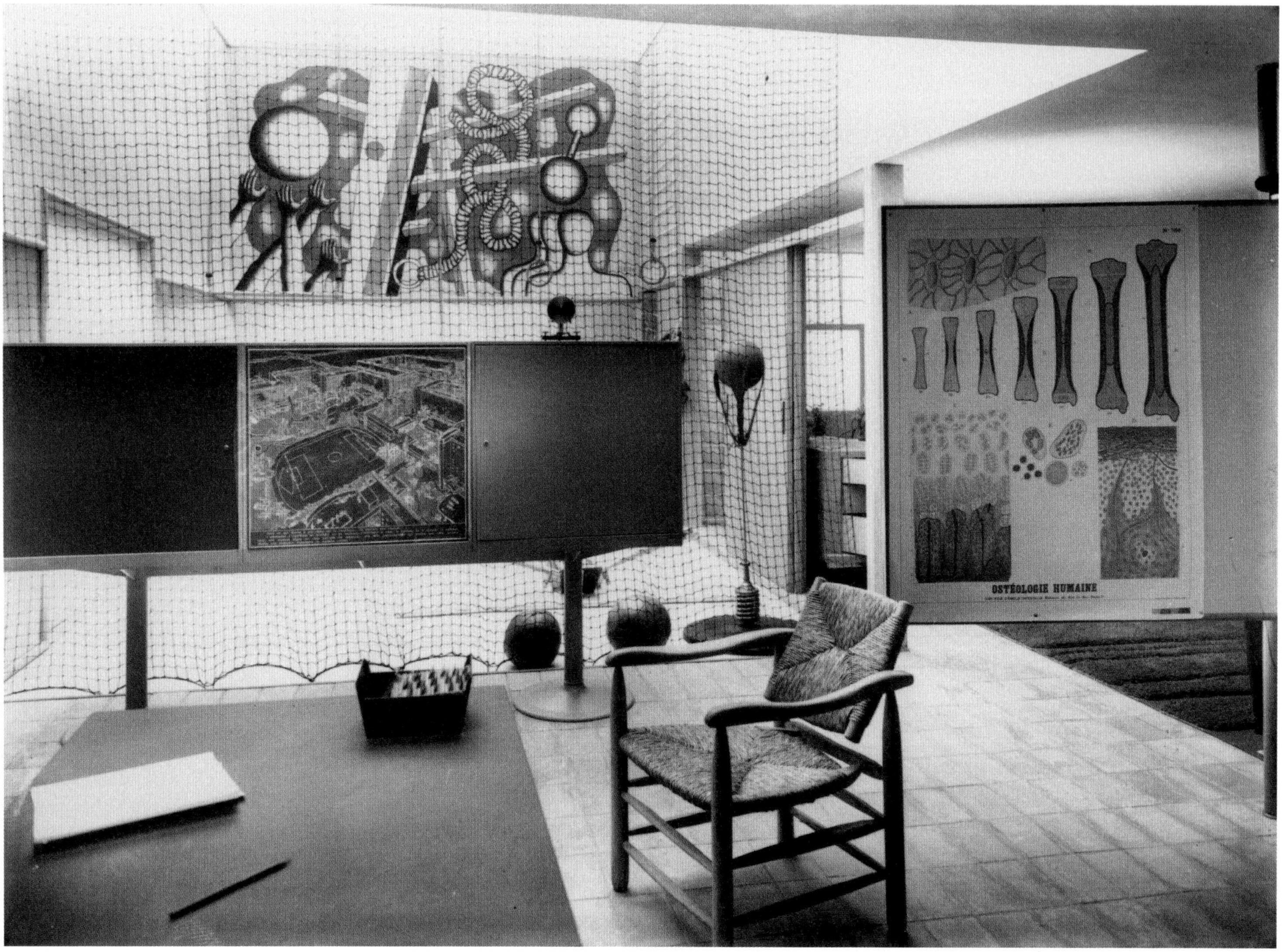

130

130 ***La Maison du jeune homme* (House for a Young Man) at the Universal Exhibition in Brussels, 1935**
Architects: Le Corbusier, Charlotte Perriand, Pierre Jeanneret, Louis Sognot, René Herbst
Archives Charlotte Perriand

View of the Gym with *La Salle de culture physique, le sport* (Gymnasium), 1935 by Fernand Léger in the background.

131 ***La Salle de culture physique, le sport* (Gymnasium), 1935**
Oil on canvas
235 × 396 cm
Private collection

132 ***Projet pour une décoration de stade-culture physique* (Project for the interior design of sports stadium), 1935**
Gouache and graphite on paper
24.53 × 36.1 cm
Musée national Fernand Léger, Biot

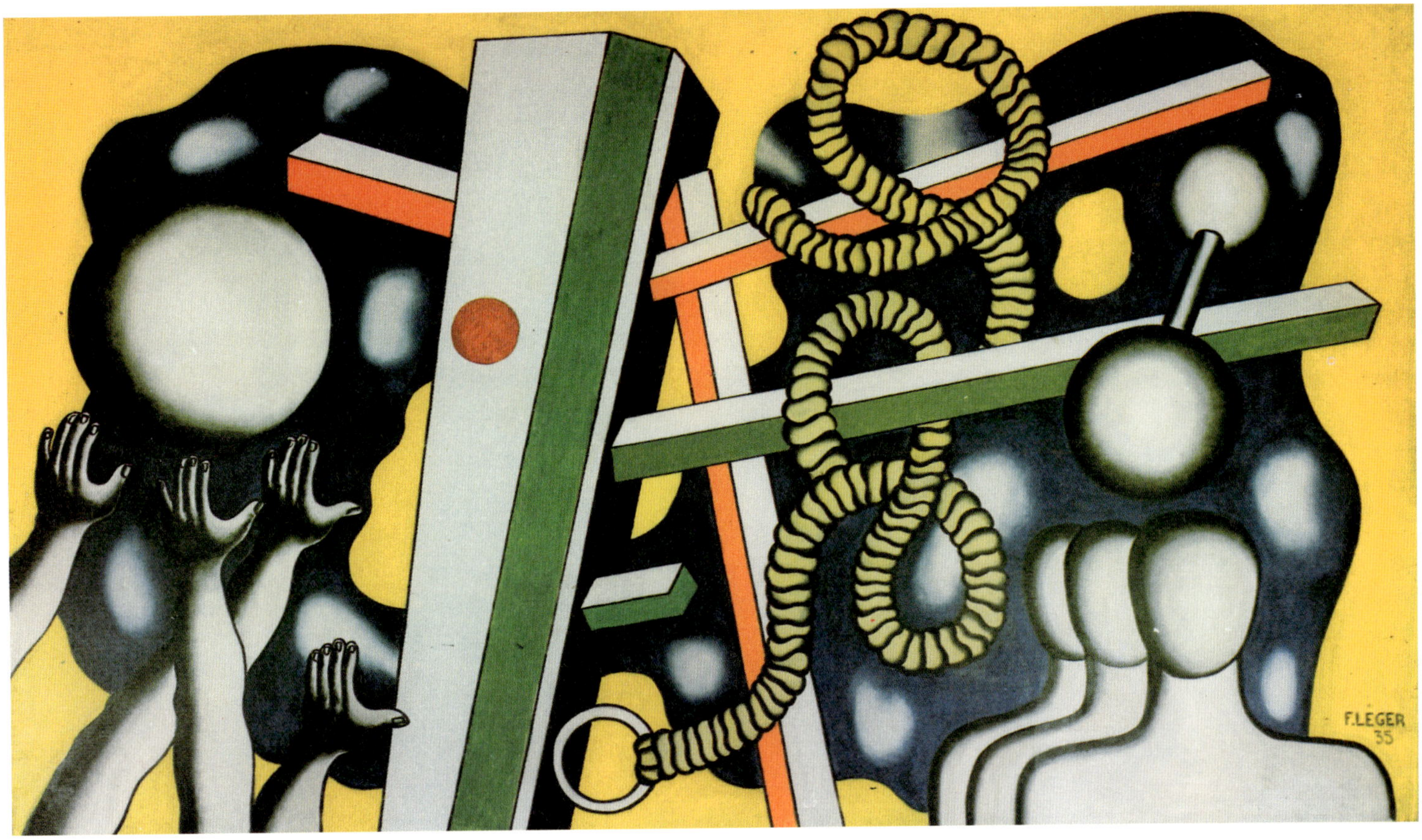
F.LEGER
35

131

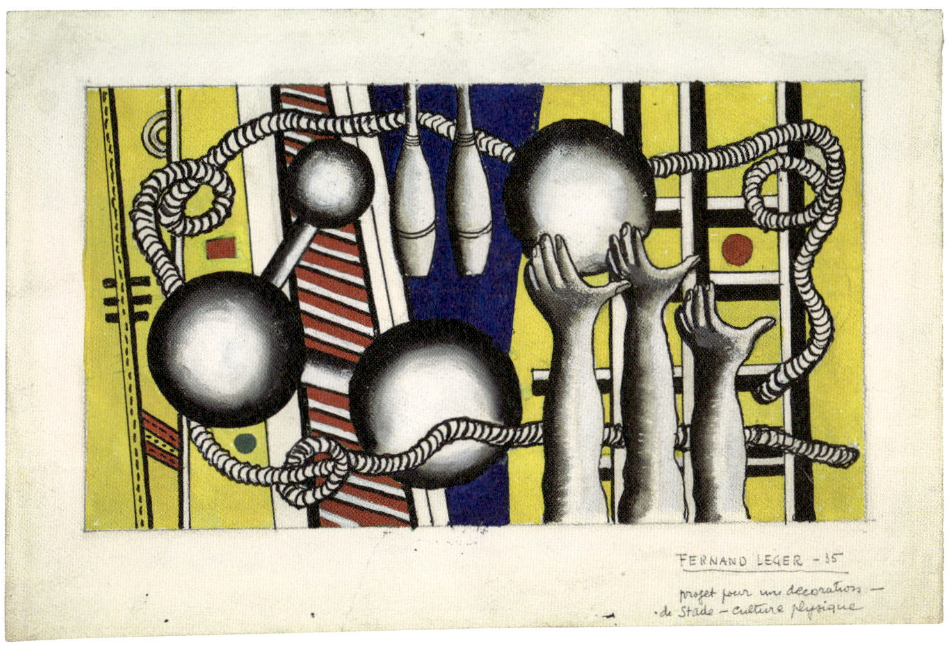
FERNAND LEGER - 35
projet pour une decoration -
de Stade - culture physique

132

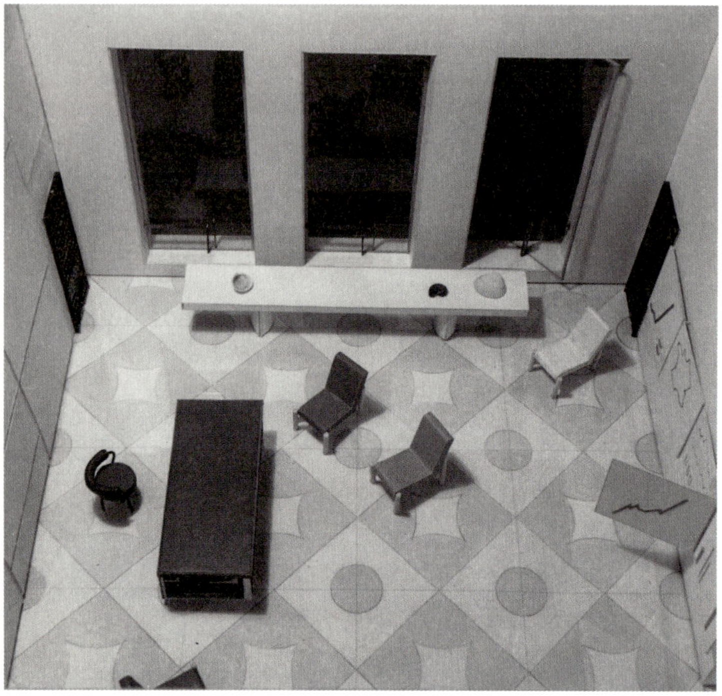

133

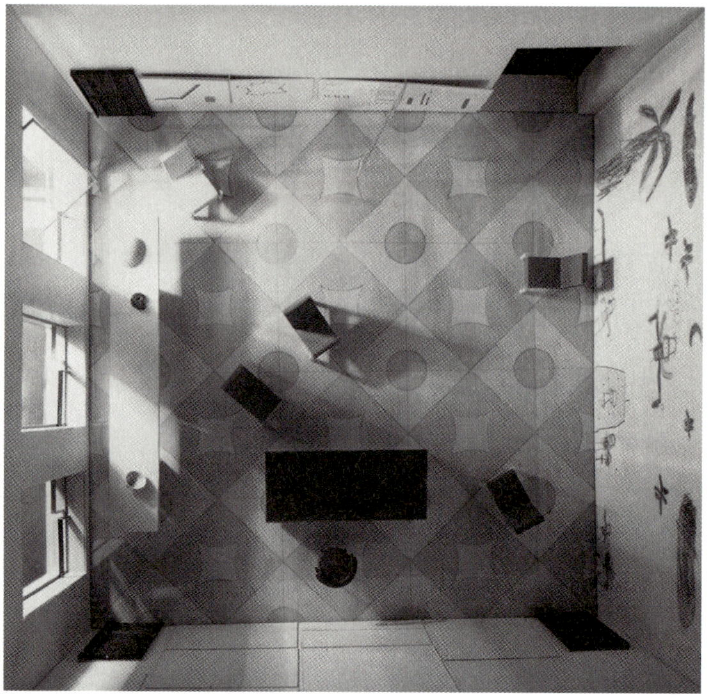

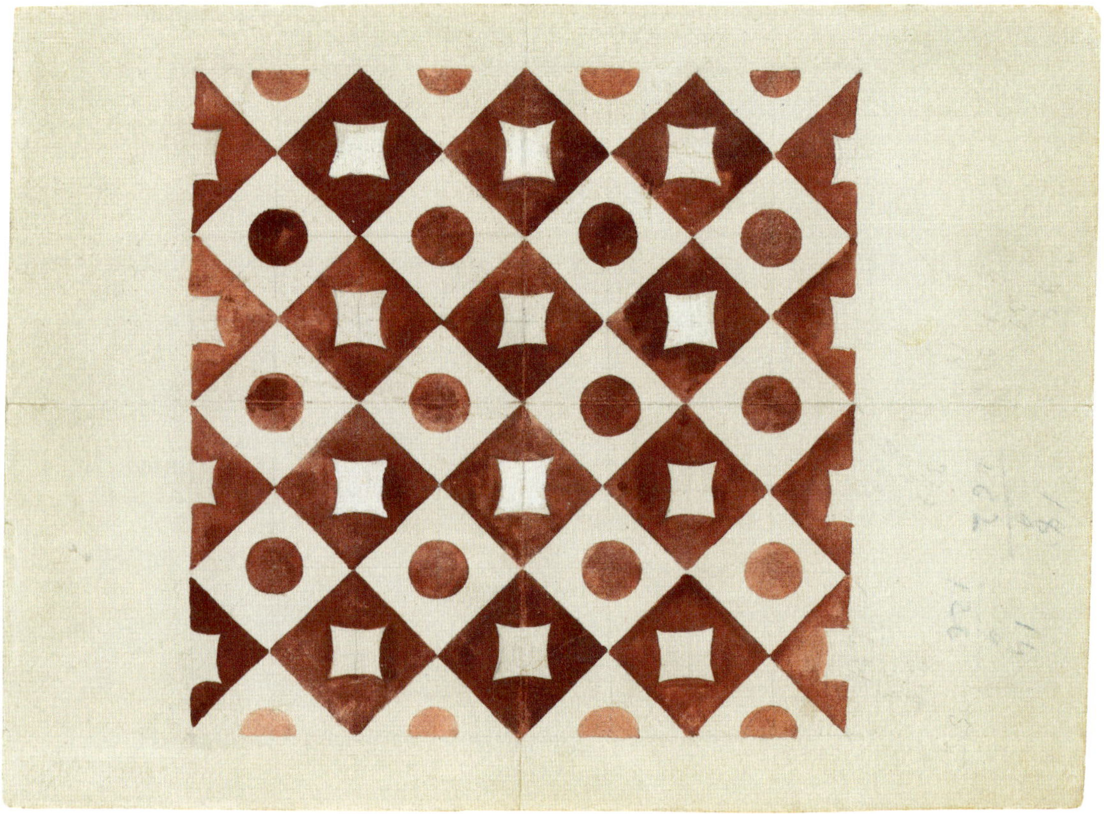

134

133 Charlotte Perriand
Competition design for the office of the Minister of National Education, Jean Zay, 1937
Floor design by Fernand Léger, drawing on the wall by Joan Miró's daughter, signed by her father
Archives Charlotte Perriand

134 ***Dessin de sol, projet pour le bureau de Jean Zay* (Floor design for the office of Jean Zay), 1937**
Gouache on paper
30.7 × 22.6 cm
Musée national Fernand Léger, Biot

135 Charlotte Perriand
Furniture for the director of the Cité universitaire in Hanoi, 1938–43, red and white tile floor based on a design by Fernand Léger, 1937
Archives Charlotte Perriand

Charlotte Perriand on Jean Zay's office design

Back in Paris I threw myself into the competition launched by the Ministry of Education: furnishing the office of the education minister, Jean Zay. A government office should not merely be a place to show off the best gilding found in private mansions; it is a representative space and should testify to the genius of Man, especially contemporary genius.

I presented a handsome mock-up of my proposals. I'd asked Fernand Léger to do the floor design, and he produced a scale model of his idea in terra-cotta slabs. Joan Miró did one of a mural fresco for the minister's offices.

I drew on two techniques to create exact reproductions of works that I viewed as pivotal, from cave paintings to modern-day artworks. First, I affixed line plates to the doors and the sides of the education minister's desk, then I laid out plaster imprints on the walls in a precise graphic arrangement. To keep national education in tune with the times, I added a Flambo revolving door, stretching from floor to ceiling, like in Brussels. Nothing came of it, but it didn't matter—I'd had fun.

Excerpt from Charlotte Perriand, *A Life of Creation* (New York: The Monacelli Press, 2003), 105–06 (originally published as *Une vie de création*, Paris, 1998).

–

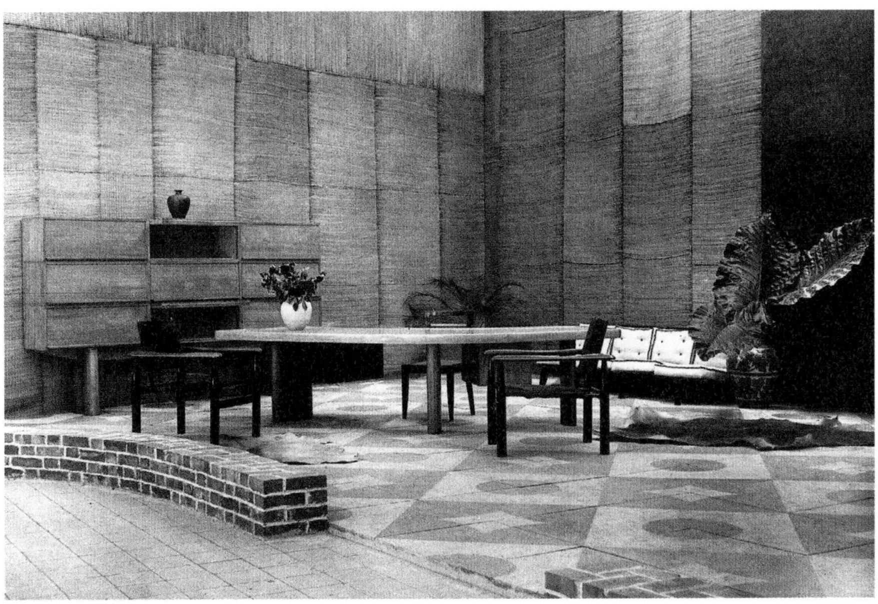

135

Revival of Mural Art (1937)
Fernand Léger

The world has known and will continue to know three main categories of artistic activity: Decorative Art, Mural Art, and Easel Painting.

Decorative Art has existed since the earliest times. It was the instinct of barbarians and primitives alike to decorate their implements of daily use: knife-handles, bows and arrows, and shields. They even tattooed their bodies, sometimes to arouse admiration, and sometimes to inspire fear. And this feeling for decoration prevailed until today. But of recent years a totally new attitude has made itself felt. Contemporary artists have claimed that objects are beautiful in themselves and are therefore in need of no decoration. Geometrical forms undoubtedly are often beautiful, and as the machine is destined to produce primarily objects of this nature, its products, based on cones, spheres and cylinders, not infrequently have been works of art. It is this incontestable, mathematical beauty which has been the modern discovery. One has only to look at the dressing of shop windows, with the wares arranged in parallel bands of colour, to see how this has been understood by the commercial world. Here we can see present-day decorative art. Stockings, groceries, even chemical products become decorative by the simple fact of their ordered presentation in brilliantly lighted displays. This is the new form of popular art, but naturally there is a great difference in the quality of the arrangements. All are not equally successful. Generally speaking, however, window displays in which objects are isolated possess an undeniable plastic and scenic value. The effect is that of a carefully planned mise-en-scène such as one is accustomed to see in music halls. Fashions in dress, coiffure and make-up are other-aspects of an ever-changing style of decoration, which is always subject to the dictates of taste alone, and which has been common to all races and all periods.

Mural art, too, can be traced back for many centuries. Its conception is inevitably purely plastic, and aesthetically it belongs to a nobler rank among expressions of Beauty. For it is concerned with artistic problems of the highest order. In the Middle Ages artists succeeded in establishing a completely successful mural art using only two important media: fresco and mosaic. The mural problem is a complex one and demands totally different solutions according to whether an external or internal wall surface is in question. This kind of painting is entirely dependent on the architecture around it; the formal unity of the building must not be broken, and the artist must take full cognisance of the surrounding construction. For the architect is the director: he it is who must supervise the realisation of his conception and bear the responsibility for the final unity of the whole.

A building contains two sorts of wall surfaces: live surfaces and dead surfaces. The mural artist is concerned with bringing to life dead surfaces by the application of colour. But first he must study the play of volumes and the sculptures (if any) decorating the building. If the play of volumes is architecturally important, the colours must be kept in a low key and not break down the plane of the wall. It is a question of the correct dose. But if on the other hand volumes play no important part, then colour can have it all its own way and can create a sense of space where none existed before; it can in other words let in light and air. By means of modelling and trompe l'oeil it can achieve the sensation of something carved. Its mood can be sad or joyful, harsh or soft, its form static or dynamic, representational or abstract. Today, however, the tendency is towards a pure form of beauty and the abandonment of representational and expressionistic works. For myself I cannot see nowadays any justification for murals setting forth the major religious, military or social issues; these can be so adequately dealt with by books, the cinema and the wireless. But I am afraid that the general public will continue to demand a representational element, for it has never had the necessary time or sufficient liberty of spirit to pursue its artistic education. And indeed for a while one many have to bear with some transitional phase. But in the construction of large public edifices, such as stadiums and aerodromes, it will shortly come to be realized that one cannot leave large areas of blank wall-space. These surfaces ought to be animated by the application of colour and by the use of beautiful natural materials such as bronze, steel, aluminum or glass, and in time it will even be realized that the breaking down of these dead surfaces is a social, not a private, responsibility.

Recently one of my friends, an architect, asked me to tackle quite a novel problem. At his house in the country, which faces north, the courtyard at the back was enclosed by a wall on which the sun never shone, so that there was no hope of ever growing any flowers or shrubs in front of it. He asked me to come with colour and destroy it. Can this really be done? you ask. I tried and, in fact, succeeded. By applying pure colours in dynamic opposition, sometimes with the aid of modelling, sometimes by a purely flat application, I found that I had given it a true dynamic value, that one no longer had the feeling of a static vertical surface on one plane only. The wall had become mobile, luminous. Its appearance changed with the variation in light, as would that of flowers or shrubs. It had brought joy; the sad monotony of the wall was gone. I believe that this problem is a pressing one and is destined to receive greater consideration. In short, the point at issue is the creation of an artificial sense of space. And this problem is typical of today, when reality and fiction are so intermingled that no one knows where one begins and the other ends. Frescoes and mosaics did not break down walls, they merely ornamented them; thus the mediaeval artist was able to set forth his religious epic without encroaching on the building. Colour possesses a force of its own which is capable of infinite variation. It is a formidable raw material, as indispensable to life as fire or water.

Once colour is divorced from a wall-surface one is faced with the third of my categories of plastic expression—easel painting. Easel painting owes its origin to the invention of mixing colours with oil and to the fact that this event happened to coincide with the growing importance of the individual: that is to say, it arose about the end of the fifteenth century. The general desire to possess a private collection of works of art forced the creative artist to desert the wall-surfaces which had served them hitherto. They abandoned, that is to say, communal artistic expression in favour of that new form which dominated the seventeenth, eighteenth, and nineteenth centuries: they adopted a more intimate form of art, which necessitated that something plastically vital should be enclosed within the narrow though adjustable limits of a frame. Easel painting is exactly the opposite of mural painting. Now one can exercise one's choice, the picture is taken home and is found particularly pleasing because, having been chosen and bought, it is to be hung on the wall: it becomes an intimate piece of furniture and belongs to someone. Art in this form is not imposed, it is selected. It is not intended to please or instruct the masses, but merely to gratify a few individuals, who do with it what they will.

But the desire for a reawakening of mural art certainly exists. And how are we going to solve that problem today? Must we return to the sentimental representationalism of the Middle Ages? I sincerely hope not. This phase should be finished and done with, there can be no excuse for retrogression. But it all depends on that dreadful word Beauty. Beauty is neither representational, nor sentimental, nor didactic. Beauty exists in an abstract quality. But we must wait for the plastic education of the masses before this thesis will be accepted. Meanwhile let us cover our walls with fresh, gay colours and so inspire optimism and joy. Then we must wait until Beauty is understood by all, and therein lies the great hope of the future.

Originally published as Fernand Léger, "Revival of Mural Art," in *The Listener*, vol. 18, no. 450 (August 25, 1937): 408–09 (translation by Douglas Lord).

Fernand Léger and the 1937 World's Fair in Paris

By Kathrin Michel

"What would you do if you had to organize the 1937 Fair?"[1] When posed with this question in 1935, Léger replied by saying he would transform the appearance of the Eiffel Tower —unaltered for fifty years—by suffusing the tower in light. Electrically lit ties and brightly lit cufflinks expanded this idea of an *atmosphère lumineuse*, accompanied by cinematic projections above the rooftops. Although Léger set out his ideas for the Eiffel Tower's new silhouette in a series of gouaches, he was unable to make his plans a reality (fig. 137). Instead, it was the architect André Granet who was tasked with transforming the Eiffel Tower's lighting (fig. 136). The exhibition, which ran from May to November 1937 in Paris, is now best remembered for first exhibiting Picasso's *Guernica* —the artist's response to the Spanish Civil War, which was raging at the time—and for the juxtaposition of the German and Soviet pavilions, which were placed directly opposite one another. This politico-historical reading aside, the 1937 World's Fair (known in French as the *Exposition Internationale des Arts et Techniques dans la Vie Moderne*) had declared art and technology in modern everyday life its main subject. Accordingly, Jacques Gréber, the exhibition's head architect, and Edmond Labbé, the commissary general, conceived a program designed to bring together art and technology as expressions of modernity.[2] The World's Fair included several projects which centered on a symbol of technological progress *par excellence*: electric light. The most prominent of these project could be found in the Palais de la Lumière et de l'Électricité, which showcased a 600 m^2 mural[3] by Raoul Dufy and examples of Robert Mallet-Stevens' sinuous architecture.[4]

The new government of the left-leaning Front Populaire, which came to power in May 1936, set up a scheme whereby artists were awarded commissions subsidized by the state. Thus the doors were opened for members of the artistic avant-garde, themselves mainly of a left-wing persuasion who, like Léger, were politically active. The idea of the collective was also brought into play, manifesting itself mainly in the collaborative production of 345 large-format murals created by 464 artists. The Salon de l'Art Mural, held in Galerie Bernheim in Paris in 1935, might well be the reason behind this large number, as was the combination of temporary architecture and painting as an approach to decoration. In addition, the World's Fair focused on revitalizing artisanal techniques such as fresco and mural painting; Léger had been campaigning for the importance of such crafts, which he saw as belonging to the public sphere, for several years. In an interview published during the World's Fair, Léger heralded "murals and big public spectacles" as the two dominant artistic trends of the moment.[5] This statement is reinforced by Léger's *Revival of Mural Art*,[6] published around that time, in which he highlights the mural artist's task as bringing dead surface layers to life through the application of color, and draws particular attention to the interplay of painting and architecture.

However steeped in tradition this approach to painting may be, it nevertheless went hand in hand with progress: many photomurals could be found alongside the murals on display at the World's Fair. Such photomurals are characterized by the use of extremely large-scale photographic reproductions created using montage techniques and often involving further graphic and artistic elements.[7] Thus the photomurals effected a programmatically direct visual language in countless pavilions, such as the Spanish pavilion, where Josep Renau's photomurals—hung alongside Picasso's *Guernica*—helped to convey the expressiveness of Picasso's monumental artwork.

Léger found many points of commonality with the ideas and design of the World's Fair. He himself had experience working in collectives, for instance in his collaboration with representatives of the Union des Artistes Modernes (Union of Modern Artists, or UAM), of which he was a member, to create the monumentally proportioned painting *La Salle de la culture physique, le sport* (Gymnasium) as part of the *La Maison du jeune homme* (The House of the Young Man) project in 1935. Alongside this group of artists, architects, and designers, Léger was also one of the active members of the Congrès Internationaux d'Architecture Moderne (the International Congresses of Modern Architecture), which engaged in topics related to modern living and organized a series of debates on urbanism at the World's Fair. Léger contributed six technically, formally, and conceptually diverse commissions. He drew on the pictogrammatic style of trade union logos in his large-scale painting *Le Syndicalisme ouvrier* (Trade Unionism), which was shown between eleven other artists' works in landscape format, all created for Robert Mallet-Stevens' *Pavillon de la Solidarité nationale* (fig. 139).[8]

On the other hand, the colorful, abstract/organic forms of the *L'Accompagnement de l'architecture* (Architecture Accompaniment) mural stretch across the wall of the UAM pavilion (figs. 144–146).[9] Léger invited artists Léopold Survage and Albert Gleizes to collaborate with him on this work; the artists' bright colors glow from within the vitrine-like glass building.

Charlotte Perriand and Léger were mainly concerned with making a political statement when they transformed the *Pavillon de l'Agriculture* into an open-air panorama of photomurals (figs. 153–155). By using oversized photomontages of motifs including rural costumes and factories, first selected by Perriand from François Kollar's 1932 publication *La France travaille*[10] before being creatively reworked by Léger, the artists placed nostalgia in opposition to the modernization of agriculture. This brought the Front Populaire's agricultural reforms into the public eye.

Of equal importance to this group of artists' political program was the *spectacle total* offered by *La naissance d'une cité* (The Birth of a City) (figs. 157, 158), for which Léger designed

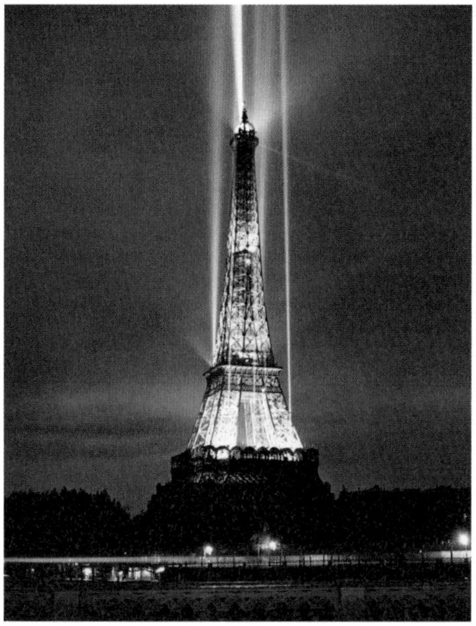

136

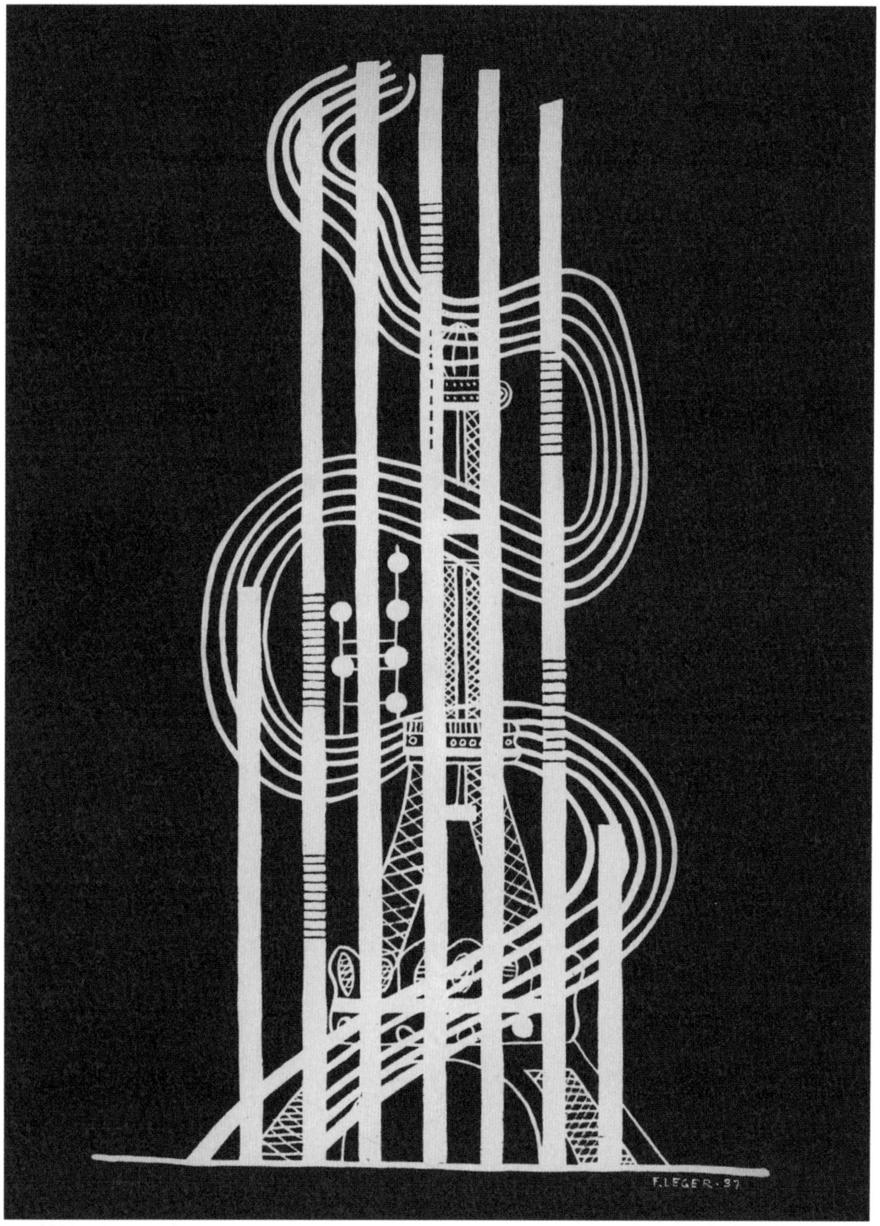

137

136 **Illumination of the Eiffel Tower by André Granet, Paris World's Fair, 1937**

137 ***Tour d'Eiffel II*** **(Eiffel Tower II), 1937**
Gouache on paper
65 × 48 cm
Whereabouts unknown

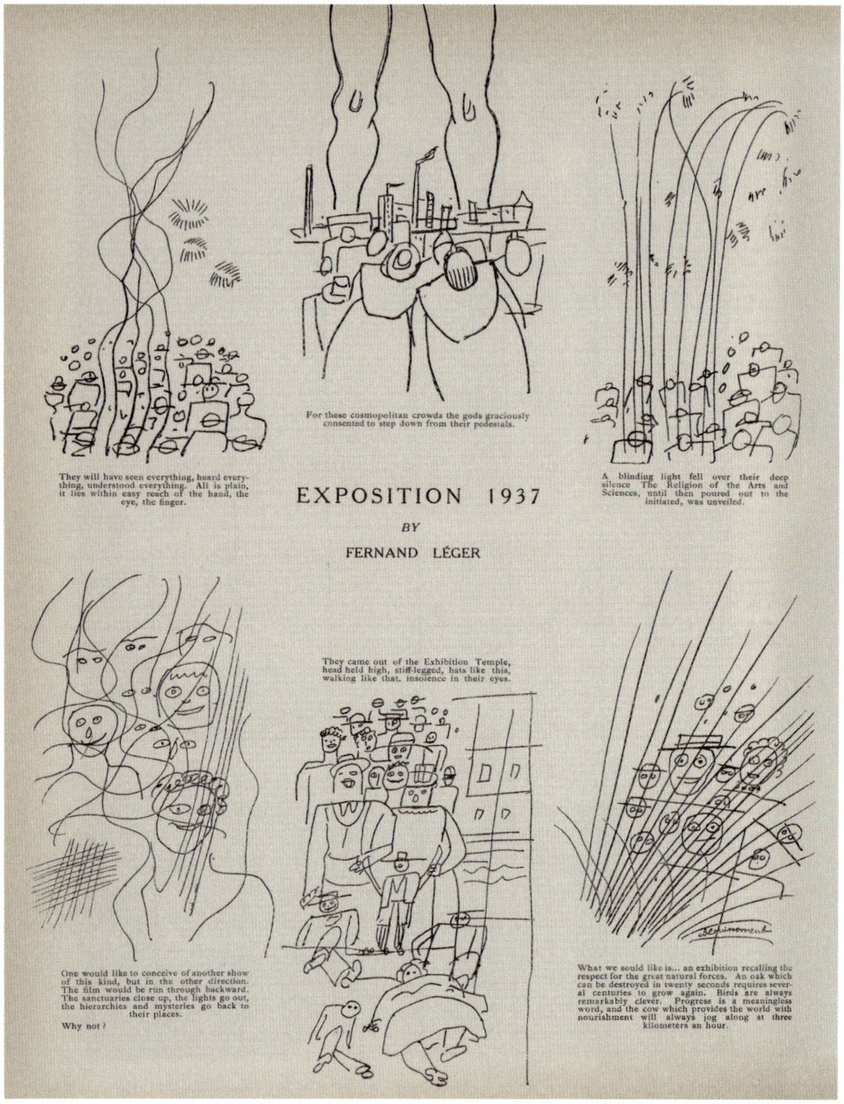
For these cosmopolitan crowds the gods graciously consented to step down from their pedestals.

They will have seen everything, heard everything, understood everything. All is plain, it lies within easy reach of the hand, the eye, the finger.

EXPOSITION 1937

BY

FERNAND LÉGER

A blinding light fell over their deep silence The Religion of the Arts and Sciences, until then poured out to the initiated, was unveiled.

They came out of the Exhibition Temple, head held high, stiff-legged, hats like this, walking like that, insolence in their eyes.

One would like to conceive of another show of this kind, but in the other direction. The film would be run through backward. The sanctuaries close up, the lights go out, the hierarchies and mysteries go back to their places.

Why not ?

What we sould like is... an exhibition recalling the respect for the great natural forces. An oak which can be destroyed in twenty seconds requires several centuries to grow again. Birds are always remarkably clever. Progress is a meaningless word, and the cow which provides the world with nourishment will always jog along at three kilometers an hour.

138

138 **Exposition internationale des Arts et des Techniques appliqués à la Vie moderne, Paris, May 25 – November 25, 1937**
Caricatures and texts by Léger published in *Verve: revue artistique et littéraire*, 1, 1937

139 ***Pavillon de la Solidarité* (Solidarity Pavilion), Paris World's Fair, 1937**
Architect: Robert Mallet-Stevens

Le Syndicalisme (Trade Unionism) by Fernand Léger in the center, flanked by murals by Robert Delaunay (left) and Le Chevalier (right). A total of twelve murals of the same size by French artists were presented in the *Hall d'Honneur* (Hall of Honor)

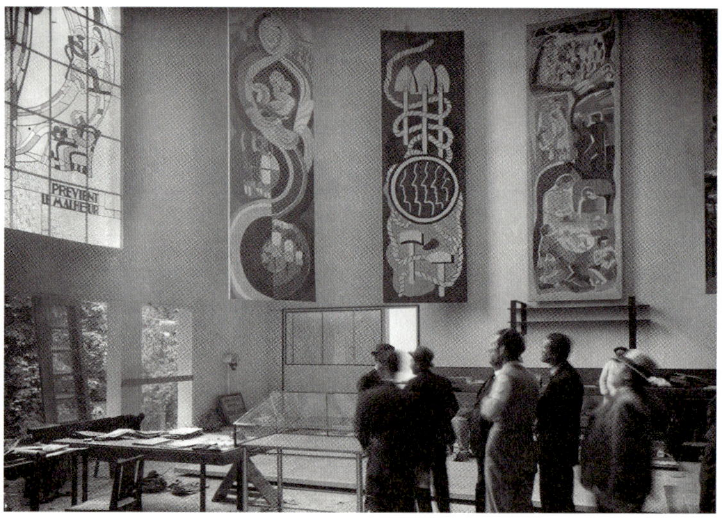

139

the mobile stage set and the costumes. This revolutionary theater piece drew on the texts of Jean-Richard Bloch, updating his themes and making them accessible to the masses. Yet two of Léger's works in particular best reflect the World's Fair's key ideas of working in a collective and spotlighting the themes of technology and industrialization: *Travailler* (Work) in the Pavillon des Temps Nouveaux, and *Le Transport des Forces* in the Palais de la Découverte.

In the tent-like Pavillon des Temps Nouveaux, Le Corbusier put together an exhibition which exemplified key ideas of architecture and urbanism (figs. 147–152), and distilled the ideas of CIAM and its members. Le Corbusier deployed his spatial concept for this pavilion to connect with Léger's interests and to incorporate Léger's works. In 1925, he had included Léger's painting *Le Balustre* (The Baluster) in his collection at the Pavillon de l'Esprit Nouveau, and his design for the Musée d'esthétique contemporaine (Museum of Contemporary Esthetics), his unsuccessful submission to the World's Fair, had included a monumental version of Léger's *Composition aux trois figures* (Composition with Three Figures) (fig. 148).[11] The project Le Corbusier was able to bring to fruition, the Pavilion des Temps Nouveaux, was "wallpapered" with large-scale photomurals by various artists, including Le Corbusier's *Habiter* (Living) and Léger's *Travailler* (fig. 151a)—living and working forming two elements in modern city planning. A photomontage comprised of pieces of an electric motor, cylinders, cables, and machines enabled Léger to portray the mechanized world of work and the use of technology in the industrial age. However, as the illustration reveals, these machines were built and maintained by human hands. Accordingly, da Vinci's *Vitruvian Man* is placed almost at the center of the machine.[12] Le Corbusier himself wrote of "tools and machines, the new slaves of men, under whose control they produce excess,"[13] thus underscoring Léger's artistic statement.

Another facet of this topic may be found in Léger's monumental painting *Le Transport des Forces* for the Palais de la Découverte, founded as a science museum on the occasion of the 1937 World's Fair and located in the western wing of the Grand Palais. Electricity was the order of the day: A great sensation was caused by the twelve-meter electrostatic loudspeaker, a machine capable of producing the world's most powerful sound waves. Léger created the painting *Le Transport des Forces* for the space near to the stairs in the Salle de physique du globe, realizing his plans with the help of his students (figs. 141–143). He portrayed mountains, water, and rainbows framed by tracks and scaffolding. Much like a photomontage,[14] the construction of the image itself evokes the technique of montage in that there is no consistent perspective, while the schematic treatment lends nature itself a technical edge. Nature and technology are shown as existing in a continuum, with the former serving as a source of coal, hydraulic energy, and electricity, thus enabling the "transference of energy."

Even if Léger was unable to realize his vision of a bright, colorful, and electrified Paris thanks to the organizers' insistence on the "cult of the old patinas, of the sentimental ruins"[15] (as Léger later described it), he was nonetheless able to create works in harmony with his central subjects, his creative process, and his political convictions.

1 Fernand Léger, "Réponse à une enquête: que feriez-vous si vous aviez à organiser l'Exposition de 1937?," *VU. L'illustré français* 387 (1935).
2 Cf. Edmond Labbé, *Exposition Internationale des Arts et Techniques. Paris 1937. Rapport général* (Paris, 1938–40), 1:56.
3 *La Fée Électricité* by Raoul Dufy was commissioned by the Parisian Electricity Group C.P.D.E. and can be found today in the collection of the Musée d'Art Moderne de la Ville in Paris.
4 Cf. Danilo François Udovicki-Selb, "The Elusive Faces of Modernity: Jacques Gréber and the Planning of the 1937 Paris World Fair," *Urban History Review / Revue d'histoire urbane* 29, no. 2 (March 2001): 20–35; 20.
5 Jean-Marc Champagne, "La Vie des arts: Avec Fernand Léger," *Marianne* (October 13, 1937): 8. For the influence of the World's Fair on the establishment of mural painting, cf. also Blandine Chavenne and Christiane Guttingen, "La peinture décorative," in ed. Betrand Lemoine, *Paris 1937. Cinquantenaire de l'Exposition internationale des arts et des techniques dans la vie moderne,* exhibition catalog, Institut français d'architecture (Paris: Institut français d'architecture, 1987), 364–91, 369.
6 Cf. Fernand Léger, "Revival of Mural Art," *The Listener* 18, no. 450 (August 25, 1937): 408–09.
7 On the establishment and identification of this format, cf. also Benjamin H.D. Buchloh, "From Fraktura to Factography," in *October* 30 (Fall 1984): 82–119.
8 Also cf. *La Revue de la Famille* (July 1 and 15, 1937): 18–19. A preliminary sketch of Léger's work, the location of which remains unknown, was printed in *L'art et les artistes*, no. 178 (June 1937): 512.
9 Cf. letter from Fernand Léger to Albert Gleizes, March 1, 1937, Centre Pompidou, Bibliothèque Kandinsky Fonds Albert et Juilette Gleizes, Paris.
10 Cf. Jacques Barsac, "The Pavilion of the Ministry of Agriculture," in *Charlotte Perriand and photography: A wide-angle eye*, exhibition catalog, Museum für Gestaltung, Zurich / Musée du Petit Palais Paris / Musée Nicéphore Niépce Chalon-sur-Saône (Milan, 2011), 312–23.
11 For a detailed look at Le Corbusier's suggestions, see Danilo François Udovicki-Selb, "Le Corbusier and the Paris Exhibition of 1937: The Temps Nouveaux Pavilion," *Journal of the Society of Architectural Historians* 56, no. 1 (May 1997): 42–63.
12 Romy Golan, "La Possibilité d'un photomural socialiste," in *Artistes et partis, esthètique et politique*, ed. Maria Stavrinaki, Œuvres et sociétés, Anthologies (Dijon: Presses du réel, 2012), 231–51; 251. Léger used one of François Kollar's photographs as a template.
13 Le Corbusier, *Des canons, des munitions? Merci! Des logis...s.v.p.* (Boulogne-sur-Seine: Éditions de l'Architecture d'aujourd'hui, 1938), 112.
14 For Léger's pursuit of photography, cf. Matthew Affron, "Léger's Modernism: Subjects and Objects," in *Fernand Léger,* ed. David Frankel, exhibition catalog, Museum of Modern Art (New York, 1998), 121–48.
15 Fernand Léger, "Modern Architecture and Color," in *American Abstract Artists* (New York: Ram Press, 1946), 207–14; 213.

Reply to a survey: What would you do if you had to organize the 1937 World's Fair? (1935)
Fernand Léger

How do I see the 37 World's Fair? Suggestions for a plan: design an all-white Paris, that is to say, all the façades scraped and cleaned, using all the unemployed people for this work (to incorporate into the Marquet plan), paid half by the city, half by the owners.

Paris is gray, foreigners say it's dirty, so there is general satisfaction.

Luminous, translucent atmosphere; Greece on the banks of the Seine! Why not?

The psychological effect on crowds of cleanliness and light (to be observed via this new event). The department stores would entrust their windows to artists, who would "sign" them… Change the color of the trams and the buses.

On the other hand, make the exhibition itself polychrome. A yellow square. A red avenue, a blue one. Dominating everything, an Eiffel Tower whose silhouette would have been camouflaged. It is important to change this silhouette, which is nearly fifty years old. As Vogel said to me: "It should have grown after all this time," so naturally a vertical camouflage. It should be made into a popular attraction. It must be eloquent, resounding. Change its color, that is to say make it the new important character in this Exhibition. This is during the day.

For the evening, it will be bathed in light, "it replaces the fireworks."

It announces shows, festivities, multicolored lines run from top to bottom. In the evening our city will help us to create a new wonderland. Instead of illuminating buildings and monuments "via their silhouette," use the streets as a backdrop to a luminous décor completely independent of the outline of the building or the monument, creating luminous lines that run along the streets, rise above them, go right down to the ground while continuing right the way along. Decorative and harmonious lines to invent. For this exhibition, the peddlers must offer us electric ties and luminous cufflinks.

By these means, we will really create a global event, we will add cinematic projections in the sky, on the gables of buildings. I cannot see anything in this plan that is "completely unrealizable." Not more expensive than anything else. We simply have to want to do it, and once again we will have amazed the world. It's about time.

Fernand Léger

Originally published as Fernand Léger, "Réponse à une enquête: que feriez-vous si vous aviez à organiser l'Exposition de 1937 ?," in *VU* (Paris), no. 387 (1935), 1102.

–

REGARDING THE WALL PAINTINGS AT THE 1937 WORLD'S FAIR (1937)
Le Corbusier

The appearance here of the usual type of mural, the one that "decorates," has already been observed. Associated with buildings of doubtful style, it provides a cladding, the effect obtained being in direct proportion to the ingenuity of the decorator.

Of greater significance is the space offered to painters of genuine reputation. They have been allotted walls large enough to hold vast works, providing an opportunity to see if it may already be possible to proffer a judgment in a debate that has only recently come to the fore.

For the bonds between the work of art and the architecture it accompanies must be insoluble; it must be a bond of extreme subtlety, a bond of a mathematical order. To make my point clearer, I might even say that the wavelengths they both emit have to be perfectly in phase, for, if not, atrocious hiatuses may appear–without necessarily any of the parties concerned (architect, painter, or sculptor) being individually at fault.

This state of harmony may be achieved by incorporating a work stumbled across by chance within the architectural oeuvre (interior or exterior) without much forethought. Thus one may come across modern pieces, paintings or sculptures, which illuminate the interior of a home or the outside of a construction wonderfully.

Rather than these fortuitous and happy meetings, here at the Exhibition we have "shotgun weddings" between architects and painters, who are not only unacquainted most of the time, but whose index of sensitivity can be quite different, alien even. Thus, the fact that the viewer often feels let down should come as no surprise.

A parenthesis: let us try to pin down the nature of this viewer. Who is the viewer? The general public? The scholar? The connoisseur? It's a bit of each and it has honestly to be admitted that what the majority seek in painting is just a bit of retinal excitation, a space filler, a little noise or entertainment. The painting Picasso dispatched to the Spanish Pavilion is a classic case: the crowd for the most part stood with their backs to it, with only a handful of visitors stopping before the work and remaining there for any length of time. To tell the truth, this is only to be expected, since there is no earthly reason why the former might enter into communion with the genius of Picasso: that would be far too easy. I'm citing here an extreme case. Contrariwise, and without any shift in the level of quality (that is to say, it's a fine painting), one could see the public lingering before Dufy's immense fresco. Here, there is a game to play: unmask the characters sporting famous names and see what kind of "mug" they have. Thus, even in what is a case of only partial attentiveness, we remain far beneath any genuine motivation for pictorial emotion.

Let us return to the painters with walls to paint, I mean the good painters. I may as well cut to the quick and state baldly that it would be a good idea for forthcoming exhibitions to offer them the opportunity to mount the scaffolding once again, because the novelty of the task assigned them, together with the gigantic leap they had to take from easel painting to wall painting, seemed to catch them unaware.

Another telltale example comes in the form of the splendid painting by Fernand Léger at the Palais de la Découverte: arbitrarily relegated to a corner of the main staircase in that dreadful Grand Palais, it strikes the attitudes of an easel work—that is the very same attitudes taken, for example, by paintings by the same artist in the hall of the Villa La Roche that they have come by chance to occupy in the course of their globe trotting existence. The effect is one of catalysis as well as irradiation. Which proves that, in spite of everything, despite all the arguments expounded for or against so-called mural painting, it remains nonetheless the case that quality alone can open the immense prospects of the mind and of the infinite, in any place it may be found, anywhere.

I'd like to push this paradox even further and confess that I am filled with apprehension when I come across art works in sites dutifully calculated to house them: I'm wary of a sculpture in a metope and a painting in a tympanum; one looks at them too quickly, so quickly in fact that one loses all ability to discover anything new. To my mind, in these circumstances, the director has failed to entrust a sufficient role to the receptive intensity of an authentic viewer.

Recently, an event has occurred with respect to the architecture of the new age that concerns painting deeply: polychromy. A value of noteworthy architectural significance, it has surfaced here and there, more or less successfully, at the World's Fair. We can judge of this by examining a case where it is in point of fact absent: the new rooms at the Palais du Trocadéro devoted to plaster casts. The tedium emanating from all this dull gray lays a pall over all the splendid pieces exhibited. These rooms could be rescued, indeed enhanced, by the skillful provision of polychromy, which, in favorable and strongly diversified conditions, would breathe fresh life into the casts, as well as allowing viewers to enter that state of plenitude that only color can induce. Color is our very lifeblood and bloodless things are depressing to contemplate. Allow me to venture further and state that, to make a house white (I am speaking of the interior here), one should place, in carefully chosen locations, the full range of all the colors of the spectrum. Only in this way will white be white.

This contention led me to halt a while in front of Robert Delaunay's contribution to the decoration of the Palais des Chemins de Fer et de l'Aviation. We stand here before a manifest demonstration (unconscious, perhaps) of the painter: architectural polychromy; it bursts out in the use of acetate film in all the hues of the rainbow, unfurling their scrolls in the aviation hall. Later one meets the painter and his excellent collaborators in enormous murals, all painted with consummate mastery, in which the phenomenon of color is organized by a chromist who understands all the resources in terms of space and lyricism afforded by color. And, by establishing judicious relations between the hues, all this expresses joy, a kind of spring-like explosion, an expansion of space.

If, at the 1937 World's Fair, I have been able to analyze various particular feelings concerning diverse aspects of polychromy and pictorial form, all the same I remain in the deepest perplexity with regard to the problem of how to deploy the mural in architecture.

May my uncertainty be forgiven; it is because I remain loyal to the arguments that rage within me. I believe though that such experiments should be pursued and that success—by which I mean rapture—may be met with whenever a spirit of concord arises between talents of the same nature: this is the only way unity can emerge from among the diverse inventions of architecture and painting.

Text dated December 14, 1937, originally unpublished. Published as Le Corbusier, "À propos des peintures murales à l'exposition 1937," in *1937. Exposition international des arts et des techniques*, exh. cat., Musée national d'art moderne, Centre Pompidou (Paris 1979), 12-13.

–

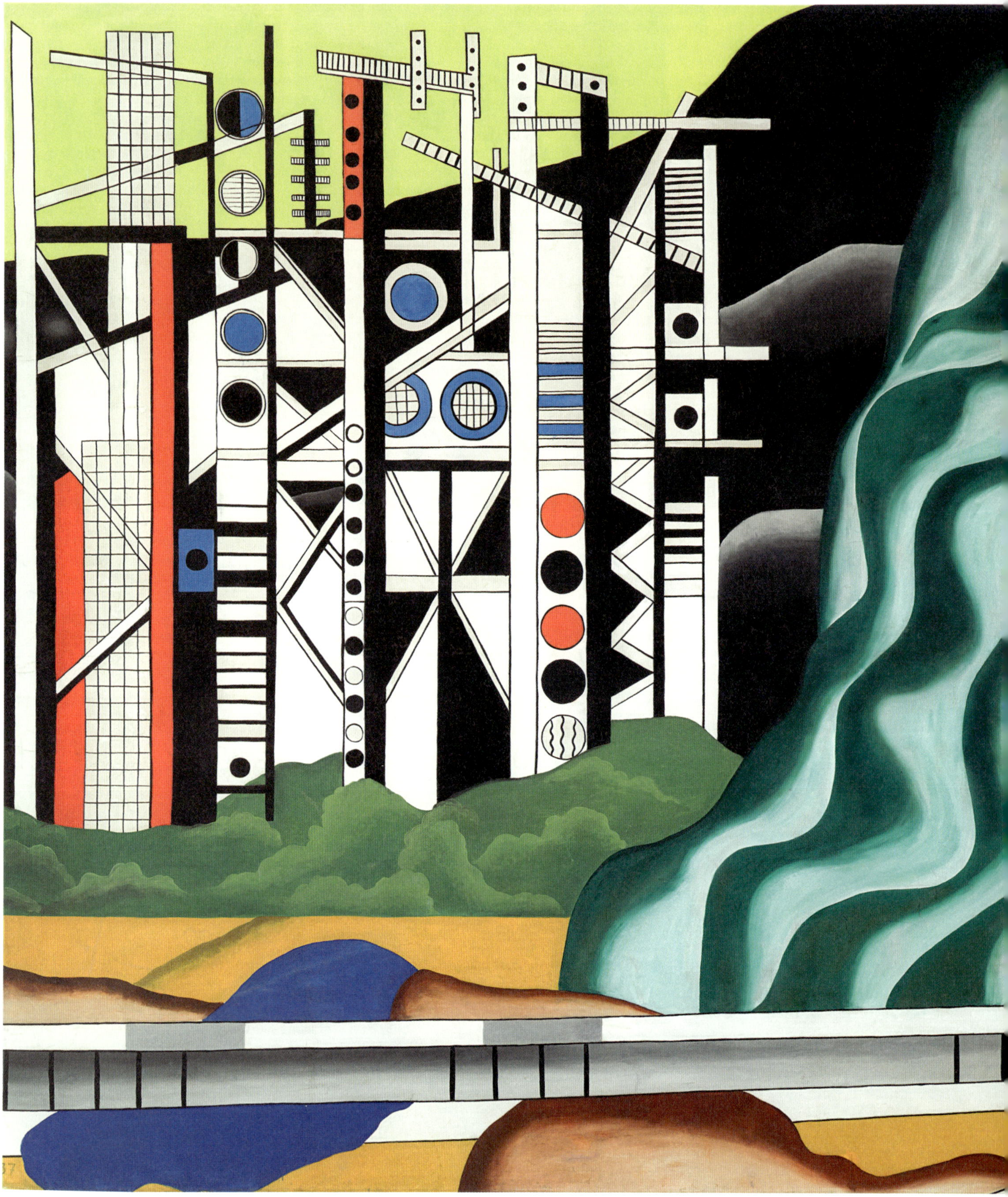

140

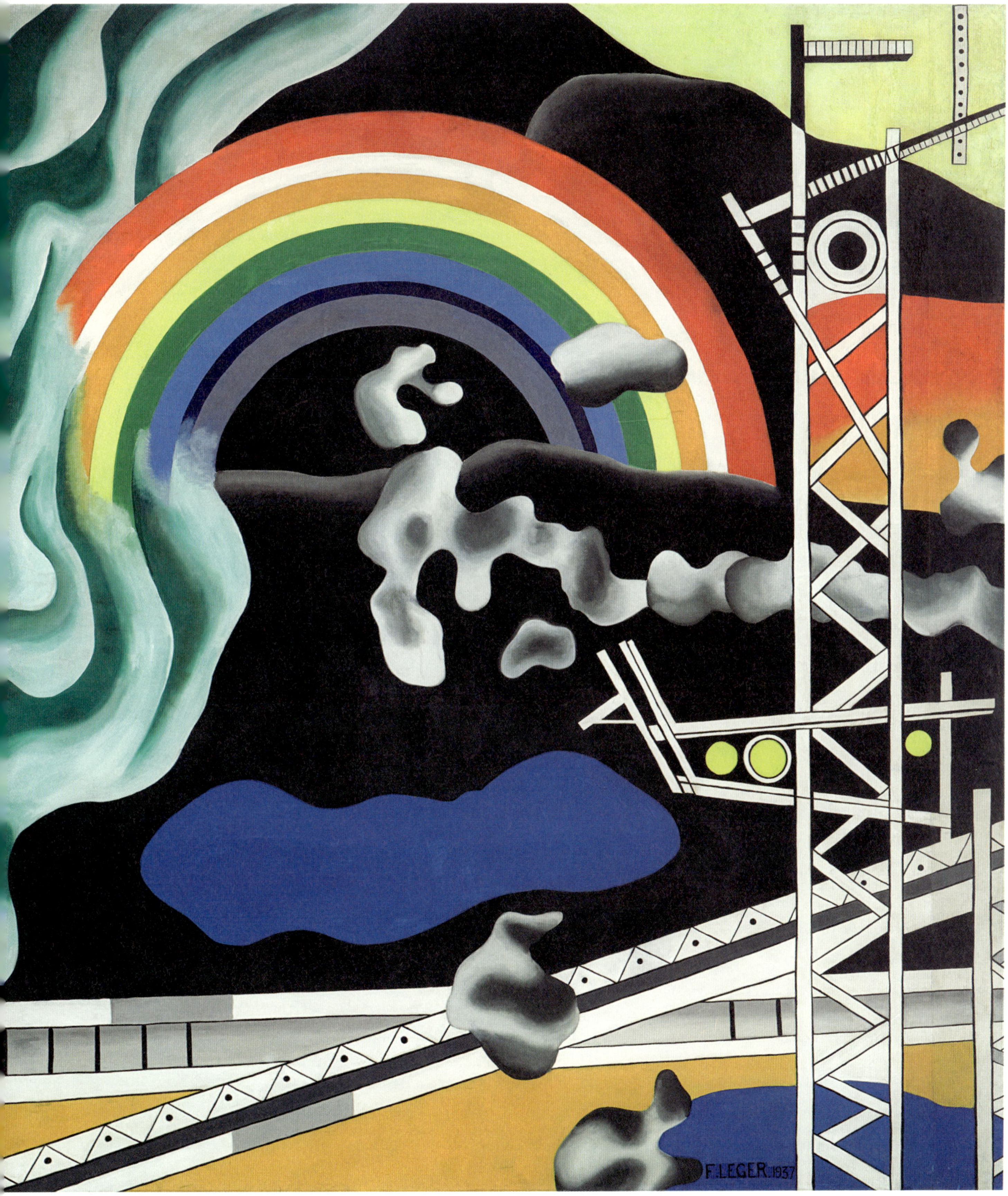
F.LEGER.1937

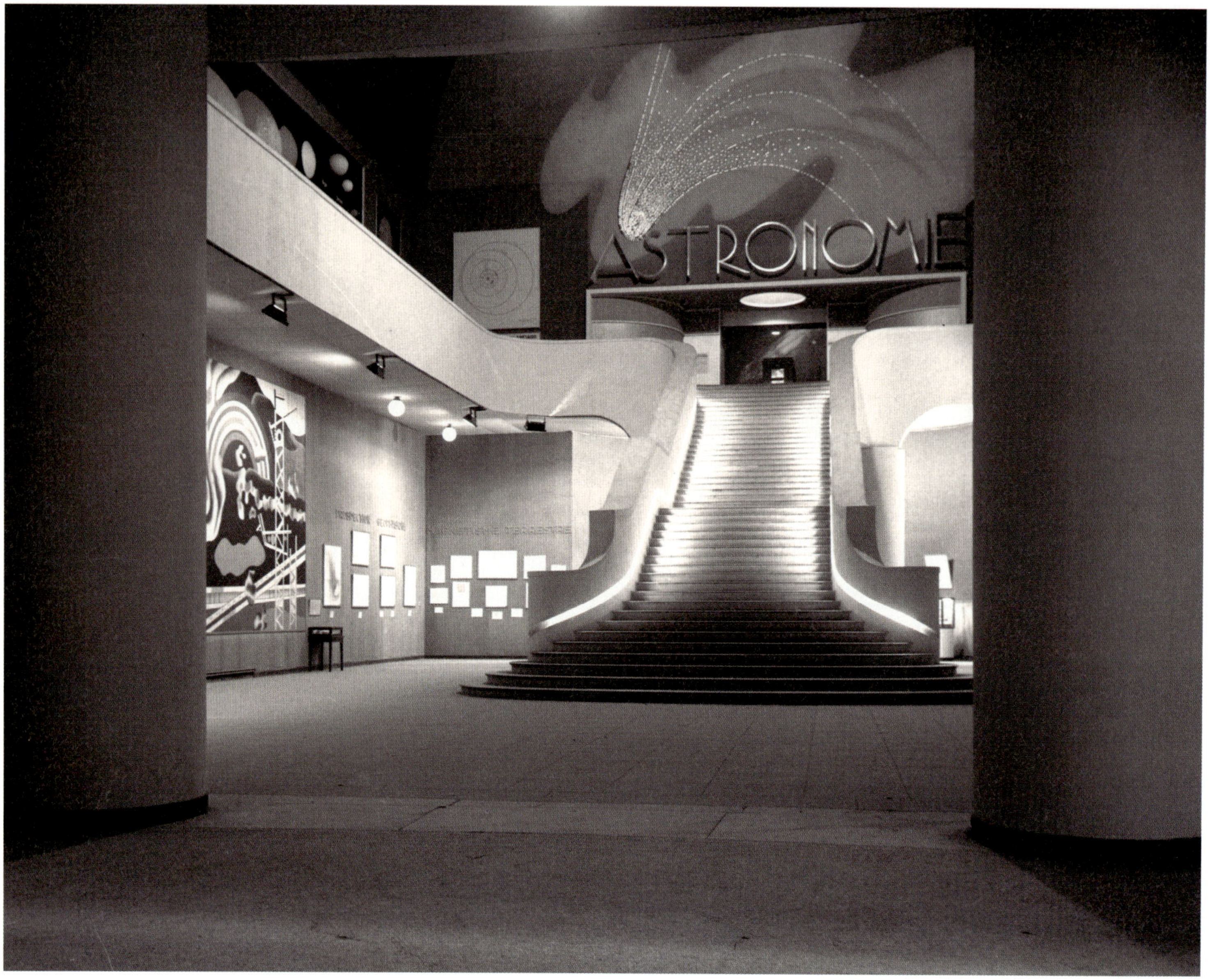

141

140 ***Le Transport des Forces*** **(Transport of Forces), 1937**
Oil on canvas
500 × 1,000 cm
Centre nationale des arts plastiques, Paris, installed in the Palais de la Découverte (Palace of Discovery), Universcience, Paris

The left and right sides of the mural were later cropped.

141 ***Le Transport des Forces*** **(Transport of Forces) by Fernand Léger, shown in the Salle de physique, next to the south side steps leading towards the Astronomy Department in the domed hall of the *Palais de la Découverte* (Palace of Discovery), *Exposition Internationale des Arts et Techniques*, Paris, 1937**

142 ***Le Transport des Forces*** **(Transport of Force), 1937**
Gouache and graphite on paper
50.9 × 100 cm
Musée national Fernand Léger, Biot

Preparatory sketch for the mural of the same name

143 ***Le Transport des Forces*** **in the making.**
Bancroft Library, Berkley

The 5 × 10 m mural was exhibited in the Salle de physique. Léger painted it with three of his students: Elie Grekoff, Pierre Wemaëre and Asger Jorn. Palais de la Découverte (Palace of Discovery), *Exposition Internationale des Arts et Techniques*, Paris, 1937

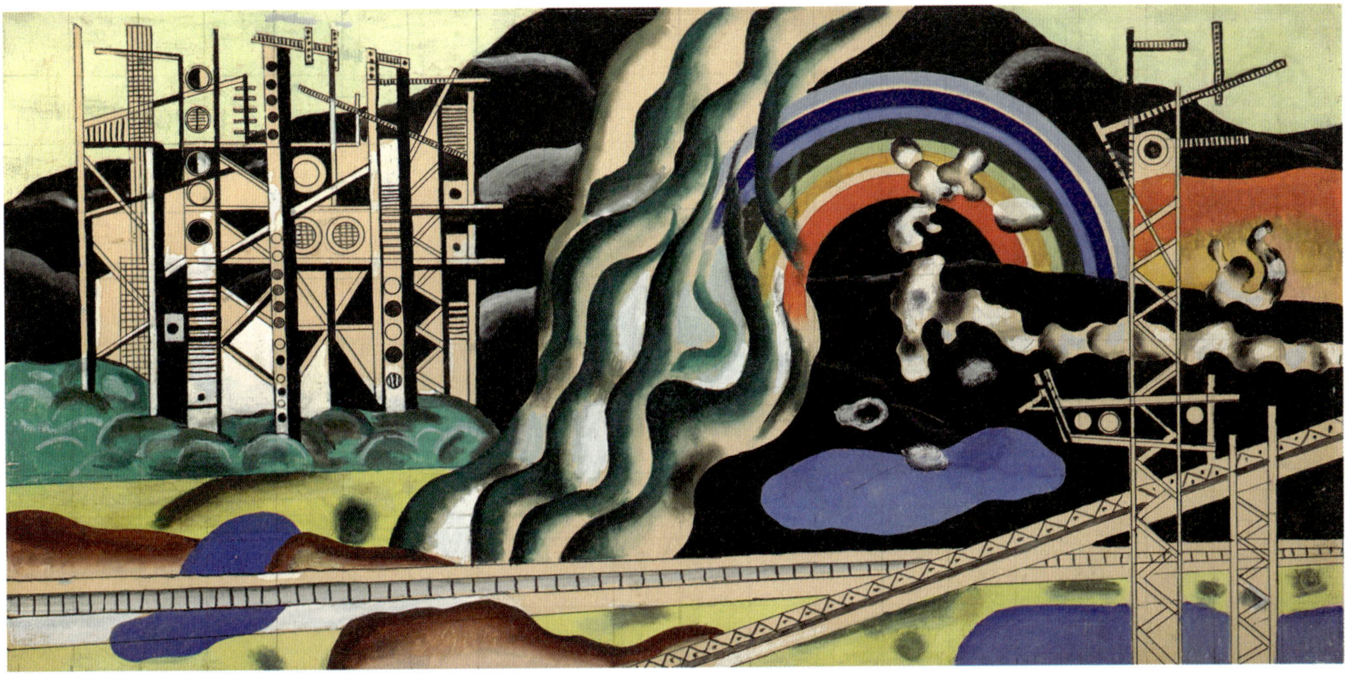

142

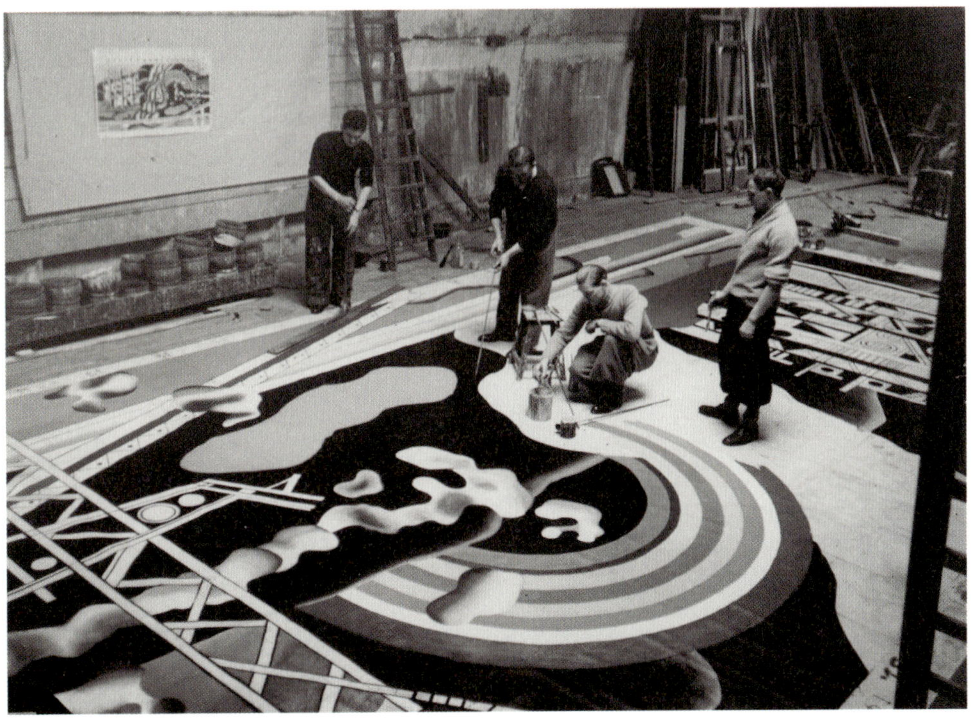

143

Letter from Fernand Léger to Albert Gleizes, March 1, 1937

My Dear Gleizes

The UAM [Union des Artistes Modernes] to which you belong would like to have a decoration for its pavilion at the 1937 exhibition. I have been requested to organize the job. There will be a panel of 23 m. by 6 on average to be covered by 3 painters, [Léopold] Survage, you, and me.

Teamwork, meaning that we need as much as possible to create a whole. Does this interest you?

Unfortunately, it's very urgent.

Could you come to Paris over the next few days?

For such a task, it's obviously indispensable that we meet up.

Send word as soon as possible

Cordially, F. Léger

Centre Pompidou, Bibliothèque Kandinsky, Fonds Albert et Juliette Gleizes, Paris. Letter reprinted in *Fernand Léger*, exh. cat., Centre Pompidou (Paris, 1997), 331.

–

144 **Fernand Léger, Albert Gleizes and Léopold Survage at work on the mural *Accompagnement d'architecture* (Architectural Accompaniment) in the Pavillon de l'Union des Artistes Modernes (UAM Pavilion), 1937**
Architect: Frantz Jourdain
Centre Pompidou, Bibliothèque Kandinsky, Fonds Juliette et Albert Gleizes, Paris

145 Fernand Léger, Albert Gleizes, Léopold Survage
***Composition pour le Pavillon de l'Union des Artistes Modernes* (Composition for the UAM Pavilion), 1937**
Gouache on paper, laminated on cardboard
24 × 119 cm
Solomon R. Guggenheim Museum, New York
Gift, Andrew Powie Fuller and Geraldine Spreckels Fuller Collection, 1999, acc. no. 2009.11

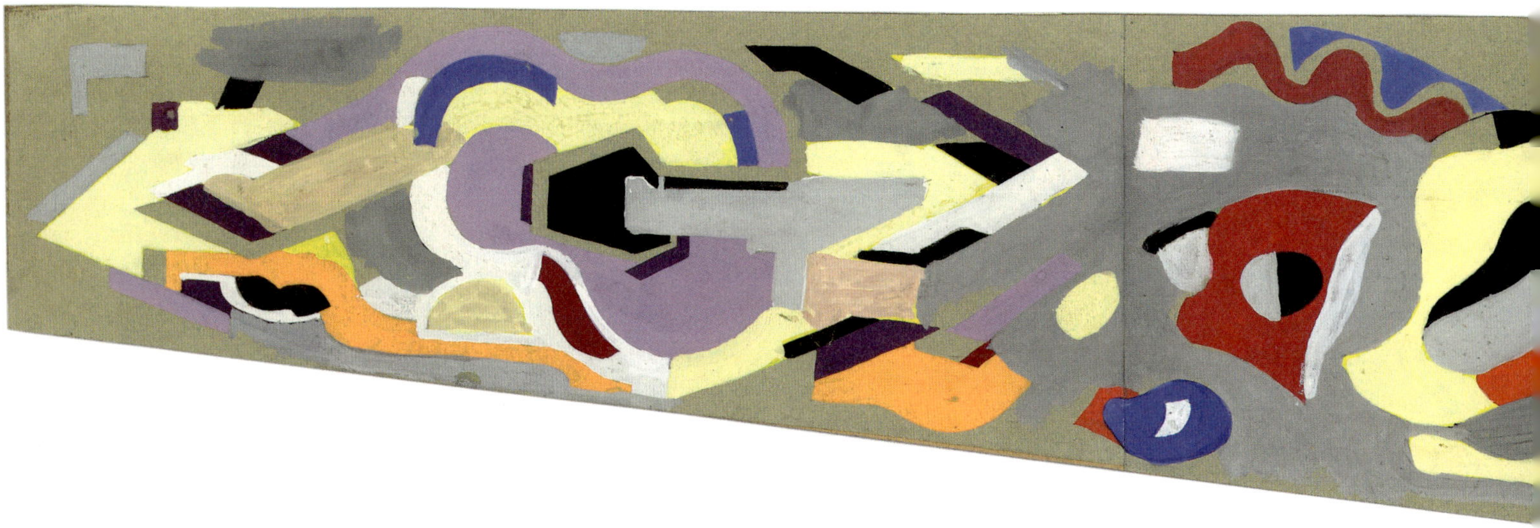

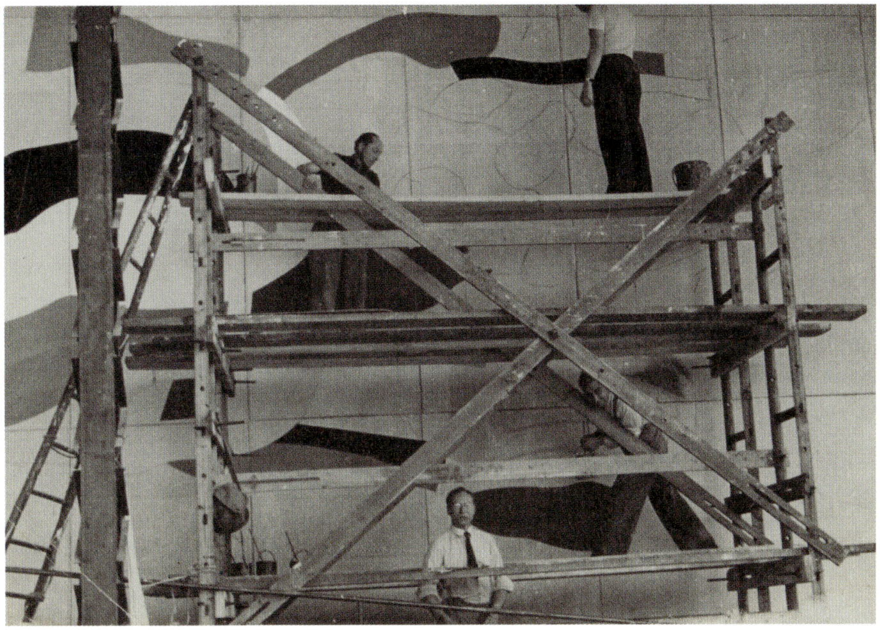

144

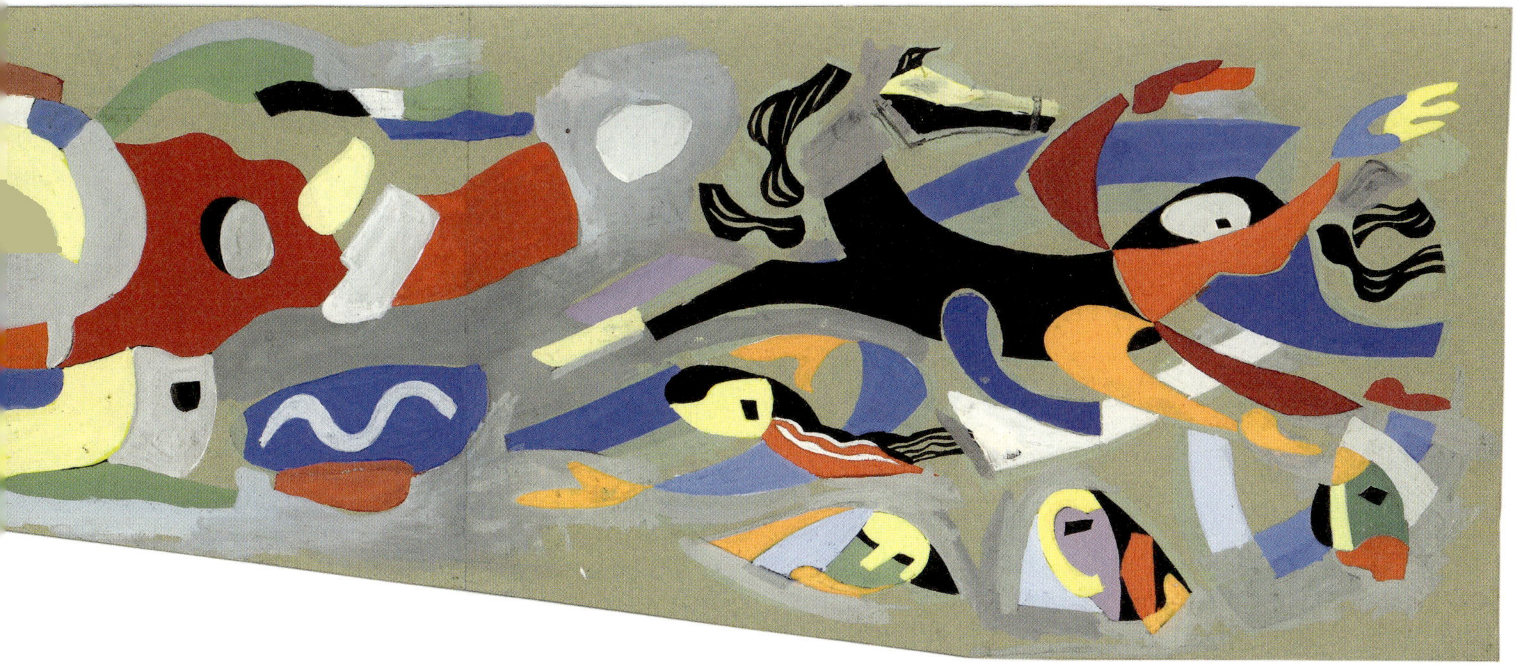

145

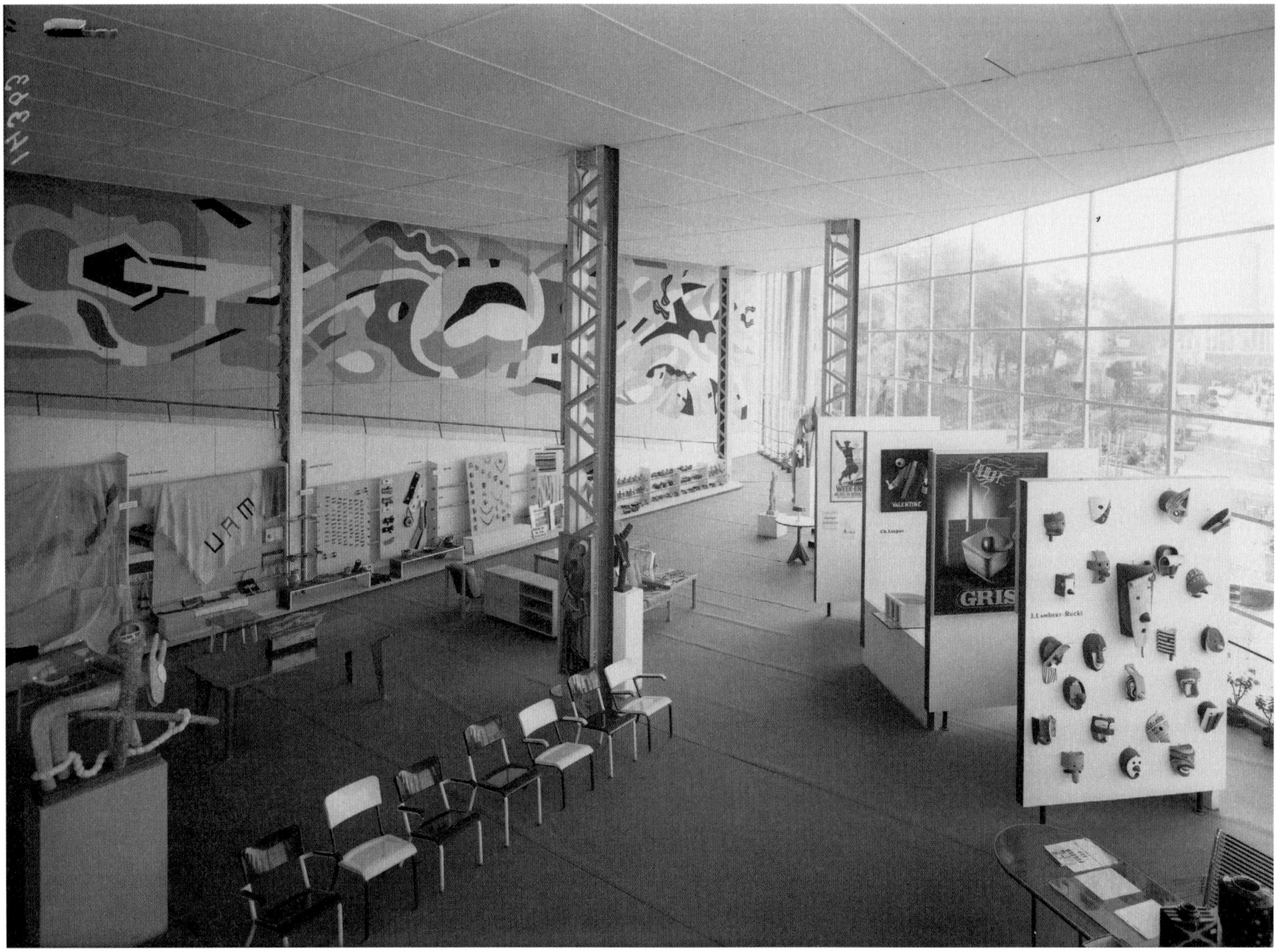

146

146 **Inside of the *Pavillon de l'Union des Artistes modernes* (UAM Pavilion), 1937. Mural *L'Accompagnement d'architecture* (Architectural Accompaniment) by Albert Gleizes, Fernand Léger and Léopold Survage**
Les Arts Décoratifs, Paris

UAM MANIFESTO (1949)
Georges-Henri Pingusson

The "U.A.M." [Union des Artistes Modernes] sprang from a spontaneous gathering of artists who were ranged against the shilly-shallying and contradictions of our time and who were eager to assert the affinities in their approach. These artists felt close to one another in terms of the spirit that animates their work and upon which their hopes were borne–the spirit of the modern age. To define this spirit amounts in fact to defining the goals of the U.A.M.

The art that the U.A.M proposed was an invitation to a particular way of life and addressed itself to the immense mass of men who are waiting for social renewal, for a revival in fellow-feeling, for a less constricted existence enriched by the discoveries of science: this was not to be an art for the few; it was aimed at everyone, it was generalizable for the masses. Reacting against the taste for opulence, for ostentation, for the "plush," it is inspired in its themes by frankness, by simplicity in life, by purity. Promoting substance over appearance, and railing against the ugliness of our public buildings, the wretchedness of our suburbs and our villages, and the bloated impoverishment of official art, it affirmed that life lies elsewhere, and that the art of our time has to start with urbanism so as to trickle down to the humblest of our everyday artifacts; that without urbanism, there is no authentic architecture; and that without architecture there can be no solid substrate to any of our artistic products.

This extended synthesis of all the arts was and remains the chief tenet of the U.A.M. It also stipulates that what is beautiful and good for one man must be so for all, and that artists ought to focus their attentions on mass production, rather than on the rare piece. It states that the gap between the art object and the everyday object must be bridged; that no useless object can be perfectly beautiful, nor any utensil incapable of possessing beauty; that art must become part and parcel of daily life and not remain the preserve of pomp and circumstance; and that it should condition not only form, but also function. The U.A.M. proposed rationalizing domestic appliances so as to lighten the chores of the housewife, organizing our homes with a view to transcending the purely artistic goals adopted at that time: everything was to obey the following dictum: a beautiful tool is an effective tool.

The U.A.M. proposes the rationalization of construction so that it attains an economic scale; standardization, so as to further the uptake of mass manufacture; the utilization of all the possibilities offered by modern science by exploiting as much the richness of natural materials–the honesty of visible woodwork, of polished stones, etc.–as the innovative use of the countless materials industry lavishes upon us (duralumin, stainless steel, plastic materials, synthetic lacquers and textiles, fiberglass, etc.). The U.A.M. wants to put to work in the service of man all the resources, all the means that human progress has placed at the disposal of creators. But serving man does not mean merely fulfilling the basic requirements of his elementary needs in the least arduous and the least onerous way: it must also satisfy his most exalted aspirations. Men are not nourished by bread alone, and the U.A.M., although sometimes critical as to this point, has always eschewed the purely primal approach. Not only does the art of the U.A.M. not exclude sensibility or *esprit de finesse*: it positively demands them. It is through its manner of tackling such rational problems, by the subtle language it adopts addressing mankind, that is, everyone, every day–the language of friendship and understanding–that it seeks to draw in the most secret and the most profound part of each one.

There exist two ways of taking mankind on a journey: the evasion into history and geography, the facile solution of pastiche and exoticism, and the source of so many aberrations; but there is also the investigation of the real in what is the deepest nature of man, the search for the new man that each bears within himself in the expectation of a new age. It is to this more laborious quest–far less rewarding in terms of "success"–that the U.A.M. has devoted itself since its inception, and with which it keeps faith. It is towards this search that it would like to direct the young of our time.

In summary, the U.A.M. stands for a modern, classical art in opposition to all the flowerings of latent false romanticism as it toils for a new humanism whose advent can be foretold everywhere.

Persuaded that it is only in so far as men act creatively, marching resolutely on towards progress, that they truly remain loyal to the past, the U.A.M., in striving for the mission it has chosen for itself, is conscious of obeying the noblest human traditions.

Originally published in *UAM Union des Artistes Modernes* (Paris: Club Mallet-Stevens, 1949). Reprinted in *Les Années UAM 1929-58*, exh. cat., Musée des arts décoratifs, Paris (1988-89), 68-71.
The UAM was founded in 1929 and published its first manifesto in 1934, "Pour l'art moderne, cade de la vie contemporaine."

–

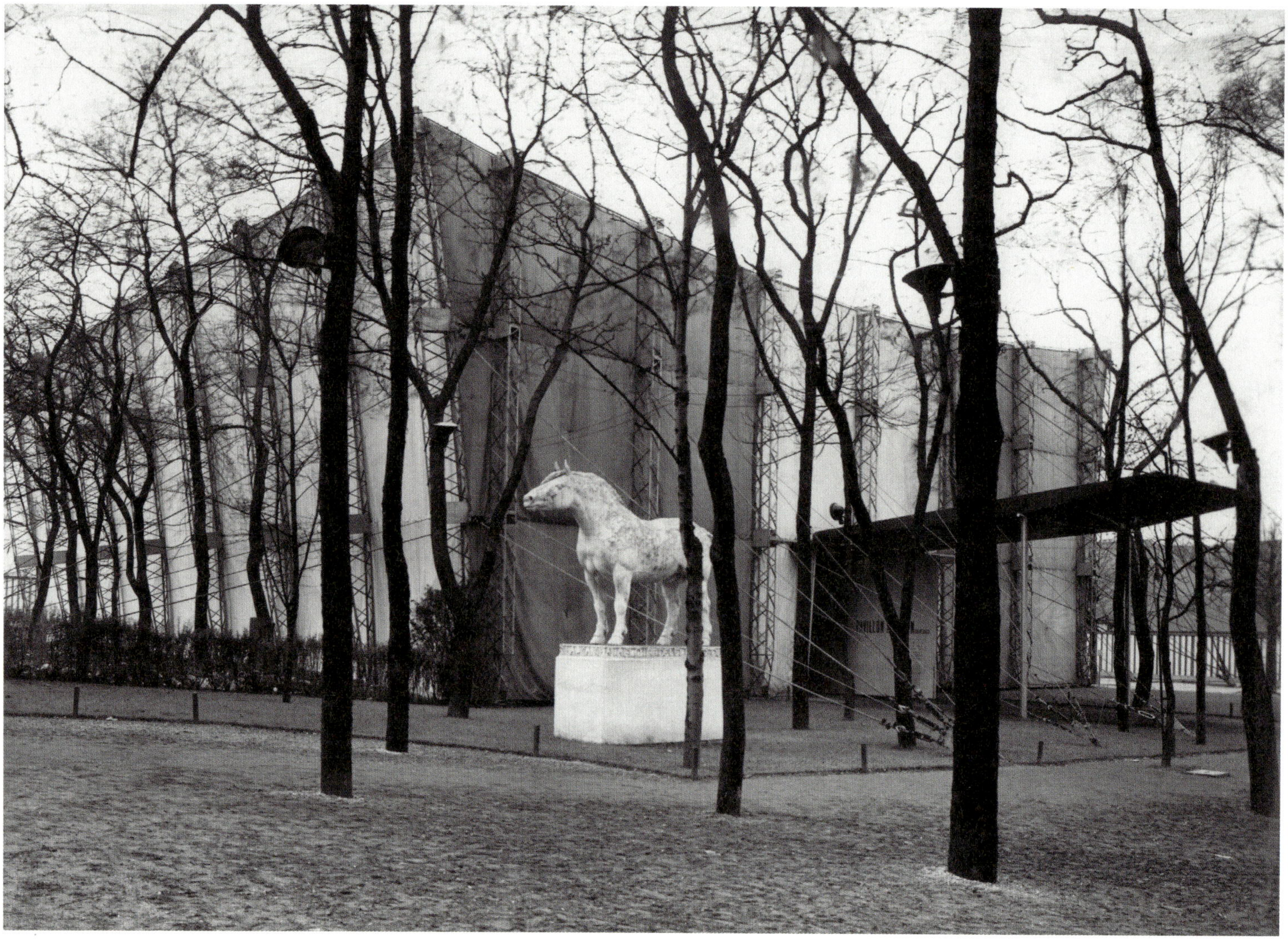

147

148 Le Corbusier, Pierre Jeanneret
***Pavillon des Temps Nouveaux, Perspective intérieure du musée avec indications* (Pavilion of the New Times, Interior Perspective of the Pavilion with Signs), February 6–7, 1936**
Print on paper
34 × 61 cm
Fondation Le Corbusier, Paris

Study for a Musée d'ésthétique contemporaine (Museum for Contemporary Aesthetics, not realized) with a sketch for a monumental painting based on Fernand Léger's painting *Composition with Three Figures* (1932)

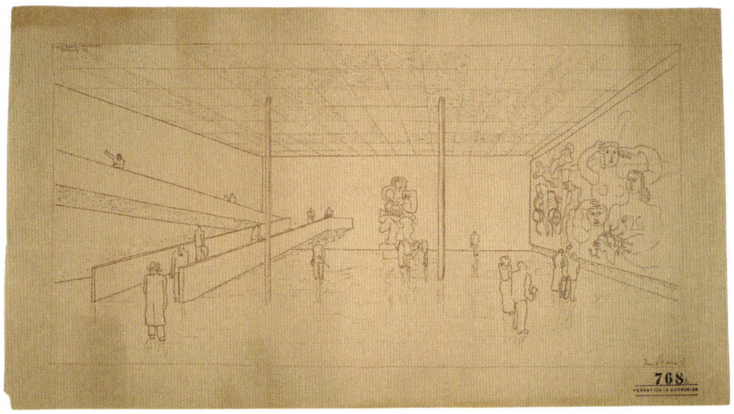

148

147 Le Corbusier, Pierre Jeanneret
***Pavillon des Temps Nouveaux* (Pavilion of the New Times) at the *Exposition Internationale des Arts et Techniques* (International Exhibition of Arts and Techniques), 1937, Pavilion with view of entrance with projecting roof**
Fondation Le Corbusier, Paris

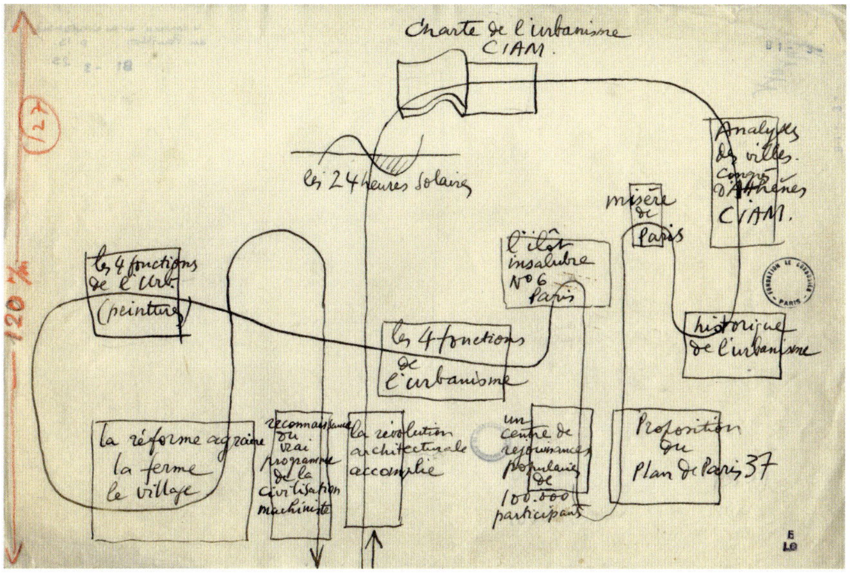

149

149 Le Corbusier
***Plan du Pavillon des Temps Nouveaux, concernant l'ouvrage de Le Corbusier "Des Canons, des munitions. Merci! Des logis... s.v.p."* Plan for the New Times pavilion for the opening, undated**
Black ink and colored pencil on paper
21 × 31 cm
Fondation Le Corbusier, Paris

150 Le Corbusier
***Pavillon des Temps Nouveaux, Perspective du bâtiment avec vue de l'entrée avec auvent* (Pavilion of the New Times, 1937 Perspective from the building with view of entrance with porch roof), undated**
Black pencil, colored ink, China ink on Canson paper, unsigned
72 × 118 cm
Fondation Le Corbusier, Paris

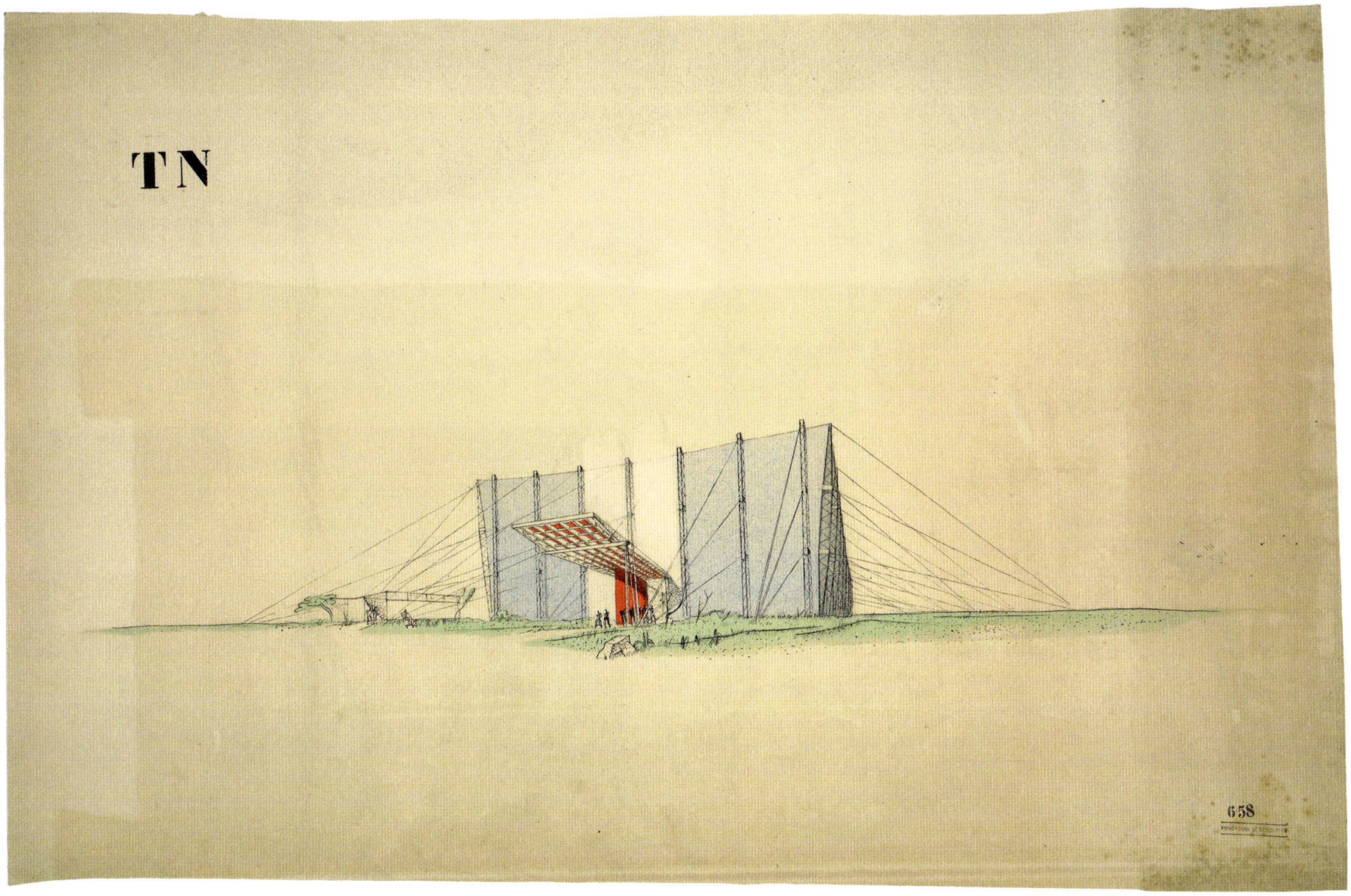

150

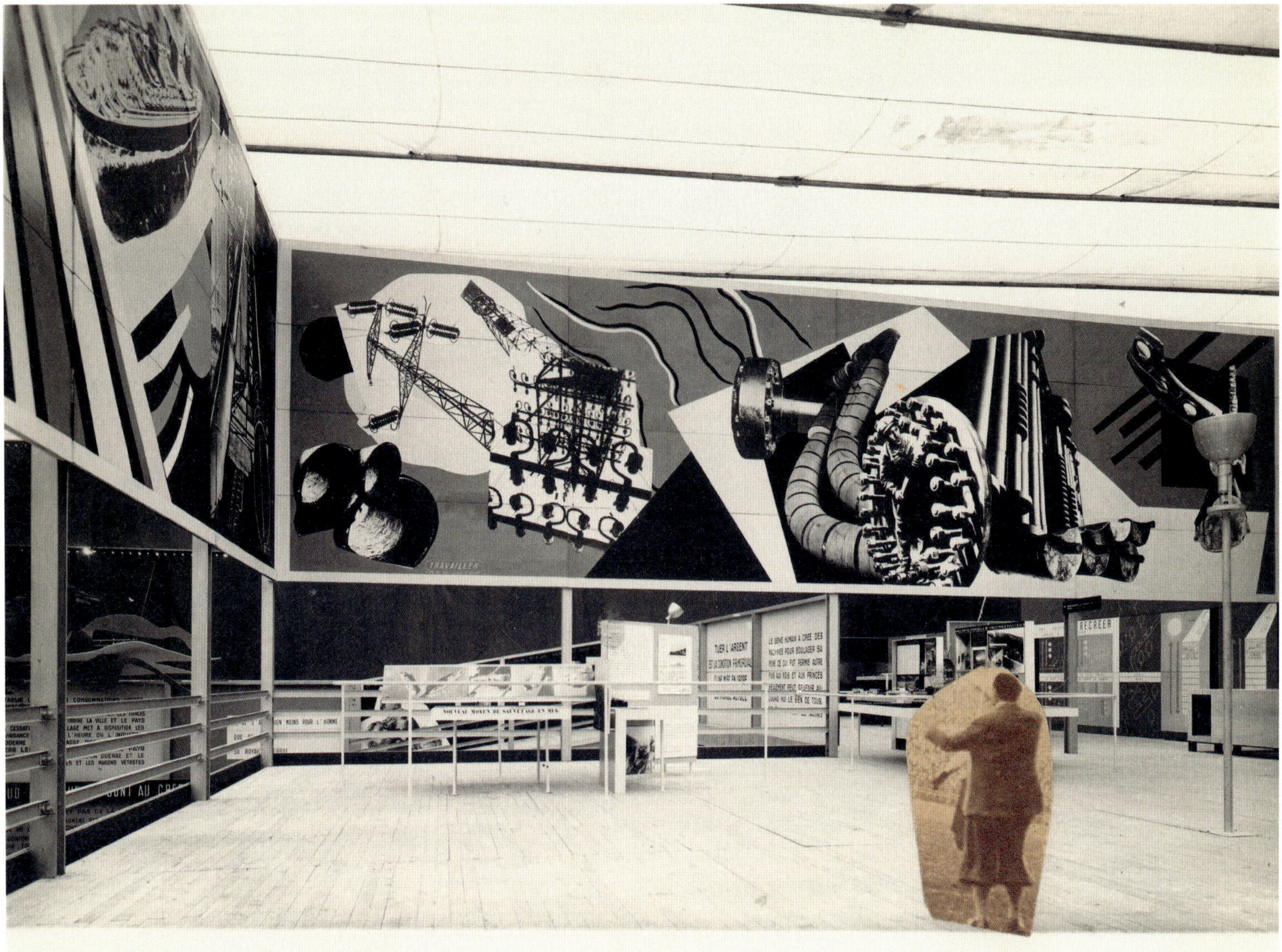

151a

151a-d Le Corbusier
Pavillon des Temps Nouveaux
(Pavilion of the New Times), 1937
Photocollage
18 × 24 cm
Fondation Le Corbusier, Paris

151a exhibition view of Léger's photomural
Travailler (Work)

152 Le Corbusier
***Pavillon des Temps Nouveaux* (Pavilion of the New Times), Paris, 1937. Illustration from *Le Corbusier: Des Canons, des munitions. Merci! Des logis… s.v.p.*, Éditions de l'Architecture d'aujourd'hui, Boulogne-sur-Seine, 1938**
24 × 30 cm
Fondation Le Corbusier, Paris

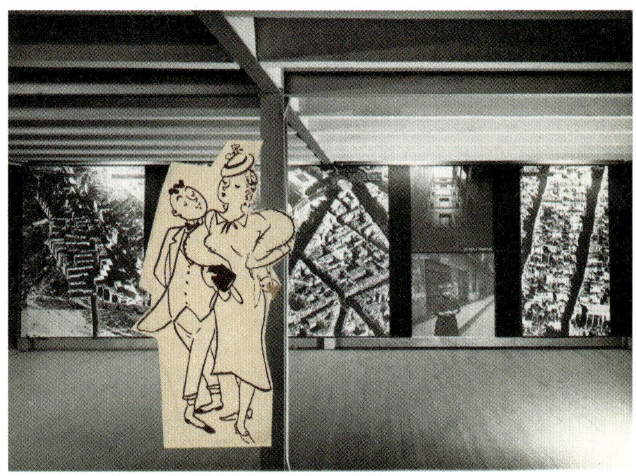

151b

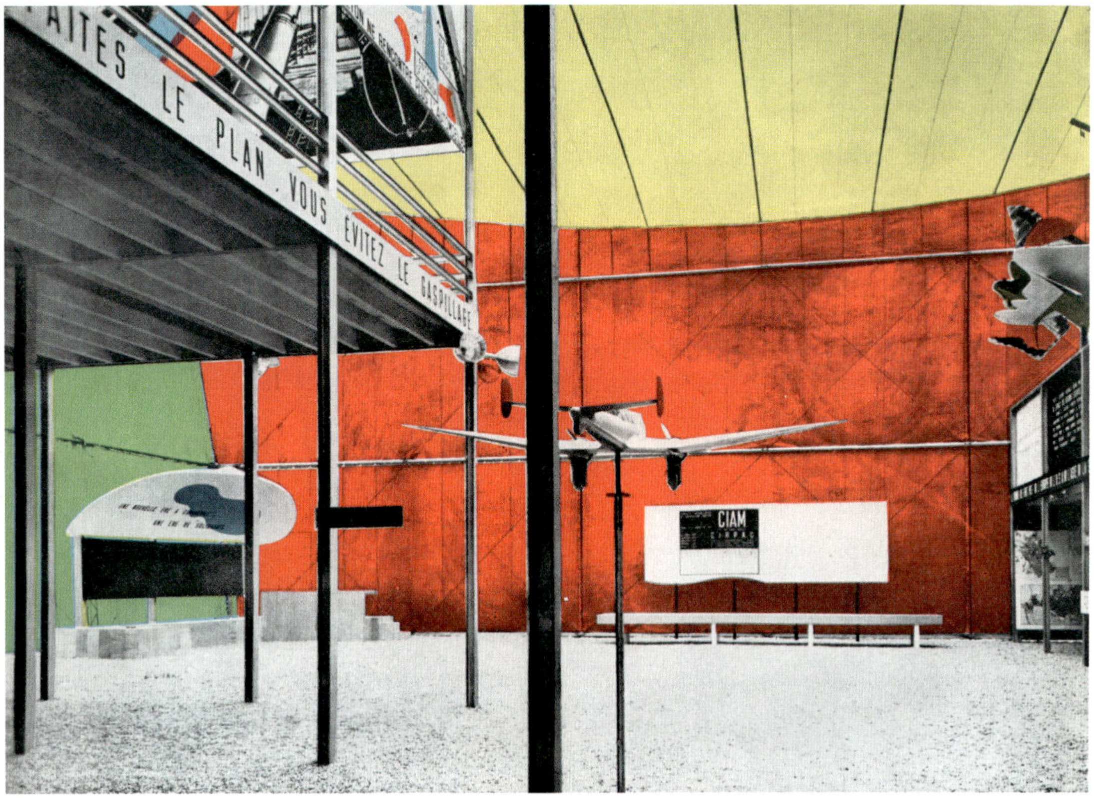

152

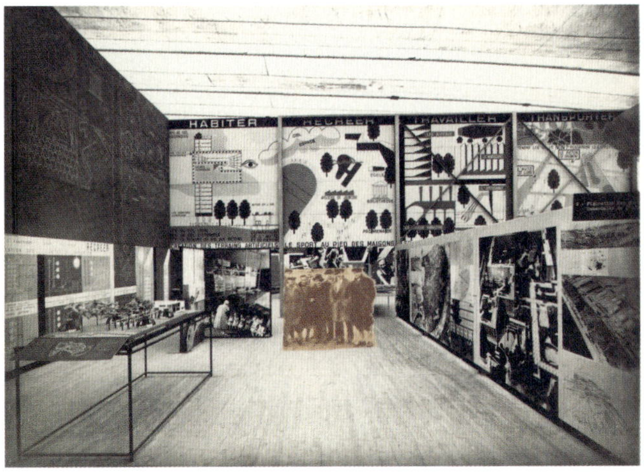

151c

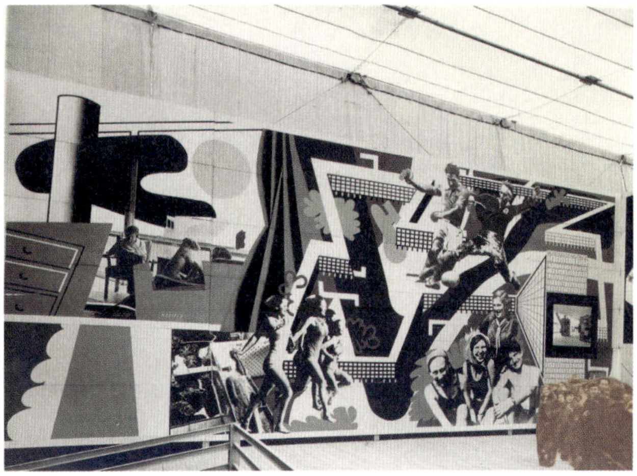

151d

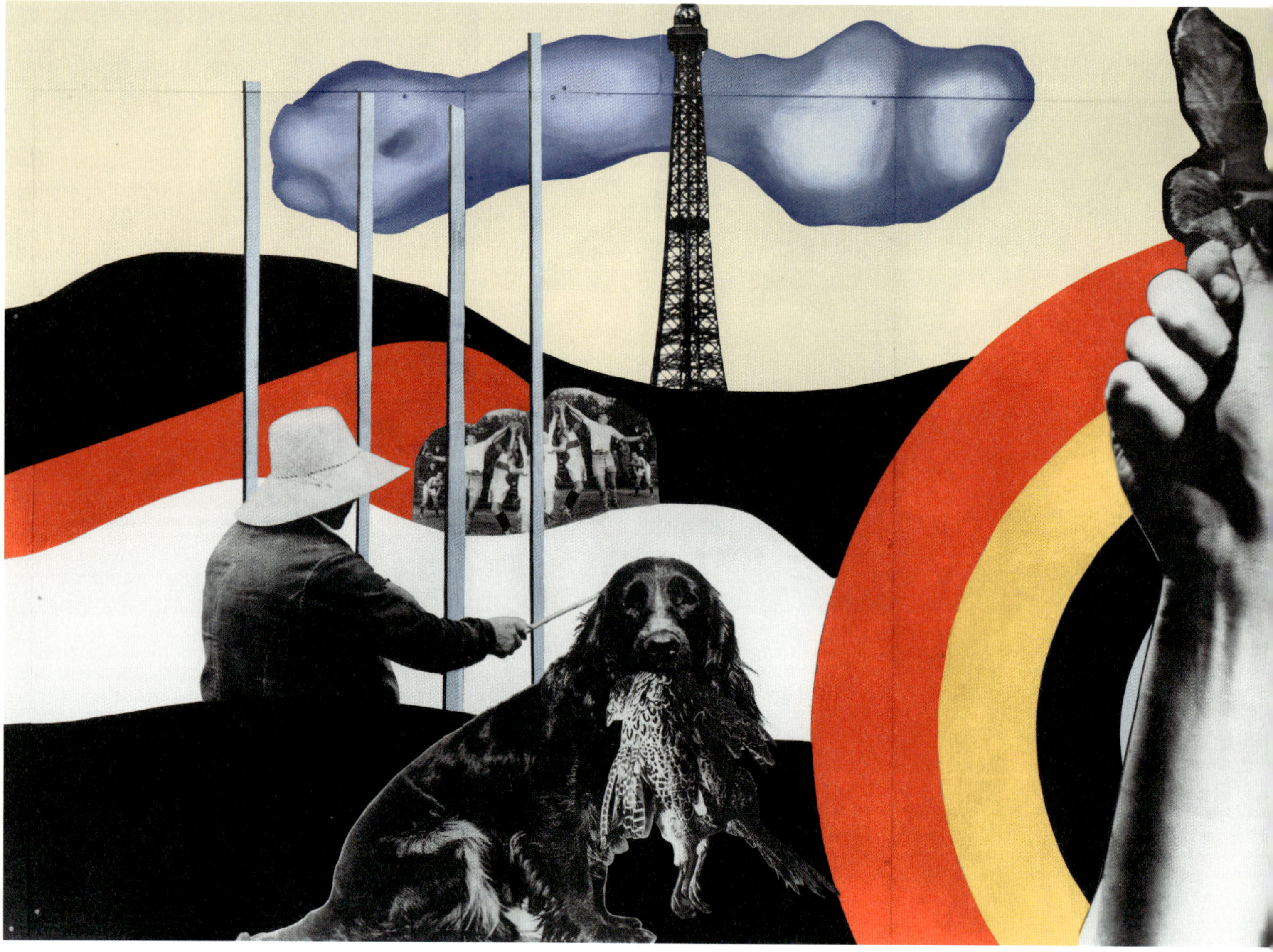

153

153 Fernand Léger, Charlotte Perriand
Joies essentielles, plaisirs nouveaux. Pavillon de l'Agriculture, Paris, Exposition Internationale
(Essential Joys, New Pleasures. Agriculture Pavilion, Paris World's Fair), 1937/2011
Acrylic, collage and print on paper and on board (original color design not known)
350 × 941 cm
Museo Nacional centro de Arte Reina Sofía, Madrid, Donated by Archives Charlotte Perriand-Pernette Perriand Barsac, Paris, 2012

Unique print, reconstruction with photomontage for the Pavilion of Agriculture by Charlotte Perriand at the Paris World's Fair, 1937, color scheme proposed by Jacques Barsac based on paintings dating from the same period by Fernand Léger.

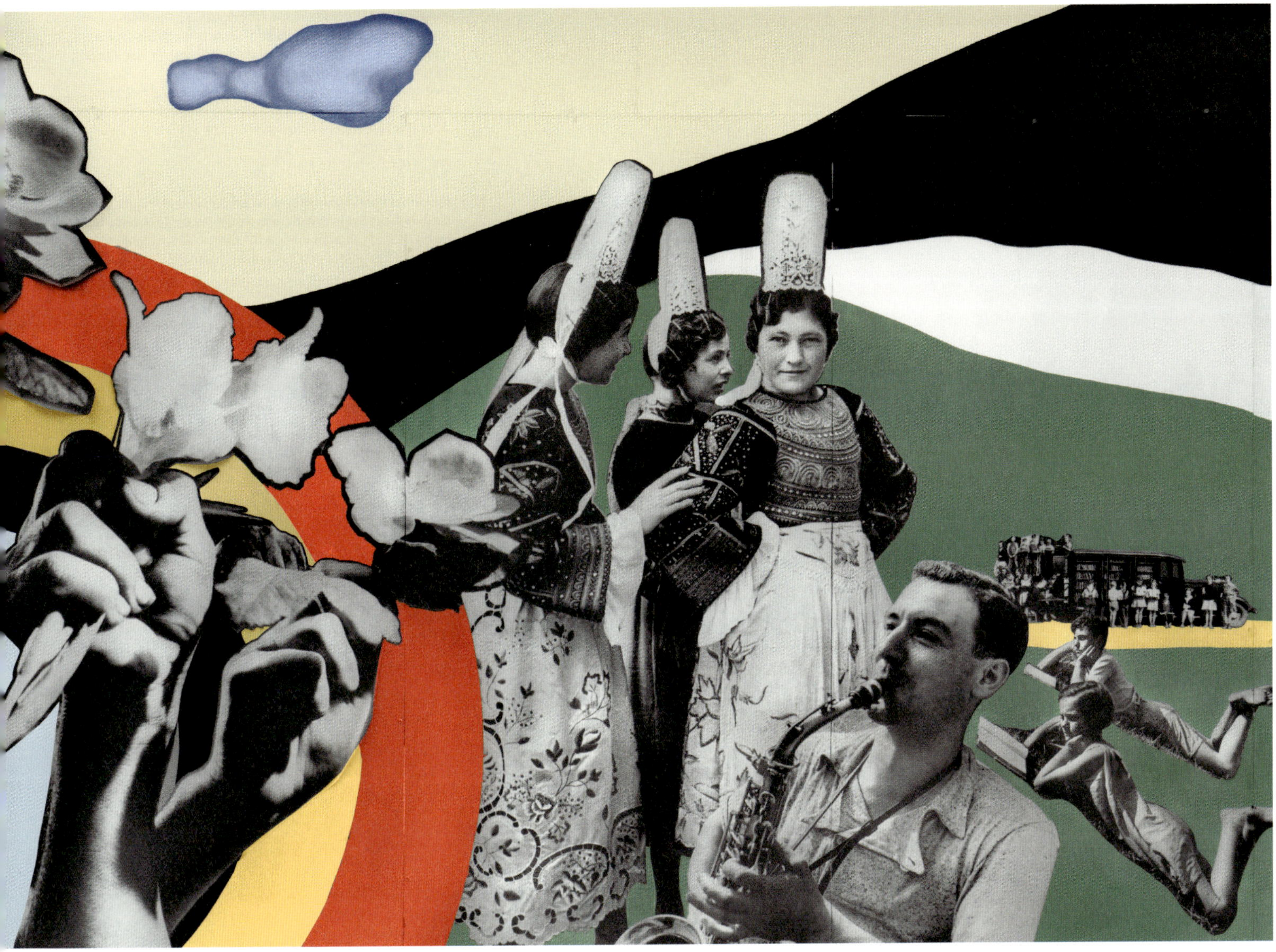

Charlotte Perriand on the Agricultural Pavilion of the 1937 World's Fair

For the 1937 Exposition Internationale des Arts et Techniques, the Ministry of Agriculture had a site at Porte Maillot. Henri Pacon and Gaston Destourbet designed the pavilion, delineating the space's enclosure and entrance with a lightweight, open structure in wooden latticework, which offered soaring views of the leafy trees. The chamfered arrangement was perfect for hanging panels depicting the benefits of Georges Monnet's program, and I was given the task of designing them.

After some thought, I realized that my black-and-white photomontages would not produce the visual effect I was seeking. I was dealing with an open-air structure; to get the message across, I decided my approach would have to be influenced by poster art—it would have to be swift, dramatic, striking, and in color, to catch the eye and capture the mind. I spoke about the project with Fernand Léger, hoping, in fact, to have the pleasure of working with him again.

A workshop was made available to us in the ministry courtyard, and we got down to the job at hand. We worked cheerfully and efficiently, our minds in sync; there was total harmony between us, an absolute degree of friendship that I would never find again.

Léger saw everything and everyone through sharp eyes; he was able to put himself in another's shoes.

[…] We started by defining the program. Then, once again, I went out hunting for relevant statistics, photographs, and slogans. I turned up at the workshop laden with documents, my head awhirl with information. Too much of everything; a sifting process was required. Fernand Léger handled the photos as if they were objects, putting the straightforward texts and graphics into abstract forms. His wonderful trademark use of color and small clouds did the rest.

[…] Léger, my faithful friend, helped me day in and day out. His quick eye was forever finding shortcuts, juggling letters and colors in a ballet of abstract forms that acted as a foil for the realism of the photographs. Our task was a joy, a celebration, an act of gratitude toward France's country dwellers, who then made up some 50 percent of the population.

Excerpts from Charlotte Perriand, *A Life of Creation* (New York: The Monacelli Press, 2003), 84-86 (originally published as *Une vie de création*, Paris, 1998).

–

154 ***Pavillon de l'Agriculture* (Agriculture Pavilion), Exposition Internationale des Arts et Techniques, Paris, 1937, painted photomontages by Fernand Léger and Charlotte Perriand.**
Left panel: *La France agricole* (Agricultural France), right panel: *La France industrielle* (Industrial France).
Architects: Henri Pacon and André Masson-Detourbet
Archives Charlotte Perriand

155 ***Pavillon de l'Agriculture* (Agriculture Pavilion), Exposition Internationale des Arts et Techniques, Paris, 1937,** inside view with the photomontage *Joies essentielles, plaisirs nouveaux* (Essential Joys, New Pleasures) in the center
Archives Charlotte Perriand

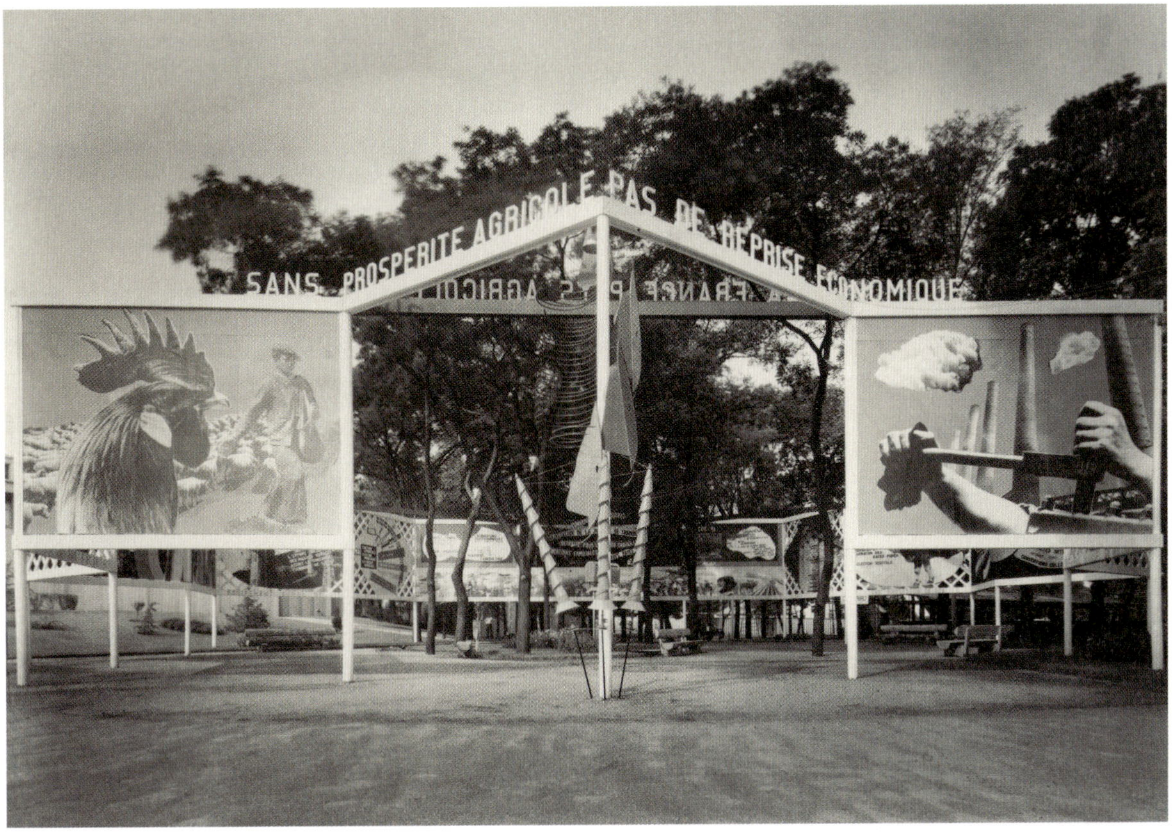
SANS PROSPERITE AGRICOLE PAS DE REPRISE ECONOMIQUE

154

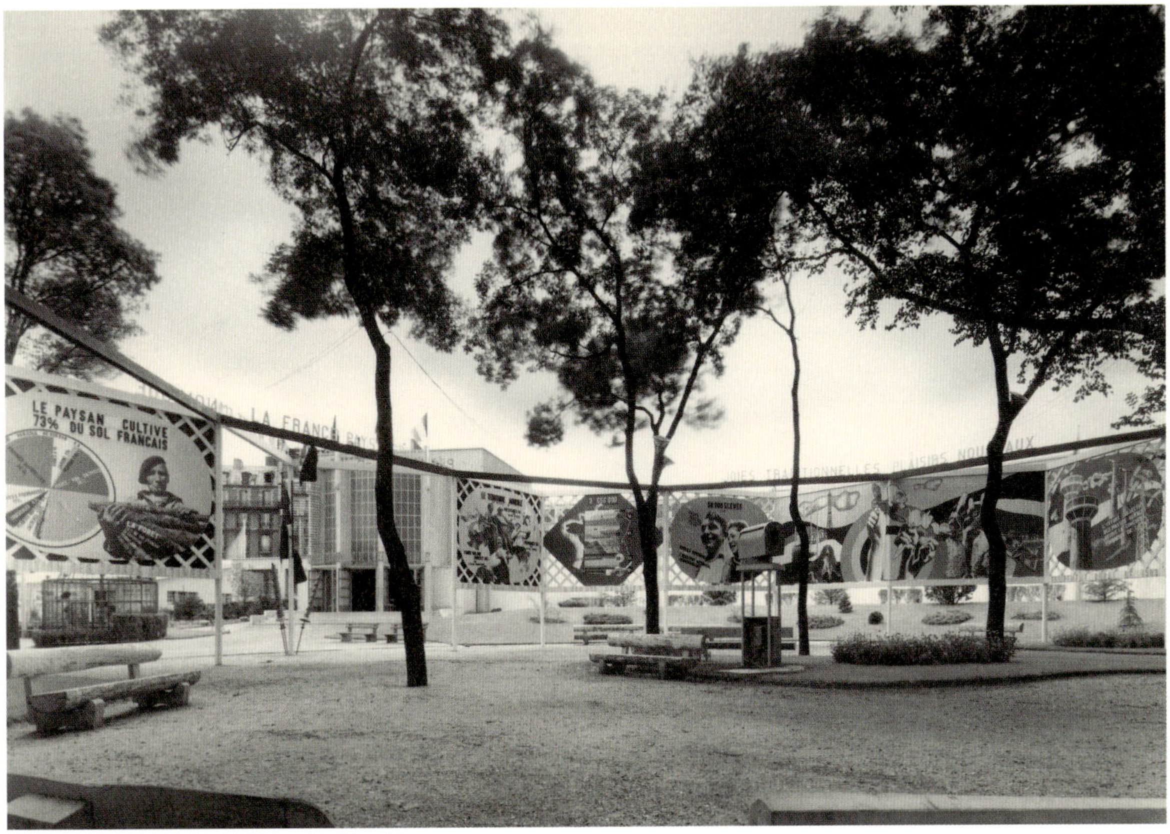
LE PAYSAN CULTIVE
73% DU SOL FRANCAIS

155

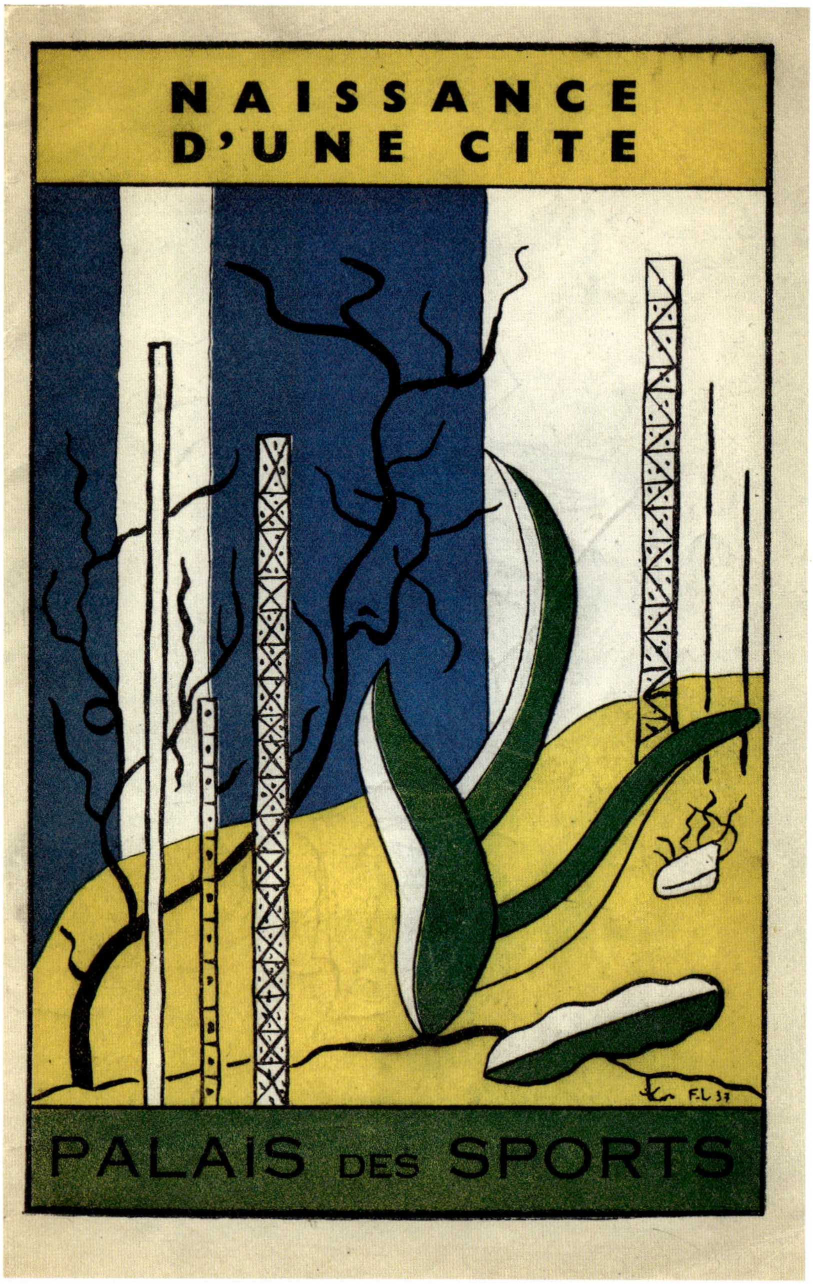

156

156 **Program for *Naissance d'une cité* (Birth of a City), 1937**
(cover designed by Fernand Léger)
Archives Charlotte Perriand

157-158 ***Naissance d'une cité* (Birth of a City) performed in the Vélodrome d'hiver (Palais des sports), Paris, October 1937,** Costume and set design: Fernand Léger; Text: Jean-Richard Bloch; Music: Darius Milhaud und Arthur Honegger

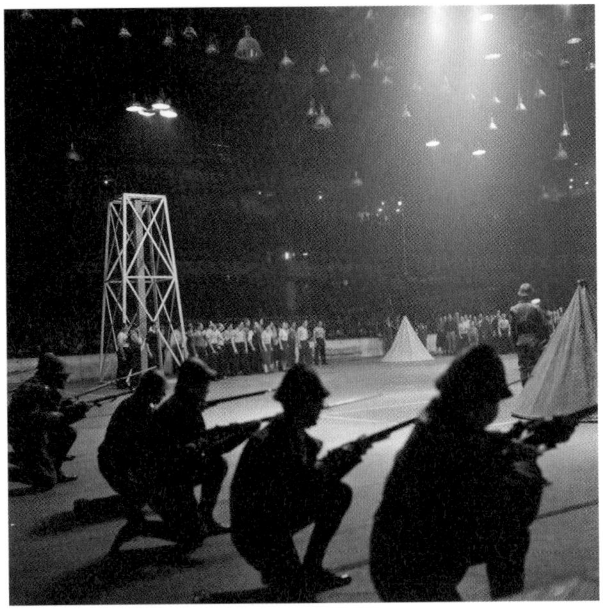

157

Fernand Léger on *Naissance d'une cité* (1937)

Caught between the loudspeakers and the footlights, the set will attempt to "situate" the important passages in the social drama by means of the rapid and mobile apparition of evocative "objects."

The bedroom, bar, subway, ship, etc., will successively appear and disappear in accordance with the requirements of the production.

The purpose of the set is to **enhance** this "birth" at certain selected moments and only where strictly necessary.

The dark blue jackets of the workmen, which are the "**sign**" of work, will be followed by the sudden blossoming of multicolored cardigans, "**signs**" of joy, celebration, and liberation.

Originally published in the playbill of *Naissance d'une cité* (Paris 1937), no page number.

–

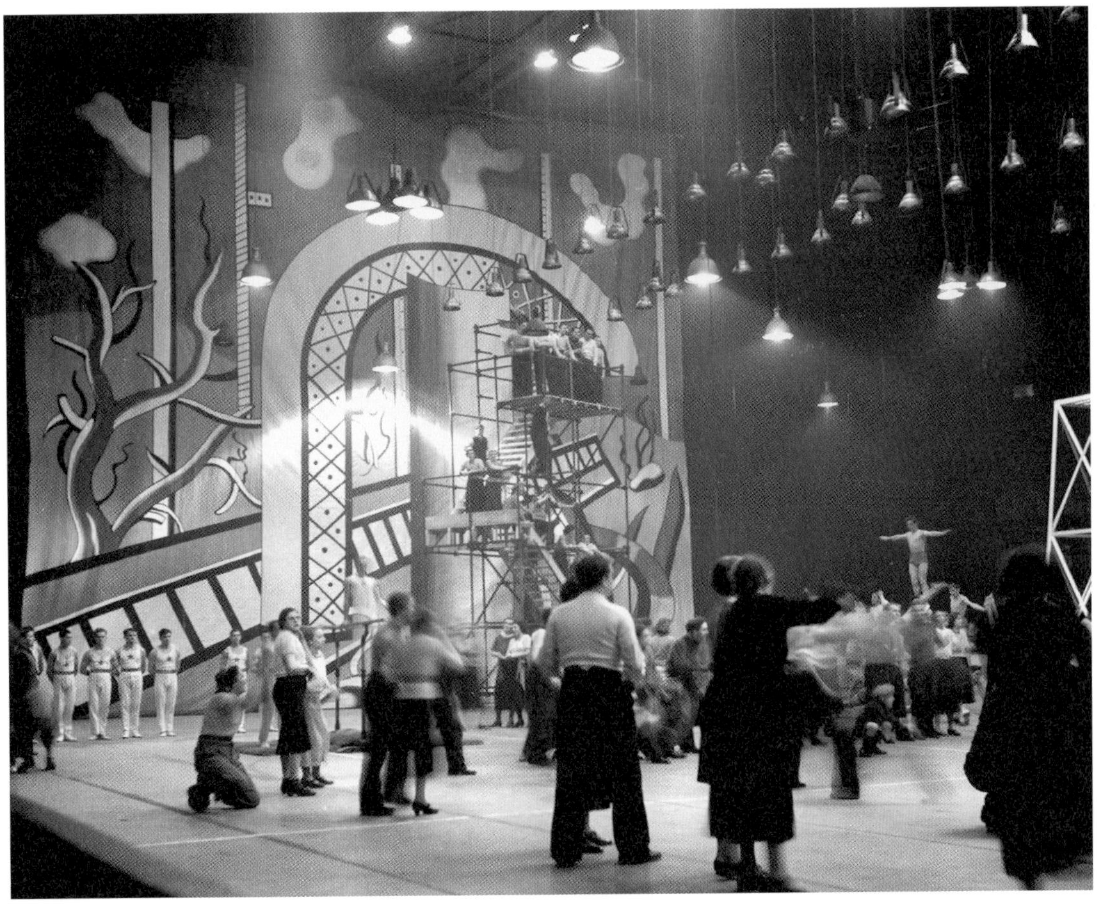

158

The Triumph of Forces: Fernand Léger and the Popular Front
By Sarah Wilson

"New York – Moscow, Moscow – New York.
Paris as spectator." Fernand Léger, 1931[1]

France's Popular Front movement experienced a euphoric moment when, in May 1936, left-wing political parties came to power for the first time in the history of the Third Republic. Their reforms had a huge impact upon the lives of the poorest—notably a forty-hour working week and two weeks' paid holiday a year. Though the Popular Front was short-lived, compromised by the fear generated by nation-wide strikes and the refusal of fraternal support for the Republicans in the Spanish Civil War, it nevertheless left a mythical imprint on the nation's psyche prior to World War II. Léger's portable mural painting *Le Transport des Forces* (Transport of Forces) (fig. 140) of 1937 belongs to this period. For Fernand Léger, too, the Popular Front was mythical. He would become the people's painter, a veritable David of the hoped-for proletarian revolution, and Popular Front iconography would dominate his late career when he returned to France from America in 1945.

Léger's 1931 pronouncement about the New York-Moscow dynamic, sidelining Paris, is astonishingly prescient of later twentieth-century tensions and the future Cold War. New York symbolized global capitalism—albeit a capitalism fragilized by the Wall Street crash of 1929 and the world economic crisis: Léger's first trip extended from September to December 1931.[2] In the USSR, Stalin, already Tsar-like, reigned in Moscow over a powerful post-revolutionary landmass of federated republics with a growing infrastructure. At the great Exposition internationale des Arts décoratifs et industriels modernes of 1925, France attracted millions of visitors to its luxurious capital, secure once again in its position as intellectual and artistic world center. Here, Léger's close friend, the poet Mayakovsky's Rosta posters and Alexandr Rodchenko's photomontages were exhibited in the Grand Palais, while all marveled at the Constructivist-style pavilion by Konstantin Melnikov. Léger's friend, Le Corbusier, won the Tsentrosoyuz building commission in Moscow: he was therefore familiar with accounts of the Revolution and its miraculous architectural aftermath.[3]

From the 1920s, Léger also collaborated with Americans, beginning with Dudley Murphy on *Ballet mécanique* in 1923 (fig. 22). We recall the well-known glimpses of a woman on a swing, the smile of Kiki de Montparnasse, the laboring laundrywoman climbing up a flight of steps, the cacophony of turning wheels, pistons, and geometric shapes.... Not only was Murphy involved, but so was Man Ray, and the poet Ezra Pound, acting as patron, suggested both Léger's participation and help from Natalie Barney. Pound chose the composer Georges Antheil, who introduced airplane propellers into his score, which he imitated with huge fans... [4] *Ballet mécanique* also influenced the Soviet filmmaker Sergei Eisenstein.[5] It demonstrated not only Léger's familiarity with American society in Paris, but offered a syncopated Jazz Age response to contemporary mechanization.

To look beyond the "machine aesthetic," however, to factory workers; to give voice and representation to the toiling masses; indeed, to bring a Marxist analysis of capitalism into the equation, was precisely the "turn" in aesthetics represented by the Popular Front. Thousands of Russian émigrés went to Paris after the Revolution—and into the film and car industries in the Billancourt suburbs. The explosion of demand for cars before World War I preceded the Renault factory's pioneering of American, Fordist principles to cope with the demand for military material, with which Léger, a veteran of the Verdun battlefield, was all too familiar. The photographer Robert Doisneau showed not only the glamour of Renault's cars (one was delivered to Mayakovsky in Moscow in 1929) and the gleaming repetition of the assembly-line process, piles of hubs or fan blades, but also the harrowing toil of workers of both sexes, uniformly dressed and plied to their work in rows: capitalism at its most alienating.[6]

As early as 1930, Léger turned away, at times, from bright abstractions to proletarian subjects. His *Trois musiciens* (Three Musicians) depict a hatted trio of cellist, trombonist, and accordion player, no doubt at a *bal populaire* (people's dancing hall). While Picasso's humanist work would always resonate with the past, Léger's affinity for popular culture and its argot was always contemporary: Charlie Chaplin and film rather than masters from Goya to Steinlen. What art was appropriate for the factory worker? For the insignificant pen-pushing clerk? Could mural painting provide the answer?

Visiting New York and Chicago in 1931, he discovered the vastness of the United States and the ambitions of mural painting. He viewed murals (which included a huge Lenin leading the Marxist Revolution) created by José Clemente Orozco for the public dining room and student lounge in Joseph Urban's radically modern New School for Social Research . Thomas Hart Benton's ten panels, *America Today*, for the school's boardroom and classroom, decorated with aluminum-leaf moldings by Urban, have since been restored and are now displayed at the Metropolitan Museum of Art in New York. It is recorded that in October 1931 Léger was working on mural project ideas himself, for the new River Club in New York.[7]

By the time of his second trip to America, the Works Progress Administration (WPA) Federal Art Project was well under way. Léger discussed mural commissions with art historian Meyer Shapiro and planned a mural for the pier of the French Line Shipping Company in New York Harbor as a group leader for a team including the young Willem de Kooning, but this project failed (fig. 165). He was keener on the Williamsburg Housing Project proposal and corresponded about this when back in Paris after his exhibitions at the Museum of Modern Art and the Art Institute of Chicago. Indeed from October

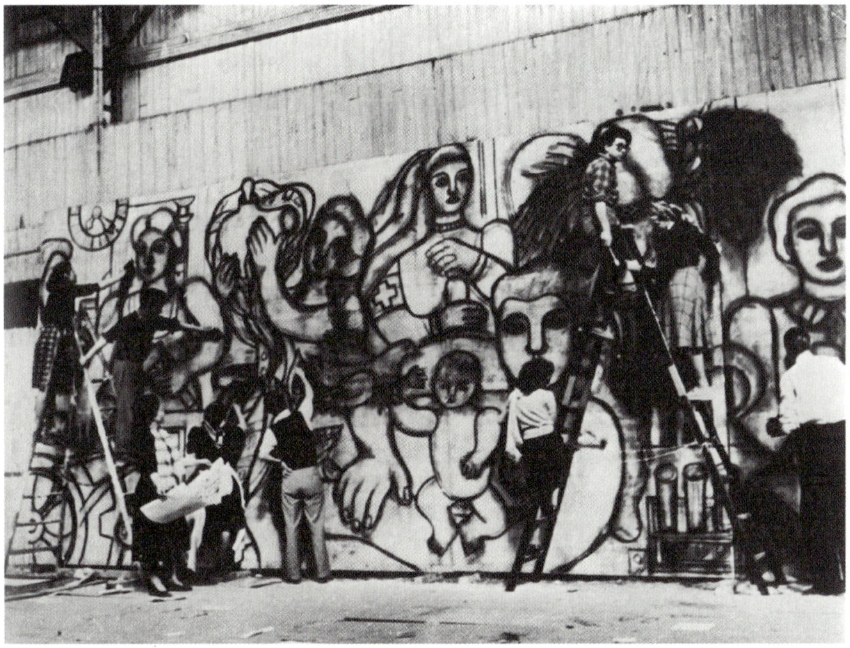

159

159 **Fernand Léger with his students completing *Les Femmes au conseil* (Women on the Board) for the Women's Congress at Porte de Versailles, Paris, 1948**

160 Nadia Khodossievitch-Léger
***Autoportrait* (Self-Portrait), 1936**
Oil on canvas
73 × 92 cm
Private collection

161 Fernand Léger,
***Maud Dale*, 1935**
Oil on canvas
100.4 × 79.7 cm
National Gallery of Art, Washington, DC

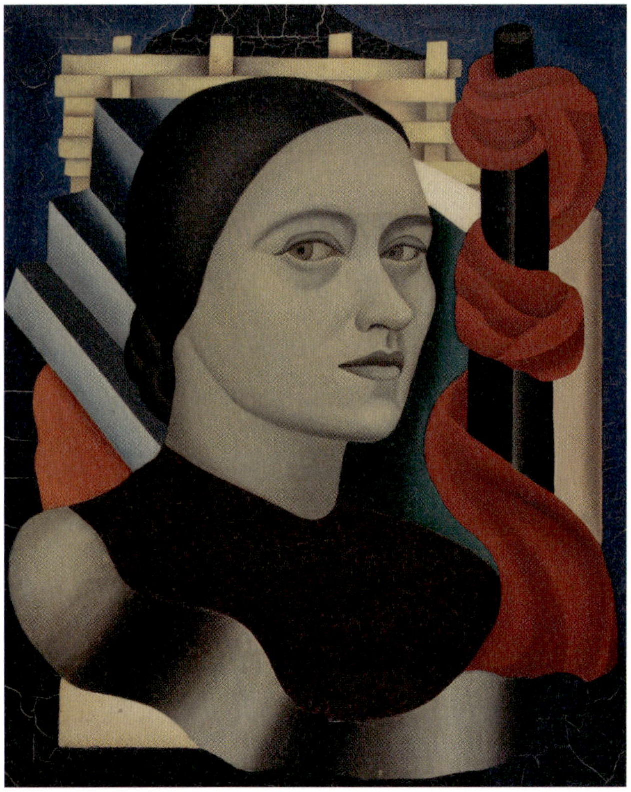

160

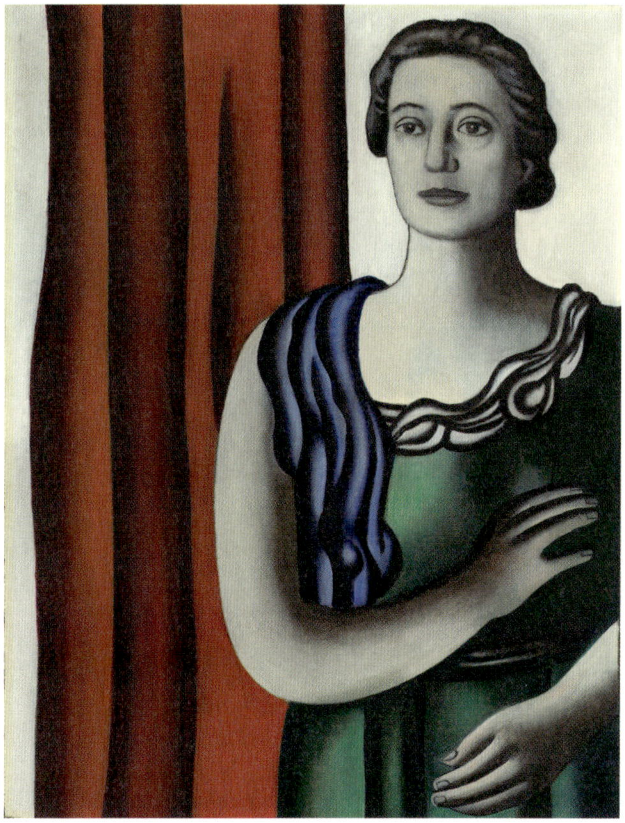

161

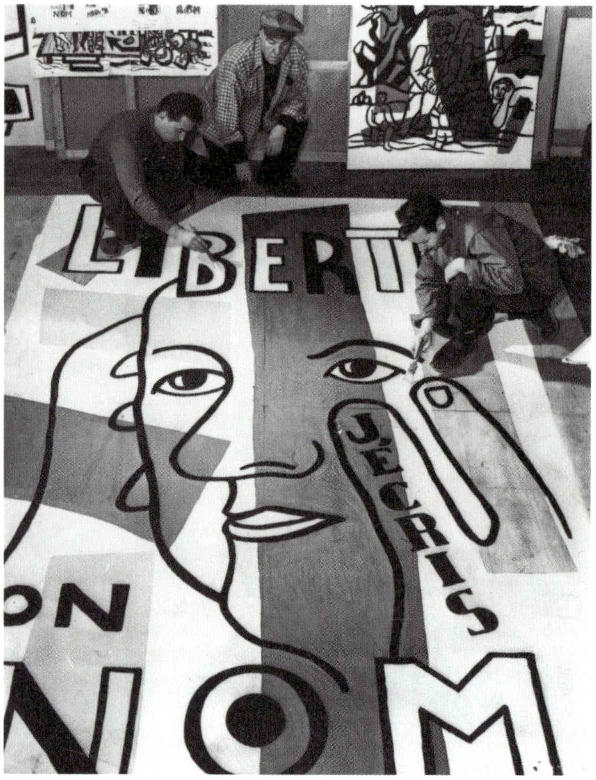

162

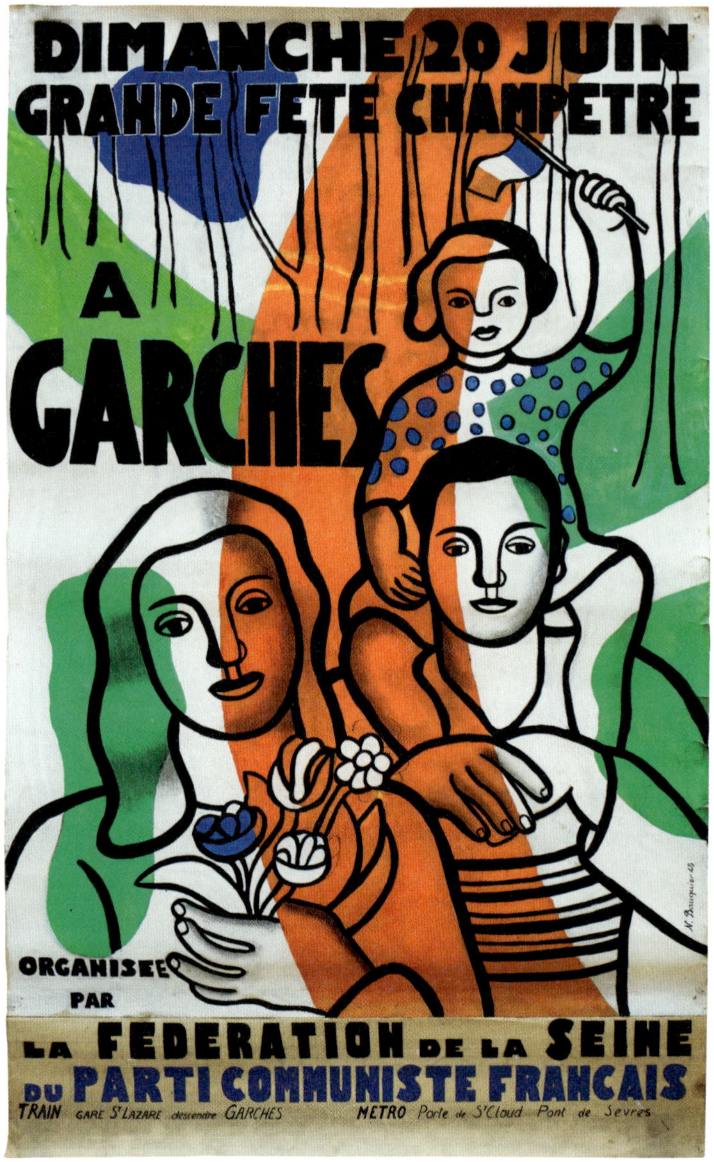

163

162 **Fernand Léger with students in his workshop in Gif-sur-Yvette working on panels for the Vélodrome d'Hiver in Paris for sale held by the Comité National des Écrivains in honor of Paul Éluard), 1953**

163 Nadia Bauquier Khodossievitch-Léger
Affiche pour le parti communiste
(Poster for the Communist Party), 1948
Gouache on paper
125 × 75 cm
Private collection

1935 to early March 1936, when Popular Front fever was at its height, Léger was absent. His seminal text, "The New Realism," was published in New York's *Art Front* in December 1935, translated by Harold Rosenberg.

There is no better illustration of Léger's social mobility, political ambiguity, and opportunism at this time than his portrait of the millionaire's wife, Mrs. Maud Chester Dale, commissioned during his second visit to America—which is challenged by the self-portrait by his disciple, Wanda Grabowska, alias Nadiezhda (Nadia) Khodossievitch (figs. 160, 161). Nadia was a former student of Streminski and Malevitch, who ran Léger's studio during her master's New York absences: Maud stands statuesque in a green evening dress with white ruched décolleté and blue stole; Nadia's hair is drawn back in a simple parting, befitting a young militant. A red Communist flag twirls around a pole beside her.[8]

The underpinnings of capitalism—an art for the masses, be it mural art or socialist realism—were at the crux of Léger's Popular Front arguments with Louis Aragon. The surrealist-turned-Communist poet returned from the USSR with his Russian wife Elsa Triolet, to promote a socialist realism in France along Communist lines. By this time the Maison de la Culture (House of Culture) was functioning as the seat of the Association des Écrivains et Artistes Révolutionnaires (Association of Revolutionary Artist and Writers) with direct affiliations to the USSR via the French Communist Party. Léger was actively engaged in its debates and published in its artists' journal; he gave talks to various worker groups and invited workers—including Roland Brice, his ceramicist in the 1950s—to join special classes in his atelier.[9] It was here that Aragon gave his lectures through 1935, published as *Pour un réalisme socialiste* (In favor of a socialist realism). Young artists responded, depicting the Popular Front processions of July 14, 1935, and the wave of strikes celebrating the Front's coming to power (see Boris Taslitzky's *The Strikes of June 1936*, Tate Modern).[10] There were ultimately two million people off work, to the dismay of captains of industry.

Coinciding exactly with the Popular Front's accession to power, the so-called artists' *querelle du réalisme* (realism debate) was staged for three evenings. Léger roundly rejected Aragon's call for socialist realism (part of the Soviet Comintern's strategy to "nationalize" their entirely Moscow-driven policy): "So what kind of representative art do you want to impose on these men? When everyday they're pursued by the cinema, radio, huge photographic montages, and advertising? What's the point of competing with these enormous modern mechanisms which give you art vulgarized to the hundredth degree?"[11] Léger's speech on the second evening was censored from *La Querelle du réalisme* of 1936:[12] "It's an outrageous thing to do to these completely new men whose only wish is to understand and march at the forefront of things… People say to them the modern isn't for us, it's for the rich; specialized art, bourgeois art, it's archi-faux [completely wrong]."[13] Aragon would keep up the onslaught however: "Slave, you paint your chains: merchandise, the sublimated product of this social order…"[14]

Youngsters such as Edouard Pignon, Jean Amblard, and Boris Taslitzky were invited to show with Picasso, Léger, Matisse, and others in the Alhambra theatre foyer in July 1936, where Romain Rolland's play *Le Quatorze Juillet* (The Fourteenth of July) of 1902 was staged to celebrate the Popular Front May triumph with a huge stage curtain by Picasso. Here Léger showed *Composition au trois figures* (Composition with Three Figures), completed in 1933, with its naked women on a yellow ground, and was joined by Matisse, Lipchitz, André Lhote, and others; he wanted a hierarchical hang but was overruled by Picasso.[15] Over two hundred professional and amateur actors were involved, in a theater seating two thousand. Restaging this immense scene in which the people of Paris seized symbolic power blurred the boundaries between art and the current political situation: The "victory of Communism" was more or less implicit.

The size of Picasso's stage curtain, over 8 × 13 meters, was certainly a challenge. By now commissions for the World's Fair of 1937 in Paris were urgent. In contrast to the *haut-bourgeois* mural commissioned for the entrance to a French Embassy produced by Robert Mallet-Stevens for the Art Deco exhibition in 1925, Léger's *Transport des Forces* (fig. 140) would be quite different. At 5 × 10 meters, it was also extremely large. And it was transportable. By this time Léger was involved in the "Art Mural" group. Founded on January 1, 1935, by the artist Saint-Maur, it had held its first salon in June of that same year. Works such as Henri Lauren's "Stella," designed for the façade of the "Bolshevik" Karl Marx school in Villejuif by André Lurçat, were exhibited here, as were mural projects *per se*. Léger joined the exhibitors at the second Salon in the Maison de la Culture in June 1936, where only maquettes (7 × 1.5 meters) could be shown.[16] "Mural art is the only really social art. Social by essence and social by destination," declared Roger Schoedelin at the opening. "Mural art or easel art?" was a question debated avidly.[17]

As opposed to the master/atelier model espoused by Léger, the Art Mural group advanced a collective idea of teamwork, which encouraged commissions by abolishing the expensive cult of the "signature" artist. Teamwork as an economic solution, as an initiative to combat unemployment, like the WPA initiative in America, would underpin the commissions for the 1937 World's Fair. The essence of mural art is its relationship to the wall—on the principle of fresco for outdoor works, or non-demountable, site-specific interior commissions (like Orozco's in New York). But the World's Fair required speed of construction and was ultimately ephemeral: all pavilions would be demolished from 1938 onwards. Thus, Léger, his team, and his contemporaries (such as Robert Delaunay and Picasso and their assistants) worked on canvas, which was later mounted. Picasso's *Guernica* and Raoul Dufy's *La Fée Éléctricité* (Electricity Fairy) with its one hundred costumed protagonists can be seen today in Madrid and Paris; similarly, Léger's *Transport des Forces* is a monument to this extraordinary moment when art and politics met.

The *Transport des Forces* was positioned to the left of the monumental staircase in the Palace of Discovery, a 1937 creation which took up half the old Grand Palais (fig. 141). The canvas itself depicts the creation of hydroelectric power, a perfect theme for the combination of industrial and natural imagery. Rectilinear structures, zigzag signs, and pylons flank the canvas, contrasting with a great rush of water, streaming diagonally across the center of the canvas, creating a huge rainbow (painted in part by Asger Jorn, the future CoBrA artist). Was Léger celebrating the mighty Barrage de Marège, a hydroelectric dam opened in the Auvergne in 1935? Was it not equally a bow to the Soviet utopia? [18]

Léger had other commissions, for example his vertical panel for the Solidarity pavilion in the spirit of the *blazon* or coat of arms: against a red ground, spades, hammers, and a medallion of profiles were linked by a twisting rope symbolized trade unions (*le Syndicalisme ouvrier*). This took its place alongside works by Lurçat, Robert Delaunay, Gromaire, Dufy, Denis, and others. In the pavilion of the militant Union des Artistes Modernes, Léger collaborated with Albert Gleizes and Léopold Survage on a large fresco called, significantly, *L'Accompagnement d'architecture* (Architectural Accompaniment) (fig. 146). Again, this was a pavilion linked to trade union struggles, this time on behalf of artists' organizations.

Most curious of all were his photomontage works for Le Corbusier's "Bolshevik" Pavillon des Temps Nouveaux (New Times pavilion) (figs.147, 151) with its tent and pylon construction. The interior was conceived as a leisure center with multiple functions with a system of internal ramps, display boards, an artificial mound, an orators' tribune, gym spaces, and so on; all, ultimately, a huge advertisement for Le Corbusier's projects and theories. A red, white, and blue national flag comprised the colorful exterior. Léger's photomontage mural for the interior—a new departure for the artist—was also based on agit-prop Soviet precedents: El Lissitsky and Sergei Senkin's photomontage murals for the USSR pavilion at the 1928 *Pressa* exhibition in Cologne and the 1929 *Film und Photo* exhibition in Stuttgart. Lucien Mazenod, whose murals complemented Léger's, had been the first to mix photomontage and painting in advertisements. Léger's *Travailler,* a companion piece to Mazenod's *Recreation*, was mounted at right-angles to it on a mezzanine supported on thin metal stilts; a slogan declared the pavilion was dedicated to the people, to understand, judge, and claim their rights (*"revendiquer"*). *Travailler* (Work) used blown-up photographs from agencies of pylons, high-tension cables, axles, pulleys, and a man at the center of a wheel-type conveyor belt. Vertiginous viewpoints collided; the flat-colored planes of the background at oblique angles increased the sensation of dynamism and dislocated autonomous movement. In contrast, Léger's twin open-air *Agriculture* panels in the Rural Center used natural imagery, with rainbow targets and fists clutching roses: a salute of hope in the spirit of the Popular Front program, as his collaborator, Charlotte Perriand, agreed. These agit-prop type panels were another departure from the idea of a simple mural or even a transportable mural: here, the agit-prop ethos of a collapsible museum space that could be to be dismantled, packed, and notionally transported through France by train.

From the simple "wall" ethos of the *Salon de l'Art* mural to these bolder ideas of transportability, Léger expanded his remit, much like other revolutionary or eighteenth-century French painters, from Jacques-Louis David to François Boucher. For the Paris Opéra in 1937 he designed costumes for Serge Lifar's ballet celebrating the biblical King David, *David Triomphant*; he created backdrops for the Vélodrome d'Hiver (Vél d'Hiv), the winter bicycle-racing track, for a *Fête des Syndicats*, a large trade union celebration organized by the Confédération Général du Travail. *La Naissance d'une cité* (Birth of a City) presented again in the Palais des Sports at the famous Vél d'Hiv, was a huge, multi-disciplinary Popular Front project created under the auspices of the Maison de la Culture with backdrops and costumes by Léger (figs. 157, 158).[19] He described "a vast fresco both realist and lyrical which will be revealed over two hours with no interruption." The origins of Léger's metro track stage were to be found not only in Frederick Kiesler's *Raumbühne*, but also in the backdrops of Alexandra Ekster and the theater of Meyerhold.[20] The electricity pylon substituting the French revolutionary Tree of Liberty (the centerpiece of many commemorative prints) is as close to the image of the newly electrified USSR as it is to any utopian vision of France.[21] Here, the portable mural is transposed to the concept of mobile décors, painted by students from Léger's and André Lhote's studios and supervised by André Fougeron. Sketches were enlarged and borne aloft, signifying, sometimes with words, the bedroom, bistro, metro, ship, and desert isles.[22] Larger elements were wheeled on and off by stagehands during the performance.[23] One year after Hitler's contested Olympic games, the scene was utopian: "Suddenly the worker's dark blue jackets, a veritable 'sign' of labor, will give way to flowering of multicolored shawls; 'sign' of joy, of fêtes, of liberation," Léger said.

By this time, the Popular Front government, rapidly compromised over non-intervention in Spain, was facing defeat. Édouard Daladier's Radical Socialists took power in April 1938. While Europe faced the Munich crisis, the Nazi-Soviet pact, and war, Léger accepted a commission—again a work on canvas—for the fireplace at Nelson A. Rockefeller's Fifth Avenue private residence (fig. 212) and made a third trip to America. He also completed exterior murals for Consolidated Edison's City of Light exhibition hall for the World's Fair of 1939 in New York (fig. 208), and in 1942, he painted a six-panel mural of *Les Plongeurs* (The Divers), ten meters long, for Wallace K. Harrison's Long Island home (fig. 245). It was an exhilarating and fertile time, but a time of exile. It was to Jean-Richard Bloch that Léger sent a telegram from America on October 18, 1945, to join the French Communist Party—following Picasso's shock decision of October 1944.

"New York - Moscow, Moscow - New York": Léger's post-war career was as ambiguous as his career in the 1930s. His studio filled with American students; he was chauffeur-driven into Paris in a large car. What a contrast to his Communist engagement, and his "proletarian" persona, with worker's cap and eternal cigarette butt… Incessantly he would return to the theme of the bicycle, the family picnic, the circus. Popular Front iconography was never as bizarre as in *Leisure (Homage to Louis David)*, where the assassinated Marat is depicted as a robust girl relaxing on the ground in front of family, friends, and bicycles, while doves of peace twitter in the clouds. His "party work," panels for fêtes and spectacles, continued with Nadia's indispensable participation. Though he attended massive rallies in stadiums from Paris to Vienna, including Prague for the Congress of the Sokols (150,000 Czechs marched in a four-hour parade in 1955), never again would the concept of the mural expand as far as it had done for him at the time of the Popular Front, from painted mural to propaganda panel, to total work of art.[24]

1 Fernand Léger, "New York vu par Fernand Léger," *Cahiers d'Art* 6, no. 9/10 (1931): 437–39.
2 See Simon Willmoth, "Léger and America," in *Fernand Léger, the Later Years*, ed. Nicholas Serota (London: Whitechapel Art Gallery; Munich: Prestel Verlag), 43–54.
3 Jean-Louis Cohen, *Le Corbusier and the Mystique of the USSR: Theories and Projects for Moscow, 1928–1936* (1987) (Princeton: Princeton University Press, 1992).
4 Mike Springer, "*Le Ballet Mécanique*: The Historic Cinematic Collaboration Between Fernand Léger and George Antheil," *Open Culture* (blog), September 4, 2012, http://www.openculture.com/2012/09/ile_ballet_mecaniquei_the_historic_cinematic_collaboration_between_fernand_leger_and_george_antheil.html
5 Sergei Eisenstein, interview with *Mon Ciné,* March 27, 1930. Eisenstein's films were shown in Paris at the Amis de Spartacus club and he corresponded with Léger in the 1930s.
6 See Claire Stoullig, ed., *Le Renault de Doisneau / Doisneau's Renault* (Paris: Somogy, 2005). Willy Ronis's photographs of the striking Citroën car factory workers are also Popular Front classics.
7 Willmoth quotes the *New York Sun,* October 24, 1931, op. cit., 54, note 11.
8 See Wilson, "Nadia Khodossievitch-Léger: la griffe du siècle," in *Hommage aux donateurs* (Biot: Musée Fernand Léger, 2010), 17–20.
9 "'Peinture 1937—Couleur dans le monde' (extrait de conférence de Fernand Léger)" was published as the first and principal article in *Peintres et sculpteurs de la Maison de la Culture,* no. 5 (May 1938).
10 Taslitzky's *The Strikes of June 1936* is a small oil sketch measuring 40.4 × 60.7; the full version was seized by the Nazis from his studio.
11 "Quel art représentatif veut–on donc imposer à ces hommes–là? Quand ils sont tous les jours sollicités par le cinéma, la T.S.F., les énormes montages photographiques et la publicité? Comment vouloir entrer en concurrence avec ces énormes mécaniques modernes qui vous donnent de l'art vulgarisé à puissance 1000?" See Fernand Léger, "Le nouveau réalisme continue," in *La Querelle du Réalisme* (Paris: Éditions Sociales Internationales, 1936), 73–79. For Le Corbusier, see 80–91; for Aragon, see 119–23.
12 Léger showed at *Le Réalisme et la Peinture*, Galerie Billiet Vorms, July 3–10, 1936, with Goerg, Gromaire, Labasque, Lhote, Lipchitz, and Lurçat; the gallery had managed the artistic Paris-Moscow exhibiting link since 1928.
13 "C'est faire outrage à ces hommes tout neufs, qui ne demandent qu'à comprendre et à marcher de l'avant.… On leur dit le moderne n'est pas pour nous, c'est pour les riches, art spécialisé, art bourgeois, c'est archifaux." The censored paragraph of Léger's text is to be found in Roger Garaudy, *Pour un Réalisme du XXe siècle, dialogue posthume avec Fernand Léger* (Paris: Bernard Grasset, 1968), 79. Le Corbusier was also censored.
14 "Esclave, vous peignez vos chaînes le produit sublimé de cet ordre social, la marchandise." Louis Aragon, "Le réalisme à l'ordre du jour," *Commune* 37 (September 1936).
15 Christian Dérouet, ed. *Fernand Léger: Lettres à Simone* (Paris: Centre Georges Pompidou / Skira, 1987), 178. Note p. 265 (letter of July 13, 1936).
16 See the newspaper format *Catalogue critique du Salon de l'Art Mural*, reproduced in René Dauthy, *Saint-Maur et l'art mural, 1935–1949, l'historique et le 1%* (Louveciennes: L'Association Les amis du peintre et sculpteur Saint Maur, 1999), 43.
17 "L'art mural est le seul art vraiment social. Social par essence et social par destination." Roger Schoedlin, "Responsabilité de l'artiste," private view talk, in *Europe* (October 15, 1936): 283. According to the review *Comoedia*, Léger exhibited with Lurçat, Lipchitz, Zadkine, Lhote, Gleizes, Souverbie, Saint-Maur, Schoedlin, Colette Rodde, A.-R. Cassou, Fasani, Lucien Lautrec, and Gili; *Saint-Maur et l'art mural*, 58–59.
18 See Henri Barbusse, *Staline* (Paris: Flammarion, 1935).
19 Léger, *Lettres à Simone*, 210, letter of July 1, 1937.
20 For the influence of Exter, Piscator, Kiesler, and Meyerhold, see Peter de Francia, *Fernand Léger* (New Haven and London: Yale University Press, 1983), 182–85.
21 "Les principaux désirs et les habitudes des foules modernes… danse, musique, sport, compétition, athlétisme, vie sociale, action corporative, réunion publique" (ibid.).
22 André Fougeron, letter to the author of August 17, 1987.
23 Jean-Richard Bloch mentions Noh theatre and the circus as influences; see "Naissance d'une cité" in *Toulon* (Paris: Gallimard, 1948).
24 Based upon my research and interview for *Fernand Léger, Art and Politics, 1935–1955* (London: Whitechapel Art Gallery, 1987). More recent material here is expanded with a fuller bibliography in *Picasso, Marx and Socialist Realism in France* (Liverpool: Liverpool University Press), 2013.

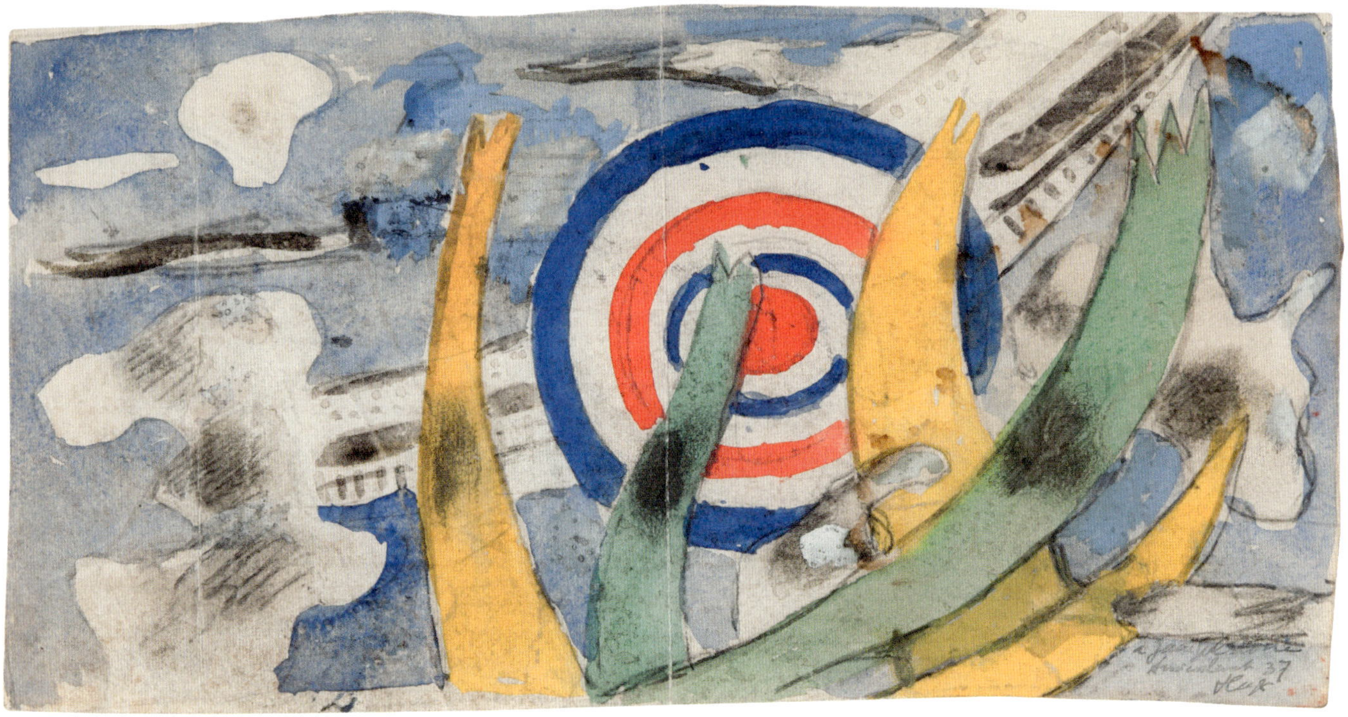

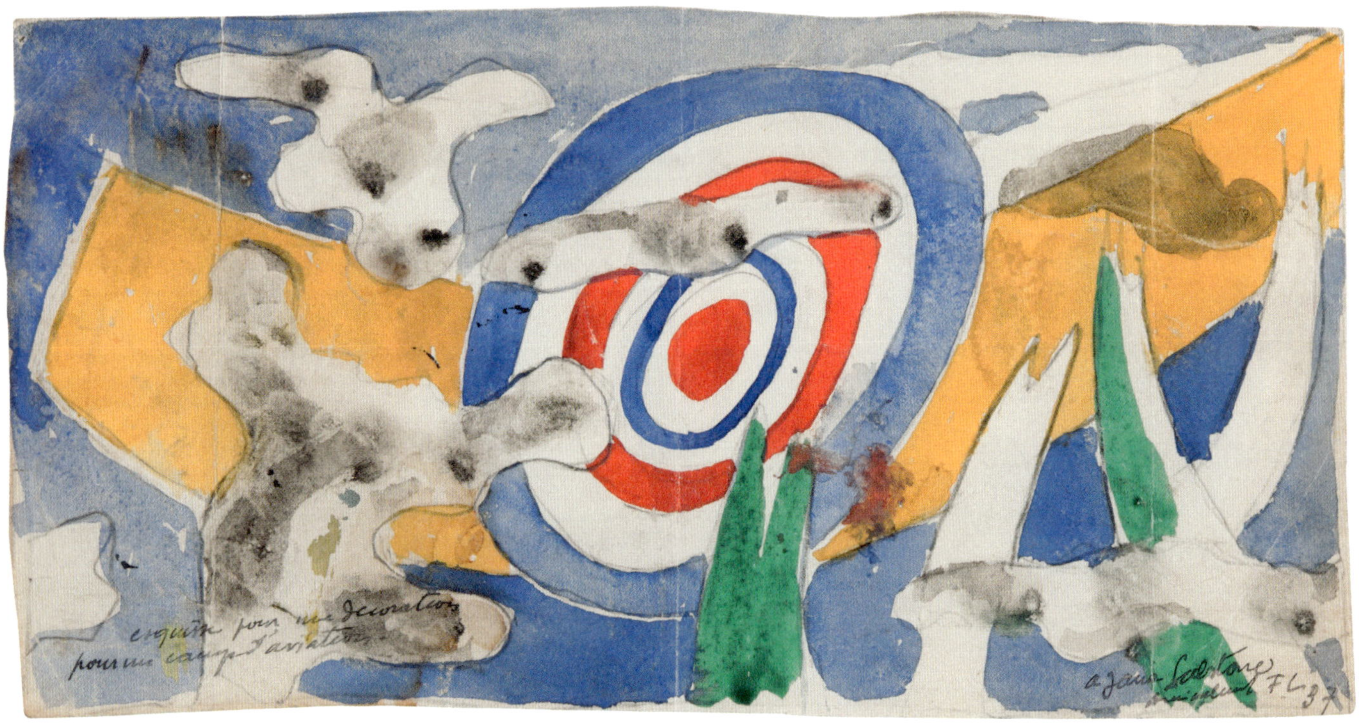

164

Burgoyne Diller on Fernand Léger's WPA (Works Progress Administration) Project (1935)

Fernand Léger wanted to paint—above all to have a mural in America. He'd never had one in Europe and they thought there was a wonderful possibility of his doing something in America. No one at the time seemed to take it upon themselves—private industry or anything of the sort… So that Léger apparently was unable to obtain that thing… They got in contact with the Project [WPA Mural Division] as a possibility, so that after their discussion with Audrey McMahon [NY Project Supervisor], who thoroughly approved of the idea that something might be done on the Project, it was turned over to me to see if it would be possible. You see, we couldn't employ him as an artist on the Project either as relief, or non-relief because he was not a citizen. But on the other hand we'd have an excuse for using him because of his name and so on, and the fact that a good many American artists might like to work with him on a mural, so, you see, it would give them employment.

We decided that it would work if we could find a place where we could do a job that would employ a group of American artists that might take the same theme that he would take… he could collaborate with them, and he could more or less establish a theme and then they could do whatever variations on that theme that they pleased… It might make an extremely interesting project. Well, it was so exciting to all of us… to do it, and dealing with Léger was a very great pleasure, and we got a group of artists to work with him. He came down to the studio area we had at the time… He worked with these artists. Then he drew lots at his own studio… until finally we developed this series of sketches for this mural for a position, a place that had been suggested somewhere along the line, that maybe the French Line pier would be good. Well, it was natural… for Léger to do in collaboration with American artists, to do decorations for the French Line pier… I went with Léger to de l'Enclet's [the director] office… I introduced Mr. de l'Enclet to Léger, and he said, "I know that man," and started off in a tirade in French… De l'Enclet had practically told him, "Well, you damn worker, you! You communist!" Léger naturally was terrifically indignant about the thing… We picked up and walked out. That was the end of the project.

Excerpt from Dr. Harlan B. Phillips, Oral history interview with Burgoyne Diller, Oct. 2, 1964, Archives of American Art, Smithsonian Institution.

–

164 ***Esquisse pour la décoration pour un camp d'aviation* (Sketch for the decoration of an airport), 1937**
Opaque watercolor and graphite on vellum (recto and verso)
13.7 × 25.9 cm
Philadelphia Museum of Art
Courtesy of the Philadelphia Museum of Art, A. E. Gallatin Collection, 1952

165 ***Esquisse pour une peinture murale* (Sketch for a mural), c. 1935**
Gouache and graphite on Canson paper
Private collection

Mural proposals for the French Line shipping company in New York Harbor, not realized. Two decades later, Léger reworked the French-American friendship theme in his mosaic mural for the Saint-Lô hospital.

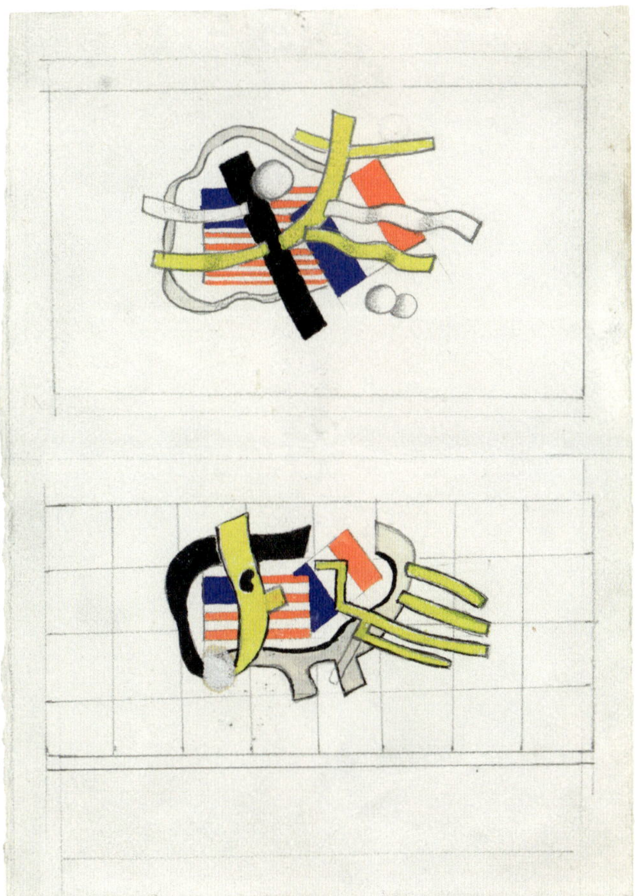

165

Painting in Space

Therapeutic Polychromy and Architecture: The Collaboration between Fernand Léger and Paul Nelson
By Donato Severo

The collaboration between Fernand Léger and the Franco-American architect Paul Nelson[1] on the building of the Franco-American Memorial Hospital in Saint-Lô (1948–56) is a fine example of a richly virtuosic relationship between architecture, the arts, and health. This cooperative venture involved the merging of two histories, with an innovative and highly significant outcome. The first of these histories is that of modern space: of constructional innovations born of the experiments of the Parisian artistic avant-garde and of American culture. The second is that of the modern hospital, that special locus of public health and physical and psychological well-being.

Paul Nelson and Fernand Léger were bound together by a long-standing friendship, a convergence of artistic interests, and shared explorations (fig. 168). Nelson's work is shot through with exchanges and collaborations with the School of Paris, and in particular Braque, Hélion, Giacometti, Miró, and Calder. Nelson was acquainted with Léger's ideas about the beneficial effects of color in hospitals. In 1924, for example, Léger had written of the polychrome urban hospital:

"Color [has] a social function, an essential function. The world of work, the only interesting one, exists in an intolerable environment. Let us go into the factories, the banks, the hospitals. If light is required there, what does it illuminate? Nothing. Let's bring in color, it is as necessary as water and fire. Let's apportion it wisely, so that it may be a more pleasant value, a psychological value; its moral influence can be considerable. A beautiful and calm environment.

Life through color. The polychromed hospital."[2]

Nelson was very much drawn to Léger's spatial painting:

"It is interesting to note the analogy between painting that leaves the wall and merges with space, and the architectural development in which the wall no longer exists. The future of architecture lies in space. Léger is in the process of making true architecture necessary."[3]

Their collaboration dates from the late 1930s. In his competition submission for the WGN radio station in Chicago in 1938 (figs. 166, 167), Nelson's "flexible acoustics" for the concert hall included partitions made of directional blades adjustable according to the desired sound quality. Léger gave him a continuous, wrap-around color composition that changed in time with the technical modeling of the sound during performances.

During the same period, Léger worked with Nelson on the Suspended House,[4] an experimental study that yielded a large metal model (figs. 169, 172). This project combined highly functional spaces with generously dimensioned areas —"useless space"—for moving about in and for the display of artworks. Nelson's goal was a form of architecture that freed the individual from the feeling of having an empirical lifestyle imposed on him. In addition to Léger, many artists including Arp, Miró, and Calder also took part. Nelson's fluid use of space readily lent itself to works of art, and in the dining room, a curved wall covered with a brightly colored decorative works by Léger fitted in perfectly.

The wall had always interested Léger as a medium for incorporating color into a city. How to liberate color? How to bring a wall to life? His ideas led him to collaborate with many architects, but his wish to work on hospitals was realized together with Nelson.

Spatializing Color

The use of color was a major subject of debate within the modernist movement. On one side were advocates of a Purist agenda—all-white architecture—and on the other, proponents of polychromy as an essential aspect of modernity. Nelson, like Theo Van Doesburg and Bruno Taut, was out to combine architecture with the experiments of the artistic avant-garde. The polychromy of the hospital at Saint-Lô broke with the traditional drab uniformity of such establishments in three significant and characteristic ways:

1) the systematic application of color to the building as a whole,
2) the use of color for medical purposes (for Nelson, this "built-in color therapy" was an integral part of modern hospital design),
3) the use of polychromy as a fusion of Léger's color spatialization approach and Nelson's quest for an architecture that would stimulate the human sensibility.

The Léger/Nelson joint venture went ahead between 1953–55 in the form of four projects for the Saint-Lô hospital: interior polychromy, exterior polychromy, a large-scale sculpture (*La fleur qui marche* [The Walking Flower]), and mosaics.

Built-in Color Therapy

The interior polychromy project included the communal and treatment areas as well as the walls of the rooms and corridors and was adapted to the function of each area (fig. 181). The color range was warm and light-hearted: lemon yellow, madder red, Veronese green and *bleu charron* (mid-blue).

The result was an extraordinary feeling of life in a building dedicated to caring for the sick. The bedheads were set against walls of madder red, while the other walls were light-colored (fig. 182). The floors were brightly colored and their hues recurred on doors and corridor walls. This interior

166 ***Perspective de l'auditorium de la WGN* (Perspective from the auditorium of WGN), 1938**
Original print
Centre Pompidou, Bibliothèque Kandinsky, Fonds Paul Nelson, Paris

167 Paul Nelson, Fernand Léger
***Salle de concert pour la station de radio WGN de Chicago* (Concert hall for the Chicago radio station WGN), 1938**
Graphite, pastel chalk and colored pencil on tracing paper
35.5 × 45.5 cm
Centre Pompidou, Musée national d'art moderne, Paris

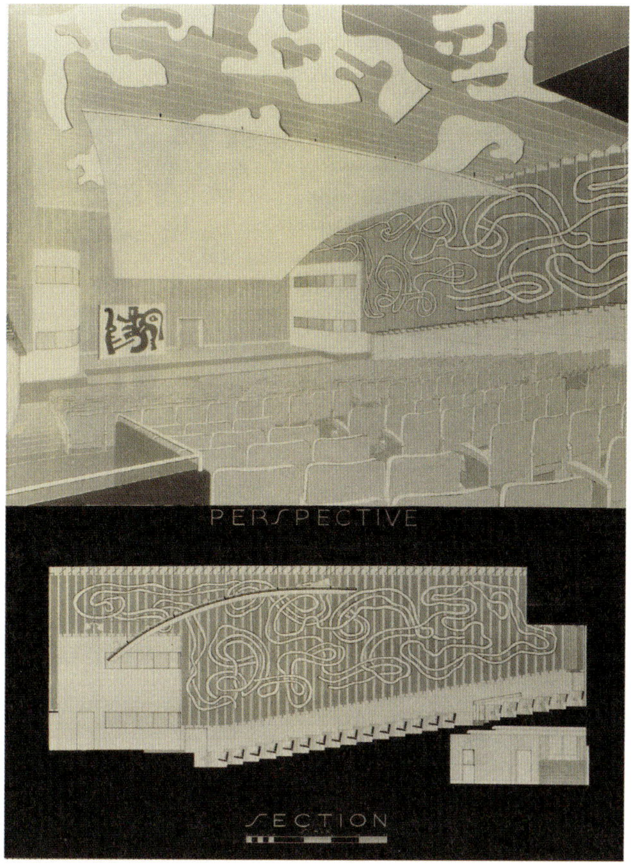

166

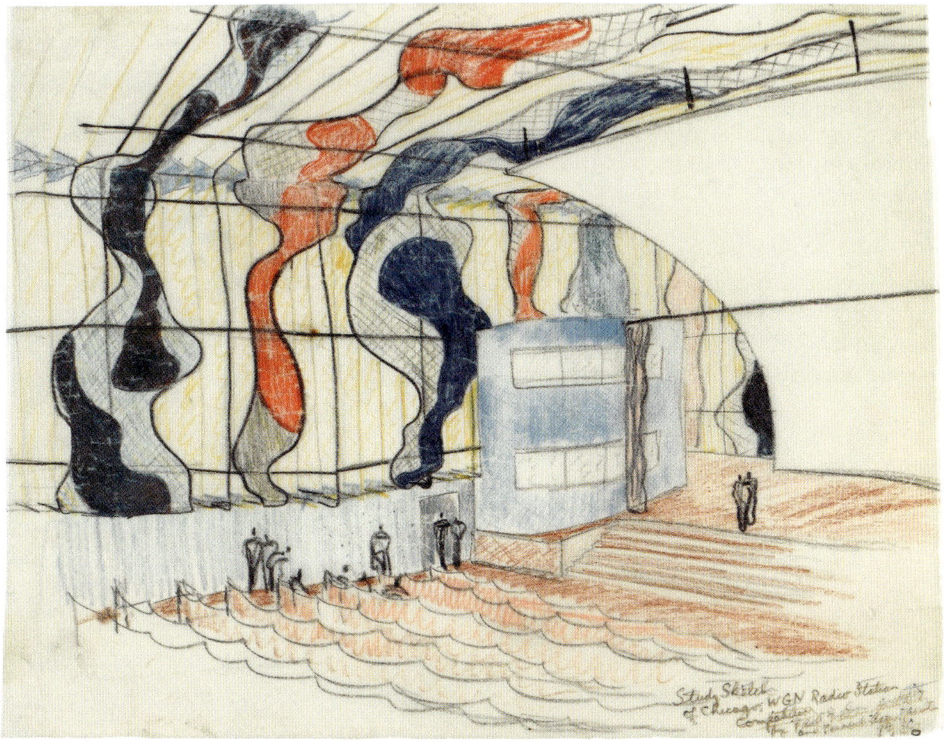

167

polychromy was a factor in the organization of space and circulation. Nelson, who had researched the concept in the United States in the 1940s, was very much aware of the importance of built-in color therapy. Therapeutic use of color can be traced back to ancient Egypt and Greece, and also has deep roots in Chinese and Indian medicine and ayurvedic healing practices. In the United States, interest in this approach had increased steadily during the first half of the twentieth century.[5] Nelson saw it as crucial, not as mere decoration, but as a psychological support to an instinctively felt ambience of relaxation, trust in life, and well-being.

Exterior Polychromy

The exterior polychromy of the building was Léger's great opportunity to try out spatial painting on a large scale. The aluminum framing for the two immense glazed areas on the south façade was vividly painted with red and *bleu charron*, with bright yellow used for the screens on the first floor (fig. 178). Léger proposed large four-sided areas of solid color of different shapes and sizes for the north (fig. 179) and east façades, together with an assertive arrangement of horizontal and vertical stripes intended to make the hospital's considerable volumes more dynamic. However, these large areas of color seemed excessively autonomous in relation to the building itself; there was probably a difference of opinion between the architects and Léger, whose idea clashed with the actual architecture,[6] and this part of his project went unrealized.

Ceramics and Mosaics

In 1952 Léger began working on three-dimensional ceramic pieces, notably *La fleur qui marche*. This sculpture of a flower some six meters high was intended to enliven the outdoor area and present and contrast with the geometrical austerity of the hospital. It was part of the 1953 mock-up of the hospital and a model can be seen in the Musée Léger (figs. 177, 180), but it was never realized due to lack of funds.[7]

Léger chose a variety of media for the decoration of the walls, including painting, mosaics, and ceramics. He created a 40-square-meter mosaic under the peristyle at the entrance (fig. 184), which was the key to the entire building's polychromy for Nelson:

"As you approach the hospital entrance, your eye is immediately caught by a very large mosaic by Fernand Léger, that great artist who died in August 1955. This is, so to speak, his last work. Measuring 14.4 meters long by 2.4 meters high, the mosaic symbolizes the liberation of Saint-Lô by the United States and France. The colors are pure and extremely bright and this is the key to all the polychromy, both exterior and interior."[8]

The mosaic shows a large American flag flanked by two French flags bearing the dates of the beginning and end of World War II, 1939 and 1945. Chromatically linked to the flags, two hands reach out towards the surrounding Cotentin region, represented by a branch of apple blossoms; a gently rolling yellow and green landscape symbolizes Normandy. The mosaic was carried out by a team of master mosaicists from the École Parisienne de Mosaïque et de Céramiques (Paris School of Mosaic and Ceramics) (fig. 185). The mosaic is an assemblage of white French and Italian marble and Venetian enamels made on the island of Murano.

Health and Art

Since the Memorial Hospital in Saint-Lô was officially declared a historical monument in 2008, a number of projects have been launched for the protection and restoration of the work of Léger and Nelson. Not only is the hospital among the most significant examples of twentieth-century architectural modernism and of Léger's art, it is also one of the most sophisticated health institutions of its kind. This dual status raises fascinating but complex issues of long-term heritage management and the relationship between the renovations of hospital departments and the restoration of the hospital's architecture and art.

The collaboration between Nelson and Léger offers an extraordinary, still-relevant opportunity to consider the interconnections between well-being, health, art, and architecture.[9]

1 Born in Chicago 1895, died in Marseille 1979.
2 Fernand Léger, "The Spectacle: Light, Color, Moving Image, Object-spectacle" (1924), in *Functions of Painting*, trans. Alexandra Anderson (London: Thames and Hudson, 1973), 46.
3 Paul Nelson, "Peinture spatiale et architecturale, à propos des dernières œuvres de Léger," *Cahiers d'Art*, no. 1-3 (1937): 86–87.
4 "La Maison suspendue. Recherche de Paul Nelson," *L'Architecture Vivante* (Paris: Éditions Albert Morancé, 1937).
5 In 1933, the Indian scientist Dinshah Ghadiali published *The Spectro Chrometry* encyclopedia, a definitive work on color therapy. This was a landmark publication and laid the foundations for much of modern color therapy. Today there are hundreds of practitioners using a wide variety of color-related therapeutic techniques in the United States, and color therapy is a well-accepted technique in complementary medicine.
6 In the opinion of Georges Bauquier, writing in *Ouest-France* (July 29, 1981).
7 The hospital set a project in motion for the production of the work in 2015.
8 Paul Nelson, "La polychromie à l'Hôpital Mémorial France-Etats Unis de Saint-Lô," contribution to a seminar on children's hospitals [copy] (June 7, 1956), 1.
9 Further sources relevant to this essay include: Roger Bordier, "Polychromie architecturale," *Aujourd'hui, Art et Architecture* no. 2 (March/April 1955); "La Maison suspendue. Recherche de Paul Nelson," *L'Architecture Vivante* (Paris: Éditions Albert Morancé, 1937), n.p.; Fernand Léger, "The Machine Ethic: The Manufactured Object, the Artisan, and the Artist" and "The Machine Ethic: Geometric Order and Truth," in *Functions of Painting* (New York: Viking, 1973); Paul Nelson, "Peinture spatiale et architecturale, à propos des dernières œuvres de Léger," *Cahiers d'Art*, nos. 1-3 (1937); Paul Nelson, "La polychromie à l'Hôpital Mémorial France-Etats Unis de Saint-Lô," contribution to a seminar on children's hospitals [copy] (June 7, 1956); Donato Severo, *Paul Nelson* (Paris: Centre des Monuments Historiques, Édition du Patrimone, 2013); and Donato Severo, *Paul Nelson et l'Hôpital de Saint-Lô. Humanisme, art et architecture* (Paris: Éditions Picard, 2015).

168 **(L-R): Christian Zervos, Fernand Léger, Paul Nelson, Mary Callery and Yvonne Marion Zervos, Centre Hospitalier Mémorial France-Etats-Unis, Saint-Lô (Memorial Hospital), 1930s**
Archives du Musée national Fernand Léger, Biot

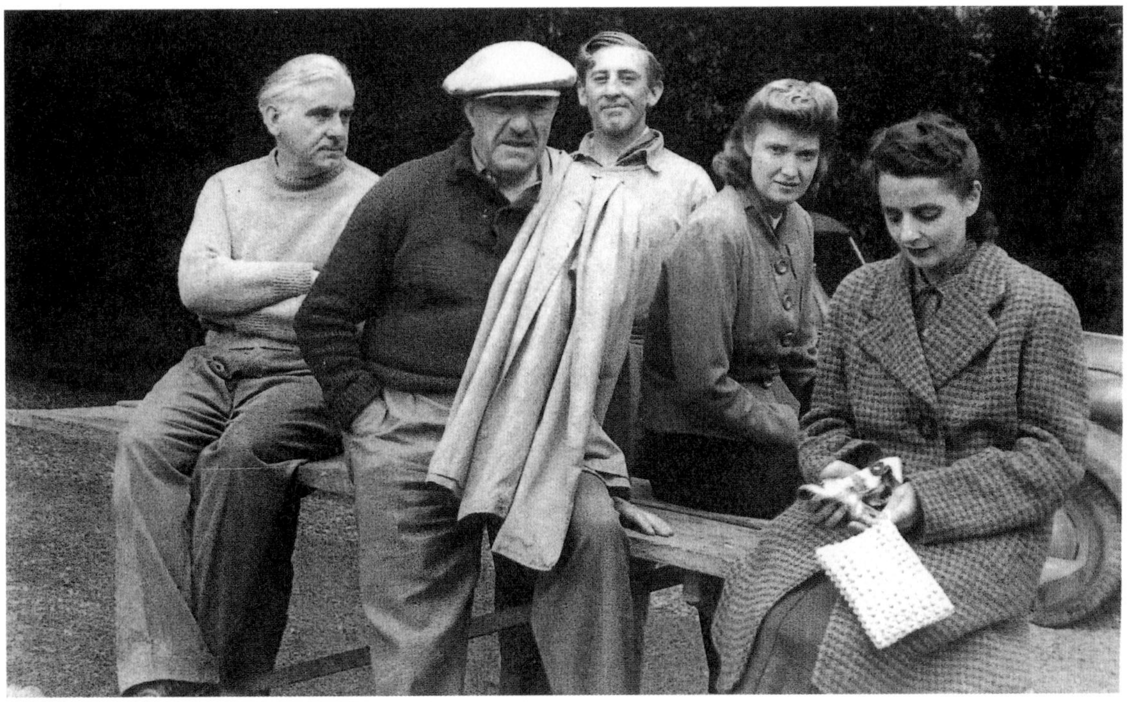

168

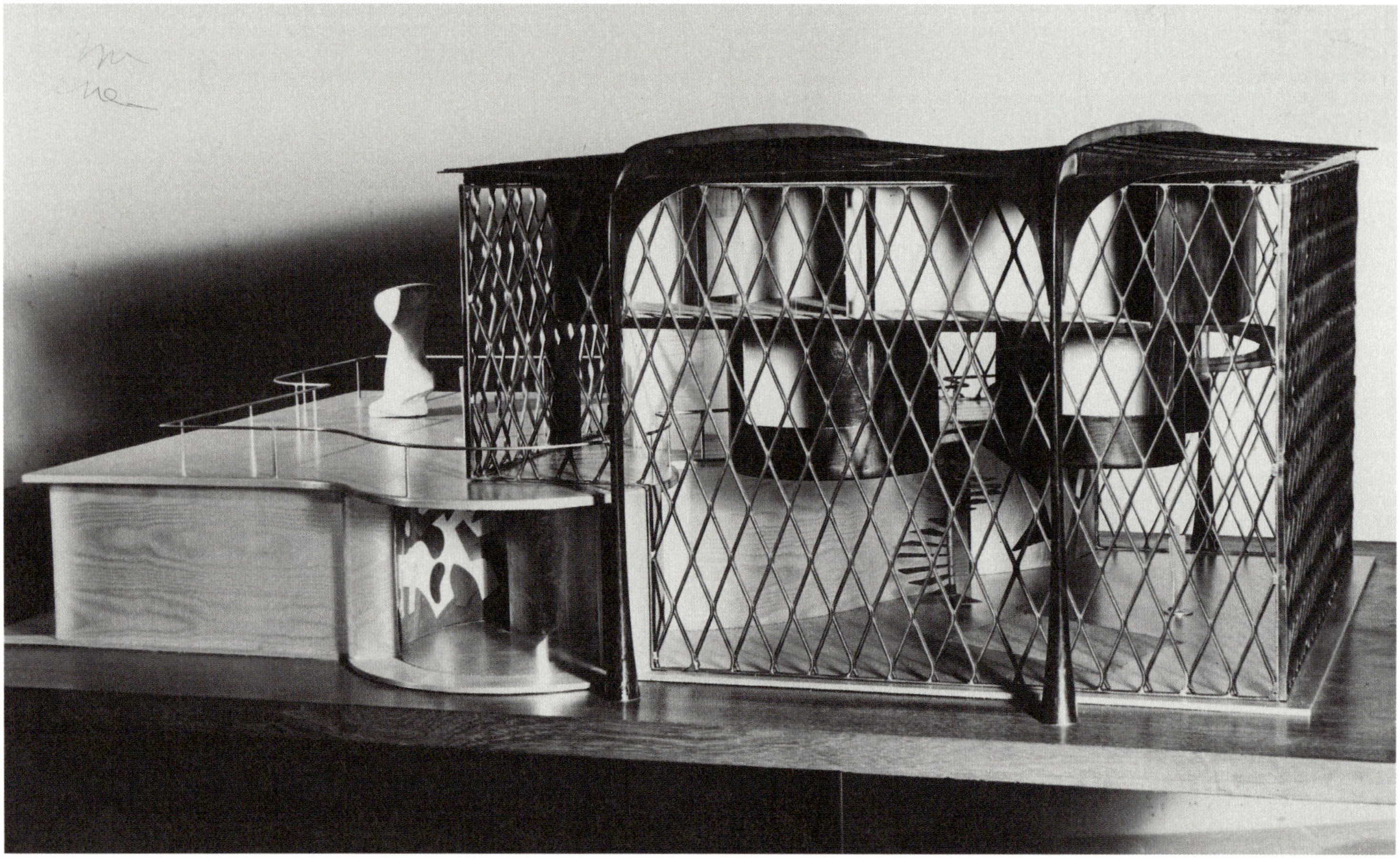

169

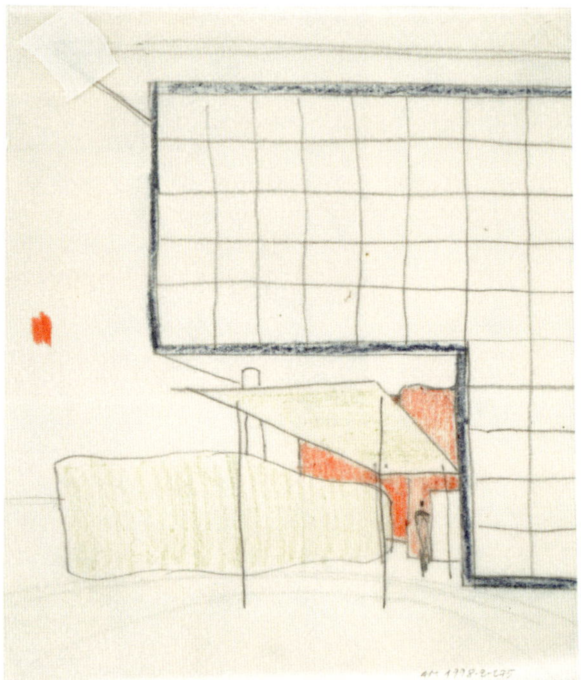

170

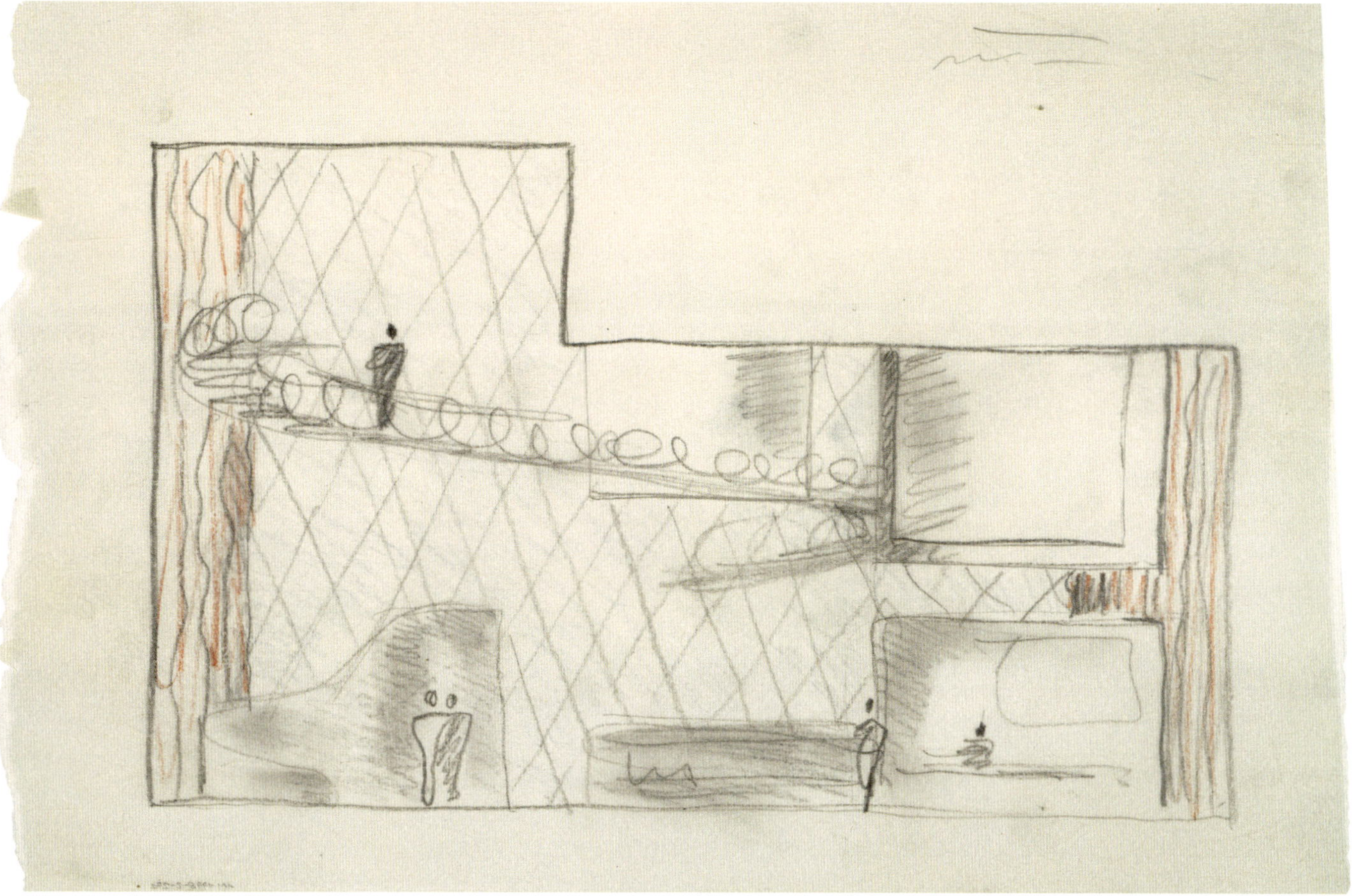

171

169 Paul Nelson with Joan Miró, Hans Arp, and Fernand Léger
***La Maison suspendue* (Suspended House), 1936–38, first model (missing) with Fernand Léger's dining room mural painting (gouache, 1936)**
Centre Pompidou, Bibliothèque Kandinsky, Fonds Paul Nelson, Paris

170 Paul Nelson
***Perspective Entrée, esquisse (Maison suspendue, Projet non réalisé, 1936-1938)* (Perspective from entrance, sketch [Suspended house, unfinished project, 1936–38]),1936**
Graphite and colored pencil on tracing paper
17.5 × 14.5 cm
Centre Pompidou, Musée national d'art moderne, Paris

171 Paul Nelson
***Plan de l'étage (Maison suspendue, Projet non réalisé, 1936-1938)* [Floor plan (Suspended House, unfinished project)], 1936**
Graphite and colored pencil on tracing paper
28 × 40 cm
Centre Pompidou, Musée national d'art moderne, Paris

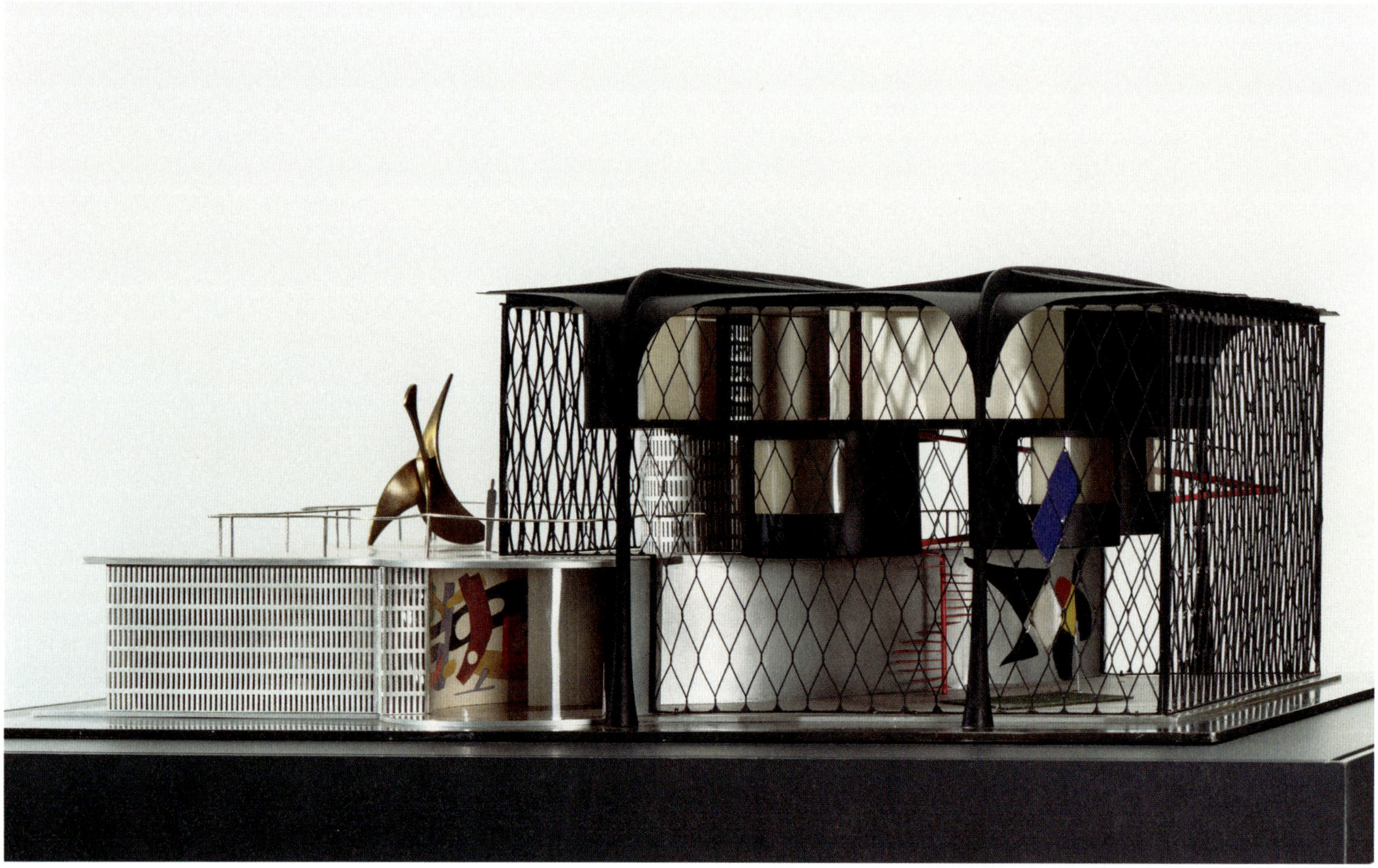

172

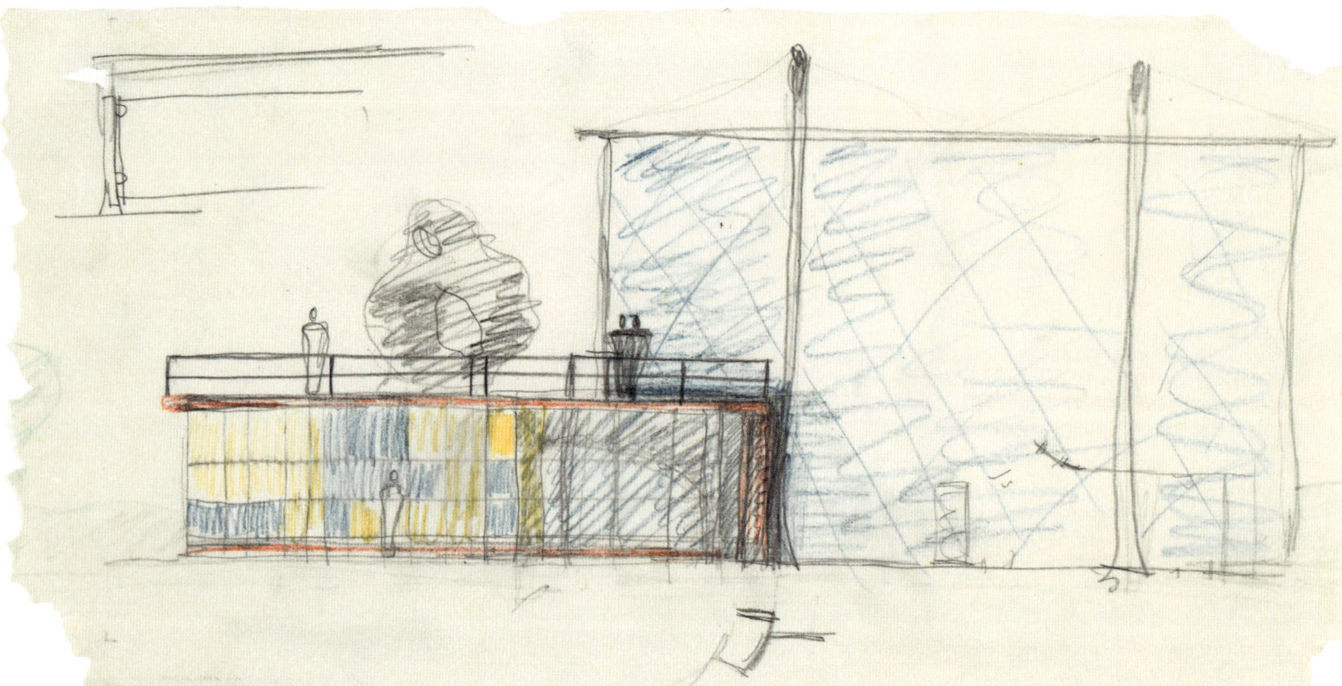

173

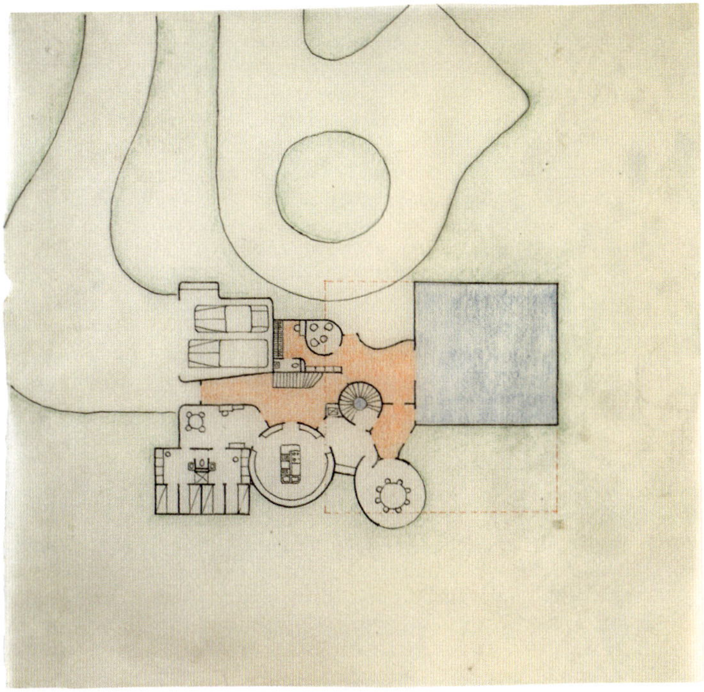

174

172 Paul Nelson with Joan Miró, Alexander Calder,
and Fernand Léger
La Maison Suspendue **(Suspended House), 1936–38, second model by Louis Dalbet with Fernand Léger's dining room mural painting (gouache, 1936)**
Model made from acrylic, metal, paint, stone, textile, wood
35.6 × 92.7 × 72.4 cm
Museum of Modern Art, New York
Gift of the Advisory Committee, acc. no. MC 14

173 Paul Nelson
Maison suspendue, Elévation Façade, esquisse **(Suspended House, façade elevation, design), 1936-1938**
Graphite and colored pencil on tracing paper
27.3 × 53.9 cm
Centre Pompidou, Musée national d'art moderne, Paris

174 Paul Nelson
Plan de niveau Rez-de-chaussée, esquisse (Maison suspendue, Projet non réalisé, 1936-1938) **(Plan of ground floor level, sketch [Suspended House, unfinished project, 1936–38]), 1936**
Architectural drawing, floorplan,
Ink and colored pencil on tracing paper
24 × 24 cm
Centre Pompidou, Musée national d'art moderne, Paris

175 Paul Nelson
Plan de niveau Rez-de-chaussée, esquisse (Maison suspendue, Projet non réalisé, 1936-1938) **(Plan of ground floor level, sketch [Suspended House, unfinished project, 1936–38]), 1936**
China ink, graphite and colored pencil on tracing paper
55 × 71.5 cm
Centre Pompidou, Musée national d'art moderne, Paris

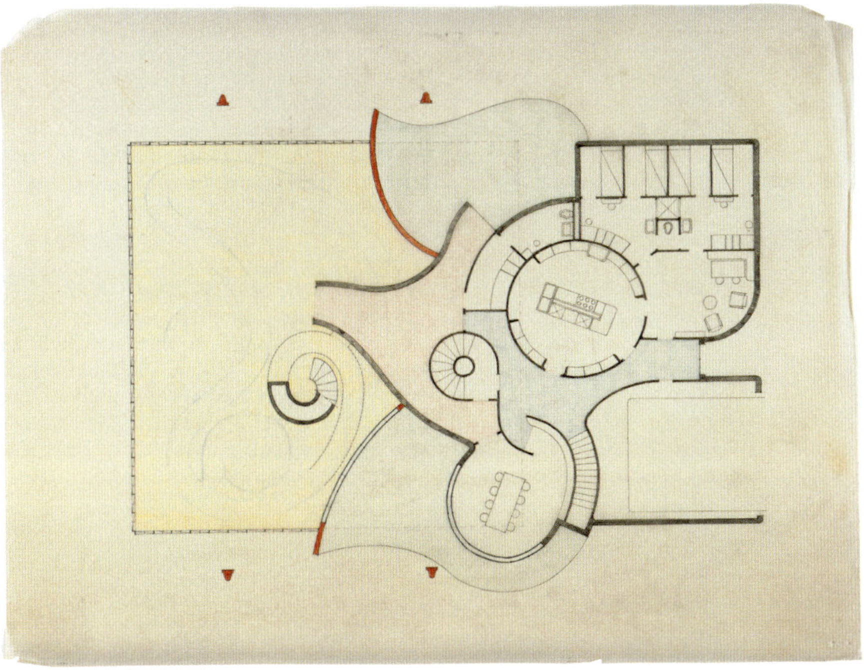

175

SPATIAL PAINTING AND ARCHITECTURE: Concerning Léger's most recent works (1937)
Paul Nelson

In the following notes I simply wish to account for my reactions to Léger's most recent paintings. As it happens, my contacts with painting tend to be rather physical. I have to touch and feel before I can judge. In my case, this fact reduces the supposed joys bestowed by literary painting, but it means that I am able to enjoy Léger's painting, composed as it is of sensual power. This power is tangible in the admirable canvases of the period erroneously dubbed "cubist" shown at the Galerie des Beaux-Arts about two years ago and in others at Paul Rosenberg's more recently. I find this power still more intense in some recent canvases that have not even left his studio yet. Gazing at them, I had the impression of becoming aware of the weight of my own body, of my arms that I tried to place firmly on the table or the back of a chair, as Léger does. Because each picture releases something solid, fully alive, and one has to have attained a certain balanced tension before being able to enter it. It bestows a sensation of wellbeing, a shudder, *"a swell feeling."*

From Léger's latest paintings there arises a novel quality one might term "spatial." And it is this which in my opinion is the key aspect in his development. For not only have his paintings stepped out of their frames (and he is wrong to use them) and become murals, but they also command the space. One is thus able, as it were, to estimate the surface area of wall that should exist around each painting. Better still, one is tempted to look, not at the wall, but at the space: that is, to turn one's back on the painting and look at its reflection, its signature as it applies to the space, and to measure the volume it projects. I have experienced this sensation of painting radiating out into space in Egyptian tombs. Their art, equally spatial, and in perfect keeping with the actual volumes, emits waves and rays to the extent that, when one closes one's eyes and no longer looks at them, it is still possible to feel them coursing through one.

A painting by Léger no longer requires a wall on which to hang it; it requires a room. It cannot be hung just anywhere. A painting or a sculpture that can be placed anywhere is not spatial.

It is interesting to note the analogy between the painting that comes off the wall to embrace the space and those developments in architecture in which the wall no longer exists. The future of architecture is in space. Léger is in the process of rendering true architecture necessary. This may represent a reversal in method, true, but such a reversal is unavoidable, since we do not possess such an architecture, and neither do we have the opportunity to build it.

If the truth be told, Léger no longer needs art dealers: he needs dealers in architecture. The day the art lover realizes that a work of painting or sculpture only acquires its true signification in a given structure, on that day he will begin to do architecture, since those of us who are architects will then be allowed to conceive of that supplement which meets the spiritual functions of man, in opposition to the narrow and purely utilitarian notion of it that has arisen in recent times, and which has culminated in the "machine for living." At the present time, our ambitions are constrained by shortages, whereas to create things useful to man, his life and his culture, architecture demands abundance.

It might be said that, up to a point, Léger marks the end of easel painting. Hence, he does away with the subject, having less use for it to develop than suitable architecture. With him, the subject disappears, without his painting becoming abstract, since, in so far as it accompanies the architecture, it impinges on the real.

Though there may be an intention with Léger, it is not primordial and it is overshadowed by the materialization of each act–with all the professional dramas this implies. We are surrounded by countless artists who no longer dare, or rather who are unable to go beyond their intentions. As an exercise, there is perhaps a certain charm in such accidents, but as a lasting work of painting, no. For the essential thing for art is not only that it make use of everything the mind and eye present in constructing an artwork, but that it should be produced from beginning to end as by a seasoned craftsman. In this our artist is in phase with the modern era. The present age of social and ethical upheaval, of profound transformation, is not to be satisfied with mere intentions: it is above all searching for things it can grasp on to. Léger is therefore in the right place. His most recent paintings are most encouraging for man. This is because man finds in them a positive, constructive painting–never minor, petty, or destructive–a type of painting he is able to enter and explore and find what he is looking for, with which he can participate, and which it is up to him to complete. A painting, finally, that possesses that sublime quality of the art of Antiquity: objectivity.

Léger is a kind of materialist. He starts off not with an idea–in which case he would have become an abstract painter, which he is not–he starts off with the real problem of painting: bringing space to life. It is my contention that the more his painting becomes spatial, and, therefore, accessory, the greater its social impact will be. I lay stress on this point because it is to my mind of prime importance in a period that has witnessed the growth of a marked tendency to demand that artists incorporate within their works propaganda subjects for the instruction of mankind. My personal conviction, on the other hand, is that, since architecture is social action par excellence, the role of painting is to join with it, to enrich the space, to become a backdrop for human life, and by that very fact elevate and liberate him. Propaganda painting is a bourgeois throwback; it's just easel painting all over again. Léger is at home in a movement that strives to embrace individualist art, but only to place it in the service of mankind.

On the face of it, Léger's most recent paintings are simplicity itself, but in reality they are becoming increasingly complex. Drawn with a sure line, composed without ponderousness, and occupying the space magnificently, they are open, radiant, direct, and powerful in their coloring. In my opinion, it is color which fills the space. More so than in the past, the literary subject is excluded. One simply enters through the artistic qualities and the just expression of spatial expanse.

Léger never seeks to amaze: he imposes his vision gradually, time is on his side.

Léger is a man of today: his oeuvre is devoid of backward-looking and retrospective effects. He is strength in action. "Léger is like a Bach sonata," to repeat the description given by an elderly lady at an exhibition of his most recent gouaches at Jeanne Bucher's, "he knows what he wants!"

Originally published as Paul Nelson, "Peinture spatiale et architecturale, à propos des dernières œuvres de Léger," in *Cahiers d'art*, no. 1-3 (June 1937): 85-88.

–

Letter from Fernand Léger to Paul Nelson, December 13, 1953

Dear Friend,

Herewith the reply to your request concerning the collaboration with architecture. Our age is confronted by two exigencies: easel painting (a value in itself), purely individual, mobile by definition and which should be at home on any wall on which it hangs. Mural painting poses an entirely different problem. It ought to be the opposite of easel painting. It loses its source in individual creativity. It enters the domain of the collective. The architect is the client and he can impose its location and even its general tonality if need be. Its execution lies in the hands of craftsmen. In the beginning, five people met up to collaborate on a work. In my opinion, it should be as much as possible with freed colors, without modulations if possible (to avoid destroying the wall), and it should be at one with the architectural space. It might even provide a sense of new space: we are hence faced by a process utterly at odds with that of easel painting, which "destroys the space" by monopolizing all interest.

The contemporary age should be able to realize this new order. Many easel artists are simply incapable of understanding how to adapt to the wall. These are two distinct paths. And one needs to be conscious of this fact from the outset.

Fernand Léger

Private collection.

–

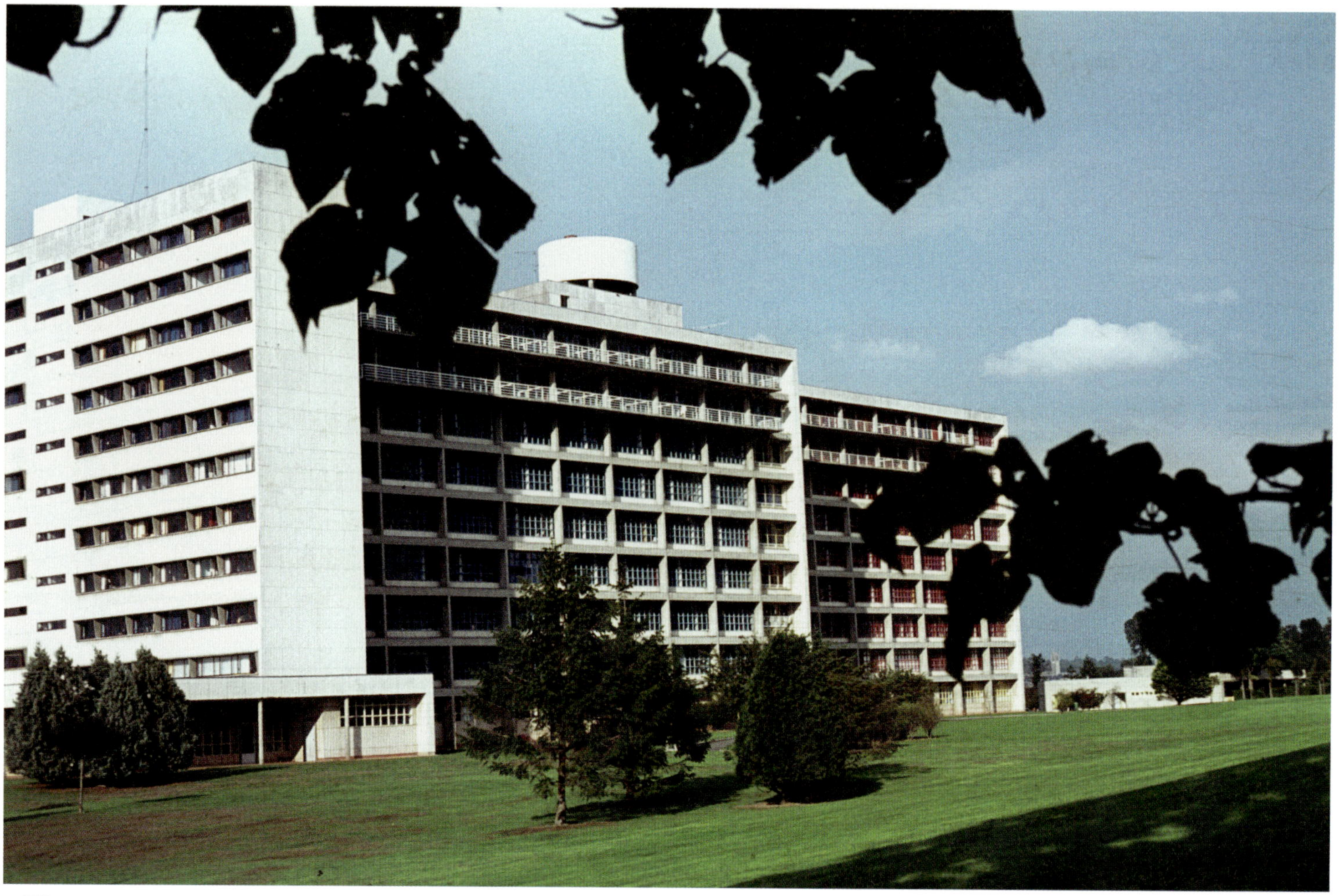

176

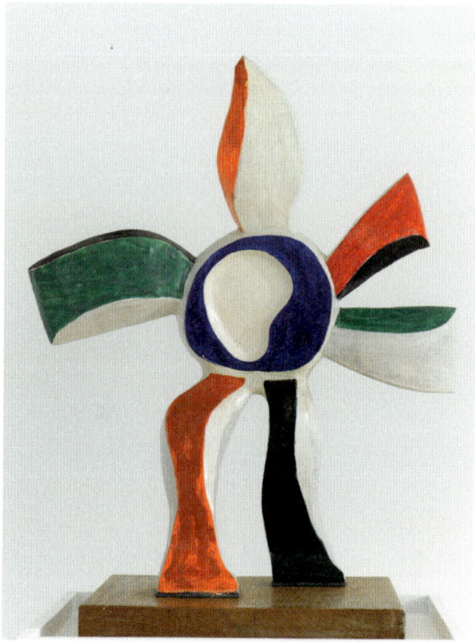

177

176 **Centre Hospitalier Mémorial France-Etats-Unis, Saint-Lô (Memorial Hospital), southern façade photo taken shortly after the building was erected**

177 ***Maquette de "La fleur qui marche"* (Model of *The Walking Flower*), c. 1952/53**
Terracotta, enamel, ceramic
64 × 59 cm
Musée National Fernand Léger, Biot

178 **Centre Hospitalier Mémorial France-Etats-Unis, Saint-Lô (Memorial Hospital), southern façade**
Postcard
Centre Pompidou, Bibliothèque Kandinsky, Fonds Paul Nelson, Paris

179–180 **Centre Hospitalier Mémorial France-Etats-Unis, Saint-Lô (Memorial Hospital), polychrome façade design by Fernand Léger (unrealized) model, 1953**
2 Postcards
Centre Pompidou, Bibliothèque Kandinsky, Fonds Paul Nelson, Paris

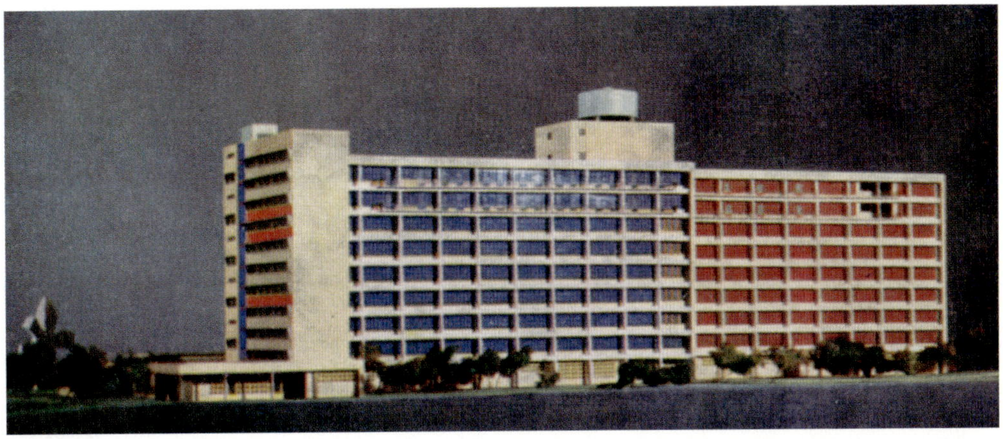

178

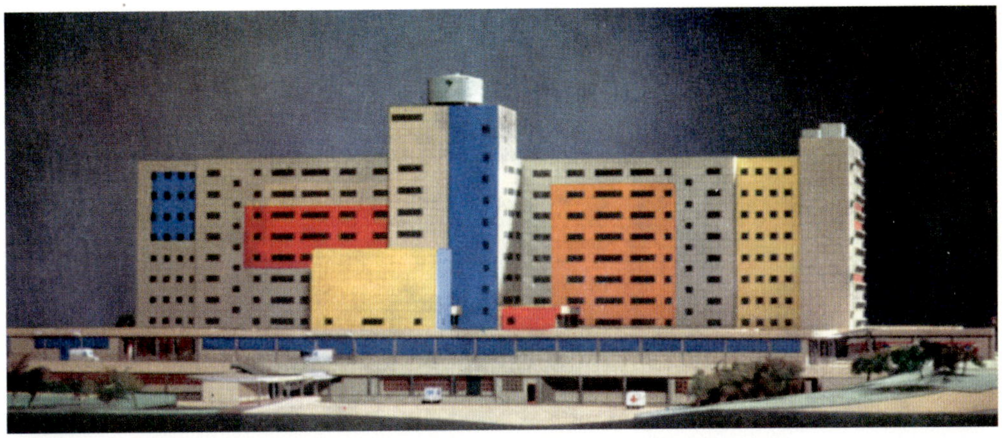

179

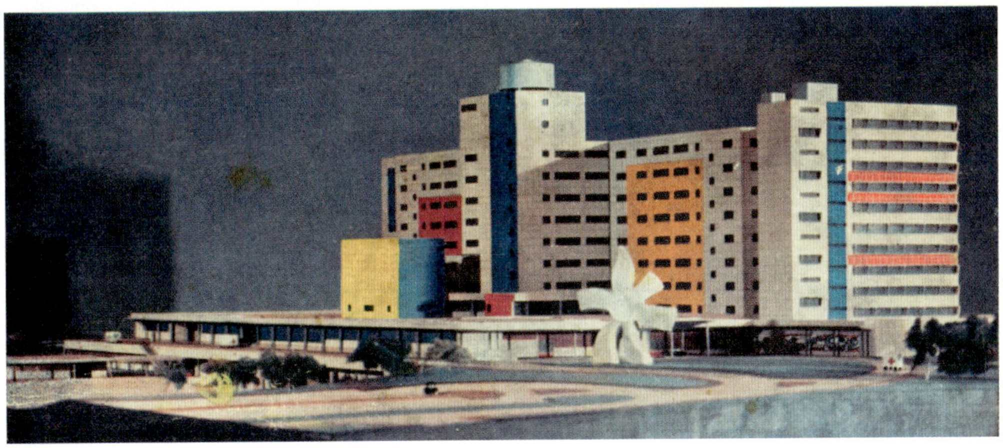

180

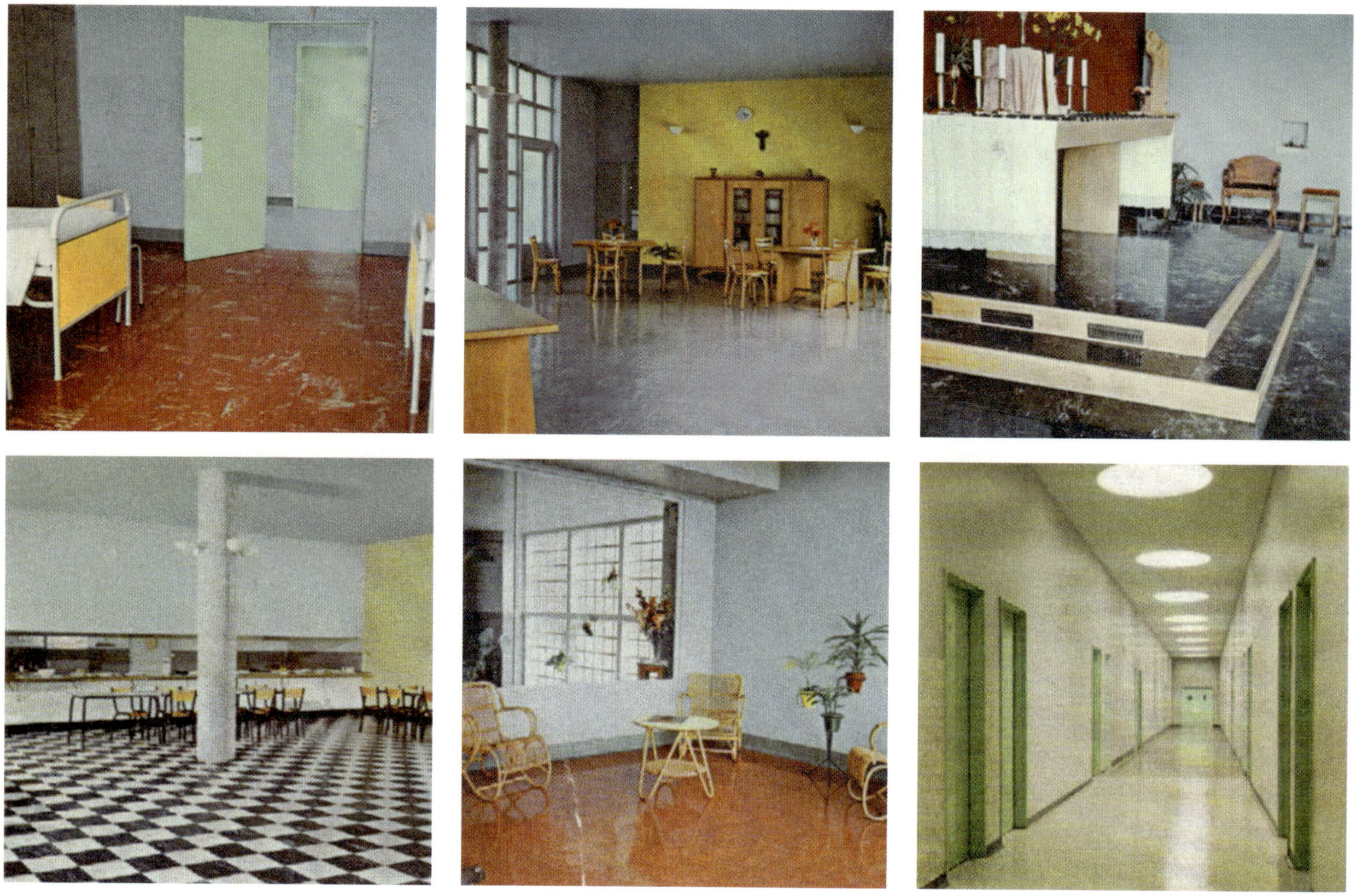

181

181 **6 photographs published in the magazine *Techniques Hospitalières*, December, 1956, Centre Hospitalier Mémorial France-Etats-Unis, Saint-Lô (Memorial Hospital).**
Polychrome: 1. Room with four beds
2. Room of the religious order
3. Chapel
4. Refectory
5. Rest area of the maternity ward
6. Hospital corridor

182 **Polychrome of a room at Centre Hospitalier Mémorial France-Etats-Unis, Saint-Lô (Memorial Hospital), 1956**

183 **Persepectival view of Centre Hospitalier Mémorial France-Etats-Unis, Saint-Lô (Memorial Hospital), published in *Handbuch für den neuen Krankenhausbau*, by Paul Vogler and Gustav Hassenpflug, Munich / Berlin, 1957**

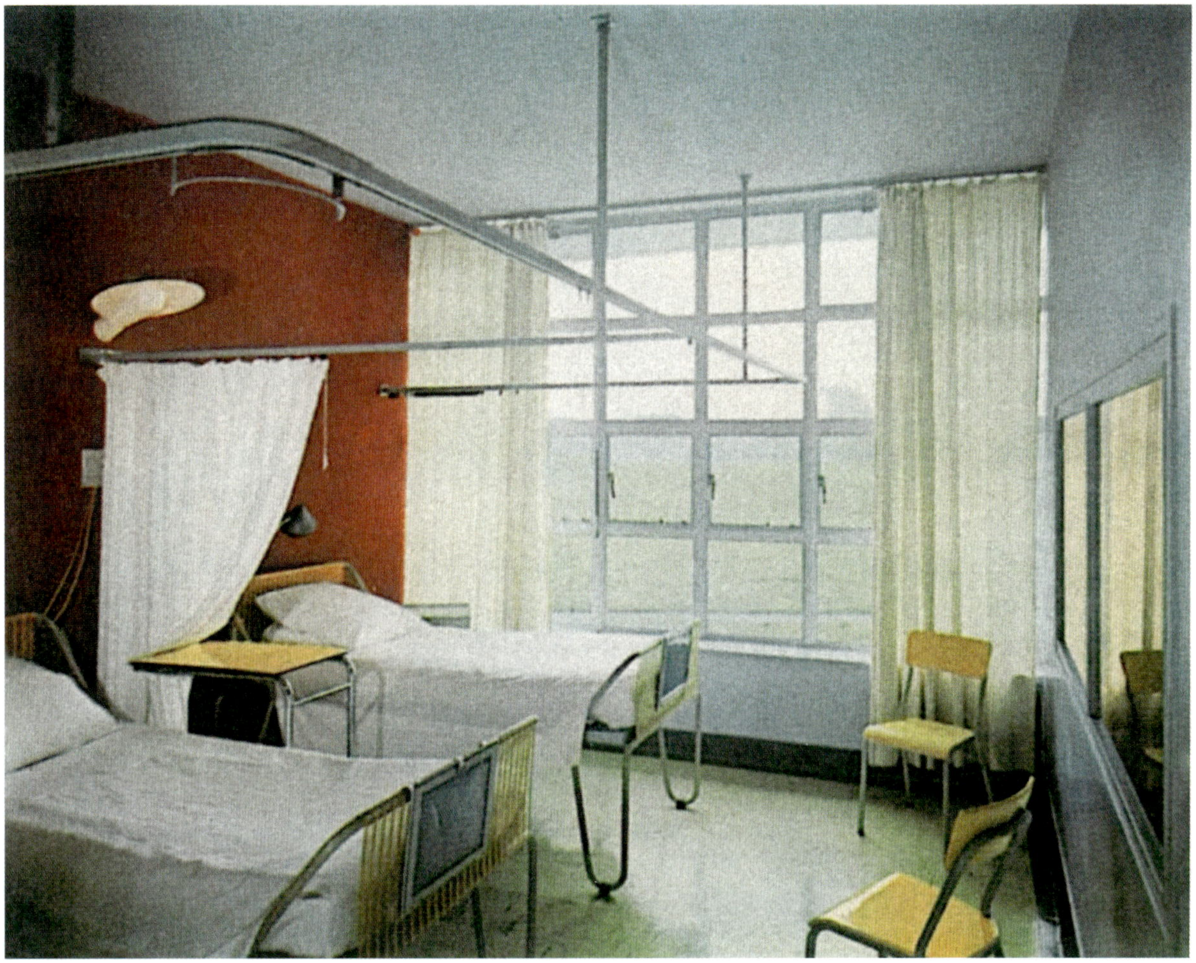

182

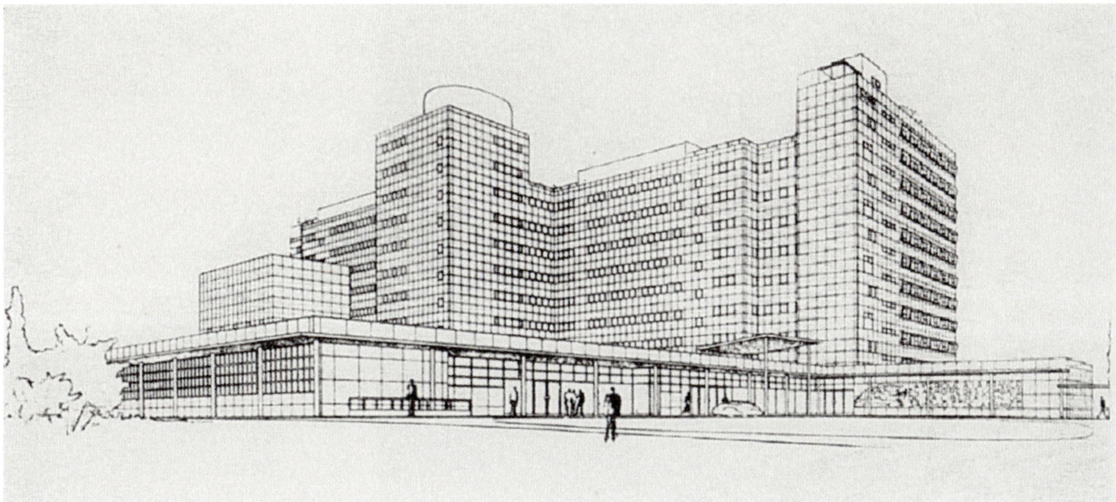

183

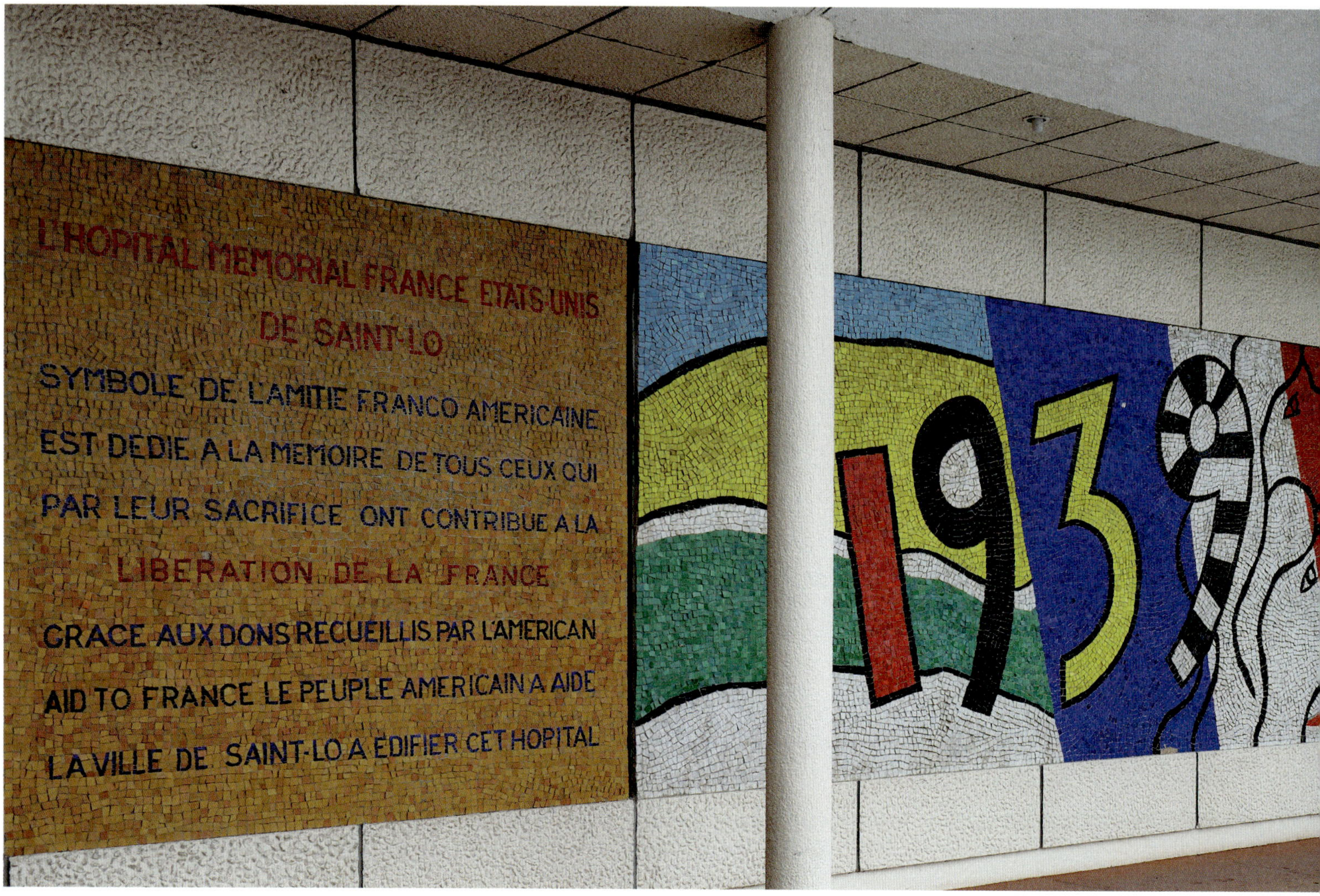
L'HOPITAL MEMORIAL FRANCE ETATS-UNIS
DE SAINT-LO
SYMBOLE DE L'AMITIE FRANCO AMERICAINE
EST DEDIE A LA MEMOIRE DE TOUS CEUX QUI
PAR LEUR SACRIFICE ONT CONTRIBUE A LA
LIBERATION DE LA FRANCE
GRACE AUX DONS RECUEILLIS PAR L'AMERICAN
AID TO FRANCE LE PEUPLE AMERICAIN A AIDE
LA VILLE DE SAINT-LO A EDIFIER CET HOPITAL
193

184

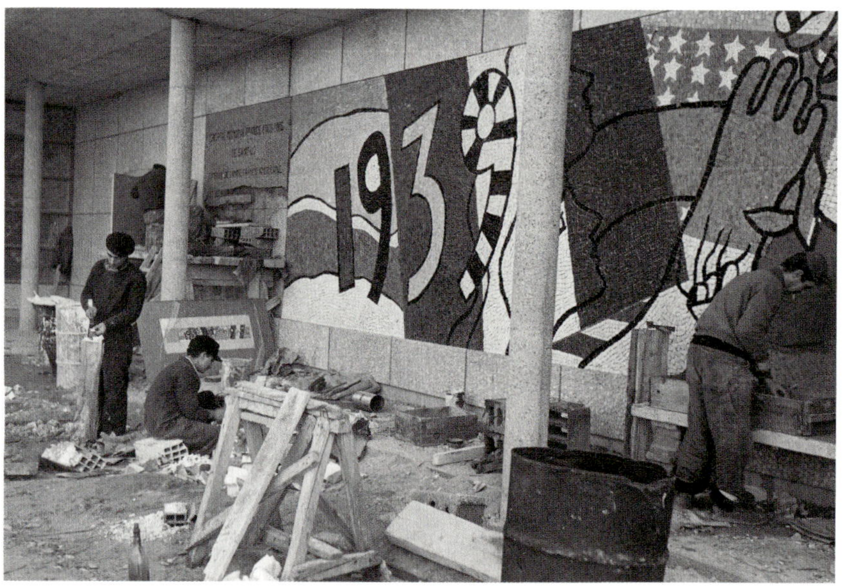

185

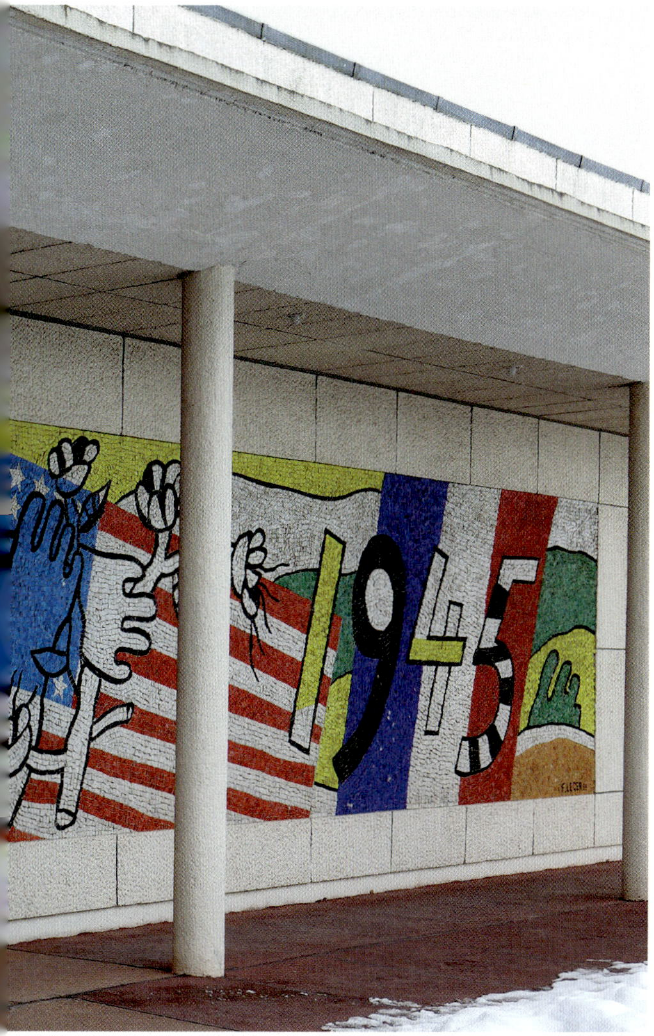

184 **Wall mosaic at Centre Hospitalier Mémorial France-Etats-Unis, Saint-Lô (Memorial Hospital), Photo: 2010, mosaic: 1956**

185 **Realization of the wall mosaic at Centre Hospitalier Mémorial France-Etats-Unis, Saint-Lô (Memorial Hospital), 1956**
Centre Pompidou, Bibliothèque Kandinsky,
Fonds Paul Nelson, Paris

186 ***Maquette Saint-Lô* (Study for Saint-Lô), 1955**
Gouache on tracing paper laminated on canvas
16 × 30 cm
Galerie Louise Leiris, Paris

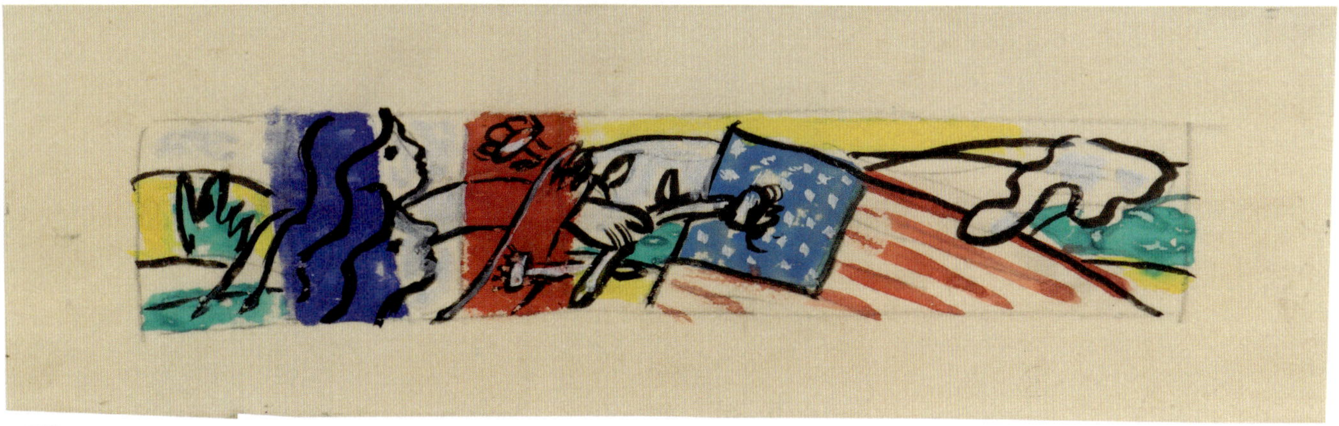

186

187 **Maison Badin (Experimental Suspended House),**
-190 **Sceaux, 1954/55**
Architect: Paul Nelson, polychrome color design for the windows: Fernand Léger, exterior and interior views shortly after the building was erected
Centre Pompidou, Bibliothèque Kandinsky, Paris

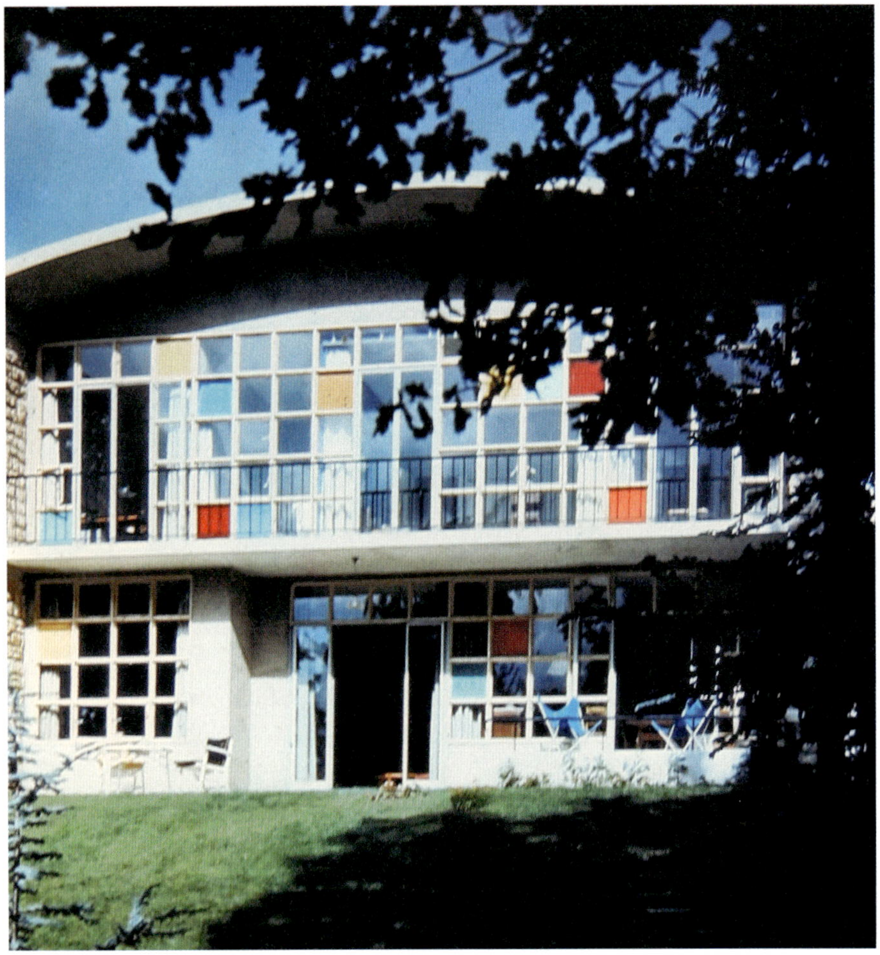

187

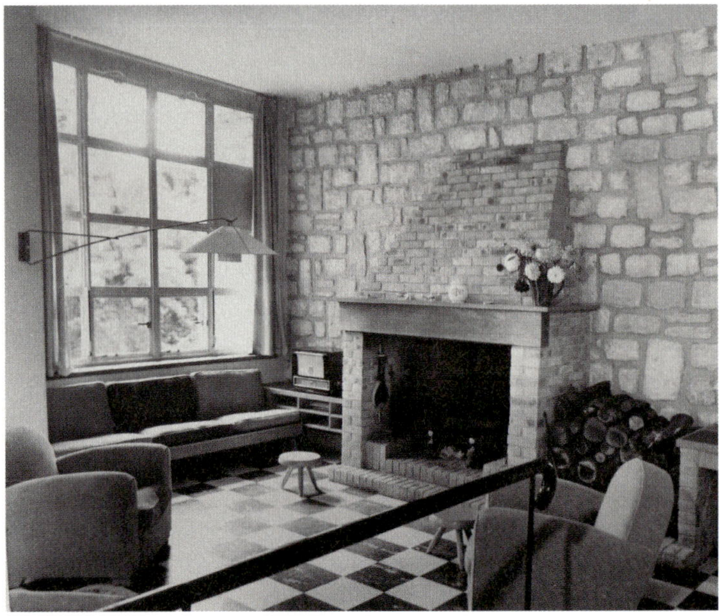

188

Paul Nelson on the Badin House (1955)
South view of the Badin House of Sceaux
by Paul Nelson, 1955

The curtain facade facing the park of Sceaux is built with the flexible window wall and colored by Fernand Léger. The floor slab which is equipped for radiant heat [?] up and down is suspended from light metal trusses leaving the ground floor completely free. The 3 of the 5 bedrooms and 1 of the 2 baths on the second floor give on the balcony all facing the beautiful view of the park. But by using a different opaque filler mosaic in the window wall of each room, variations on a given theme become possible for one of the first times

Paul Nelson's notes on the back of a photograph of the House Badin, Centre Pompidou, Bibliothèque Kandinsky, NEL 45, Fonds Paul Nelson, boîte 2, 3921 NEL 59-5, Paris

–

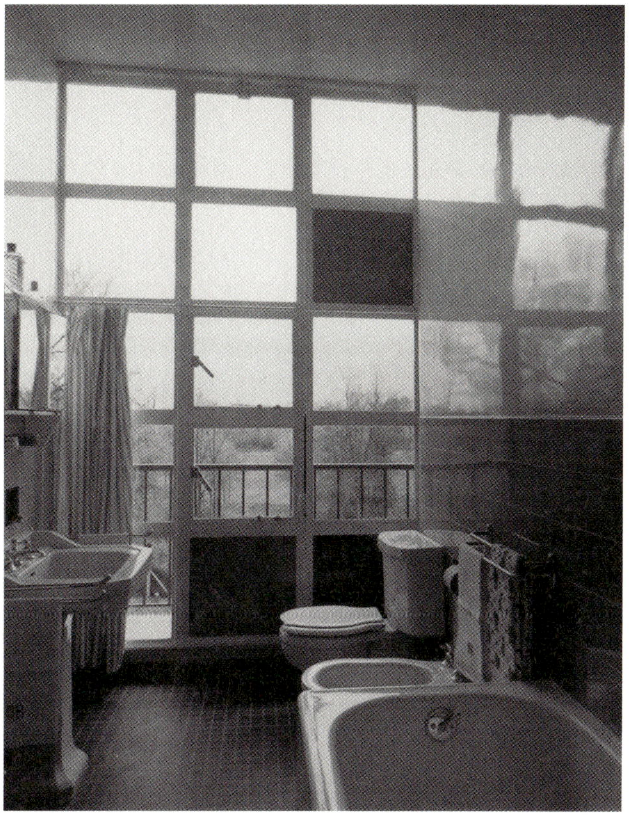

189

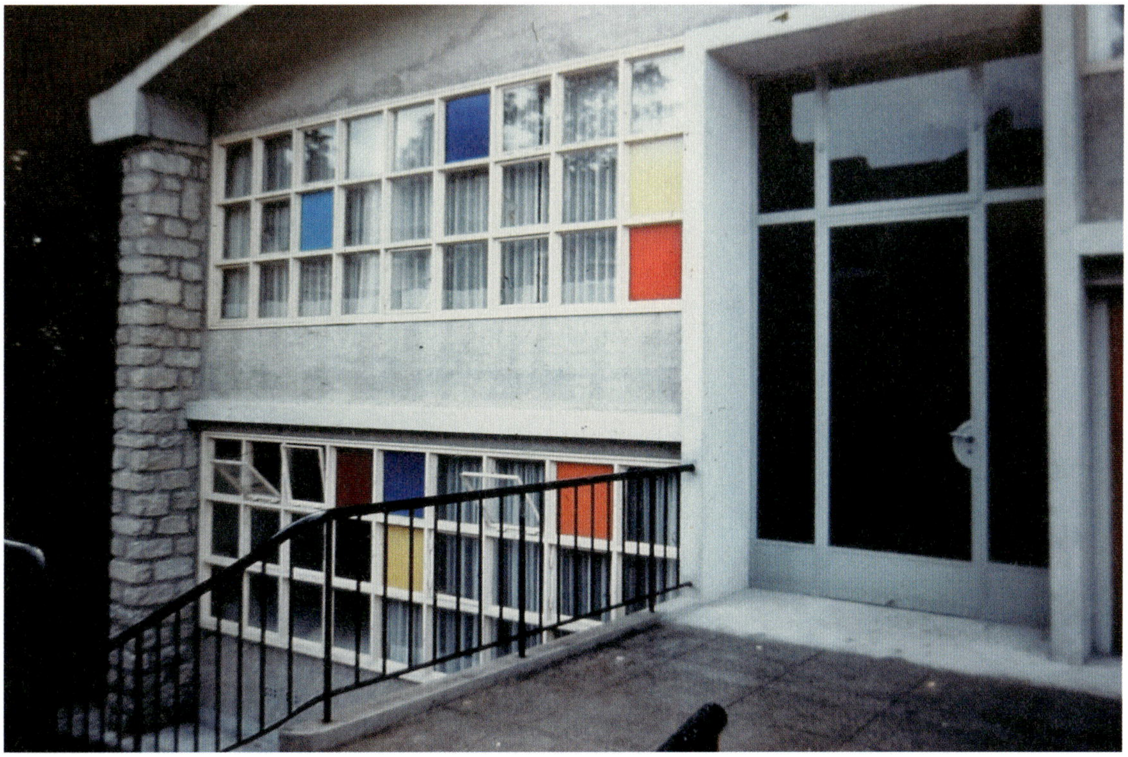

190

Fernand Léger and Wallace K. Harrison: An American Dream Come True
By Katia Baudin

"[…] painters are put into this world in order to destroy lifeless surfaces, to make them livable […]" – Fernand Léger[1]

"When we come to painters, I have to admit, I'm stumped. It seems to me that we have many very promising young men and women, but, there seems very little chance for them to practice at the apex of their profession, i.e., mural decoration. We had a period from 1932 to 1938 when the Federal Government gave the painter a chance—but since then there have not been many walls waiting for the brush strokes of the master. Certainly there have been few 1950 De Medici's waiting to command the work of the future Michelangelo's." – Wallace K. Harrison[2]

Léger had been chasing after Le Corbusier for decades, repeatedly offering his services to the great modernist architect—but to no avail, as Le Corbusier preferred to play the role of painter and muralist himself. An American architect finally answered the French artist's prayers: Wallace K. Harrison (1895–1981).[3]

While the name Harrison may not ring any bells today, many of the public buildings he designed, notably in New York, are familiar landmarks. Several buildings within Rockefeller Center, the 1939 World's Fair theme park, the Metropolitan Opera House in Lincoln Center, La Guardia airport, the CIA headquarters in Langley, Virginia, and even the the United Nations headquarters in New York—as director of planning —are among the prime achievements of the architect, who was featured on the cover of *Time* magazine on September 22, 1952. Harrison was also active in residential projects, where he let himself experiment more freely, and where his modernist heritage can most keenly be felt. Projects range from his own home in Huntington, Long Island—one of the first examples of the International Style in America (1932)— to the numerous homes and apartments Harrison worked on for his close friend and ally, Nelson Rockefeller in Manhattan, Tarrytown (on the Hudson River), Seal Harbor, Maine, and elsewhere.

Harrison—who studied at the École des Beaux-Arts in Paris from 1919 to 1923—was a European at heart, adhering to modernism's principles and ideals, and sharing the core values of his "Old World" counterparts—including Léger's French architect friends Le Corbusier, Perriand, Bruyère, Mallet-Stevens, and the Union des Artistes Modernes group (Union of Modern Artists, or UAM)—who aimed to integrate the fine arts of painting and sculpture within architectural projects. In line with Harrison's deeply ingrained attitude captured in the quotation of his words above, he solicited artists to participate in his projects and convinced his patrons —notably Rockefeller—to include art commissions in their architectural commissions. No other artist benefitted more from this than Fernand Léger, who worked on a dozen projects—both realized and unrealized—for or via Harrison between 1938 and 1952.

Although according to some sources, the painter and the American architect first met around 1927—possibly through the artist and collector Mary Callery—it seems more probable that the two met via Le Corbusier in the mid-1930s.[4] However, the pivotal moment in their relationship can be traced to a day in early August 1938, when Harrison came to visit Léger in Paris in order to persuade him to come to New York, offering the French painter a mural commission for Rockefeller's Manhattan apartment. In addition, Harrison—who was Rockefeller's preferred architect, as well as his art advisor— invited Léger to take up a teaching stint at Yale on the subject of mural painting, in conjunction with Harrison's own architectural seminar.[5] During this August trip to Paris, Harrison also invited Léger to take on a public project: a mural commission for Radio City; the inspired painter produced a series of ten sketches within two days to Harrison's apparent satisfaction.[6] In early September, Léger happily stated in a letter, "Decoration project accepted by Nelson Rockefeller. Harrison is begging me to come over and do it on site. I'm leaving—."[7]

Léger had previously made two trips to New York—a city that fascinated him—in 1931 and in 1935–36, during which his multiple attempts to secure mural commissions had remained unsuccessful. On the first trip, his discussions with Hilla Rebay and Solomon Guggenheim for a mural in the latter's estate on Long Island's Gold Coast never came to fruition. His second trip brought him one step closer to realizing a mural within the framework of the New Deal's newly instated Works Progress Administration public mural program, which commissioned public murals and invited him to make a series of sketches for the French Line pier in New York Harbor (fig. 165).[8]

During the six months of Léger's third visit to America, he worked on several projects for both Rockefeller and Harrison and found them both to be charming: "Rockefeller really nice. Not at all decadent—sturdy, massive, and very modest. A good billionaire—Harrison delightful—."[9] Contrary to his previous experiences with architects, most of these permanent projects actually materialized.

A Winning Team: Léger, Harrison, and Rockefeller

His first task was to paint a mural above a fireplace in the living room on the twelfth floor of Rockefeller's Fifth Avenue apartment, which Harrison had recently redesigned in a classical style. Léger's painting would be facing another mural situated above a fireplace on the opposite site of the room, *Le chant* (The Song) by Matisse, who, contrary to Léger, had not made his mural on site (fig. 214). The mural design Rockefeller selected from Léger's proposals (at least five, figs. 215–217) builds on the painter's animated landscape series of 1937, assembling flowing biomorphic shapes based on aloe plants and tree trunks together with more static architectural shapes (figs. 212, 213). While the figurative elements remain recognizable, the general composition echoes certain abstracted designs for murals without a specific site which the artist had worked on earlier that year (fig. 221). Léger's key advantage of actually seeing the site motivated him to increase the color intensities. Rockefeller's satisfaction with the result was such that he had Léger work on another site-specific project around the newly created circular staircase extending from the twelfth to the fourteenth floors and the twelfth-floor hallway.[10] For Léger, "The decoration even posed some tricky problems. We had to put ourselves in the place of the man who would be seeing the same painting for years. So around the staircase, I tried to make a nice arrangement of colors."[11] (figs. 222–224) Léger developed a completely abstract composition for this space: an interplay of colors and biomorphic shapes which evoke his flint and root sketches of the early 1930s (figs. 119, 120). He created several sketches for the project in Harrison's office.[12] He was able to concretize his views that abstract art is best adapted to architectural projects in that the painting accompanies the wall—bringing to mind the monumental, abstract mural he painted for the UAM pavilion at the 1937 World's Fair in Paris together with Albert Gleizes and Léopold Survage, aptly entitled *L'Accompagnement d'architecture* (Architectural Accompaniment, fig. 146).

Léger's interventions in Rockefeller's apartment attest to his sensitivity to and deep understanding of architectural contexts, as each proposal is adapted to a specific situation. With the fireplace mural, he created a mural closer in spirit to a *tableau de chevalet* (easel painting)—to be viewed from a more static, frontal position—whereas his more abstract composition, which filled the entire space around the staircase, took into account the viewer's movement and occasional glances. One might note that Léger painted both the fireplace and the staircase murals on canvas pasted onto the wall. Indeed, over the decades, Léger rarely painted his privately commissioned, site-specific murals directly onto walls.[13] The reason seems to reside in the collector's wish to retain the option of removing the work without destroying it. This hypothesis seems to be confirmed when one considers the subsequent lives of the two Rockefeller murals. The staircase mural was removed in 1964 when the second floor of the apartment was given up; it was then sold in 1973 to the dealer Harold Diamond, and has since been dismantled into smaller canvases which have been sold separately—disfiguring the work and Léger's original intention.[14] The fireplace mural was placed in storage in 1950, and then lent to Harrison the following year, only to be reinstalled in its original location in 1969. It is now in the Museum of Modern Art's collection.[15]

During this trip, Léger worked on another project for a newly built home belonging to Nelson Rockefeller: the Hawes Guest House in Pocantico, New York. Designed by Harrison in 1939, the house consists of two small fieldstone pavilions—a rectangular pavilion housing the bedrooms, a circular one for the living room—connected by a roof. In this case, the collaboration between artist and architect went a step further: for the first time, Léger's intervention structurally modified the architecture. Harrison asked Léger to design a cutout in the roof to provide more light for the entryway.[16] Rather than creating a rounded skylight, as Le Corbusier had for the 1925 Pavillon de l'Esprit Nouveau (Pavilion of the New Spirit) and the 1935 Maison du jeune homme (Home for a Young Man)—both projects Léger participated in (figs. 89, 129)—Léger designed a bird-like shape, which is projected through the skylight opening onto the slate floor, moving across it in slow animation with the passage of daylight (figs. 234, 235).

Harrison and Rockefeller were actively engaged in developing a public art program at Rockefeller Center during this period, for which they approached Léger. The artist had met one of the Center's original architects, Harvey Wiley Corbett, via Austrian architect Frederick Kiesler back in 1931.[17] In a speech Léger delivered at the Museum of Modern Art in 1935, he lauded Radio City, part of Rockefeller Center, as "the most representative monument of the modern age. Naturally we would need to discuss this magnificent project, and a painterly, decorative design equal to the building as a whole. I have some very clear ideas in this respect. Mosaic should have played a part, but that's another story and for another time."[18] Léger had appealed to Le Corbusier to help him secure a commission and asked Le Corbusier to talk to Harrison about him: "I found out this evening that Harrison will continue with Radio City, or that he has important things to do there. Is there room for any decorations? Could you talk to him about this and arrange a meeting when I get back from Chicago?"[19]

One can thus imagine and even better understand Léger's enthusiasm when Harrison mentioned the Rockefeller Center commission during his visit to Paris in 1938. Léger's analysis of both site and context is reflected in his proposal for the site: an animated film based on a series of studies paying homage to Manhattan with multiple references to the Statue of Liberty, billboards, skyscrapers, ships in the harbor, etc. to be projected onto the wall of the International Building's lobby (figs. 196–202). A moving mural would indeed best reflect his perception of Manhattan, as captured in his very first impressions of the city back in 1931: "I 'took in' the lights of New York last night. It really is the greatest spectacle in the world—all the more surprising in that everything is strictly utilitarian, and the movies are quite incapable of conveying this limitless world [...] it's a vertical city [...] Everything is upright climbing elongated";[20] "everything's moving, fidgeting leaping."[21] Harrison, who was in charge of designing the International Building, described it as:

"[a] moving mural that would have gone at the same rate that the escalators went up ... the whole thing would have been going together. It would have been wonderful. [...] We actually built the wall of white marble on which Léger's mural would have been shown. [...] [W]e even built the projection booth down in the lobby. Léger had done a number of drawings for the project and these were to be given to a writer

191 **Fernand Léger and Wallace K. Harrison, c. 1940**
Avery Architectural & Fine Arts Library, Columbia University, New York, Wallace K. Harrison architectural drawings and papers, Series II: Collection II; Box 6, Folder 31

192 **Portrait of Fernand Léger in his studio on October 7, 1941, New York**
Avery Architectural & Fine Arts Library, Columbia University, New York, Wallace K. Harrison architectural drawings and papers

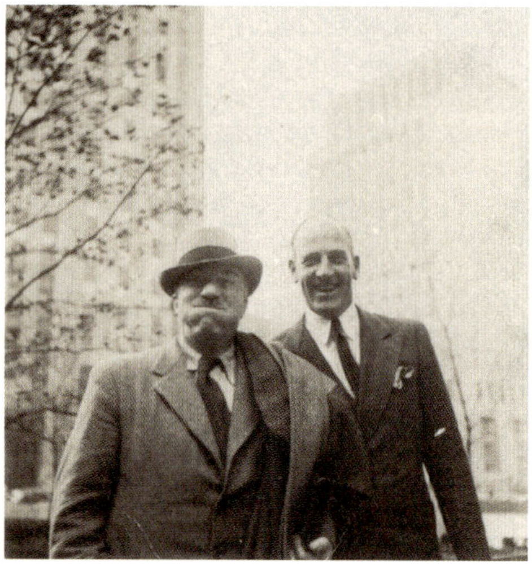

191

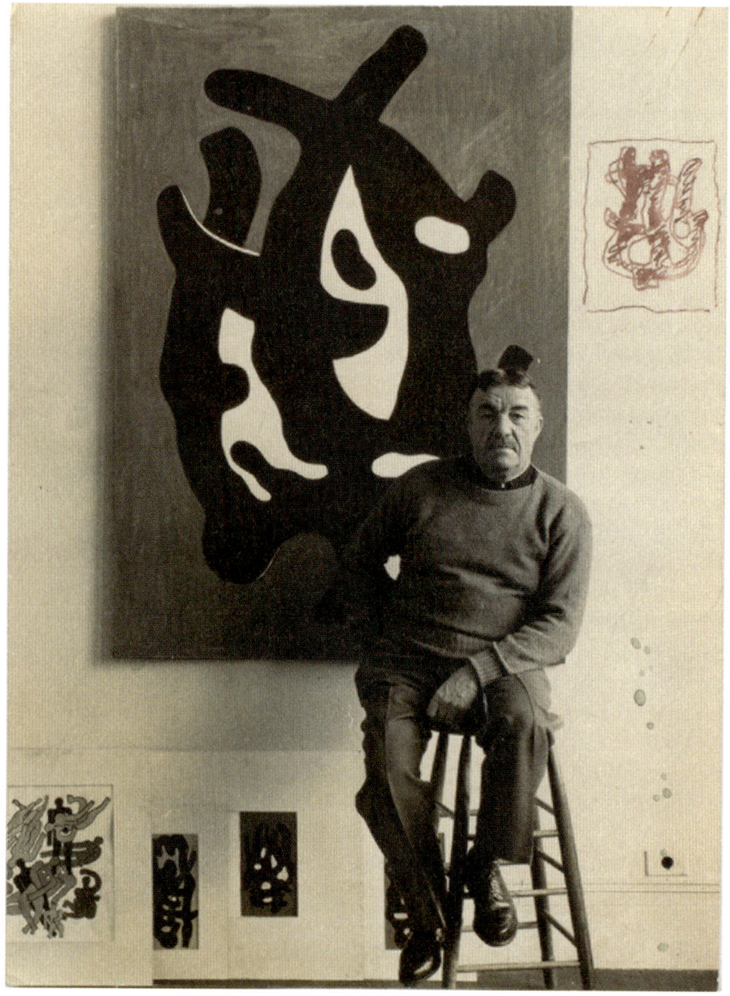

192

who would put together the scenario according to Léger's directions and from looking at the drawings."[22]

Unfortunately, this particularly experimental and novel idea met with opposition from both management and the conservative art committee, and was thus not realized.[23]

The cinematic mural would have enabled Léger to apply his interest in and exploration of the time-based medium of film (cf. *Le Ballet mécanique* [Mechanical Ballet]) to murals (figs. 22). It also reflected a dream that had intensified over the years of projecting light and color in space, particularly in urban environments. He had thus proposed illuminating the Eiffel Tower for the 1937 World's Fair, and was fascinated by Manhattan by night, illuminated as it was by a dynamic interplay of light and color from billboards and neon signs (fig. 137). The painter deplored the grayness of New York under cloudy skies, leading him to propose bringing color to Manhattan streets in 1931: "Fifth Avenue could be red; Madison, blue; Park Avenue, yellow."[24] He later planned the same interplay of primary colors for his cinematic mural.

Harrison—who was certainly familiar with Léger and had probably seen Léger's murals for the 1937 World's Fair in Paris—approached the artist to work on his plans for the 1939 World's Fair in New York, which included a theme center conceived with a futuristic, emblematic Trylon and Perisphere (with his architectural firm Harrison & Fouilhoux), as well as several buildings, including one for Consolidated Edison (fig. 205). Léger worked on two projects for the latter building, a mural and a fountain (figs. 208, 211). The artist made numerous sketches for both projects, some of which were done on Harrison's company letterhead—indicating that Léger probably made them at Harrison's office (figs. 209, 210). The architect would later recall Léger's "exuberant manner of sketching ideas for the project as they kept popping into his head."[25] The mural—with its multiple references to electricity—was painted by workers following Léger's return to Paris, and lacked the vibrancy of the artist's initial sketches. The fountain project was—unfortunately, one might add—abandoned. According to the sketches and the model, Léger appears to have planned a fountain displaying a dynamic interplay of color and movement in space and heralding the kinetic art of the future.

Léger and Harrison Take the Plunge

World War II occasioned Léger's fourth and final trip to the United States. Léger fled France when it was under German occupation in November 1940—which led to his being labeled a degenerate artist—and was able to make his way to New York, thanks to Harrison, who tried to secure him a teaching job at Yale, building on the eight lectures the artist had given there on color in the world and on architecture and painting during his previous stay. Once again, both Rockefeller and Harrison played instrumental roles in Léger's life, albeit in different capacities.

This would be Léger's longest stay in the States, for he would only return to France at the end of World War II, in December 1945. During this stay, Léger—who spoke little English—developed close ties to other expats from the art and architecture fields, including core Congrès Internationaux d'Architecture Moderne (International Congresses of Modern Architecture, known as the CIAM) members Sigfried Giedion and Josep Lluís Sert—with both of whom he co-wrote a manifesto ("Nine Points on Monumentality") in 1943—as well as the American architect Paul Nelson, who invited Léger to present his ideas on the role of color in town planning to the United States Housing Authority committee in 1942.[26] It is somewhat surprising that, contrary to his comparatively brief yet highly productive third trip just a few months earlier, Léger realized few murals during this fourth, much longer stay. The reason is certainly his precarious status as an immigrant, for, although Rockefeller's intervention had enabled Léger to extend his visa, he was not allowed to accept commissions and fees for his work as an artist from August 1941 onwards.[27] However, teaching at an American university was permitted, enabling Léger to pursue this activity, in particular at the Harvard School of Architecture (thanks to Walter Gropius, who invited him to give lectures on color in architecture in 1943 and 1945), and at Mills College in San Francisco (summer 1941).

During his stay at Mills College, Léger completed a series of twenty drawings and sketches around the theme of *plongeurs* (divers), which obsessed the artist during his entire stay in the United States (figs. 237–241, 243). A few months later, Léger wrote in a letter to Le Corbusier, "Personally I've been doing a lot of work on a very dynamic theme, *Les Plongeurs* [The Divers], which is freer and more violent than *Les Perroquets* [The Parrots/The Acrobats], which you saw in Paris. I've been battling with the human body and pure color for fifteen months. Already done gouaches and drawings, and fifteen or twenty canvases."[28] Léger's interest in the subject was piqued back in Marseille: "In 1940, I was in Marseille working on my *Divers*, five or six persons in the act of diving. I had the idea for the picture in the South of France. Later, I left for the United States and one day I went to a swimming pool there. The divers were no longer five or six, but two hundred there at once. What do I see? To whom belonged a head, a leg, some arms, one could not tell, one could not make a distinction. So I scattered the limbs in my picture. I think I was far closer to the truth in that than Michelangelo was when he studied the detail in each of the muscles."[29]

Léger was haunted by a dream: that of painting a monumental version of his diver theme. His inscription on one drawing of a constellation of divers can be read as a cry for help: "Who will give me this wall? I need a wall to carry out Men in Space." (fig. 247) One sketch for a mural sets the divers theme around an opening—perhaps a fireplace, door or window—on a fieldstone wall (1942, fig. 236). Here, Léger appears to have adapted his *Étoile de Mer* composition (Starfish, 1942, fig. 239) to an architectural context. The fact that Harrison was in possession of this sketch can be taken as confirmation that Léger developed the idea for one of his buildings. Harrison used stone walls on two occasions during this period, both for houses commissioned by Rockefeller: the aforementioned Hawes Guest House (1939)—for which Léger made the skylight—and the Anchorage in Seal Harbor, Maine (1941). It seems probable that Léger developed the proposal for this latter house set on a cliff above the bay, which dates from the same period as the sketch. The commission probably fell through due to the recent work restrictions imposed on Léger; it was obviously impossible for Rockefeller, with his increasing political responsibilities and ambitions, to carry it through.[30]

Ultimately, it was Harrison himself who enabled Léger to realize his dream in the architect's own home in Huntington, on Long Island's north shore. Léger was thoroughly familiar with the site, having already spent some time here during his previous trip to America.[31] The house was designed by the architect in 1932 as "an exercise in how to fit circles together," with a round living room (10.45 meters in diameter) flanked by a round dining room half its size and a quarter-circle shaped bathroom, with round concrete paving stones leading towards a round swimming pool in the garden (figs. 256–261). A rectangular bedroom wing was added onto the structure in 1940.[32] The Harrison house and estate provided Léger the ideal location for three site-specific interventions: a mural in the living room, followed by a mural on the floor of the swimming pool—both variations on the theme of divers—and an indoor skylight in the shape of a cloud (figs. 253–255).[33]

Two vivid accounts recount the realization of the *Les Plongeurs* mural in the living room (figs. 244–246). In Ruth Meyer's account of a 1975 conversation with Harrison, she later wrote that Harrison had told her:

"Léger was a frequent visitor to the house and they had many art and architectural projects under discussion. Harrison knew that Léger was always looking for a wall to paint. Léger proposed the mural and during a lengthy stay with the Harrison family it was undertaken. A sketch was made, squared off and enlarged for transfer to the wall. Canvas strips were applied to the wall to receive it. Harrison, his wife and daughter worked in his words 'as Léger's assistants'. He made no mention of any others being present. When the great black line drawing was done the collaborators, patron and artist, looked at it and, although color had been contemplated, decided it was great and complete."[34]

In Hester Diamond's account of a conversation with Harrison in 1974, the year she and her husband purchased the home from him, she writes:

"Harrison was a close friend of Léger's. He had helped him get at least one commission [...] In 1942, Léger told him he wanted to do a wall decoration for Harrison's living room in Huntington. In preparation for this, Léger made some preparatory sketches, as he always did for large works, and Harrison had the canvas put up on the wall. Léger came out to the country for a long weekend and did the mural in the course of the weekend."[35]

These two accounts convey the collaborative approach the painter preferred for murals. While his murals were usually painted with the help of his students, in this case, far from home, the exiled artist had to find help elsewhere. For Harrison and his wife, this must have been a dream come true, since both were amateur artists, painting in the style of Léger. They apparently did not only collaborate on the living room mural, but also on the pool mural (fig. 254).[36]

In the living room mural, the black paint drips that extend below certain lines on the canvas confirm that *Les Plongeurs* was painted in rapid streaks, with the canvas apposed onto the wall. Here again, the artist painted the mural on canvas rather than directly on the wall; as in the case of Rockefeller's home, this seems to reflect the collector's wish. While the white, undulating shape flanking the fireplace from above is echoed in Léger's sinuous lines, the central part of the composition—three human forms moving in space—is directly inspired by Léger's painting *La danse* (The Dance, 1942, fig. 241).[37] As in *La danse* and other *plongeur* paintings of this period (figs. 239, 243), in which Léger separated the lines and contours from the color planes, the preliminary sketch for the mural proves that Léger planned red, yellow, blue, and green color planes (fig. 248). He even sketched the contours for the colors onto the canvas. While he limited his palette in other related works—such as his *Les Plongeurs sur fond jaune* (Divers on a Yellow Background, 1941, fig. 237) and *Les acrobats en gris* (Acrobats in Grey, 1942–44, fig. 238)—he used different hues of black, gray, and white in these cases to give his figures a sense of volume. *Les Plongeurs* is the only mural in his oeuvre in which color—which played such an existential role for him as a painter—is totally absent. What led the painter to this decision?

A photo of Harrison and city planner Robert Moses sitting in the living room in front of the mural (fig. 245), gives one the impression that the two are sitting on a stage, in front of a monumental set design. A remark Léger made back in 1918—four years before he embarked on his first murals—seems prophetic: "To me, 'the opposite of a wall' is a picture with its verve and movement. For example, in a flat, I'm satisfied if my picture controls the room, if it dominates everything and everyone, people and furniture. It must be the most important character."[38] If the color fields had been filled, the effect of the mural would have been overpowering and out of proportion with the moderately sized living room. The mural with its architectural setting—nestled in between a wood-paneled ceiling and hardwood floors surrounded by black and white tiles—must have created a dynamic interplay of biomorphic and geometric shapes. Color within the mural would have been superfluous, since nature provided the colors—which changed over the seasons—through the monumental wall-to-floor windows on the south side of the room. One can imagine that the play of light and shadows on the wall would have further animated the mural.[39]

The mural is part of the Museum Ludwig's collection; since 1986, it has often been given pride of place and hung prominently in the lobby. Viewing it in this context, one is nevertheless left with an aftertaste that Léger's dream was only partially realized, and that the artist would have liked to see *Les Plongeurs* in a more monumental, public space—and then, most probably, in color. It is certainly no coincidence that Léger's close friend, the architectural historian Sigfried Giedion, concluded his text in a 1945 publication on Léger's Plongeurs series with the following appeal: "Where are the walls of public buildings in the United States and Canada that might lend themselves to such a language? Yes, where are these walls? I can't see them."[40] (fig. 289)

Harrison and Léger Reach New Summits

In 1947, Harrison was appointed director of planning the new United Nations headquarters in Manhattan, following John D. Rockefeller's gift of the location.[41] Here again, the architect fought for the integration of top-quality art in the new, emblematic building, and, here again, his choice for the prime space—the General Assembly Hall—was Léger. The challenge of financing a mural in this space, which had not been accounted for in the budget, was resolved thanks to Nelson Rockefeller, who anonymously donated the artists' fees.[42] Harrison's proposal of Léger was not the easiest to realize in the throes of McCarthyism, and the artist was ultimately denied entry into the United States due to his membership in the Communist party.[43] Léger submitted a first series of sketches—some of which echoed paintings from his abstract *peintures murales* or "mural paintings" series—for the east and west wall spaces reserved for murals, but these were not suitable due to the artist's erroneous interpretation of the space. In 1952, the artist was provided with a scale model of the hall, which allowed him to propose the sketches that were retained and realized (figs. 312, 314, 315).[44] As Léger would later explain and recollect:

"In my opinion, abstract art is perfectly suited for large mural decorations. I have discussed it, for example, as a possibility for the United Nations. Mr [Wallace] Harrison said to me: 'We would like something from you for the UN Building in New York.' He came to see me with his model, and we discussed more or less representative pictures. We settled on something abstract, and I did two large panels, about thirty-three feet by thirty-three, for the UN."[45]

Léger proposed a former student of his, Bruce Gregory, to do the job. Upon first visiting the site, Gregory recalls:

"I could quickly see how Léger's work and sense of architectural scale would fit beautifully. [...] The gouaches of the designs to be executed were approximately 8"× 8". They were abstract in nature, but organic in feeling, and were an example of Léger's belief that abstract art functioned beautifully with the volumes of modern architecture."[46]

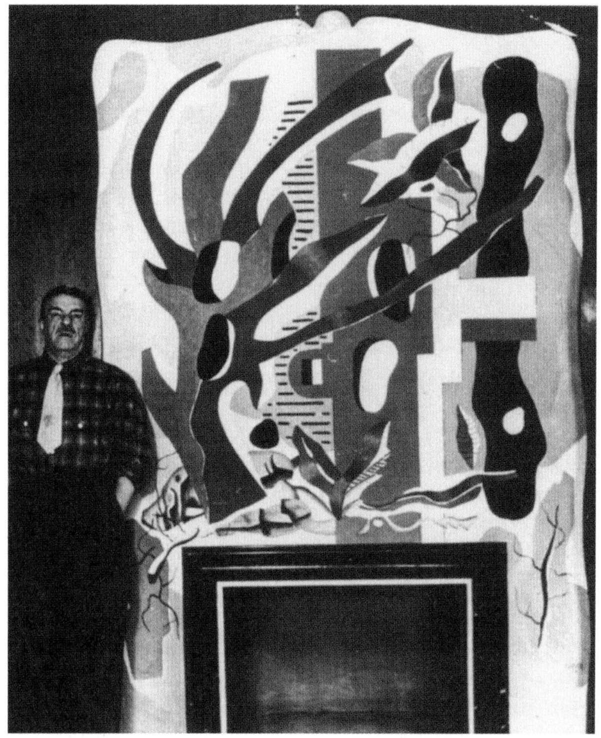

193

193 **Fernand Léger in front of his fireplace mural painting in Nelson A. Rockefeller's apartment, New York, 1938**
Archives Georges Bauquier

Gregory's account of the mural-making process shows that Harrison attentively followed the realization of the murals—demanding that his approval be sought before even the slightest modifications to Léger's plans were made. For the most part, Gregory faithfully executed Léger's designs; the adjustments he proposed reflected his deep understanding of Léger's work and intentions. Gregory sought and obtained Léger's approval to lessen the intensity of the orange originally proposed for the west wall mural.[47]

Léger considered the UN murals among his key achievements: "It is the most recent major thing that I have created; it was something that really had to be done."[48] Although many—from taxicab drivers to Harry Truman—dubbed the murals "fried-egg art"—the highly visible UN murals opened new doors for the painter. The long awaited commissions finally began pouring in for other large-scale public projects—a new phase that would abruptly come to an end with the artist's death on August 17, 1955.[49]

Wallace K. Harrison was more than "just" an architect friend and ally. He was an avid collector of Léger's work, and ultimately, perhaps, his most devoted patron: helping the artist in times of need, securing not only commissions but also teaching jobs for the artist, and granting Léger the necessary platform and conditions to be able to paint those private and public murals he so strived to create all his life. In Harrison, Léger had finally found his Medici.

1 Fernand Léger, "The Wall, the Architect, the Painter," in *Functions of Painting*, trans. Alexandra Anderson (London: Thames and Hudson, 1973), 96.
2 Wallace K. Harrison, "Must Art be Sterile?," transcript of speech given at a discussion forum at the Architectural League, New York, October 18, 1950, with annotations by the author, 3, held in Wallace K. Harrison architectural drawings and papers, 1913–86, coll. 2, box 4, file 5, Archival Collections, Department of Drawings and Archives, Avery Architectural & Fine Arts Library, Columbia University, New York. Consulted in December 2014; I have taken the liberty of making minor spelling corrections in the citation.
3 Léger's correspondence with Le Corbusier (held in the Fondation Le Corbusier, Paris) attests to his frustration with the fact that Le Corbusier never engaged him for a project (see in particular Léger's letter to Le Corbusier of September 17, 1951). In particular, Léger's speech to the architects at the 1933 CIAM conference (also included in the present publication, see page 107–10) was directed at Le Corbusier.
4 Contradictory information exists regarding the first time Léger and Harrison met. The artist Mary Callery was a close friend of Harrison's wife, and Léger collaborated with her in painting sculptures. According to Newhouse, Harrison and Le Corbusier first met in New York in 1933 (Victoria Newhouse, *Wallace K. Harrison, Architect* [New York: Rizzoli, 1989], 29, 112). According to Ruth K. Meyer, who interviewed Harrison within the framework of her doctoral dissertation, Harrison met Léger in the 1930s (Ruth Ann Krueger Meyer, *Fernand Léger's Mural Paintings 1922–55* [Ph.D. dissertation, University of Minnesota, 1980], 224). An undated letter on stationery from the Gotham hotel in New York from Léger to Le Corbusier (probably dating from 1935/36, when both Léger and Le Corbusier were in New York), in which Léger asks Le Corbusier to set up a meeting with Harrison, confirms this hypothesis (letter E2-8-68, consulted on April 10, 2015, by the author at the Fondation Le Corbusier, Paris).
5 According to a letter from Léger to Simone Herman, Callery accompanied Harrison on this first visit and strongly supported the commission. Fernand Léger, *Lettres à Simone* (Paris: Centre Georges Pompidou/Skira, 1987), 222 (letter of August 17, 1938). Léger picks up on the competitive spirit between Harrison and Gropius, with Harrison inviting many architects and artists to take part in his seminar.
6 Cf. letter from Fernand Léger to Simone Herman, in Léger, *Lettres à Simone* (1987), 226 (letter of August 28, 1938). The term Radio City was used at the time to denote the Rockefeller Center.
7 Postcard from Léger to Simone Herman, in Léger, *Lettres à Simone* (1987), 227 (postcard of September 9, 1938).
8 The director of the French Line pier ultimately rejected Léger's proposal. See Burgoyne Diller's account of this incident, included in the present publication, page 165. For more information on Léger's other mural projects and leads during these first two trips, see Simon Willmoth, "Léger and America," in *Fernand Léger: The Later Years*, exhibition catalog (London: Whitechapel Art Gallery, 1987), 45.
9 Letter from Léger to Simone Herman, in Léger, *Lettres à Simone* (1987), 229 (letter of September 27, 1938). See also Fernand Léger, "Choses d'Amérique," *La Nouvelle Revue Française* 27, no. 308 (May 1, 1939): 902–03.
10 See Nelson Rockefeller, introduction to *The Nelson A. Rockefeller Collection: Masterpieces of Modern Art* (New York: Hudson Hills Press, 1981), 16. Rockefeller's account is reproduced in the present publication, see page203. The Rockefeller Archive Center in Sleepy Hollow, New York, holds files on these murals, which date the staircase mural to 1939–41, implying that Léger reworked it during his fourth trip to America. The author consulted these archives in December 2014.
11 Pierre Imbourg, "Fernand Léger pendant son séjour en Amérique a fait des conférences à l'université de Yale et décoré l'intérieur de Rockefeller Jr.," *Beaux-arts: chronique des arts et de la curiosité* 76, no. 326 (March 31, 1939).
12 According to the collection sheets and files under NAR RE4/Cancelled Photo File Leger/Art subseries 6/box 16/folder 92 held in the Rockefeller Archive Center, Sleepy Hollow, New York.
13 Two notable exceptions are Léger's outdoor fresco for Badovici's home in Vézelay (1934–36) and the mural he painted on Kahnweiler's dining room wall in Saint-Hilaire (1954).
14 According to the staircase mural file under NAR RE4/Cancelled Photo File Léger/Art subseries 6/box 16/folder 92 held at the Rockefeller Archive Center, Rockefeller sold the mural to the dealer Harold Diamond—who later purchased Harrison's home on Long Island. See also Meyer, *Fernand Léger's Mural Paintings*, 227.
15 According to annotations in the fireplace mural file under NAR RE4/Cancelled Photo File Léger/Art subseries 6/box 16/folder 91 at the Rockefeller Archive Center. Rockefeller had been a trustee of the MoMA since 1932, and was named its president in 1939.
16 Newhouse, *Wallace K. Harrison*, 68.
17 Cf. Fernand Léger, "New York" (1931), in Fernand Léger, *Functions of Painting*, 84–90. Corbett had left the Rockefeller Center Project to work on Metropolitan Life's north building; Léger was fascinated by the vertical circulation challenges that confronted the architect in planning what was intended to be the tallest building in the world (due to the Great Depression, only twenty-nine of the planned one hundred floors were built).

18 Fernand Léger, "Un nouveau réalisme, la couleur pure et l'objet" (1935), *Fonctions de la peinture* (Paris: Gallimard, 2004), 192. The English edition of this text (Functions of Painting, 109–13) differs from the French.
19 Léger in a letter to Le Corbusier (c. 1935/36), consulted by the author at the Fondation Le Corbusier, Paris (letter E2-8-68), cf. note 4. Radio City was the generic term used at the time for Rockefeller Center.
20 Postcard from Léger to Simone Herman, in Léger, *Lettres à Simone* (1987), 29 (postcard of September 27, 1931).
21 Léger in a letter to Simone Herman, in Léger, *Lettres à Simone* (1987), 34 (letter of October 16, 1931).
22 Meyer, *Fernand Léger's Mural Paintings*, 232. Harrison later gave seven gouache studies for the mural to the MoMA. According to Victoria Newhouse, the artist planned on collaborating with Walt Disney (see Victoria Newhouse, *Wallace K. Harrison, Architect* [New York: Rizzoli, 1989], 49)—however, I have not encountered primary source evidence of this.
23 See Meyer, *Fernand Léger's Mural Paintings*, 232, and Newhouse, *Wallace K. Harrison*, 49.
24 Léger, "New York," (1931), 87.
25 See Meyer's recollection of an interview with Harrison, in Meyer, *Fernand Léger's Mural Paintings*, 229. Wallace Harrison later gave a selection of Léger's sketches for the two projects to the university museums of Cornell and Dartmouth. Harrison also invited Alexander Calder, another artist he was close to, to develop a water ballet for the façade of the Con Ed building. This fountain, also illuminated by night through different colors, received much public attention and praise—while Léger's mural on the rear of the building went unnoticed.
26 See Willmoth, "Léger and America," 47.
27 Kristen Erickson, "Chronology," in Carolyn Lanchner, *Fernand Léger*, exhibition catalog, Museum of Modern Art (New York: Harry N. Abrams, 1998), 279.
28 Cited from an undated letter from Léger to Le Corbusier, conserved in the Fondation Le Corbusier archives, Paris, and reproduced in *Fernand Léger*, exhibition catalog (Paris: Centre Georges Pompidou, 1997), 340.
29 Léger cited in Dora Vallier, "La vie fait l'oeuvre de Fernand Léger. Propos de l'artiste recueillis," *Cahiers d'Art* 2 (1954): 156. English translation by Ruth Meyer in her PhD Dissertation *Fernand Léger's Mural Paintings 1922–55*, 247–48.
30 Nelson Rockefeller served at the time as member of the Westchester County Board of Health, and had been named in 1940 by President Roosevelt Coordinator of Inter-American Affairs. He would become Roosevelt's Assistant Secretary of State in 1944.
31 In a letter dated October 2, 1938, from "Mon Souci, Huntington, Long Island," Léger wrote to Simone Herman "I have just returned from a lovely weekend with Harrison [...] – in the area where the terrible storm hit – heaps of Harrison's oaks were knocked down – it was terrible." See Léger, *Lettres à Simone* (1987), 229 (letter of October 2, 1938).
32 See Newhouse, *Wallace K. Harrison*, 60–63. Harrison purchased eighty-five acres of land in 1931, and first lived in the Aluminaire house (by A. Lawrence Kocher and Albert Frey)—prototype for a prefabricated aluminum house, inspired by Le Corbusier—before building his own home from 1932 onwards, in several phases. Harrison sold his home to art dealer Harold Diamond in 1974; it was then sold again in 1984 (in 1985 all but 3.5 acres remained). The current owners purchased the house—which had been deliberately left to fall into disrepair by its previous owner—in 2003, restored it to its original condition, and added a wing.
33 Harrison had told Hester Diamond that Léger designed the skylight. See Kenneth Wayne, "Long Island Moderns: Artists on the North Shore from Edward Steichen to Cindy Sherman," in Kenneth Wayne and Erik Neil, eds, *Long Island Moderns: Art and Architecture on the North Shore and Beyond*, exhibition catalog (New York: The Heckscher Museum of Art/University Press of New England, 2009), 54, footnote 11. Harrison told Ruth K. Meyer that they (Léger and the Harrisons) had painted the swimming pool mural together as well. See letter from Ruth K. Meyer to Kurt Delbanco of October 26, 1984. A photocopy of this letter is in the collection file on Léger's *Les Plongeurs*, Museum Ludwig, Cologne. The design on the swimming pool floor has disappeared. The skylight has been moved by the present owners to the new wing they had built.
34 Letter from Ruth K. Meyer to Kurt Delbanco, October 26, 1984, cf. note 33.
35 Letter from Hester Diamond to Kurt Delbanco, October 25, 1984. A photocopy of this letter is held in the collection file on Léger's *Les Plongeurs*, Museum Ludwig, Cologne.
36 The Harrison archives at the Avery Architectural & Fine Arts Library, Columbia University hold several gouaches by Harrison close in spirit to Léger. Harrison reportedly kept paint cans next to his bed in case he woke up at night and wanted to paint. See Newhouse, *Wallace K. Harrison*, 57.
37 The sculptural form above the fireplace seems to be an element from a plaster cast used by Alfred Janniot for the relief on La Maison Française, Rockefeller Center. For a more detailed account of Léger's mural from a conservator's viewpoint, please refer to Petra Mandt's essay in the present publication.
38 Léger in a letter to Rosenberg, quoted in Meyer, *Fernand Léger's Mural Paintings*, 59.
39 These observations are based on my visit to the house in January 2015. I wish to thank Lori Spiegel for her generosity.
40 Sigfried Giedion, "L'art se prépare à la vie publique," in *Léger, la forme humaine dans l'espace* (Montreal: Les Éditions de l'Arbre, 1945), 50–52.
A letter from Léger to Père Couturier proves that Léger was very involved in this publication, and personally invited the different authors (cf. letter of February 12, 1944, reproduced in the present publication, see page 240). Léger gave Harrison a copy of the book, which he signed with "À Ellen Harrison, à Wallace Harrison Très amicalement F. Léger" (Harrison archives, Avery Architectural & Fine Arts Library, Columbia University, New York).
41 See Newhouse, *Wallace K. Harrison*, 112.
42 Ibid., 142. Harrison also created a review committee for art gifts.
43 See Meyer, *Fernand Léger's Mural Paintings*, 274. Harrison gave eight of these sketches to Dartmouth.
44 Cf. ibid., 274. In the fall of 1952, following the completion of the murals, Harrison gave Rockefeller ten of Léger's sketches from the second group, including those which served for the murals. Photographs of these sketches were consulted by the author in December 2014 under NAR RE4/Cancelled Photo File Léger/Art subseries 6/box 16/folder 92 in the Rockefeller Archive Center.
45 Fernand Léger, "Color in Architecture" (1954), in *Functions of Painting*, 186. According to Bruce Gregory, it was Michael Harris, Deputy Chief of Planning, who was sent to Paris with the model. Cf. Bruce Gregory, "Léger's United Nations' Murals," *Art Journal* 23, no. 1 (Fall 1963): 35. Consulted on January 3, 2015, http://www.jstor.org./stable/774636.
46 Gregory, "Léger's United Nations' Murals," 35.
47 Ibid., 35–36. Gregory had one month to paint the two murals.
48 Léger, "Color in Architecture" (1954), in *Functions of Painting*, 186.
49 See the editorial, "Strange Shapes in Eggs, Art and Nature," *Life* 3, no.18 (November 3, 1952): 21. Léger exclaimed "ca commence à venir" ("It's starting to come") regarding the post-UN commissions to Pierre Descargues, in Pierre Descargues, *Fernand Léger* (Paris: Cercle d'Art, 1955), 141.

Léger's Remarks on Rockefeller and Harrison (1939)

During my five months' stay in New York, I grew to like two Americans, two young men, both bustlingly active in the world of business: Nelson Rockefeller Jr., "responsible for Radio City," and his architect and friend Wallace Harrison, who designed "the Ball and the Spire" (the Perisphere and the Trylon), which is the architectural marker of their 1939 World's Fair. Together, these two forces of nature will carry out astonishing things in the future. I could witness them as they took action, moved about and worked. Their kindness, their tact amid their octopus-like telephones they have managed to tame. They know how to devote the right amount of time to worthwhile subjects, neither more nor less. They are by no means machines, on the contrary, they are new men, neat, clear, precise, exactly like the atmosphere they breathe.

Excerpt, originally published as F. Léger, "Choses d'Amérique," in *Nouvelle Revue Française*, no. 308 (May 1, 1939). Reprinted in F. Léger, *Lettres à Simone* (Geneva and Paris: Skira, 1987), 179–80.

–

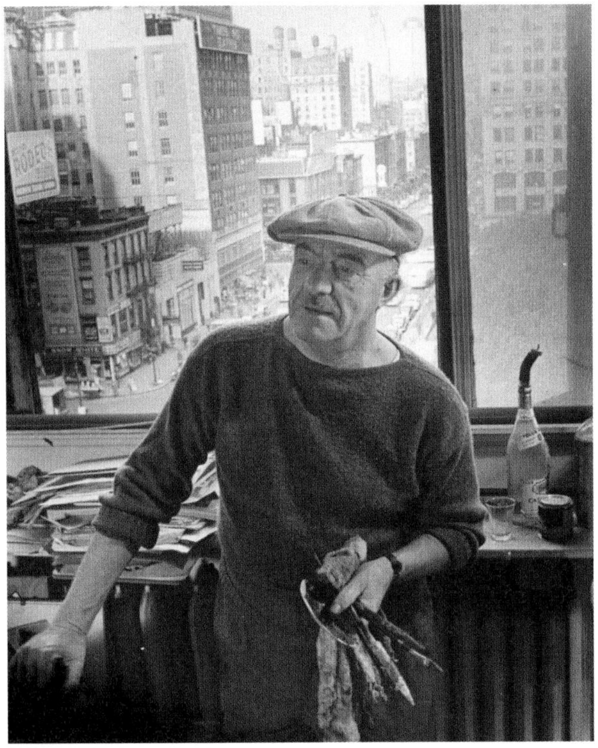

194

New York (1931)
Fernand Léger

The most colossal spectacle in the world. Neither film nor photography nor reportage can dim the amazing spectacle that is New York at night, seen from the fortieth floor. This city has been able to withstand all the vulgarizations, all the curiosity of men who have tried to describe her, copy her. She retains her freshness, her unexpectedness, her surprise for the traveler who is seeing her for the first time.

[…] This the apotheosis of vertical architecture: a bold collaboration between architects and unscrupulous bankers pushed by necessity. An unknown, unplanned elegance emerges from the geometric abstraction. Squeezed into two metal angles, these are figures, numbers that climb stiffly toward the sky, controlled by a distorting perspective.

[…] The architectural severity is broken up by the myriad fantasy of colored lights. The great spectacle begins when they go on, and this radiant vision has that special something that no artist, however inspired, has captured, nor has any theater director had a hand in it. No one has "managed" its action. This moving play is performed by the houses inhabited by tenants like you and me. Those thousands of lights that astonish us are lighted by people who work humbly at their unrewarding daily jobs. Those huge buildings are strictly utilitarian, rational; their vertical thrust reflects economic reasons.

[…] During the day New York is too severe. It lacks color, and if the sky is gray, it is a city of lead.

Why not put color on the houses? Why this oversight in the country with all these inventions?

Fifth Avenue could be red; Madison, blue; Park Avenue, yellow. Why not? And the lack of vegetation? New York has no trees. Medicine decreed a long time ago that green in particular is a color that is indispensable to life. We must live with color around us; it is as necessary as water and fire.

Clothing manufacturers could be compelled to put out a group of green dresses and green suits…

Every month, a dictator of color would decree the monthly or quarterly colors–the blue quarter, the pink fortnight! Trees could be taken out for rides in the street for those who can't get to the country. Moving landscapes decorated with tropical flowers pulled slowly along by plumed horses.

[…] Visit the office of Corbett the architect with [Friedrich] Kiesler. He is one of the greatest figures in American building. A fine, good-natured man, tall, uncomplicated. He tells me: "Accommodating 20,000 people living in one building, that is my current work." Don't think that the solution is only a question of floor space! No, it's more complicated; it's a matter of the elevators. Maneuvering this army vertically! Bring them down every day to the four dining rooms that are located sixty-five feet underground… and making all that work in the desired times.

The second thing is like a game, nothing more. Getting them outside without stopping traffic. … Six months of work. Ten specialized engineers haven't found the solution yet.

A specifically American problem–they are unbeatable in reasoning, in mass production, in numbers. Starting from numbers in order to make the whole comfortable. A New World!

Originally published as "New York vu par F. Léger," in *Cahiers d'Art* (Paris) 6, no. 9/10 (1931): 437–39.
English translation (excerpts) from "New York," in Fernand Léger, *Functions of Painting* (New York: Thames and Hudson, 1973), 84–90.

–

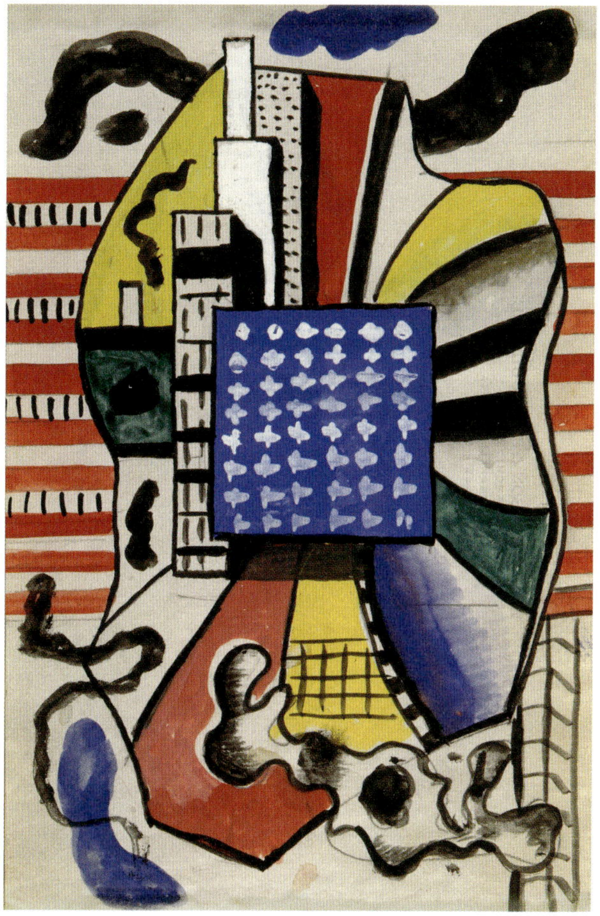

195

194 **Fernand Léger in his studio, New York, c. 1940–45**

195 ***New York*, 1944**
Gouache on paper (Letterhead from Wallace K. Harrison's architecture firm)
21.5 × 14 cm
Musée franco-américain du Château de Blérancourt

Fernand Léger's Remarks on Radio City (Rockefeller Center) (1935)

America has not taken a backward step in the construction of Radio City, far from it. Its architectural conception is very pure, very modern American, and the comprehension of interior decoration has resulted in the correct application and arrangement of beautiful, natural materials–if I exclude a few decorations by artists about whom I shall say nothing. The fact is that Radio City is a modern monument and a lesson to the entire world.

It is a very luxurious social enterprise, in the grand American taste that is quite unlike the taste of any other country.

It is the most representative monument of the modern age.

Naturally we would need to discuss this magnificent project, and a painterly, decorative design equal to the building as a whole. I have some very clear ideas in this respect.

Mosaic should have played a part, but that's another story and for another time.

Based on a lecture delivered in 1935 at the Museum of Modern Art New York and published in *Art Front* II, no. 8 (1935): 10–11 (translated by Harold Rosenberg). English translation (excerpts) by Alexandra Anderson in F. Léger, "The New Realism," in Fernand Léger, *Functions of Painting* (New York: Thames and Hudson, 1973), 109–13. The above excerpts translated from F. Léger "Un nouveau réalisme, la couleur pure et l'objet," in Fernand Léger, *Fonctions de la peinture* (Paris: Denoël, 1965), 192. The English edition of the conclusion of this text differs from the French.

–

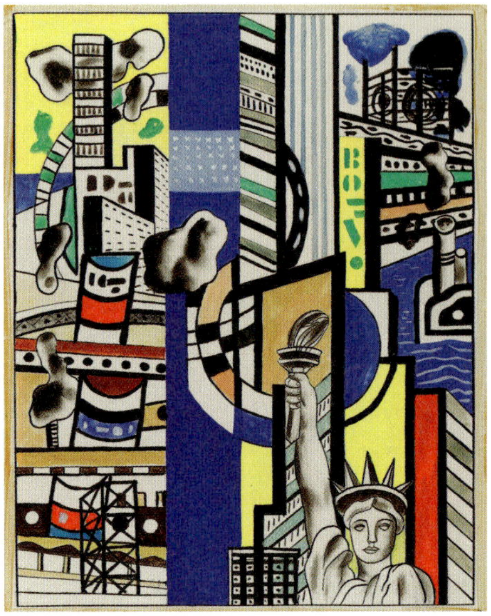

196

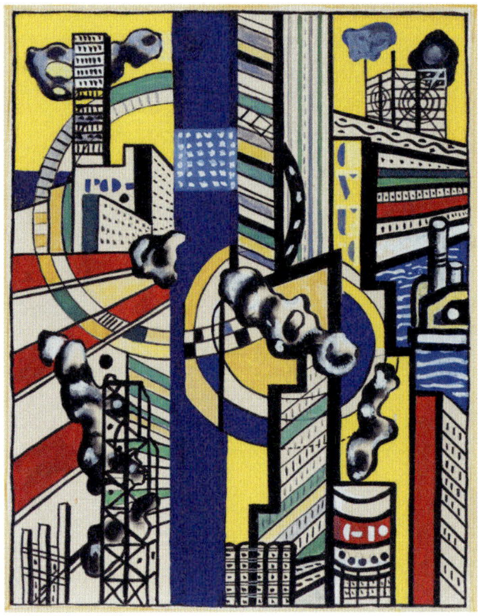

200

196 **Study for Cinematic Mural I, 1938/39**
Gouache and pencil on wood
50.7 × 40.5 cm
Museum of Modern Art, New York
Given Anonymously, acc. no. 738.1966

197 **Study for Cinematic Mural II, 1938/39**
Gouache and pencil on board
50.2 × 38 cm
Museum of Modern Art, New York
Given Anonymously, acc. no. 741.1966

198 **Study for Cinematic Mural III, 1938/39**
Gouache and pencil on board
50.7 × 37.8 cm
Museum of Modern Art, New York
Given Anonymously, acc. no. 743.1966

199 **Study for Cinematic Mural IV, 1938/39**
Gouache and pencil on wood
50.7 × 38 cm
Museum of Modern Art, New York
Given Anonymously, acc. no. 737.1966

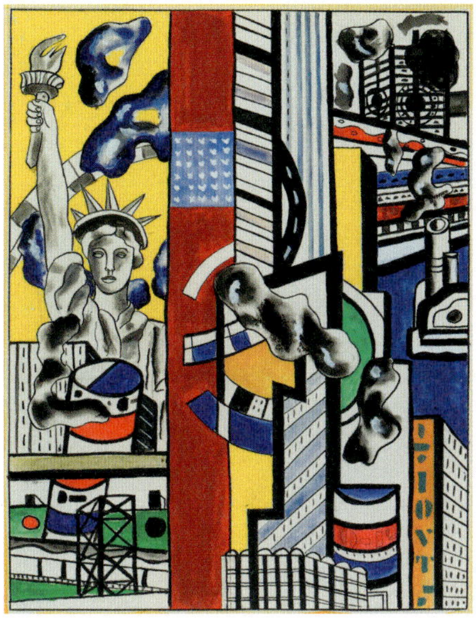

197

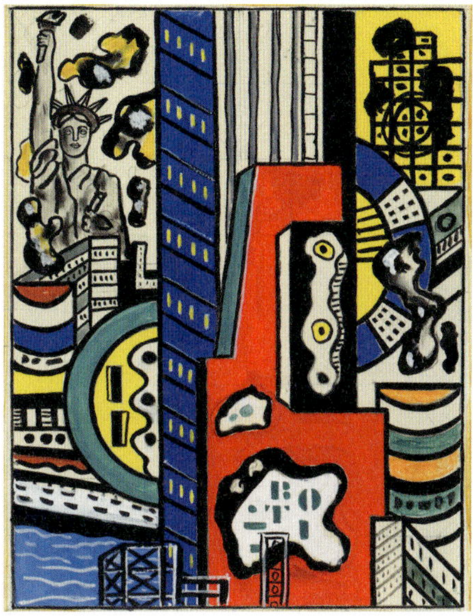

198

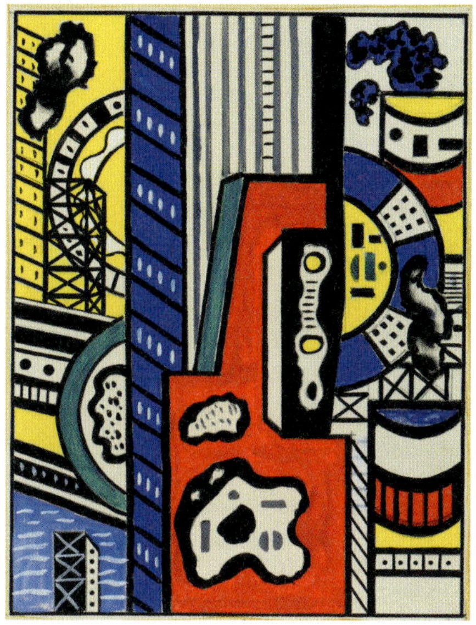

199

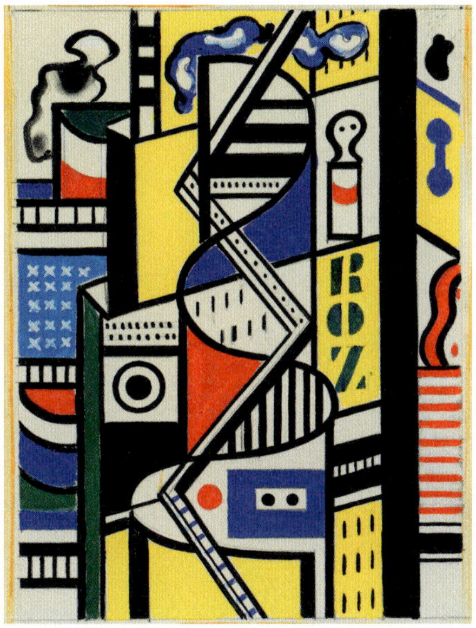

201

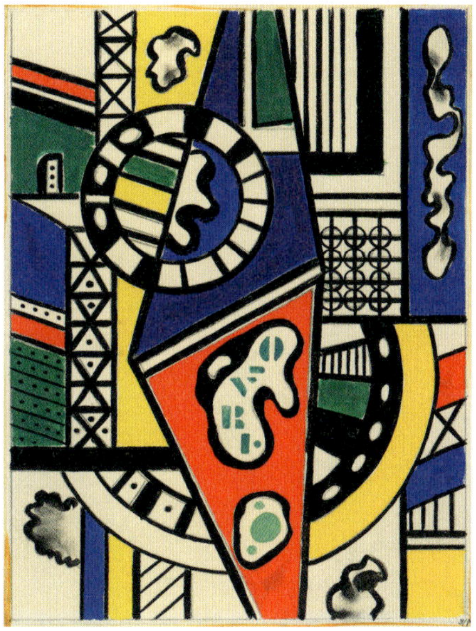

202

200 **Study for Cinematic Mural V, 1938/39**
Gouache and pencil on wood
50.7 × 40.4 cm
Museum of Modern Art, New York
Given Anonymously, acc. no. 739.1966

201 **Study for Cinematic Mural VI, 1938/39**
Gouache and pencil on board
50.7 × 37.9 cm
Museum of Modern Art, New York
Given Anonymously, acc. no. 740.1966

202 **Study for Cinematic Mural VII, 1938/39**
Gouache and pencil on board
50.6 × 37.7 cm
Museum of Modern Art, New York
Given Anonymously, acc. no. 742.1966

Two postcards from Fernand Léger to Le Corbusier, undated, c. 1939

(Postcard 1)
Dear chap–

Received note. We did what had to be done.
But don't forget that I am in the land of
slowness. Traffic, decisions
etc. Very slow–everything is sensible and
well thought out and cold
as soon as things go over 10 dollars.
I'm going to nudge Bar [Alfred Barr]–because
Nelson got himself into a
big business mess–
For us, all is going well here.
mural finished–beginning painting in living room
a Matisse at the end and
me on the side + project
evoking NY in the marble panel
above the mobile staircases
in the entrance of Radio [City, Rockefeller Center]
5th Ave–a big thing I've
been wanting to do–
difficult–but it's gotten off to a good start

(Postcard 2)
with all that, when I'm coming back,
I don't know. At
Harrison's I was
able to look at everything
that was being done for the exhibition.
You can imagine how much work it is!
Saw Baronne [Hilla von Rebay]. You should not
have written when I spoke to her
about it she told me in a superior way
yes I have a letter from Corbusier
Here you have to have the patience
to wait and
touch indirectly.
Best wishes to all
F Léger

Here, success for Nelson's
suspended house–
They say it's a
new departure
what comes before is regarded
as fixed! SEE YOU friend

Warm regards to Yvonne
Received catalog – Good, but don't forget
architecture

Fondation Le Corbusier, Paris.

–

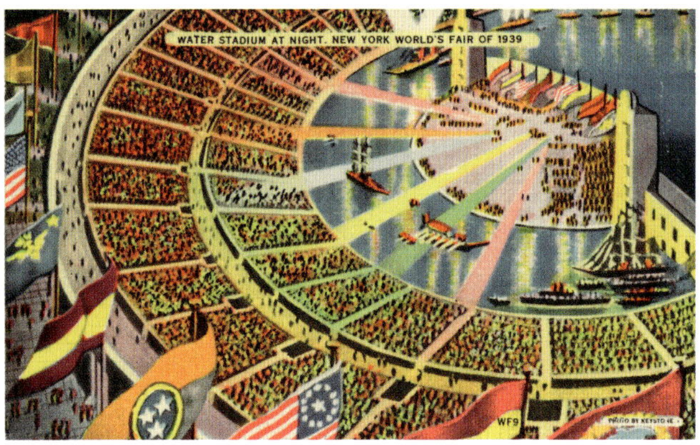

203

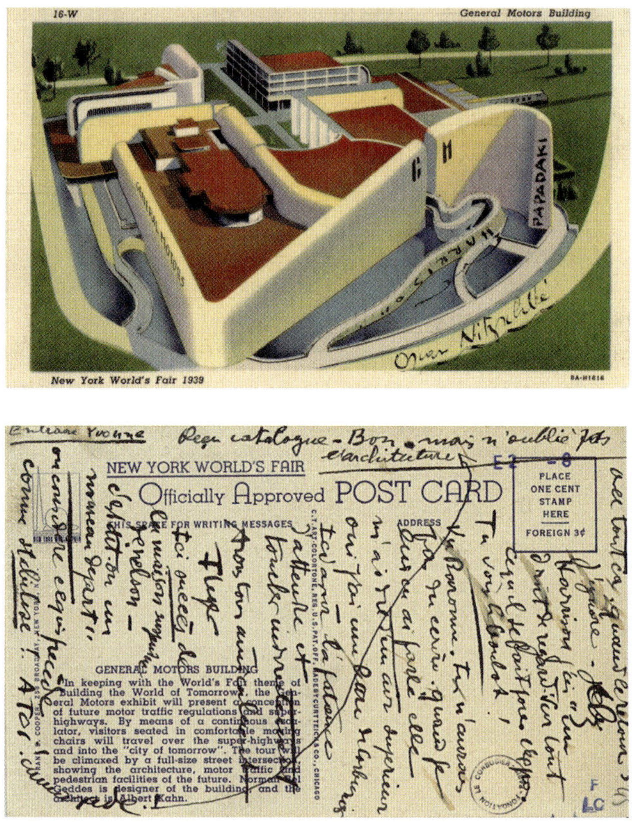

204

203–204 **Two Postcards from Fernand Léger to Le Corbusier with images of the New York World's Fair, c. 1939**
Fondation Le Corbusier, Paris

205 **Exterior view of the Consolidated Edison Pavilion with *Trylon* and *Perisphere* at the New York World's Fair, 1939**
Architecture: Harrison & Fouilhoux
Museum of the City of New York, acc. no. 2010.7.118027

206 **Postcard to Wallace K. Harrison with drawings by Fernand Léger on the theme of the New York World's Fair, 1939**
Avery Architectural & Fine Arts Library, Columbia University, New York, Wallace K. Harrison architectural drawings and papers, Box 1: Folder 17

207 **Postcard to Wallace K. Harrison with drawings by Fernand Léger on the theme of the New York World's Fair, 1939**
Avery Architectural & Fine Arts Library, Columbia University, New York, Wallace K. Harrison architectural drawings and papers, Box 1: Folder 17

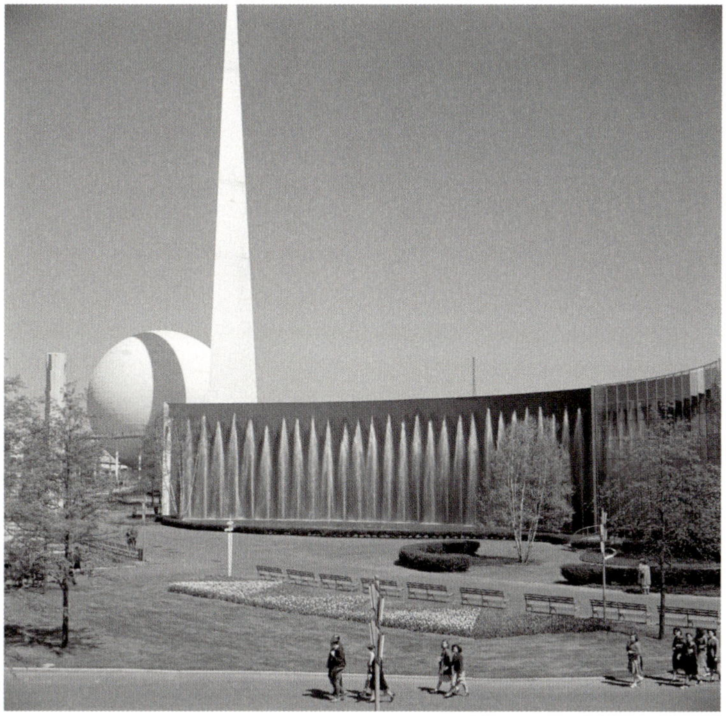

205

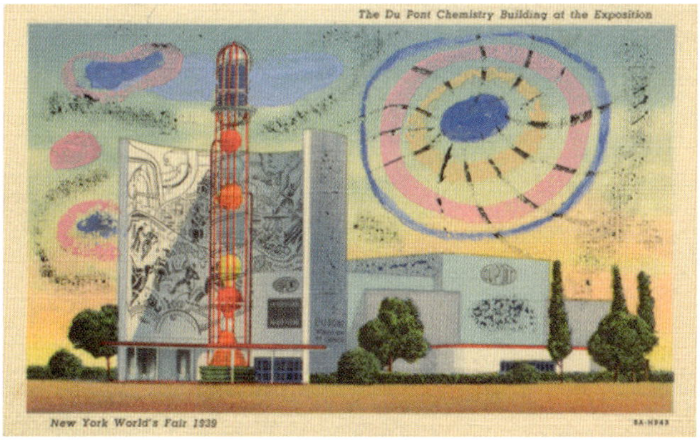

206

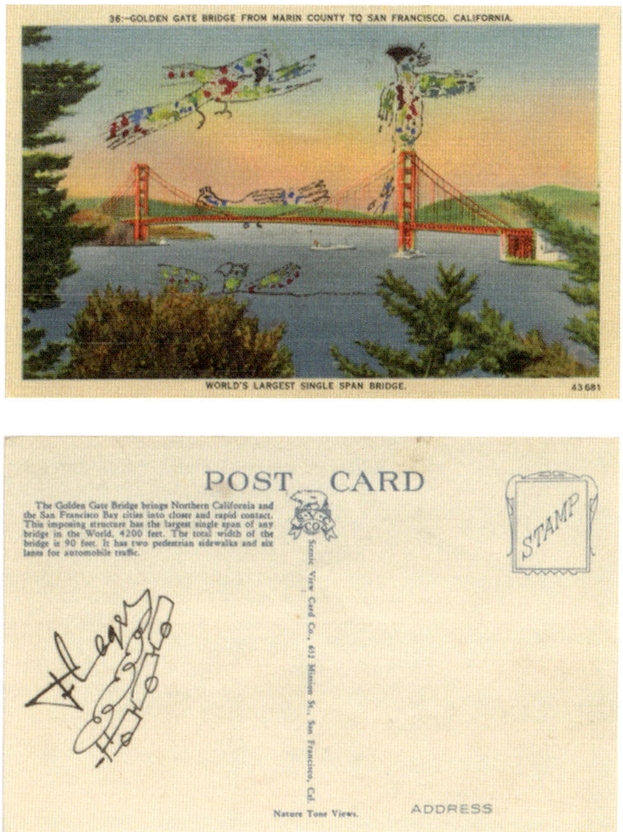

207

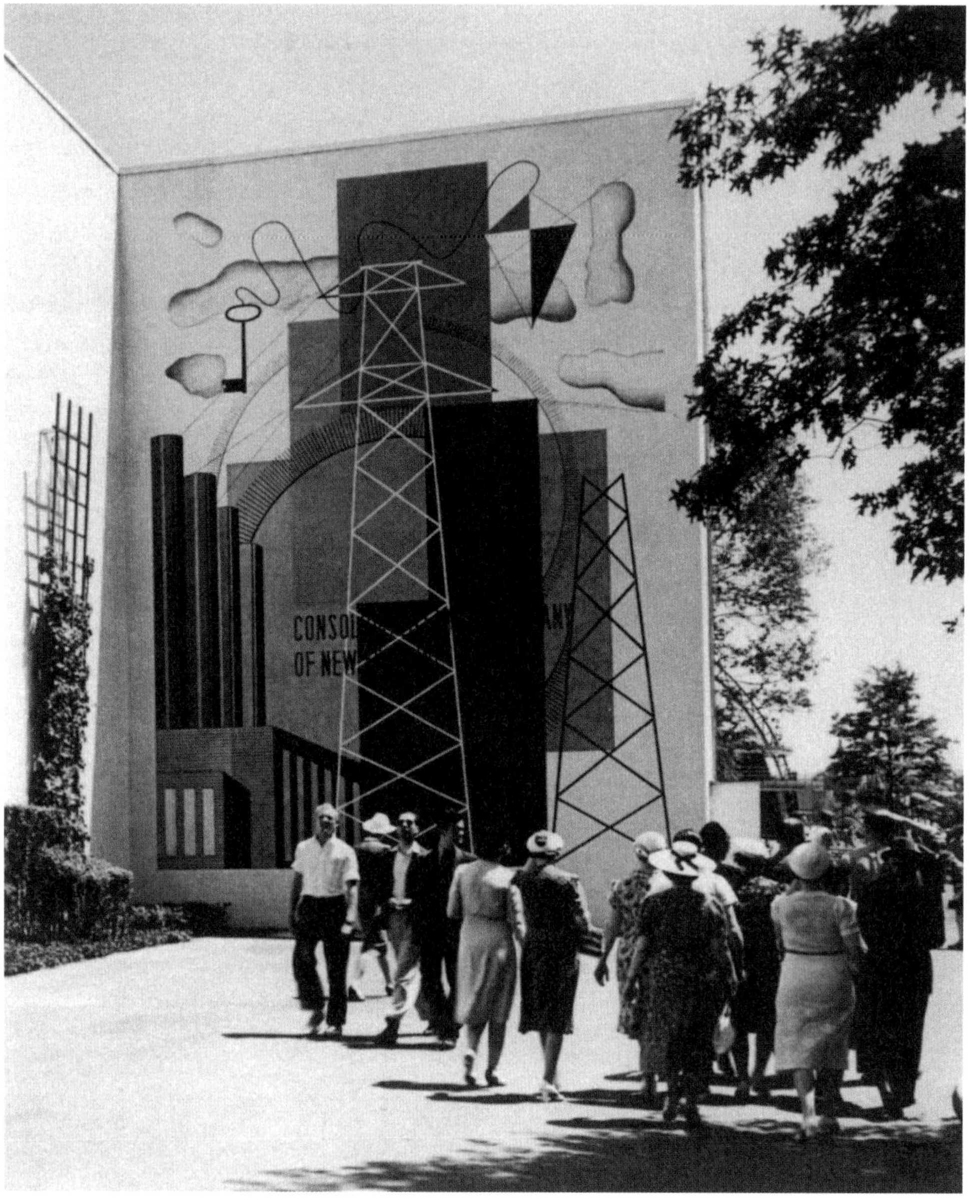

208

208 **Consolidated Edison Pavilion with mural painting *City of Light*, executed according to a design by Fernand Léger, New York World's Fair, 1939**

209 **Untitled, 1938**
Double-sided drawing: Gouache and pencil on paper
24.1 × 15.4 cm
Herbert F. Johnson Museum of Art, Cornell University
Anonymous Gift, acc. no. 72.108.028

Preliminary studies for the design of the consolidated Edison Pavilion, New York World's Fair, 1939.

210 **Untitled, 1938**
Pencil on paper
47 × 34.1 cm
Herbert F. Johnson Museum of Art, Cornell University
Anonymous Gift, acc. no. 72.108.006

211 **Model for a fountain for the Consolidated Edison Pavilion by Theodore Conrad based on drafts by Fernand Léger**
Brushed aluminum, brass, copper, plastic, painted wood, and with a piping system within a wooden base
113.7 × 78.8 cm
The Collection of Richard H. Driehaus, Chicago, Illinois

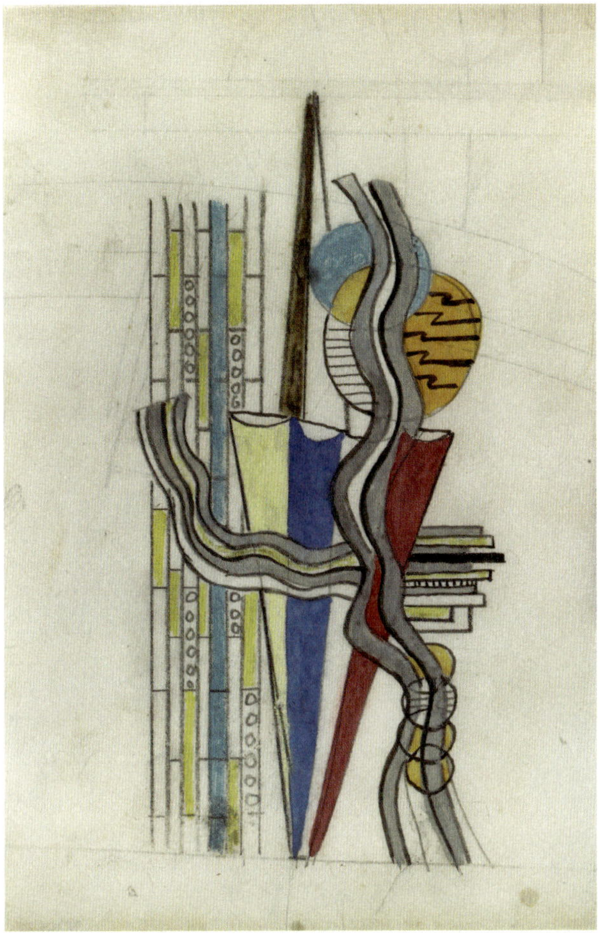

209

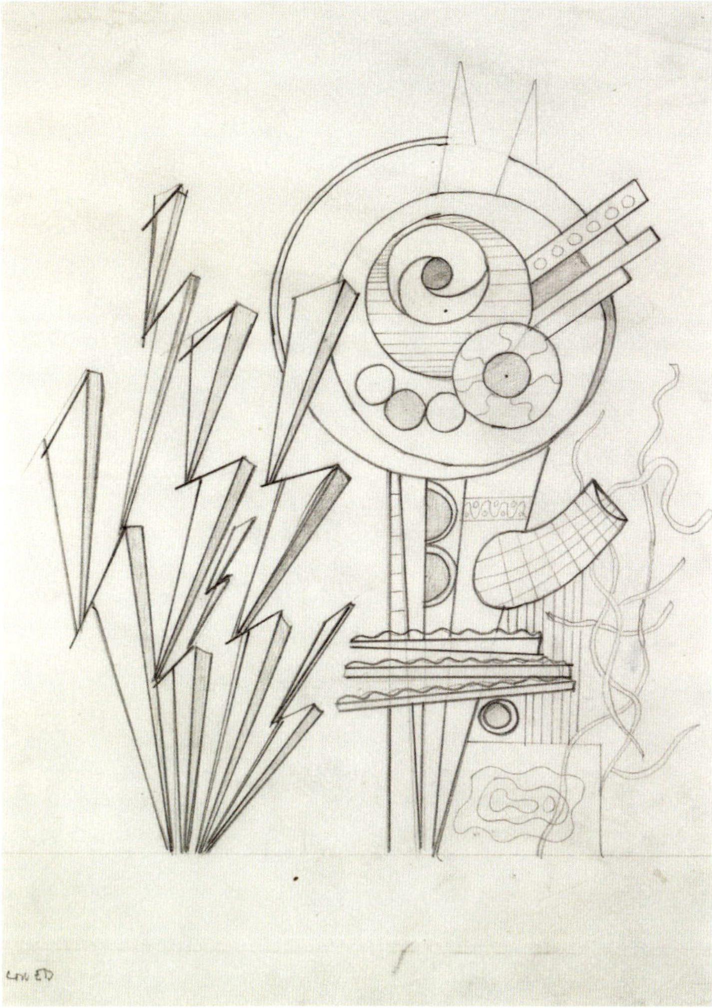

210

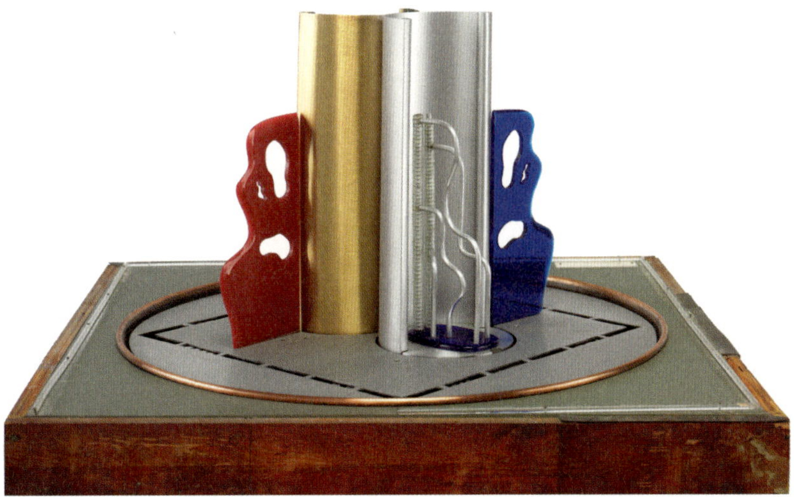

211

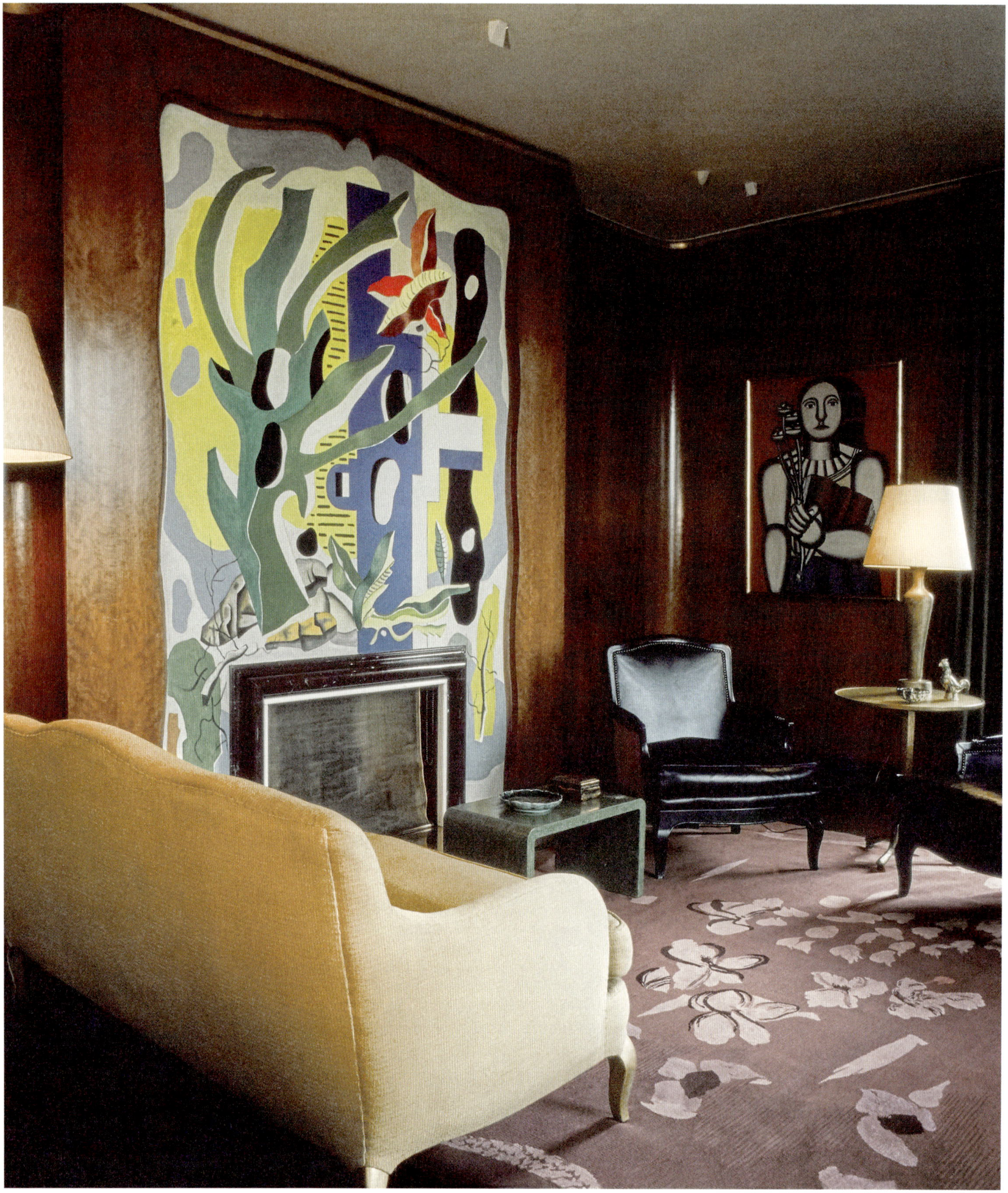

212

Nelson A. Rockefeller's recollections of Léger painting the murals in his apartment (1938-39)

Thus, when I had purchased a new apartment in 1936, I decided to decorate it in the modern style. I worked with Wallace K. Harrison, my close friend and a brilliant architect, who designed very simple wood paneling with a Louis XIV influence in order to provide a warm and inviting background. We asked Jean-Michel Frank, one of the outstanding French designers of the period, to design the interior. He commissioned distinguished young artists to do the furnishings, including the lamps and tapestries for the rugs and chair coverings. These artists included the Giacometti brothers, Alberto and Diego, and Christian Bérard.

Wally designed two fireplaces in the living room with space for great murals around them, and our friends Henri Matisse and Fernand Léger accepted commissions to undertake the murals. Matisse did the mural in Paris from full-scale drawings of the fireplace, but Léger came over to New York and actually did the painting in the apartment.

I used to watch Léger with fascination as he painted and the details of the mural unfolded. After he had finished, we liked it so much that we persuaded him to do additional murals for the circular stairwell and the hallways, both upstairs and down. Léger was a wonderful human being, and we remained friends until his death.

I was constantly working with artists on commissions for various projects. Thus, modern art for me was not only the most rewarding aesthetic experience, but also a warm personal experience because of my friendship with artists.

Excerpt from Nelson A. Rockefeller, "Introduction," in ed. Dorothy Canning Miller, *The Nelson A. Rockefeller Collection: Masterpieces of Modern Art* (New York: Hudson Hills Press, 1981), 12–19.

–

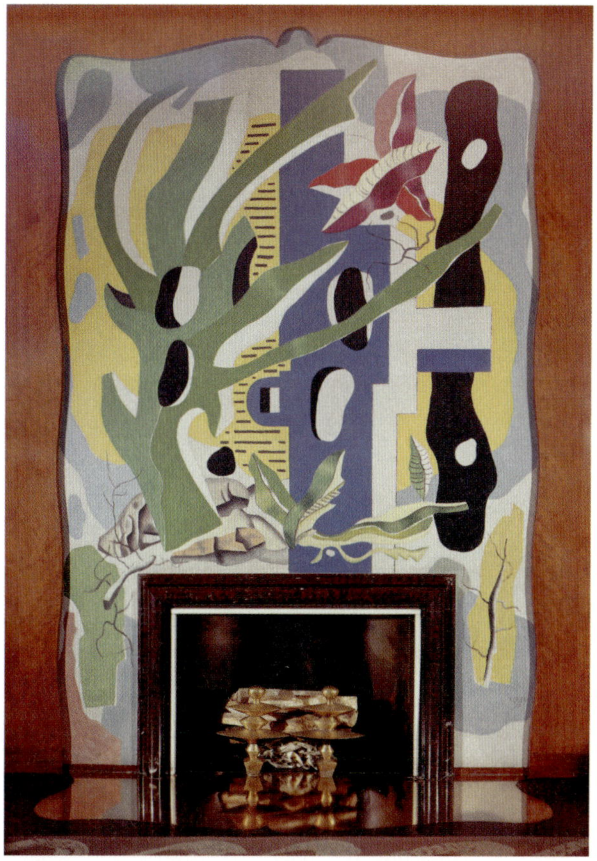

213

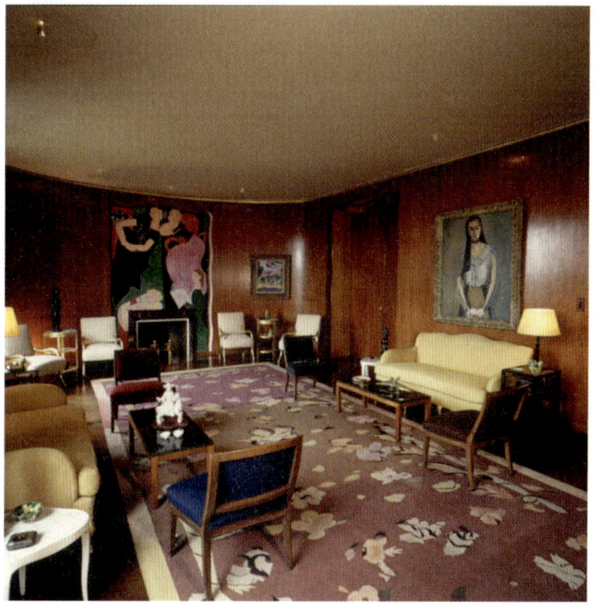

214

212-213 **The living room of Nelson A. Rockefeller's apartment, New York. Fireplace mural (untitled), 1938 by Fernand Léger.**
Architect: Wallace K. Harrison
Interior design: Jean-Michel Frank, 1937

214 **The living room of Nelson A. Rockefeller's Fifth Avenue apartment in New York. Fireplace mural *Le Chant* (Song), 1938 by Henri Matisse.**

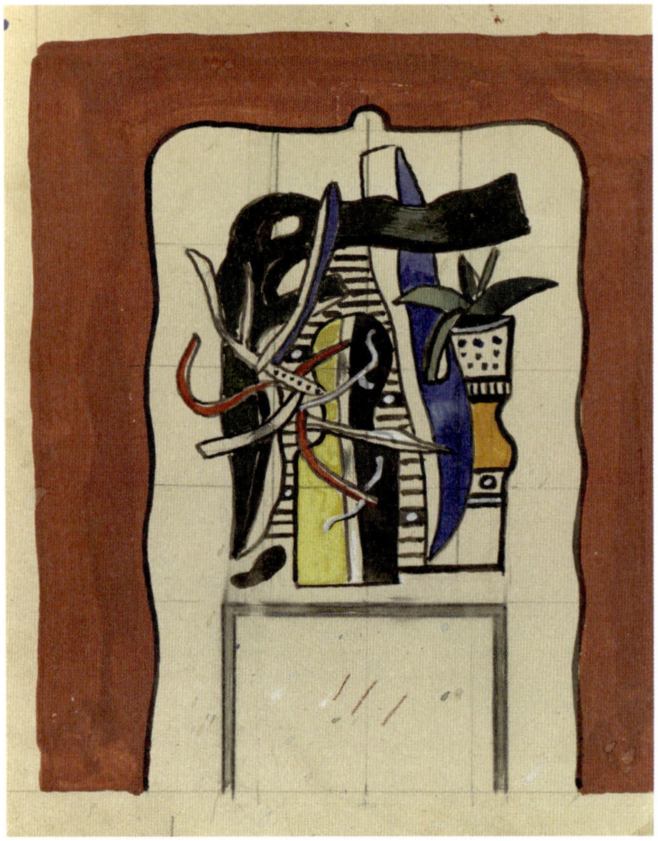

215

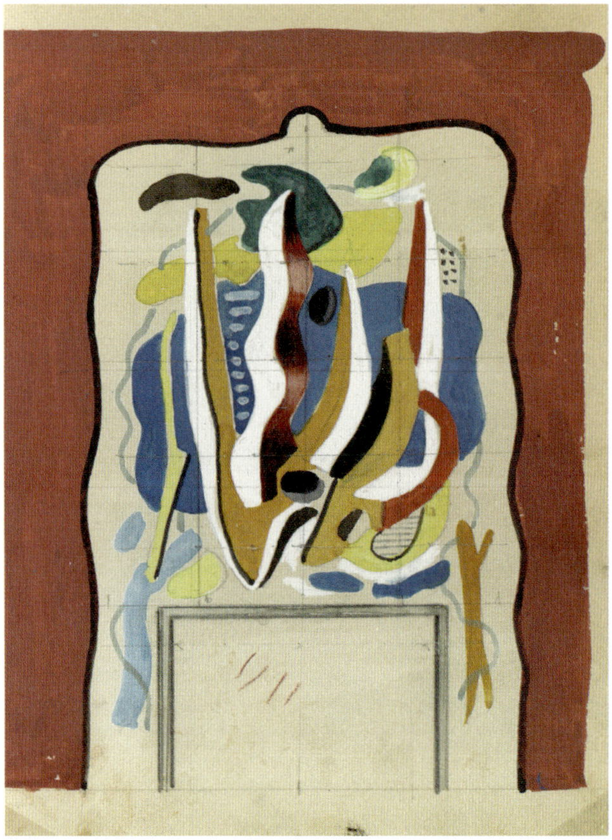

216

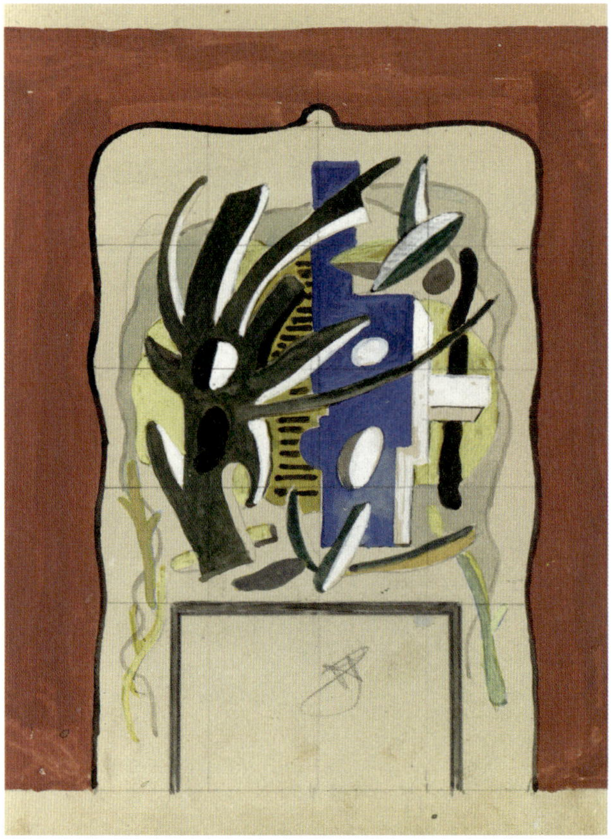

217

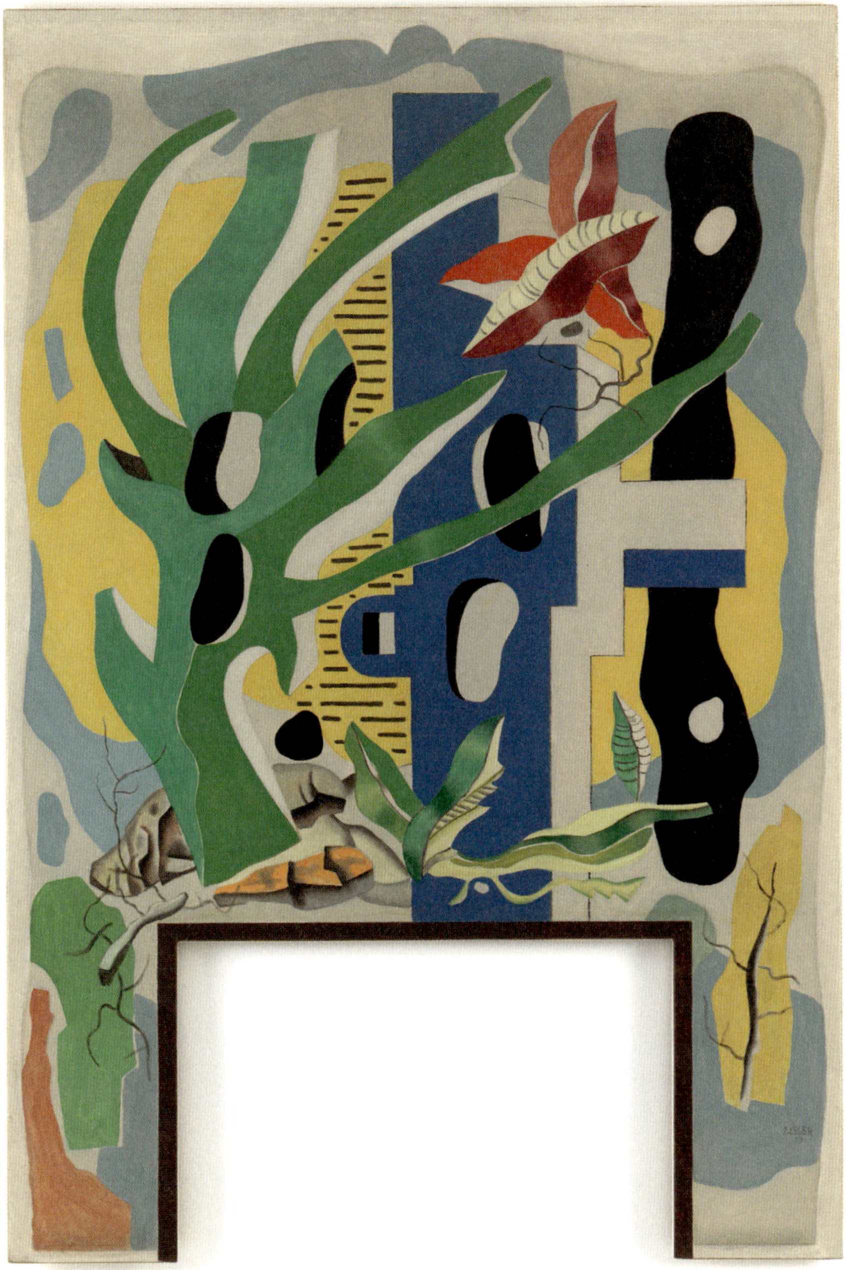

218

215 **Study for the fireplace mural in Nelson A. Rockefeller's New York apartment, 1938/39**
Gouache and pencil on composition board
26 × 18.3 cm
Herbert F. Johnson Museum of Art, Cornell University
Anonymous gift

216 **Study for the fireplace mural in Nelson A. Rockefeller's New York apartment, 1938/39**
Gouache and pencil on composition board
26 × 16.2 cm
Herbert F. Johnson Museum of Art, Cornell University
Anonymous Gift, acc. no. 74.098.003

217 **Study for the fireplace mural in Nelson A. Rockefeller's New York apartment, 1938/39**
Gouache and pencil on composition board
26 × 15.9 cm
Herbert F. Johnson Museum of Art, Cornell University
Anonymous Gift, 74.098.012

218 **Mural composition for fireplace of Nelson A. Rockefeller's apartment, 1939**
Oil on canvas
287.3 × 189.2 cm
Museum of Modern Art, New York, acc. no. TR6327

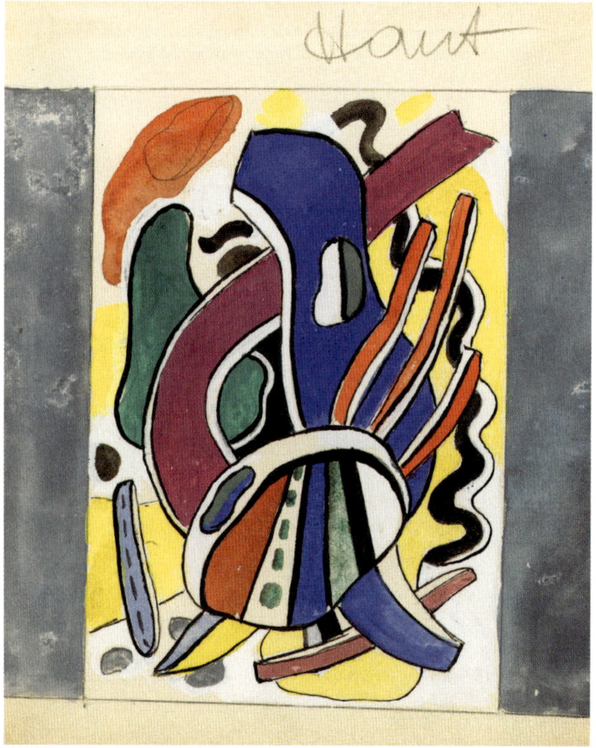

219

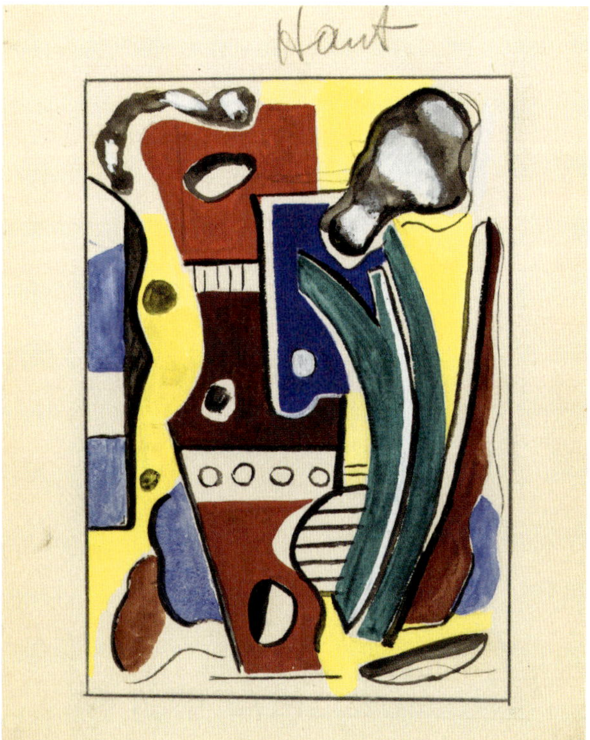

220

Letter from Fernand Léger to Nelson A. Rockefeller, January 27, 1939

BARBIZON-PLAZA-HOTEL
101 West 58th Street-Central Park South-New York

January 27, 1939

Dear Mr. Rockefeller
Your letter has arrived - I'm glad if I have been able to bring you satisfaction -
I consider the painting for the living room as finished, but if you would like us to look over it again together, it will be a pleasure. Send me word.

Yours faithfully
FLéger

I take the liberty of itemizing our accounts:
Wall painting. settled
The 8 gouaches – settled
There remains the painting in
the living room 2500 d.
Received today in part payment 1000 d.
Remaining due 1500 d.

Regarding the magnificent project for the entrance to Radio, be so kind as to inform me of your decision as soon as possible –
FL.

-

Letter from Nelson A. Rockefeller to Fernand Léger, January 30, 1939

January 30, 1939

Dear M. Leger:

I can't tell you how pleased I am with the final work which you did on the mural in our living room. I have been enthusiastic about it all along but somehow those slight changes in colors seem to have strengthened the painting and pulled it together in a way that is quite extraordinary. We are simply thrilled with it and I can't tell you how much I appreciate the thought and consideration which you have given this matter. I know it is going to be the source of the greatest possible pleasure to both Mrs. Rockefeller and me.
I am enclosing herewith my check to your order in the amount of $1,600, which represents final payment in connection with this work.

Again with many thanks, and very best wishes.
Sincerely yours,

Nelson A. Rockefeller

Monsieur Ferdinand [sic] Leger,
c/o Mr. Wallace K. Harrison,
830 Fifth Avenue, New York City.

Rockefeller Archive Center, New York.

-

219 **Untitled, 1940**
Gouache and pencil on paper
22.5 × 22.7 cm
Herbert F. Johnson Museum of Art, Cornell University
Anonymous Gift, acc. no. 74.098.023

220 **Untitled, 1938**
Pencil on paper
25.4 × 20.3 cm
Herbert F. Johnson Museum of Art, Cornell University
Anonymous Gift, acc. no. 72.108.015

221 ***Maquette pour une peinture murale***
(Study for a mural painting), 1938
Oil on canvas
162 × 114.5 cm
Lille métropole, musée d'art moderne, d'art contemporain et d'art brut, Villeneuve d'Ascq
Donation from Geneviève et Jean Masurel en 1979

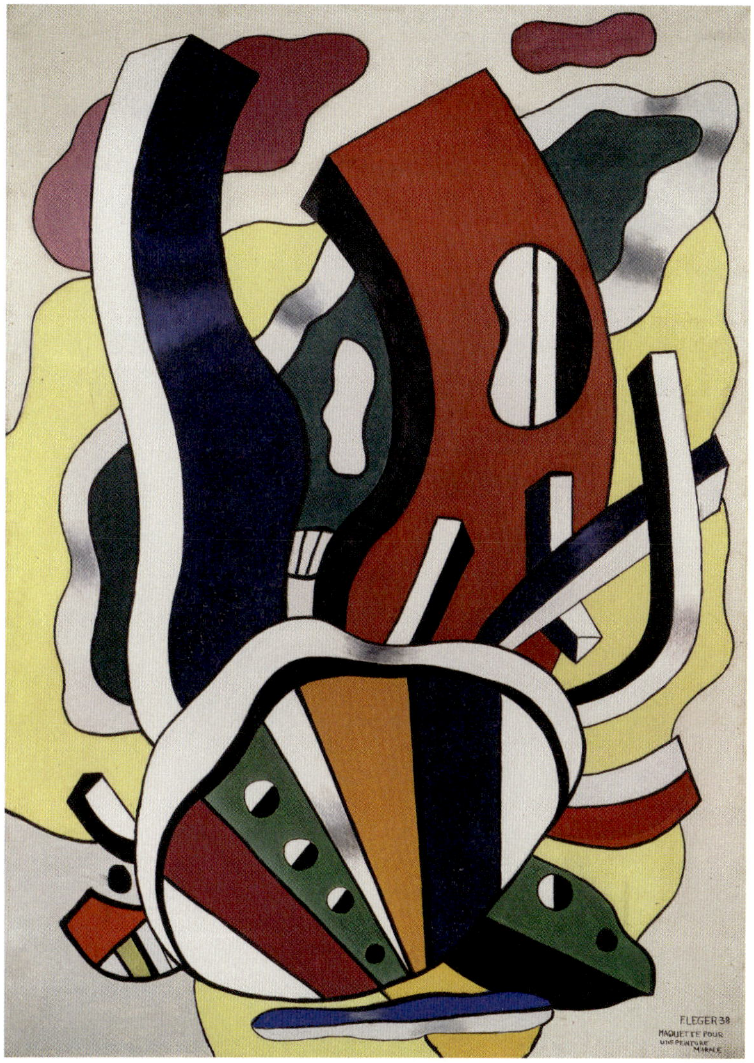

221

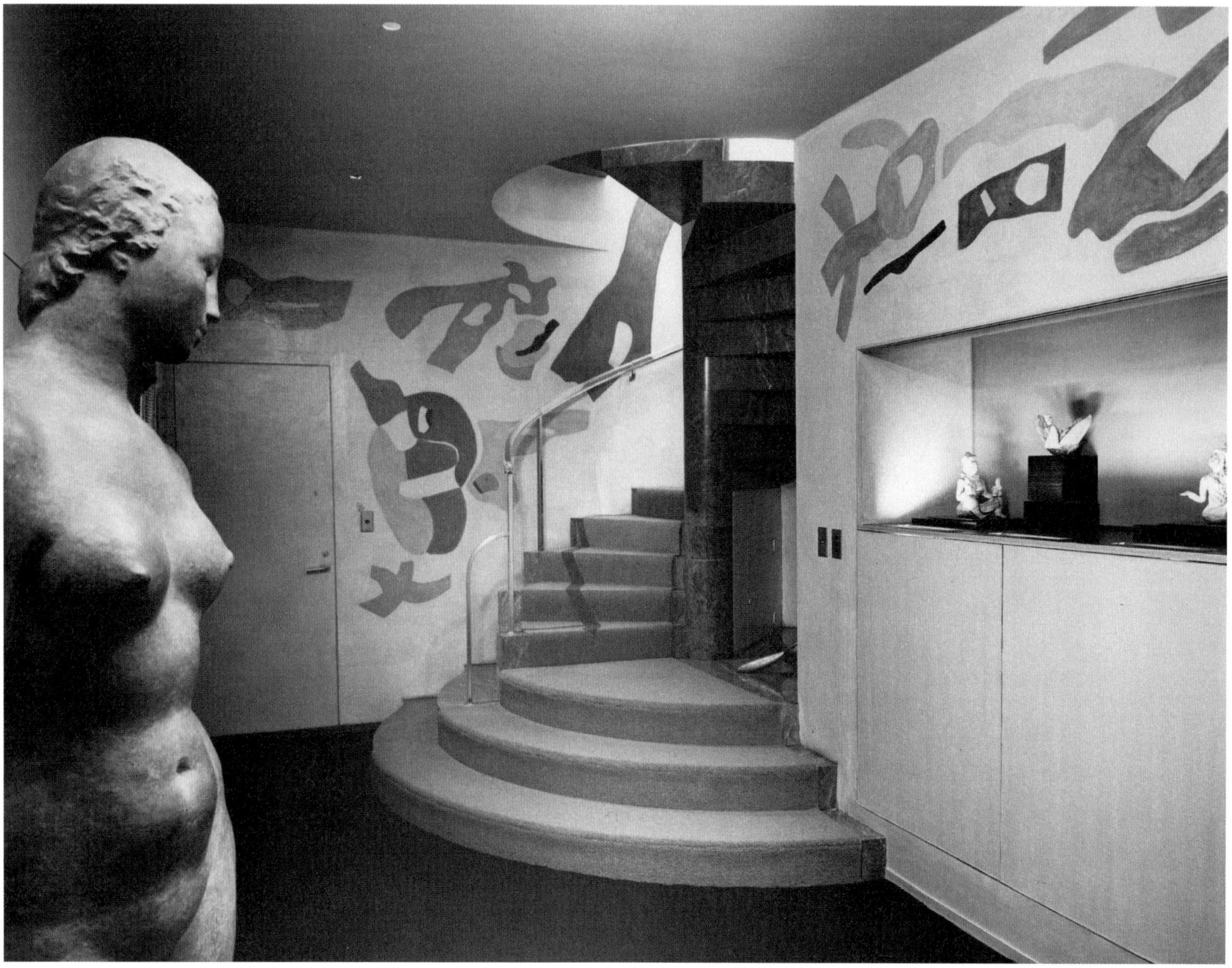

222

222–224 **Mural painting for the staircase of Nelson A. Rockefeller's apartment, New York, 1938/39**
Rockefeller Archive Center, Sleepy Hollow

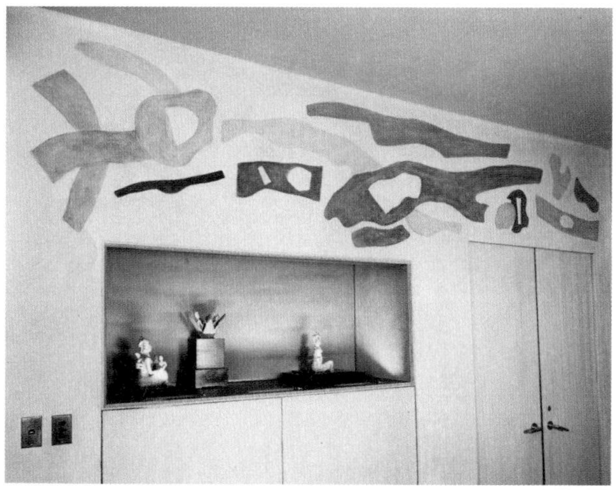

223

Fernand Léger during his stay in America held conferences at Yale University and decorated Rockefeller Jr.'s interiors (1939)
Pierre Imbourg

Almost as soon as he had returned from America, Fernand Léger got back to work. We found him the other morning in his studio on Rue Notre-Dame-des-Champs, amid numerous canvases, piles of documents, and a table laden with colors dominated by the blue and yellow that he is so partial to.

"What did you do in America?" we asked him.
Fernard Léger sat down and adjusted his cap.
"Last summer, Mr. Harrison, one of the most famous architects in New York, and who is head of the architecture course at Yale, asked me to go and give a few lectures at this university. I gave eight lectures on the role of color in architecture, that is to say on the different uses of colored space."

"What was the students' reaction?"
"Out of fifty students, a third turned out to be very understanding, others were very slow to understand, the final third turned out to be vigorously recalcitrant."

"Do you speak English?" we asked.
"No, it was of no importance. I had an excellent translator with me."

Fernand Léger then told us that the universities of Yale and Harvard were beginning to fight openly against our École des Beaux-Arts and that American architects were looking at the problem of low-cost metal houses.

"A house entirely made out of metal, that you can pay for every month. The factories are ready and are just waiting for final plans in order to start mass-production."

"You also decorated Rockefeller's home?"
"Yes, I decorated with murals the home of Rockefeller Jr. on Fifth Avenue."

"What do they represent?"
"Nothing. I simply wanted to create a colorful ambiance," replied our apostle of Cubism.

He specifies:
"Rockefeller Jr. is a thirty-year-old man who loves modern art–probably because he was raised amid his father's collections of 18th-century and Chinese art."

"His father does not understand us," added Fernand Léger, "but his son is not bothered by something that is distorted."

"Did you show him some models?"
"Of course, Rockefeller does not like surprises. The decoration even posed some tricky problems. We had to put ourselves in the place of the man who would be seeing the same painting for years. So around the staircase, I tried to make a nice arrangement of colors. For the living room, one side of which is decorated with a vigorous Matisse symbolizing music, I used even stronger colors that are arranged around a sort of plant."

Fernand Léger's remarks end there.

Originally published as Pierre Imbourg, "Fernand Léger pendant son séjour en Amérique a fait des conférences à l'université de Yale et décoré l'intérieur de Rockefeller Jr.," in *Beaux-arts: Chronique des arts et de la curiosité*, vol. 76, no. 326 (March 31, 1939).

–

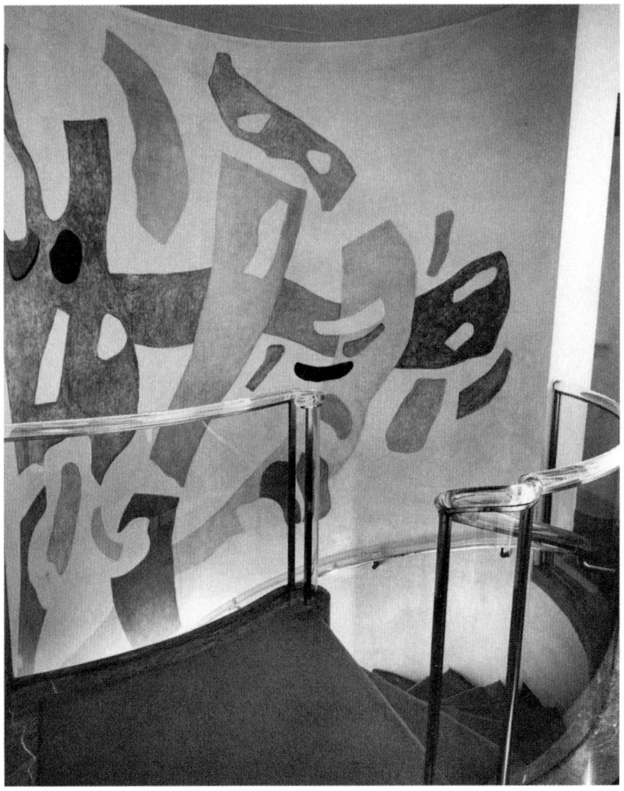

224

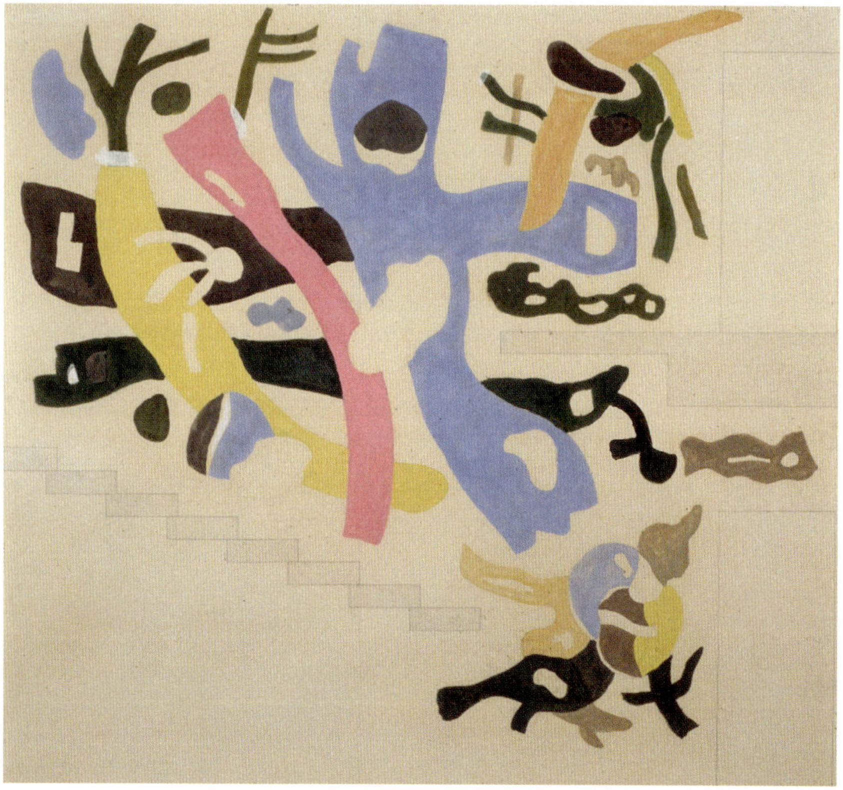

225

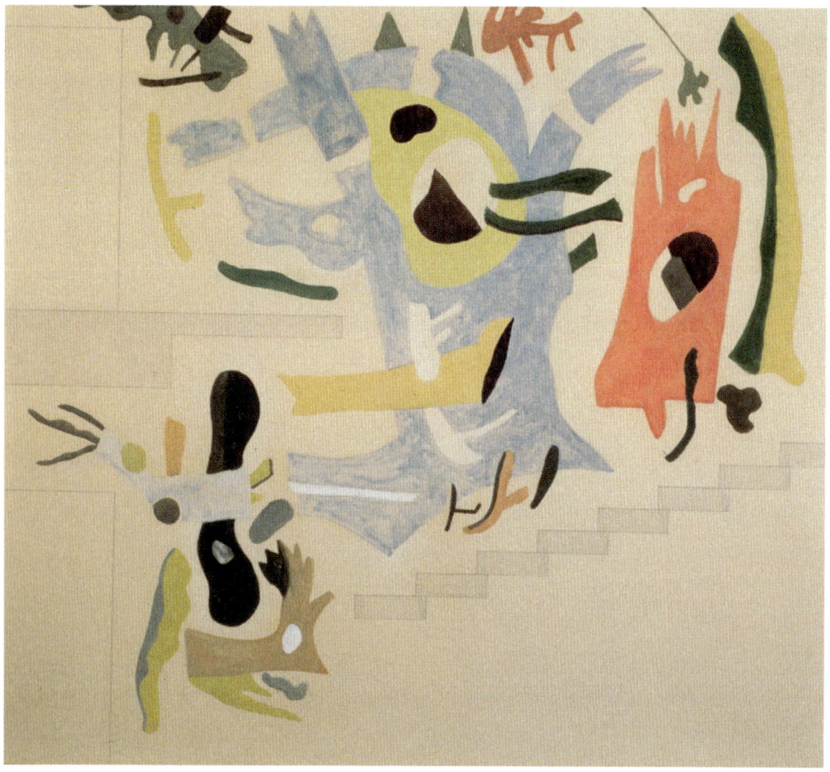

226

225 **Study for a mural painting for the foyer and staircase of Nelson A. Rockefeller's New York apartment, 1938**
Gouache and pencil on paper
75.6 × 80.6 cm
Herbert F. Johnson Museum of Art, Cornell University
Anonymous Gift, acc. no. 75.043.001

226 **Study for the foyer and staircase mural paintings for Nelson A. Rockefeller's New York apartment, 1938**
Gouache and pencil on paper
75.2 × 80.6 cm
Herbert F. Johnson Museum of Art, Cornell University
Anonymous Gift, acc. no. 75.043.002

227 **Six Studies for a mural painting for the staircase of Nelson A. Rockefeller's apartment, c. 1938/39**
Graphite, watercolor, and gouache on tissue paper
38.58 × 62.23 cm
Portland Museum of Art, Maine
Anonymous gift

228 **Six studies for abstract wall decorations, c. 1940–55**
Gouache and graphite
42.2 × 70.1 cm
The Metropolitan Museum of Art, New York
Gift of Wallace K. Harrison, 1972, acc. no. 1972.730.2

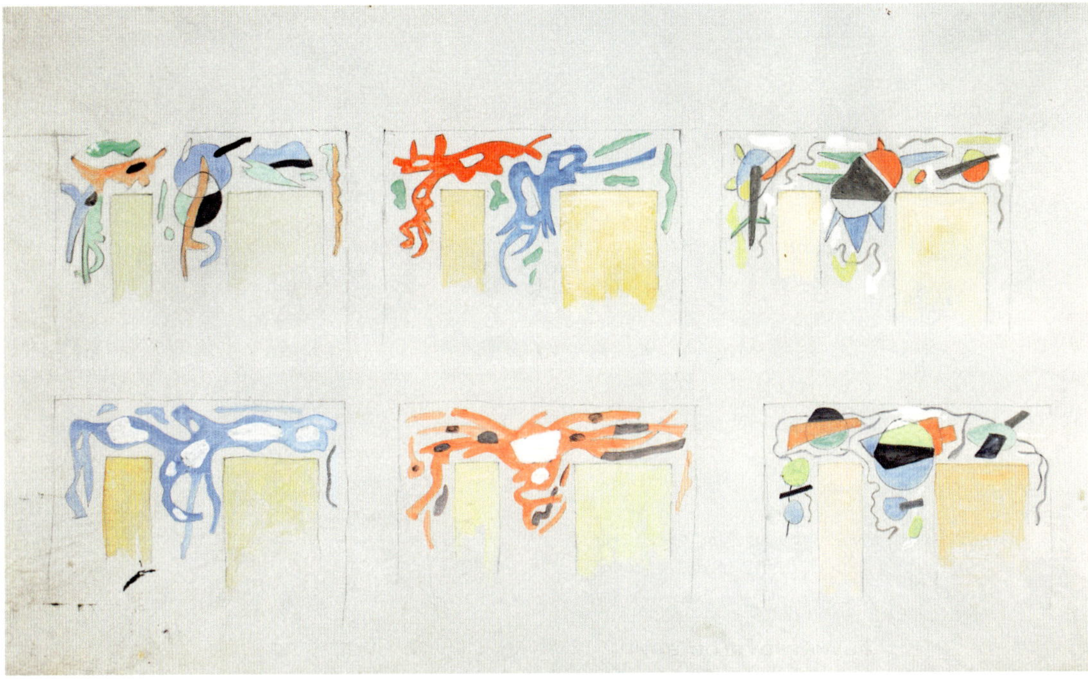

227

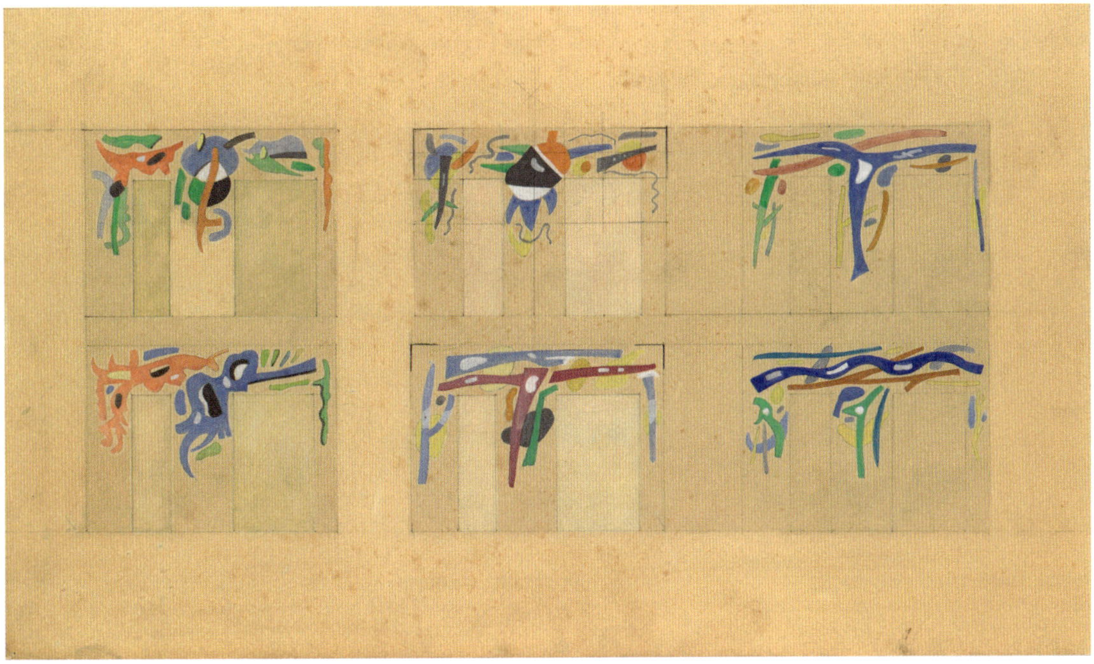

228

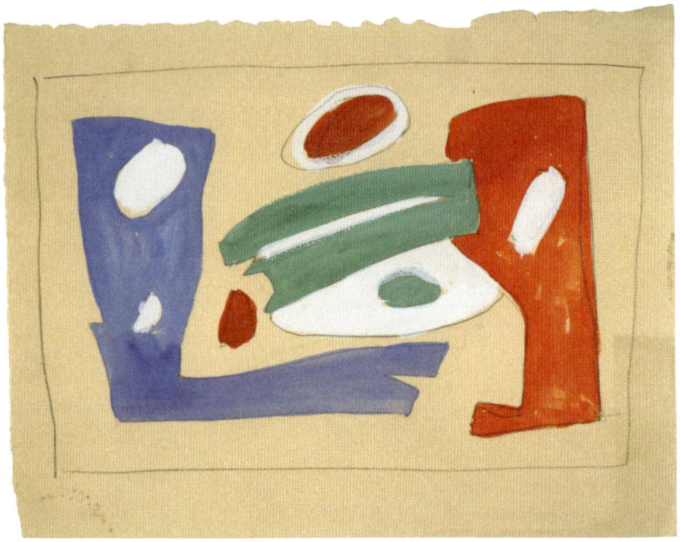

229

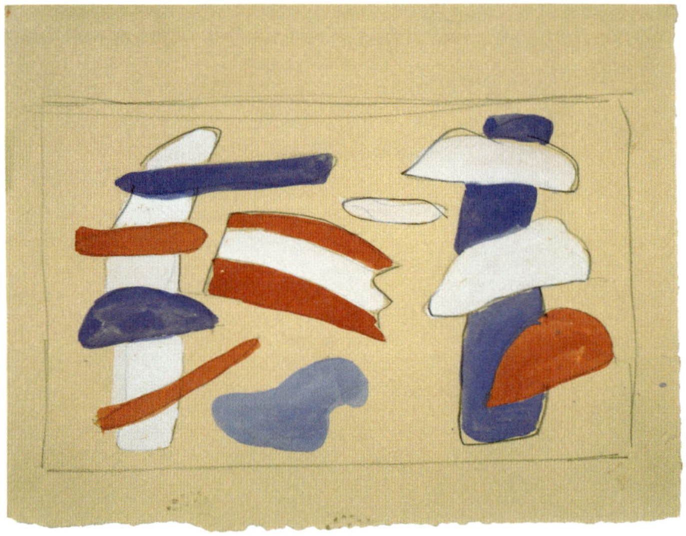

230

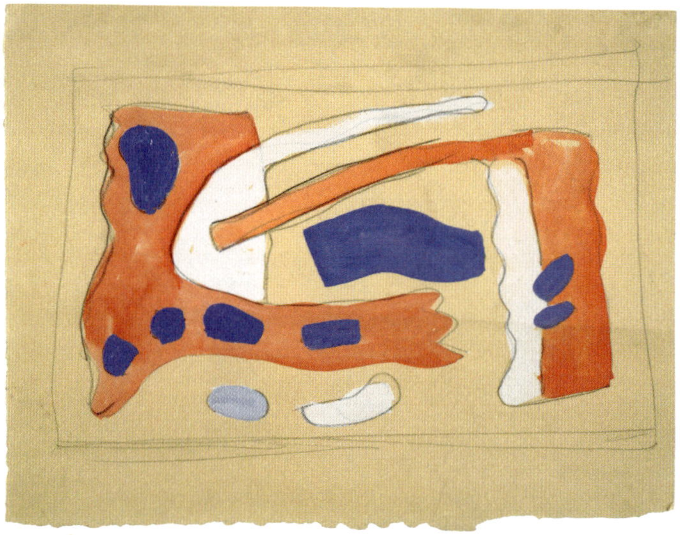

231

229 ***Projet de décoration murale* (Study for a mural decoration), c. 1939**
Gouache and pencil on Canson paper
25.6 × 32.5 cm
Centre Pompidou, Musée national d'art moderne, Paris

230 ***Sans Titre (Projet de décoration murale)* (Untitled [Study for a mural decoration]), c. 1939**
Gouache and graphite on Canson paper
25.6 × 32.5 cm
Centre Pompidou, Musée national d'art moderne, Paris

231 ***Projet de décoration murale* (Study for a mural decoration), c. 1939**
Gouache and pencil on Canson paper
25.2 × 32.6 cm
Centre Pompidou, Musée national d'art moderne, Paris

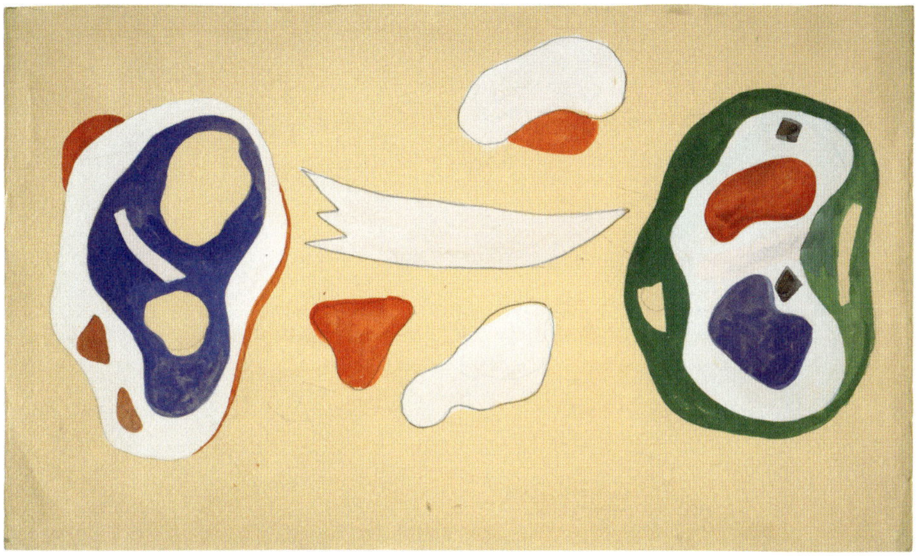

232

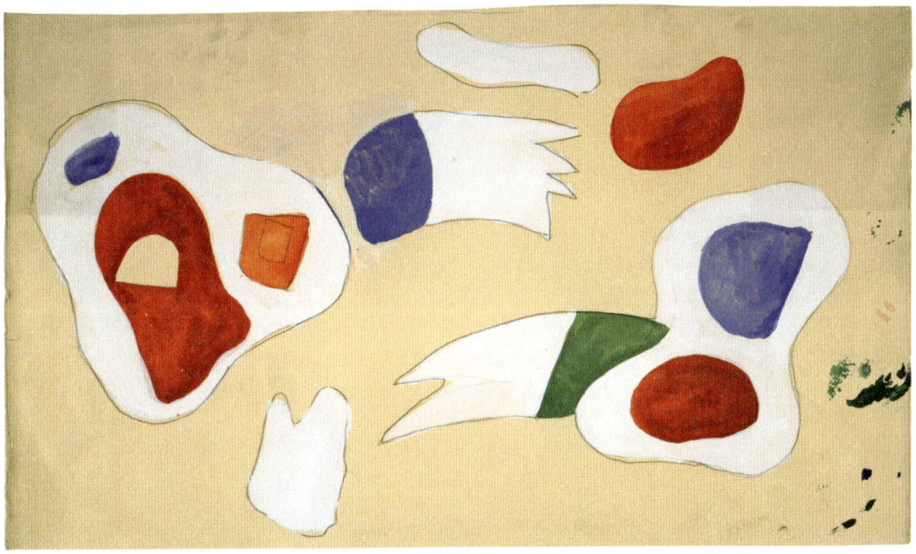

233

232 ***Projet de décoration murale***
(Study for a Mural Decoration), c. 1936
Gouache and pencil on Canson paper
30.5 × 50 cm
Centre Pompidou, Musée national d'art moderne, Paris

233 ***Projet de décoration murale***
(Study for a Mural Decoration), c.1936
Gouache and pencil on Canson paper
30.2 × 50 cm
Centre Pompidou, Musée national d'art moderne, Paris

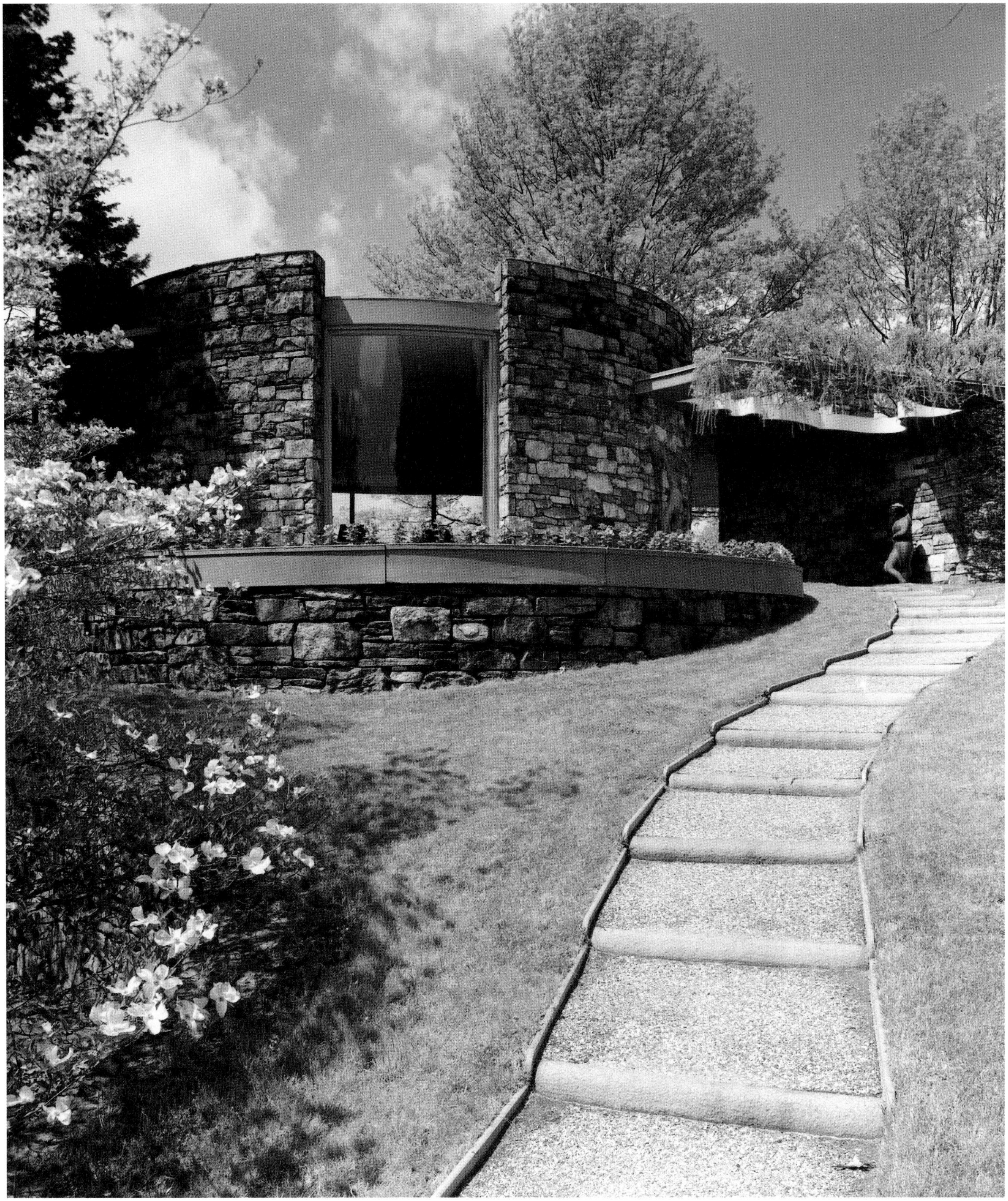

234

234 **Nelson A. Rockefeller's Hawes Guest House, Pocantico, New York, 1939**
Architect: Wallace K. Harrison

235 **Skylight by Fernand Léger between the two pavilions**
Avery Architectural & Fine Arts Library, Columbia University, New York, Wallace K. Harrison architectural drawings and papers, Box 6, Folder 43

236 ***L'Étoile de Mer et les plongeurs* (Starfish and Divers [design for a mosaic or mural painting]), 1942**
Brush, yellow, red, green and beige wash and graphite
13.3 × 44.5 cm
The Metropolitan Museum of Art, New York
Gift of Wallace K. Harrison, 1972, acc. no.1972.730.1

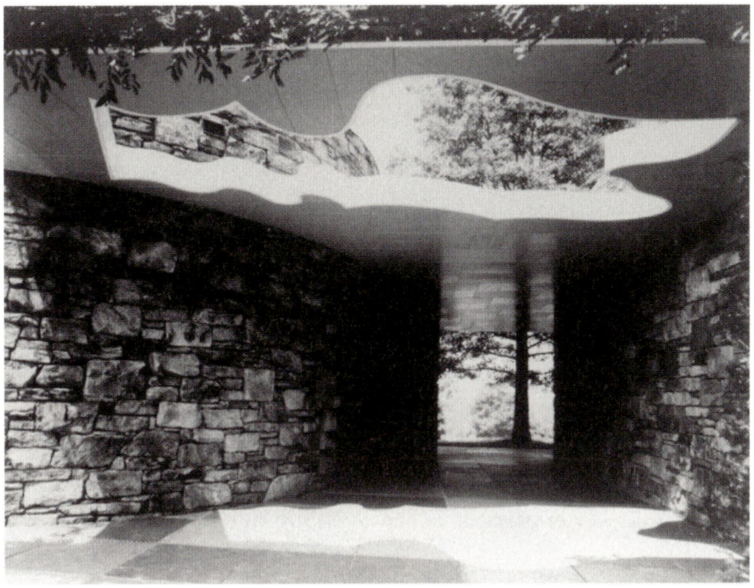

235

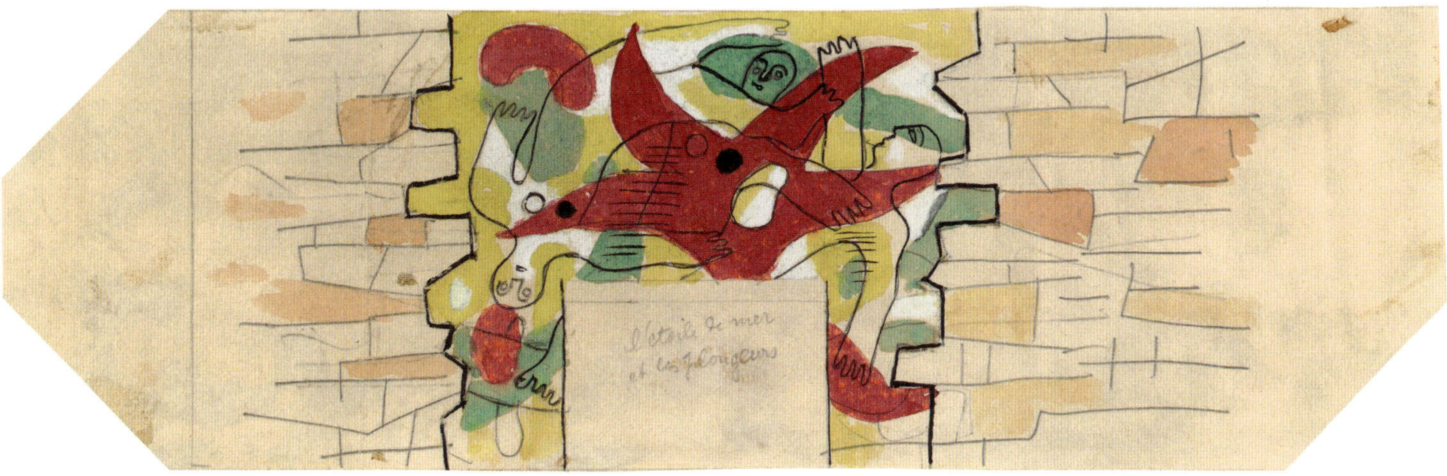

236

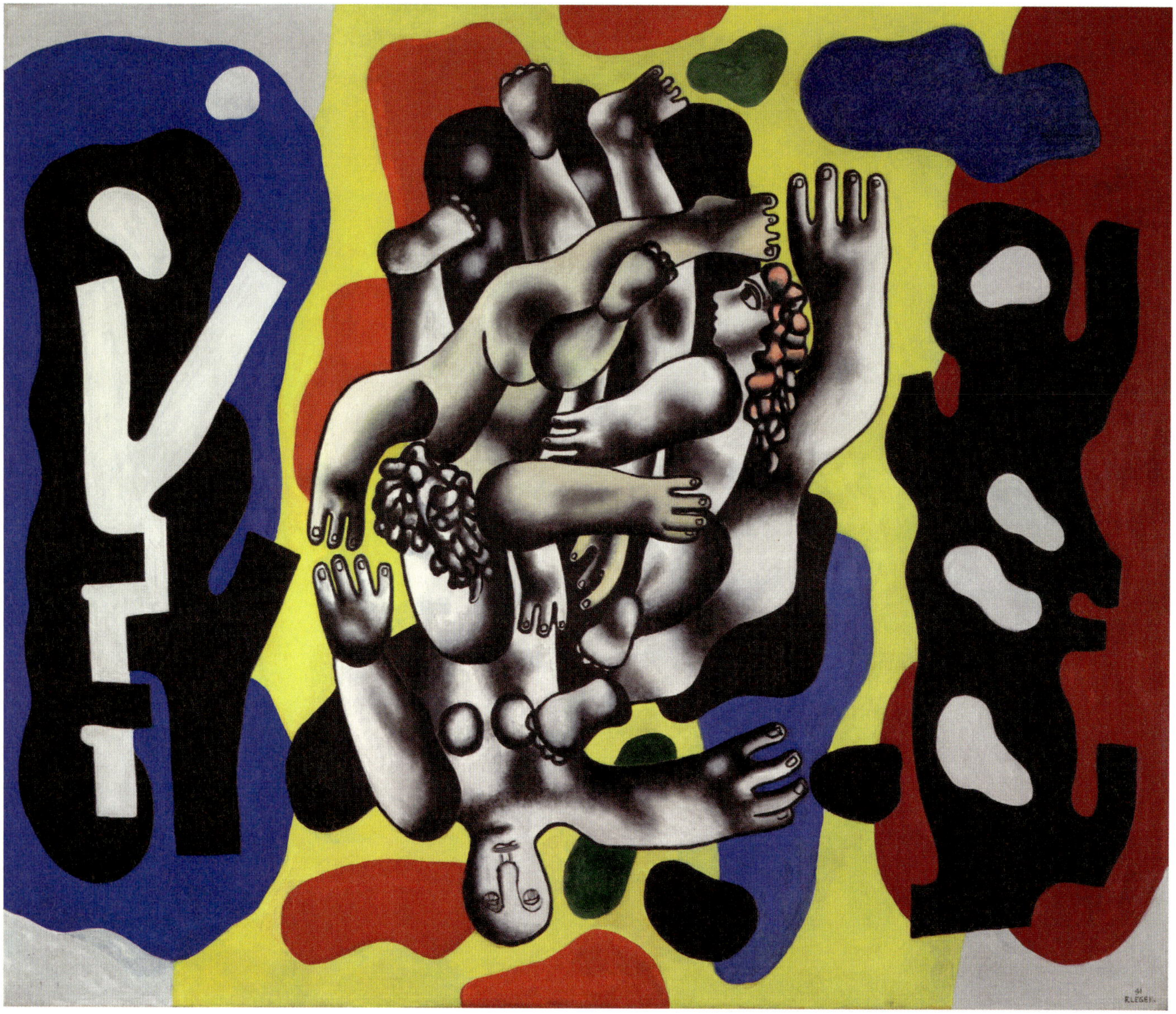

237

237 ***Les Plongeurs sur fond jaune* (Divers on a Yellow Background), 1941**
Oil on canvas
186.7 × 217.8 cm
The Art Institute of Chicago
Gift of Mr. and Mrs. Maurice E. Culberg

238 ***Les acrobates en gris* (Acrobats in Gray), 1942–44**
Oil on canvas
183 × 147 cm
Centre Pompidou, Musée national d'art moderne, Paris

On the human body considered as an object (1945)
Fernand Léger

In modern painting today, the object ought to become the *main character* and replace the subject. If, in its turn, the individual, the figure, the human body also becomes an object, then considerable freedom is afforded to the modern artist. At this time it has become possible for him to employ the law of contrasts, which, in its complete extension, is *the* constructive law.

This law of contrasts is nothing new; if one casts a look back, one sees that the old masters have, if not utilized it, at least sensed it in the composition of their pictures.

[…] We now come to our own era. The subject no longer being the *main character*, it has been replaced by the object, a new element. At this juncture, in the mind of the modern artist, a cloud, a machine, a tree have become elements of an interest equal to that of the individual or the figure. Hence, one will be able to carry out new pictures and large compositions from a wholly different viewpoint.

The law of contrasts dominates human life in all its emotional, spectacular, and dramatic aspects. […]

Abstract Art

Among the various directions that have evolved in the fine arts over the last twenty-five years, abstract art is the most significant, the most interesting.

[…] If, to me, its creative development appears fulfilled, the same cannot be said of its pictorial potential in architecture. Mural art, which flourished in the Middle Ages and during the Renaissance, has undergone an eclipse. The 19th and 20th centuries have been dominated by easel painting.

Certain painters, both social and artistic, though, seem to foretell a revival in mural art. By enlarging them, monumental art can and should use these novel ideas.

The young architects who will rebuild a devastated Europe should turn their eyes in this direction. This art has to be placed in large structures. It is static in its very expression; it respects the wall, in conjunction with a dynamic conception that destroys the wall.

It will be its measure and its equilibrium.

FERNAND LÉGER

Excerpt from F. Léger, "À propos du corps humain considéré comme un objet," in *Fernand Léger, la forme humaine dans l'espace* (Montreal: Les Éditions de l'Arbre, 1945), 65–75.

–

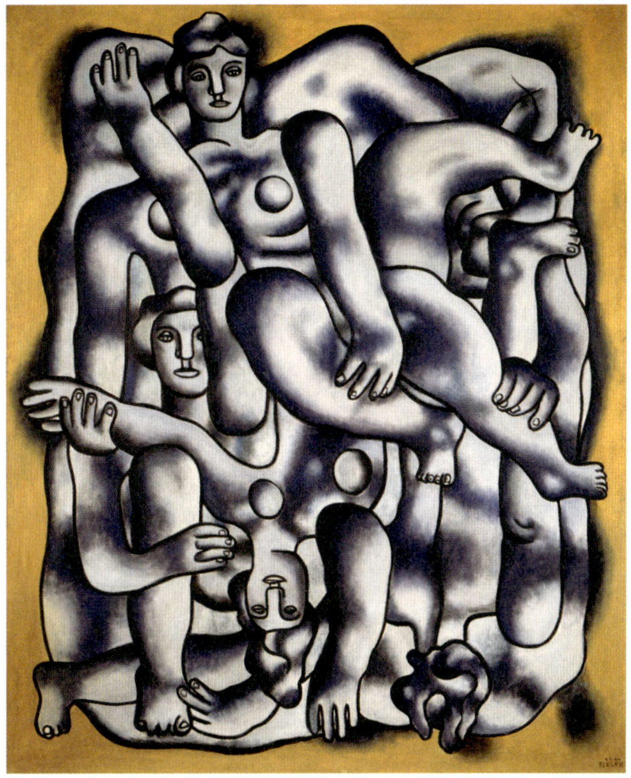

238

Letter from Fernand Léger to Le Corbusier, New York (undated)

My dear chap, I hear through friends that you're still alive and keeping busy. How exactly? I'd really like to know how you're handling things in the midst of the fray. I'm interested because here I'm just a refugee patiently awaiting a possible return. Maybe I made a mistake in leaving, convinced that my line of work was screwed until the turmoil was over. I hear that everyone's hard at work in Paris, and what's more (talking of painters) selling their stuff pretty well. Naturally I hadn't foreseen this, and if I had, I might have done otherwise. Naturally life here is pretty easy for me, without being extraordinary. I'm doing a lot of work. Maybe the imagination is more creative and faster here. I've written saying this to R[ex] Martienssen in Johannesburg (I've just had a letter from him). Interest in painting is still enormous here, which means it's a good place for a guy like me. But the old Normandy boy in me lives on; after all, it's not the same grass here!

At my age you don't assimilate and, mainly, you're not as pliable as you used to be. Despite having made some very good friends in a nice circle of people including Sert and Calder and Sweeney and lots of others, home lingers on my mind. I would really love some news of you and what's going on around you. Here the war has put a stop to any ideas of doing architecture–if there were any to start with. The engineer takes precedence over the architect, as you'd expect.

Personally I've been doing a lot of work on a very dynamic theme, *Les Plongeurs* [The Divers], which is freer and more violent than *Les Perroquets* [The Parrots/The Acrobats], which you saw in Paris. I've been battling with the human body and pure color for fifteen months. Already done gouaches and drawings, and fifteen or twenty canvases. You can write to me as long as you don't catch the eye of the censors. Letters get through. All the best, old chap, and love to Yvonne. Fernand Léger

Fondation Le Corbusier, Paris. Reprinted in *Fernand Léger*, exh. cat., Centre Pompidou (Paris, 1997), 340.

–

Fernand Léger on *Les Plongeurs* (The Divers) (1954)

In 1940, I was in Marseille working on my *Divers*, five or six persons in the act of diving. I had the idea for the picture in the South of France. Later, I left for the United States and one day I went to a swimming pool there. The divers were no longer five or six, but two hundred there at once. What do I see? To whom belonged a head, a leg, some arms, one could not tell, one could not make a distinction. So I scattered the limbs in my picture. I think I was far closer to the truth in that than Michelangelo was when he studied the detail in each of the muscles. I have seen the figures painted in the Sistine Chapel: they don't fall, they stay put in all the corners of the building. One can distinguish their toenails. I can assure you that when those fellows in Marseille jumped into the water I had no time to observe the details and my divers really fall.

Excerpt, originally published in Dora Vallier, "La vie fait l'œuvre de Fernand Léger," in *Cahiers d'Art* 2 (1954): 156.
English translation by Ruth Ann Krueger Meyer in Ruth Ann Krueger Meyer, *Fernand Léger's Mural Paintings 1922–55*, Ph.D. Diss. University of Minnesota (1980), 247–48.

–

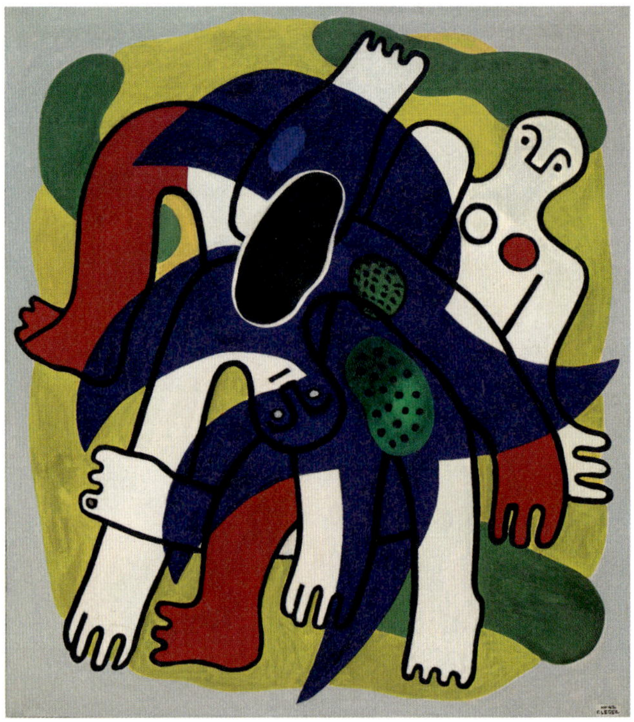

239

239 ***L'Étoile de Mer* (Starfish), 1942**
Oil on canvas
147.3 × 127 cm
Solomon R. Guggenheim Museum, New York, acc. no. 77.2669

240 ***Esquisse pour les plongeurs* (Sketch for The Divers), 1945**
Oil on canvas
194.8 × 146 cm
Kunsthalle Mannheim
On loan from the state of Baden-Württemberg since 1963

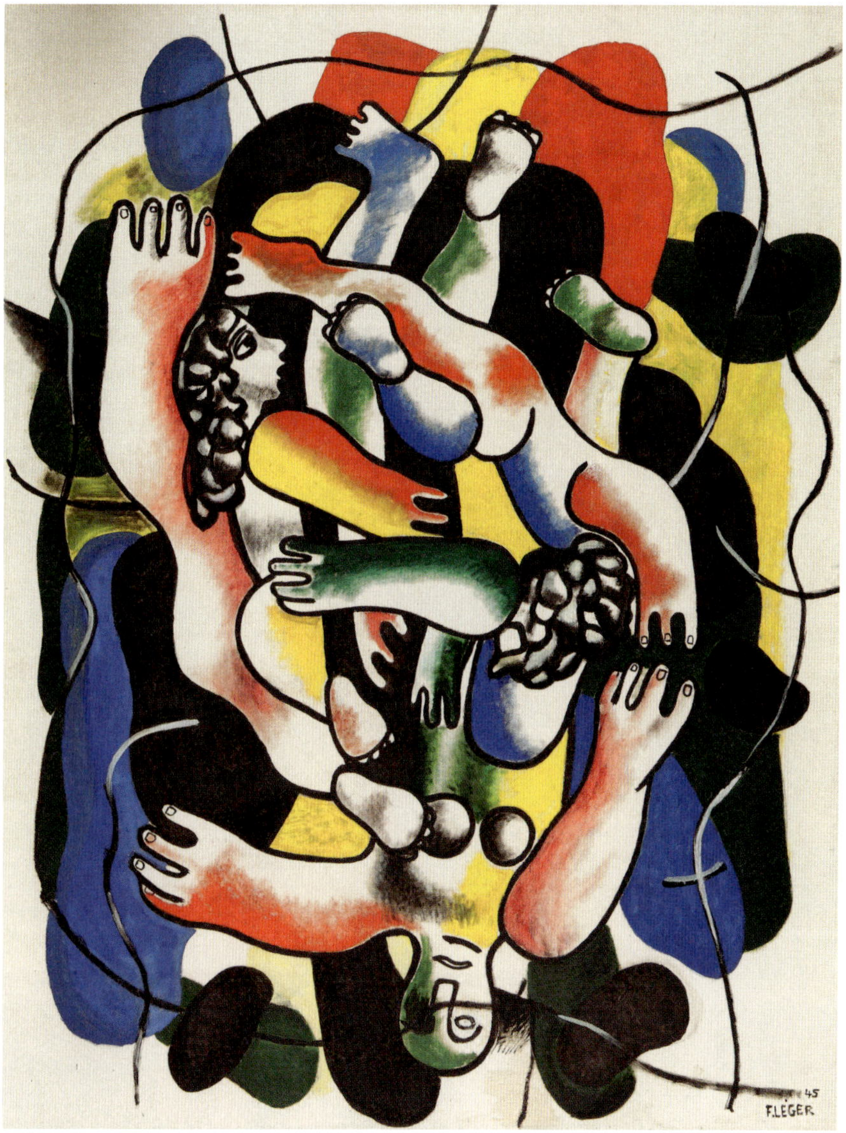

240

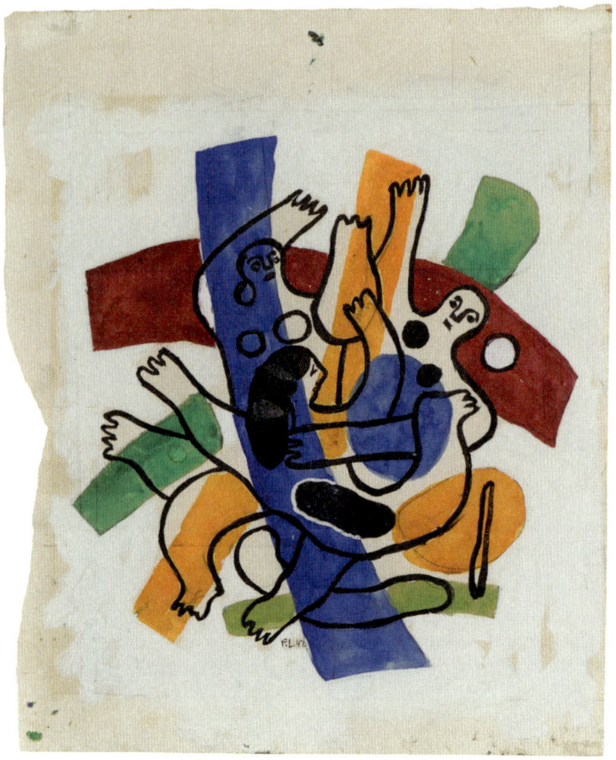

241

Fernand Léger on Experiencing Color in Space on Broadway (1954)

In 1942, when I was in New York I was struck by the advertising projectors on Broadway which played upon the street. There you are. You're talking to someone and all of a sudden he becomes blue. As soon as that color passes another comes and he becomes red or yellow. That kind of color, the color of the projector is free; free in space. I would like to have the same thing in my canvases. It is very important for mural painting because that has no scale, but I have also used them in my easel paintings. I have not invented it. I didn't imagine it.

Excerpt, originally published in Dora Vallier, "La vie fait l'œuvre de Fernand Léger," in *Cahiers d'Art* 2 (1954): 154.
English translation by Ruth Ann Krueger Meyer in Ruth Ann Krueger Meyer, *Fernand Léger's Mural Paintings 1922–55*, Ph.D. Diss. University of Minnesota (1980), 250.

–

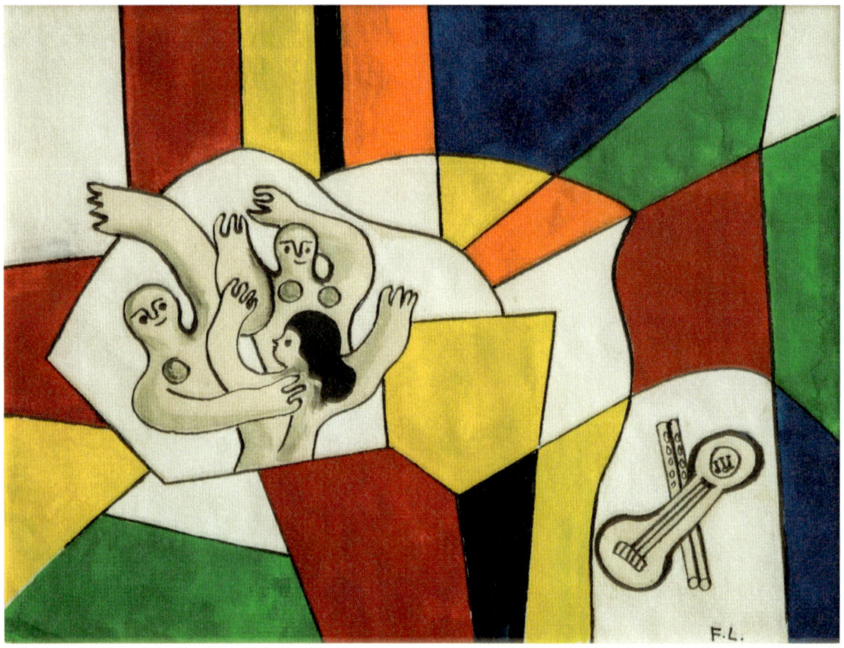

242

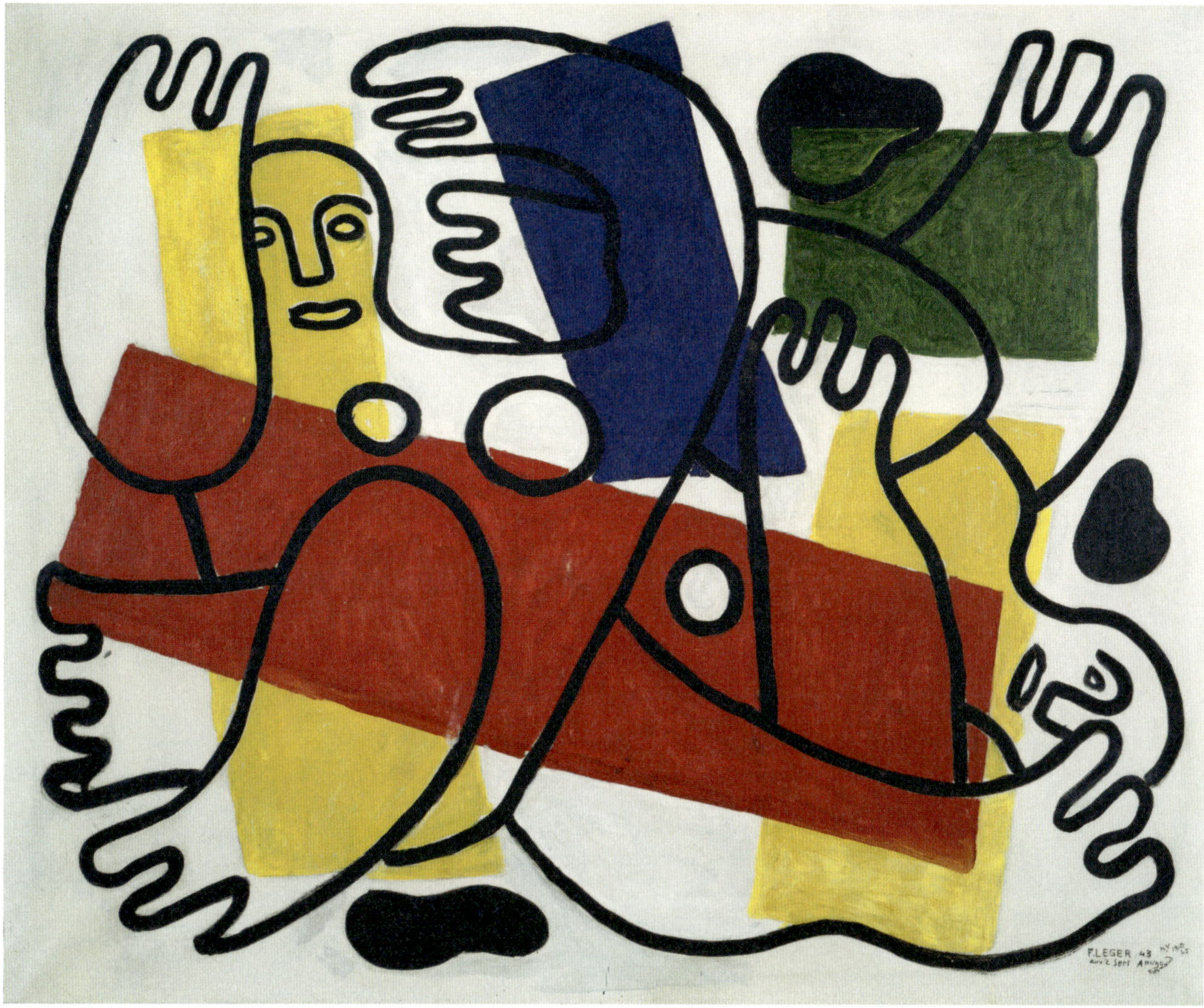

243

241 ***Étude pour La danse* (Study for The Dance), 1942**
Pencil, gouache and India ink on paper
36.8 × 29.7 cm
Galerie Louise Leiris, Paris

242 **Study for Saõ Paolo, c. 1952**
Gouache on paper
18.5 × 24.5 cm
Private collection

Mural sketch for an auditorium designed by Oscar Niemeyer in São Paulo (not realized).

243 ***Les Plongeurs* (The Divers), 1943**
Oil on canvas
88.9 × 106.68 cm
Harvard Art Museums/Fogg Museum
Gift of Mr. and Mrs. Josep Lluís Sert, acc. no. 1964.60

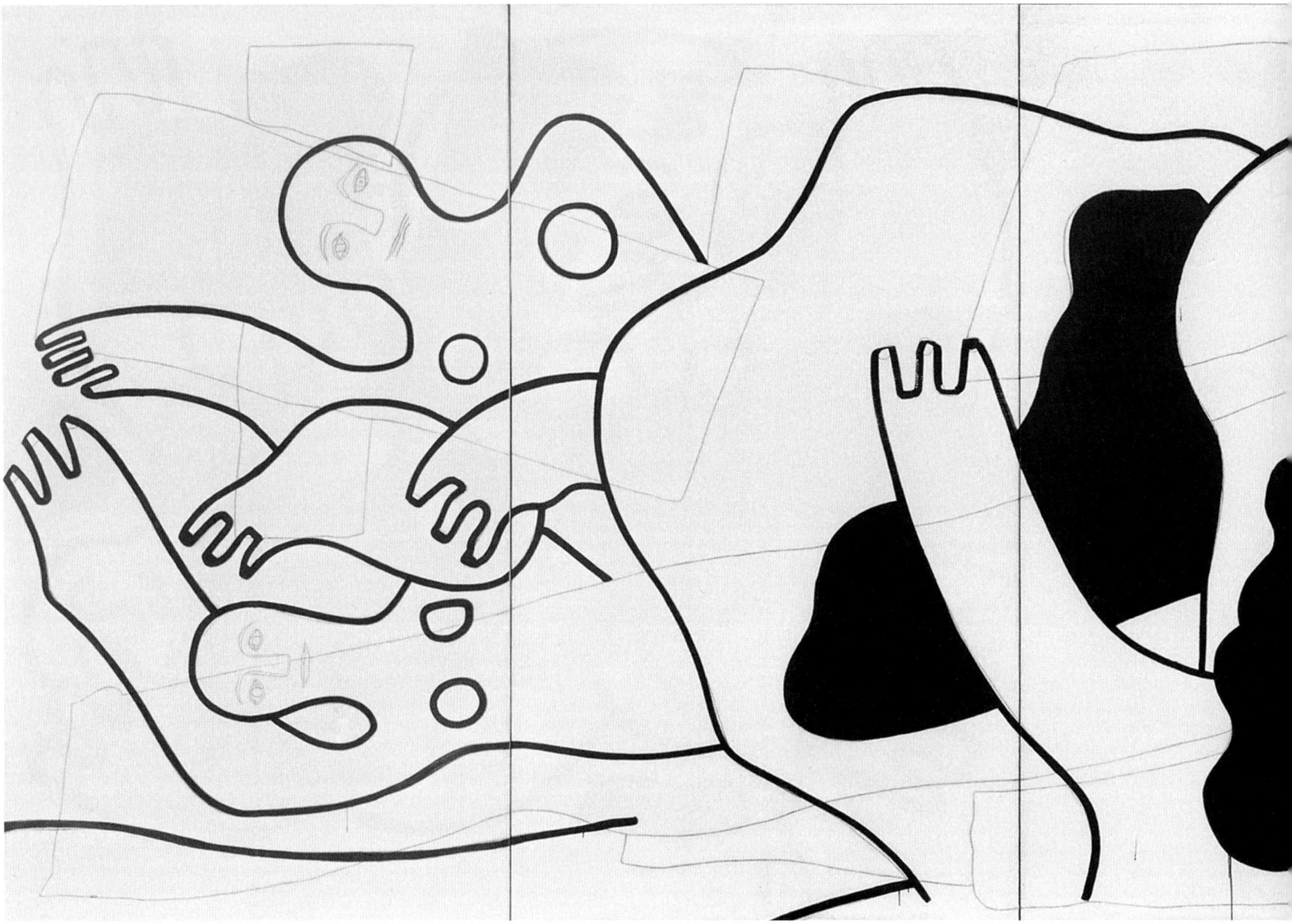

244

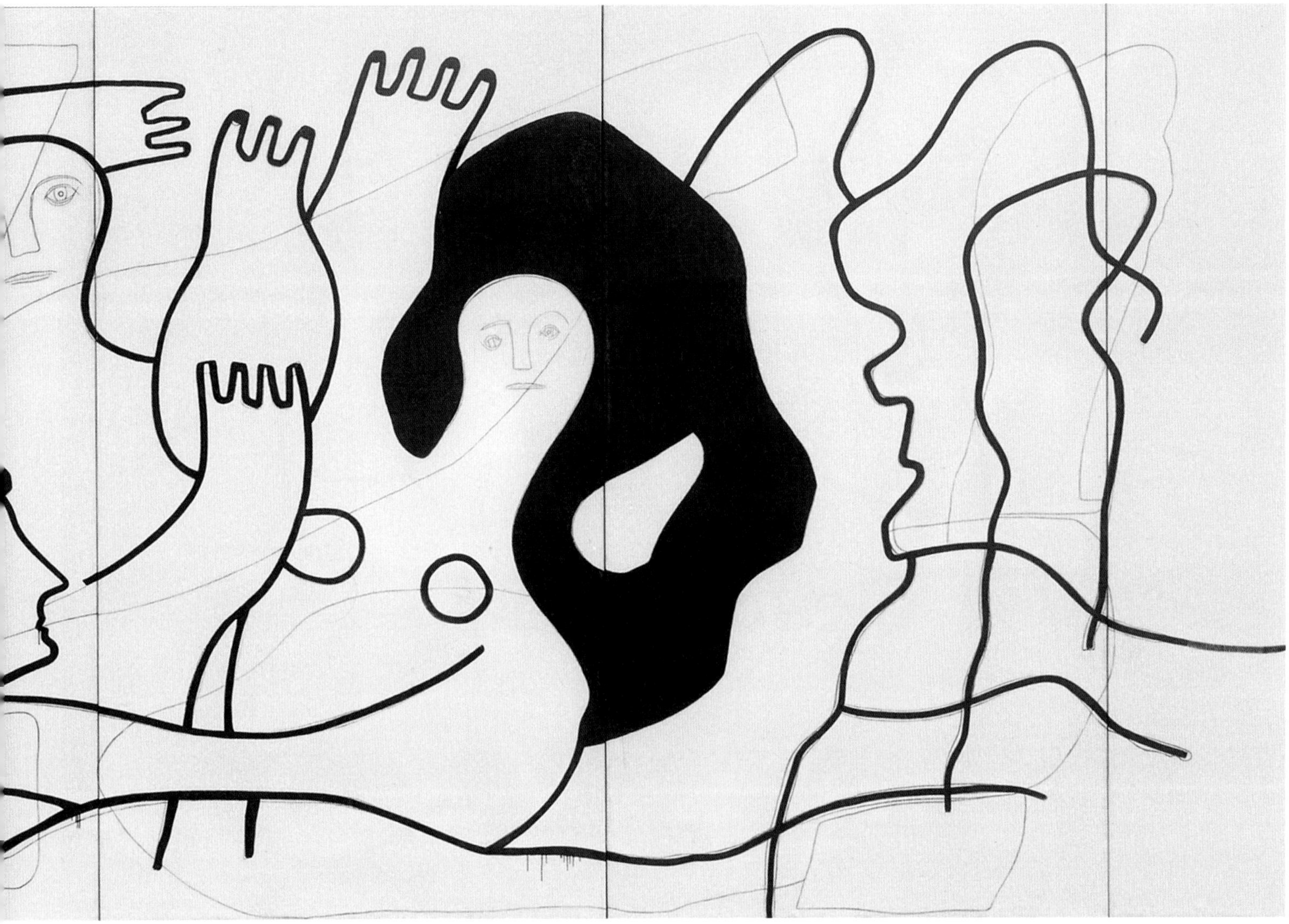

244 ***Les Plongeurs*** **(The Divers), 1942**
Oil and charcoal on canvas
372 × 1092 cm
Museum Ludwig, Cologne

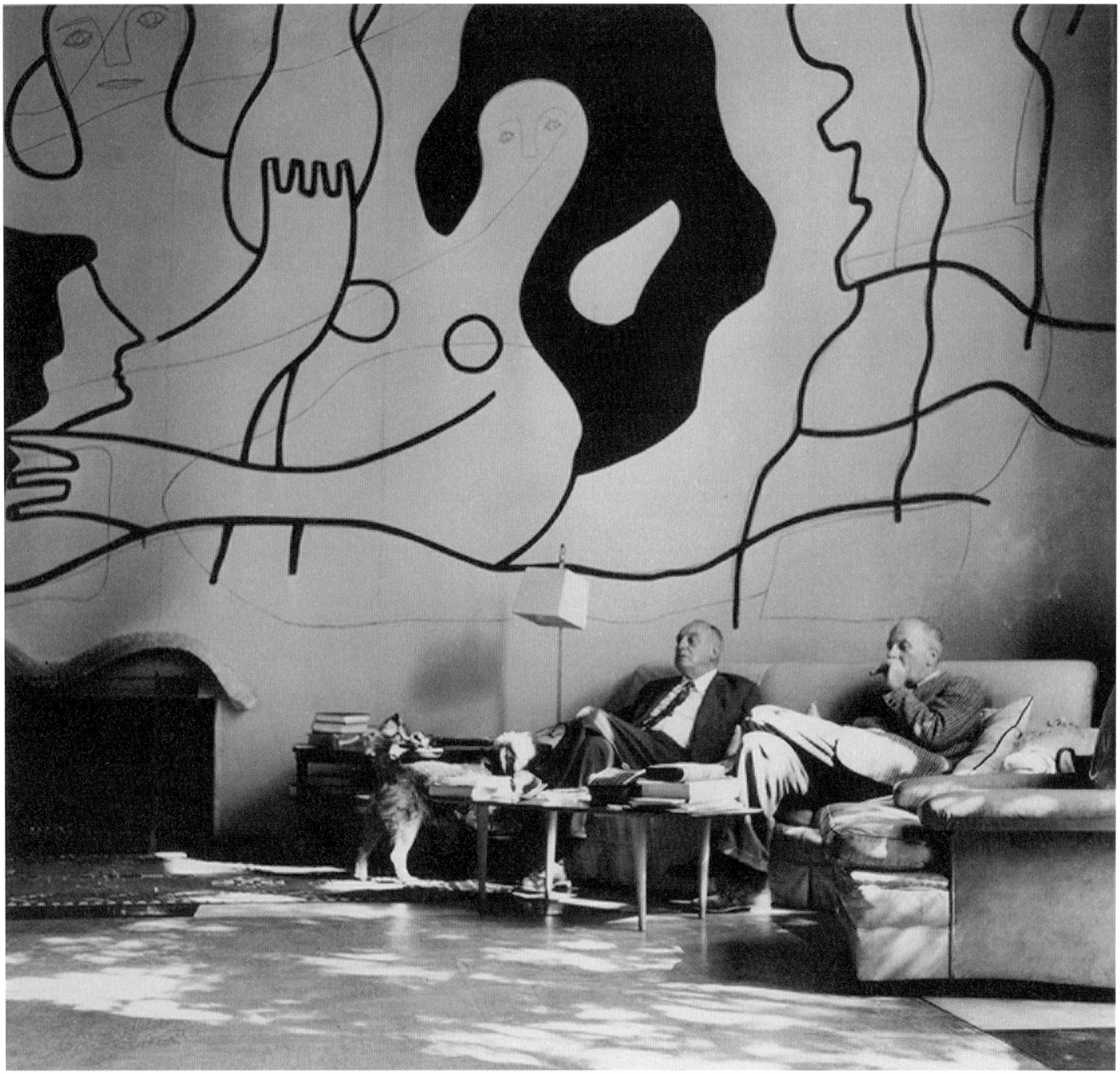

245

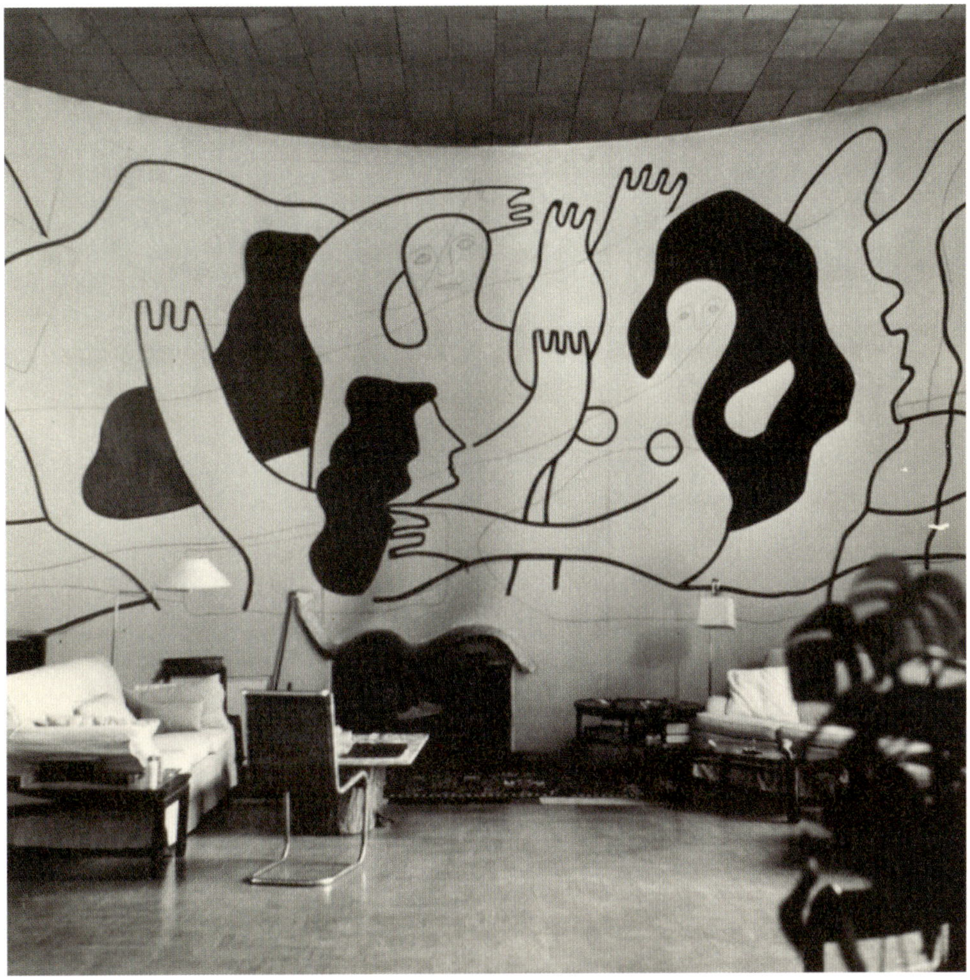

246

245 **Mural painting *Les Plongeurs* (The Divers) in the home of Wallace K. Harrison, Huntington, Long Island, circa late 1940s, Wallace K. Harrison with Robert Moses**
Avery Architectural & Fine Arts Library, Columbia University, New York, Wallace K. Harrison architectural drawings and papers, Series II: Collection II; Box 6, Folder 31

246 **Photograph of the mural painting *Les Plongeurs* (The Divers) in the house of Wallace K. Harrison, Huntington, Long Island, circa late 1940s**
Avery Architectural & Fine Arts Library, Columbia University, New York, Wallace K. Harrison architectural drawings and papers, Series II: Collection II; Box 7, Folder 31

247 ***Les hommes dans l'espace* (Men in Space), c. 1942**
India ink on paper
24 × 18 cm
Whereabouts unknown

248 **Study for the Mural for the home of Mr. and Mrs. Wallace Harrison, c. 1942**
Graphite, ink, and gouache on paper
55.56 × 76.52 cm
Portland Museum of Art, Maine
Anonymous Gift, 1986.2

249 ***Plongeurs. Étude pour le projet de São Paolo* (*Divers*, study for the São Paulo project), c. 1942**
Gouache on paper
29.5 × 66.3 cm
Private collection, Geneva

Most likely a study for the mural *Les Plongeurs*.

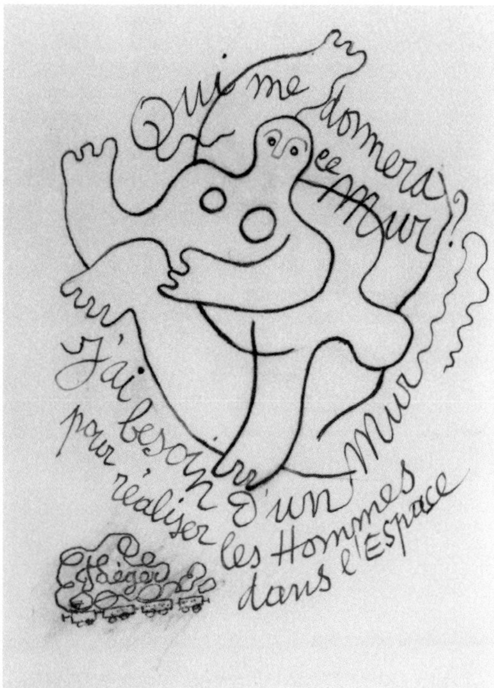

247

THE DIVERS OR MOVEMENT IN SPACE (1945)
Sigfried Giedion

Fernand Léger is one of the very few painters of our time whose work, since its inception, has striven to reach out to the people. This book records a phase in his evolution towards simplification and a monumental language. This is the meaning behind the series of *Divers* Léger started in Marseille (1940) and developed further in New York. In these illustrations, one can observe the power of condensation he deploys, as well as the abbreviated forms and the solution to a problem that has long intrigued the artist: *the representation of movement in a mass*. Already in Marseille, inarticulate forms on a beach can be seen. Soon the horizontal base disappears, being transposed to a vertical plane. The bathers reclining on the sand have become divers. Divers: a name, nothing more. But it indicates that the elements are placed in the "space" and on a vertical plane. Massing like bees on their nuptial flight, the volumes are increasingly simplified, being reduced to their essence.

Here are the *Divers on a Yellow Ground*, with straining forms in bold black outlines. This cloud of movement against a yellow background, accompanied to the right and left by surfaces of blue and red colors, is penetrated by irregular black objects, perhaps stylized roots. It is just as if the mass was flying through the sky and the sea simultaneously. Motion is present statically! Everything is readily grasped. Yet an enigma can arise if ever one tries to stop the movement with some stereotyped interpretation. The more the *Divers* series progresses, the more simplified the shapes and the number of figures become. They are condensed and purified. Just two entities are enough to personify motion in a mass. Transparent planes of color traverse their shapes guided by other contrasts. The contours drawn on the field of the canvas are reduced to marks of an absolute firmness, drawn freely in space, like an airplane writing in the stratosphere.

Where are the walls of public buildings in the United States and Canada that might lend themselves to such a language?

Yes, where are these walls?

I can't see them.

First published as S. Giedion, "Les Plongeurs ou mouvement dans l'espace," in *Fernand Léger, la forme humaine dans l'espace* (Montreal: Les Éditions de l'Arbre, 1945), 50-52.

–

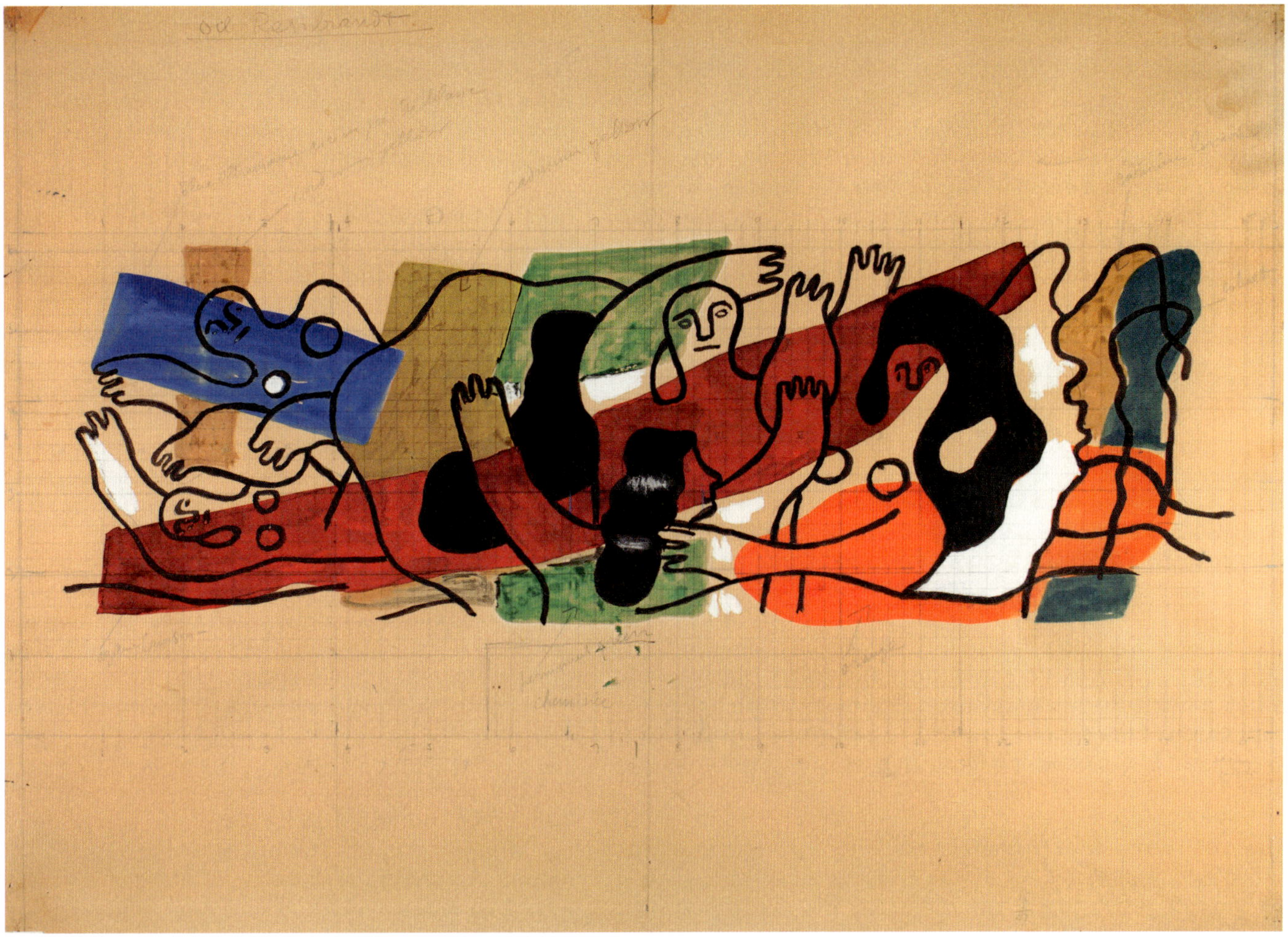

248

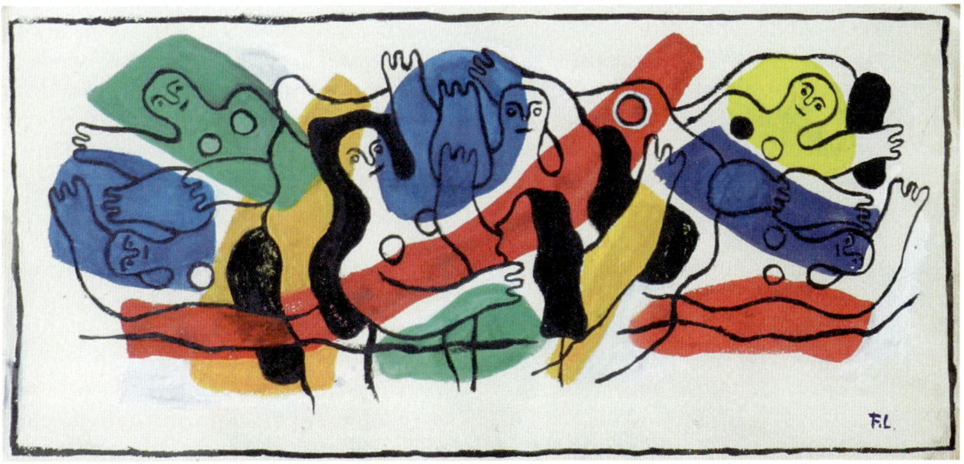

249

From Mural to Canvas

By Petra Mandt

Fernand Léger's painting *Les Plongeurs* (The Divers) was purchased by Peter and Irene Ludwig in 1984, and was gifted to the Ludwig Museum in 1986 to mark the opening of the new building (fig. 244). The painting took pride of place in the stairwell in the summer of 1987, where it would go on to be displayed for years to come. Spanning a total of 3.71 × 10.84 meters, what appears to be a single, monumental picture is actually several aligned canvases. It is difficult to imagine how it was originally conceived: as a mural created with one specific room in mind.

Les Plongeurs was painted in 1942 for the American architect Wallace K. Harrison (1895–1981) and was previously displayed in the living room of his summerhouse in Huntington on Long Island.[1] The surviving historical photographs do not, however, shed sufficient light on the mural's original effect in the room or its dimensions (figs. 245, 246).

The older of the two photographs shows the room shortly after the painting was created (fig. 246). With a diameter of 10.45 meters, the mural takes up slightly less than half of the wall space of the circular room.[2] The individual canvas sheets were fixed to the wall, one flush up against the next, running from floor to ceiling.[3]

The small-scale draft of the final painting[4] indicates that the piece's position in the room was a key consideration, even in its early stages. A gap of approximately 110 centimeters was to be left between the mantelpiece and the entire composition. The detailed draft sketch even specifies the colors for the abstract shapes upon which the figures are superimposed (fig. 248).

The outlines of the figures and colored planes shown in the sketch were first replicated in charcoal on the canvases, which had been commercially primed in white. Then, the outlines were gone over in black, using paintbrushes of varying size. Some parts of the painting were colored completely black, for example the hair of the female figure shown in profile at the center of the picture. However, at this stage, the charcoal lines of the faces, as well as the outlines of the planned colored shapes, were still visible. In an interview from 1975, the architect Harrison told art historian Ruth K. Meyer that the painting was created over the course of a long weekend, with the help of Harrison's family. Having gone over the initial lines in charcoal, contoured the figures, and filled in the black shapes, the decision was made to leave the work as it stood.[5]

A full-color version as per the draft sketch[6] would probably have further emphasized the enormous amount of space taken up by the mural. Even the room's color scheme and the materials used to decorate it were said to have influenced the decision. The circle of large terrazzo floor tiles, for example, provided the black-and-white contrast. But perhaps the most important architectural element is the trimming around the fireplace. The mantelpiece, shaped like an abstract white wave, highlighted the central group of figures in the painting, and made direct reference to the theme of *Les Plongeurs*. The mural is part of the architecture.

In 1974, the house was sold to the New York art dealer Harold Diamond (1926–1982). A photograph from 1978 shows the state of the room after renovations had been carried out (fig. 255), which involved alterations to the mural's format. The canvas sheets, which had originally reached the floor, were trimmed to the height of approximately 110 centimeters. The painting's overall composition, however, was retained, save for two of the black contour lines along the new lower edge of the canvas, which were slightly reduced, and the addition of a narrow white trim.[7] These changes to the picture's format and framing resulted in the creation of an entirely new piece.

In addition, there were changes to the room's decor. The wooden coffered ceiling was removed and replaced with a white plaster ceiling, complete with spotlights that lit the picture. The terrazzo tiles and parquet flooring were exchanged for a lighter flooring material, and the mantelpiece was removed.

In 1984, the painting was taken down for good with the intention of putting it up for sale,[8] and comprehensive conservation and restoration measures ensued. These were carried out under the direction of Margaret M. Watherston,[9] a New York-based restorer, and their effects can be seen even today.

A photograph shows the painting being removed from the wall (fig. 252). In order to roll the whole painting onto a vertical rotating roller, the edges of the individual canvas panels were secured with adhesive strips and gradually detached from the wall. Their removal was far from straightforward: some parts were more firmly attached than others, while several areas of the canvas were substantially degraded due to mold and this needed to be dealt with.[10] The mold first had to be removed from the affected fabric, which was then thoroughly treated. The parts that were beyond repair had to be completely replaced and patched with primed pieces of canvas.

The original canvas sections were fitted together in twos and the resulting seams were secured on the back with fabric strips. All the outer edges were reinforced with a strip-lining: this allowed for the canvas to be stretched on a frame (the expansion-bolt stretcher based on James J. Lebron's model).[11] The result was five separate canvas paintings of the same size, supplemented by a narrower section on the right-hand side of the image. The consolidation treatment of the black-color areas, a surface treatment of the white priming coat, followed by fillings and retouching, formed the final steps of the process.

The multi-part, transportable canvas painting that resulted from this work has often been on display in the stairwell of the Museum Ludwig in recent years, where visitors can admire it from afar. The painting was once again displayed on a semicircular wall as part of the exhibition *Our Century* (Museum Ludwig, 1995).[12] The current 2016 exhibition also uses this same presentation (fig. 250). By displaying the work on a semicircular wall in combination with the floor plan of the circular room, it is possible to recreate the painting's original positioning, allowing the viewer a glimpse of how the monumental piece was first intended to appear.

1 Erik Neil and Kenneth Wayne, with an essay by Sandy Isenstadt, *Long Island Modern: Art and Architecture on the North Shore and Beyond* (Huntington, NY: Heckscher Museum, 2009), 16–25 for Harrison's house.
2 The former director of the restoration, Christa Steinbüchel, took exact measurements of the room in situ in 1985.
3 The original width of an individual canvas panel was around 101.5 cm, as indicated by the selvages on both sides. Wallpaper glue was used as an adhesive.
4 Fernand Léger, *Study for the Mural in the home of Mr. and Mrs. Wallace Harrison*, c. 1942: graphite, ink, gouache on paper, c. 55 × 76.5 cm, Portland Museum of Art, Maine.
5 As reported in a letter from Ruth K. Meyer (26 October 1984), Museum Ludwig image file.
6 See fig. 248.
7 The identity of the person responsible for these alterations remains unknown.
8 The painting was purchased by the Gmurzynska Gallery.
9 The restorer Margaret M. Watherston was a specialist in the conservation and restoration of contemporary art. Her papers from 1965 to 2005 are housed in the library of the Winterthur Museum in Winterthur, Delaware (http://findingaid.winterthur.org/html/HTML_Finding_Aids/col0935.htm). They do not document her work on *Les Plongeurs*; copies of invoices indicate around 700 hours of work. The private notes of a member of staff provide more exact details about the measures taken and the materials used.
10 The adhesive used, together with the environmental conditions on the site, created the perfect breeding ground for microorganisms.
11 This form of stretcher was developed c. 1957/58 by James J. Lebron. See Barbara A. Buckley, "Stretchers and Strainers," *AIC Wiki*, March 27, 2014, http://www.conservation-wiki.com/wiki/Paintings#Strechers_and_Strainers
12 It was displayed together with the sculpture *Black Nana* by Niki de Saint Phalle.

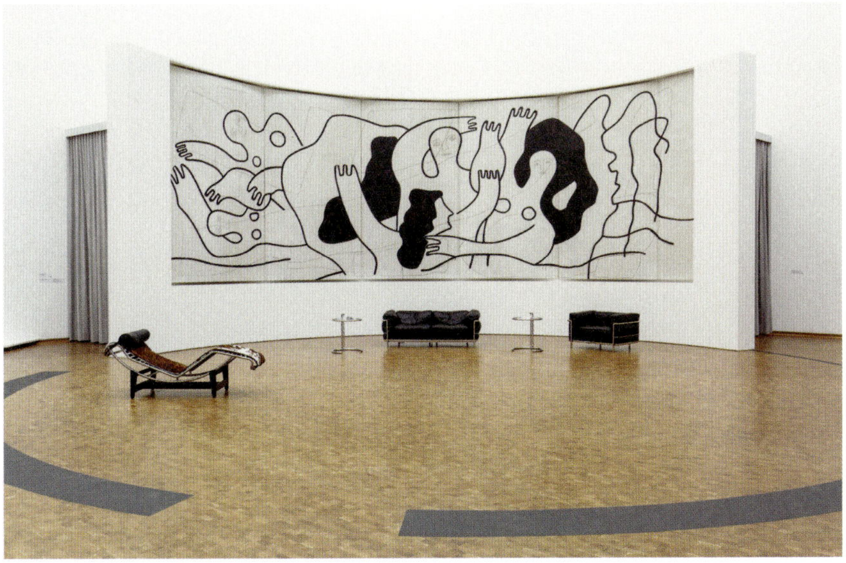

250

250 **Exhibition view: *Fernand Léger: Painting in Space*, Museum Ludwig, Cologne, 2016**
Partial reconstruction of Wallace K. Harrison's living room. The floor marking shows the dimension of the space.

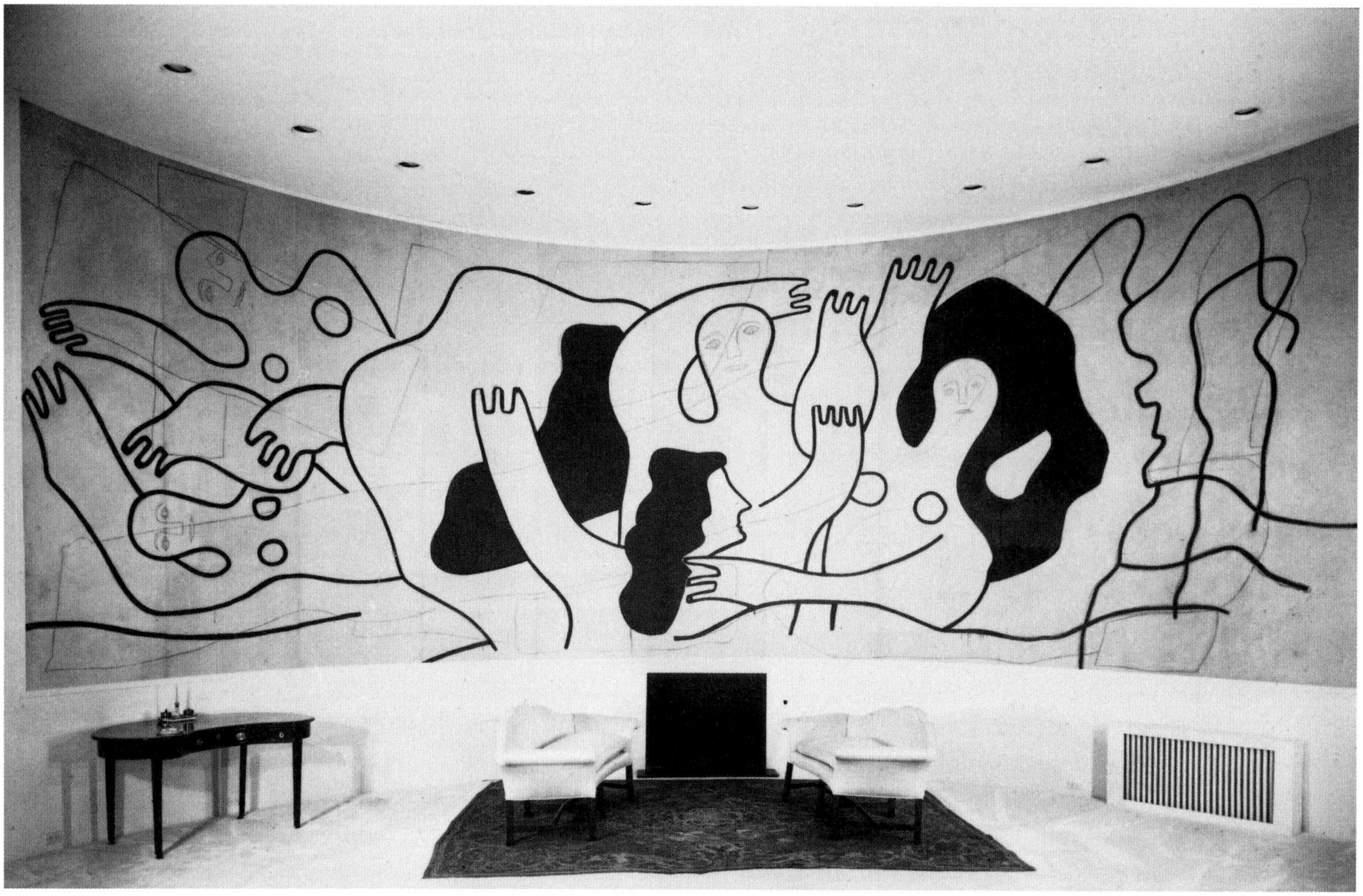

251

251 **Mural painting *Les Plongeurs* installed in the home of Wallace K. Harrison, Huntington, New York, early 1980s**
Courtesy Galerie Gmurzynska

The house was owned at the time by art dealer Harold Diamond and his wife Hester

252 **Removal of the mural painting *Les Plongeurs* from the home of Wallace K. Harrison, 1984**
Museum Ludwig archive, Cologne

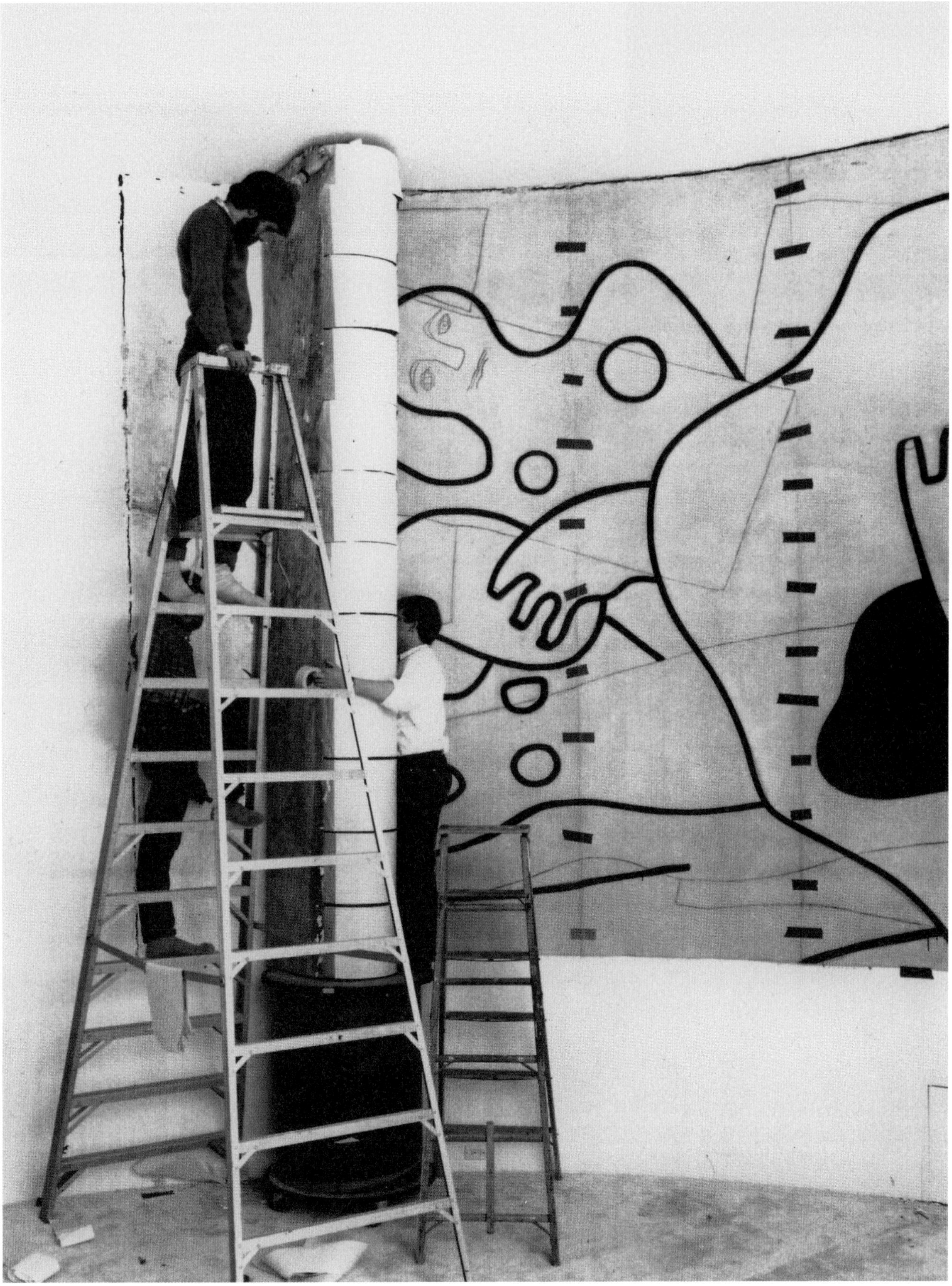

252

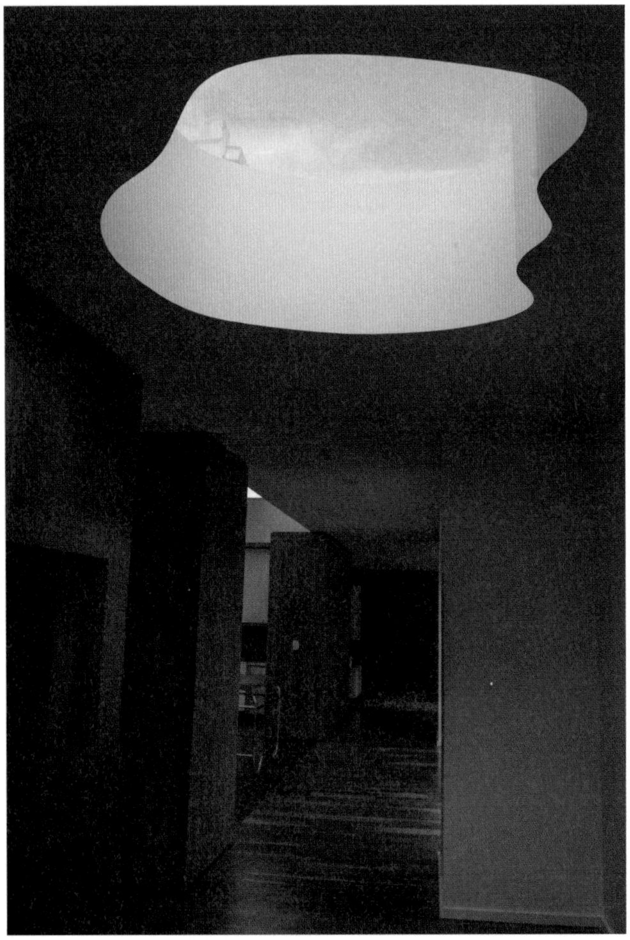

253

253 **Skylight by Fernand Léger in Harrison's home, Huntington, Long Island**
(current status, in the new extension by the current owners), photo: 2009

254 **Swimming pool with diver motif by Fernand Léger in the garden of Wallace K. Harrison, Huntington, New York, later removed**
Avery Architectural & Fine Arts Library, Columbia University, New York, Wallace K. Harrison architectural drawings and papers, Series II: Collection II
Box 7, Folder 21

255 ***Les Plongeurs*** **(The Divers) mural at the former home of Wallace K. Harrison, Huntington, New York, photo 1978**
(following modifications in the room by the then owners Harold and Hester Diamond)

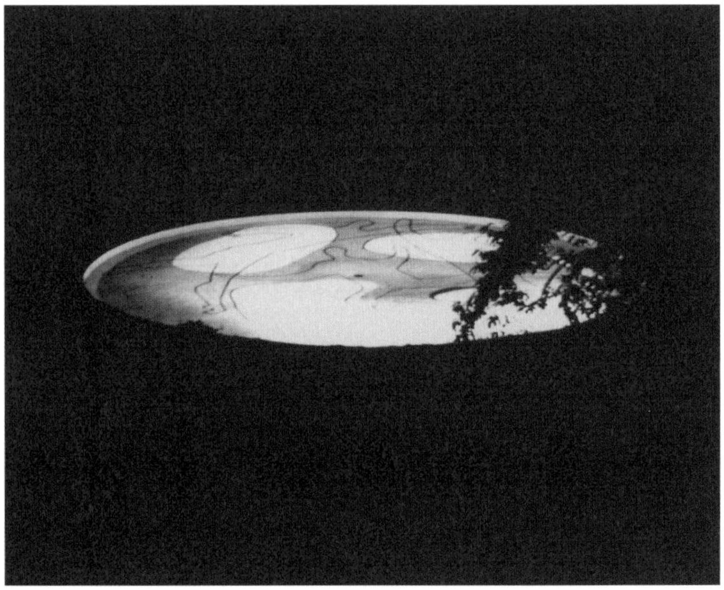

254

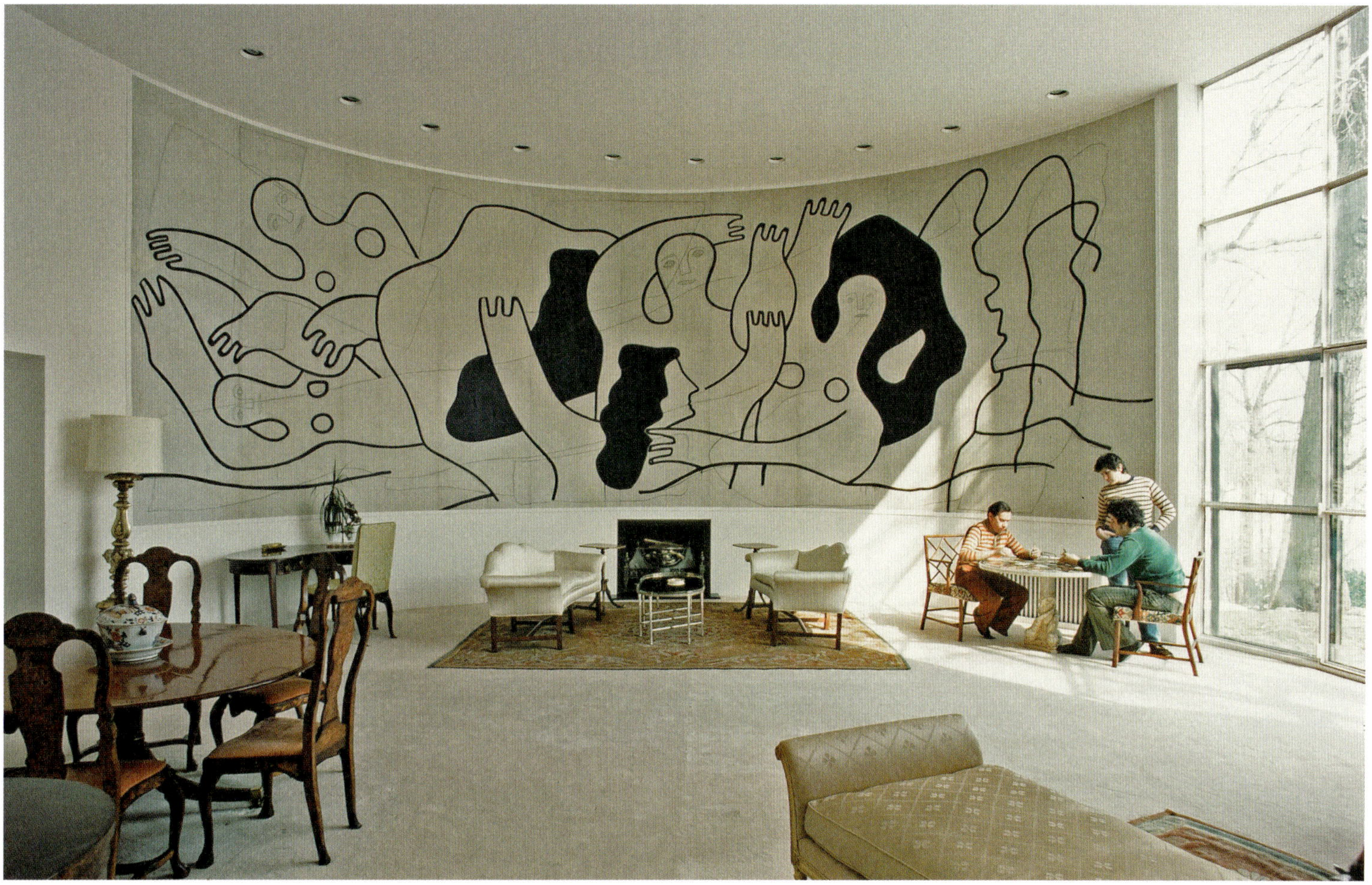

255

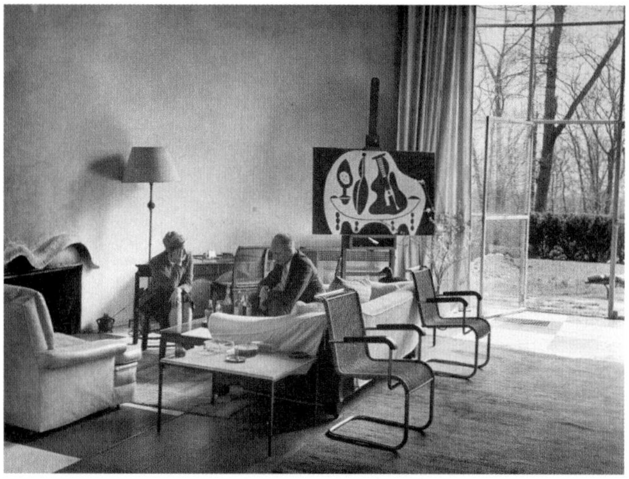

256

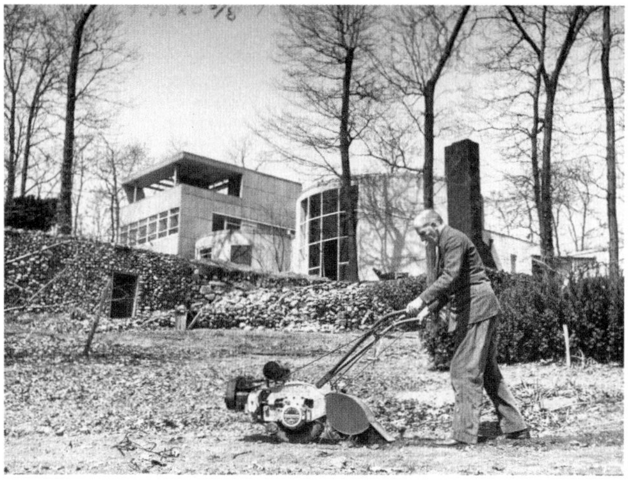

257

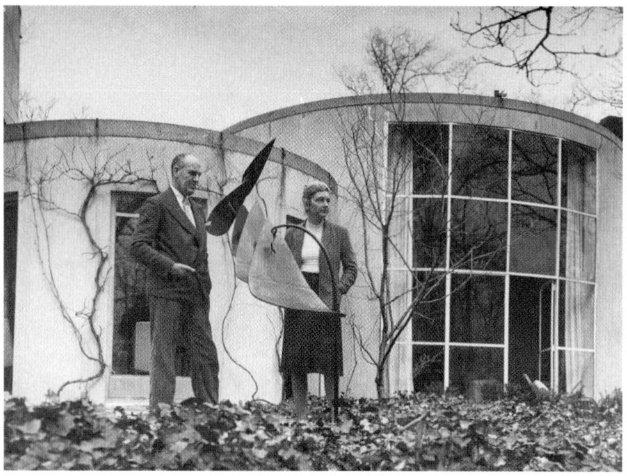

258

256 **Architect Wallace K. Harrison and his wife in their living room, c. 1941**
In the background: Pablo Picasso's *Compotier, bouteille, guitare* (Fruit Bowl, Bottle, Guitar), 1925, oil on canvas

257 **The architect Wallace K. Harrison, mowing the lawn. His home is in the background, c. 1941**

258 **Architect Wallace K. Harrison and his wife in the garden, c. 1941**

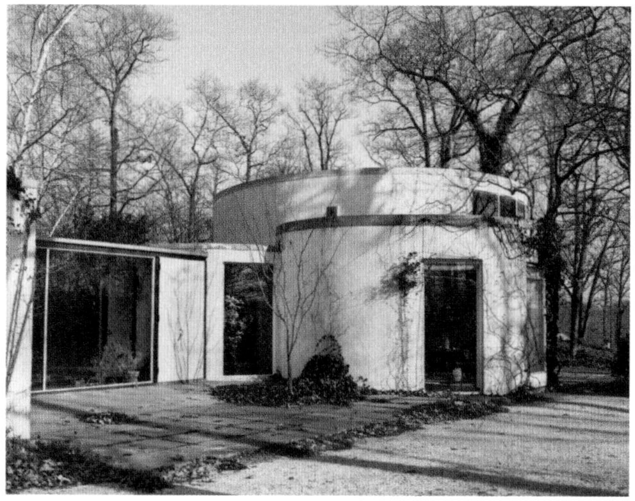

259

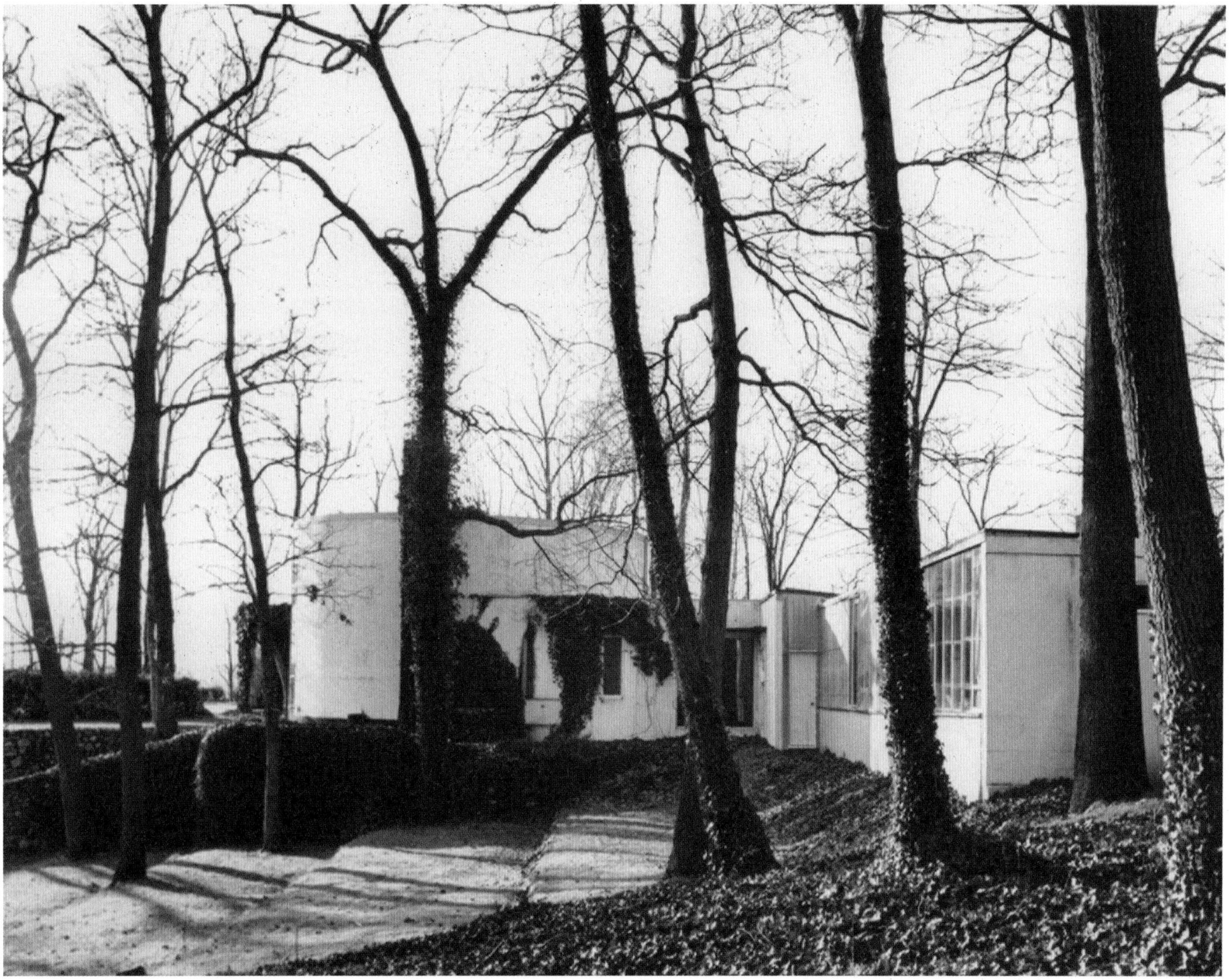

260

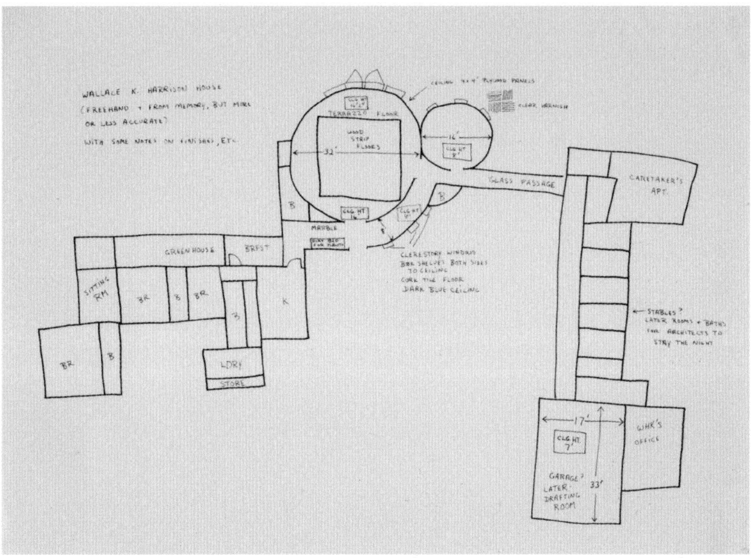

261

259 **Harrison's home, Huntington, New York, dining room, 1932**
Avery Architectural & Fine Arts Library, Columbia University, New York, Wallace K. Harrison architectural drawings and papers, Box 6, Folder 43

260 **Harrison's home, Huntington, New York**
Avery Architectural & Fine Arts Library, Columbia University, New York, Wallace K. Harrison architectural drawings and papers, Box 6, Folder 31

261 **Plan for the home of Wallace K. Harrison, Huntington, drawn by Hester Diamond (second owner of the house), c. 1940**
Avery Architectural & Fine Arts Library, Columbia University, New York, Wallace K. Harrison architectural drawings and papers, NYDA.1989.003.00126

Fernand Léger and the Reconstruction Period

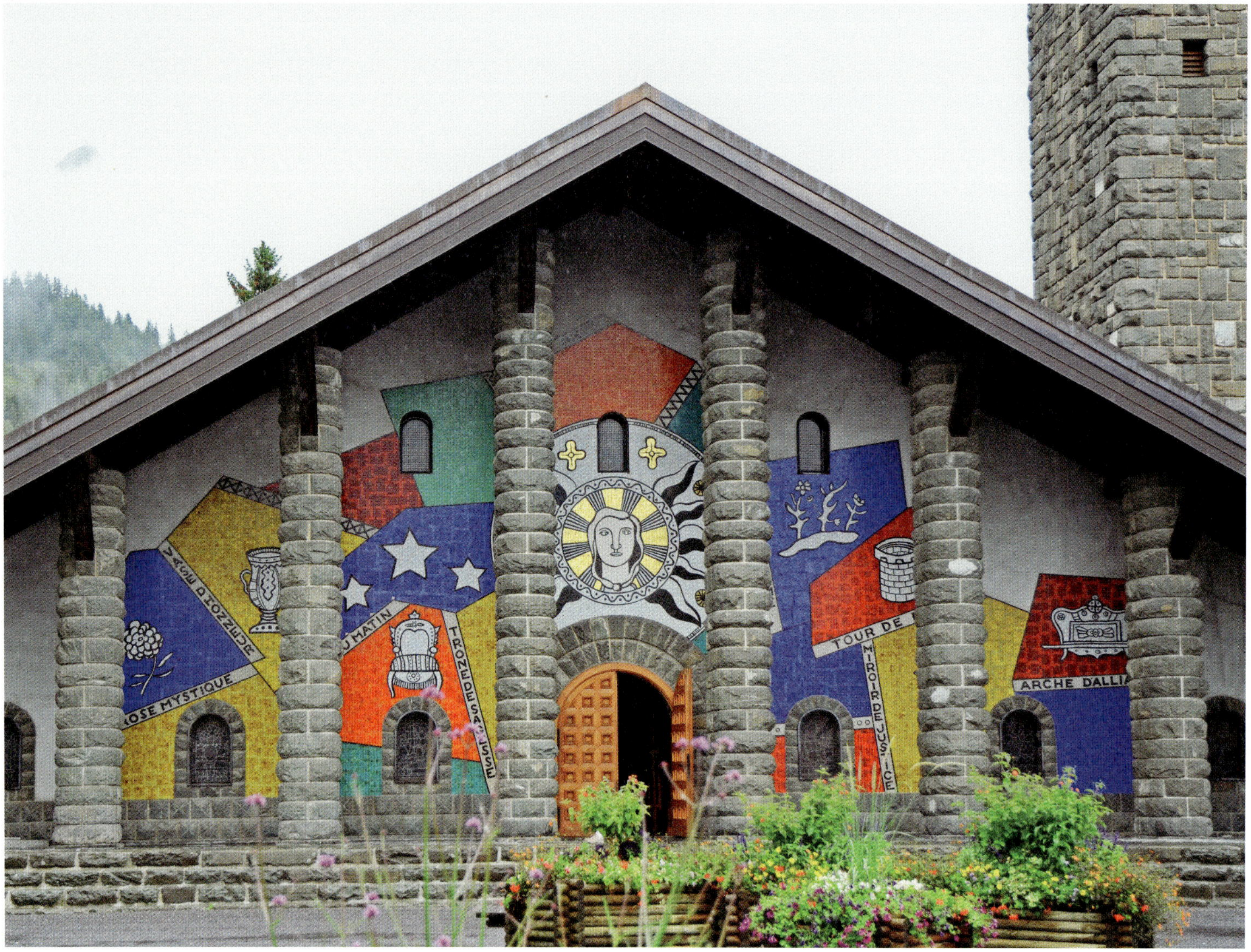

262

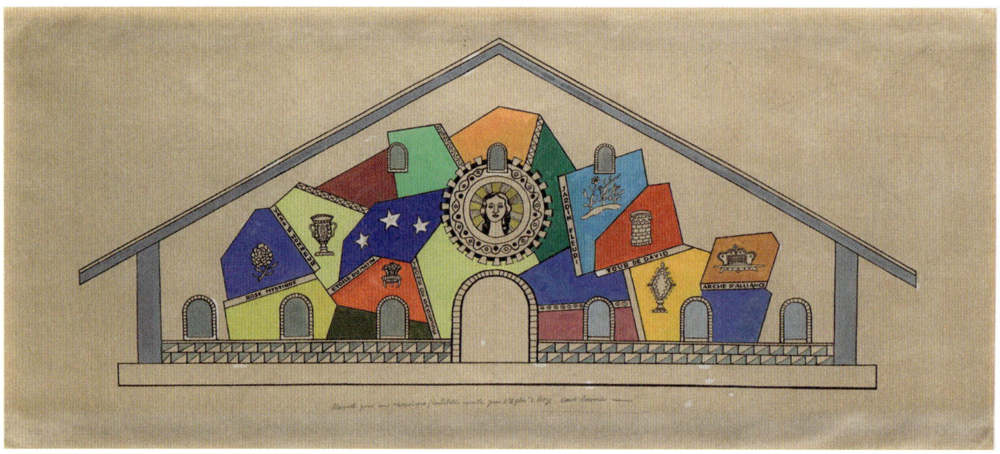

263

Fernand Léger on the Church Notre-Dame-de-Toute-Grâce in Assy

The realization of the façade of the church in Assy was a major event in my life as an artist. I'd been waiting for the opportunity to produce a mural work in an architectural material for a long time. It became possible to do one "in mosaic" thanks to the decision taken by Abbé Deveny and Father Couturier. I was able to compose this ensemble of pure colors without, for all that, destroying the architecture. It's done. The considerable worldwide impact of this remarkable church in which some of the foremost modern artists have participated proves that the time has come for the three arts, architecture–painting–sculptor, to collaborate extensively.

It marks the first time in our era, I think, that such a collaboration has found its rightful place. It is traditional in that I believe we have "linked" this work back to that of the Middle Ages. For us, the Romanesque and Gothic periods were the "reference" to follow with the tools of the present-day that have enabled us to completely renew that venerable "tradition."

Excerpt, originally published in Georges Bauquier, *Fernand Léger, Vivre dans le vrai* (Paris: Maeght, 1987), 321.

–

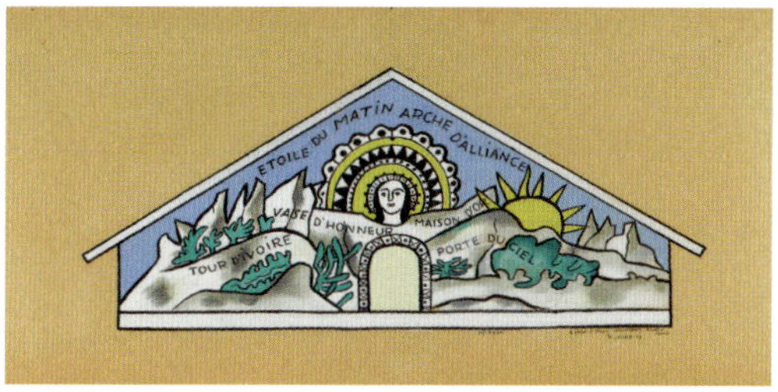

264

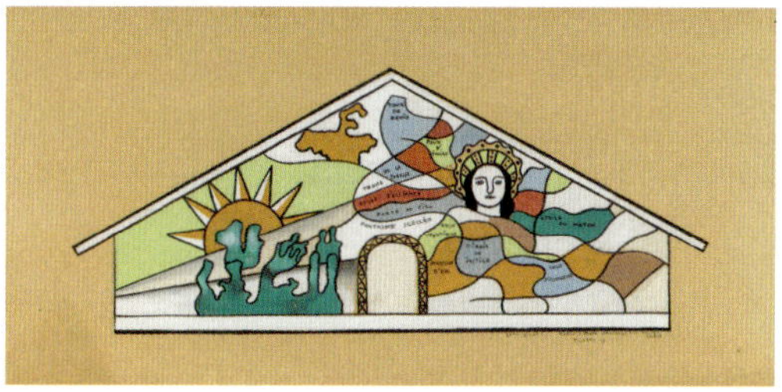

265

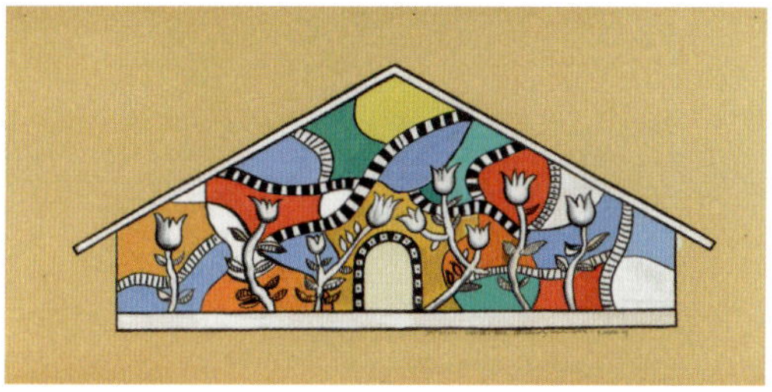

266

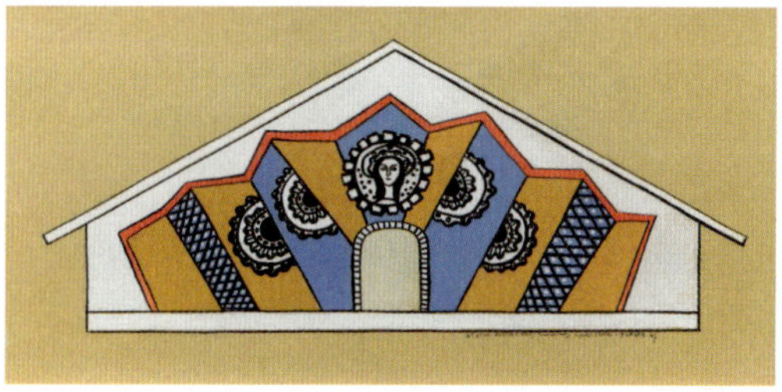

267

262 **Mosaic *Litanies de la Vierge* (Litanies of the Virgin) on the façade of the church of Notre-Dame-de-Toute-Grâce, Assy, Haute-Savoie], 1947/48**
Architect: Maurice Novarina

263 ***Maquette pour la mosaïque de l'église Notre-Dame-de-Toute-Grâce, Plateau d'Assy, Haute Savoie* (Study for the mosaic in the church of Notre-Dame-de-Toute-Grâce), 1947**
Gouache on paper
82.9 × 181.2
Musée national Fernand Léger, Biot

264 ***1er état,* Église d'Assy (First State, Church of Assy), Sancellemoz, Haute-Savoie, 1947**
46.5 × 102.5 cm

265 ***2me état,* Église d'Assy (Second State, Church of Assy), Sancellemoz, Haute-Savoie, 1947**
46.5 × 102 cm

266 ***3me état,* Église d'Assy (Second State, Church of Assy), Sancellemoz, Haute Savoie, 1947**
45.9 × 122 cm

267 ***4me état,* Église d'Assy (Second State, Church of Assy), Sancellemoz, Haute-Savoie, 1947**
46.5 × 118 cm

All: Gouache on paper
Musée national Fernand Léger, Biot

Letter from Fernand Léger to Father Marie-Alain Couturier, February 12, 1944 (New York)

February 12, 44

My Dear Friend -

Les Editions de l'Arbre in Montreal are publishing a new book about my work–35 to 40 reproductions. These reproductions will feature solely my work in New York and in particular "Human Shapes in Space" (*The Divers*). A certain number of writers and artists will provide me with articles–I hope for one from you, naturally–Owing to the narrow subject, I have to give all of you a general direction in order to avoid repetition. Thus, for you, dear Friend, I'd like your contribution to focus on the Gothic and Romanesque tradition you have so rightly sensed in my work - on the tradition of <u>stained glass windows</u>– on pure color, etc., well, you can surely sense the favorable terrain for you–hand me over 4 or 5 or 6 typed pages, as you like. You'll understand that the publishers and I will be delighted to have your article.

How's it going?… we never see each other–

Cordially yours
F. Léger

Archives Père Couturier, Bibliothèque du Saulchoir - Province dominicaine de France.

–

Léger and the Middle Ages (1945)
Marie-Alain Couturier

And yet now I will no longer forget the sudden impression made on me by the ten large canvases he exhibited in 1942, in New York, at Paul Rosenberg's. The quiet power, the joyful colors and lines, and, on an even deeper level, the felicitous choices made filled the place with their power, banishing doubt and mediocre intentions, and the slightly morbid anxiety often induced by the art of the past twenty years. That day I had the unexpected feeling that something that had disappeared since the Middle Ages had been revived. At any event, I could see that since the Middle Ages, such noble, dazzling colors and large forms with their familiar solemnity had not been spread across walls in such a simple fashion. The desire for monumentality was evident, yet it did not result in any coldness because the joy of painting shone out.

[…] First of all, I should point out that Léger's painting does not evoke 14th- or 15th-century art, but rather 12th- and 13th-century forms, Romanesque frescoes, the large stained-glass windows of the early 13th century, and the large transept windows at Chartres, for example. The kinship with such works seems undeniable.

I would say it is characterized by the following elements. Firstly, the very "abstraction" that today seems to pose difficulties. For a long time I used to think that abstract art as such could not be religious, because the meaning of works is enclosed within them, whereas "religious" art essentially involves reference to another reality, to another world. But such a view remains very superficial: the "religious" character of a work does not necessarily, nor even primarily, stem from the representation of a sacred subject, but, on a deeper level, from the character, the very *quality* of the visual forms. And "that very quality" comes to them directly, spontaneously, from the intimate dispositions of the mind and the heart–and not from the subject represented or from some more or less hieratic formula. Because if that had been the case, how could the arts that do not involve the representation of a subject, such as music or architecture, be religious or sacred?

On the contrary, I have observed that a certain "abstraction" will always be necessary for religious art, for sacred art: indeed "consecration," in the true sense, is removal from the natural order and transfer to the supernatural order.

[…] So it must be admitted that, in that sense, abstract art involves spiritual and religious potentialities that naturalistic art lacks. And it is in this respect, in this loosening, this untying of the close links with material reality, that Fernand Léger's abstract art is able to take us back to the great works of the hieratic periods, in which the representation of natural realities is limited to the minimum required for the intelligible expression of sacred realities.

This gives rise, in very different forms, to aspects which, in Léger's work, appear inacceptable within the terms of a narrow concept of religious art, but which in reality it has in common with Romanesque and early Gothic art, and that we would no doubt find again in all the archaic periods in which religious feeling is at its most intense: for example, the little importance attached by artists of these periods to facial features, to the psychological expression of the mouth, the gazes and gestures. Similarly in figuration, the elimination of elements that are picturesque or even simply too specific–the elimination also of aspects that are too accidental, of vanishing or three-quarter profiles–figures constantly depicted in profile or frontally. The reduction of poses or gestures to precise, schematic forms. Finally, a casual indifference to archeological detail and local color.

I don't have to point out the similarities with the art of Fernand Léger: the geometric forms, the flat tints, the schematic symbolism, and, in the drawing and modeling of human forms, precision reduced to possible resemblance or even simple allusion. I simply want to point out that, on both sides, in both Léger's work and that of anonymous medieval masters, everything that tends to remove visual forms from the perpetual instability of the shifting world in which we live fixes them in a timeless plane that obviously must not be confused with that of eternal realities, but which at least shares with it the common character of being protected from the undefined changes of duration.

[…] In addition, I know that in affirming this parallel I am not at odds with his own personal feelings. So to be quite clear, I would say that from a strictly Christian point of view, such works, no matter how beautiful or noble they are, are currently purely "profane," but they now have, as a result of their abstraction, everything required to become "religious." Moreover, they have the architectural, monumental qualities that church walls demand: it is significant that the most recent of them could immediately serve as admirable cartoons for stained-glass windows, perfectly in accordance with the highest tradition of this difficult art. Furthermore, the recent introduction of human forms brings them even closer to this Christian art, which is always an "art of Incarnation." "I have just discovered the human," he says to us. No doubt abstraction, whose importance to sacred art we have nonetheless emphasized, might impair that emotional tension without which no great art could be truly mystical.

But it might be thought that a living flame could spring from personal contact with dogmas and the great subjects of Christianity. We will have to rebuild a lot of churches in France. Especially in Normandy, where Léger was born: let us hope that one day we will be able to see there the admirable frescoes and stained-glass windows that are to be expected from a great artist of such gifts.

Excerpts from M.-A. Couturier, "Léger et le moyen-âge," in *Fernand Leger, la forme humaine dans l'espace* (Montreal: Éditions de l'Arbre, 1945), 15–23.

–

Free Objects amidst Rhythm and Tension: Light in Fernand Léger's Colorful Sacred Space in Audincourt
By Friedhelm Mennekes

A noteworthy modern church is to be found in the suburb of Audincourt in eastern France. The local priest, Abbé Louis Prenel, an affable man and a great appreciator of art, was conscious of the necessity of building a new church in his town. With little money, an openness to a clever project advisor, and a great talent for organization, he succeeded in realizing the Sacré-Cour in Audincourt in just two years, now one of France's cultural treasures (fig. 279).

The well-known unfrocked Dominican Marie-Alain Couturier (1897–1954), who was a notable artist in his own right prior to joining the Church, gave his advice, while Maurice Novarina (1905–2002) lent his support as an architect. During the war, Couturier and Novarina had already built a church, the Notre-Dame-de-Toute-Grâce in Assy beneath the Mont Blanc massif, which had quickly garnered considerable attention due to the involvement of many artists in its design, including Pierre Bonnard, Marc Chagall, Léger, Jacques Lipchitz, Jean Lurçat, Henri Matisse, Germaine Richier, and Georges Rouault (fig. 262). Novarina's new design was once again intended to be simple and offer scope for powerful artistic features in a compact architectural space.

The result was a rectangular building with a semicircular choir area and a crypt underneath, built out of hewn slabs of quarry rock and concrete. A tall, slender bell tower is found to the right of the façade, and a cylindrical baptistery made entirely out of glass is found to the left. The flat roof of the church protrudes slightly over the entrance to form a kind of vestibule, supported by two pillars. Three artists were called in to carry out the decoration of the church: Jean René Bazaine (1904–2001) for the baptistery and mosaic above the entrance, Jean Le Moal (1909–2007) for the crypt, and Léger for the windows in the interior (fig. 279).

Upon entering the church, the visitor needs some time to adjust to the dim lighting; one is surrounded on all sides by faintly lit, dark-brown wood forming the gently arched paneled ceiling, the wood-paneled walls, and built-in pews. The semicircular choir area is the only surface that is left white. A band of light, 1.75 meters in height and seventy meters in length, traverses the entire room with the exception of the wall by the entrance. The line of windows appears to be part of the wall. It runs from the back left to the rounded center of the front part of the church, then continues right and back into the dark brown of the organ and the matroneum. This band of light is the only light source in the church.

The altar does not face east, as is usual, but instead northward. As a result, light from the south is blocked by the closed entrance front. Seen from within, the east is to the right, the west to the left, so that there is no unobstructed beam of light shining into the room. The light is restricted, an effect underlined by the technical construction of the window. Instead of using light in the Gothic style (as if filtered through a glass membrane to create a mystical, illuminated, diaphanous glow), the light here is reduced to a cool austerity. This was a result of the then-new and common method of constructing concrete glass windows, which was promoted with a missionary zeal.

This glass construction technique was a new and popular post-war development that harked back to the earlier, innovative origins of stained glass, when the glass was not painted beforehand but inserted directly like a brick. In order to maintain the required tension between different construction materials such as glass and stone (and later glass and concrete), the colored glass had to be at least three centimeters thick, whether red, blue, yellow, or green, pink, gray, or white. To this end, the colored plates of glass were produced in large sizes.

The tracery of such windows is initially poured in concrete and prefabricated. The artist then makes a design for the open fields drawn in a ratio of 1:1 and arranges the various pieces of glass (which are broken off from larger colored panes) according to his template. New lines and networks are created between the pieces of glass, and the resulting joins are later filled with liquid concrete. In this way even the details of the sketch are realized and the concrete glass window is given form and completed.

The construction process is fairly crude, as is the effect of the result. Light finds its way into the church through tube-like openings and therefore appears "naked," unadorned by any kind of line or illustration or modulation of color. Nor does it project anything but simply shows itself: light as light, lacking a narrative or symbolism, formed simply by a hole in the stone and the color of the glass. Thus viewed, it appears to be a part of the wall that glows, that moves through the atmosphere of the sacred space and into the inner chambers of whomever observes it. Through a total of seventeen individual windows, the bright energy of the sun flows into the room, restrained yet wide. It creates a gentle mood and delicately rests on the "sleeping" brown of the wood. Over time, subtle highlights reveal themselves: mirroring effects and reflections appear languorously, while small flecks of color seem to play across the benches and floor. When the eye sweeps over the band of light, details of the background colors and the objects in the foreground appear depending on the viewer's stance and angle of sight. All the colors are clear, but between them run the straight black lines of the tracery and meandering streams of poured concrete. They join to form a network and a supporting structure; everything melds together at dusk.

The formal and thematic features of the individual windows are surprising. The central image is displayed behind the altar as the center of the altar space. A set of eight windows runs along each side from this point towards the entrance at the back. Each window has its own structure, divided into five zones of equal size. The middle three most often form a thematic center that is repeated abstractly or ornamentally in the side sections. As is often the case in Léger's work, he frequently varies or even dispenses entirely with this underlying formal pattern. This is most apparent in the middle image, which occupies a particular thematic and formal role: it is here that the artist evokes the name of the church, dedicated to the Sacred Heart of Jesus (fig. 273).

Following their first meetings in America, a close friendship formed between the well-known Léger and the much younger priest and artist, Couturier. Couturier valued Léger's great creativity, while Léger, who was consistently active both socially and politically, was impressed by the formal openness of the Dominican. Here was a man of the Church who respected the freedom of art, and indeed, considered it an end unto itself; there was a left-leaning artist moved by the social reality of a Christian community in a working-class suburb.

In designing the church's band of light, Léger wanted to remain true to his orientation towards objects and moreover to avoid any narrative or interpretative references to the religious space itself. Léger and Couturier quickly came up with a concept for the content, namely the motif of the Arma Christi, or the instruments of the Passion. These are the concrete objects of the Passion story: whips and ropes, hammers and nails, tongs and stakes, lances or daggers, purple robes and shrouds (figs. 269–278). They all play a role in the final hours of Jesus Christ as they are employed to torture and eventually kill him. To the informed observer, these objects subtly signal a higher literary or symbolically charged meaning of imprisonment, interrogation, ridicule, scourging, crucifixion, consolation, sympathy, fear, and death. The motif of the Arma Christi emerged at the time of an iconoclastic shift in storytelling using images in churches, whereby the observer could place a pictorially depicted object in a verbal context.

Léger makes an unusual interpretation of the history of piety in the central image above the altar (fig. 273). It serves to venerate the Sacred Heart, a practice developed in convents during the Middle Ages by which solemn contemplation allows an individual to commune with something of the suffering in Jesus Christ's inner world. Thus one may feel the power of God's presence in a world in which love has grown cold; one may be consoled, strengthened, and given a new Spirit active in transforming all darkness. For people in the Middle Ages, this secret of the bleeding heart was the symbolic core to understanding the Passion, Death, and Resurrection of Christ, and the process of transformation into the Risen Jesus.

In the tradition of medieval worship of the Instruments of Christ, each individual wound was given special consideration: the hands, feet, and sides. In the wound created by the lance, the pierced heart becomes a source of holiness, from which one can be reborn. In the Baroque period, the "five sacred wounds" appeared to the mystic Margareta Maria Alacoque (1647–1690) in a vision as five blazing suns. Léger took inspiration from this vision for his design. Inlaid in the surrounding red background is a further, somewhat smaller section. Blue in color, it bears resemblance to a magic carpet. It displays the image of five suns, appearing as if in cosmic space, alongside two red footprints to the right and the left, and all overlaid with a dominating red sun. The smaller suns each contain a red fragment of glass at their center. Only the sun in the middle of the image has a heart rather than a wound in its center. White lines traversing the image lend it a dynamism.

The window directly to the right is all the more concrete and austere. Alongside centrally positioned rings of color in white, blue, red, yellow, green, and black, it depicts three tools: a white hammer, six blue nails, and three gray tongs. This motif extends across the three inner image planes; the outer panels echo the motif in abstract planes of red, blue, black, and white set against straight and winding red lines at right angles. Within each one is the trace of a hole, as a nail would leave. Léger once elaborated on the painterly quality of everyday objects in his work:

"The beauty of the object to be painted no longer counts, but the way in which the painter brings it into being, even if it is nothing more than a nail. Even a nail must take on the dignity of something that 'exists.' In painting, a nail can be worthy of just as much interest as a face."[1]

The sixth window on the left as viewed from the entrance displays a motif of particular interest. Its design consists of abstract, purely primary colors on a white background. At the center there are three red and yellow letters–*pax*, the Latin word for peace –underlined in yellow against a blue background. The line beneath the word undulates slightly, perhaps suggestive of a kind of banner. It is affixed to the left and right by perpendicular crosses, which may even be a reference to placards like those found at demonstrations. The word does not occur in the story of the Passion, but in John's gospel it is repeated after Easter Sunday as the first greeting uttered by the Jesus when he appears to the apostles: "'Peace be with you!' And when He had said this He showed them His hands and His side." (John, 20:19:26)

In this context, there is a photo from the studio which shows Léger looking solemn and critically surveying his initial designs as they lay on the floor *en bloc*. In the foreground there is a sketch that was never produced, depicting the face of Christ with his right hand raised in the sign of peace. The windows he ultimately created make clear that the artist had to struggle during the process to remain true to himself and his work. This was the only way this group of works could be understood as art.

Fernand Léger presents a stirring array of images and values from our time within numerous everyday objects, which achieve the effect of an awakening precisely by virtue of their removal from any kind of iconography.

Georg Baselitz once said that one cannot see a picture one already knows, thus steering our gaze towards the vital quality in art, towards art as art. Here, the truth of this insight may be grasped with our eyes and our hands.

1 "Fernand Léger, Maschinenästhetik und geometrische Ordnung," in *Fernand Léger 1881–1955*, ed. Dieter Ruckhaberle, exhibition catalog, Staatliche Kunsthalle Berlin (Berlin, 1980), 274–88.

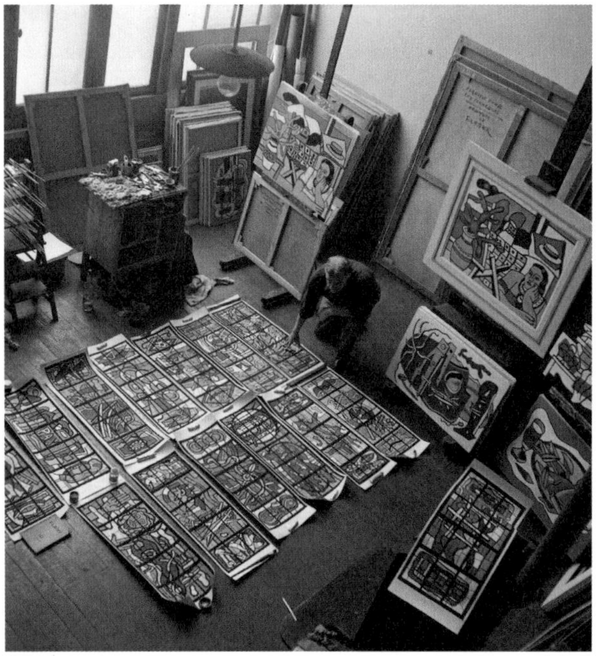

268

268 **Fernand Léger with drafts for the church windows at Audincourt, 1951**
Archives Lucien Hervé

Designs for the stained glass windows of the Sacré-Coeur church in Audincourt.

269 ***La tunique du Christ* (The Tunic of Christ, not realized), 1950**
36 × 84.5 cm

270 ***La lance* (The Lance), 1950**
37 × 91 cm

271 ***Les calices et l'éponge* (The Chalices and the Sponge), 1950**
37 × 92 cm

272 ***La croix* (The Cross), 1950**
34 × 97 cm

273 ***Les cinq plaies du Christ* (The Five Wounds of Christ), 1950**
37 × 94 cm

274 ***Le calvaire* (Calvary), 1950**
33 × 92 cm

275 ***Remets en place ton glaive* (Put Your Sword Back In Its Place), 1950**
33.4 × 89 cm

276 ***Les fouets* (The Whips), 1950**
37 × 94 cm

277 ***Les deux arbres de vie* (The Two Trees of Life), 1950**
34 × 92 cm

278 ***La tunique du Christ* (The Tunic of Christ), 1950**
34 × 98 cm

All: Gouache on paper
Centre Pompidou, Musée national d'art moderne, Paris

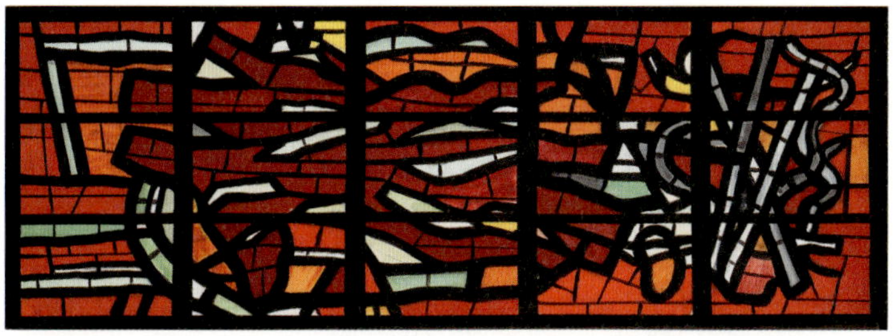
269

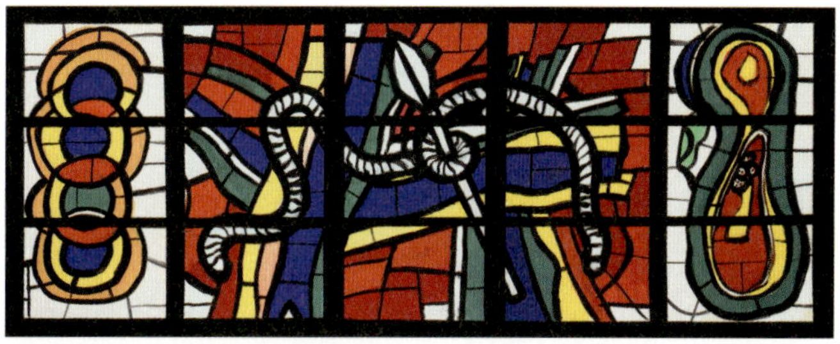
270

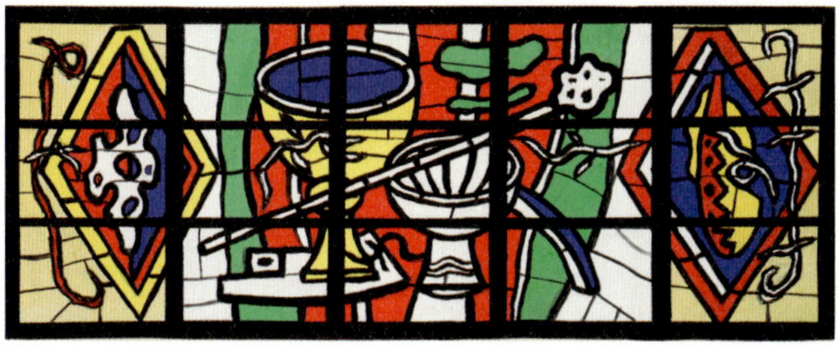
271

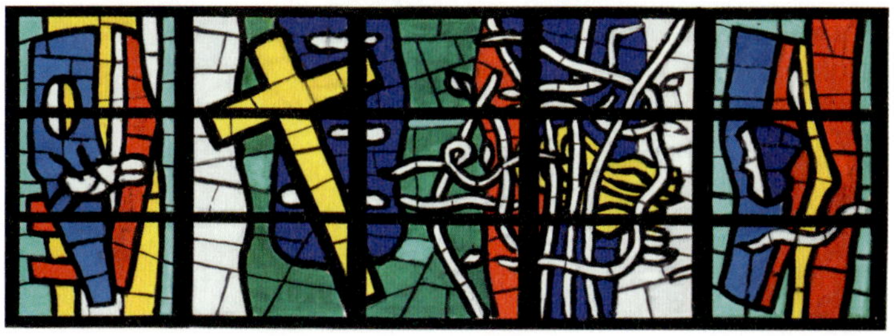
272

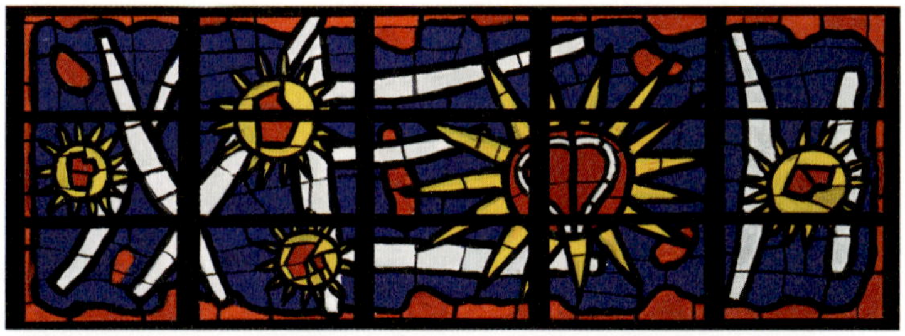
273

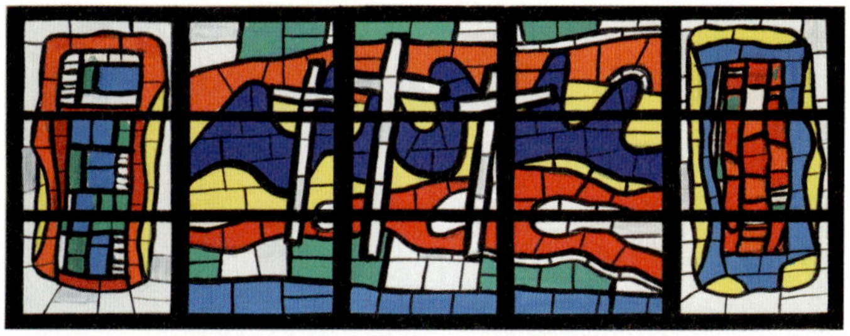
274

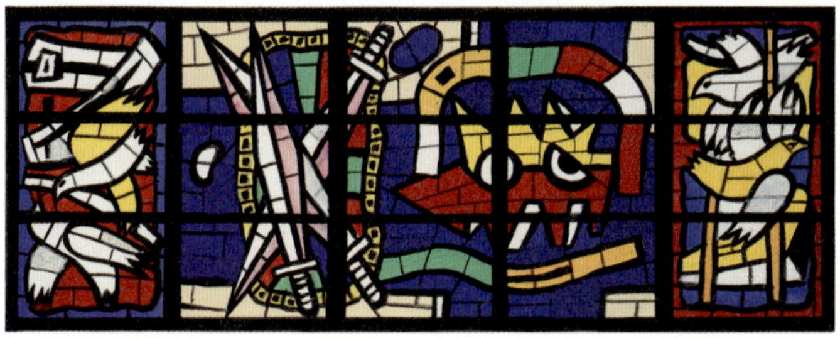
275

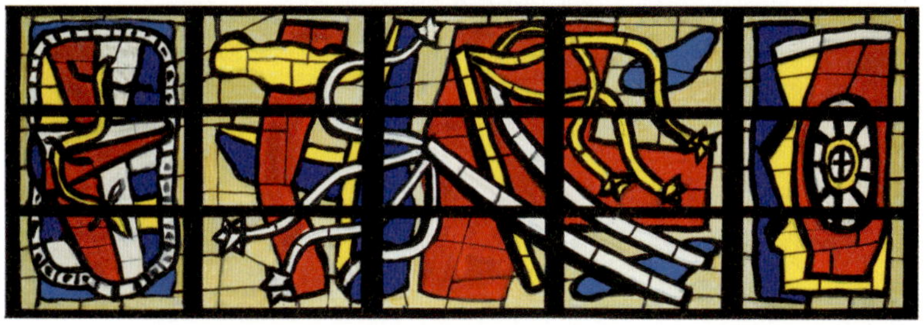
276

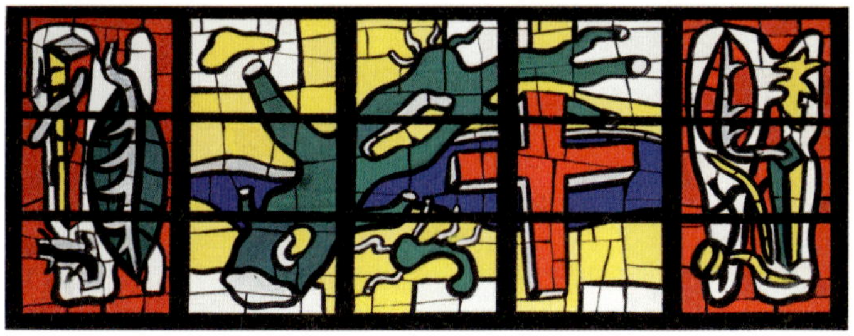
277

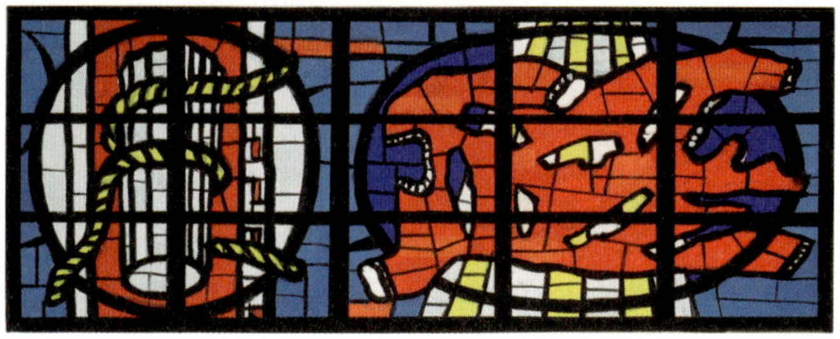
278

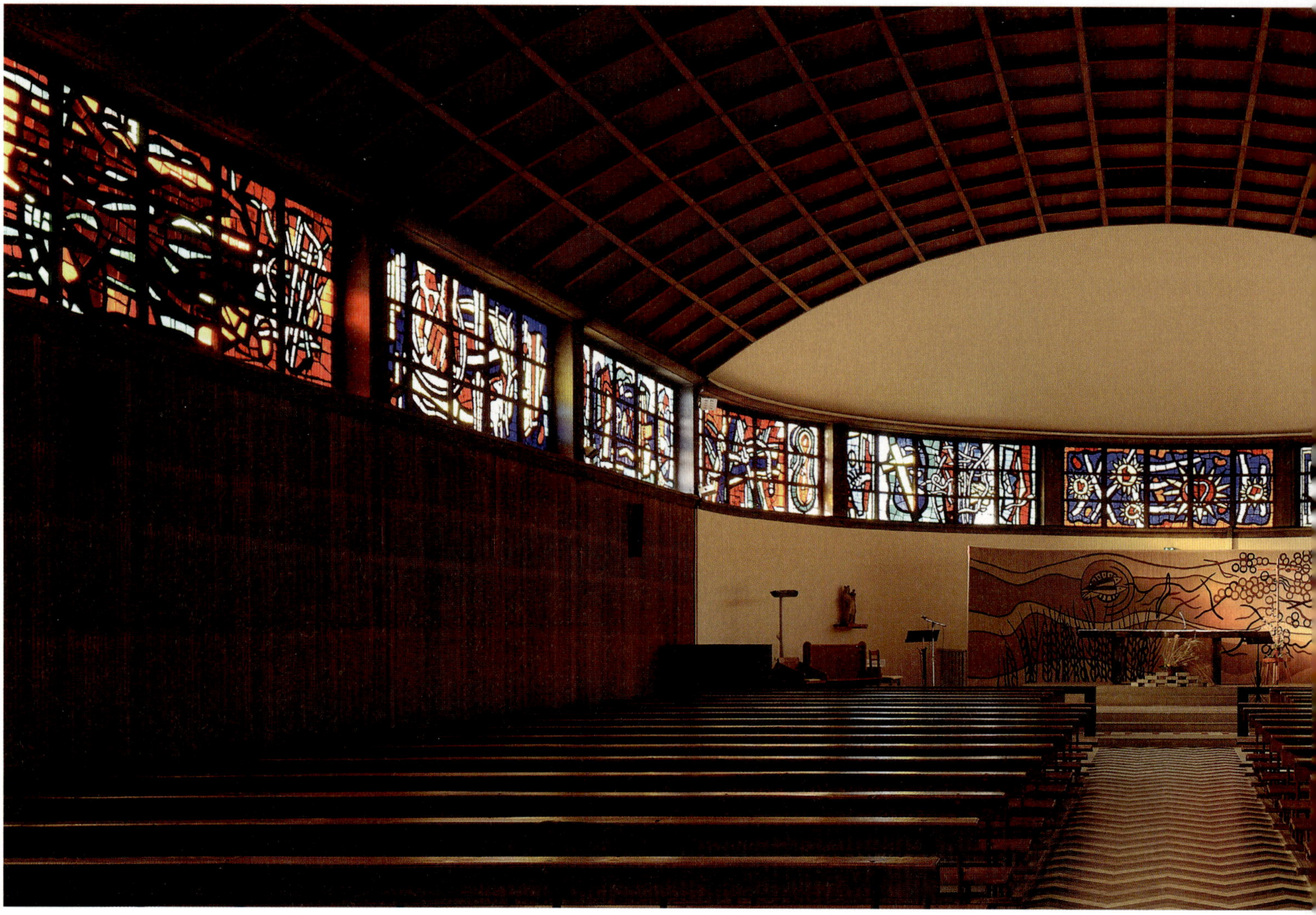

279

279 **Interior of the church of Sacré Coeur, Audincourt, windows and tapestry behind altar by Fernand Léger, 1951**
Architect: Maurice Novarina

280 **Study for the tapestry for the church in Audincourt, c. 1953**
Gouache on paper
25.3 × 64.4 cm
The Menil Collection, Houston

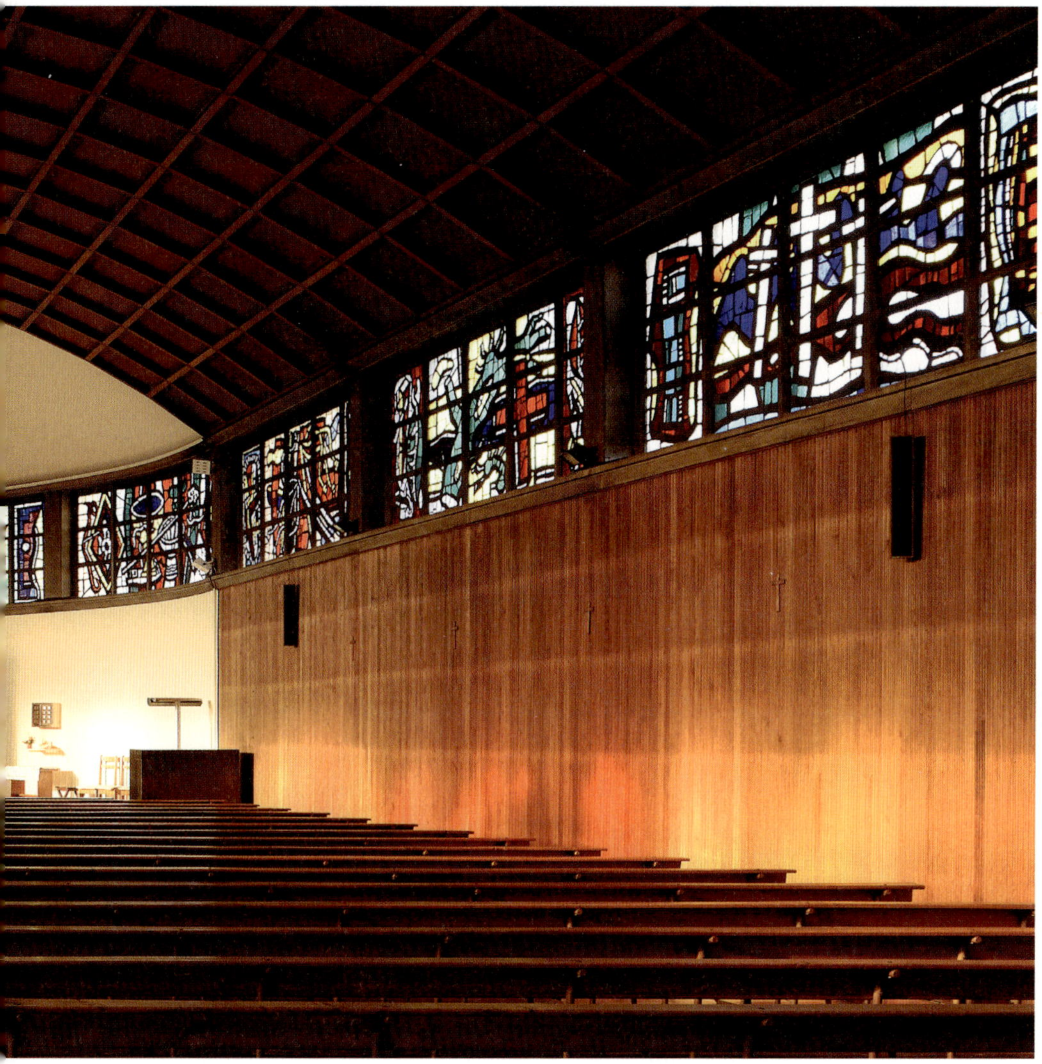

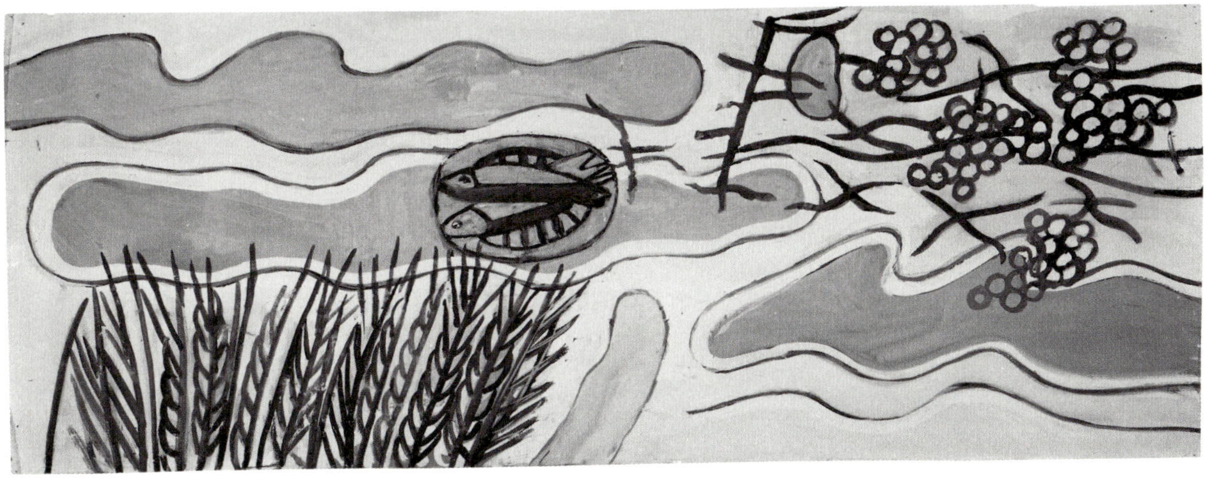

280

Letter from Fernand Léger to Father Marie-Alain Couturier, November 6, 1951

Nov. 6, 51

Dear Friend

Back from Audincourt. I'm impressed by the terrific result. This glass paste is wonderful—I'm very happy—We need to get hold of the two models that are circulating in the USA, in addition, the (very nice) priest wants something on the wall behind the altar—two tapestries of mine have just been very well made. I thought of choosing a different material and decorating the wall with a tapestry motif. What do you think? Perhaps in a free shape to contrast with the surrounding geometry, or oval or round. He would like to have a Virgin or the face of the Virgin. He mentioned a "Virgin worker" to me because the blue-collar workers are his parishioners. What does he mean by that? Help me with that. You are always a winner in this domain. I know a thing or two about that.

The Bazaine mural is lively. I think it should have been kept in check by the architecture—that is to say, framed, it goes "outside"—and extends beyond the wall. That's my view. I was there with Jeanne Laurent and B.A. Jardot: historic monuments and Kahnweiler's Galerie Leiris. Everyone was enthusiastic. A photographer specializing in color is being asked for reproductions from all quarters.
How are you? Well I hope. Let me have your news.
Best wishes to you and to the parish priest of Assy.

F. Léger

The architecture is better than I thought it's clear and simple and anonymous.

Archives Père Couturier, Bibliothèque du Saulchoir – Province dominicaine de France.

–

Letter from Fernand Léger to Father Marie-Alain Couturier, February 26, 1952

Tuesday - 26.II.52

Hello Dear Friend,

Barillet tells me that you do not like the red coat model. What don't you like about it? First of all, this model was difficult to make. I made four changes before the large one and I told my two students to bring the model back to me before the enlargement. They did not do so—or perhaps they came when I was not there. I had my students make 3 large panels in the "Art Ménager" [domestic art trade fair] Restaurant. They did a good job—a model made by them under my supervision as agreed with the Art Ménager director. All the same, it required fairly close supervision by me to make it.

I have decided to call upon my former students regarding everything dealing with decorative murals—architectural adaptations. I have a workshop for that. It is a return to the large projects of the pre-Renaissance and Renaissance artists. Right now we have to initiate a collective enterprise. A man's life is not enough to accomplish these sorts of things. For our works, tell me what is wrong.

As for the tapestry. For my part, I don't think it goes very well in this curved space between the altar and the wall.

This is also the opinion of my [colleague's ?] tapestry. We need a little model before getting started with this project.

Have you seen the stained-glass window with thorns? I think you have. (This whole Art Ménager business has really been troubling me this whole time)

How are you? I thought I could see you in Paris at the end of the month.

I had two students make a trip to Audincourt to make a note of the dominant colors to situate the last two stained-glass windows. I enclose their architectural survey with the last two in progress left empty. Take a look at that.

Regards and good health and see you soon

F.L.

Archives Père Couturier, Bibliothèque du Saulchoir – Province dominicaine de France.

–

Letter from Marie-Alain Couturier to Fernand Léger, undated

Dear Friend

Our letters crossed. Our thoughts too. The church choir and even the altar definitely need to be given more solemnity. The parish priest mentioned mural painting to me. I don't agree with that at all. Here's why: in this rainy region, in this church that will only be heated on Sundays, on walls that are not prepared for it, no painting will resist—and furthermore, what "painting" will survive alongside the radiant stained-glass windows: everything will look inferior. That's why, like you, I thought of a tapestry, quite a big tapestry with large black drawings on a white background that will completely enclose the altar. The wool material would be a magnificent and natural match for the glass. Before I left Paris, I had seen at Mme Cuttoli's an admirable tapestry of yours broadly in that vein and immediately I thought that this is what was needed at Audincourt: a tapestry and nothing else. I see that we are in agreement.

But a word of warning! You were surely struck, as we all were, by the sacred grandeur of this ensemble. I think that the sacred, solemn character comes from abstraction, it is your shapes, your style with no concession to sentimentality that gives us that. I must emphasize this, because I think that is where your real greatness lies; indeed, you know this better than I do: the "human" value of a work of art is not based on its representation of the human, but on the very quality of its forms, in themselves. So no concessions on that! By the way, I have a brilliant subject in mind in the spirit of the stained-glass windows; I will tell you about it.

For the stained-glass windows, the Ministry of Foreign Affairs has been warned and is doing what is required. I received a letter yesterday. Let me know if we are in agreement.
Best wishes

Fr. Couturier

Published in Georges Bauquier, *Fernand Léger, Vivre dans le vrai* (Paris: Maeght, 1987), 329.

–

Fernand Léger on the Church of Sacré-Cœur in Audincourt

I wish to clarify that there is not one iota of difference between the person who created the murals for the UN, and the stained-glass windows for the church in Audincourt. In both cases, I was a free agent. I did not split myself in two. The glorification of holy items, nails, chalices, and crowns of thorns, and the portrayal of the Passion of Christ: none of this was an act of escapism for me. I am well, my spirit does not need crutches. I was simply presented with the unexpected opportunity to decorate these large surfaces according to the strict principles of my vision of form.

I was not placed under any pressure; I was free to take it or leave it. My goal was simple: to create a vibrant rhythm of shape and color that everyone, believers and non-believers alike, could use and appreciate purely for the way it kindled light and joy in their hearts.

Bringing my ideas to life was difficult at first. For example, the pastor in Assy wanted nothing to do with it. Couturier, the Dominican priest, always fully supported me…

Excerpt, originally published in ed. Christoph W. David, *Moderne Kirchen. Henri Matisse Vence, Fernand Léger Audincourt, Le Corbusier Ronchamp* (Zurich: Peter Schifferli, 1957), 46.

–

1954, A Heterotopia in Biot: Fernand Léger and Groupe Espace

By Diana Gay

In summer 1954, Groupe Espace organized its first outdoor exhibition, *Architecture Formes Couleur* (Architecture Forms Color), in Biot, France. Comprising architects and visual artists, this group championed the synthesis of the arts.[1] Their joy at having survived World War II expressed itself in a collective action that heralded a critical rereading of modernist theories. It was the beginning of a redefinition of artistic practices: an expansion of the field of materials, the territory itself as project, the ephemeral as a mode of experiencing art. Since 1951,[2] Fernand Léger had served as vice-chairman of the group, which was founded by André Bloc[3] and Félix Del Marle.[4] By analyzing their relationships, it becomes possible to identify the issues at stake in the reconstruction effort in France. Did progressive art have a place in a society in crisis?

Reinventing Modern Space

Biot was a rural village famous for its pottery. The experience of the Resistance had united its inhabitants around an ideal of social progress. Political debates were lively in this heavily Communist area. Sixty-four visual artists and architects, including members of Groupe Espace and invited guests, exhibited in a 3,000-square-meter communal field made up of terraces planted with olive trees (fig. 283).[5] This exhibition preceded the advent of an actual synthesis of the arts, which was the real objective of Groupe Espace.[6] The immediate priority was to gain visibility by taking part in exhibitions, to take concrete action that would raise awareness of the art of the day among the public and the government. The exhibition in Biot represented a continuation of the Anglo-Saxon and Austrian experiments with total art in parks and garden cities initiated by the Arts and Crafts movement and the Wiener Werkstätte. It involved an alternative space of thinking through action,[7] organized around the interaction between materials and environment, which made it possible to explore the relativity of perceptions. Like Matisse and Paul Nelson, Léger was convinced of the therapeutic effect of color. Certain designs not specifically conceived for the exhibition were less effective than others better adapted to the local context, such as Jean Leppien's painted reed screens. The artists experimented freely with planes, volumes, and color in an effort to devise new exhibition vehicles with the help of the set designer André Bruyère (fig. 282). Beyond the bucolic aspect of this exhibition, the problem of art's reception was a central concern.[8]

The works were realized with sustainable materials, traditional and innovative. Exhibited beneath metal sheds that resembled the emergency dwellings of the time were photographs by Denis Brihat and Étienne Bertrand Weill (fig. 281) as well as architectural projects by Pierre Vago, Georges Dedoyard, Claude Parent, and Jean Sebag. The exhibitors worked alone or sought advice from others, as in the case of *Régulation Spatiale* (Spatial Regulation) by Antoine Fasani, who, with the help of Parent, devised a system of ropes by which polychrome panels were hung, creating a sheltered space among the olive trees. A stroll through the grounds made for poetic encounters with the simple forms of Jean Arp, Morice Lipsi, and Émile Gilioli. It was still too early for a full-fledged dialogue among the arts, but that would come soon. Other events were advertised for 1955, including the exhibition *Bau und Bild. Architektur-Malerei-Plastik* (Constructions and Images: Architecture, Painting, Sculpture) at the Kunstgewerbemuseum in Zurich (now the Museum für Gestaltung) or the first exhibition of equipment, construction, and public works at the Saint-Cloud national park.[9] Thanks to Bloc, the group's strategy for expansion led to the creation of outposts in Great Britain, Switzerland, Italy, and Sweden. The search for an exhibition setting that would allow for a genuinely disinterested appreciation of art was made explicit in an editorial in which Bloc denounced the commercialized art widespread on the Côte d'Azur, especially in Vallauris.[10] Bloc had owned property in Biot since 1935 and had built a house there where he made sculptures, most frequently during his exile in the war years. The choice of Biot as a proving ground thus seemed foreordained.

Fernand Léger Outside the Frame

Contrast—between speed and slowness, culture and nature—was the engine of Léger's creative production. All around him, he saw a society in the midst of rapid transformation. How could the painter influence his or her time? Deployed in the engineering corps in 1914, Léger discovered the Other in the trenches and wondered about the conditions for a positive reception of his Cubo-Futurist painting. Lacking artistic education, ordinary people did not understand abstraction. On returning from the front, Léger had them in mind when he produced his paintings with figurative compositions. His mural painting was inherently abstract, because where decoration was concerned he drew inspiration from the notion of "furniture art," devised by Erik Satie on the basis of elevator music.[11]

Before joining Groupe Espace, Léger participated in a number of movements that championed the synthesis of the arts, including Cercle et Carré (Circle and Square, 1929); Abstraction-Création (Abstraction-Creation, 1931); the Union des Artistes Modernes (Union of Modern Artists, 1929–1958); the Union pour l'Art (Union for Art), founded by Bloc in 1936; and an association for the synthesis of the major arts planned with Bloc, Matisse, and Le Corbusier in 1950 and ultimately aborted. He also took part in the IX Triennale in Milan in 1951 with Charlotte Perriand. With his distinction between easel and mural painting,[12] Léger was a close ally of modernist architects. At the Exposition internationale des Arts décoratifs et Industriels modernes in Paris (International Exposition of Modern Decorative and Industrial Arts, 1925),

281 ***Architecture Formes Couleur* (Architecture Forms Color), Groupe Espace, July 10 – September 10, 1954**
Shelter for photographs designed by André Bruyère

282 ***Architecture Formes Couleur* (Architecture Forms Color), Groupe Espace, July 10 – September 10, 1954**
First row (L-R): sculptures by André Bloc, Nicolas Schöffer, and Aargaard Andersen; second row (L-R): mission cross from 1824 and bench-sculpture by André Bloc; third row behind cross: sculpture by Maxime Descombin

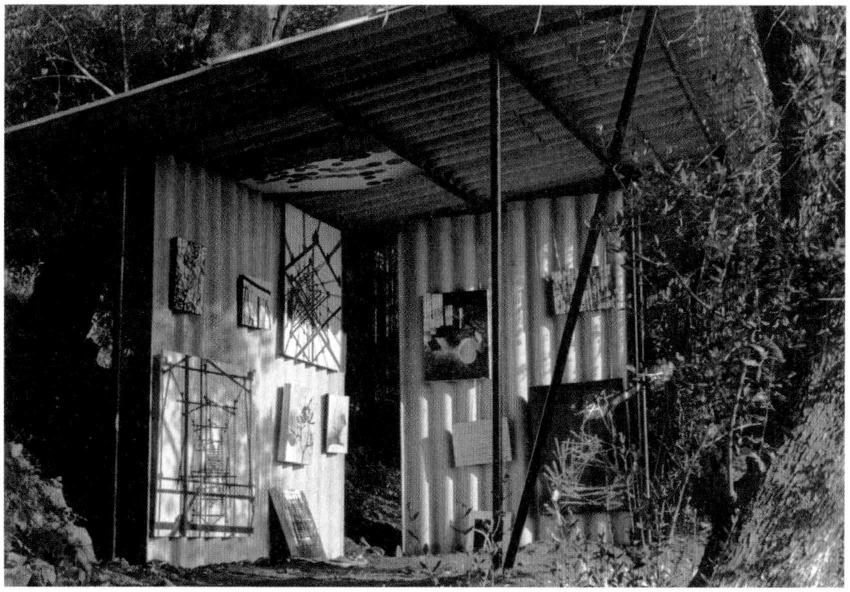

281

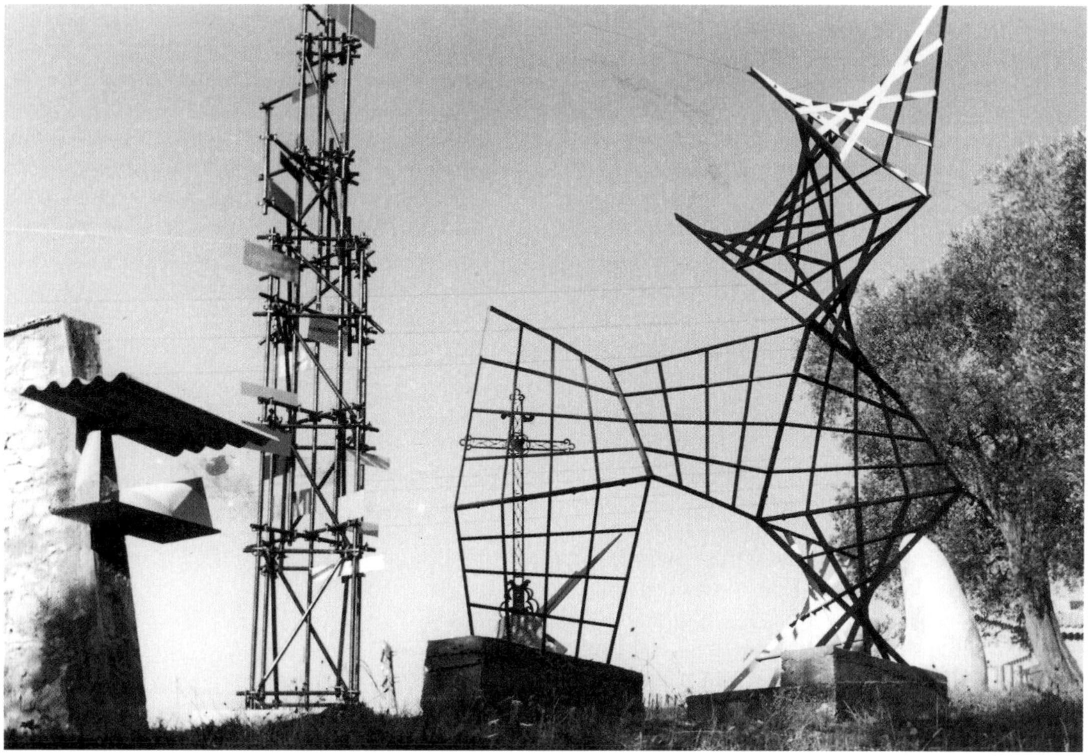

282

Le Corbusier displayed a painting by Léger in his Pavillon de l'Esprit Nouveau (Pavilion of the New Spirit) (fig. 87). Robert Mallet-Stevens used an abstract composition by Léger that was influenced by De Stijl (a series of *peintures élastiques* or "flexible paintings") to decorate his project of a lobby for a French embassy (fig. 52). In the 1950s, Léger worked with Paul Nelson, Wallace Harrison, André Bruyère, and Maurice Novarina (figs. 176, 187, 279, 285). He was a friend of Sigfried Giedion, who founded the Congrès Internationaux d'Architecture Moderne (International Congresses of Modern Architecture, known as the CIAM) in 1928. At the fourth CIAM congress in Athens in 1933, Léger gave a lecture in which he warned the architects against the temptation of working alone. During their years of exile in the United States, José-Luis Sert, Léger, and Giedion published "Neuf Points sur la Monumentalité" (Nine Points on Monumentality),[13] in which they asserted their determination to go beyond architectural functionality and zoning plans, which were enshrined as dogmas by the Athens Charter published the same year. They called for an approach to urban planning that would bring architects and visual artists together to serve the residents and to meet their physiological, psychosocial, and emotional needs. In "Intégration des Arts Plastiques dans la Vie" (Integrating the Visual Arts into Life), his preface for the *Architecture Formes Couleur* catalog, Bloc in turn described a need for urgent action: "We now call upon the authorities and all builders of good will to help facilitate a collaboration between artists and architects beginning at the stage of the preliminary project studies."[14]

Widely regarded as a champion of the machine, beginning in the 1930s Fernand Léger dreamed of returning to the age of the cathedrals, when artists and artisans collaborated on public structures under the direction of an architect.[15] In his illustrated book *Cirque* (Circus), published by Tériade in 1950, he decries the alienation caused by machines and champions a vision of sustainable development based on a harmonious relationship with nature. This position makes it easier to understand why he spent time producing ceramics in a village untouched by the touristic development of the Côte d'Azur. Léger regularly left the Paris region to work with Roland Brice, his ceramist in Biot. He was searching for materials capable of entering into a dialogue with architecture, in an effort to free art from its elitist confinement. In the catalog of the *Architecture Formes Couleur* exhibition, Fernand Léger lists a number of models now preserved at the Musée national Fernand Léger. However, only the two paintings on fiber cement can be seen in the archival photographs (fig. 284). Like other exhibitors in 1954,[16] Léger employed this material, which was commonly used in the construction industry but seldom employed in the artistic realm. Lacking funding, the exhibition was financed by the exhibitors themselves and by advertising inserts as well as by a personal donation from the Venezuelan architect Carlos Villanueva, also a member of Groupe Espace. The artists probably used materials provided by these advertisers, which included the company Elo, a fiber cement and coatings manufacturer based in Poissy.[17]

After Utopia: A Failed Reception or the Emergence of Postmodernity?

The press conference in Nice on July 9, 1954, received only scant attention in the media. In 1965, a public housing complex was constructed on the site of the 1954 exhibition. Groupe Espace entered a period of serious crisis in 1956 with the resignation of the Neo-Plasticists Jean Gorin, Servanes, and Georges Folmer. Bloch turned over the chairmanship to the painter Georges Breuil in the same year. His accidental death in 1966 sounded the death knell of the association. By then, however, the dialogue between social and cultural history was well underway and moving toward a post-modern rereading of art that would incorporate increasingly wide-ranging practices and territories.

There are indications in Léger's work that he was influenced by Groupe Espace. Two weeks before his death, the painter purchased a plot of land on the hill located opposite the exhibition location in Biot. He too now wished to populate it with works that stood in dialogue with Mediterranean nature. The previous year, he had produced a model of a habitable sculpture for children. Realized by his family when the Musée Léger was built, the *Jardin d'Enfants* (Children's Garden) is a wading pool seven meters high and made of brightly colored ceramics. Was it inspired by the "archi-sculptures" of André Bloc and Alain Le Breton, exhibited in 1954? Bloc favored monumental sculpture, but Léger gave priority to color. His colorful contrasts, however, were not well received. A number of monumental projects were realized after his death by his widow Nadia and by Georges Bauquier, his friend and assistant, including his decoration for a stadium in Hanover (carried out at the Musée Léger in Biot) as well as his bas-relief for the Gaz de France administrative building in Alfortville. Paradoxically, he had his greatest successes with religious rather than civil commissions. The first stone was laid for his museum three years after the exhibition of 1954. In a setting far removed from large urban areas, the Musée Léger continues to pursue the utopia first initiated by the exhibition *Architecture Formes Couleur*.

1 "Manifeste du Groupe Espace," *L'Architecture d'aujourd'hui*, no. 37 (October 1951). It was published at the same time in *Art d'aujourd'hui*, no. 8 (October 1951), and posted in the streets of Paris.
2 Honorary chair: Eugène Claudius-Petit, Minister of Labor and former Minister of Reconstruction and Urban Planning; acting chair: André Bloc; vice-chairs: Paul Herbé, Bernard Zehrfuss, Fernand Léger; secretary general: Sonia Delaunay; treasurer: Bernard Lafaille; members in charge of propaganda: Luc Arsène-Henry and Edgar Pillet; secretary: Renée Diamant-Berger. See the exhibition catalog *Architecture Formes Couleur* (Paris: Groupe Espace, 1954), 7.
3 André Bloc (b. 1896 Alger, d. 1966 New Delhi). Engineer, sculptor, painter, editor of the journals *L'Architecture d'aujourd'hui* (from 1930), *Art d'aujourd'hui* (1949–54), and *Aujourd'hui, art et architecture* (1955–67).
4 Félix Del Marle (b. 1889 Pont-sur-Sambre, d. 1952 Bécon-les-Bruyères). Abstract painter and theorist of abstraction. Helped to create the Salon des Réalités Nouvelles (Salon of New Realities). Founded Groupe Espace in 1951 together with André Bloc.
5 See the list published in the 1954 catalog. Certain works can be seen in the photographic archives but are not on the list of works exhibited; these include the Dane Sven Hauptmann's brightly colored mobile as well as Nicolas Schöffer's twenty-four-meter high "spatiodynamic tower." Groupe Espace mentions eighty exhibitors in its journals.
6 Pierre Guéguen, "Une démonstration du groupe Espace: l'exposition Architecture Formes Couleur à Biot (Côte d'Azur)," *Art d'aujourd'hui* 5, no. 6 (September 1954): 18–21.
7 According to Eric Mangion, "one must not overlook the specificity of a region blessed with a climate and landscape that surely impelled the artists to occupy numerous territories, whatever the season"; *A la vie délibérée: Une histoire de la performance sur la Côte d'Azur de 1951 à 2011* (Nice: Villa Arson-La Strada, 2012), 8.
8 See the book *Art as Experience* (1934) by the American Pragmatist John Dewey. It influenced the experimental pedagogy at Black Mountain College, where artists exiled during World War II (including Fernand Léger) gave lectures.
9 In Saint-Cloud, a number of works were once again exhibited outdoors, including the paintings on fiber cement by Fernand Léger and Alberto Magnelli, which can be seen in the report published by *Aujourd'hui art et architecture,* no. 4 (September 1955): 19.
10 André Bloc, "Peut-on le dire?," *Art d'aujourd'hui* 2, no. 8 (October 1951): 1.
11 Fernand Léger, "Color in the World" (1937), in *Functions of Painting,* ed. Edward F. Fry, trans. Alexandra Anderson (New York: Viking, 1973), 119–31, esp. 123–24.
12 Fernand Léger, "Mural Painting and Easel Painting," in *Functions of Painting*, 160–64.
13 J.L. Sert, F. Léger, S. Giedion, "Nine Points on Monumentality" (1943), in S. Giedion, *Architecture, You and Me: The Diary of a Development*, ed. and trans. Jaqueline Tyrwhitt (Cambridge, MA: Harvard University Press, 1958), 48–51.
14 André Bloc, "Intégration des arts plastiques dans la vie," in exhibition catalog *Architecture Formes Couleur*, 4–5.
15 Fernand Léger, "Color in Architecture" (1954), in *Functions of Painting*, 183–88.
16 Painters utilizing fiber cement in 1954 included Étienne Béothy, Natalia Dumitresco, Alexandre Istrati, Joseph Jarema, Edgar Pillet, Paul Etienne-Sarissson, Marie Sperling, Nicolaas Warb, and Jean Weinbaum; see exhibition catalog *Architecture Formes Couleur*, 18–19.
17 All of the paintings on fiber cement exhibited in summer 1954 had the same dimensions, which suggests that they all came from the same source. A study of the use of fiber cement in twentieth-century art is currently being conducted by Alain Colombini at the Centre Interdisciplinaire de Restauration et de Conservation du Patrimoine in Marseille.

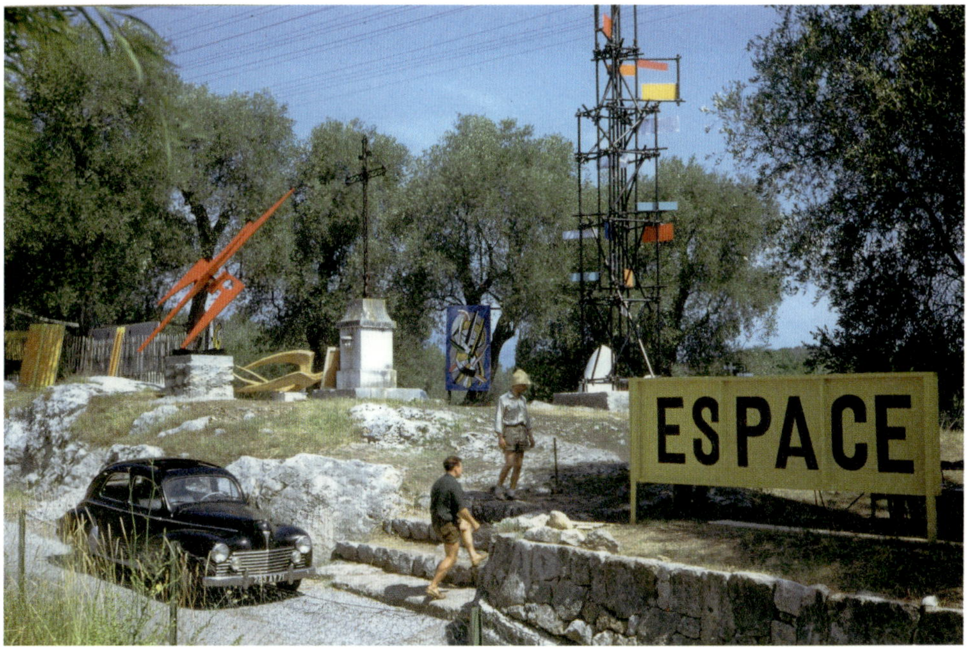

283

283 **Entrance to *Architecture Formes Couleur* exhibition, Groupe Espace, Biot, July 10 - September 10, 1954**

Manifesto Groupe Espace (1951)

MANIFESTO

To cleanse themselves utterly of certain harmful residues that still permeate a large number of artists, as well as the general public, the undersigned Architects, Constructors, and Visual Artists establish:

THE GROUPE ESPACE

they recommend

a nonfigurative Art derived from modern technologies and methods for unprecedented aims

an Art inscribed in real space that meets man's functional necessities and all his other needs, from the most basic to the most elevated

an Art concerned with living conditions, private and collective, an Art that would become indispensable, even to those least concerned with aesthetic values

a constructive Art, which, through efficient realizations, will participate actively and directly with the human community

an Art that becomes spatial by the perceptible and modulated penetration of light into every work, an Art the conception and execution of which are based on the simultaneity of every aspect in all three dimensions that are not merely suggested, but made tangible

an Art, finally, in which color and form are indissolubly bound by intrinsic and architectural qualities into ideal expressions of ratio and proportion

they observe

that immense tasks of construction have too often been entrusted to people totally unqualified to conceive of a group of dwellings, a city, and even of a country for the future

that town-planning and city construction demand of those responsible for them not only technical aptitude, but also a knowledge of psychology and social life, as well as a certain artistic culture

that this knowledge and this culture are generally lacking, and that all too often one sees our cities rebuilt after imperfect plans and with questionable modeling

that the majority of Architects have not been prepared to meet these new challenges

that those charged with the responsibility of creating the environment in which future generations will live must make sure they are assisted by technicians and visual artists familiar with spatial problems, and, furthermore, they must be backed and aided by laws and regulations

they propose

the forging of closer links between all those who might be called upon to contribute to the great tasks of our age, and in particular as regards:

Studies in Urbanism and Layout plans, Studies in Architectural Modeling, including all its ramifications in everyday life; the impact of color in Architecture

And hence, so as to familiarize the public with the necessary plastic innovations, it would be desirable for the Artists of the Groupe Espace to be called upon to lend their aid, in particular on the occasion of Festivals and Exhibitions, and at the time of major public events. Artistic demonstrations on a large scale are more feasible during such events and they would pave the way for more permanent realizations

The following Committees will be set up immediately for the study of specific problems, each including Architects, Painters, Sculptors, and Visual Artists

URBANISM, LAYOUT PLANS, COLOR, EXHIBITIONS, FESTIVALS, PLASTIC FORM APPLIED TO OBJECTS

they demand

THE HARMONIOUS DEVELOPMENT OF EVERY HUMAN ACTIVITY

T H E F U N D A M E N T A L P R E S E N C E
O F P L A S T I C F O R M S

Originally published simultaneously in *L'Architecture d'Aujourd'hui*, no. 37 (Oct. 1951) and *Art d'Aujourd'hui*, Series 2, no. 8 (Oct. 1951).

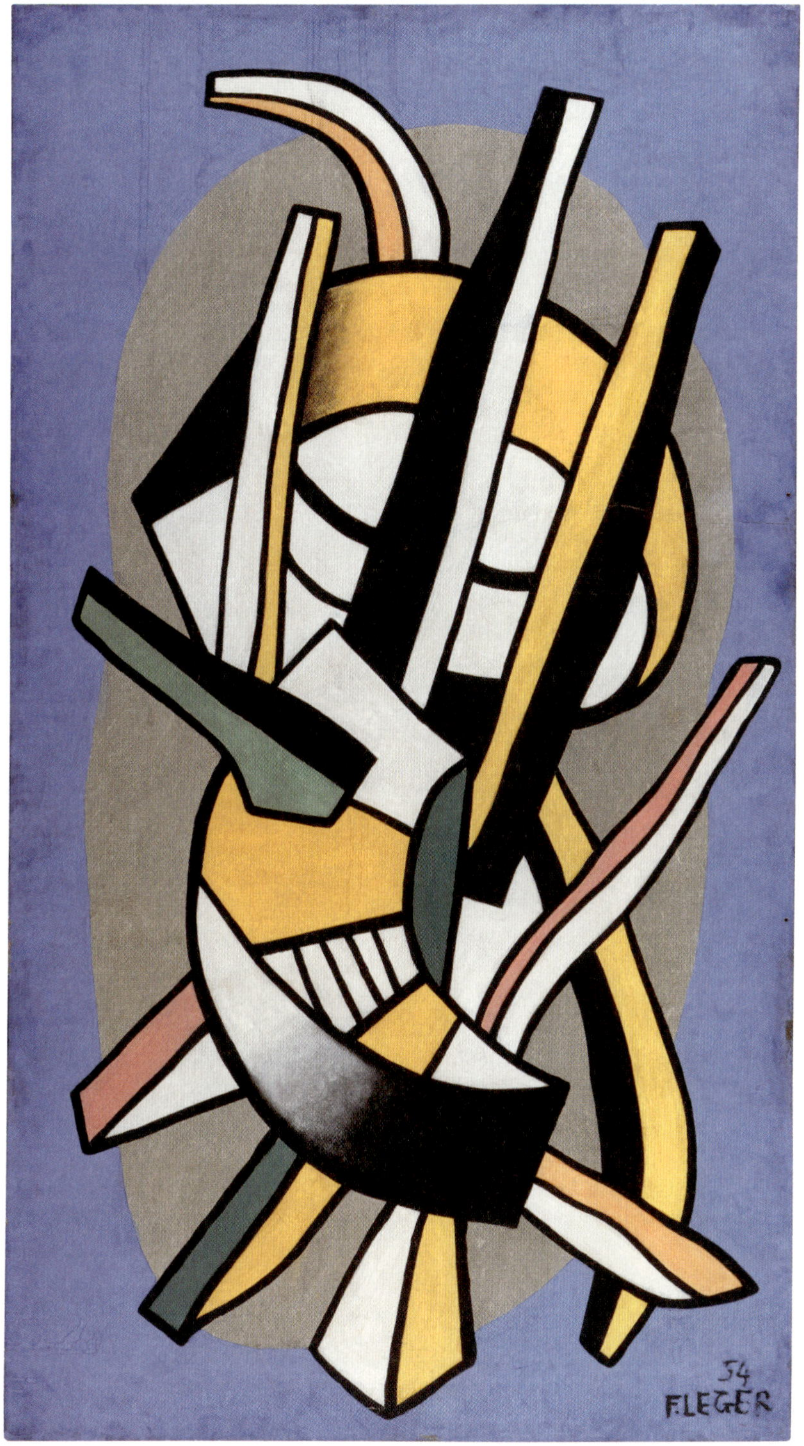

284

284 ***Sans Titre Peinture Murale* (Untitled mural painting), 1954**
Paint, gouache, fiber cement
220 × 120 cm
Gift of Nadia Léger and Georges Bauquier, Musée National Fernand Léger

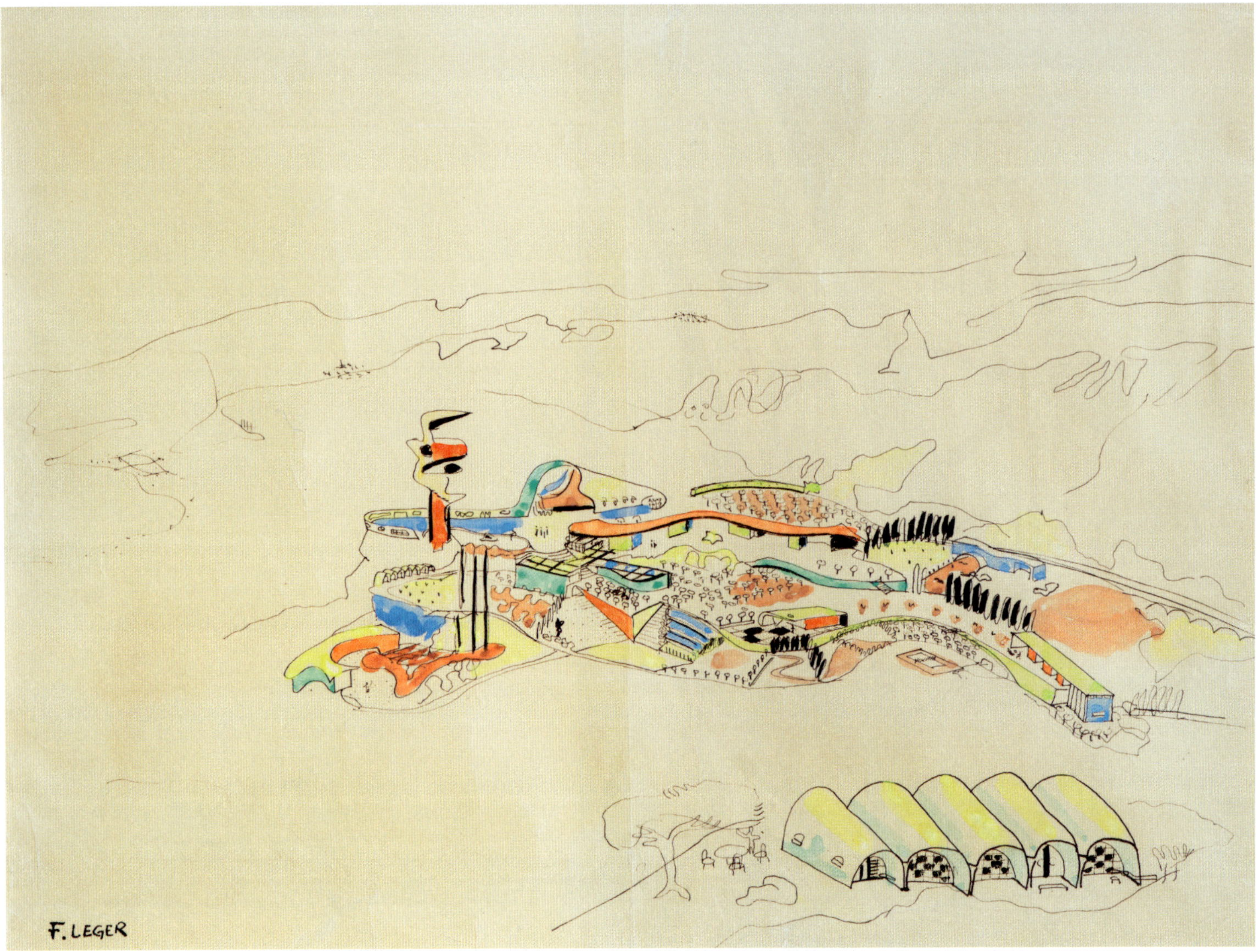

285

285 André Bruyère, Fernand Léger
Village Polychrome **(Polychrome Village), near Biot, 1952/53**
Gouache and India ink on paper
40 × 55 cm
Private collection

286 André Bruyère, Fernand Léger
Village Polychrome **(Polychrome Village), perspectival view of a villa with three workshops, near Biot, 1953**
Pastel chalk on tracing paper
37.3 × 55.5 cm
Collection Centre Canadien d'Architecture/ Canadian Centre for Architecture, Montreal
Gift in memory of Daniel Robbins

287 André Bruyère, Fernand Léger
Village Polychrome **(Polychrome Village) perspectival view of a guest villa with terrace and façades, near Biot, France, 1952**
Graphite and pastel chalk on tracing paper
42.4 × 54.6 cm
Collection Centre Canadien d'Architecture/ Canadian Centre for Architecture, Montreal
Gift in memory of Daniel Robbins

288 André Bruyère, Fernand Léger
Village Polychrome (Polychrome Village), **perspectival view of guest villa showing the terrace, near Biot, 1953**
Pastel chalk on tracing paper
37 × 55.3 cm
Collection Centre Canadien d'Architecture/ Canadian Centre for Architecture, Montreal

The polychrome village, in collaboration with Fernand Léger (1953)
André Bruyère

Fernand Léger's studio was on rue Notre-Dame-des-Champs [Paris], while my house is located on the route he took mornings and evenings between his country place in Gif-sur-Yvette and the aforementioned studio.

Returning from Biot one day in 1951, he told me how, after a good lunch, Mr. Assy de Chateaubriand, a South American press baron, had thrown big banknotes to children in the streets of a village on the Côte d'Azur.

Léger, with whom he was sharing his difficulties, retorted: "One starts by asking for a project. With Bruyère, I'll get busy realizing my dream: to compose, on a neutral site, on the gray rock, a painting worthy of the scale of the landscape."

We sought to lay out a pedestrian village in which, to reach home, one has to pass beneath a neighbor's house; in which everything radiates out from a little square; whence things can be made out without making a show, with everything serving color, or else a series of dark places, with other, brighter areas allowing the tonal properties to be accentuated.

Due to its richness, the space was sometimes cavalierly deployed, more especially since it was used by fewer people and since color there found its voice.

There would be ten houses for Mr. de Chateaubriand's billionaire friends, a museum, bistros, and a hall for 200 students.

The Brazilian currency crumbled and the project was swept away with the crumbs.

Originally published as A. Bruyère, "Le village polychrome en collaboration avec Fernand Léger," in André Bruyère, *Pourquoi des architectes?* (Paris, 1968), 145–46.

–

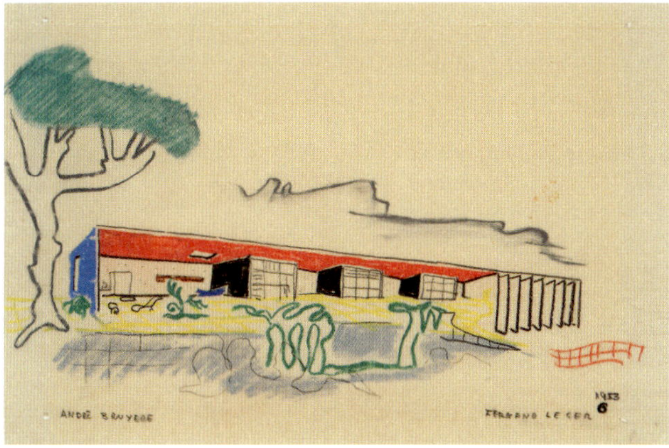

286

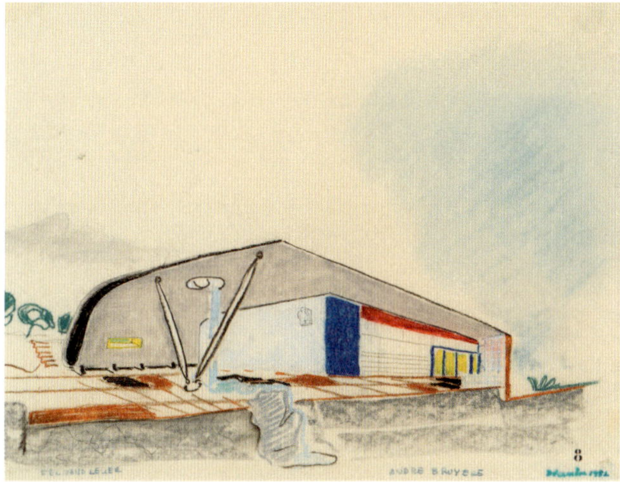

287

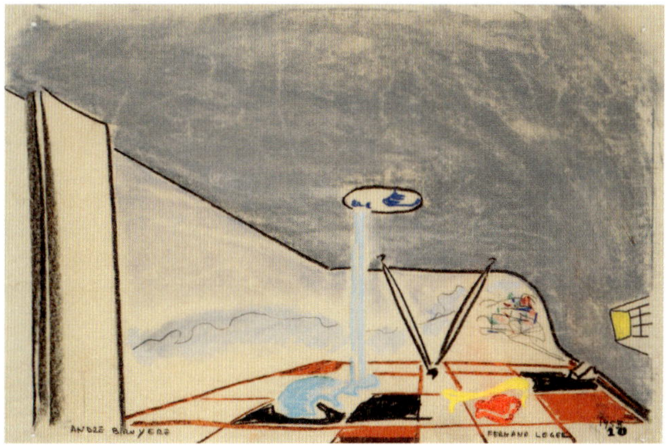

288

Nine Points on Monumentality (New York, 1943)
J.L. Sert, F. Léger and S. Giedion

Que donneriez vous ma belle
Pour revoir votre mari ?
Je donnerai Versailles, Paris et Saint Denis
Les tours de Notre Dame
Et le clocher de mon pays.
Auprès de ma blonde
Qu'il fait bon, fait bon, fait bon.

(From an old French song, "Auprès de ma blonde")

(1) Monuments are human landmarks which men have created as symbols for their ideals, for their aims, and for their actions. They are intended to outlive the period which originated them, and constitute a heritage for future generations. As such, they form a link between the past and the future.

(2) Monuments are the expression of man's highest cultural needs. They have to satisfy the eternal demand of the people for translation of their collective force into symbols. The most vital monuments are those which express the feeling and thinking of this collective force–the people.

(3) Every bygone period which shaped a real cultural life had the power and the capacity to create these symbols. Monuments are, therefore, only possible in periods in which a unifying consciousness and unifying culture exists. Periods which exist for the moment have been unable to create lasting monuments.

(4) The last hundred years have witnessed the devaluation of monumentality. This does not mean that there is any lack of formal monuments or architectural examples pretending to serve this purpose; but the so-called monuments of recent date have, with rare exceptions, become empty shells. They in no way represent the spirit or the collective feeling of modern times.

(5) This decline and misuse of monumentality is the principal reason why modern architects have deliberately disregarded the monument and revolted against it.

Modern architecture, like modern painting and sculpture, had to start the hard way. It began by tackling the simpler problems, the more utilitarian buildings like low-rent housing, schools, office buildings, hospitals, and similar structures. Today modern architects know that buildings cannot be conceived as isolated units, that they have to be incorporated into the vaster urban schemes. There are no frontiers between architecture and town planning, just as there are no frontiers between the city and the region. Correlation between them is necessary. Monuments should constitute the most powerful accents in these vast schemes.

(6) A new step lies ahead. Post-war changes in the whole economic structure of nations may bring with them the organization of community life in the city which has been practically neglected up to date.

(7) The people want the buildings that represent their social and community life to give more than functional fulfillment. They want their aspiration for monumentality, joy, pride, and excitement to be satisfied.

The fulfillment of this demand can be accomplished with the new means of expression at hand, though it is no easy task. The following conditions are essential for it. A monument being the integration of the work of the planner, architect, painter, sculptor, and landscapist demands close collaboration between all of them. This collaboration has failed in the last hundred years. Most modern architects have not been trained for this kind of integrated work. Monumental tasks have not been entrusted to them.

As a rule, those who govern and administer a people, brilliant as they may be in their special fields, represent the average man of our period in their artistic judgments. Like this average man, they experience a split between their methods of thinking and their methods of feeling. The feeling of those who govern and administer the countries is untrained and still imbued with the pseudo-ideals of the nineteenth century. This is the reason why they are not able to recognize the creative forces of our period, which alone could build the monuments or public buildings that should be integrated into new urban center which can form a true expression for our epoch.

(8) Sites for monuments must be planned. This will be possible once replanning is undertaken on a large scale which will create vast open spaces in the now decaying areas of our cities. In these open spaces, monumental architecture will find its appropriate setting which now does not exist. Monumental buildings will then be able to stand in space, for, like trees or plants, monumental buildings cannot be crowded in upon any odd lot in any district. Only when this space is achieved can the new urban centers come to life.

(9) Modern materials and new techniques are at hand: light metal structures; curved, laminated wooden arches; panels of different textures, colors, and sizes; light elements like ceilings which can be suspended from big trusses covering practically unlimited spans.

Mobile elements can constantly vary the aspect of the buildings. These mobile elements, changing positions and casting different shadows when acted upon by wind or machinery, can be the source of new architectural effects.

During night hours, color and forms can be projected on vast surfaces. Such displays could be projected upon buildings for purposes of publicity or propaganda. These buildings would have large plane surfaces planned for this purpose, surfaces which are non-existent today.

Such big animated surfaces with the use of color and movement in a new spirit would offer unexplored fields to mural painters and sculptors.

Elements of nature, such as trees, plants, and water, would complete the picture. We could group all these elements in architectural ensembles: the stones which have always been used, the new materials which belong to our times, and color in all its intensity which has long been forgotten.

Man-made landscapes would be correlated with nature's landscapes and all elements combined in terms of the new and vast facade, sometimes extending for many miles, which has been revealed to us by the air view. This could be contemplated not only during a rapid flight but also from a helicopter stopping in mid-air.

Monumental architecture will be something more than strictly functional. It will have regained its lyrical value. In such monumental layouts, architecture and city planning could attain a new freedom and develop new creative possibilities, such as those that have begun to be felt in the last decades in the fields of painting, sculpture, music, and poetry.

Excerpt from S. Giedion, *Architecture, You and Me: The Diary of a Development* (Cambridge, MA: Harvard University Press, 1958), 48–51

–

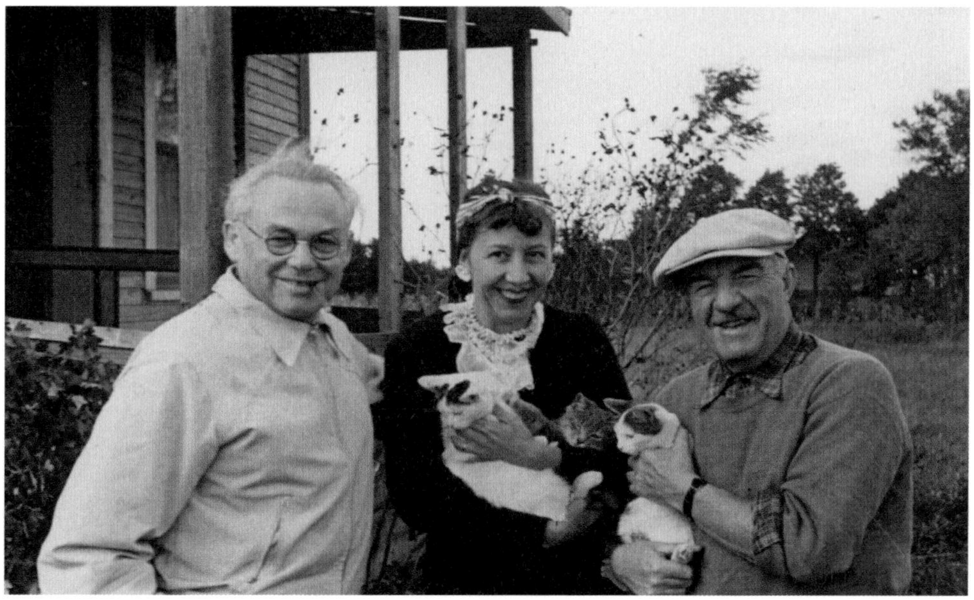

289

289 **Sigfried Giedion, Fernand Léger and his wife Jeanne-Augustine Lohy at Rouses Point, 1945**
ETH Zurich, estate of Sigfried Giedion

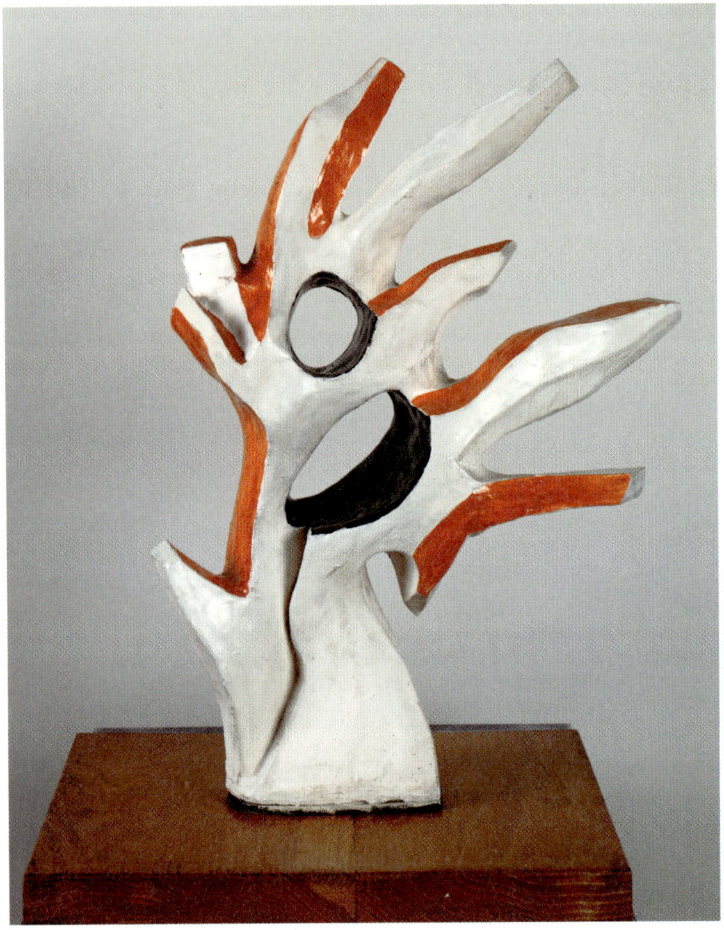

290

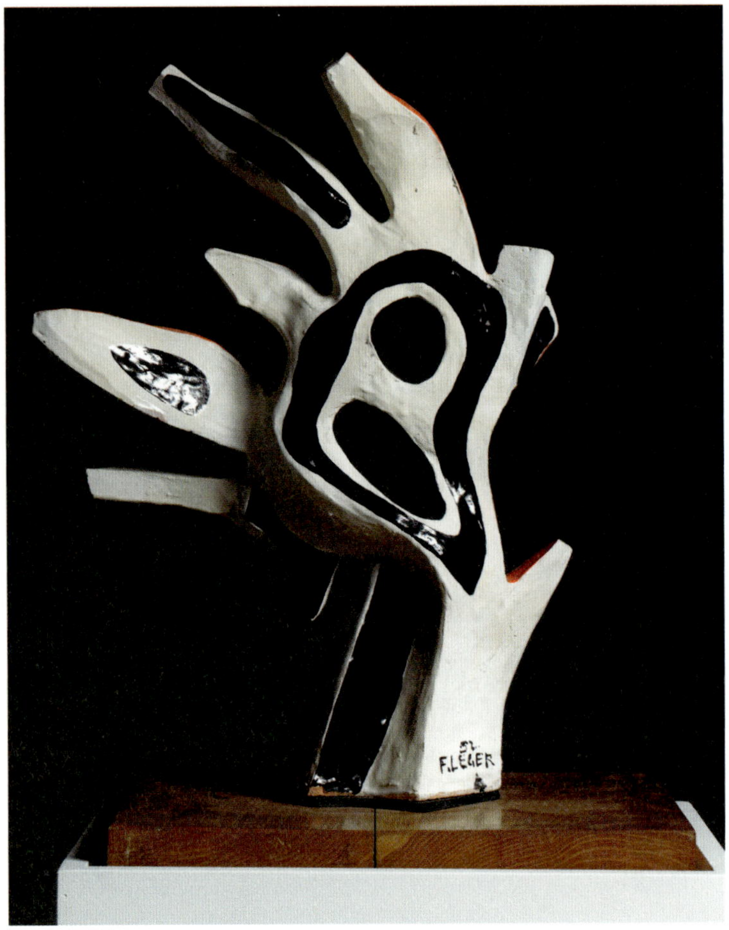

290 ***La branche Rockefeller***
(The Rockefeller Branch), 1952
Glazed ceramic
48.5 × 3.5 × 11 cm
Musée national Fernand Léger, Biot

In this work, Léger reworks the central motif of the Rockefeller fireplace mural into a three-dimensional composition.

291 ***Le Tournesol* (The Sunflower) c. 1952/53**
Glazed ceramic
41.5 × 46.5 cm
Private collection

292 ***Léger et le Tournesol* (Léger and the Sunflower), artist Fernand Léger in his studio in the 1950s**

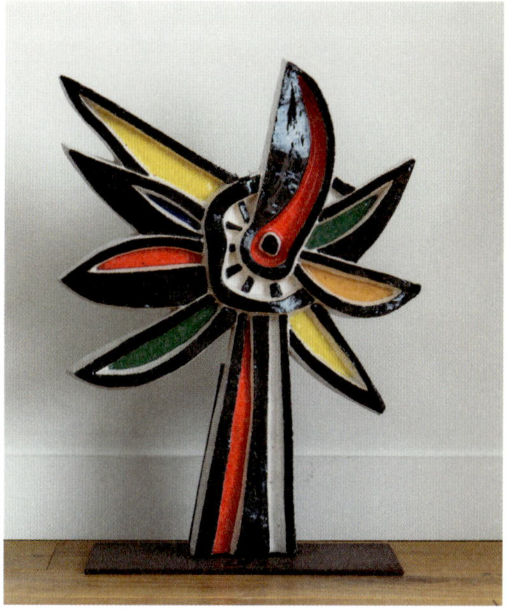
291

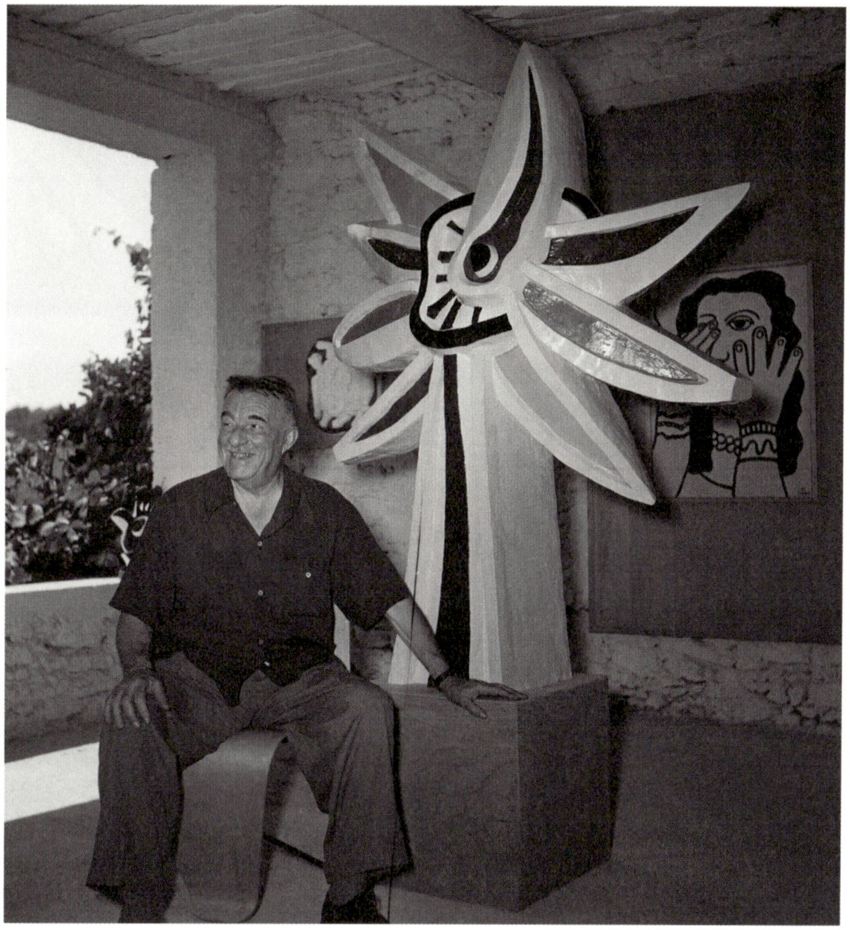
292

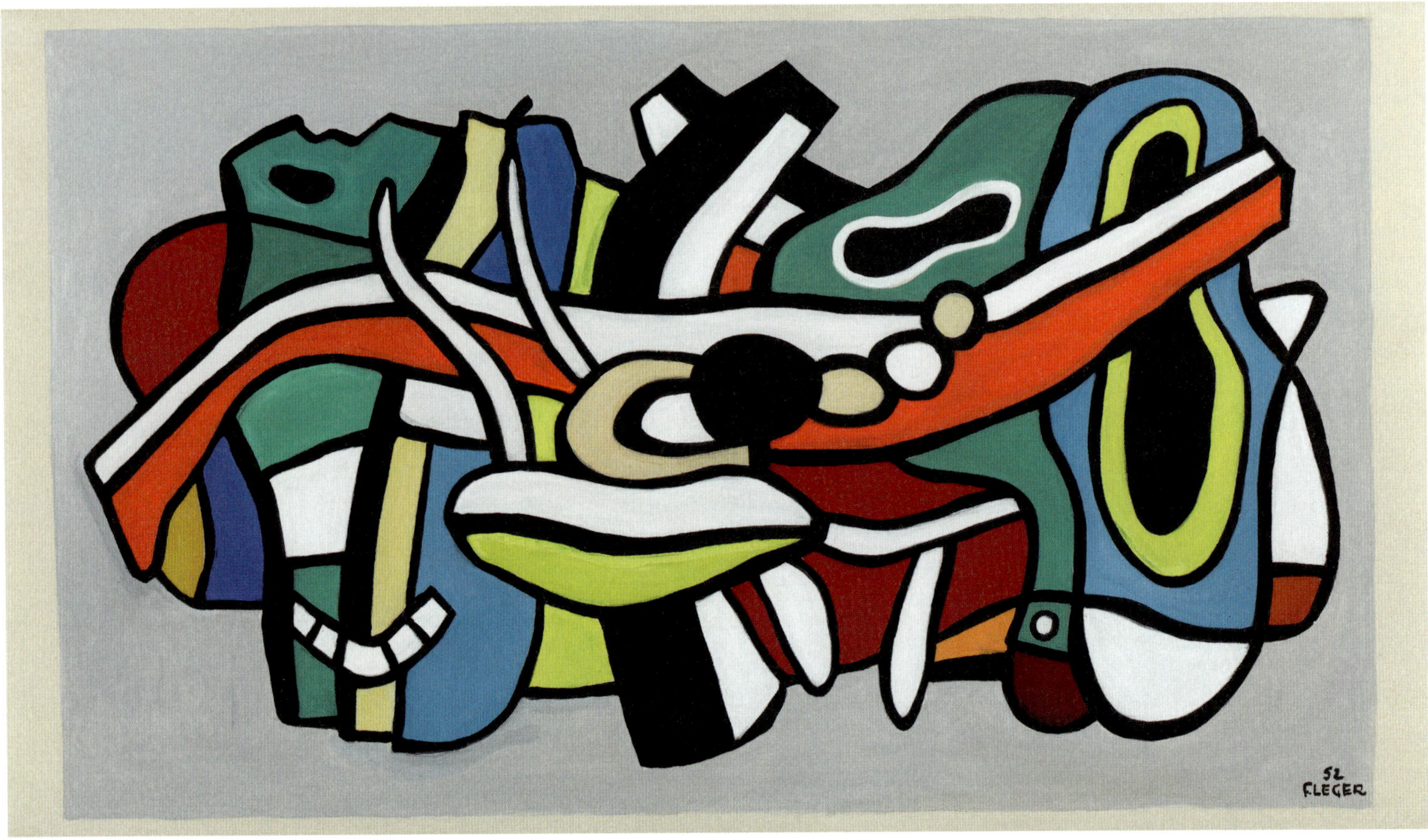

293

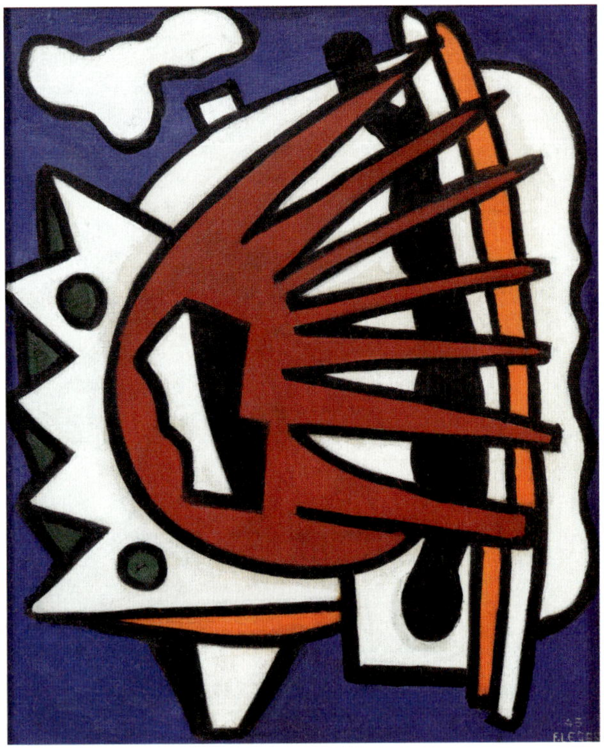
294

293 ***Projet pour une peinture murale* (Plan for a Mural Painting), 1952**
Oil on canvas
114 × 195 cm
Musée national Fernand Léger, Biot

294 ***Composition pour une peinture murale* (Composition for a Mural Painting), 1945**
Oil on canvas
50.7 × 40.5 cm
Musée national Fernand Léger, Biot

295 ***Peinture murale* (Mural Painting), 1953**
Oil on canvas
92 × 65.2 cm
Musée national Fernand Léger, Biot

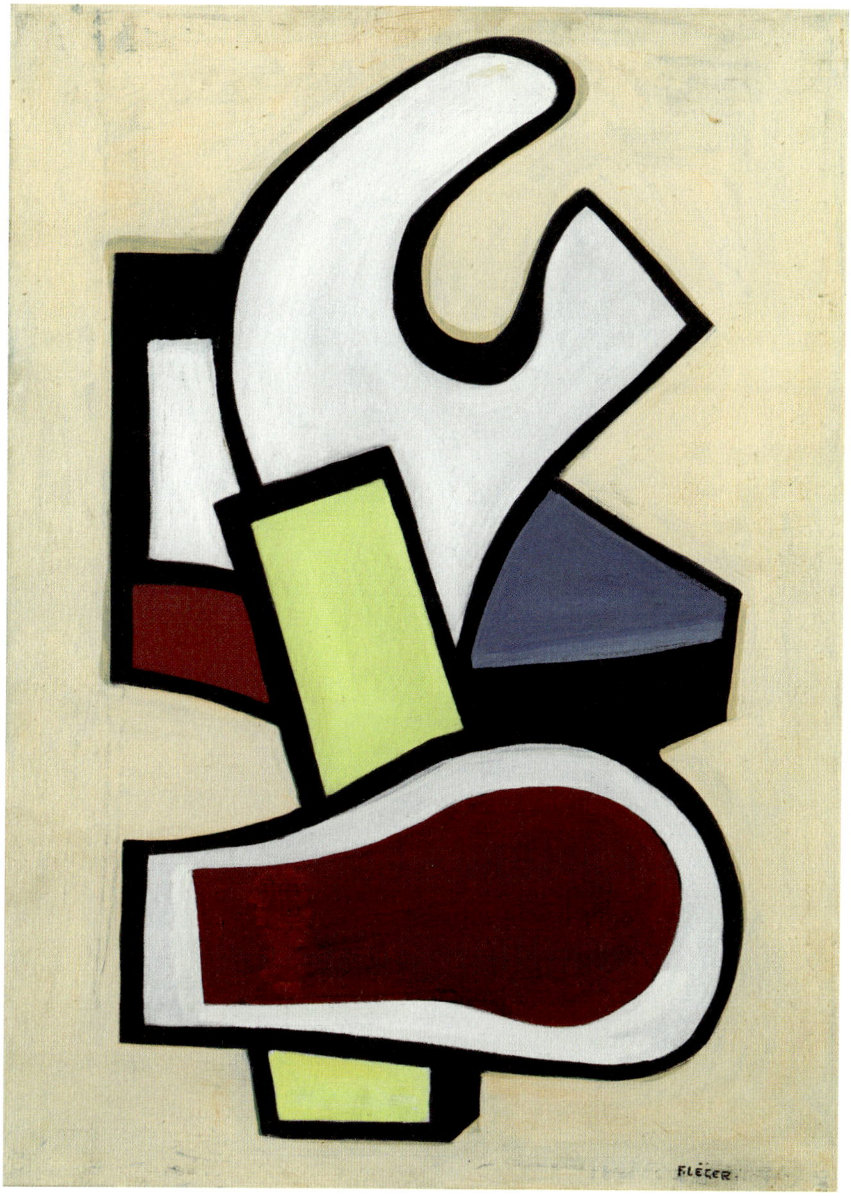

295

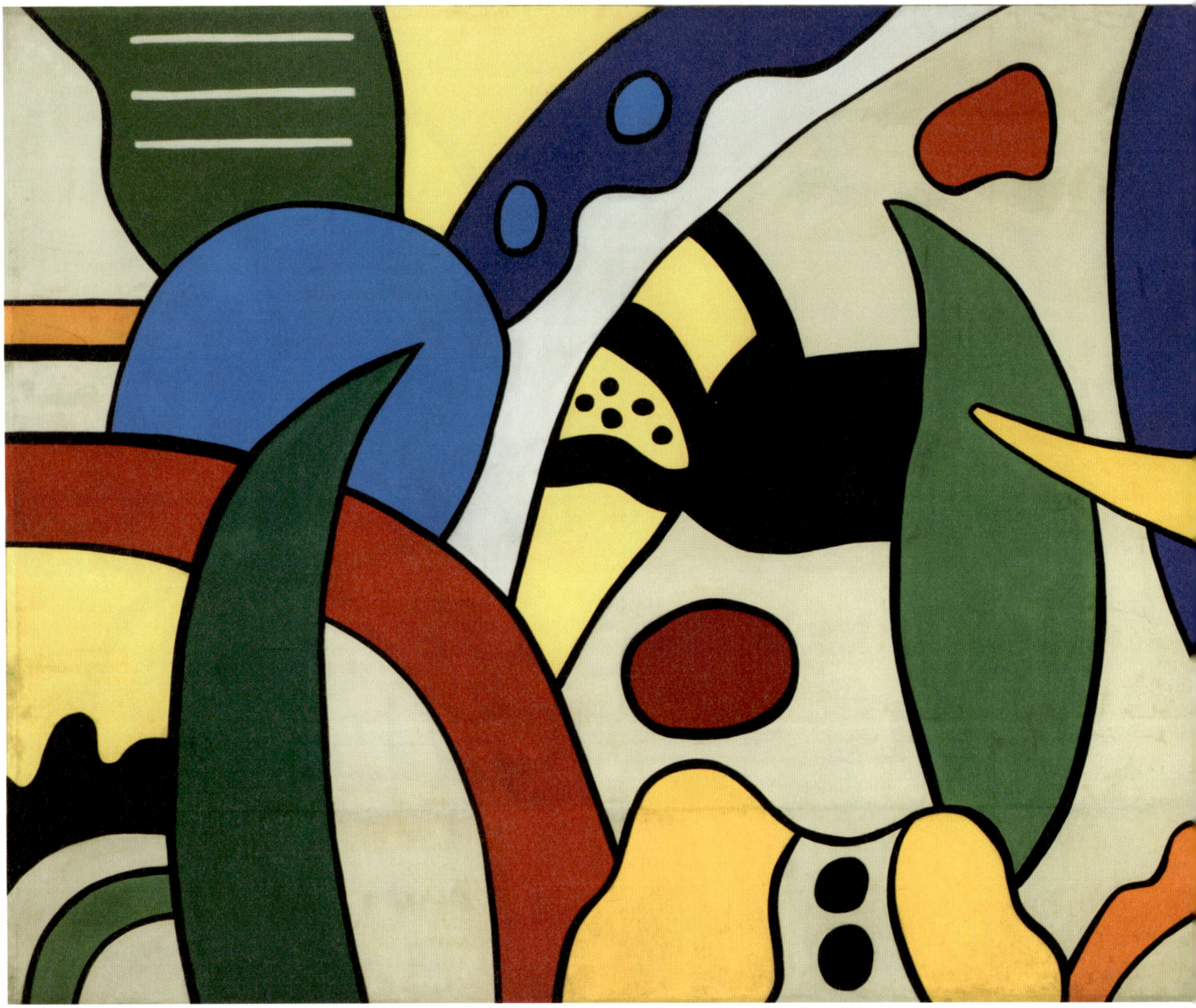

296

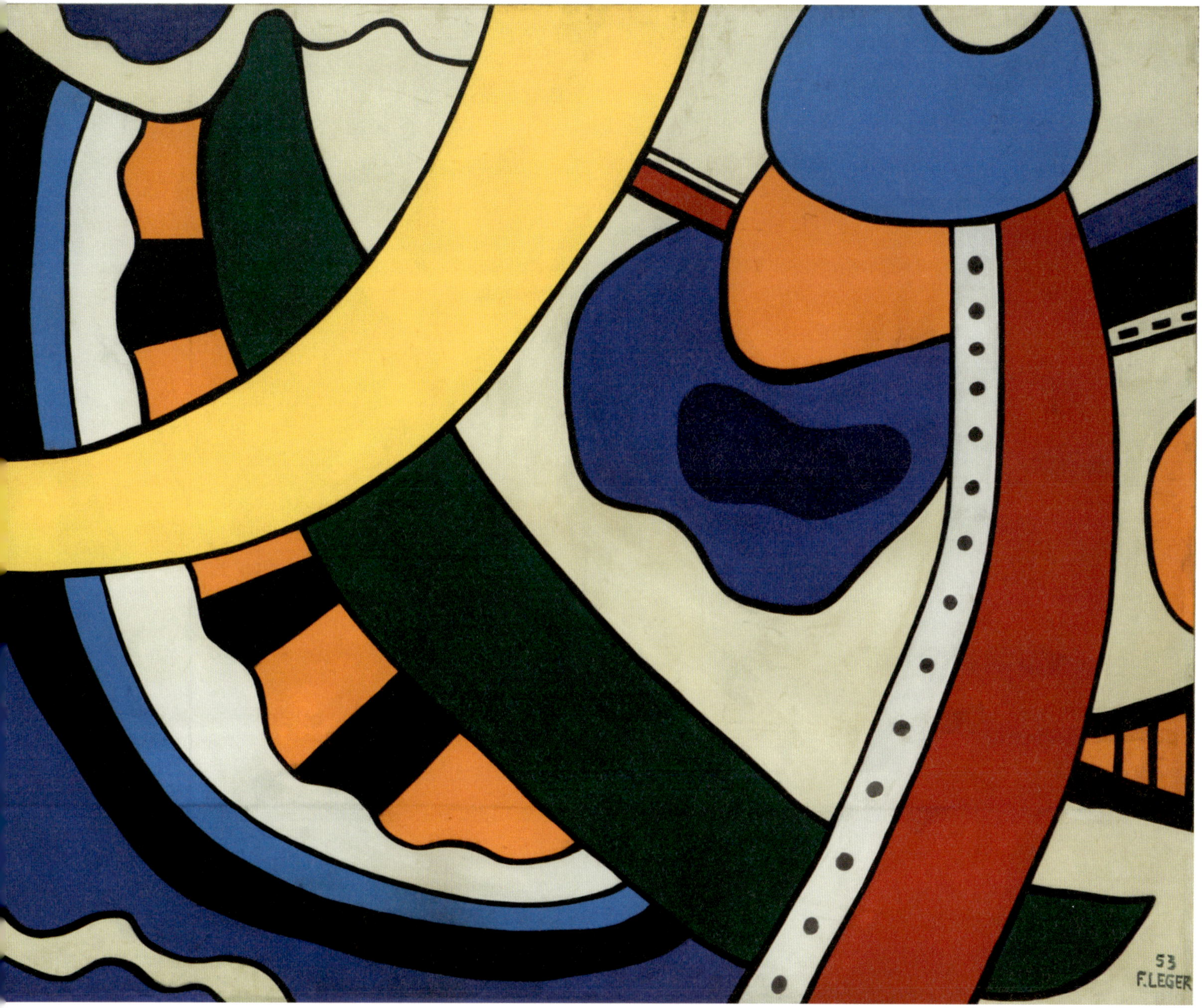
53
F.LEGER

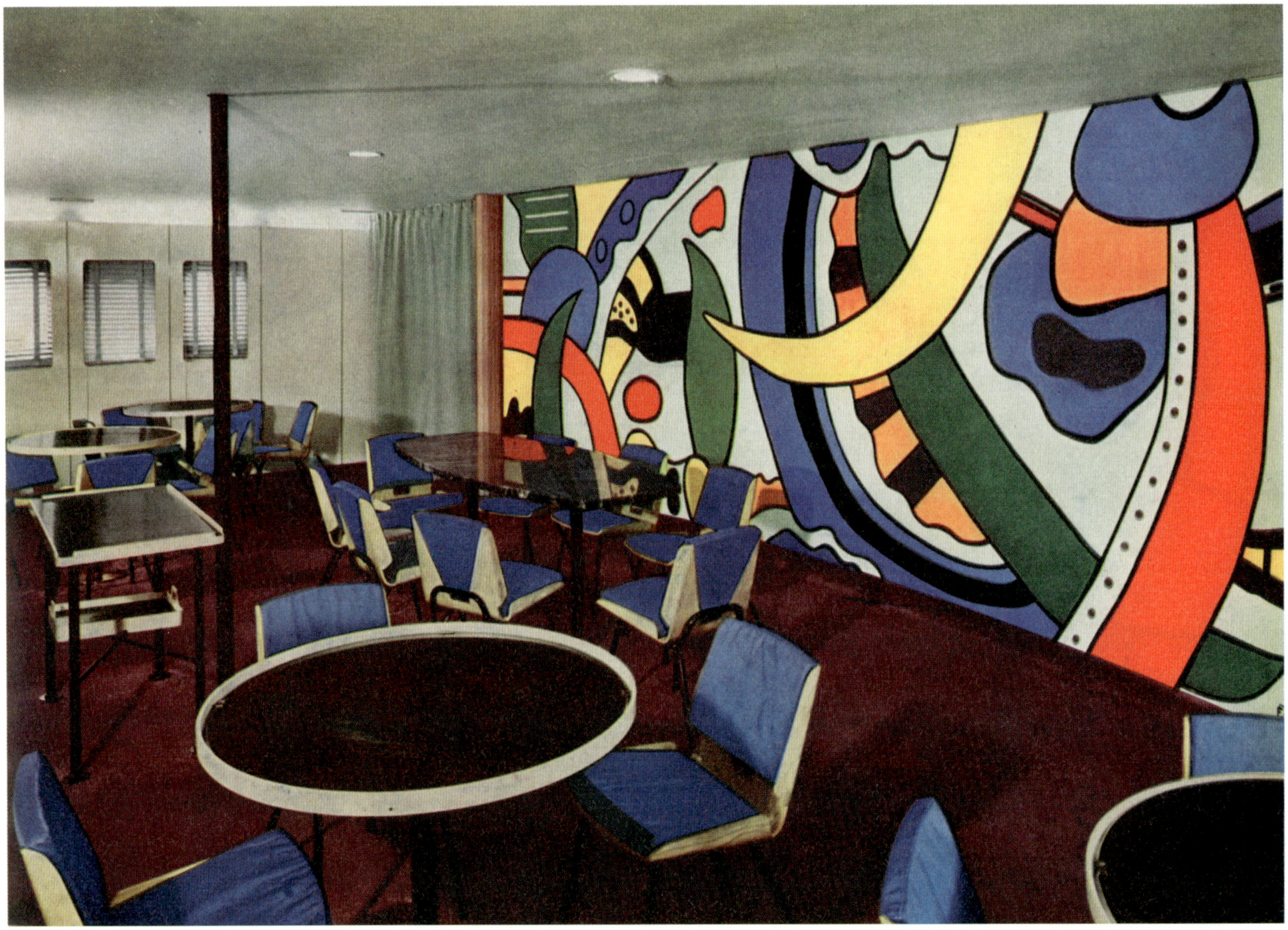

297

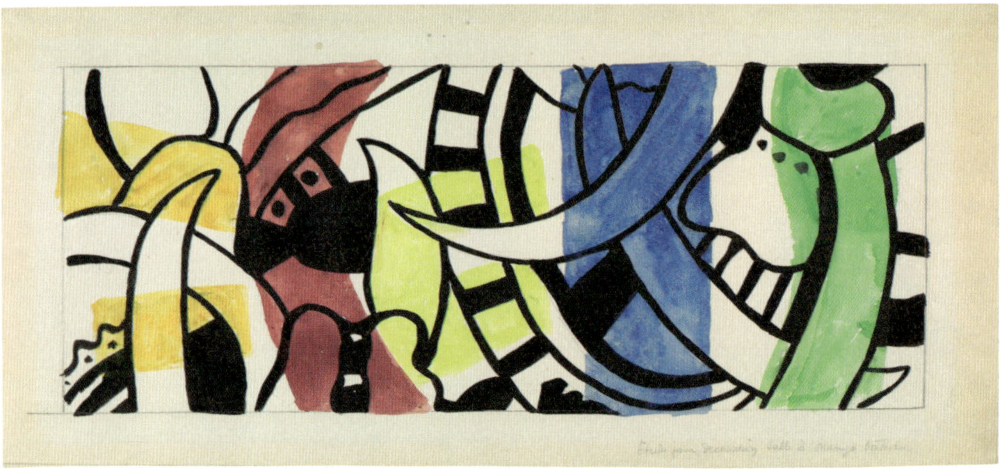

298

The Interior Design of the "Lucania" (1953)
Gio Ponti

[…] Across from these displays, we see the natural presence of the large Léger panel. This episode, too, it should be pointed out, is not a Léger placed on a wall; here Léger himself has collaborated, supporting the aim of the architecture, with a wall that involves a breaking through of the space, and not a final closing: his design, incomplete, explosive, has been implemented after various attempts; and the colors of the furnishings, flooring and curtains, in parts have been influenced by it, and in parts have influenced it, as happens with a living collaboration.

Excerpt from Gio Ponti, "Interni della 'Lucania'," in *Domus* (1953): 21–23.

–

296 ***Composition* (Composition), 1953**
Oil on canvas
210 × 510 cm
Museu Coleção Berardo, Lisbon, acc. no. UID 102-334

Mural painting for the dining room of Lucania, cruise ship, interior design: Giancarlo de Carlo, Enzo Mariani.

297 **Mural painting *Composition* onboard the *Lucania*, 1953**
From *Domus*, October 1953, p. 21
Colorized photograph

298 ***Projet de décoration pour la salle à manger du paquebot »Vulcania«* (Study for the decoration of the dining room of the *Vulcania* passenger ship [Lucania]), c. 1951**
Gouache and pencil on vellum
31.3 × 65.2 cm
Musée national Fernand Léger, Biot

299 ***Projet de décoration pour la salle à manger du paquebot »Vulcania«* Study for the decoration of the dining room of the *Vulcania* passenger ship [Lucania]), c. 1951**
Gouache and pencil on paper
31.3 × 65.2 cm
Musée national Fernand Léger, Biot

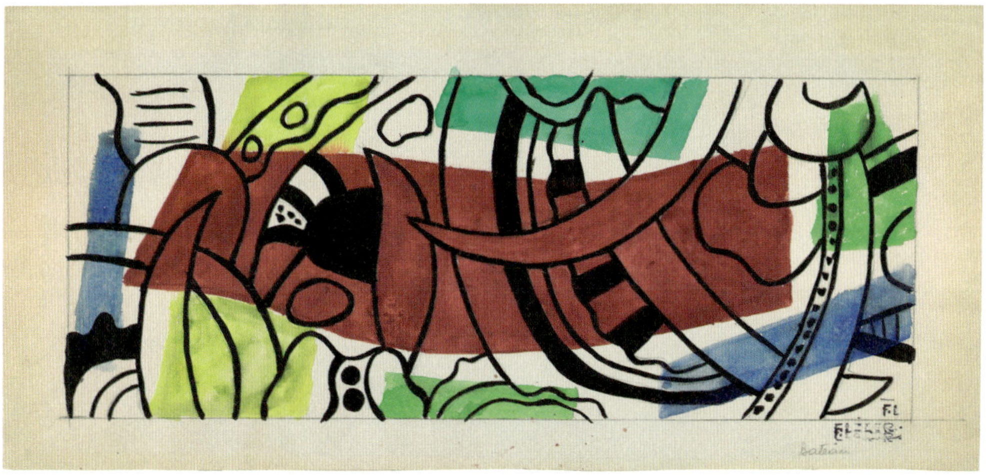

299

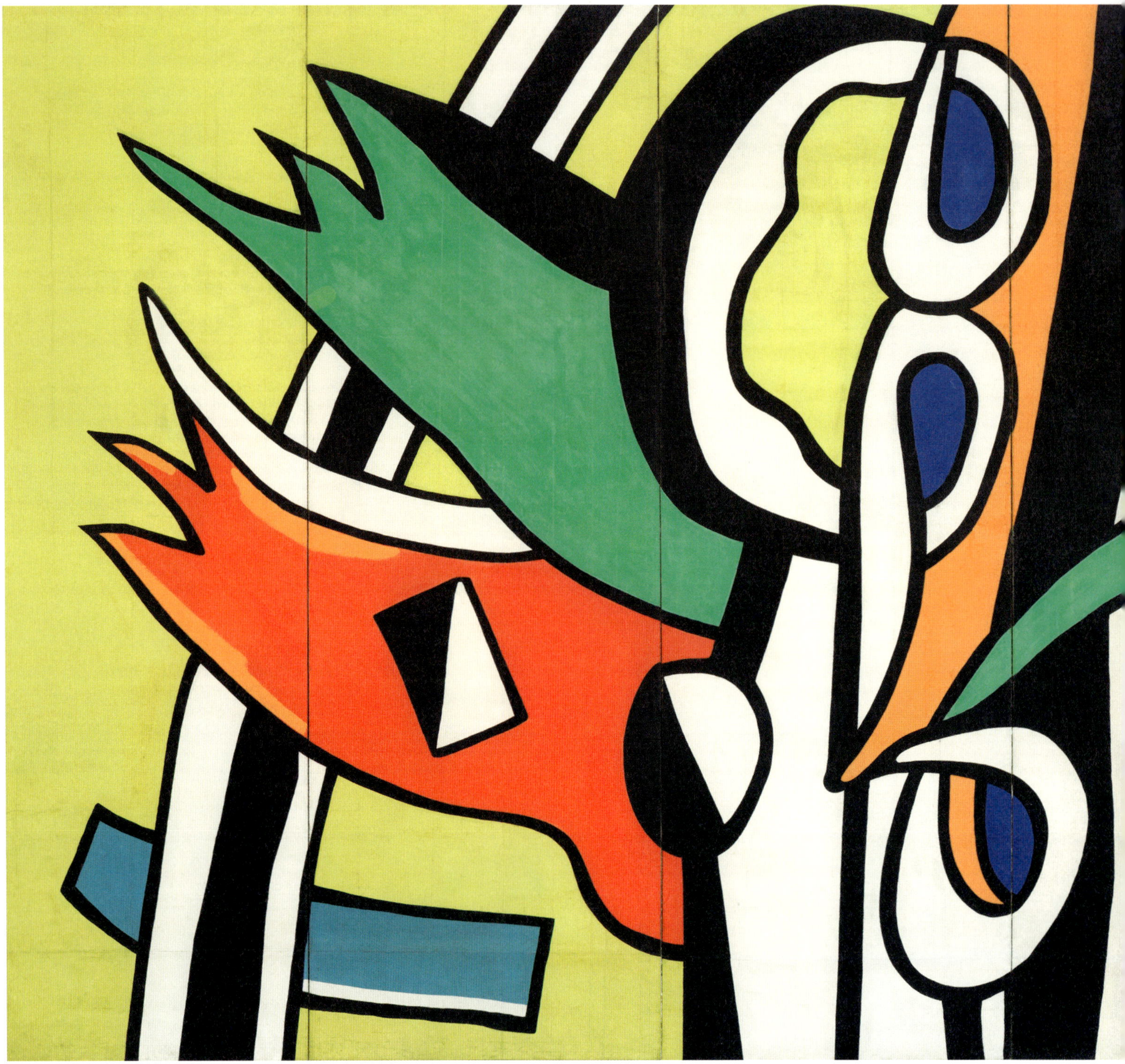

300

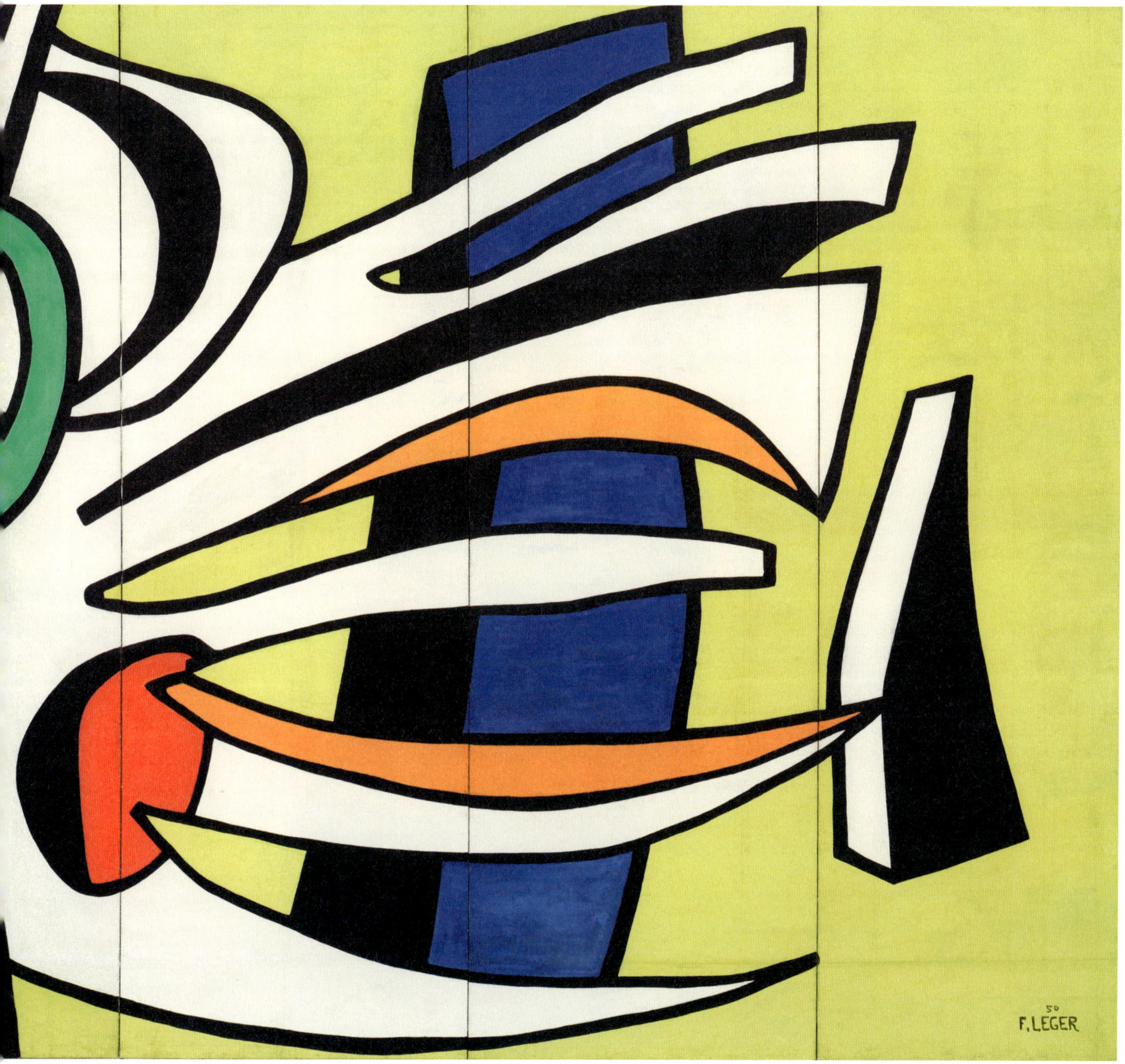
50
F. LEGER

Charlotte Perriand on the ninth Milan Triennale (1951)

I put *Formes Utiles* on center stage at the ninth Milan Triennale, held in 1951 and organized under the patronage of the Association Française d'Action Artistique. I had been approached by the commissioner-general of French participation in the Triennale, Tony Bouilhet, who asked me to make some proposals. "Only modern works boasting originality and quality can be shown in our French exhibitions held abroad", he said.

[…] I proposed that Henri Prouvé, Jean's brother, design the architecture display. He was in charge of creating the metal framework structure that consisted of a mezzanine, poles, window supports, and screens; the design was modular to create a coherent link between the various displays.

The planning display had a separate stand, where the Ministry of Reconstruction and Urbanism presented a series of models for Toulon and Le Havre, student residence halls at Antony, Corbu's Unité d'Habitation, and Jean Prouvé's prefabricated structure. The exhibition area was huge, with everything placed at ground or eye level.

There was a huge bare wall at the back, which I nabbed. I was hoping to ask Fernand Léger to brighten it up with a large fresco, to make it the high point of the show. But, as always, there was no money in the coffers. I was completely free to promote ideas, but without resources. We had to sponsor ourselves.

Fernand and I went to beg the Lefèvre-Foinet and Lefranc stores for a free canvas and paint. But we didn't even have enough to pay the guys who would produce the fresco on site. In the end, Fernand gave us some of his lithographs that we could sell to cover costs.

I was directly responsible for the *Formes Utiles* display.

Excerpts from Charlotte Perriand, *A Life of Creation* (New York: The Monacelli Press, 2003), 237-38 (originally published as *Une vie de création*, Paris, 1998).

–

300 ***La Triennale de Milan*** **(Milan Triennial, mural painting for the French section of the IX Milan Triennial, realized by Léger's students), 1951**
Oil on canvas
625 × 1,340 cm
Musée national Fernand Léger, Biot

301 **Mural La Triennale de Milan, 1951 for the French section of the Milan Triennial, 1951**
Curator: Charlotte Perriand. In the foreground: a model of Toulon by Jean de Mailly

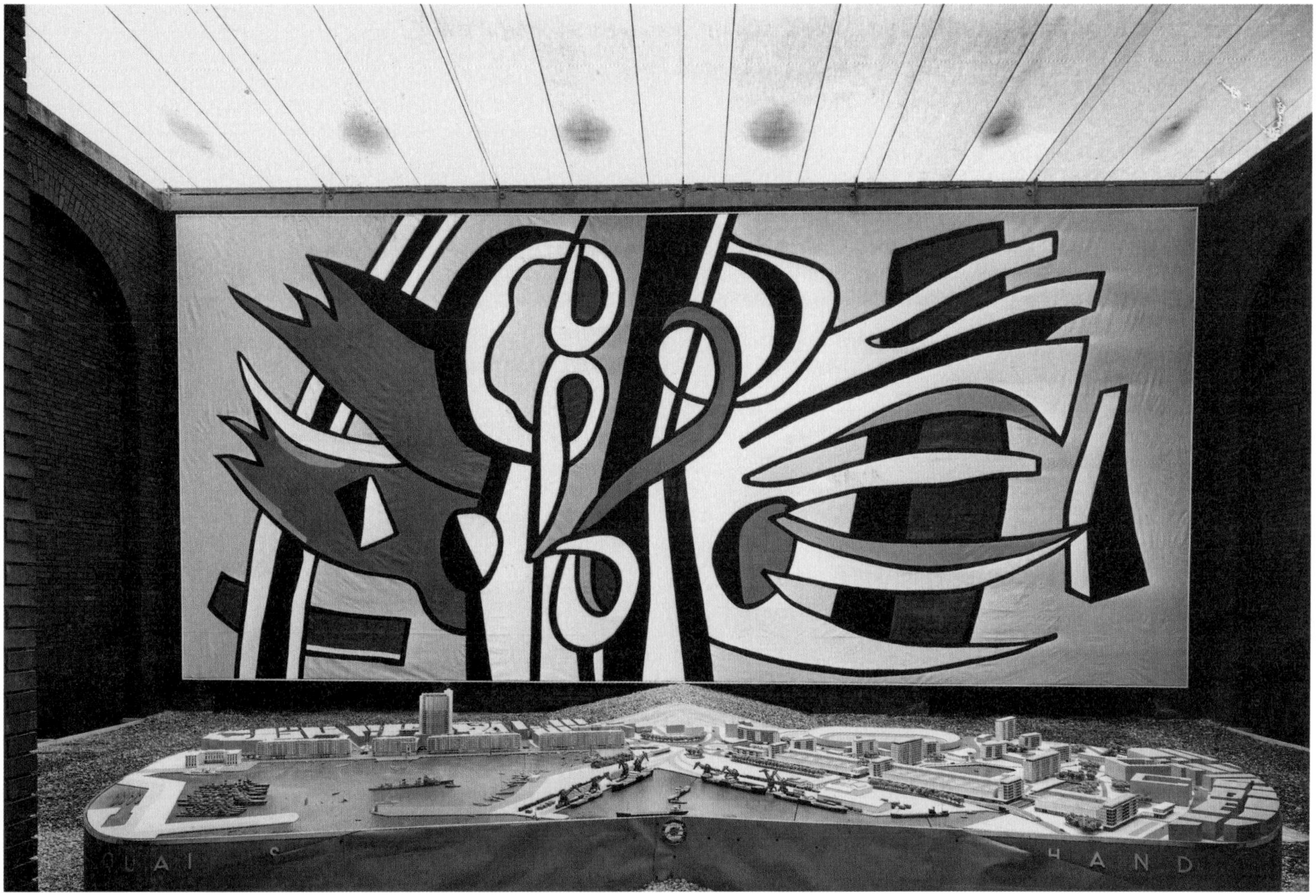

301

Charlotte Perriand on the UAM Exhibition *Formes utiles, objets de notre temps* (1949-50)

After my return to France in 1946, I got back in contact with my friends from the Union des Artistes Modernes (UAM)—René Herbst, Georges Henri Pingusson, André Hermant, and others. We were looking for ways to update UAM initiatives.

[…] The UAM set up an exhibition at the Pavillion de Marsan, with the backing of the Union Centrale des Arts Décoratifs. We selected ordinary commercial objects we considered useful for everyday living, based on our criteria of "function, technique, and savings," which also bestowed a certain beauty. In the long run, we hoped this would spark artist-industry partnerships, thereby promoting the fields of design and manufacturing. Our exhibition needed a title, and André Hermant came up with *Formes Utiles* (Useful Forms). It was accompanied by the slogan "Useful (and beautiful) forms are those that highlight the harmony between materials and the aspirations of the mind."

[…] I hadn't forgotten that the UAM championed synthesis. As a supplement to the *Bazaar* exhibition demonstrations, I designed ensembles of selected objects—a children's bedroom and an office. I separated the two with a large stretch of white sand, on which I set up a mobile by Alexander Calder and the blade of an airplane propeller. Walls and screens structured the space, and on them I hung a Miró painting and a cardboard-mounted tapestry by Corbu, as well as a superb enlargement of a bas-relief of the Borobudur in Java.

A painting by Fernand Léger (*Les Deux Soeurs*, 1935) could be seen from the entrance. It depicted two sisters set against a yellow background. François Mathey, the Musée des Arts Décoratifs curator, was somewhat puzzled by it.

There is art in everything, whether it can be an action, a vase, a saucepan, a glass, a piece of sculpture, a jewel, a way of being. My ever-present friends encouraged me.

Excerpts from Charlotte Perriand, *A Life of Creation* (New York: The Monacelli Press, 2003), 235–38 (originally published as *Une vie de création*, Paris, 1998).

–

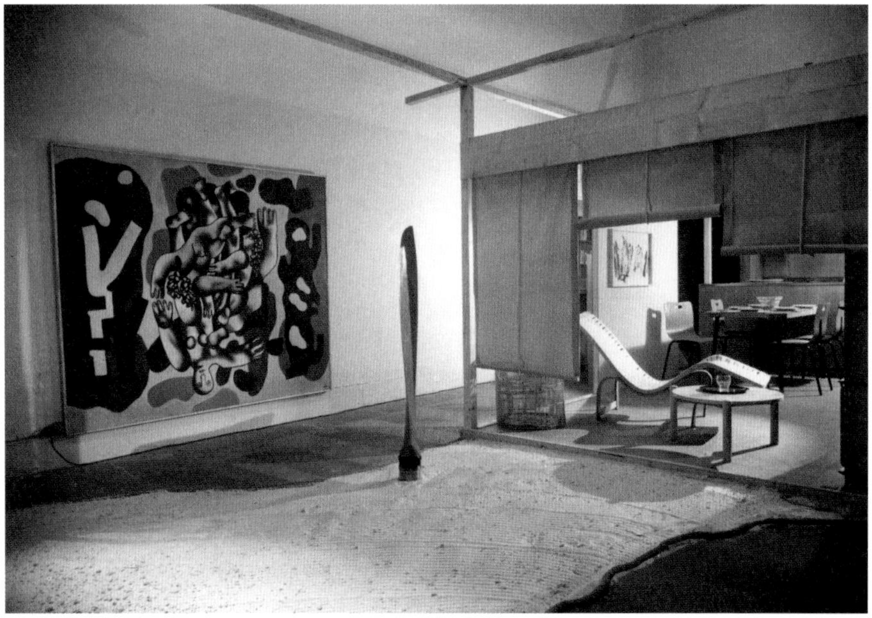

302

302 ***Formes utiles, objets de notre temps*** **exhibition (Useful Forms, Objects of Our Time), Paris, December, 1949–February, 1950**
Scenography by Charlotte Perriand, *Les Plongeurs sur fond jaune* (Divers on a Yellow Background) by Fernand Léger in the Synthesis of the Arts section
Archives Charlotte Perriand

Charlotte Perriand's introduction in the exhibition catalog *Proposition d'une synthèse des arts, Paris, 1955: Le Corbusier - F. Léger - Ch. Perriand*

The exhibition that opens on March 31st in Tokyo will be more or less the one devised when Le Corbusier and F. Léger lent me their unhesitating support on my return from a trip to Japan.

[…] In reality, this exhibition must show the trends and preoccupations of the West with regard to the visual arts and housing. It is based on two topical themes, which were already part of the Triennale, namely:

"Illustrating the collaboration between artists and industrial manufacturers."

"Reaffirming the Unity between architecture, painting, and sculpture."

[…] F. Léger calls for walls because his easel paintings are not enough. He creates stained-glass windows, mosaics for churches, tapestries; thanks to his polychrome sculptures, he has found a new mural form of expression for the art of ceramics.

A synthesis of the Arts? They include all of these elements–architecture, furniture, everyday objects, tapestries, polychrome sculptures, canvases for the walls–which by complementing each other will aim for unity.

I know that all these works can be seen as luxury items. But should we allow these artisanal technical companies to disappear, or on the contrary should we protect and find a new expression for this magnificent artistic heritage, which will be at home in buildings for collective use? Through the harmonious interplay of forms, it will fulfill everyone's need for art. This exhibition will present living elements that are being perpetually renewed.

Excerpt from *Proposition d'une synthèse des arts, Paris, 1955: Le Corbusier - F. Léger - Ch. Perriand*, exh. cat., Grand Magasin Takashimaya, Tokyo (1955), curated by Charlotte Perriand.

–

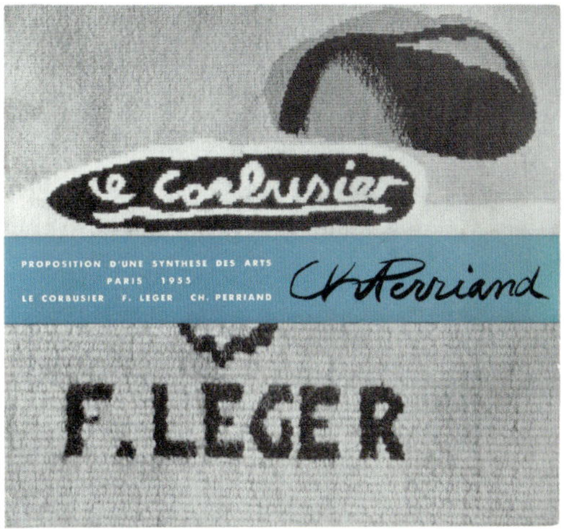

303

303 **Catalog cover for the exhibition *Proposition d'une Synthèse des Arts, Paris, 1955* (Proposition for a Synthesis of the Arts), Tokyo, 1955**
Archives Charlotte Perriand

304 **View of the exhibition from the entrance**
Interior design by Charlotte Perriand and Pierre Jeanneret, ceramic relief and *Les deux femmes aux fleurs* (Two Women with Flowers) by Fernand Léger
Archives Charlotte Perriand

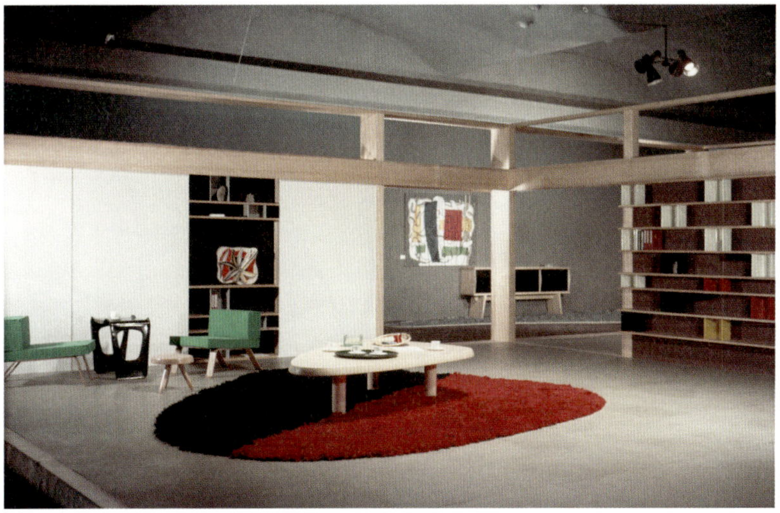

304

Letter from Fernand Léger to Carlos Raúl Villanueva, July 10, 1953

Paris, July 10, 1953

My Dear Villanueva,

I enclose 12 sketches for our project. I have kept a moveable space between the two decorative elements. So you can space them yourself or close them up in the best interests of the presentation. As I shall not be present, it is up to you to decide according to the light or the visual distance.

As soon as you have made your choice, return the 12 models to me indicating which ones you have chosen. Then I will quickly look for the relief elements to make to your choice if you still want them.

Mr. Barillet should have sent you the two stained-glass maquettes yesterday. He saw them and they are in order from the point of view of making them. It's the same for the mosaic maquettes. They have been seen by MM; Gaudin. The reliefs will present no difficulties provided you make them by following the exact outline of a colored element without cutting into it with a line of drawing.

Warmest regards and answer as quickly as possible,

F. LEGER

Fundación Villanueva, Caracas.

-

Fernand Léger on the University of Caracas by Villanueva (1954)

When Villanueva came to find me with the plans and the model of his project for the university campus under his arm, I felt that this project, if it had been built, would be a modern event from an architectural point of view. So I agreed to collaborate on it with a mural work (mosaic) and glass-paste stained-glass window.

Although I haven't seen the layout of the elements and their relationships on the plan of Caracas, I have no doubts that the complex designed and executed by Villanueva will be a big success and as I have already said an important event in international architecture.

Excerpt from a letter by Fernand Léger to Carlos Raúl Villanueva, February 11, 1954, Fundación Villanueva, Caracas.

-

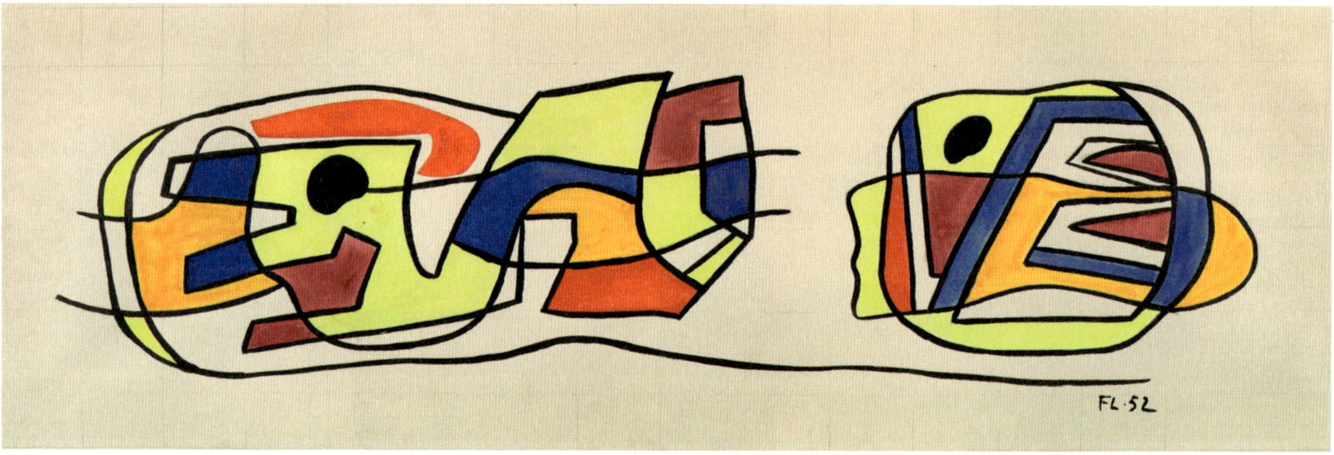

305

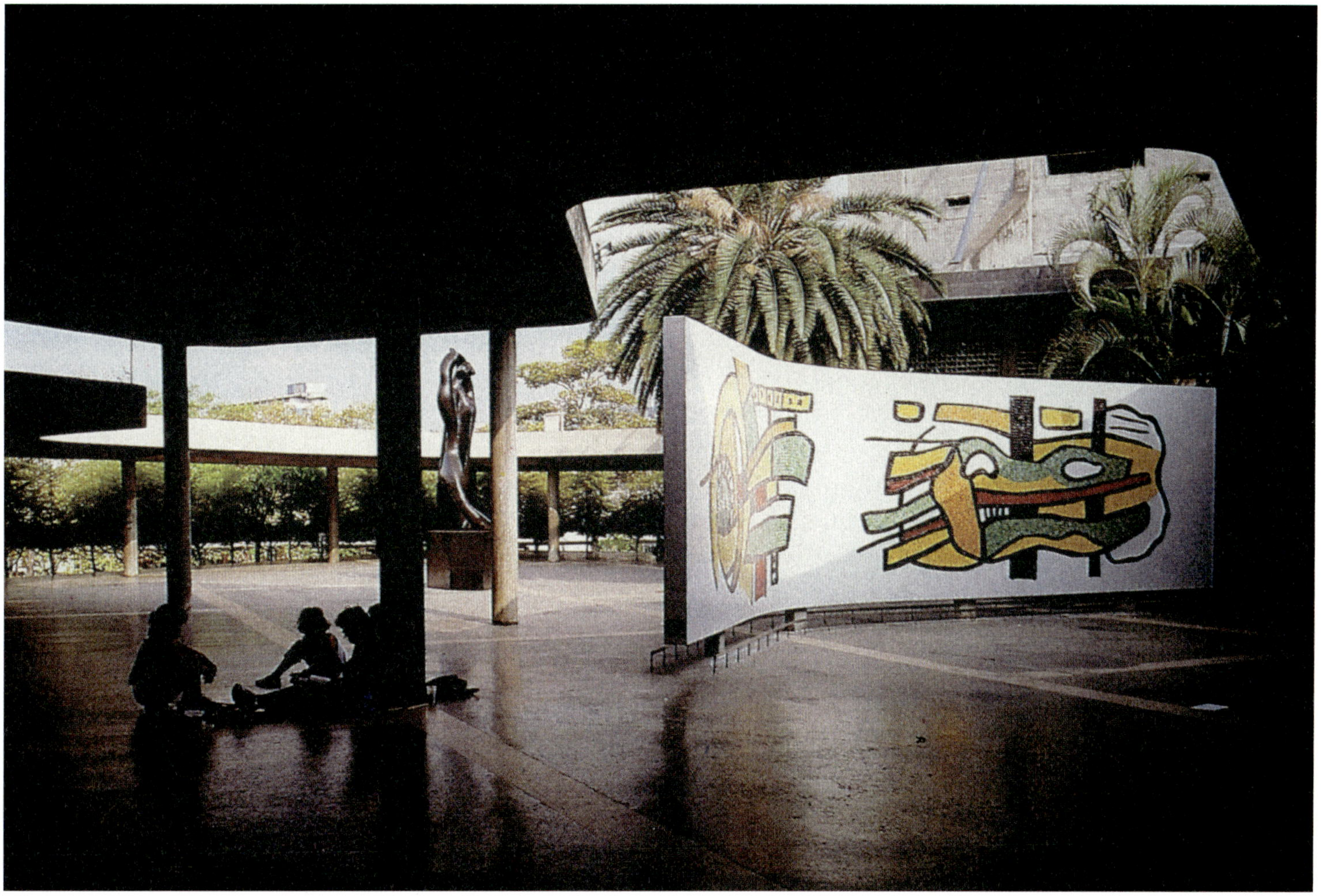

306

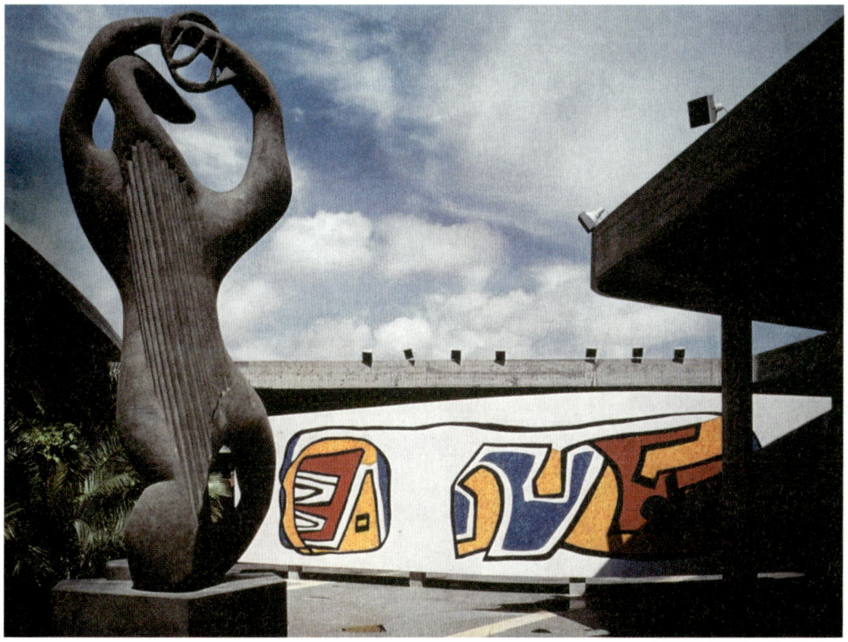

307

305 ***Maquette, projet pour une mosaïque de l'université de Caracas***
(Design for a mosaic for the University of Caracas), 1952
30 × 89.5 cm
Gouache and India ink on paper
Musée national Fernand Léger, Biot

306–307 **Mosaic by Fernand Léger on the campus of the University of Caracas, c. 1954**
Architect: Carlos Raúl Villanueva
Archivo Fundación Villanueva, Caracas

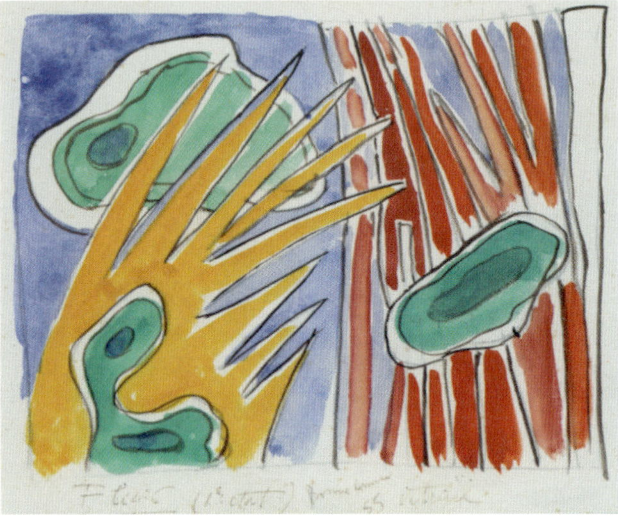

308

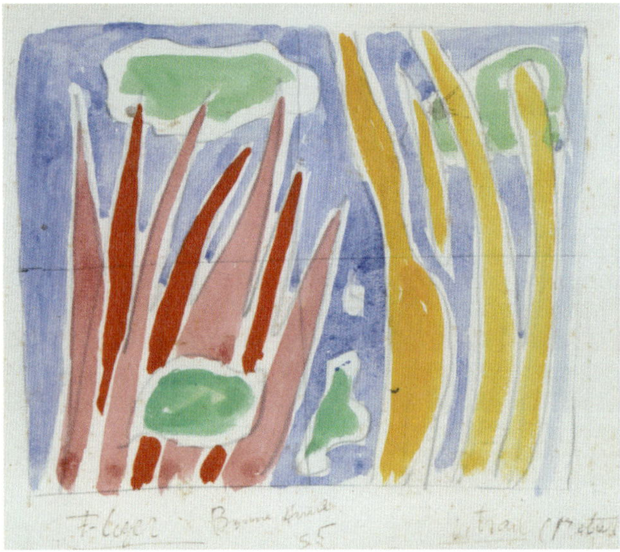

309

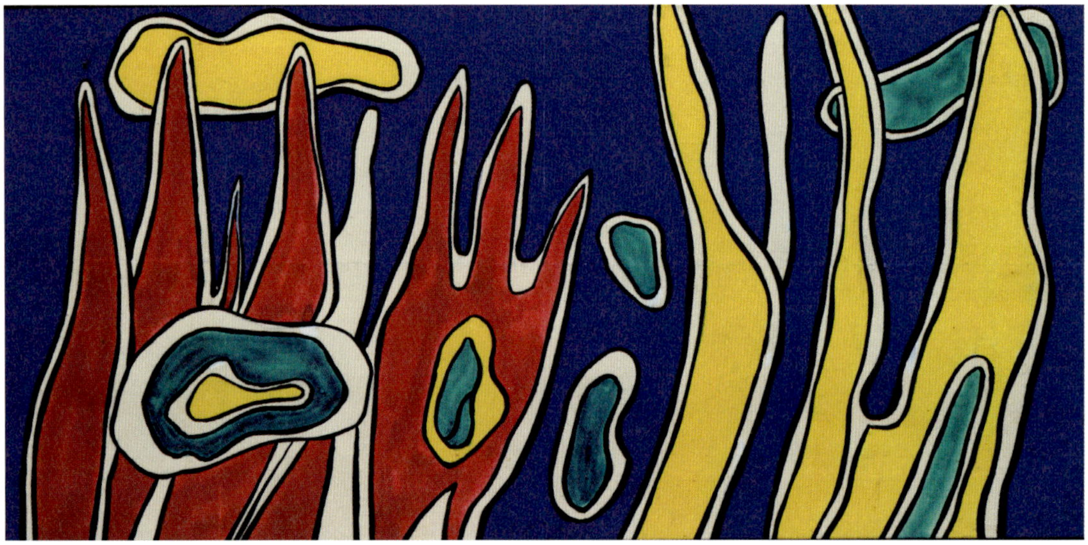

310

308 **Study for the painting of a window at the University of Caracas, 1955**
Gouache on paper
20 × 23.5 cm
Fundación Villanueva, Caracas

309 **Study for the painting of a window at the University of Caracas, 1955**
Gouache on paper
20 × 21.5 cm
Fundación Villanueva, Caracas

310 **Study for the painting of a window at the University of Caracas, 1954**
Gouache on paper
45 × 91 cm
Fundación Villanueva, Caracas

311 **Window design by Fernand Léger in the library at the University of Caracas, c. 1954**
Architect: Carlos Raúl Villanueva
Archivo Fundación Villanueva, Caracas

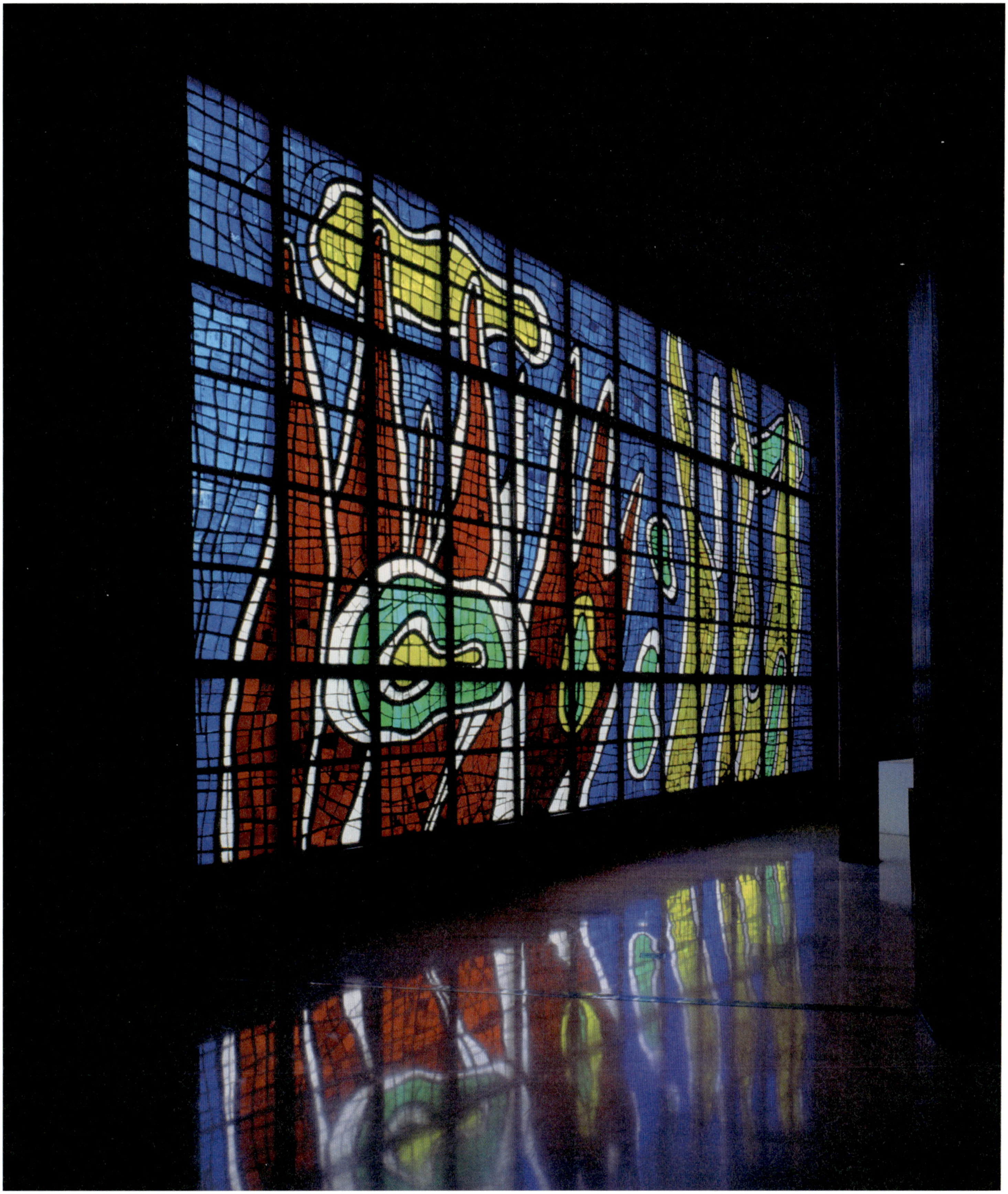

311

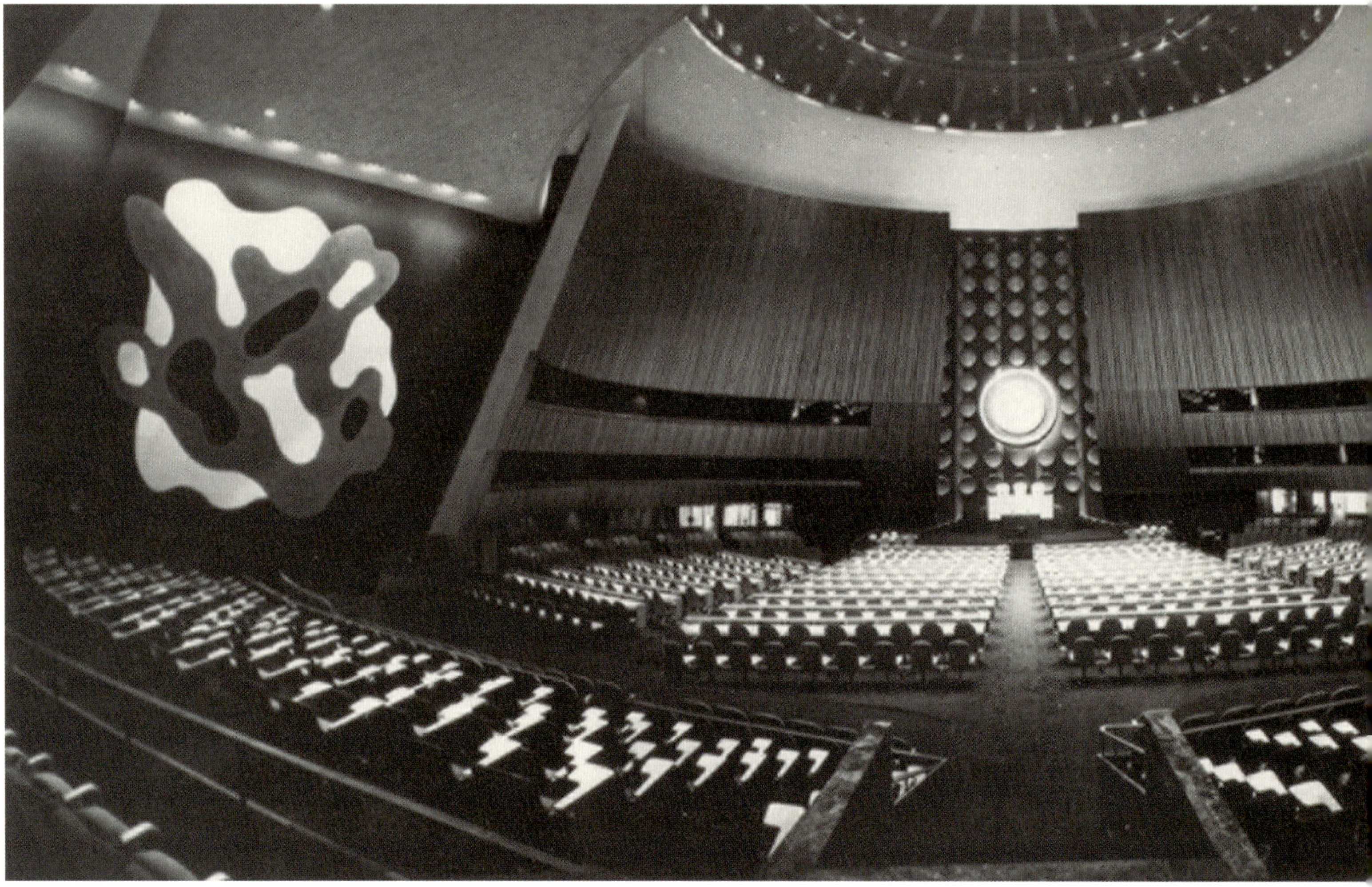

312

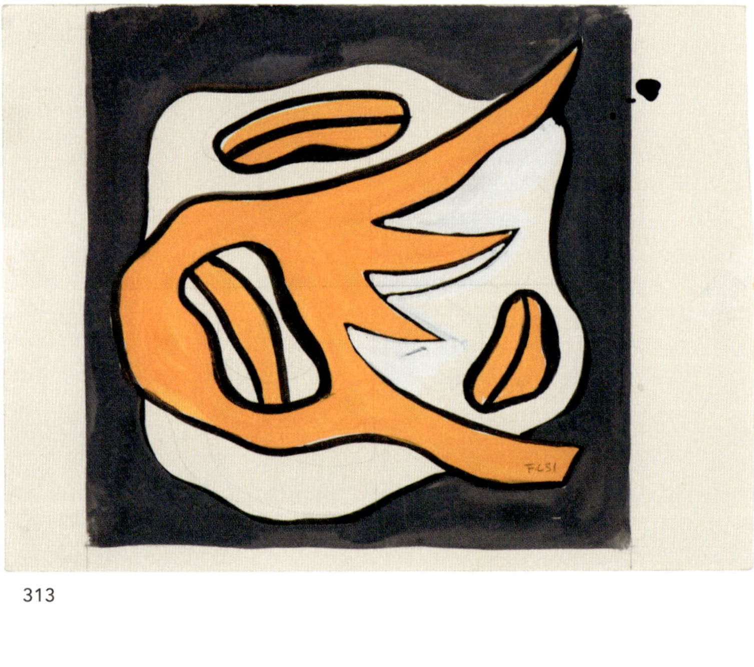

313

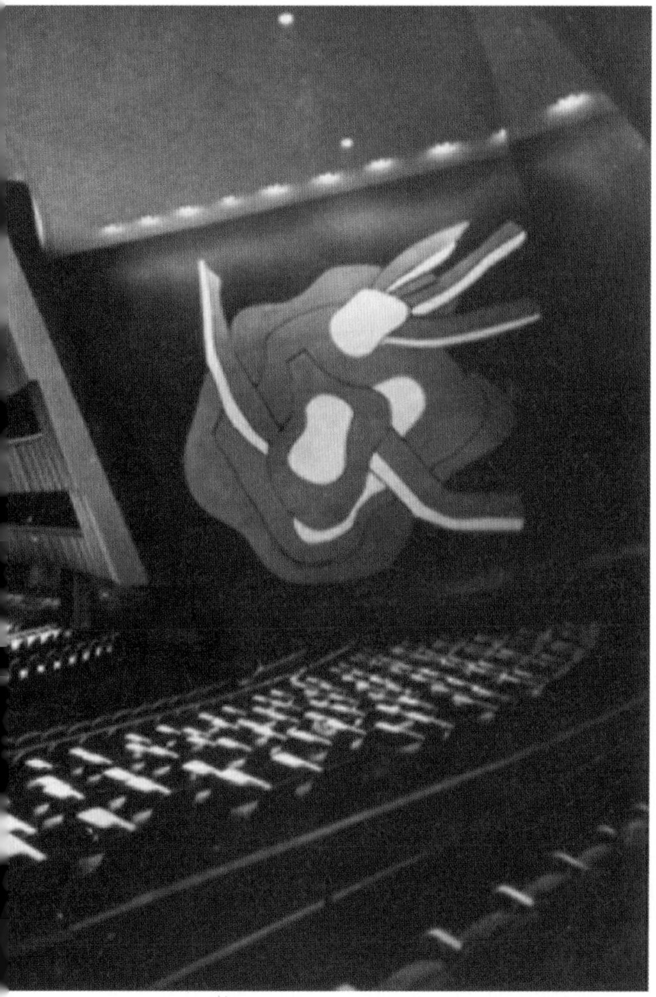

Fernand Léger on the UN murals (1952)

In my opinion, abstract art is perfectly suited for large mural decorations. I have discussed it, for example, as a possibility for the United Nations. Mr. [Wallace] Harrison said to me: "We would like something from you for the UN Building in New York." He came to see me with his model, and we discussed more or less representative pictures. We settled on something abstract, and I did two large panels, about thirty-three feet by thirty-three, for the UN. It is the most recent major thing that I have created; it was something that really had to be done.

Excerpt from F. Léger, "Color in Architecture,". English translation by Alexandra Anderson in Fernand Léger, Functions *of Painting* (New York: Thames and Hudson, 1973), 186. Originally published as F. Léger, "La couleur dans l'architecture," (1954) in ed. Ignace Meyerson, *Problèmes de la couleur, exposés et discussions*, Colloque du Centre de Recherches de psychologie comparative (Paris: S.E.V.P.E.N., 1957), 135–40.

–

312 Bruce Gregory after a design by Fernand Léger
Mural painting on the eastern and western walls of the meeting hall of the General Assembly of the United Nations Headquarters in New York, 1952
Avery Architectural & Fine Arts Library, Columbia University, New York, Wallace K. Harrison architectural drawings and papers, Harrison I, Box 17, Folder 14

313 **Study sketch for the UN Mural Painting, 1951**
Gouache and pencil on cardboard
21 × 27.5 cm
Sprengel Museum, Hannover/Kurt and Ernst Schwitters Stiftung

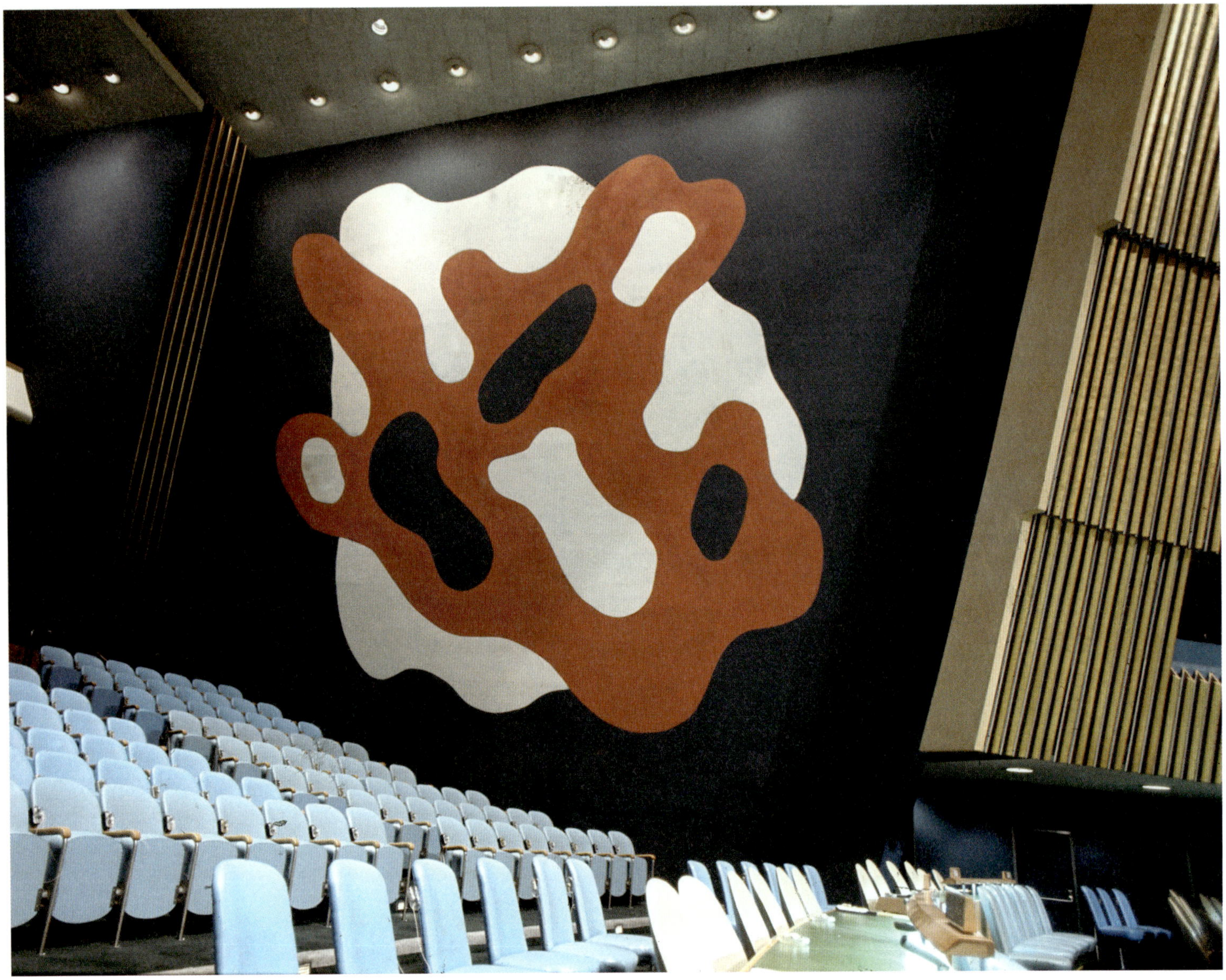

314

314–315 Bruce Gregory after a design by Fernand Léger
Mural painting on the eastern and western walls of the meeting hall of the General Assembly of the United Nations Headquarters in New York, 1952, Photo: 1971

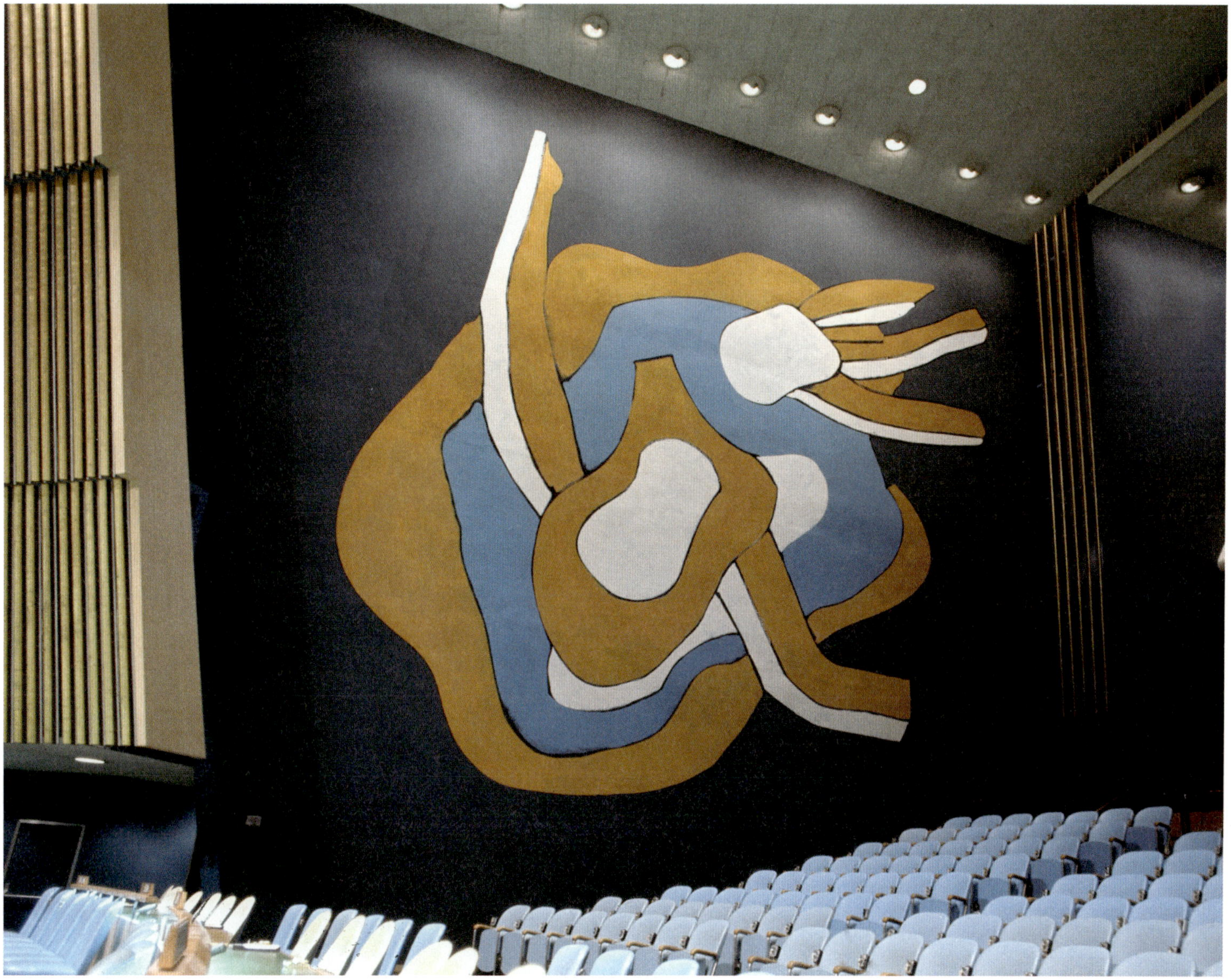

315

Appendix

The Life of Fernand Léger

1881 Joseph Fernand Henri Léger is born in Argentan, Normandy. His father dies in 1884.

1897–99 Apprenticeship with an architect in Caen.

1903–05 Attends the École des Arts Décoratifs and the Académie Julian in Paris. Also works as an architectural draftsman.

1908 Takes a studio at La Ruche, a Parisian building in which Amedeo Modigliani, Henri Laurens, Alexander Archipenko, Jacques Lipchitz, Marc Chagall and Robert Delaunay also have studios. Becomes friends with several writers, including Guillaume Apollinaire, Ilya Ehrenburg and Blaise Cendrars, with whom he will work on several occasions.

1913 Takes part in the *Armory Show* in New York and in the *Erster Deutscher Herbstsalon* in Berlin. Moves to a studio in the Montparnasse neighborhood, which he keeps until his death. Signs a contract with art dealer Daniel-Henry Kahnweiler.

1914–17 Mobilized as a soldier during World War I and fights on the Western Front, including at Verdun. Sees his first Charlie Chaplin film while on leave in Paris.

1919 First solo exhibition in the Galerie de l'Effort Moderne, owned by Léonce Rosenberg, his dealer since 1918. Marries his first wife, Jeanne Lohy.

1920 In Paris, meets Charles-Édouard Jeanneret-Gris, who takes on the pseudonym Le Corbusier, with whom he will develop a lifelong friendship as well as an artistic rivalry. Makes the acquaintance of Theo van Doesburg. Takes part in the *Festival Dada* in Paris.

1922 Premiere of *Skating Rink* and, a few months later, *La Création du monde* with Ballets Suédois in the Théâtre des Champs-Elysées, both with costumes and sets designed by Léger. Designs the engineer's laboratory for Marcel L'Herbier's film *L'Inhumaine* (1924). Influenced by the *Les Architectes du Groupe de Stijl* exhibition at the Galerie de l'Effort Moderne. Inspired by the works of de Stijl artists, he develops his *peintures murales* series (1924–26) of abstract wall murals not intended for specific locations, which he will continue to develop throughout his life.

1924–30 Teaches at the Académie Moderne, located in the same building as his studio, in Rue-Notre-Dame-des-Champs.

1924 Travels through Italy with Léonce Rosenberg. Léger is particularly impressed by the mosaics in Ravenna. Premiere of the film *Ballet mécanique* by Léger and Dudley Murphy.

1925 At the *Exposition internationale des Arts décoratifs et industriels modernes* in Paris, an abstract mural by Léger is included in the entrance hall designed by Mallet-Stevens for the French embassy. Another painting by Léger is showcased in Le Corbusier's Pavillon de l'Esprit Nouveau.

1930 Meets Charlotte Perriand, with whom he develops a lifelong friendship and creative dialogue. Begins a relationship with Simone Herman, a former student.

1931 First US trip to New York and Chicago (September–December).

1932 Resumes teaching at the Académie Moderne, now located in the Académie de la Grande Chaumière.

1933 Retrospective in the Kunsthaus Zürich. Attends and delivers a speech at the CIAM IV (Fourth International Congress for Modern Architecture) in Athens, also attended by Le Corbusier, Charlotte Perriand, Josep Lluís Sert and Alvar Aalto.

1934 His Académie Moderne is renamed Académie d'Art Contemporain. Delivers the lecture *From the Acropolis to the Eiffel Tower* at the Sorbonne. Joins the Union des Artistes Modernes (UAM), which brings together artists, architects and designers.

1935 Creates two murals for the *Maison du jeune homme* by Le Corbusier, Charlotte Perriand, Pierre Jeanneret, Louis Sognot and Réne Herbst at the World's Fair in Brussels. Second trip to America (October 1935–March 1936) on the occasion of his exhibition at the Museum of Modern Art in New York. He most likely meets the architect Wallace K. Harrison through Le Corbusier during this trip. Harrison later becomes Léger's most important patron in the United States and goes on to secure several mural commissions for the artist.

1936 Léger paints a fresco in the inner courtyard of Jean Badovici's home in Vézelay; Le Corbusier makes a fresco for the interior of the house.

1937 Creates five large-scale murals for different pavilions at the World's Fair in Paris, as well as the set design and costumes for Jean-Richard Bloch's *Naissance d'une cité*.

1938 Third trip to America (September 1938–March 1939) thanks to Wallace K. Harrison, in order to paint two murals for Nelson A. Rockefeller's Manhattan apartment. Delivers lectures to Harrison's students at Yale University, which include *Color in the World* and *Architecture and Painting*.

1940–45 Fourth and longest stay in America (November 1940–December 1945), during World War II. Lives in New York and travels to other cities in the US and Canada. Teaches intermittently, most notably at Mills College in Oakland, California, and at Harvard University. Begins the *Plongeurs* series upon his arrival, painting a mural on this theme at Harrison's home on Long Island (1942).

1945 Joins the Communist Party. Returns to France. His art academy is reopened.

1947 Approached by Father Marie-Alain Couturier to design a mosaic for the façade of the Notre-Dame-de-Toute-Grâce church in Assy, Haute-Savoie (consecrated in 1950). Other artists working on designs for the church include Henri Matisse, Georges Rouault, Marc Chagall and Germaine Richier.

1948 Premiere of the ballet *Le Pas d'acier* at the Théâtre des Champs-Elysées in Paris with costumes and a set with reflective metal sculptures by Léger. Takes part in a UNESCO peace congress in Wrocław.

1949 Retrospective at the Musée national d'art moderne in Paris.

1950 First ceramic sculptures and reliefs with his former student Roland Brice; he continues to experiment with the technique until his death. The artist's designs for monumental outdoor sculptures in ceramic are realized posthumously. Designs stained glass windows and a tapestry for the Church of the Sacré-Cœur in Audincourt, organized by Marie-Alain Couturier. Retrospective at the Tate Gallery, London. In December, his wife Jeanne dies.

1951 Designs a large-scale mural for the French section of the IX Triennale in Milan (direction and invitation: Charlotte Perriand). Founding of the Groupe Espace, which advocates a synthesis of the arts; Léger is vice chairman.

1952 Marries Nadia Khodossievitch, an artist who plays a key role in Léger's academy, and moves to Gif-sur-Yvette, near Paris. Designs murals for the General Assembly Hall of the United Nations in New York, which attract international attention and result in many commissions for murals. Attends a peace congress in Vienna.

1953 Creates a mural for the first-class dining room on board the Italian cruise ship *Lucania*. The exhibition *Léger: A Survey of his Art* is shown in Chicago, San Francisco, and New York.

1954 Creates a mosaic and the outer and inner color designs for architect Paul Nelson's Franco-American hospital in Saint-Lô.

1955 Awarded the Grand Prix at the São Paulo Biennial. Léger dies of a heart attack on August 17 in Gif-sur-Yvette.

Brazil

São Paulo

1954
Opera São Paulo
Mural proposal
Architect: Oscar Niemeyer

Venezuela

Caracas

1954
University of Caracas
Library windows design and two exterior mosaic murals
Architect: Carlos Raúl Villanueva

USA

Chicago

1938
Competition for the decoration of the WGN Radio studio-theater
Design proposal with Paul Nelson, architect

New York

1935
Pier of French Line Shipping Company in New York Harbor
Façade mural proposal

1938
International Building, Rockefeller Center, New York City
Proposal for an animated film: *Cinematic Mural*
Architect: Wallace K. Harrison

1938–39
Apartment of Nelson A. Rockefeller, 5th Avenue, New York City
Fireplace mural in the living room and mural for the circular staircase
Architect: Wallace K. Harrison

1939
Hawes House of Nelson A. Rockefeller, Pocantico
Cut-out in the roof
Architect: Wallace K. Harrison

World's Fair, Flushing Meadows, Long Island Consolidated Edision Pavilion
Mural: *City of Light*
Fountain design proposal
Architect: Wallace K. Harrison

1942
Home of Wallace K. Harrison, Huntington, Long Island
Mural *Les Plongeurs* in the living room, floor mural in the swimming pool and interior skylight
Architect: Wallace K. Harrison

1952
United Nations, New York City
Two murals for the General Assembly Hall
Architect: Wallace K. Harrison

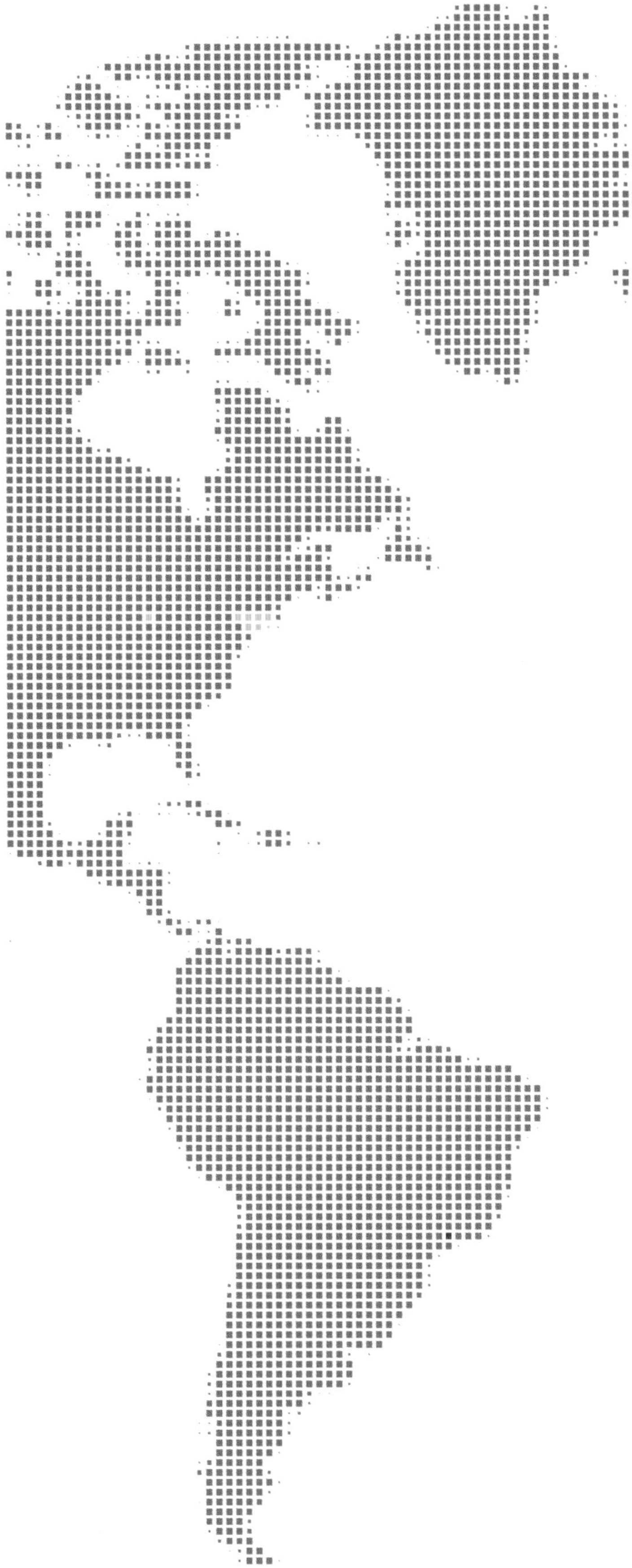

Fernand Léger
Architecture- and Space-related Projects

Lists realized works and non-realized proposals, excluding stage-related projects. Architects are only mentioned if they solicited or collaborated with Léger on the project.

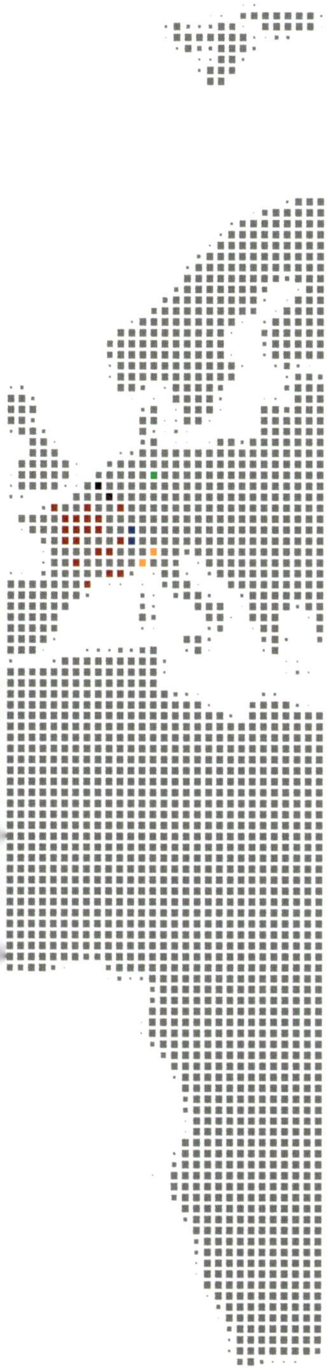

France

Alfortville

1954
Gaz de France
Ceramic mosaic for building façade

Antibes

Circa 1930
Villa of Gerald and Sara Murphy
Screen

Assy

1946
Église Notre-Dame-de-Toute-Grâce
Façade mosaic: *Les Litanies de Vierge*

Audincourt

1951
Église du Sacré-Coeur
Stained glass windows and tapestry

Biot

1952–53
Village Polychrome
Urban design proposal with André Bruyère, architect

1954
Open-air exhibition Groupe Espace: Architecture Formes Couleurs
Free-standing fiber cement mural

Briey

1937
Centre d'Aviation Populaire (Airport)
Mural proposal

Paris

1923
Salon des Indépendants
Design proposal for a hall in the house of Jacques Doucet, with József Csáky, sculptor

1925
Exposition internationale des Arts décoratifs et industriels modernes

Une Ambassade française (Pavillon de la Société des Artistes Décorateurs)
Mural for the entrance hall
Architect: Robert Mallet-Stevens

Pavillon de l'Esprit Nouveau
Two paintings: *Composition*, 1924 replaced with *Le Balustre*, 1924
Architects: Le Corbusier, Pierre Jeanneret

1928
Apartment of Léonce Rosenberg
Four murals: *Les Quatre Saisons*

1937
Exposition internationale des Arts et des Techniques appliqués à la Vie moderne

Palais de la Découverte
Mural: *Le Transport des Forces*

Pavillon UAM (Union des Artistes Modernes)
Mural: *L' Accompagnement d'architecture*

Pavillon des Temps Nouveaux
Photomontage mural: *Travailler*
Architect: Le Corbusier

Pavillon de l'Agriculture
Painted photomontage panels, with Charlotte Perriand, Architect/Designer

Pavillon de la Solidarité
Mural: *Le Syndicalisme ouvrier*
Architect: Robert Mallet-Stevens

Project proposal for lighting the Eiffel Tower

1937
Competition design for the office of Jean Zay, Minister for National Education
Floor designs for Charlotte Perriand's competition design proposal

1948
L'Exposition internationale des femmes, Portes de Versailles
Mural: *Les Femmes au conseil*

1950
Comité national des écrivains, Vélodrome d'Hiver
Large-scale portraits of writers

Saint-Hilaire

1954
House of Daniel-Henry Kahnweiler
Fresco mural in the dining room

Saint-Lô

1954
Centre hospitalier Mémorial France-Etats-Unis (Hospital)
Mosaic for the building façade, interior and exterior color design, monumental outdoor sculpture proposal (*La fleur qui marche*)
Architect: Paul Nelson

Saint-Paul-de-Vence

1952
Hôtel de la Colombe d'Or
Monumental ceramic bas-relief: *La Femme au Perroquet*

Sceaux

1954–55
Badin house
Color design for the windows
Architect: Paul Nelson

Vézelay

1934–36
House of Jean Badovici
Fresco on courtyard wall

Switzerland

Chailly

1930
House of Dr. Franz Reber
Three part mural for the dining room

Courfaivre

1953–54
Saint Germain d'Auxerre
Stained glass windows

Germany

Hanover

1955
Lower Saxony stadium in Hanover
Mural proposal

Belgium

Brussels

1935
L'Exposition universelle (World's Fair)
La Maison du jeune homme
Two murals: *Composition à l'aloës* and *La Salle de culture physique, le sport*
Architects: Charlotte Perriand, Le Corbusier, Pierre Jeanneret, Louis Sognot, René Herbst

Bastogne

1950
Mardasson Memorial
Three mosaics for the American war memorial

Italy

Mailand

1951
French section, IX Triennale di Milano
Large-scale mural
Curator: Charlotte Perriand

1953
***Lucania* cruise ship**
Mural for the first-class dining room
Interior designers: Giancarlo De Carlo, Enzo Mariani

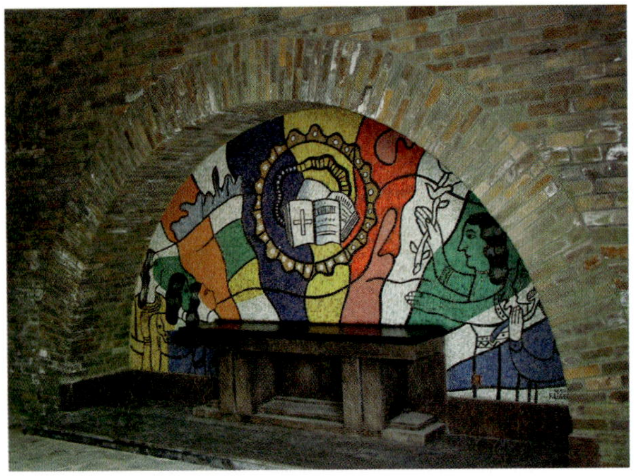

316

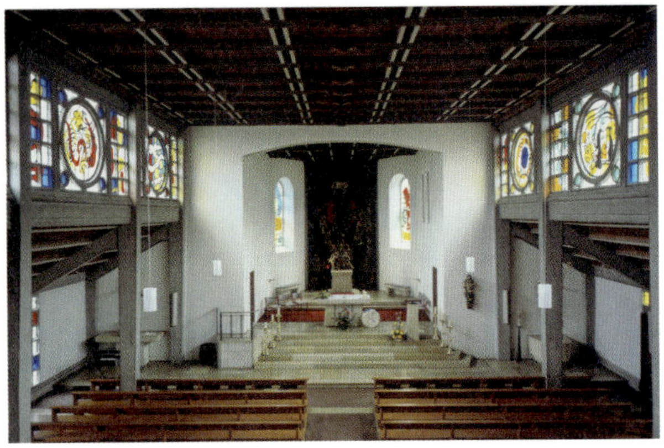

317

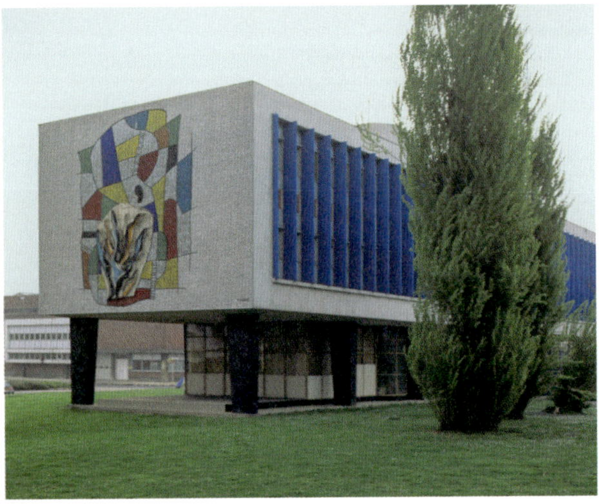

318

316 **One of three mosaics in crypt of Mardasson monument, the American war memorial in Bastogne, Belgium, 1950**

317 **Interior view of the church in Courfaivre, Switzerland, window by Fernand Léger, 1954**

318 **Gaz de France building in Alfortville with mosaic based on a design by Fernand Léger, 1954**

319 ***Décoration pour la salle á manger de la maison de D.H. Kahnweiler á Saint Hilaire* (Decoration for dining room in home of D.H. Kahnweiler at Saint-Hilaire), 1954**
Gouache and pencil on plaster
138 × 260 cm
Centre Pompidou, Musée national d'art moderne, Paris

320 Robert Doisneau
Fernand Léger in his studio in Gif-Sur Yvette, c. 1954

321 **Fernand Léger and his wife Nadia in front of Léger's ceramic wall relief *Femme au Perroquet* (Woman with Parrot) at the Hôtel La Colombe d'Or in Saint-Paul-de-Vence, 1954**

322 ***Sans titre, maquette pour la stade vélodrome de Hanovre* (Untitled, design for the stadium in Hanover), c. 1955**
Gouache on paper
21.3 × 90 cm
Musée national Fernand Léger, Biot

323 Paul Nelson
First sketch for the Musée national Fernand Léger Biot, 1956

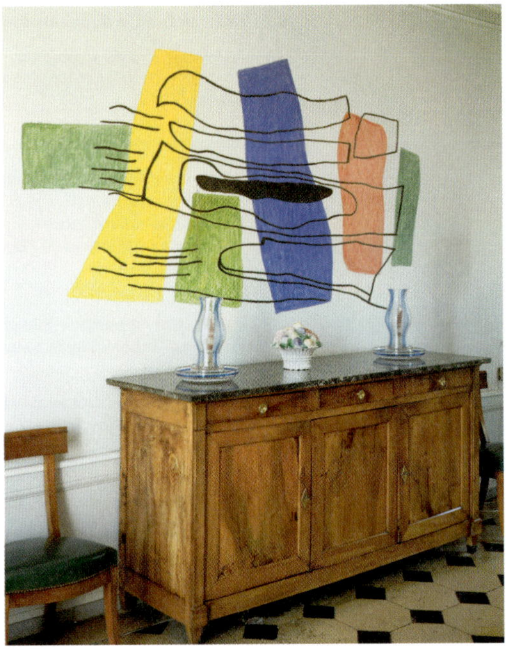

319

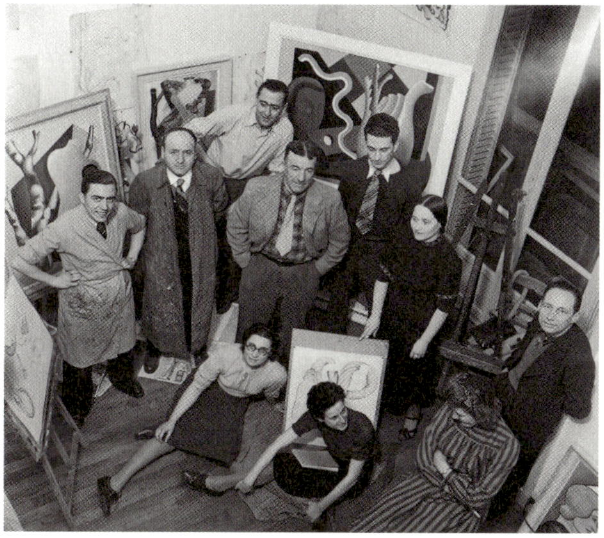
320

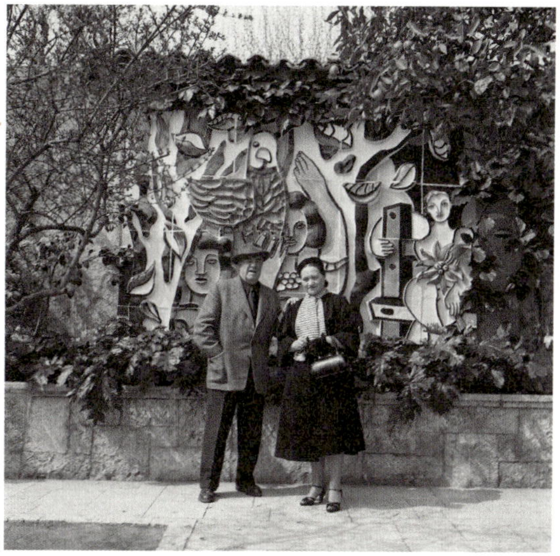
321

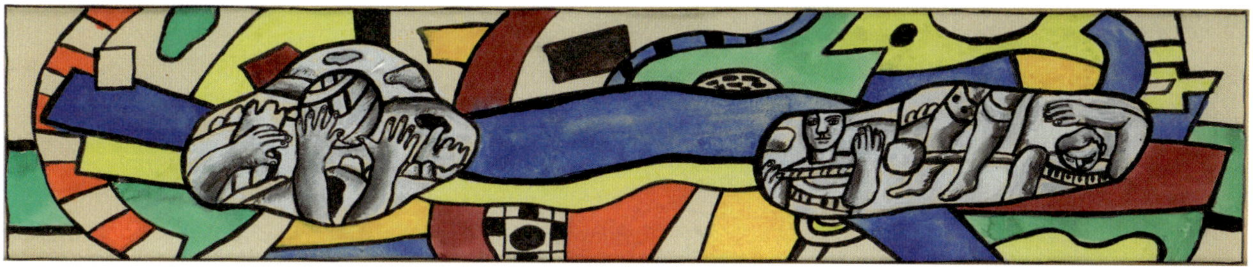
322

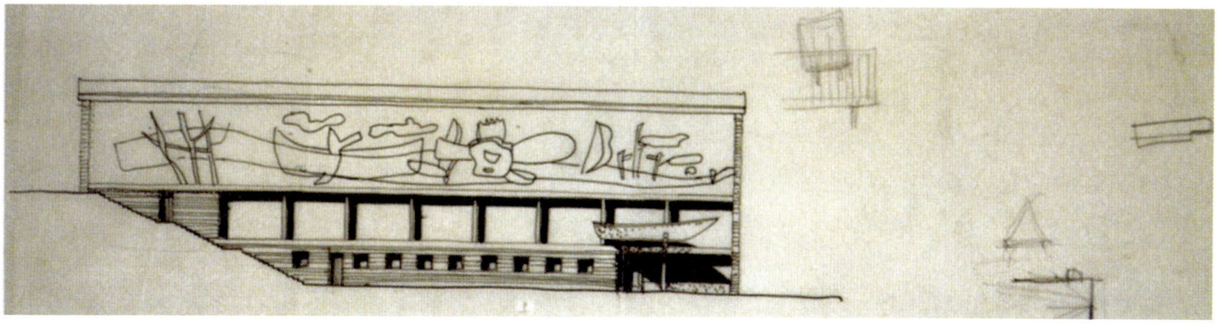
323

Bibliography

The arrows with page numbers refer to texts reproduced in the catalog.

Texts by Fernand Léger (in chronological order)

"Les Origines de la peinture contemporaine et sa valeur representative," lecture, Académie Wassilieff, Paris, 1913, in *Montjoie!* 1.8 (May 29, 1913): 7.

"L'Origine de la peinture actuelle et sa valeur representative," in *Montjoie!* 1.9/10 (June 14–29, 1913): 9–10.

"Les Réalisations pictuales actuelles," lecture, Académie Wassilief, Paris, 1914, in *Les Soirées de Paris* 3.25 (June 15, 1914): 349–56.

"La Couleur dans la vie," in *Promenoir* (1921).

"À propos du Congrès de Paris," in *Comoedia* (February 7, 1922).

"Correspondance" (March 1922), in *Bulletin de l'Effort moderne* 4 (April 1924): 10–12.

"La Roue, sa valeur plastique," in *Comoedia* (December 16, 1922): 5.

"À propos de l'élément mécanique" (1923), first published in F. L., *Fonctions de la Peinture* (Paris, 2004): 81–85. First published 1965.

"L'Esthétique de la machine", lecture, Baraque de la Chimère, Paris, June 1, 1923, published as "The Esthetics of the Machine: Manufactured Objects, Artisan and Artist," in *The Little Review* 9.3 (Spring 1923): 45–49, and in *The Little Review* 9.4 (Autumn/Winter 1923/24): 55–58.

"L'Esthétique de la Machine," in *Les Nouvelles Littéraires* 2.37 (June 30, 1923): 4.

"Notes sur la réglemention de la mise en scène," in *L'Esprit Nouveau* 18 (November 1923).

"Kurzgefasste Auseinandersetzung über das aktuelle künstlerische Sein (Notes sur la vie actuelle)," in *Das Kunstblatt* 7 (1923): 1.

"Au Salon des Indépendants," in *Montparnasse* 9.28 (December 1, 1923).

"Réponse à notre enquête: Où va la peinture moderne?," in *Bulletin de l'Effort moderne* 2 (February 1924): 5.

"L'architecture Polychrome," in *L'Architecture Vivante* 2.4 (Fall/Winter 1924): 21–22. → see 48

"Les Bals populaires," in *La Vie des Lettres et des* Arts 15 (1924): 50–52.

"Le Spectacle: Lumière – Couleur – Image mobile – Objet-Spectacle" (lecture, Sorbonne, Paris, May 1924), in *Bulletin de l'Effort Moderne* 7 (July 1924): 4–7, in 8 (October 1924): 5–9, and in 9 (November 1924): 7–9. → see 32–34

"Chez les cubistes: Notre enquête – I.," in *Le Bulletin de la Vie Artistique* 5.21 (November 1, 1924): 486.

"Vive Relâche," in *L'Action* (December 18, 1924).

"Autour du Ballet mécanique" (n.d.), in F. L., *Fonctions de la peinture* (Paris, 2004): 133–39. First published 1965.

"Mechanical Ballet" (July 1924), in *The Little Review* 10.2 (Fall/Winter 1924/25): 42–44. Also published as "Ballet Mécanique," in *L'Esprit Nouveau* 28 (January 1925): 2336–37.

"L'Affaire de l'exposition des arts décoratifs," in *Les Nouvelles Littéraires* (June 6, 1925). → see 57

"Peinture et Cinéma," in *Les Cahiers du mois* 16.16 (October 1925): 107–08.

"Notations on Plastic Values," in *Fernand Léger*, exhibition catalog, Anderson Galleries, New York, organized by the Société Anonyme (New York, 1925): 10–11.

"A New Realism – The Object (Its Plastic and Cinematographic Value)," trans. by Rosamond Gilder in *The Little Review* (New York) 11.2 (Winter 1926): 7–8.

"Charlie Chaplin," in *Chroniques du jour* 7/8 (1926): 243–44.

"Meine Berliner Ausstellung," in *Der Querschnitt* 8.1 (January 1928): 35–37.

"Notre courier," in *La Presse* (January 29, 1928).

"Voyage d'artiste: Berlin 1928," in *L'Intransigeant* (April 16, 1928).

"Au Salon de l'automobile: Gloire du metal," in *L'Intransigeant* (October 8, 1928).

"La Roue: Objets, Spectacle," in *Vers un Paris nouveau? Cahiers de la République des Lettres, des Sciences et des Arts* 12 (1928): 102–04.

"Pensées sur l'art" (1928), in George Waldemar, *Fernand Léger* (Paris, 1929), 14.

"Actualités," in *Variétés* 1.10 (15 February 1929): 522–25.

"Paris-Objets-Spectacle-Paris" (Response to an article by Jean Cocteau), in *L'Intransigeant* (February 25, 1929) (altered version of "La Roue: Objets, Spectacle").

"Voyage d'artiste: Music-Hall-France-Côte d'Azur," in *L'Intransigeant* (June 10, 1929).

"Si tu n'aimes pas les vacances," in *L'Intransigeant* (October 21, 1929).

"L'École de Paris au Brésil," in *Montparnasse* 58 (January 1930): 1.

"Deus ex machina," in *L'Intransigeant* (January 27, 1930).

"Vouloir construire," in *Cercle et Carré* 1 (March 15, 1930): 139.

"Voyage d'artiste: Sur les routes d'Espagne," in *L'Intransigeant* (November 3, 1930).

"À Propos du cinema," in *Plans. Organe de doctrine et d'action* 1 (January 1931): 80–84.

"New York vu par F. Léger," in *Cahiers d'Art*, 6.9/10 (1931): 437–39. → see 194–95

"Notre Paysage," in *L'Intransigeant* (May 18, 1931).

"Erik Satie illustré par Calder. Pourquoi pas?," in *Alexander Calder Volumes – Vecteurs – Densités/Dessins – Portraits*, exhibition catalog, Galerie Percier (Paris, 1931).

"De l'art abstrait (II): Réponse de Fernand Léger," in *Cahiers d'Art* 6.3 (1931): 151–52.

"Voyage d'artiste: Wall Street," in *L'Intransigeant* (December 28, 1931).

"Introduction," in *Paris: 80 Photographies de Moï Ver* (Paris, 1931).

"Chicago," in *Plans* 2.11 (January 1932): 68. Excerpts also published as "Voyage d'artiste: Vingt-quatre heures ou la vie d'un journal à Chicago," in *L'Intransigeant* (January 4, 1932): 5.

"Concours chorégraphique international au théâtre des Champs-Élysées," in *Cahiers d'Art* 7.6/7 (July 1932): 288.

"L'Amérique et le chiffre 3" (1932), in *Orbes* 2.1 (Spring 1933): 30–34.

"De la peinture dansée à la danse sans peinture, spectacle sans décors," in *L'Intransigeant* (July 11, 1932): 7.

"Introduction," in *12 Paintings by Elisabeth Blair*, exhibition catalog, John Becker Gallery, Inc. (New York, 1933).

"Fernand Léger precise," in *Beaux-Arts* 18 (May 5, 1933).

"Voyage d'artiste: Au pays de Jean-Jacques," in *L'Intransigeant* (May 15, 1933).

"Art est entré en cambrioleur," in *Mouvement* 1 (June 1933).

"Discours aux architectes" (lecture, Congrès International d'Architecture Moderne, August 1933), in *Quadrante* 11.5 (September 1933): 44-47. Also in *Annales Techniques* (1933): 1159-62 (republished with textual alterations as "Mauern, Architekten und Maler" in F. L., *Mensch, Maschine, Malerei* (Bern, 1971), 132-44). → see 107-10

"Avènement de l'objet," in *Le Mois* 41 (June 1934): 217-24.

"Le Beau et le vrai" (excerpt from the lecture "De L'Acropole à la Tour Eiffel," Sorbonne, Paris, February 8, 1934), in *Beaux-Arts* 73.58 (February 9, 1934): 2.

"Mystique de l'objet," in *Beaux-Arts* 81 (July 20, 1934).

"Stockholm," trans. by Otto Carlsund in *Svenska Dagbladet* (September 30, 1934).

"Où va la peinture? (Conversations recueillies par Jean Cassou, René Crevel, Aragon, Champfleury, etc.)," in *Commune* 2.21 (May 1935): 944-46.

"L'Invasion polychrome," in *La Bête noire* 3 (June 1, 1935).

"Londres," in *La Nouvelle Revue Française* 258 (June 1935) and 264 (September 1935).

"Enquête," in *Cahiers d'Art* 10.1-4 (1935): 66-67 (Léger's response is outlined by Christian Zervos).

"La Couleur et le sentiment," in *Pour Vous* 358 (September 26, 1935): 2.

"The New Realism", lecture, The Museum of Modern Art, New York, October 4, 1935, trans. by Harold Rosenberg, excerpts in *Art Front* 2.8 (December 1935): 10. → see 120, 196

"Réponse à une enquête: que feriez-vous si vous aviez à organiser l'Exposition de 1937?," in *VU. L'illustré français* 387 (1935): 1102. → see 138

"Propos sur la couleur dans la vie moderne et au cinéma, sur l'art et la mesure," in *Pour Vous* (1935).

"Le Nouveau Réalisme continue" (from a debate between Fernand Léger, Louis Aragon and Le Corbusier, Maison de la Culture, Paris, May 1936), in Jean Lurçat, et al., *La Querelle du Réalisme* (Paris, 1936), 73-79. Also as "Painting and Reality: a discussion," trans. by Maria Jolas in *Transition* 25 (Autumn 1936): 104-08.

"Apropos of colour," trans. by James Johnson Sweeney in *Transition* 26 (New York, 1937): 81.

"L'Art mural de Victor Servranckx," in *Clarté* 10.7 (July 1937): 20.

"Sur la peinture," in *L'Exposition 1937 et les artistes à Paris* (Paris, 1937).

"Revival of Mural Art," trans. by Douglas Lord in *The Listener* 18, no. 450 (August 25, 1937): 408-09.

"Jean-Marc Champagne, La Vie des arts: Avec Fernand Léger," in *Marianne. Grand hebdomadaire littéraire illustré* (October 13, 1937): 8.

"Exposition 1937 by Fernand Léger," in *Verve: revue artistique et littéraire*, 1 (1937): 106.

"Beauty in Machine Art," in *Design* 39.9 (March 1938): 6-7.

"Préface," in *Fernand Léger*, exhibition catalog, Palais des Beaux-Arts (Brussels, 1938).

"Couleur dans le monde" (based on a lecture in Antwerp, November 1937), in *Europe* 47.4-7 (May 1938): 99-113. Also in *Peintres et sculpteurs de la Maison de la Culture* 5 (May 1938), in F. L., *Fonctions de la peinture* (Paris, 2004), 205-25. First published 1965.

"The Question of Truth," in *Architectural Forum* 70.2 (February 1939): 137.

"Choses d'Amérique," in *La Nouvelle Revue Française* 27.308 (May 1, 1939): 902-03. → see 194

"Enquête (L'Acte créateur se ressent-il de l'influence des événements environnants...)," in *Cahiers d'Art* 14.1-4 (1939): 70-72.

"New York-Paris, Paris-New York," in *La Voix de France* (November 1, 1941).

"Découvrir l'Amérique," in *La Voix de France* (May 15, 1942).

Sert, José-Luis, Fernand Léger, and Sigfried Giedion, *Nine points on Monumentality* (1943), in S. Giedion, *Architecture, You and Me: The Diary of a Development* (Cambridge, MA, 1958), 48-51. → see 258-59

"Byzantine Mosaics and Modern Art," in *Magazine of Art* 37.4 (April 1944): 144.

"À propos du corps humaine considéré comme un objet," in Marie-Alain Couturier, et al., *Fernand Léger, la forme humaine dans l'espace* (Montreal, 1945), 63-75. → see 217

"Modern Architecture and Color," in *American Abstract Artists* (New York, 1946), 207-14. Also as "L'architecture moderne et la couleur, ou la creation d'un nouvel espace vital" (1946) in F. L., *Fonctions de la Peinture* (Paris, 2004), 239-45 (with textual alterations). → see 74-75

"Color in Architecture," in Stamos Papadaki, ed., *Le Corbusier: Architect, Painter, Writer* (New York, 1948), 78-80. → see 90-91

"L'Art abstrait," in *Derrière le miroir* 20.21 (May 1949).

"Un nouvel espace en architecture," in *Art d'aujourd'hui* 3 (October 1949): 19. Also in F. L., *Fonctions de la peinture* (Paris, 2004), 257-61. First published 1965.

"Peinture murale et peinture de chevalet" (1950), in F. L., *Fonctions de la peinture* (Paris, 2004), 277-83. First published 1965.

"Calder," in *Calder Mobiles and Stabiles*, exhibition catalog, Galerie Maeght Paris (Paris, 1950).

"Notes de Fernand Léger sur Bolivar," in *Arts* 260 (April 28, 1950): 7.

"Situation de la peinture dans le temps actuel 1951," in *La Biennale de Venezia* 5 (August 1951): 19.

"Témoignages: Fernand Léger," in *XXe Siècle, Nouvelle Série Nr. 2, Nouvelles Conceptions de l'Espace* (January 1952): 67-68.

"La peinture moderne devant le monde actuel", lecture, Maison de la Pensée française, Paris, March 1952, in *Les Lettres Françaises* 405 (March 1952).

"Une Ère nouvelle s'ouvrira pour la peinture lorsque le choix aura été fait entre le figuratif et l'abstrait," in *Arts* 401 (March 6-10, 1953): 7.

"Vers l'architecture," in *Fernand Léger*, exhibition catalog, Galerie Louis Carré (Paris, 1953).

"La couleur dans l'architecture" (1954), in Ignace Meyerson, ed., *Problèmes de la couleur, exposés et discussions du Colloque du Centre de Recherches de psychologie comparative* (Paris, 1957), 135-40. → see 279

"L'Adieu de ses amis, les artistes," in *Hommage au Père Couturier* (special issue of *L'Art Sacré*) 7.8 (March/April 1954): 6.

"La Marche vers le mur," in *Les Lettres Françaises* 582 (August 1955).

"De la peinture murale" (1952), in *Derrière le miroir*, 107-09 (1958).

Collections of writings with texts by Fernand Léger

Léger, Fernand, *Fonctions de la peinture* (Paris, 1965), extended version with notes by Sylvie Forestier (Paris, 2004).

Léger, Fernand, *Mensch, Maschine, Malerei*, trans. and ed. by Robert Füglister (Bern, 1971).

Léger, Fernand, *Functions of Painting*, ed. Edward F. Fry, trans. by Alexandra Anderson, (London and New York, 1973). → see 32-34, 74-75, 120, 194-95, 196, 279

Fernand Léger, 1881-1955, exhibition catalog, Staatliche Kunsthalle Berlin (Berlin, 1980).

Derouet, Christian, ed., Fernand Léger, *Lettres à Simone* (Geneva and Paris: Skira, 1987). → see 194

Derouet, Christian, ed., *Une correspondance d'affaires, Fernand Leger-Léonce Rosenberg 1917-1937*, les cahiers du Musée national d'art modern, Hors-série Archives (Paris, 1996).

Léger, Fernand, *Mes Voyages* (Paris, 1960, reprinted 1997).

Derouet, Christian, ed., *Une correspondance poste restante, Fernand Léger, lettres à Simone, 1931-1941* (Paris, 1997) (Les cahiers du Musée national d'art moderne. Hors-série Archives).

Selected publications on Fernand Léger (in chronological order)

Couturier, Marie-Alain, et al., *Fernand Léger, la forme humaine dans l'espace* (Montreal, 1945). → see 226, 240-41

Cooper, Douglas, *Fernand Léger et le nouvel espace* (Geneva, 1949).

Kuh, Katharine, *Fernand Léger* (Chicago, 1953).

Jardot, Maurice, *Léger* (Paris, 1956).

Mathey, François, *Fernand Léger*, exhibition catalog, Musée des Arts décoratifs (Paris, 1956).

Verdet, André, *Fernand Léger. Bekenntnisse und Gespräche mit André Verdet. Mit Zeichnungen und Photos* (Zurich, 1957).

Vallier, Dora, *Kunst und Zeugnis: Gespräche mit Georges Braque, Joan Miró, Fernand Léger, Brancusi, Jacques Villon. Mit Photos und Zeichnungen* (Zurich, 1961). → see 218, 220

Garaudy, Roger, *Pour un Réalisme du XXe siècle, dialogue posthume avec Fernand Léger* (Paris, 1968).

Léger and Purist Paris, exhibition catalog, The Tate Gallery (London, 1970).

Richet, Michele, ed., *Fernand Léger*, exhibition catalog, Grand Palais (Paris, 1971).

Le Noci, Guido, ed., *Fernand Léger: Sa vie, son œuvre, son rêve* (Milan, 1971).

Cassous Jean, and Jean Leymarie, *Fernand Léger. Das grafische Werk* (Tübingen, 1973).

Green, Christopher, *Leger and the Avant-Garde* (New Haven and London, 1976).

Saphire, Lawrence, *Fernand Léger: The Complete Graphic Work* (New York, 1978).

McQuillan, Melissa Ann, "Painters and the Ballet, 1917–1926: An Aspect of the Relationship between Art and Theatre," PhD diss., New York University, 1979.

Krueger Meyer, Ruth Ann, *Fernand Léger's Mural Paintings 1922–55*, PhD diss., University of Minnesota, 1980.

Derouet, Christian, ed., *Fernand Léger et la poésie de l'objet, 1928–1934*, exhibition catalog, Musée national d'art moderne, Centre Pompidou (Paris, 1981).

F. Léger. 1881–1981, exhibition catalog, Galerie Beyeler Basel (Basel, 1981).

Contensou, Bernadette, ed.,*Léger et l'esprit moderne. Une alternative d'avant-garde à l'art non-objectif (1918–1931)*, exhibition catalog, Musée d'Art Moderne Paris / Museum of Fine Arts, Houston / Musée Rath, Geneva 1982/83 (Paris, 1982).

Francia, Peter, *Fernand Léger* (New Haven and London, 1983).

Bauquier, Georges, *Fernand Léger, Vivre dans le vrai* (Paris, 1987). → see 239, 249

Serota, Nicholas, ed., *Fernand Léger: The Later Years*, exhibition catalog, Whitechapel Art Gallery, London / Staatsgalerie Stuttgart (Munich, 1987).

Fernand Léger, exhibition catalog, Kunsthalle der Hypo-Kulturstiftung München (Munich, 1988).

Bauquier, Georges, Irus Hansma, Nelly Maillard, and Claude Lefebvre du Preÿ, eds, *Fernand Léger: Catalogue Raisonné de Œuvre Peint*, vols 1–10 (Paris, 1990–2013).

Fernand Léger, exhibition catalog, Musée d'Art Moderne de Villeneuve d'Ascq 1990 (Milan, 1990).

Affron, Matthew, "Fernand Léger and the Spectacle of Objects," PhD diss., Yale University, 1994.

Kosinski, Dorothy M., *Fernand Léger. Der Rhythmus des modernen Lebens*, exhibition catalog, Kunstmuseum Wolfsburg / Kunstmuseum Basel (Munich and New York, 1994).

Fernand Léger et l'architecture: l'hymne à la ville, exhibition catalog, Musée d'Art et d'Histoire de Belfort (Belfort, 1995).

Samson-Hédel, Brigitte, ed., *Fernand Léger et le spectacle*, exhibition catalog, Musée national Fernand Léger, Biot (Paris, 1995).

Derouet, Christian, ed., *Fernand Léger*, exhibition catalog, Musée national d'art moderne, Centre Pompidou (Paris, 1997).

Frankel, David, ed., *Fernand Léger*, exhibition catalog, Museum of Modern Art New York (New York, 1998).

Fernand Léger: la céramique, exhibition catalog, Musée national Fernand Léger, Biot (Paris, 2000).

Verdet, André, *Entretiens notes et écrits sur la peinture. Braque, Léger, Matisse, Picasso, Chagall* (Nantes, 2000).

Maillard, Nelly, ed., *Fernand Léger et les Arts décoratifs*, exhibition catalog, Musée national Fernand Léger Biot / Musée départemental de la tapisserie Aubusson (Biot, 2002).

Fage, Gilles, *Fernand Léger*, exhibition catalog, Musée des Beaux-Arts Lyon (Lyon, 2004).

Brunhammer, Yvonne, *Léger. The Monumental Art* (Milan, 2005).

Max Beckmann – Fernand Léger – Unerwartete Begegnungen, exhibition catalog, Museum Ludwig Köln (Cologne, 2005).

Derouet, Christian, "La première peinture murale de Fernand Léger (Vézelay, 1936)," in *Les Cahiers du Musée national d'art moderne* 95 (Spring 2006): 63–77.

Beyeler Museum AG, Delia Ciuha, and Raphaël Bouvier, eds, *Fernand Léger: Paris–New York*, exhibition catalog, Fondation Beyeler Riehen (Ostfildern, 2008).

Teixeira de Barros, Regina, and Brigitte Hedel-Samson, *Fernand Léger: relações e amizades brasileiras*, exhibition catalog, Pinacoteca do Estado de São Paulo (São Paulo, 2009).

Bovet, Henri, *Disques et sémaphores. Le langage du signal chez Léger et ses contemporains*, exhibition catalog, Musée national Fernand Léger, Biot (Paris, 2010).

Vallye, Anna, *Léger: Modern Art and the Metropolis*, exhibition catalog, Philadelphia Museum of Art (New Haven and London, 2013).

André Bruyère (selection)

Bruyère, André, *Pourquoi des architectes?* (Paris, 1968). → see 257

Chaslin, François, *Andre Bruyère. La Tendresse des Murs* (Paris, 2016).

Le Corbusier (selection)

Le Corbusier, and Amadée Ozenfant, *Après le cubisme* (Paris, 1918).

Le Corbusier, "L'architecture au Salon d'automne," in *L'Esprit Nouveau* 19 (December 1923).

Le Corbusier, "Notes à la suite," in *Cahiers d'art* 3 (1926): 46–52.

Le Corbusier, "L'architecture et Fernand Léger," in *Sélection: Chronique de la vie artistique* 5 (1929): 21–24.

Boesinger, Willy, Max Bill, and Oscar Stonorov, eds, *Le Corbusier et Pierre Jeanneret, œuvre complète 1910–1965*, 8 vols (Erlenbach/Zurich, 1948–70).

Moos, Stanislaus von, and Le Corbusier, *Elemente einer Synthese* (Frauenfeld, 1968).

Le Corbusier "A propos des peintures murales à l'exposition de 1937," printed in *1937. Exposition internationale des arts et des techniques*, exhibition catalog, Musée national d'art modern, Centre Pompidou (Paris, 1979). → see 138–39

L'Esprit Nouveau: Le Corbusier und die Industrie, 1920–1925, exhibition catalog, Museum für Gestaltung Zürich / Bauhaus Archiv Berlin (Berlin, 1987).

Cohen, Jean-Louis, *Le Corbusier and the Mystique of the USSR: theories and projects for Moscow, 1928–1936* (Princeton, 1992).

Udovički-Selb, Danilo, "Le Corbusier and the Paris Exhibition of 1937: The Temps Nouveaux Pavilion," in *Journal of the Society of Architectural Historians* 56.1 (March 1997): 42–63.

Vegesack, Alexander von, ed., *Le Corbusier: The Art of Architecture*, exhibition catalog, Nederlands Architectuurinstituut Rotterdam / Vitra Design Museum Weil am Rhein / The Crypt, Metropolitan Cathedral of Christ the King, Liverpool / Barbican Art Gallery London (Weil am Rhein, 2007).

Heer, Jan de, *The Architectonic Colour: Polychromy in the Purist Architecture of Le Corbusier* (Rotterdam, 2009).

Rüegg, Arthur, and Fondation Le Corbusier Paris, eds, *Arthur Rüegg, Le Corbusier. Möbel und Interieurs 1905–1965* (Zurich, 2012).

Hall, Emily, ed., *Le Corbusier – an atlas of modern landscapes*, exhibition catalog, Museum of Modern Art New York / Caixa Forum Barcelona / Caixa Forum Madrid 2013/14 (London, 2013).

Derouet, Christian, *Le Corbusier à Vézelay*, exhibition catalog, Musée Zervos Vézelay (Vézelay, 2015).

Migayrou, Frédéric, and Olivier Cinqualbre, eds, *Le Corbusier, mesures de l'homme*, exhibition catalog, Musée national d'art modern, Centre Pompidou (Paris, 2015).

Wallace K. Harrison (selection)

Thank You, Wallace K. Harrison, exhibition catalog, Hood Museum of Art, Dartmouth College (Hanover, 1985).

Newhouse, Victoria, *Wallace K. Harrison, architect* (New York, 1989).

Robert Mallet-Stevens (selection)

Mallet-Stevens, Robert, "Les décors au cinéma," in *La Gazette des sept arts* 2 (January 25, 1923): 12.

Mallet-Stevens, Robert, "Architecture moderne," in *L'Architecture d'aujourd'hui* 8 (1932): 2.

Deshoulières, Dominique, and Hubert Jeanneau, eds, *Robert Mallet-Stevens: Architecte* (Brussels, 1980).

Pinchon, Jean-Francois, *Robert Mallet-Stevens: Architecture, mobilier, décoration* (Paris, 1986).

Penz, François, ed., *Cinema & Architecture: Méliès, Mallet-Stevens, Multimedia* (London, 1997).

Cinqualbre, Olivier, and Aurélien Lemonier, eds, *Robert Mallet-Stevens: l'œuvre complète* (Paris, 2005) (published to mark the occasion of the exhibition *Mallet-Stevens, Architecte (1886–1945)*).

Klein, Richard, *Robert Mallet-Stevens: agir pour l'architecture moderne* (Paris, 2014).

Paul Nelson (selection)

Nelson, Paul, *Architecture hospitalière. Deux études de Paul Nelson. Maison de santé et pavillon de chirurgie* (Paris, 1936).

Nelson, Paul, "Peinture spatiale et architecturale, à propos des dernières œuvres de Léger," in *Cahiers d'Art* 1–3 (1937): 85–88. → see 176–77

Nelson, Paul, *La Maison suspendue: Recherche de Paul Nelson* (Paris, 1939).

Bordier, Roger, "Polychromie architecturale," in *Aujourd'hui, Art et Architecture* 2 (March/April 1955).

Nelson, Paul, *La polychromie à l'Hôpital Mémorial France-Etats Unis de Saint-Lô, Mitteilung im Seminar über Kinder-krankenhäuser*, photocopied text dated June 7, 1956.

Nelson, Paul, "From an Integrated Approach to Design: a 'Hospital for Life'," in *Journal of the American Heart Association* 33 (June 1959): 34–36.

Riley, Terence, and Joseph Abram, *The Filter of Reason: Work of Paul Nelson*, exhibition catalog, Ross Architectural Gallery Buell Hall (New York, 1990).

Robert, Jean-Paul, "La maison suspendue," in *L'architecture d'aujourd'hui* 316 (April 1998): 37–70.

Cinqualbre, Olivier, and Paul Nelson, "'Faire vivre l'espace': chronique d'une recherche partagée," in *Les Cahiers du Musée national d'art moderne* 95 (Spring 2006): 78–89.

Un architecte, des artistes, Paul Nelson, Léger, Calder, Brassaï, Hélion, Braque, Miró, exhibition catalog, Musée des Beaux-Arts Gaillac / Musée des Beaux-Arts de Saint-Lô (Saint-Lô, 2007).

Severo, Donato, *Paul Nelson, Edition du Patrimoine*, Centre des Monuments Historiques (Paris, 2013).

Severo, Donato, *Paul Nelson et l'Hôpital de Saint-Lô: Humanisme, art et architecture* (Paris, 2015).

Charlotte Perriand (selection)

Perriand, Charlotte, "L'habitation familiale, son développement économique et social," in *L'Architecture d'aujourd'hui* (January 1935).

Charlotte Perriand – Un art de vivre, exhibition catalog, Musée des arts décoratifs (Paris, 1985).

Hédel-Samson, Brigitte, ed., *Charlotte Perriand, Fernand Léger, Une connivence*, exhibition catalog, Musée national Fernand Léger, Biot (Paris, 1999).

Perriand, Charlotte, *Une vie de création* (Paris, 1998); English edition: *A Life of Creation* (New York, 2003).
→ see 131, 154, 270, 272

Barsac, Jacques, *Charlotte Perriand, un art d'habiter 1903–1959* (Paris, 2005).

Jousset, Marie-Laure, *Charlotte Perriand*, exhibition catalog, Musée national d'art moderne, Centre Pompidou (Paris, 2005).

Charlotte Perriand and photography: a wide-angle eye, exhibition catalog, Museum für Gestaltung Zürich / Musée du Petit Palais Paris / Musée Nicéphore Niépce Chalon-sur-Saône (Milan, 2011).

Barsac, Jacques, *Charlotte Perriand, Complete Works*, vol. 1, 1903–1940 (Zurich, 2014).

Barsac, Jacques, *Charlotte Perriand, Complete Works*, vol. 2, 1940–1955 (Zurich, 2015).

Barsac, Jacques, *Charlotte Perriand, Complete Works*, vol. 3, 1966–1999 (Zurich, forthcoming).

Carlos Raúl Villanueva (selection)

Moholy-Nagy, Sibyl, *Carlos Raúl Villanueva und die Architektur Venezuelas* (Stuttgart, 1964).

Villanueva, Paulina, and Maciá Pintó, *Carlos Raúl Villanueva* (Basel, 2000).

Secondary literature

Guéguen, Pierre, "Une démonstration du groupe Espace: l'exposition Architecture Formes Couleur à Biot (Côte d'Azur)," in *Art d'aujourd'hui* 6 (September 1954).

Rubin, William, *Modern Sacred Art and the Church of Assy* (New York,1961).

Robbins, Daniel, "From Symbolism to Cubism: the Abbaye of Créteil," in *Art Journal* 23.2 (Winter 1963/64): 11–16.

Cinquantenaire de l'exposition de 1925, exhibition catalog, Musée des arts décoratifs (Paris, 1976).

1937. Exposition international des arts et des techniques, exhibition catalog, Musée national d'art moderne, Centre Pompidou (Paris, 1979).

Harrison, Helen, *Dawn of a New Day: the New York World's Fair, 1939/40*, exhibition catalog, Queen's Museum (New York, 1980).

Canning Miller, Dorothy, ed., *The Nelson A. Rockefeller Collection: Masterpieces of Modern Art* (London, 1981). → see 203

Lionel-Marie, Annick, Marie-Claire Llopès, and Michèle Thomas, eds, *Paris – Paris, 1937/1957: creations en France*, exhibition catalog, Musée national d'art moderne, Centre Pompidou (Paris, 1981).

Troy, Nancy J., *The De Stijl Environment* (Cambridge, MA, 1983).

Lemoine, Bertrand, ed., *Paris 1937: Cinquantenaire de l'Exposition internationale des arts et des techniques dans la vie moderne*, exhibition catalog, Institut français d'architecture (Paris, 1987).

Les Années UAM 1929–58, exhibition catalog, Musée des arts décoratifs (Paris, 1988).

Menil, Dominique de, and Pie Duployé, eds, *Sacred Art: Texts by Marie Alain Couturier* (Austin, 1989).

Goguel, Solange, *Réne Herbst* (Paris, 1990).

Häger, Bengt, *Ballets Suédois* (London, 1990).

Norman Baer, Nancy van, *Paris Modern: The Swedish Ballet 1920–1925*, exhibition catalog, Fine Arts Museums of San Francisco (San Francisco, 1995).

Blau, Eve, and Nancy Troy, *Architecture and Cubism* (Cambridge, MA, 1997).

Costa, Xavier, and Guido Hartray, *Sert. Arquitecto en Nueva York*, exhibition catalog, Museu d'Art Contemporani de Barcelona (Barcelona, 1997).

Schmidt, Katharina, and Hartwig Fischer, *Ein Haus für den Kubismus: die Sammlung Raoul La Roche. Picasso, Braque, Léger, Gris – Le Corbusier und Ozenfant*, exhibition catalog, Kunstmuseum Basel (Ostfildern-Ruit, 1998).

Reunion des musees nationaux, ed., *L'Esprit Nouveau. Le purisme à Paris 1918–1925*, exhibition catalog, Musée Grenoble / Los Angeles County Museum of Art (Paris, 2001).

Udovički-Selb, Danilo François, "The Elusive Faces of Modernity: Jacques Gréber and the Planning of the 1937 Paris World Fair," in *Urban History Review* 2 (March 2001): 20–35.

Wilk, Christopher, *Modernism: Designing a New World 1914–1939*, exhibition catalog, Victoria and Albert Museum (London, 2006).

Bouvier, Yves, *Audincourt, le sacre de la couleur: Fernand Léger, Jean Bazaine, Maurice Novarina, Jean Le Moal au Sacré-Cœur* (Besançon, 2007).

Golan, Romy, *Muralnomad: The Paradox of Wall Painting, Europe 1927–1957* (New Haven, 2009).

Leleu, Véronique, ed., *Dis-moi, Blaise. Léger, Chagall, Picasso et Blaise Cendrars*, exhibition catalog, Musée national Fernand Léger Biot / Musée National Marc Chagall Nice / Musée National Pablo Picasso, La Guerre et la Paix Vallauris (Paris, 2009).

Näslund, Erik, *Rolf de Maré: art collector, ballet director, museum creator* (Alton, 2009).

Wayne, Kenneth, and Erik Neil, eds, *Long Island Moderns: Art and Architecture on the North Shore and Beyond*, exhibition catalog, Heckscher Museum of Art, Huntington (Long Island, 2009).

Paulvé, Dominique, ed., *Marie Cuttoli, Myrbor et l'invention de la tapisserie modern* (Paris, 2010). (To mark the occasion of the exhibition *Renaissance et Métamorphoses de la Tapisserie à Aubusson dans la Première Moitié du XXe Siècle*, Musée Départemental de la Tapisserie d'Aubusson 2010).

Encounters with the 30s, exhibition catalog, Nacional Centro de Arte Reina Sofía, Madrid (Madrid, 2012).

Wilson, Sarah, *Picasso/Marx and Socialist Realism in France* (Liverpool, 2013).

Dietrich, Karin, *Die Schwedischen Ballette – Les Ballets Suédois. Getanzte Visionen im Paris der 1920er Jahre* (Frankfurt, 2015).

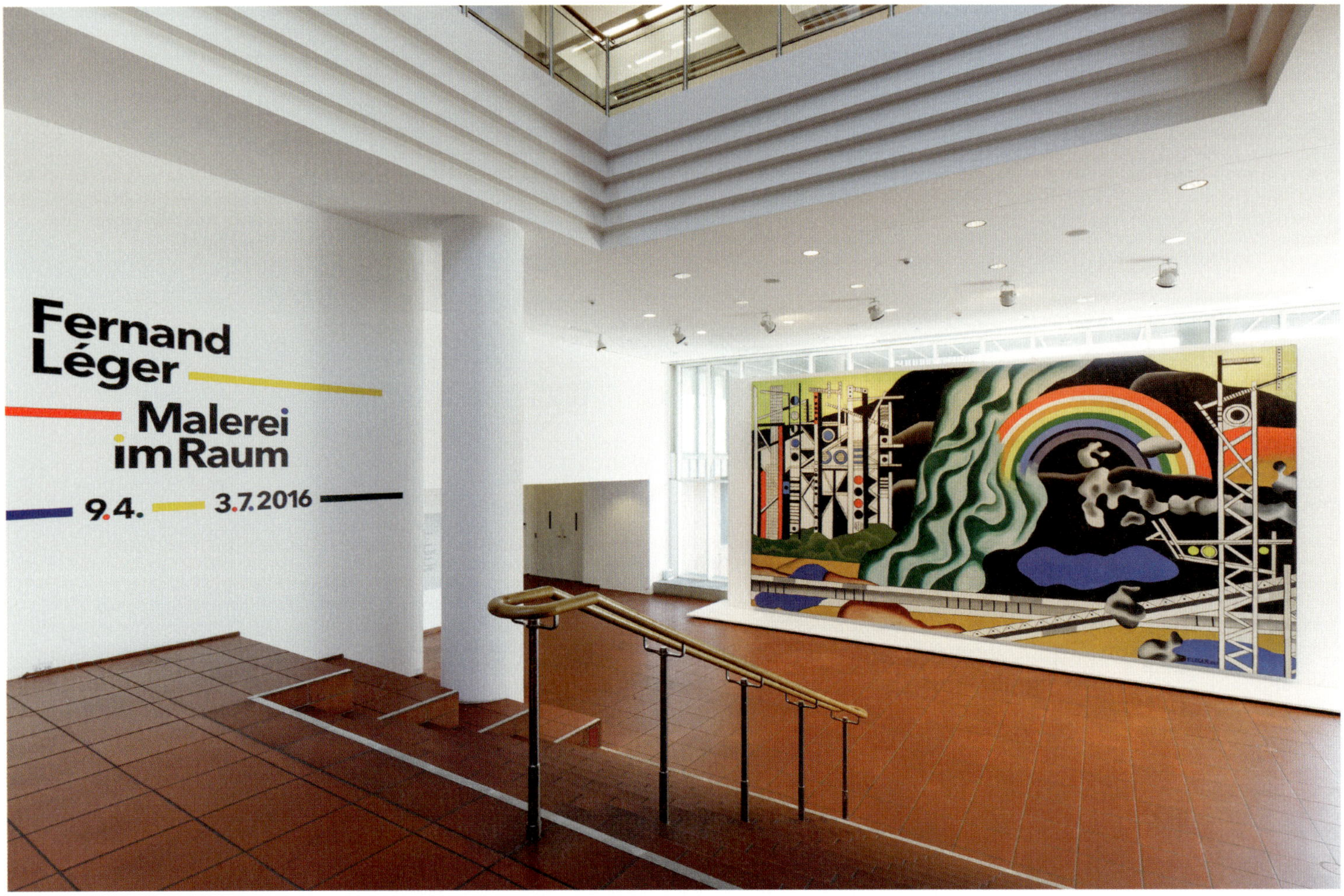

324

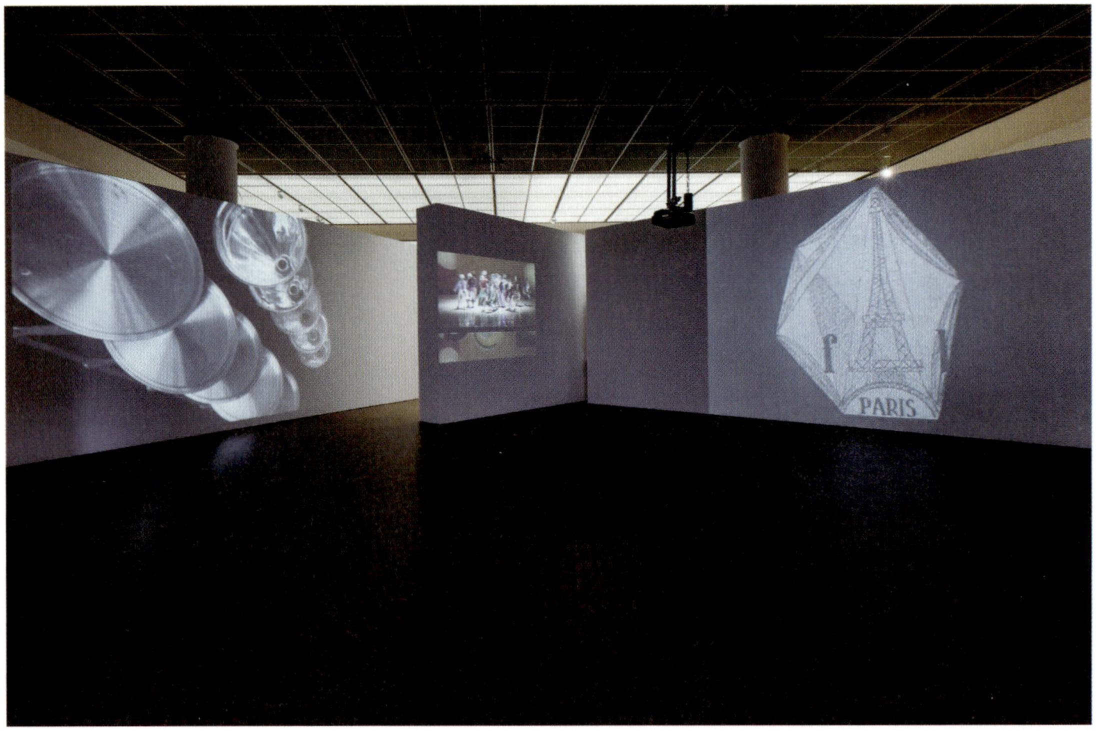

325

Exhibition List of Works and Documents

The following order corresponds to the layout of the exhibition. Photographic reproductions projected onto the wall or exhibited digitally have not been included. The superscript numbers refer to the image numbers in the catalog.

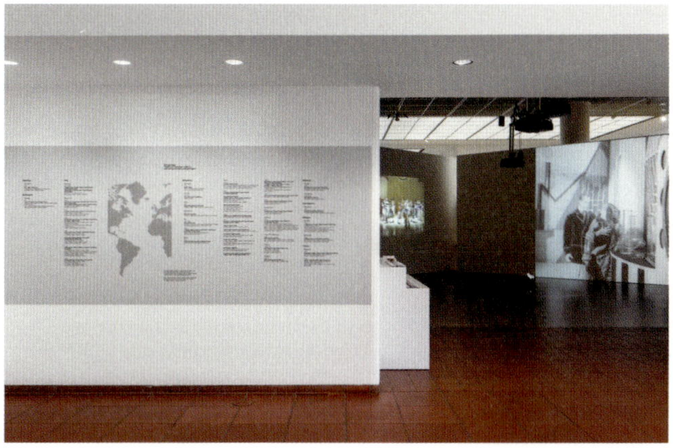

326

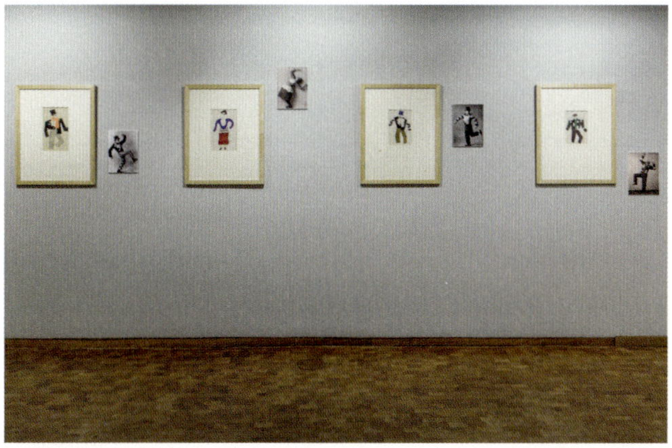

327

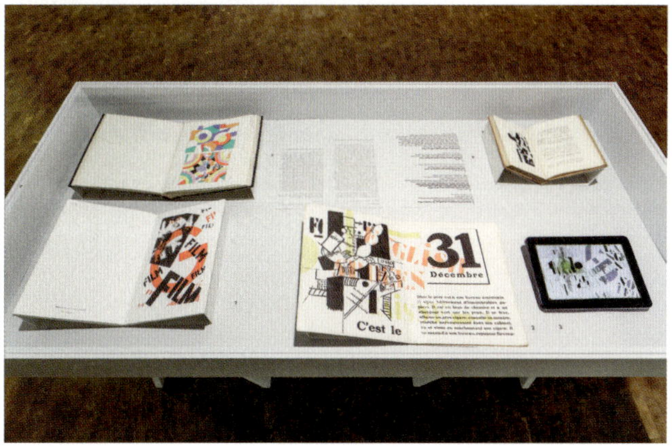

328

Entrance Hall [324]

***Le Transport des Forces* (Transport of Forces), 1937** [140]
Oil on canvas
500 × 1,000 cm
Centre nationale des arts plastiques, Paris, installed in the Palais de la Découverte (Palace of Discovery), Universcience, Paris

Paintings, Sets, and Films [325]

Fernand Léger in collaboration with Dudley Murphy
***Le Ballet mécanique (version Kiesler)* (The Mechanical Ballet [Kiesler version]), 1923/24** [21]
35mm film, black and white, silent
19 min 50 sec
Centre Pompidou, Musée national d'art moderne, Paris

Fernand Léger in collaboration with Dudley Murphy
***Le Ballet mécanique (version Film-museum)* (The Mechanical Ballet [film museum version]), 1923/24** [22]
35mm film, black and white, colorized, silent
17 min
Centre Pompidou, Musée national d'art moderne, Paris

Marcel L'Herbier
***L'Inhumaine* (The Inhuman Woman), 1923** [26]
Laboratory: Fernand Léger; exteriors: Robert Mallet-Stevens; furniture: Pierre Chareau; garden: Claude Autant-Lara; sets: Alberto Cavalcanti; costumes: Paul Poiret; music: Darius Milhaud; dancers: Ballets suédois
35mm film, black and white, silent
132 min
Excerpts from the edition restored and colorized in 2015 (Lobsterfilms)

Performance of *Skating Rink*, 1996
Dance and Design by Millicent Hodson and Kenneth Archer after a choreography by Jean Börlin; set design, costumes (reconstruction): Fernand Léger; music: Arthur Honegger
Recording of a performance by the Ballet Zurich, 1996
18:30 min

***Hommage à la danse* (Homage to Dance), 1925** [1]
Oil on canvas
158.5 × 120.5 cm
Collection Galerie Maeght, Paris

Skating Rink [326, 327]

Curtain design for *Skating Rink*, 1921 [14]
Graphite, watercolor, gouache and India ink on paper
41.5 × 49 cm
Dansmuseet, Stockholm

Letter from Fernand Léger to Rolf de Maré, November 21, 1921, with costume sketches
Dansmuseet, Stockholm

Costume design for the Man in blue top hat in *Skating Rink*, 1921 [8]
Graphite, watercolor, gouache and India ink on paper
25 × 16 cm
Dansmuseet, Stockholm

Costume design for Jean Börlin as the Madman in *Skating Rink*, 1921 [9]
Graphite, watercolor, and India ink on paper
30 × 18 cm
Dansmuseet, Stockholm

Costume design for the Woman in red skirt and blue top in *Skating Rink*, 1922 [10]
Graphite, watercolor, gouache and India ink on paper
25 × 17 cm
Dansmuseet, Stockholm

Costume design for the Man in checked hat and green and brown costume in *Skating Rink*, 1921 [11]
Graphite, watercolor and gouache on paper
22.5 × 14.5 cm
Dansmuseet, Stockholm

Set design for *Skating Rink*, 1921 [12]
Graphite and watercolor on paper
23.5 × 31.5 cm
Dansmuseet, Stockholm

Sketch for program cover for *Skating Rink*, with the figure of the Madman, c. 1922
Graphite, watercolor, and India ink on paper
10 × 3.3 cm
Dansmuseet, Stockholm

Choreographic notes by Jean Börlin for *Skating Rink*, 1921–22
Graphite on paper
22 × 46 cm
Dansmuseet, Stockholm

Backdrop design for *Skating Rink*, 1922 [13]
Graphite, watercolor, gouache and India ink on paper
29 × 60 cm
Dansmuseet, Stockholm

Sketch for back cover of program Stockholm-Paris, 1923 [15]
Pencil, watercolor, gouache and India ink on paper
32.5 × 24.5 cm
Dansmuseet, Stockholm

***Skating Rink, Danseuses, rideau de scène pour le ballet* (Skating Rink, dancers, stage curtain for the ballet), 1922–24** [16]
Gouache on paper
22.5 × 24 cm
Collection Galerie Maeght, Paris

Archival material and documents:

Program for Ballets Suédois, *Skating Rink,* 1922 [3]
(front and back cover designed by Fernand Léger)
32 × 24.5 cm
Dansmuseet, Stockholm

Painting and Graphics [328]

***Le remorqueur rose* (The Pink Towboat), 1918** [37]
Oil on canvas
66.5 × 92 cm
Museum Ludwig, Cologne

***L'arret d'autobus* (The Bus Stop), c. 1919** [39]
India ink on paper
42.5 × 32 cm
Grafische Sammlung Museum Ludwig, Cologne

***La Roue* (The Wheel), poster design, 1922** [27]
Gouache on paper
31.3 × 24.2 cm
Galerie Louise Leiris, Paris

***Charlot cubiste* (Cubist Charlie Chaplin), 1924** [23]
Montage on wood
70 × 30 × 5 cm
Musée Pierre-Noël, Saint-Dié-des-Vosges

Archival material and documents:

Blaise Cendrars
***La fin du monde filmée par l'ange N. D.* (The End of the World Filmed by the Angel of Notre Dame), 1919** [28]
Print on Lafuma vellum document paper
31.7 × 25.4 × 0.5 cm
Lille métropole, Musée d'art moderne, d'art contemporain et d'art brut, Villeneuve d'Ascq
(Title and double-page spreads with color compositions by Fernand Léger, Paris, Éditions de la Sirène, 1919)

Ivan Goll, *Le Nouvel Orphée, Aux Éditions de la Sirène*, Paris, 1923
(drawings by Fernand Léger for Ivan Goll's "Chaplinade")
Private collection

***Zeitschrift für elementare Gestaltung*, 5/6 (April 1926),** ed. by Hans Richter (with cover design by Fernand Léger and an article by Georges Antheil entitled "Zeit. Mein Ballet mécanique. Zu dem Film von Léger")
Reprint
Kunst- und Museumsbibliothek Köln

First Murals [328]

***Eléments mécaniques* (Mechanical Elements), 1922** [42]
Pencil, China ink, quill and brush on paper
27.4 × 21.1 cm
Musées royaux des Beaux-Arts de Belgique, Brussels, acc. no. 7338

***Eléments mécaniques* (Mechanical Elements), 1922** [43]
Pencil, China ink, quill and brush on paper
27.2 × 21 cm
Musées royaux des Beaux-Arts de Belgique, Brussels, acc. no. 7339

Documents:

***L'Architecture Vivant* (Fall/Winter 1924), ed. by Jean Badovici** [40, 41]
(Plate 9 with sketches by Léger *Fresque pour Music Hall* and *Fresque (extérieur) pour une Hall d'Hôtel,* illustrated with Jean Badovici's article "Projet décoratif et fresques par F. Léger")
Staatsbibliothek zu Berlin

Painting for Architecture [329, 331]

***Peinture murale* (Mural Painting), 1924** [56]
Oil on canvas
180.3 × 79.2 cm
Museum of Modern Art, New York, acc. no. 49.1965

***Composition architecturale* (Architectural Composition), 1924–26** [62]
Gouache on paper
54.5 × 38.5 cm
Courtesy Galerie Gmurzynska

Study for a mural painting, 1925 [54]
Opaque watercolor and black ink over graphite on vellum
Image: 24.1 × 8.3 cm,
sheet: 36.8 × 21.1 cm
Philadelphia Museum of Art, A. E. Gallatin Collection, 1952-61-60

Purist composition, 1926 [61]
Gouache on paper
26 × 13.4 cm
Collection J.-M. Decrop, Hong Kong

***Composition murale* (Mural Composition), 1926** [63]
Oil on canvas
130.4 × 97 cm
Musée national Fernand Léger, Biot

***Peinture murale* (Mural Painting), 1926** [55]
Oil on canvas
180 × 80 cm
The Menil Collection, Houston

***Le petit cheval n'y comprend rien* (The Little Horse Doesn't Understand It), c. 1924/25** [75]
Collage, oil and gouache on paper
23 × 26.5 cm
Galerie Louise Leiris, Paris

***Les gémeaux* (The Twins), 1929/30** [74]
Oil on canvas
73 × 92 cm
Museum Ludwig, Cologne

***Composition I (Décoration pour une salle à manger)* (Composition I [Mural decoration for a dining room]), 1930** [77]
Oil on canvas
141 × 291 cm
Fondation Beyeler, Riehen/Basel
Collection Beyeler

***Tapis »blanc«* (white rug), c. 1930, later edition (c. 1950–62)** [60]
Wool, knotted
262 × 138 cm
Private collection

Archival material and documents:

***Une Ambassade française* (organized by the Société des Artistes Décorateurs), Éditions Charles Moreau, 1925** [53]
Stencil print
25 × 32.4 cm
Les Arts Décoratifs Paris, library

***Catalogue Général Officiel: Exposition internationale des arts décoratifs et industriels modernes,* Paris, April–October 1925 (Official catalog, ed. by Ministère du Commerce et de l'industrie des postes et des télégraphes)**
Kunst- und Museumsbibliothek Köln

Abstraction and Figuration [330, 332]

***Le Printemps (du cycle: les quatre saisons)* (Spring [from the "Four Seasons" cycle]), 1928** [64]
Oil on canvas
185.3 × 79.8 cm
Kunstmuseum Basel
Gift of Dr. h. c. Raoul La Roche

***L'Été (du cycle: les quatre saisons)* (Summer [from the "Four Seasons" cycle]), 1928** [65]
Oil on canvas
185.5 × 62 cm
Kunstmuseum Basel
Gift of Dr. h. c. Raoul La Roche

***L'Automne (du cycle: les quatre saisons)* (Fall [from the "Four Seasons" cycle]), 1928** [66]
Oil on canvas
185.4 × 80 cm
Kunstmuseum Basel
Gift of Dr. h. c. Raoul La Roche

***L'Hiver (du cycle: les quatre saisons)* (Winter [from the "Four Seasons" cycle]), 1928** [67]
Oil on canvas
185.5 × 76 cm
Kunstmuseum Basel
Gift from Dr. h. c. Raoul La Roche

Untitled, study for a rug (realized with assistance from his student Théodora Bücking-Klute), 1929 [70]
Gouache and pencil on paper
30.7 × 23 cm
Musée national Fernand Léger, Biot

Untitled, study for a rug (realized with assistance from his student Théodora Bücking-Klute), 1929 [71]
Gouache and pencil on paper
30.5 × 22.5 cm
Musée national Fernand Léger, Biot

Untitled, study for a rug (realized with assistance from his student Théodora Bücking-Klute), 1929 [72]
Gouache and pencil on paper
30.5 × 22.5 cm
Musée national Fernand Léger, Biot

Untitled, study for a rug (realized with assistance from his student Théodora Bücking-Klute), 1929 [73]
Gouache and pencil on paper
30.5 × 22.5 cm
Musée national Fernand Léger, Biot

Untitled, study for a rug (realized with assistance from his student Théodora Bücking-Klute), 1929
Gouache and pencil on paper
30.7 × 23 cm
Musée national Fernand Léger, Biot

Untitled, study for a rug (realized with assistance from his student Théodora Bücking-Klute), 1929
Gouache and pencil on paper
30.5 × 22.5 cm
Musée national Fernand Léger, Biot

Untitled, study for a rug (realized with assistance from his student Théodora Bücking-Klute), 1929
Gouache and pencil on paper
30.5 × 22.5 cm
Musée national Fernand Léger Biot

Untitled, study for a rug (realized with assistance from his student Théodora Bücking-Klute), 1929
Gouache and pencil on paper
30.5 × 22.5 cm
Musée national Fernand Léger, Biot

***Sans titre, projet de costume* (Untitled, study for a costume, realized with assistance from his student Théodora Bücking-Klute), 1929** [68a, 68b]
Gouache and pencil on paper
30.5 × 22.5 cm
Musée national Fernand Léger, Biot

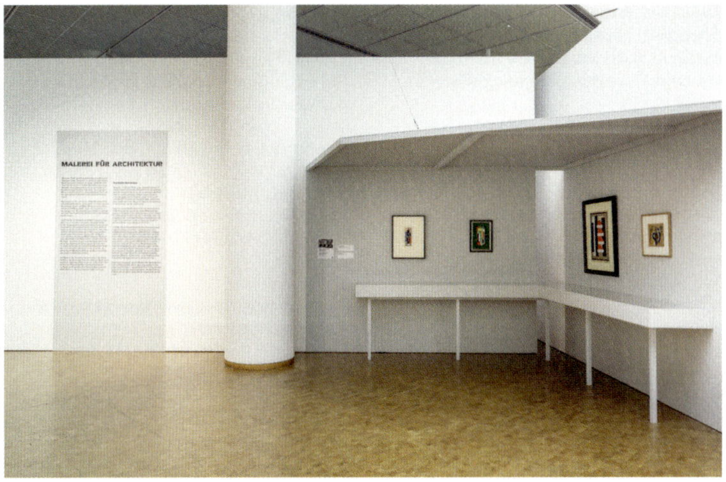

329

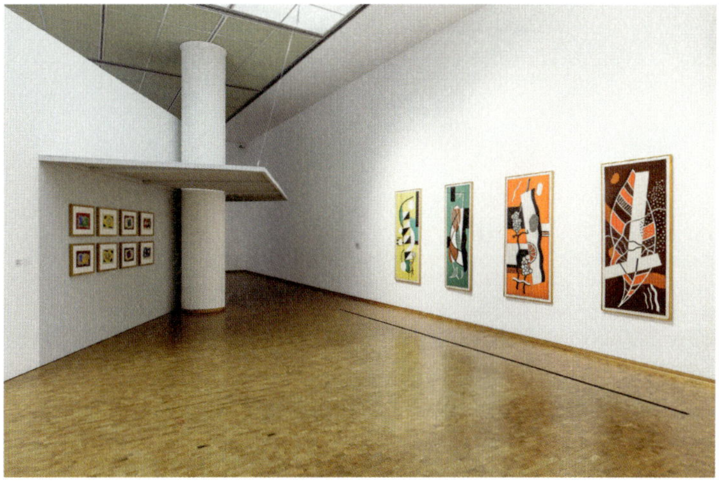

330

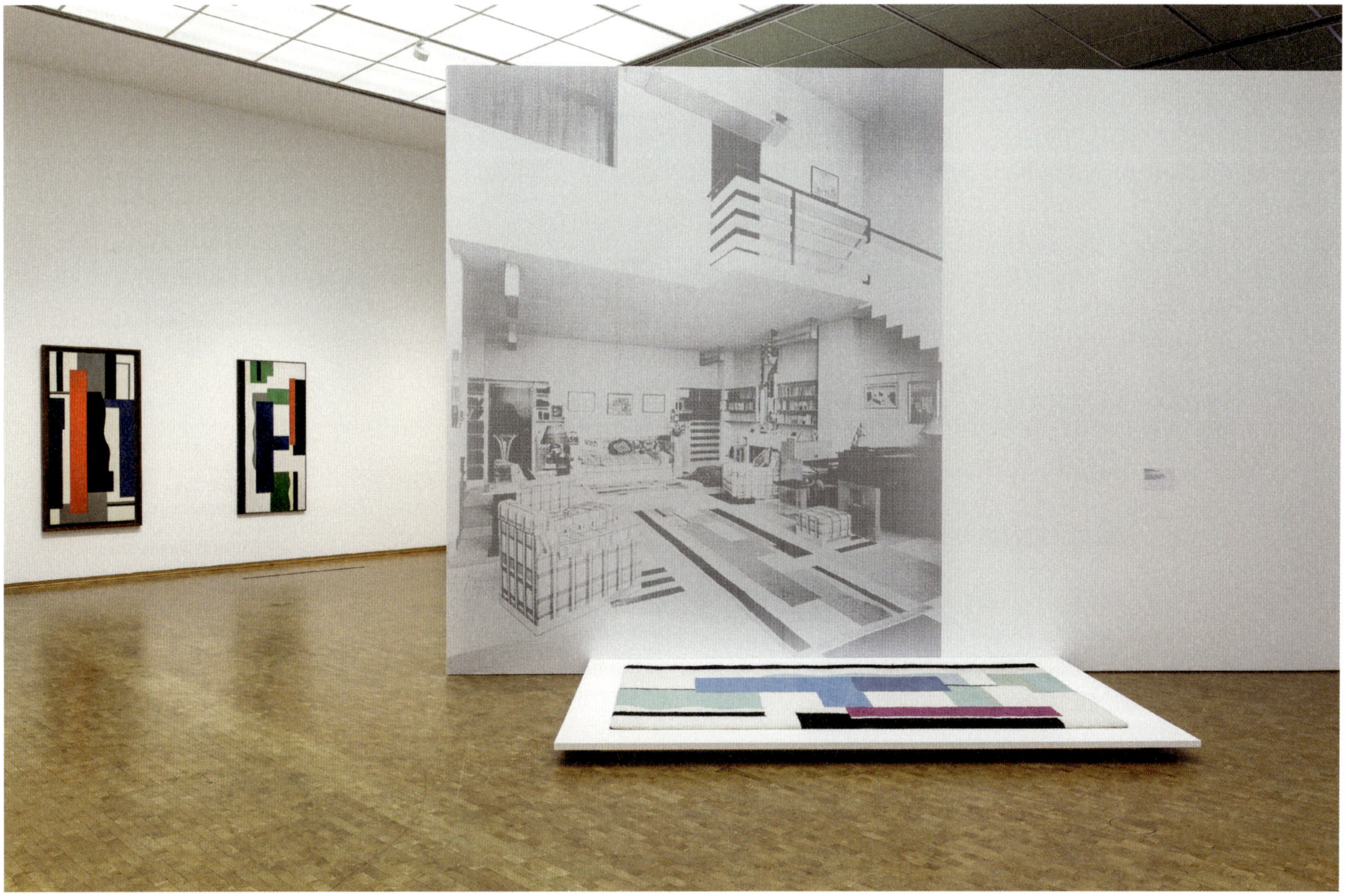

331

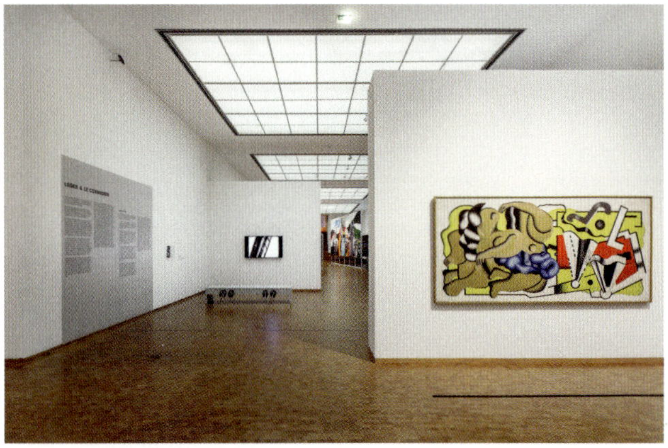

332

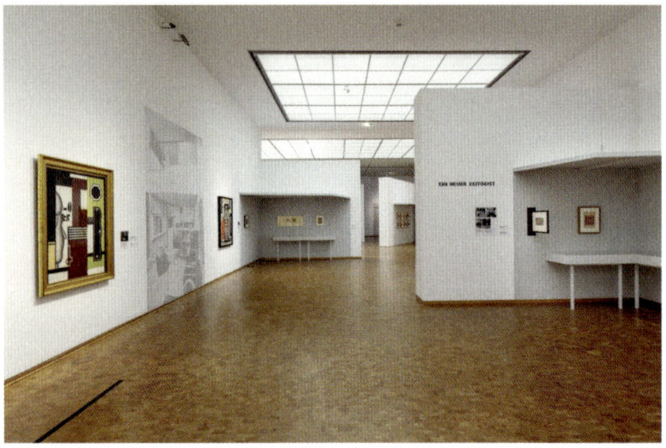

333

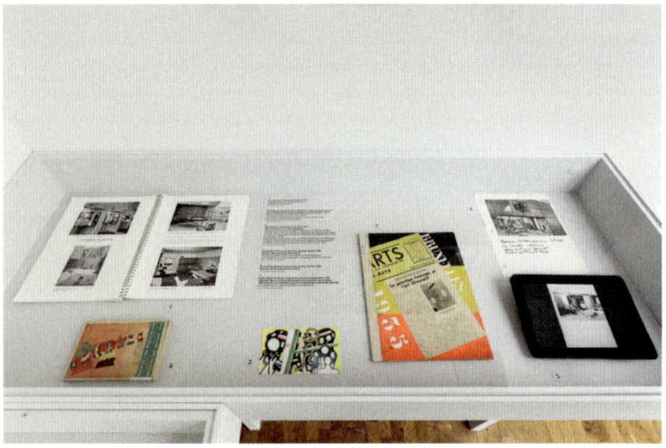

334

***Sans titre, projet de costume* (Untitled, study for a costume, realized with assistance from his student Théodora Bücking-Klute), 1929** [69a, 69b]
Gouache and pencil on paper
30.5 × 22.5 cm
Musée national Fernand Léger, Biot

Students in Fernand Léger's Paris studio, 1938, annotated photograph
Archives Charlotte Perriand

Léger and Le Corbusier [333]

Cover design for the magazine *L'Esprit Nouveau*, c. 1922 [91]
Watercolor on paper
25.4 × 16.8 cm
Fondation Le Corbusier, Paris

Le Corbusier, Pierre Jeanneret
***Pavillon de l'Esprit Nouveau, Paris, étude de façade* (Pavilion of the New Spirit, Paris, design for the façade), 1924** [90]
Black pencil and pastel chalk on paper
60.5 × 111.6 cm
Fondation Le Corbusier, Paris

***Le balustre* (The Baluster), 1925** [85]
Oil on canvas
129.5 × 97.2 cm
Museum of Modern Art, New York
Mrs. Simon Guggenheim Fund,
acc. no. 179.1952

Compass and Paint Tubes, 1926 [79]
Gouache on paper
26.7 × 36.2 cm
Museum of Modern Art, New York
Gift of Edward M. M. Warburg,
acc. no. 4071941

***Composition avec profil* (Composition with Profile), 1926** [96]
Oil on canvas
139 × 97 cm
Von der Heydt Museum, Wuppertal

***Nature Morte* (Still Life), 1928** [100]
Oil on canvas
69.5 × 96.5 cm
Fondation Le Corbusier, Paris

***La Baigneuse* (The Bather), 1932** [103]
Oil on canvas
98 × 130
Musée national Fernand Léger, Biot

László Moholy-Nagy
Architects' Congress, 1933
35mm film, black and white, silent
29 min
Centre Pompidou, Musée national d'art moderne, Paris

***Discours aux Architectes*, 1933**
Speech to the Architects, speech by Fernand Léger during CIAM IV (International Congress of Modern Architecture), August 1933 in Athens, orig. publ. in: *Quadrante*, no. 5, September 1933, Milan, pp. 44–47, also in: *Annales Techniques*, Athens 1933, pp. 1159–62
25 min (audio loop in German and English translation)

Le Corbusier
***Femme couchée, cordage et bateau à la porte ouverte* (Reclining Nude, Rope and Boat with Open Door), 1935** [101]
Oil on canvas
129.9 × 162.4 cm
Kunstmuseum Basel
Gift of Dr. h. c. Raoul La Roche

Le Corbusier
***Étape pour le Mural de Cap Martin* (Study for a mural painting in Cap Martin), 1937**
Gouache and watercolor on paper on cardboard
20.7 × 30.6 cm
Centre Pompidou, Musée national d'art moderne, Paris

Archival material and documents:

***L'Esprit Nouveau, Revue Internationale Illustré de l'Activité Contemporaine. Arts. Lettres. Sciences* 4 (January 1921), 17 (June 1922), 19 (Winter 1923/24)**
Archives Charlotte Perriand

***L'Architecture Vivante* (Fall/Winter 1925), ed. by Jean Badovici**
Staatsbibliothek zu Berlin

A New Zeitgeist [333, 334]

***Composition* (Composition), 1935** [128]
Oil on cardboard
38 × 46 cm
Fundación Joan Miró, Barcelona
Gift of Josep Lluís Sert

***Dessin de sol, projet pour le bureau de Jean Zay* (Floor design for the office of Jean Zay), 1937** [134]
Gouache on paper
30.7 × 22.6 cm
Musée national Fernand Léger, Biot

***Esquisse pour la décoration pour un camp d'aviation* (Sketch for the decoration of an airport), 1937** [164]
Opaque watercolor and graphite on vellum
13.7 × 25.9 cm
Philadelphia Museum of Art
Courtesy of the Philadelphia Museum of Art, A. E. Gallatin Collection, 1952

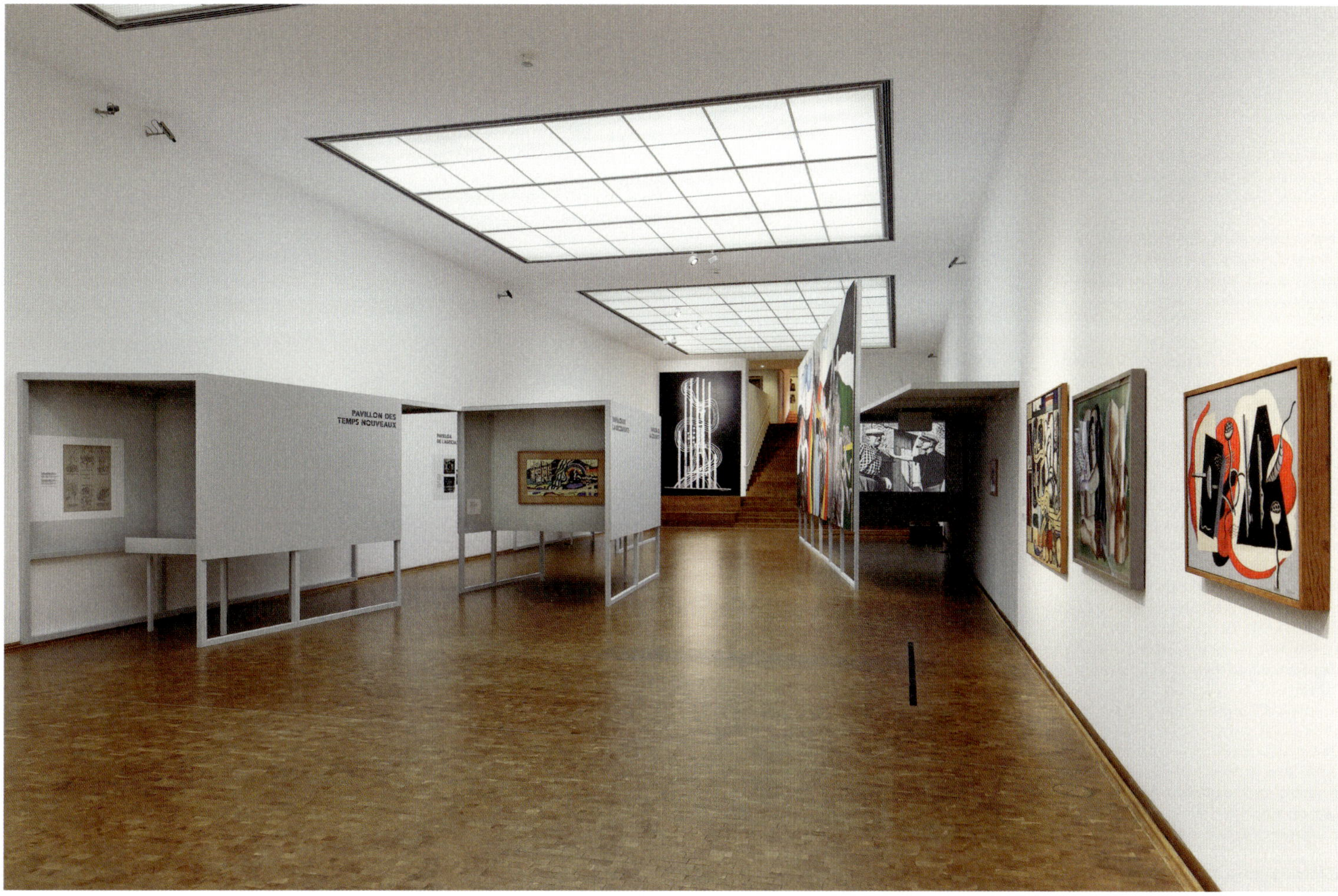

335

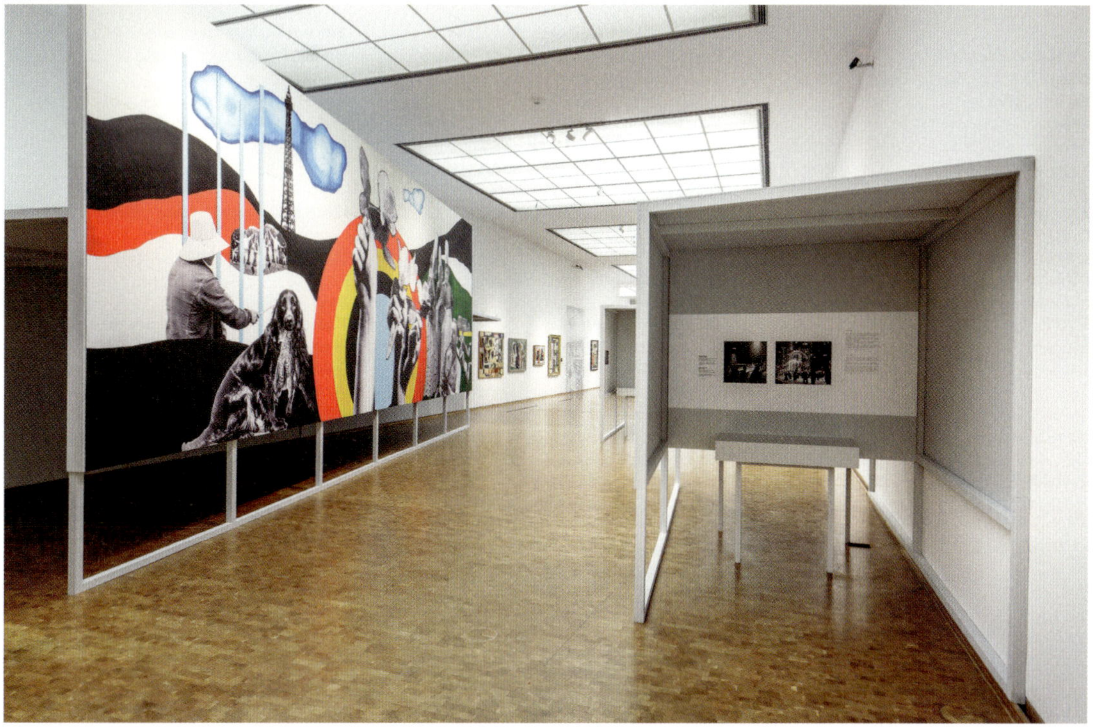

336

Archival material and documents:

Postcard from Simone Herman to Charlotte Perriand, dated December 2 (year unknown)
Archives Charlotte Perriand

Postcard from Fernand Léger to Charlotte Perriand, undated
Archives Charlotte Perriand

Letter from G. H. Pingusson to Fernand Léger, October 17, 1934, inviting him to join the UAM (Union des Artistes Modernes)
Bibliothèque des Arts décoratifs, Paris

Typescript of a lecture by Fernand Léger in Yale, 1935
Archives Charlotte Perriand

Guide Officiel & Plan de l'exposition universelle de Bruxelles 1935
Official guide and exhibition map for the Exposition universelle, Brussels, ed. by Marcel van der Donck
Kunst- und Museumsbibliothek Köln

Postcard of *La Salle de culture physique, le sport* by Fernand Léger Produced in conjunction with *La Maison du jeune homme* at the Exposition universelle, Brussels, 1935
Archives Charlotte Perriand

Personal album made by Réne Herbst with newspaper articles, photographs, and postcard from Fernand Léger, 1935 [(127)]
Bibliothèque des Arts décoratifs, Paris

L'Architecture d'aujourd'hui* (October 1935), ed. by André Bloc, *La Maison du jeune homme
Archives Charlotte Perriand

School furniture at the Salon d'Automne 1936, Paris, exhibition by UAM in collaboration with l'Office Technique pour l'Utilisation de l'Acier; in the background: *La Salle de culture physique, le sport* by Fernand Léger, 1935
Bibliothèque des Arts décoratifs, Paris

1937 World's Fair [(335, 336)]

Jean Carlu
***Exposition Internationale des Arts et Techniques 1937,* Paris**
(Official poster for the 1937 Paris World's Fair)
Lithograph
26.5 × 39.5 cm
Private collection

Le Transport des Forces
(Transport of Forces), 1937 [(142)]
Gouache and graphite on paper
50.9 × 100 cm
Musée national Fernand Léger, Biot

Le Corbusier, Pierre Jeanneret
Pavillon des Temps Nouveaux, Perspective intérieure du musée avec indications
(Pavilion of the New Times, interior perspective of the pavilion with signs), February 6–7, 1936 [(148)]
Print on paper
34 × 61 cm
Fondation Le Corbusier, Paris

Le Corbusier, Pierre Jeanneret
***Pavillon des Temps Nouveaux, Perspective du bâtiment avec vue de l'entrée avec auvent* (Pavilion of the New Times, building perspective with view of porch roof entrance), undated** [(150)]
Black pencil, colored ink, China ink on Canson paper, unsigned
72 × 118 cm
Fondation Le Corbusier, Paris

Le Corbusier, Pierre Jeanneret
Pavillon des Temps Nouveaux
(Pavilion of the New Times), 1937 [(151)]
Five photo collages (including exhibition view with Léger's photomural *Travailler*)
18 × 24 cm
Fondation Le Corbusier, Paris

Fernand Léger, Charlotte Perriand
Joies essentielles, plaisirs nouveaux. Pavillon de l'Agriculture, Paris, Exposition Internationale
(Essential Joys, New Pleasures. Agriculture Pavilion, Paris World's Fair), 1937/2011 [(153)]
Photomural (Acrylic, collage and print on paper and on board)
350 × 941 cm
Museo Nacional centro de Arte Reina Sofía, Madrid, Donated by Archives Charlotte Perriand-Pernette Perriand Barsac, Paris, 2012

Charlotte Perriand
Bench for the Agriculture Pavilion, 1937/2016
Wood
Reconstruction authorized by Archives Charlotte Perriand

Fernand Léger, Albert Gleizes, Léopold Survage
Composition pour le Pavillon de l'Union des Artistes Modernes
(Composition for the UAM Pavilion), 1937 [(145)]
Gouache on paper, laminated on cardboard
24 × 119 cm
Solomon R. Guggenheim Museum, New York
Gift, Andrew Powie Fuller and Geraldine Spreckels Fuller Collection, 1999, acc. no. 2009.11

Paris 1937, L'Exposition Internationale des Arts et Techniques
(*World's Fair*)
Anonymous, 1937
21 min
Coll. Ciné-Archives, fonds audiovisuel du PCF - Mouvement ouvrier et démocratique
Film restauré par les Archives françaises du film du CNC - Ministère de la Culture

Archival material and documents:

Fernand Léger, 1930, taken by Michel Seuphor
Photograph
Museum Ludwig Köln

***Exposition Internationale des Arts et Techniques 1937,* Paris**
Map of the World's Fair
Bibliothèque des Arts décoratifs, Paris

***Les Pavillons Français, Exposition Internationale des Arts et Techniques 1937,* Paris, ed. by Jacques Gréber, Henri Martin, Éditions Art et Architecture**
Bibliothèque des Arts décoratifs, Paris

Le Corbusier
Des Canons des munitions? Merci! Des Logis ...S.V.P.
Éditions de l'Architecture d'aujourd' hui, Boulogne-sur-Seine, 1938 [(152)]
Fondation Le Corbusier, Paris

***L'Architecture d'aujourd'hui 9* (September 1937), ed. by André Bloc (Article on the World's Fair in Paris and the *Pavillon des Temps Nouveaux*)**
Universitätsbibliothek Johann Christian Senckenberg Frankfurt

Letter from Charlotte Perriand to René Herbst, Paris, July 5, 1935
Bibliothèque des Arts décoratifs, Paris

Program for *Naissance d'une cité* (Birth of a City), 1937 [(156)]
(cover designed by Fernand Léger)
Archives Charlotte Perriand

Nature, Object, and Abstraction [(337)]

Queues de comètes (Étude pour un paravent)
(Comet Tails [Study for a screen]), c. 1930 [(123)]
Oil on canvas
70 × 92 cm
Musée national Fernand Léger, Biot

Paravent, Composition sur fond marron, trois feuilles
(Screen, composition on brown background, three leaves), original reverse side, c. 1930 [(125)]
Oil on canvas
201 × 275 cm
Musée national Fernand Léger, Biot

Branches (racine)
(Branches [root]), 1930
Pencil on paper
28.5 × 21.5 cm
Galerie Louise Leiris, Paris

Les troncs d'arbres (Tableau)
(The Tree Trunks), 1931 [(120)]
Oil on canvas
92 × 65 cm
Musée d'art moderne, Belfort

***Planète* (Planet), 1931** [(122)]
Graphite on paper
43.5 × 30.2 cm
Centre Pompidou, Musée national d'art moderne, Paris

***Composition* (Composition), 1931** [(121)]
White chalk and graphite on gray-green paper
63.2 × 49.5 cm
Centre Pompidou, Musée national d'art moderne, Paris

Fernand Léger, Charlotte Perriand, Pierre Jeanneret
Les Objets à Réaction Poetique
(Objects with Poetic Effect), 1931–36 [(118)]
25 photographs, gelatin silver print on paper
Each: 5.4 × 5.4 cm
Tate: Purchased with assistance from the Photography Acquisitions Committee, Konstantin Grigorishin and the Art Fund 2013

Silex jaune sur fond beige
(Yellow Flint on Beige Background), 1932 [(119)]
Gouache (drawing) on paper
49 × 67 cm
Musée d'art moderne, Belfort
Donation from Maurice Jardot

***Silex bleu sur fond blanc* (Blue Flint on White Background),** 1932
Gouache on paper
60 × 46 cm
Galerie Louise Leiris, Paris

Color, Surface, Space [(338, 339)]

(Maison suspendue Section)

Paul Nelson
Coupe Esquisse (Maison suspendue, Projet non réalisé, 1936–1938)
(Floor plan, sketch, [Suspended House, unfinished project, 1936–38]), 1936
Pencil and colored pencil on tracing paper
28 × 50 cm
Centre Pompidou, Musée national d'art moderne, Paris

Paul Nelson
***Maison suspendue, Elévation Façade, esquisse* (Suspended House, façade elevation, design), 1936–38** [(173)]
Graphite and colored pencil on tracing paper
27.3 × 53.9 cm
Centre Pompidou, Musée national d'art moderne, Paris

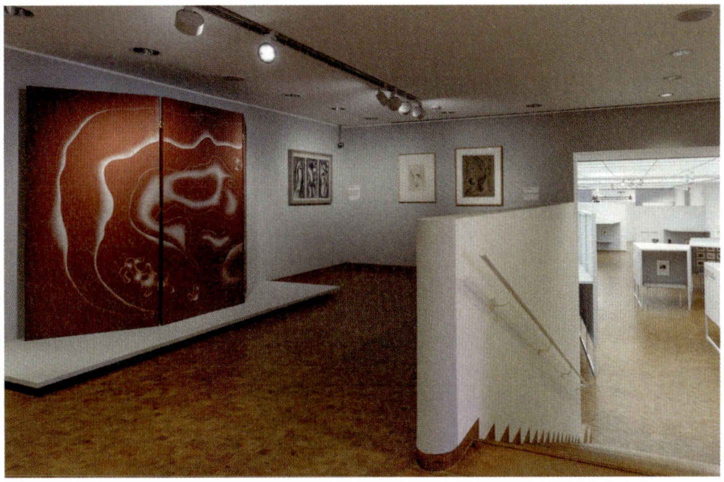

337

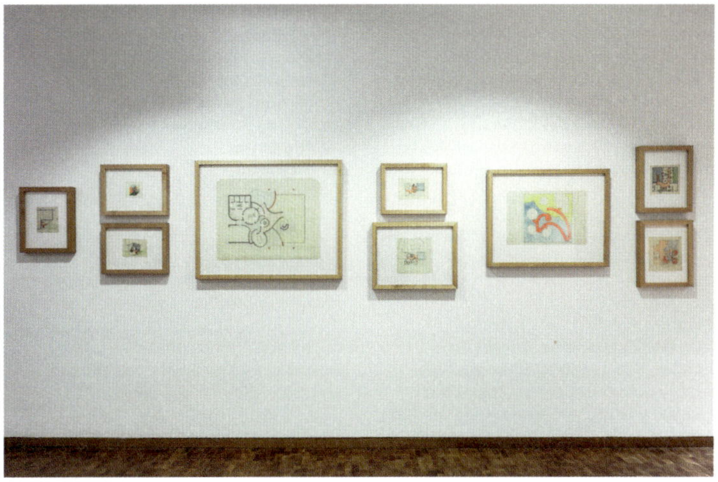

338

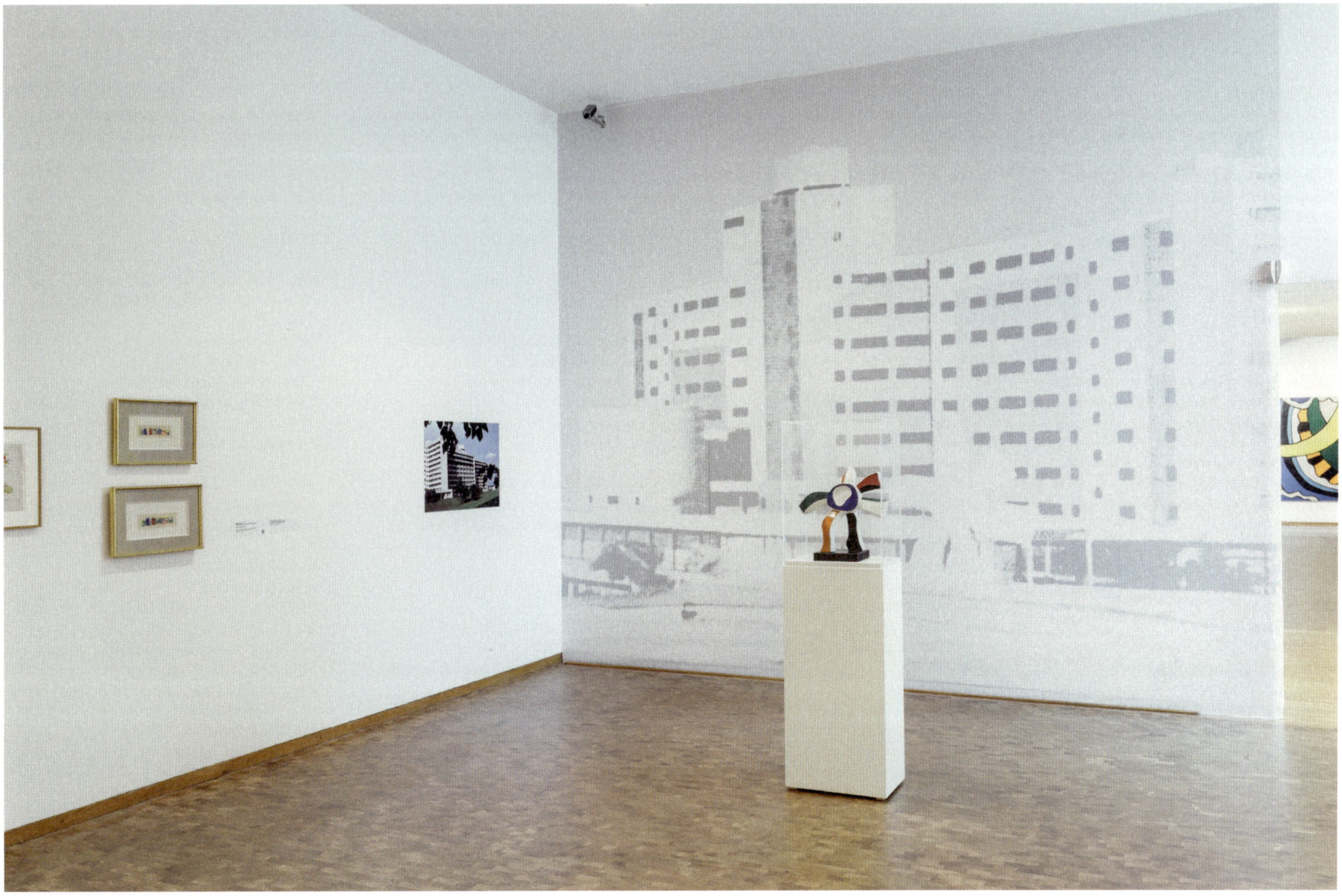

339

Paul Nelson
***Axonométrie Esquisse (Maison suspendue, Projet non réalisé, 1936–1938)* (Axonometric projection [Suspended House, unfinished project, 1936–38]), 1936–38**
Architectural drawing, axonometric projection, pencil and colored pencil on paper
10.9 × 12 cm
Centre Pompidou, Musée national d'art moderne, Paris

Paul Nelson
***Perspective Entrée, esquisse (Maison suspendue, Projet non réalisé, 1936–1938)* (Perspective from entrance, sketch [Suspended house, unfinished project, 1936–38]), 1936** (170)
Graphite and colored pencil on tracing paper
17.5 × 14.5 cm
Centre Pompidou, Musée national d'art moderne, Paris

Paul Nelson
***Plan de niveau Rez-de-chaussée, esquisse (Maison suspendue, Projet non réalisé, 1936–1938)* (Plan of ground floor level, sketch [Suspended House, unfinished project, 1936–38]), 1936** (174)
Ink and colored pencil on tracing paper
24 × 24 cm
Centre Pompidou, Musée national d'art moderne, Paris

Paul Nelson
***Plan de niveau Rez-de-chaussée, esquisse (Maison suspendue, Projet non réalisé, 1936–1938)* (Plan of ground-floor level, sketch [Suspended House, unfinished project, 1936–38]), 1936** (175)
China ink, graphite and colored pencil on tracing paper
55 × 71.5 cm
Centre Pompidou, Musée national d'art moderne, Paris

Paul Nelson
***Esquisse du plan du Rez-de-chaussée (Maison suspendue, Projet non réalisé, 1936–1938)* (Sketch for plan of ground-floor level [Suspended House, unfinished project, 1936–38]), 1936**
Pencil and colored pencil on tracing paper
14.5 × 20.7 cm
Centre Pompidou, Musée national d'art moderne, Paris

Paul Nelson
***Croquis de salle à manger (Maison suspendue, Projet non réalisé, 1936–1938)* (Sketch for the dining room [Suspended House, unfinished project, 1936–38]), 1936**
Pencil and colored pencil on tracing paper
13 × 8 cm
Centre Pompidou, Musée national d'art moderne, Paris

Paul Nelson
***Plan d'étage (Maison Suspendue, Projet non réalisé, 1936–1938)* (Floor plan [Suspended House, unfinished project, 1936–38]), 1936**
Graphite and colored pencil on tracing paper
21.5 × 23 cm
Centre Pompidou, Musée national d'art moderne, Paris

Paul Nelson
***Plan de l'étage (Maison suspendue, Projet non réalisé, 1936–1938)* (Floor plan [Suspended House, unfinished project]), 1936** (171)
Graphite and colored pencil on tracing paper
28 × 40 cm
Centre Pompidou, Musée national d'art moderne, Paris

Paul Nelson
***Plan d'étage (Maison suspendue, Projet non réalisé, 1936–1938)* (Floor plan [Suspended House, unfinished project, 1936–38]), 1936**
Pencil and colored pencil on tracing paper
19.5 × 19.5 cm
Centre Pompidou, Musée national d'art moderne, Paris

Paul Nelson
***Plan de niveau Balcon (Maison suspendue, Projet non réalisé, 1936–1938)* (Plan for balcony [Suspended House, unfinished project, 1936–38]), 1936–38**
Architectural drawing, floor plan, pencil and colored pencil on tracing paper
36 × 53.4 cm
Centre Pompidou, Musée national d'art moderne, Paris

(Polychrome Village Section)

André Bruyère, Fernand Léger
***Village Polychrome* (Polychrome Village), perspectival view of a villa with three workshops, near Biot, 1953** (286)
Pastel chalk on tracing paper
37.3 × 55.5 cm
Collection Centre Canadien d'Architecture/Canadian Centre for Architecture, Montreal
Gift in memory of Daniel Robbins

André Bruyère, Fernand Léger
***Village Polychrome* (Polychrome Village) perspectival view of a guest villa with terrace and façades, near Biot, France, 1952** (287)
Graphite and pastel chalk on tracing paper
42.4 × 54.6 cm
Collection Centre Canadien d'Architecture/Canadian Centre for Architecture, Montreal
Gift in memory of Daniel Robbins

André Bruyère, Fernand Léger
***Village Polychrome (Polychrome Village),* perspectival view of guest villa showing the terrace, near Biot, 1953** (288)
Pastel chalk on tracing paper
37 × 55.3 cm
Collection Centre Canadien d'Architecture/Canadian Centre for Architecture, Montreal

André Bruyère, Fernand Léger
***Village Polychrome* (Polychrome Village), Biot, 1952/53** (285)
Gouache and India ink on paper
40 × 55 cm
Private collection

André Bruyère
Elevation for *Village Polychrome* (Polychrome Village), Biot, December 1952/53
Reprographic copy, Diazotype
34.3 × 55 cm
Collection Centre Canadien d'Architecture/Canadian Centre for Architecture, Montréal

André Bruyère
Bird's-eye perspective for *Village Polychrome* (Polychrome Village), Biot, 1952/53
Reprographic copy, Diazotype
49.4 × 63.6 cm
Collection Centre Canadien d'Architecture/Canadian Centre for Architecture, Montréal

André Bruyère
Specifications for *Village Polychrome* (Polychrome Village), Biot, May 1953
Reprographic copy, Diazotype
37.8 × 52.4 cm
Collection Centre Canadien d'Architecture/Canadian Centre for Architecture, Montreal

(Saint-Lô Section)

***La fleur qui marche* (The Walking Flower), c. 1952/53**
(posthumous edition)
Glazed ceramic
41.5 × 56.5 cm
Private collection

***Maquette Saint-Lô* (Study for Saint-Lô), 1955** (186)
Gouache on tracing paper laminated on canvas
16 × 30 cm
Galerie Louise Leiris, Paris

***Maquette Saint-Lô* (Study for Saint-Lô), 1955**
Gouache on tracing paper laminated on canvas
18 × 35 cm
Galerie Louise Leiris, Paris

***Esquisse pour une peinture murale* (Sketch for a mural), c. 1935** (165)
Gouache and graphite on Canson paper
Private collection

Archival material and documents:

***Cahiers d'Art* (Paris) 1–3, 1937**
(Article: Paul Nelson, "Peinture spatiale et architecturale, à propos des dernières œuvres de Léger")
Universitäts- und Stadtbibliothek Köln

Letter from Fernand Léger to Paul Nelson, December 13, 1953, facsimile
Private collection

Léger and Wallace K. Harrison (340-344)

(Les Plongeurs Section)

***Les Plongeurs* (The Divers), 1942** (244)
Oil and charcoal on canvas
372 × 1092 cm
(Mural painting for the home of Wallace K. Harrison)

***Les acrobates en gris* (Acrobats in Gray), 1942–44** (238)
Oil on canvas
183 × 147 cm
Centre Pompidou, Musée national d'art moderne, Paris

***Les Plongeurs* (The Divers), 1943** (243)
Oil on canvas
88.9 × 106.68 cm
Harvard Art Museums/Fogg Museum
Gift of Mr. and Mrs. Josep Lluís Sert, acc. no. 1964.60

***Esquisse pour les plongeurs* (Sketch for The Divers), 1945** (240)
Oil on canvas
194.8 × 146 cm
Kunsthalle Mannheim
On loan from the state of Baden-Württemberg since 1963

***Les Plongeurs sur fond jaune* (Divers on a Yellow Background), 1941** (237)
Oil on canvas
186.7 × 217.8 cm
The Art Institute of Chicago
Gift of Mr. and Mrs. Maurice E. Culberg

***L'Étoile de Mer* (Starfish), 1942** (239)
Oil on canvas
147.3 × 127 cm
Solomon R. Guggenheim Museum, New York, acc. no. 77.2669

***Étude pour La danse* (Study for The Dance), 1942** (241)
Pencil, gouache and India ink on paper
36.8 × 29.7 cm
Galerie Louise Leiris, Paris

***Plongeurs. Étude pour le projet de São Paolo (Divers,* study for the São Paulo project), c. 1942** (249)
Gouache on paper
29.5 × 66.3 cm
Private collection, Geneva
(Most likely a study for the mural *Les Plongeurs*)

Study for the mural for the home of Mr. and Mrs. Wallace Harrison, c. 1942 (248)
Graphite, ink, and gouache on paper
55.56 × 76.52 cm
Portland Museum of Art, Maine
Anonymous gift, 1986.2

Study for São Paolo, c. 1952 (242)
Gouache on paper
18.5 × 24.5 cm
Private collection

***L'Étoile de Mer et les plongeurs* (Starfish and Divers [design for a mosaic or mural painting]), 1942** (236)
Brush, yellow, red, green and beige wash and graphite on paper
13.3 × 44.5 cm
The Metropolitan Museum of Art, New York, Gift of Wallace K. Harrison, 1972, acc. no. 1972.730.1

Archival material and documents:

***Fernand Léger, la forme humaine dans l'espace,* Montreal 1945, Les Éditions de l'Arbre, with texts by Fernand Léger, Marie-Alain Couturier, Sigfried Giedion. Léger personally selected the authors.**
Private collection

Mural painting *Les Plongeurs* installed in the home of Wallace K. Harrison, Huntington, New York, early 1980s (251)
Courtesy Galerie Gmurzynska

Letter from Hester Diamond to Kurt Delbanco, October 25, 1984 (copy)
Museum Ludwig archive, Cologne

Removal of the mural painting *Les Plongeurs* from the home of Wallace K. Harrison, 1984 (252)
Museum Ludwig archive, Cologne

Peter Ludwig's index card for Fernand Léger's mural *Les Plongeurs*
Museum Ludwig archive, Cologne

***TIME*: *The Weekly News Magazine* 12, September 22, 1952 (Cover with Wallace K. Harrison)**
Institut für Zeitungsforschung, Dortmund

(Nelson A. Rockefeller Section)

***Maquette pour une peinture murale* (Study for mural painting), 1934**
Gouache on cardboard
43.4 × 36.9 cm
Kunstmuseum Basel; Schenkung Marguerite Arp-Hagenbach 1968, acc. no. 1968.410

***Projet de décoration murale* (Study for a mural decoration), c. 1936** (232)
Gouache and pencil on Canson paper
30.5 × 50 cm
Centre Pompidou, Musée national d'art moderne, Paris

***Projet de décoration murale* (Study for a mural decoration), c. 1936** (233)
Gouache and pencil on Canson paper
30.2 × 50 cm
Centre Pompidou, Musée national d'art moderne, Paris

Untitled, 1937
Oil on canvas
65 × 93.7 cm
Portland Museum of Art, Maine
Bequest of Ellen Hunt Harrison, 1996.8.14

***Maquette pour une peinture murale* (Study for a mural painting), 1938** (221)
Oil on canvas
162 × 114.5 cm
Lille métropole, musée d'art moderne, d'art contemporain et d'art brut, Villeneuve d'Ascq
Donation from Geneviève and Jean Masurel in 1979

Study for a mural painting for the foyer and staircase of Nelson A. Rockefeller's New York apartment, 1938 (225)
Gouache and pencil on paper
75.6 × 80.6 cm
Herbert F. Johnson Museum of Art, Cornell University, Anonymous gift, acc. no. 75.043.001

Study for the foyer and staircase mural paintings for Nelson A. Rockefeller's New York apartment, 1938 (226)
Gouache and pencil on paper
75.2 × 80.6 cm
Herbert F. Johnson Museum of Art, Cornell University, Anonymous gift, acc. no. 75.043.002

Six studies for a mural painting for the staircase of Nelson A. Rockefeller's apartment, c. 1938/39 (227)
Graphite, watercolor, and gouache on tissue paper
38.58 × 62.23 cm
Portland Museum of Art, Maine
Anonymous gift

Study for the fireplace mural in Nelson A. Rockefeller's New York apartment, 1938/39 (215)
Gouache and pencil on composition board
26 × 18.3 cm
Herbert F. Johnson Museum of Art, Cornell University, Anonymous gift, acc. no. 74.098.013

Study for the fireplace mural in Nelson A. Rockefeller's New York apartment, 1938/39 (216)
Gouache and pencil on composition board
26 × 16.2 cm
Herbert F. Johnson Museum of Art, Cornell University, Anonymous gift, acc. no. 74.098.003

Study for the fireplace mural in Nelson A. Rockefeller's New York apartment, 1938/39 (217)
Gouache and pencil on composition board
26 × 15.9 cm
Herbert F. Johnson Museum of Art, Cornell University, Anonymous gift, acc. no. 74.098.012

Mural composition for fireplace of Nelson A. Rockefeller's apartment, 1939 (218)
Oil on canvas
287.3 × 189.2 cm
Museum of Modern Art, New York, acc. no. TR6327

***La branche Rockefeller* (The Rockefeller Branch), 1952** (290)
Glazed ceramic
48.5 × 3.5 × 11 cm
Musée national Fernand Léger, Biot

Untitled, 1940 (219)
Gouache and pencil on paper
22.5 × 22.7 cm
Herbert F. Johnson Museum of Art, Cornell University, Anonymous gift, acc. no. 74.098.023

***Projet de décoration murale* (Study for a mural decoration), c. 1939** (229)
Gouache and pencil on Canson paper
25.6 × 32.5 cm
Centre Pompidou, Musée national d'art moderne, Paris

***Sans Titre (Projet de décoration murale)* (Untitled [Study for a mural decoration]), c. 1939** (230)
Gouache and graphite on Canson paper
25.6 × 32.5 cm
Centre Pompidou, Musée national d'art moderne, Paris

***Projet de décoration murale* (Study for a mural decoration), c. 1939** (231)
Gouache and pencil on Canson paper
25.2 × 32.6 cm
Centre Pompidou, Musée national d'art moderne, Paris

Archival material and documents:

Letter from Simone Herman to Charlotte Perriand, October 7, 1938
Archives Charlotte Perriand

Letter from Fernand Léger to Nelson A. Rockefeller, January 27, 1939
The Rockefeller Archive Center, Sleepy Hollow

Letter from Nelson A. Rockefeller to Fernand Léger, January 30, 1939
The Rockefeller Archive Center, Sleepy Hollow

Archival document regarding staircase mural by Fernand Léger in Nelson A. Rockefeller's New York apartment, undated
The Rockefeller Archive Center, Sleepy Hollow

Photograph with information relating to the fireplace mural by Fernand Léger in Nelson A. Rockefeller's New York apartment
The Rockefeller Archive Center, Sleepy Hollow

Inventory sheet for Léger's fireplace mural in Nelson A. Rockefeller's New York apartment
The Rockefeller Archive Center, Sleepy Hollow

(New York Section)

Untitled, 1938 (210)
Pencil on paper
47 × 34.1 cm
Herbert F. Johnson Museum of Art, Cornell University, Anonymous gift, acc. no. 72.108.006

Untitled, 1938 (220)
Pencil on paper
25.4 × 20.3 cm
Herbert F. Johnson Museum of Art, Cornell University, Anonymous gift, acc. no. 72.108.015

Untitled, 1938 (209)
Double-sided drawing: Gouache and pencil on paper
24.1 × 15.4 cm
Herbert F. Johnson Museum of Art, Cornell University, Anonymous gift, acc. no. 72.108.028

Study for Cinematic Mural I, 1938/39 (196)
Gouache and pencil on wood
50.7 × 40.5 cm
Museum of Modern Art, New York
Anonymous gift, acc. no. 738.1966

Study for Cinematic Mural II, 1938/39 (197)
Gouache and pencil on board
50.2 × 38 cm
Museum of Modern Art, New York
Anonymous gift, acc. no. 741.1966

Study for Cinematic Mural III, 1938/39 (198)
Gouache and pencil on board
50.7 × 37.8 cm
Museum of Modern Art, New York
Anonymous gift, acc. no. 743.1966

Study for Cinematic Mural IV, 1938/39 (199)
Gouache and pencil on wood
50.7 × 38 cm
Museum of Modern Art, New York
Anonymous gift, acc. no. 737.1966

Study for Cinematic Mural V, 1938/39 (200)
Gouache and pencil on wood
50.7 × 40.4 cm
Museum of Modern Art, New York
Anonymous gift, acc. no. 739.1966

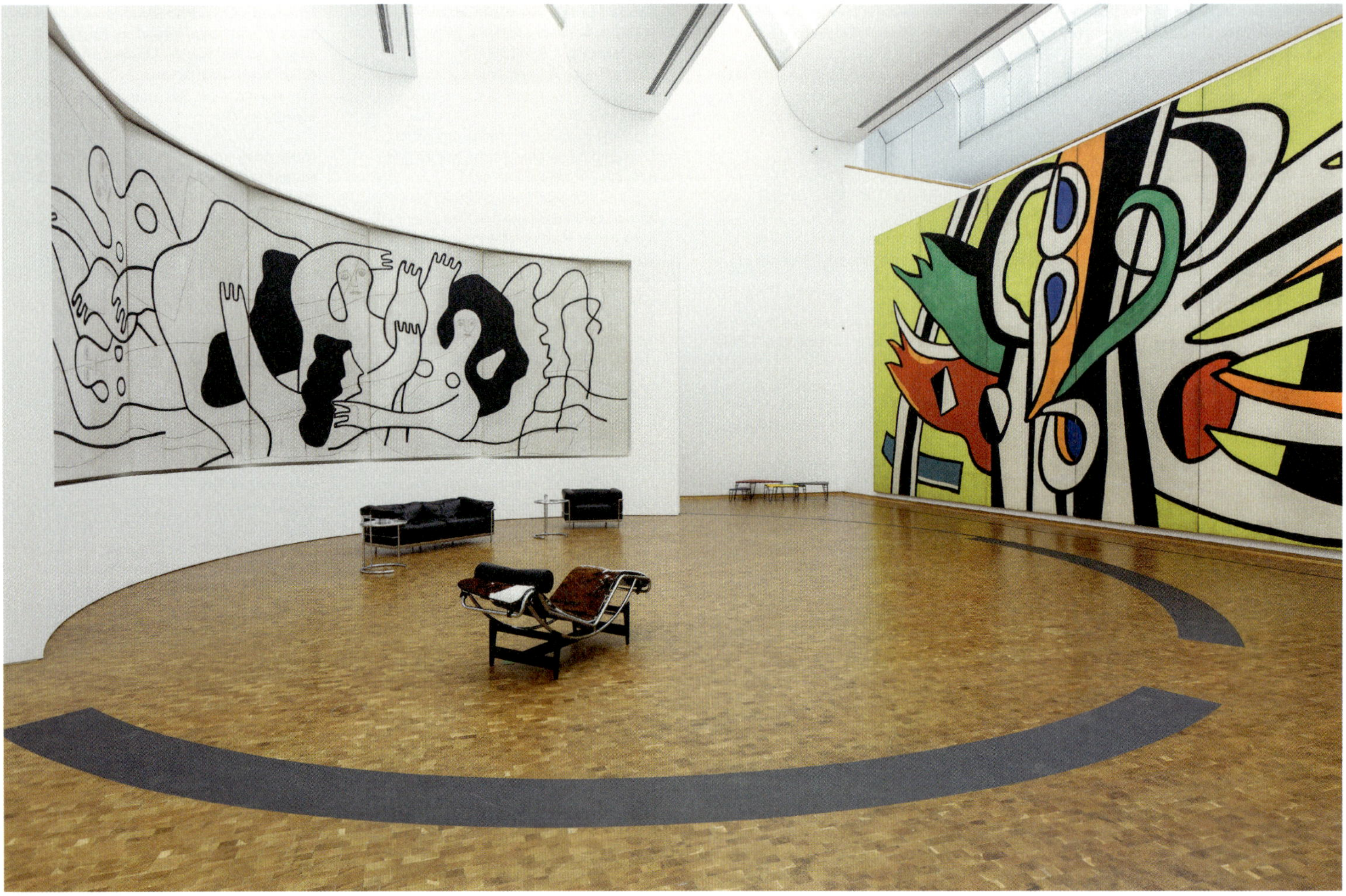

340

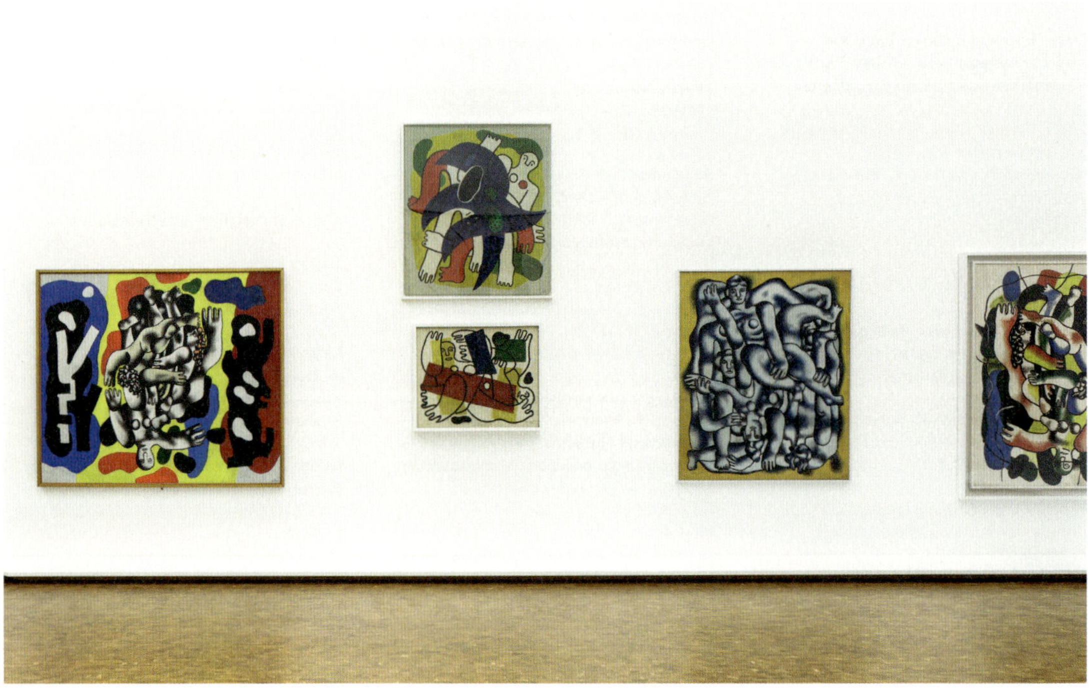

341

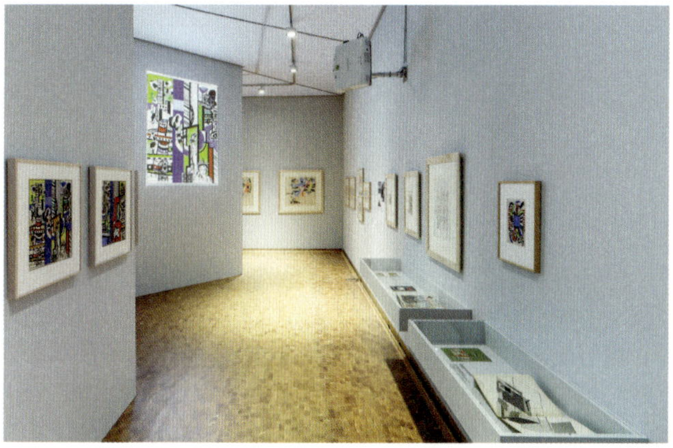

342

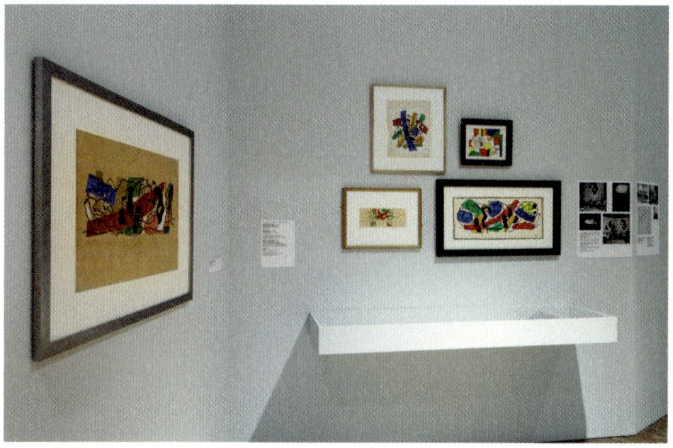

343

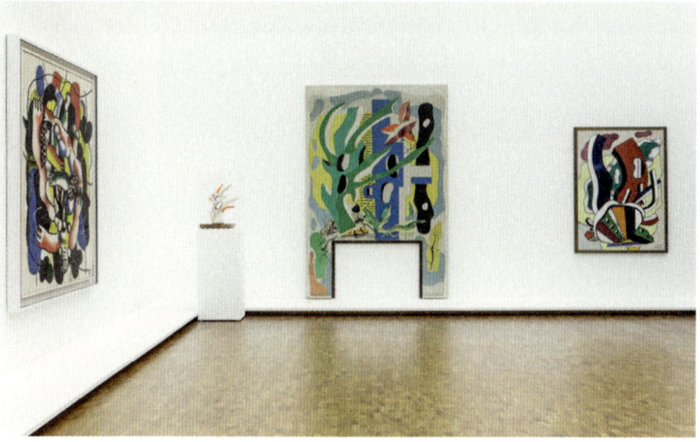

344

Study for Cinematic Mural VI, 1938/39 (201)
Gouache and pencil on board
50.7 × 37.9 cm
Museum of Modern Art, New York
Anonymous gift, acc. no. 740.1966

Study for Cinematic Mural VII, 1938/39 (202)
Gouache and pencil on board
50.6 × 37.7 cm
Museum of Modern Art, New York
Anonymous gift, acc. no. 742.1966

***New York*, 1944** (195)
Gouache on paper (Letterhead from Wallace K. Harrison's architecture firm)
21.5 × 14 cm
Musée franco-américain du Château de Blérancourt

Archival material and documents:

Two postcards from Fernand Léger to Le Corbusier with images from the New York World's Fair, 1939 (203, 204)
Fondation Le Corbusier, Paris

Official guidebook to the New York World's Fair 1939, ed. by Expositions Publications / Thos. R. Gardiner, New York 1939
Kunst- und Museumsbibliothek Köln

IX Milan Triennial (340)

***La Triennale de Milan* (Milan Triennial, mural painting for the French section of the IX Milan Triennial, realized by Léger's students), 1951** (300)
Oil on canvas
625 × 1,340 cm
Musée national Fernand Léger, Biot

Archival material and documents:

Exhibition program for the IX Milan Triennale, 1951
Archives Charlotte Perriand

***Des Arts appliqués à la vie quotidienne*, 1951**
Catalog for the IX Milan Triennial
Archives Charlotte Perriand

Seats in the room: (340)
(Provided by Cassina, Pesch International Interiors, Cologne)

Eileen Gray
***Adjustable Table* E1027 side table, 1927**

Le Corbusier, Pierre Jeanneret, Charlotte Perriand
LC4 lounger, LC3 sofa, LC3 armchair, 1928

Charlotte Perriand
Five nesting Petalo tables, 1951

A Synthesis of the Arts (345)

***Composition pour une peinture murale* (Composition for a mural painting), 1945** (294)
Oil on canvas
50.7 × 40.5 cm
Musée national Fernand Léger, Biot

***Projet de décoration pour la salle à manger du paquebot »Vulcania«* (Study for the decoration of the dining room of the *Vulcania* passenger ship [Lucania]), c. 1951** (298)
Gouache and pencil on vellum
31.3 × 65.2 cm
Musée national Fernand Léger, Biot

***Projet de décoration pour la salle à manger du paquebot »Vulcania«* Study for the decoration of the dining room of the *Vulcania* passenger ship [Lucania]), c. 1951** (299)
Gouache and pencil on paper
31.3 × 65.2 cm
Musée national Fernand Léger, Biot

***Composition* (Composition [Mural painting for the dining room of *Lucania* passenger ship]), 1953** (296)
Oil on canvas
210 × 510 cm
Museu Colecção Berardo, Lisbon, acc. no. UID 102-334

***Projet pour une peinture murale* (Plan for a mural painting), 1952** (293)
Oil on canvas
114 × 195 cm
Musée national Fernand Léger, Biot

***Peinture murale* (Mural Painting), 1953** (295)
Oil on canvas
92 × 65.2 cm
Musée national Fernand Léger, Biot

***Maquette, projet pour une mosaïque de l'université de Caracas* (Design for a mosaic for the University of Caracas), 1952** (305)
30 × 89.5 cm
Gouache and India ink on paper
Musée national Fernand Léger, Biot

***Le Tournesol* (The Sunflower) c. 1952/53** (291)
Glazed ceramic
41.5 × 46.5 cm
Private collection

Archival material and documents:

Letter from Fernand Léger to Le Corbusier, September 17, 1951
Fondation le Corbusier, Paris

Invitation card for the annual exhibition in Fernand Léger's studio, December 11–27, 1951
Fondation Le Corbusier, Paris

***Art d'aujourd'hui*, October 1951 (Manifesto of the Groupe Espace)**
Kunst- und Museumsbibliothek Köln

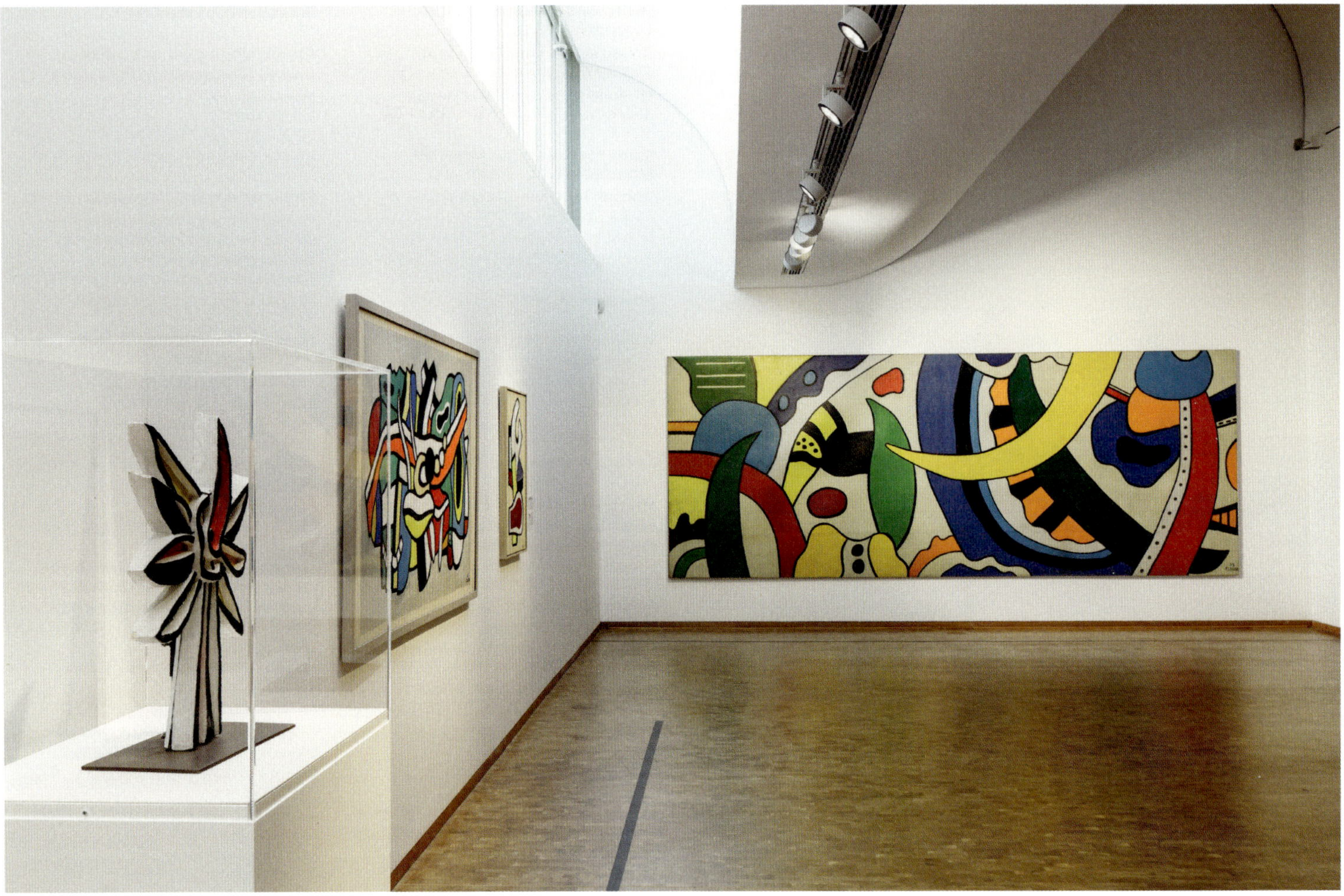

345

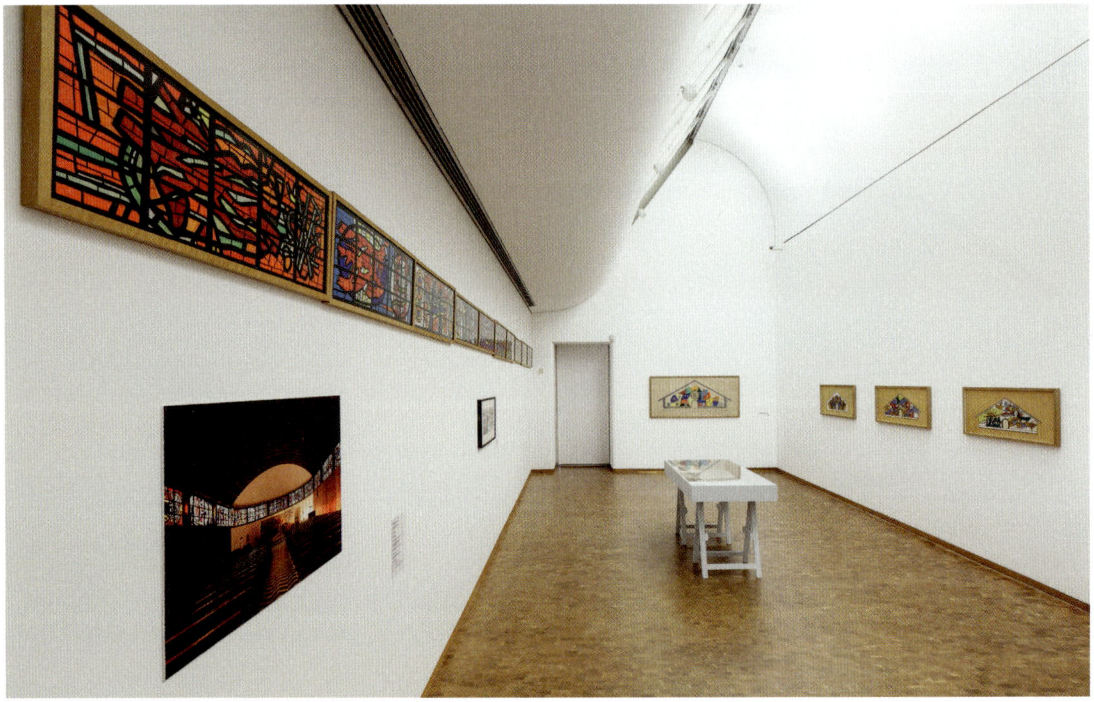

346

***Formes Et Vie* 1, 1951 (Article: Fernand Léger, "L'architecture moderne et la couleur")**
Private collection

***LIFE 3*, November 1952 (Article: "Strange Shapes in Eggs, Art and Nature")**
Kunst- und Museumsbibiothek Köln

***Architecture d'aujourd'hui*, 53, March /April 1954 (Article: Pierre Guéguen, "Une démonstration du Groupe Espace. L'exposition 'architecture couleur formes' à Biot (Côte d'Azur)")**
Universitätsbibliothek Johann Christian Senckenberg Frankfurt

Catalog of the exhibition by Le Corbusier, Fernand Léger and Charlotte Perriand: *Proposition d'une Synthèse des arts, Paris, 1955*, Tokyo 1955 (303)
Archives Charlotte Perriand

Sacred Space (346)

***Maquette pour la mosaïque de l'église Notre-Dame-de-Toute-Grâce, Plateau d'Assy, Haute Savoie* (Study for the mosaic in the church of Notre-Dame-de-Toute-Grâce), 1947** (263)
Gouache on paper
82.9 × 181.2
Musée national Fernand Léger, Biot

***1er état*, Église d'Assy (First State, Church of Assy), Sancellemoz, Haute-Savoie, 1947** (264)
Gouache on paper
46.5 × 102.5 cm
Musée national Fernand Léger, Biot

***2me état*, Église d'Assy (Second State, Church of Assy), Sancellemoz, Haute-Savoie, 1947** (265)
Gouache on paper
46.5 × 102 cm
Musée national Fernand Léger, Biot

***3me état*, Église d'Assy (Second State, Church of Assy), Sancellemoz, Haute Savoie, 1947** (266)
Gouache on paper
45.9 × 122 cm
Musée national Fernand Léger, Biot

***4me état*, Église d'Assy (Second State, Church of Assy), Sancellemoz, Haute-Savoie, 1947** (267)
Gouache on paper
46.5 × 118 cm
Musée national Fernand Léger, Biot

Designs for the stained glass windows of the Sacré-Coeur church in Audincourt

***La tunique du Christ* (The Tunic of Christ), 1950** (278)
Gouache on paper
34 × 98 cm
Centre Pompidou, Musée national d'art moderne, Paris

***La tunique du Christ* (The Tunic of Christ, not realized), 1950** (269)
Gouache on paper
36 × 84.5 cm
Centre Pompidou, Musée national d'art moderne, Paris

***La lance* (The Lance), 1950** (270)
Gouache on paper
37 × 91 cm
Centre Pompidou, Musée national d'art moderne, Paris

***La croix* (The Cross), 1950** (272)
Gouache on paper
34 × 97 cm
Centre Pompidou, Musée national d'art moderne, Paris

***Les cinq plaies du Christ* (The Five Wounds of Christ), 1950** (273)
Gouache on paper
37 × 94 cm
Centre Pompidou, Musée national d'art moderne, Paris

***Remets en place ton glaive* (Put Your Sword Back In Its Place), 1950** (275)
Gouache on paper
33.4 × 89 cm
Centre Pompidou, Musée national d'art moderne, Paris

***Les calices et l'éponge* (The Chalices and the Sponge), 1950** (271)
Gouache on paper
37 × 92 cm
Centre Pompidou, Musée national d'art moderne, Paris

***Les fouets* (The Whips), 1950** (276)
Gouache on paper
37 × 94 cm
Centre Pompidou, Musée national d'art moderne, Paris

***Les deux arbres de vie* (The Two Trees of Life), 1950** (277)
Gouache on paper
34 × 92 cm
Centre Pompidou, Musée national d'art moderne, Paris

***Le calvaire* (Calvary), 1950** (274)
Gouache on paper
33 × 92 cm
Centre Pompidou, Musée national d'art moderne, Paris

Study for the tapestry of the church in Audincourt, c. 1953 (280)
Gouache on paper
25.3 × 64.4 cm
The Menil Collection, Houston

***Mosaïque La mère et l'enfant* (Mother and Child mosaic), c. 1955**
Glass
72.5 × 92.5
Musée national Fernand Léger, Biot

Archival material and documents:

***L'Art Sacré*, November–December 1951, Article about the church in Audincourt**
Universitäts- und Landesbibliothek Bonn

***L'Art Sacré*, May–June 1952, cover page on the church in Assy**
Universitäts- und Landesbibliothek Bonn

***L'Art Sacré*, March–April 1953, article about the church in Assy**
Universitäts- und Landesbibliothek Bonn

Letter from Fernand Léger to Father Couturier, February 12, 1944
Archives Père Couturier, Bibliotheque du Saulchoir - Province dominicaine de France

Letter from Fernand Léger to Father Couturier, November 6, 1951
Archives Père Couturier, Bibliotheque du Saulchoir - Province dominicaine de France

Letter from Fernand Léger to Father Couturier, February 26, 1952
Archives Père Couturier, Bibliotheque du Saulchoir - Province dominicaine de France

Films by and about Léger:

***Fernand Léger in America. His New Realism*, 1945**
Director: Thomas Bouchard
Music: Edgard Varèse
27 min
The Harvard Film Archive

Segment by Fernand Léger: *The Girl with the Prefabricated Heart*, from: *Dreams That Money Can Buy*, 1947
Director: Hans Richter,
Producers: Kenneth Macpherson, Peggy Guggenheim
35mm, sound, color and black and white
99 min
Contributions by Fernand Léger, Alexander Calder, Marcel Duchamp, Max Ernst, Man Ray, Darius Milhaud
Music: John Cage, Louis Applebaum, Paul Bowles, David Diamond, Darius Milhaud, Josh White

Authors' Biographies

Jacques Barsac
Jacques Barsac is a historian, exhibition curator, and documentary filmmaker with a focus on art and history from 1976 to 2001. His films include documentaries on Charlotte Perriand, Le Corbusier, Winston Churchill, Jean Cocteau, and Clovis, as well as feature films that have been awarded upwards of twenty prizes at international festivals, such as *L'aigle et le sphinx*, *l'An Mil*, and *Le Roman du visage*. Since 2002 he has worked as the biographer of Charlotte Perriand, focusing on her oeuvre. Author of five reference works on the designer, including her catalogue raisonné, he has served as both scientific advisor and joint curator for key exhibitions of her work at venues including the Centre Pompidou and the Musée d'Art Moderne in Saint-Étienne.

Katia Baudin
Since 2008, Katia Baudin has been Deputy Director of the Museum Ludwig, and she is curator of the exhibition *Fernand Léger: Painting in Space*. A French-born, American-raised art historian, she previously directed the Fonds Régional d'Art Contemporain Nord Pas-de-Calais in Dunkirk (1997–2004) and the École supérieure des arts décoratifs in Strasbourg (2004–07). Baudin specializes in interdisciplinary issues, in particular between the fine and the applied arts, as well as questions relating to identity and the social role of the arts. She has published extensively on these subjects and has curated over forty exhibitions on modern and contemporary art and design.

Diana Gay
Diana Gay is the curator of the Musée National Fernand Léger in Biot. She previously worked at the Musée Départemental Henri Matisse in Cateau-Cambrésis and at the Musée d'Art Contemporain du Val-de-Marne in Vitry-sur-Seine. A specialist in modern and contemporary art, she is especially interested in investigating the cultural history of art from the perspective of axiology (the theory of values), including the professional ethics of art restoration.

Jan de Heer
Jan de Heer is a Dutch architect and publishes on architecture and applied arts. He wrote his doctoral dissertation on Le Corbusier and polychromy, which has been one of his main research topics since 1986.

Roxane Jubert
In addition to her teaching and research, Roxane Jubert is a graphic designer and typographer. Based in Paris, she has taught at the École nationale supérieure des arts décoratifs (ENSAD) since 1997. Flammarion published an English translation of a book based on her PhD dissertation under the title *Typography and Graphic Design: From Antiquity to the Present*. Educated at the École Estienne, she went on to study at ENSAD, ANRT, and the Universities of Paris I and IV, where she completed her PhD.

Giovanni Lista
A resident of Paris since 1969, Giovanni Lista is an Italian art historian. A former Director of Research at the National Center for Scientific Research, he specializes in the study of the early twentieth-century avant-garde. The author of many critical works on modern artists and writers including Boccioni, Medardo Rosso, Russolo, De Chirico, Loïe Fuller, Paladini, Léger, Herbin, Ionesco, and Marinetti, he has also dealt with movements and broader subjects such as the "modern scene," Futurism, Dada, "happenings," and avant-garde photography. Additionally, he has curated significant international exhibitions held in Paris, Tokyo, Rome, Munich, London, and New York among other locations.

Petra Mandt
Petra Mandt completed her master's degree in art history, theater studies, and education at the Universität Köln and trained as a conservator in several museums and private studios in Germany. Following her work at the Schweizer Institut für Kunstwissenschaft in Zurich, she served as a conservator of paintings and sculpture at the Wallraf-Richartz-Museum/Museum Ludwig from 1996, and at the Museum Ludwig since the separation of the two museums in 2000. Her research focus is the conservation history of the nineteenth century. Since 2010, she has carried out art-technological research on the museum's Russian avant-garde collection.

Friedhelm Mennekes
Friedhelm Mennekes is a Jesuit priest who studied philosophy, Catholic theology, political science, and modern history at the universities of Bonn and Munich. Moreover, he was a student at priest training colleges in Pullach and Frankfurt am Main. He completed his habilitation and holds a Licentiate of Theology. From 1979 to 2008 he was Professor of Practical Theology and Religious Sociology in Frankfurt, and headed the Kunst-Station Sankt Peter Köln between 1987 and 2008, where he organized numerous exhibitions of major contemporary artists. Mennekes is Honorary Professor at the Hochschulen der Bildenden Künste in Mainz and Brunswick, and has taught at the Kunsthistorische Institut der Universität Bonn (A.-M. Bonnet Chair) since 2008. He is an advisor to the primates of Mexico on matters relating to art and the Church.

Kathrin Michel
Kathrin Michel holds a degree in art history, classical archeology and ethnology and is a doctoral candidate at the Rheinische Friedrich-Wilhelms-Universität Bonn. She has worked in the areas of museum education and communication at the Kunstmuseum Bonn and other institutions. She is Curatorial and Research Assistant for the *Fernand Léger: Painting in Space* exhibition at the Museum Ludwig.

Donato Severo
The architect and historian Donato Severo was awarded a PhD in architectural history from Université Paris I Panthéon-Sorbonne, and holds a habilitation to supervise research. He teaches at the École nationale supérieure d'architecture Paris-Val de Seine and is a researcher at the Laboratoire EVCAU. His activities center on the history, theories, and practices of architectural heritage, as well as issues relating to the concepts of health and well-being. His publications include *Paul Nelson* (Paris, 2013) and *Paul Nelson et l'hôpital de Saint-Lô: Humanisme, art et architecture* (Paris, 2015).

Anne Vallye
Anna Vallye is Postdoctoral Research Associate at the School of Arts and Sciences and the Sam Fox School of Design and the Visual Arts at Washington University in St. Louis, Missouri, where she is currently working on a book entitled *The Management of Modernity: Modern Architecture and the Politics of State Governance*. Vallye holds a PhD in art history from Columbia University. Previously, she was Andrew W. Mellon Postdoctoral Fellow at the Philadelphia Museum of Art, where she curated the interdisciplinary exhibition *Léger: Modern Art and the Metropolis*, which was awarded the 2014 Dedalus Foundation Exhibition Catalogue prize. Her work has been published in several edited anthologies and museum catalog, as well as in journals such as *arq: Architecture Research Quarterly*, *Constructs*, and *Grey Room*.

Sarah Wilson
Sarah Wilson is Professor of Modern and Contemporary Art at the Courtauld Institute of Art, University of London. Her recent publications include *The Visual World of French Theory* (Yale, 2010) and *Picasso/Marx and Socialist Realism in France* (Liverpool, 2013). In 2015, she co-curated the First Asian Biennale/Fifth Guangzhou Triennale, and was awarded the AICA international prize for distinguished contributions to art criticism.

This catalog is published in conjunction with the exhibition *Fernand Léger: Painting in Space* Museum Ludwig: April 9–July 3, 2016

The exhibition and publication have been made possible with the generous support of

Peter und Irene Ludwig Stiftung

RheinEnergie

DS Automobiles

Freunde des Wallraf-Richartz-Museum und Museum Ludwig e.V.

Gesellschaft für Moderne Kunst am Museum Ludwig e.V.

Bankhaus Sal. Oppenheim jr. & Cie. AG & Co. KGaA

Pesch International Interiors, Cologne

Cooperation partner: Institut Français, Cologne

Our thanks go to all the lenders:

Archives Père Couturier Bibliothèque du Saulchoir - Province dominicaine de France; Archives Charlotte Perriand; The Art Institute of Chicago; Bibliothèque des Arts décoratifs, Paris; Centre de documentation des musées des Arts décoratifs, Paris; Photothèque des Arts décoratifs, Paris; Canadien Centre for Architecture, Montréal; Centre national des arts plastiques, Paris, avec le concours du Palais de la découverte, Universcience; Ciné Archives Paris; Dansmuseet Stockholm-Musée Rolf de Maré; J.M. Decrop, Hong Kong; Die Stadt Dortmund – Institut für Zeitungsforschung; Fondation Beyeler, Riehen/Bale; Fondation Le Corbusier, Paris; Fundació Joan Miró, Barcelona; Galerie Gmurzynska AG, Zug; Galerie Antoine Laurentin, Paris; Galerie Louise Leiris, Paris; Galerie Maeght, Paris; Johann Wolfgang Goethe Universität, Universitätsbibliothek Johann Christian Senckenberg, Frankfurt; Solomon R. Guggenheim Museum, New York; Harvard Art Museums/Fogg Museum; The Harvard Film Archive; Von der Heydt-Museum Wuppertal; Millecent Hodson and Kenneth Archer, London; Herbert F. Johnson Museum of Art, Cornell University; Kunsthalle Mannheim; Kunstmuseum Basel; Kunst- und Museumsbibliothek Köln; Lille Métropole musée d'art moderne, d'art contemporain et d'art brut, Villeneuve d'Ascq; The Menil Collection, Houston; The Metropolitan Museum of Art, New York; Musée franco-américain du Château de Blérancourt; Musée national d'art moderne/Centre de création industrielle, Centre Pompidou, Paris; Musée Pierre-Noël, Saint-Dié-des-Vosges; Musées de Belfort; Musées nationaux du XXème siècle des Alpes-Maritimes, Musée national Fernand Léger Biot; Musées Royaux des Beaux-Arts de Belgique, Bruxelles; Museo Nacional Centro de Arte Reina Sofía, Madrid; Museu Colecção Berardo, Lisbon; Museum of Modern Art, New York; Philadelphia Museum of Art; Portland Museum of Art, Maine; Rheinische Friedrich-Wilhelm-Universität Bonn; The Rockefeller Archive Center, Sleepy Hollow; Staatsbibliothek zu Berlin – Preußischer Kulturbesitz; Tate; Universitäts- und Landesbibliothek Bonn; Universitäts- und Stadtbibliothek Köln; and all the lenders whom it is not possible to mention by name.

We would also like to thank those who supported us in researching and preparing the exhibition and catalog, in particular:

Emma Abadi, Universcience, Paris; Nadia Abbas (Sotheby's); Stefan Bachmann, Michaela Kretschmann, Andrea Imler, Jakob Leo Stark, Justus Maier, Henriette Nagel, Nicolas Streit, Schauspiel Köln; Gilles Barnaud und Frère Jean-Michel Potin (Bibliothèque du Saulchoir - Province dominicaine de France, Paris); Gabriele und Detlef Bierbaum; Aude Bodet, Xavier-Philippe Guiochon, Violaine Daniels (CNAP, Paris); Donatella Cacciola, Tanzarchiv Köln; Christian Derouet (Musée Zervos – Maison Romain-Rolland, Vézelay); Hester Diamond; Anne Dopffer, Diana Gay, Nelly Maillard (Musée national Fernand Léger, Biot); Gudrun Dröghoff (Christie's); Jean du Chatenet; Andrew Eschelbacher (Portland Museum of Art, Maine); Amy Fitch (The Rockefeller Archive Center, Sleepy Hollow); Isabelle Fournel, Elise Barzun, Laurence Bartoletti, Laure Haberschill (Bibliothèque et Photoèque des Arts décoratifs, Paris); Sonja Gandert (Herbert F. Johnson Museum of Art, Cornell University); Catherine Giraud (Cité de la Tapisserie Aubusson); Isabelle Godineau, Delphine Studer (Fondation Le Corbusier, Paris); Daniel Kramer (Fondation Beyeler, Riehen/Bale); Quentin Laurens (Galerie Louise Leiris, Paris); Perrine Le Blan (Malingue S.A.); Marie-Ange L'Herbier, Mireille Beaulieu; Olga Makhroff, (Musée national d'art moderne, Centre Pompidou, Paris); Erik Näslund, Dansmuseet Stockholm; Ugo Nelson; Janet Parks und Nicole Richard (Avery Architectural & Fine Arts Library, Columbia University, NY); Cristina Pérez Bueno (Josep Lluís Sert Archive - Fundació Jean Miró, Barcelona); Pernette Perriand, Jacques Barsac (Archives Charlotte Perriand, Paris); Melanie Pfeiffer und Jeannette Weiss (Galerie Gmurzynska); Cora Rosevear (The Museum of Modern Art, NY); Xavier-Francois Roth, Johannes Wunderlich, Patrick Hahn, Gürzenich-Orchester Köln; Nathalie Samoilov; Didier Schulmann, Brigitte Vincens, Karine Bomel und Véronique Borgeaud (Bibliotheque Kandinsky – Centre de documentation et de recherche du Musée national d'art moderne – Centre de creation industrielle, Centre Pompidou, Paris); Isabel Schulz (Kurt Schwitters Archiv, Sprengel Museum, Hanover); Lori Spiegel; Nicolas Surlapierre, Musées de Belfort; Paulina Villanueva und Cecilia Castrillo (Fundación Villanueva, Caracas); Claude Wrobel; Ines Zalduendo (Josep Lluís Sert Collection - Frances Loeb Library / Harvard University Graduate School of Design, Boston); Gerd Zillner (Kiesler Archiv - Österreichische Friedrich und Lillian Kiesler-Privatstiftung, Vienna),

as well as all the catalog authors:

Jacques Barsac, Diana Gay, Jan de Heer, Roxane Jubert, Giovanni Lista, Friedhelm Mennekes, Donato Severo, Anna Vallye, Sarah Wilson.

A special thank you goes to Tino Graß, Meyer Voggenreiter and Nicole Hüttner.

Exhibition

Curated by
Katia Baudin, Deputy Director

Research Assistant
Kathrin Michel

Director
Yilmaz Dziewior

Administration
Ursula Hübner

Registrar
Christin Wähner

Conservation
Kathrin Keßler, Petra Mandt, Sophia Elze, Yvonne Garborini, Alicia Fisch, Carla Frechen, Katja de Grussa-Bernard, Philipp Kochendörfer, Arnau Monsonis, Svenja Tempich, Carmen Seuffert, Natalie Strauß

Press and Public Relations
Sonja Hempel, Anne Niermann, Kirsten te Brake, Katharina Fugmann

Partnerships and Fundraising
Lisa Nadig, Dagmar von der Burg

Education
Angelika von Tomaszewski

Exhibition Coordination
Iris Maczollek

Object Management
Axel Kuhn, Alfred Glasner

Documentation
Beate Bischoff, Anina Baum, Ulrich Tillmann

Exhibition Installation
Sven Bormes, Paul Esser, Jürgen Koll, Saffet Sen
D'Art, ®ART HANDLING Spedition GmbH, Cologne

Display Construction
Michael Bangert, Leif Lenzner, Milan Scharf, Basileios Chronz, Johannes Gabler

Building Superintendants
Lukas Hofmann, Dirk Otter

Technical Equipment
Guido Fassbender, Andreas Wischum, Michael Zorn, Thomas Loerzer, Thomas Sydlik, Ingo Weber, Peter Pier

Administration
Angela Coenen, Marion Funken, Pia Christoph, Ursula Meyer-Krömer, Karsten Zinner, Susanne Brentano

Interns
Krisztina Csaba, Nele Guinand, Kristina Kreutzwald, Lola Lorant, Janine Muckermann, Simone Schmahl

Audio Guide
soundgarden audioguidance GmbH, Pia Linden

Wall Texts
Katia Baudin, Pia Linden, Angelika von Tomaszewski

Media Technology
235 Media GmbH

Photo Editors
picture worx – Monika Bergmann, Leonie Pfennig

Exhibition Design
mvprojekte – Nicole Hüttner, Meyer Voggenreiter

Graphic Design and Communication
studio tino graß

Catalog

Editor
Katia Baudin

Editorial Office
Katia Baudin, Kathrin Michel

Catalog Management
Iris Maczollek

Text Editors
Ellen Mey, Leonie Pfennig

Photo Editors
picture worx – Monika Bergmann, Barbara Linz, Leonie Pfennig
Kathrin Jurgenowski (assistant)

Project supervision Hirmer
Kerstin Ludolph

Project management Hirmer
Karen Angne, Katja Durchholz

Copy Editors
Sylee Gore, Chris Murray

Translators
German-English: Sylee Gore
French-English: James Gussen, David Radzinowicz, John Tittensor, Bernard Wooding
Italian-English: Veronica O'Neill, Galway
Dutch-English: Sue McDonnell

Design
studio tino graß

Lithography
REPROMAYER Medienproduktion GmbH, Reutlingen

Paper
Profibulk 1,3, 115 g/m²

Font
Avenir Next LT Pro, Pitch

Production
Katja Durchholz

Print and Binding
Printer Trento S.r.l., Trento

Printed in Italy

Bibliographic information of the Deutsche Nationalbibliothek
The Deutsche Nationalbibliothek records this publication in the Deutsche Nationalbibliografie; detailed bibliographic data is available at http://www.dnb.de.

ISBN 978-3-7774-2594-8

www.hirmerpublishers.com

The numbering refers to the catalog numbers.

Archiv Museum Ludwig: 252. Archives Charlotte Perriand: 106, 112–115, 133, 135, 155–156, 302–304; Henrot 117; C. Vanderberghe 129–130; Albin Salaün 97; François Kollar 154. Archives municipales d'Ivry-sur-Seine: 162. Archivio Fotografico © La Triennale di Milano: 301. Archivo Fundación Villanueva/ Paolo Gasparini 306–311. Art Institute of Chicago: 237. Avery Architectural & Fine Arts Library, Columbia University: 191–192, 206–207, 234, 261, 312; Katrina Thomas for Harrison & Abramovitz Architects 245–246, 254, 259–260. The Bancroft Library University of California, Berkeley/Thérèse Bonney: 143. Belfort, Musée d'art moderne, Donation Jardot: 119–120. Bibliothèque des Arts décoratifs, Paris: 127. Board of Trustees, National Gallery of Art, Washington, DC: 161. bpk/CNAC-MNAM: 121–122, 175, 319; Jacqueline Hyde 269–278; Georges Meguerditchian 167; Philippe Migeat 108, 170, 173, 229–233; Jean-Claude Planchet 171; Jean-Claude Planchet/Georges Meguerditchian 174; Image Centre Pompidou, MNAM-CCI/Hervé Véronèse 20–21, 25; Dist. RMN/Jacques Faujour 238. bpk/RMN-Grand Palais: Estate Brassaï 99; Gérard Blot 24, 63, 68–73, 103, 125, 134, 177, 264–265, 267, 284, 290, 293–295; Adrien Didierjean 38, 123, 132, 142, 263, 266, 298–299, 305, 322. bpk: The Metropolitan Museum of Art/ Art Resource, NY 228, 236; RMN 195; Solomon R. Guggenheim Foundation 57, 145, 239; Sprengel Museum Hannover/Michael Herling/Benedikt Werner/Aline Gwose 313. Bridgeman Images: Amélie Granet-Garosciol 136; Christie's Images 211. Cantz Medienmanagement, Ostfildern: 77. Giorgio Casali/ Domus Oktober 1953: 297 Collection Centre Canadien d'Architecture/Canadian Centre for Architecture, Montreal Gift in memory of Daniel Robbins: 286–288. Centre Pompidou, Bibliothèque Kandinsky: 144, 166, 176, 180, 185, 187–190; Hugo P. Herdeg mit freundlicher Genehmigung von Christian Herdeg 169. Consolidated Edison Company of New York City, Inc., 2004: 208. Dansmuseet – Musée Rolf de Maré Stockholm: 2–15; 17–20. Nicolas Dewitte & Philip Bernard/LaM: 28. Courtesy of Doyle, Auctioneers & Appraisers: 247. Estate of Nadia Khodossievitch-Léger: 160. Ezra Stoller/Esto: 235. Fondation le Corbusier: 82, 86, 88, 90–91, 94, 98, 100, 102, 104, 149–150, 152, 203–204; Olivier Martin Gambier 92; Albin Salaün 147–148, 151; Peter Willi 93, 95. Fundació Joan Miró, Barcelona: 138. Courtesy Galerie Gmurzynska: 62, 251. Galerie Laurentin, Paris: 61, 249. Collection Galerie Maeght, Paris, PHOTO MAEGHT, 2015: 1, 16. Getty Images: Robert Doisneau/Gamma-Rapho 320; Herrmann/The LIFE Picture Collection 194; Arnold Newman Collection 192; Reporters Associes/Gamma-Rapho 292; Frank Scherschel/The LIFE Picture Collection 256–258. gta Archiv/ETH Zürich/Nachlass Sigfried Giedion: 289. Indiana University Art Museum/Kevin Montague: 83. Harvard Art Museums/Fogg Museum, Cambridge/ Imaging Department, Courtesy of President and Fellows of Harvard College: 243. Herbert F. Johnson Museum of Art, Cornell University: 209–210, 215–217, 219–220, 225–226. Lucien Hervé: 268. Horst P. Horst/Architectural Digest © Condé Nast: 212, 214. IAM/akg-images: 48. J.S./Artedia/Opale/Leemage/ laif: 317–318. Michael Krasowitz: 253. Kunsthalle Mannheim/Cem Yücetas: 240. Kunstmuseum Basel/ Martin P. Bühler: 64–67, 101. Michel Legret: 262. Leiris Paris: 27, 75, 186, 241. Les Arts décoratifs, Paris: 51, 53; Jean Collas 146; Editions Albert Lévy/Jacques Thibaud 89; Jean Tholance 59. Lille métropole, musée d'art moderne, d'art contemporain et d'art brut, Villeneuve d'Ascq, Donation de Geneviève et Jean Mansurel en 1979/Philip Bernard: 221. Lobsterfilms: 26. Magyar Nemzeti Galéria, Budapest: 54. Lucas Matagne, mit freundlicher Genehmigung von Patrice Novarina: 279. Norman McGrath, New York: 255. The Menil Collection, Houston: Paul Hester 55; Gift of Abbé Prenel/F. Wilbur Seiders 280. Digital image, The Museum of Modern Art, New York/Scala, Florence: 47, 56, 79, 85, 172, 196–202, 218. Collection du Musée Pierre-Noël: 23. Museu Coleção Berardo/Jose Manuel Costa Alves: 296. Museum of the City of New York: 205. Nachlass André Bruyère/Dimitri Tibislawsky: 281–282. Niedersächsische Staats- und Universitätsbibliothek Göttingen: 138. Palais de la découverte/Universcience/P. O'Doyé: 141. Courtesy of the Philadelphia Museum of Art: 164. Photographic Archives Museo Nacional Centro de Arte Reina Sofia: 153. Portland Museum of Art: 227, 248. Rheinisches Bildarchiv Köln: 37 (rba_d000066), 39 (rba_c014478), 74 (rba_c000984), 140 (rba_d040067), 165 (rba_d040070), 244 and cover (rba_ c005586), 300 (rba_d040066); Britta Schlier: 250 (rba_d040124_045), 324 (rba_d040124_011), 325 (rba_d040124_014), 326 (rba_d040124_060), 327 (rba_d040124_062), 328 (rba_d040124_069), 329 (rba_d040124_075), 330 (rba_d040124_025), 331 (rba_d040124_023), 332 (rba_d040124_028), 333 (rba_d040124_030), 334 (rba_d040124_089), 335 (rba_d040124_006), 336 (rba_d040124_036), 337 (rba_d040124_040), 338 (rba_d040124_114), 339 (rba_d040124_042), 340 (rba_d040124_051), 341 (rba_d040124_003), 342 (rba_d040124_133), 343 (rba_d040124_147), 344 (rba_d040124_047), 345 (rba_d040124_056), 346 (rba_d040124_058). Bertrand Rieger/Hemis/laif: 184. Courtesy of Rockefeller Archive Center: 213; Charles Uht 222-224. Royal Museums of Fine Arts of Belgium, Brussels/J. Geleyns: 42–43. Donato Severo: 178–179, 181–183, 323. TATE, London 2015: 118. Christian Ueding/www. vergessener-beton.de: 316. UN Photo: 314–315. Roger-Viollet: Albert Harlingue 139; Boris Lipnitzki 157–158; Gaston Paris 105. Von der Heydt-Museum Wuppertal/Sierra Günnel-Kaag: 96.

Cover:
***Les Plongeurs* (The Divers), 1942**
Oil and charcoal on canvas
372 × 1092 cm
Museum Ludwig, Cologne